Rethinking American History
in a Global Age

Rethinking
American History
in a Global Age

EDITED BY
Thomas Bender

UNIVERSITY OF CALIFORNIA
PRESS
Berkeley   Los Angeles   London

University of California Press
Berkeley and Los Angeles, California

University of California Press, Ltd.
London, England

© 2002 by the Regents of the University of California

Library of Congress Cataloging-in-Publication Data

Rethinking American history in a global age / edited by Thomas Bender.
    p.   cm.
Includes index.
    ISBN 0-520-23057-4 (cloth : alk. paper).—ISBN 0-520-23058-2 (paper :
alk. paper)
    1. United States—Historiography.   2. United States—History—
Philosophy.   3. Globalization.   I. Bender, Thomas.
E175 .R48 2001
973'.07'2—dc21   2001002388

Manufactured in the United States of America
10 09 08 07 06 05 04 03 02 01
10 9 8 7 6 5 4 3 2 1

CONTENTS

PREFACE

Modern historiography is inextricably linked with the modern nation. That connection has both given focus to historical inquiry and won for it a place in civic life. But it has also been disabling, silencing stories both smaller and larger than the nation. Today, at the beginning of the twenty-first century, in an era of intense discussion of multiculturalism and globalism, it may be easier than ever before to recognize the plenitude of historical experiences and narratives imbricated in a national history. To historicize the nation is to relate its dominant narrative, its national narrative, to other narratives that refer to both smaller histories and larger ones. That means understanding the historical production of the nation and locating it in a context larger than itself. That is the work of this volume. It asks a big question and begins the work of answering it: How does one frame the narrative of American history in the context of a self-consciously global age?

This book is the product of a complex collaborative project; many individuals and institutions thus deserve thanks. The Project on Internationalizing the Study of American History involved seventy-eight scholars, both from the United States and abroad (listed in the appendix), and was a joint endeavor of New York University, through its International Center for Advanced Studies, and the Organization of American Historians. It received enthusiastic support, valuable suggestions, and generous funding from several foundations and institutions: The Gladys Kriebel Delmas Foundation, particularly Patricia La Balme; The Rockefeller Foundation, particularly Lynn Szwaja and Thomas Ybarra Frausto; The Ford Foundation, particularly Alison Bernstein and Toby Volkman; The Andrew W. Mellon Foundation, particularly Richard Ekman; the American Council of Learned Societies, particularly Stanley N. Katz and Steven Wheatley; and the Faculty of Arts and Sciences at NYU, particularly Philip Furmanski, dean of the faculty.

Holding the project's conferences outside of the United States seemed symbolically to make an important point about the value of stepping outside of the nation, if only temporarily, to write a fresher account of it. That fantasy became real, and pleasantly so, in 1997, when New York University welcomed the first of the series of conferences to its campus in Florence, Italy, the extraordinarily beautiful and peaceful Villa La Pietra. Surely the consistently good spirits of the conference, even when conflicting points of view were being proposed, owed something to the Tuscan sun, the delightful gardens of the villa, and the formal but comfortable meeting rooms where we spent the better part of our days. For this opportunity, I wish to thank especially the late Debra James, vice president of New York University, and Cecilia Guarnaccia at La Pietra itself.

David Thelen and Linda Kerber were quick to support the idea for this project when I first broached it, and they helped develop the first outline of the project, which was presented to the executive board of the Organization of American Historians. At the time this project began, Linda Kerber was president of the OAH, and I want to thank her both for her wise counsel at the beginning and her diplomatic skills at other times. Two past presidents and the two presidents-elect at the time of the establishment of the project were active and helpful participants, and I wish to thank Gary B. Nash, Eric Foner, George Fredrickson, and William H. Chafe. At the beginning, Arnita Jones was executive director of the OAH, and her assistance was unstinting and invaluable, as was that of John Dichtl in the OAH office. At the beginning of the project, I was NYU's dean for the humanities, and my assistant, Shirley Riddell, was indispensable in getting the work under way. At the International Center for Advanced Studies, I wish to thank Tanya Serdiuk, who helped with the logistics of the first conference; Saverio Giovacchini, for the second; Sula Haska, for the third; and Mark Elliott, for the fourth.

Mainly, however, I want to thank all of the participants. I have never participated in a single conference that was so consistently stimulating, let alone a series of four conferences. Special fields and approaches, different institutional locations and statuses, U.S. scholars and foreign scholars, research university faculty and community college and high school teachers, public historians, senior leaders and graduate students became an intellectual community, recognizing one another as equals at the conference table—historians all, serious, committed, and civil. From among the very large number of excellent papers presented at the various conferences, this book offers a selection that collectively and coherently represents the work of the project. But each discussion and each paper, written in a cumulative process, builds upon every other paper, and I want to thank the authors of both the papers in this book and those not included. All equally contributed to the success of the project, even if practicality dictated that only some of the papers could be published.

The chapters that follow do not cover all aspects of the issue of internationalization nor all the important themes and periods of American history. But they do cover a great deal, addressing many of the big issues in American historiography. The different sections have varying purposes and different work to do within the context of the whole volume. Parts 1 and 2 are the most theoretical. Moreover, they are for the most part statements of advocacy; they urge historians to consider a very different relationship to the nation and national history. The chapters in part 3 *do* rather than advocate. Put differently, they seek to exemplify the kind of history being urged in this volume. In part 4, there is a certain stepping back. If parts 1 and 2 are unreservedly promoting a new kind of history, the chapters in part 4 are cautionary, urging a moderate historiographical revolution. They raise hard questions about structures and constraints on change, and they warn against mischaracterizing traditional history and mistaking the dimensions of change. They reaffirm that the point here is not a postnational history but a richer and more historical narrative of the nation, more clearly distinguishing what is part of the national history but either large or smaller than the nation.

The historiographical innovations being proposed here are incremental and plural. The book does not advance a cut-and-burn approach to the historiographical past. The claim I would make for the volume is that it invites our colleagues to consider a new and important framing, or contextualization, for the history of the United States. It does not specify a single form for the new narratives implied by this reframing, but the ideas and examples it offers ought to provide sufficient orientation to those who recognize the present opportunity, and, I would argue, obligation, to think afresh about the relation of the narratives we present to audiences in the United States and abroad in our increasingly self-conscious global age.

Thomas Bender

INTRODUCTION

Historians, the Nation, and the Plenitude of Narratives

Thomas Bender

Lived history is embedded in a plenitude of narratives. Those narratives come in all sizes, shapes, and degrees of social and political consequence. Historiography necessarily reduces them, emphasizing those that seem more important, those that speak to us, while ignoring or marginalizing—and rightly so—the greater number of them. Of course, over time, different themes or concepts, different narratives, will be deemed significant and emphasized. These privileged narratives, at least on the scale that concerns me here, are in a vital way the product of a quite serious conversation between the historical experience of the present and the histories available in the past. The making of nations and national histories exemplifies this process.

The nation (like a national history) represents a particular narrative of social connection that celebrates a sense of having something in common. A history in common is fundamental to sustaining the affiliation that constitutes national subjects. The achievement of such a history, as Ernest Renan observed more than a century ago, in his classic essay on the nation, depends upon the capacity for disregarding. "Forgetting," he wrote in 1882, "is a crucial factor in the creation of a nation, which is why progress in historical study often constitutes a danger for nationality." Understanding the nation as a "historical result," Renan expected that it would have an end point as well as a beginning, but he did not imagine that its historical career would soon come to an end, and neither, a century later, do I.[1] Nor is it the purpose of this work to subvert the nation. But it does aim to rethink its nature and its relations to alternative solidarities and social connections. It seems important at this moment in our own history, when there is a heightened awareness of both transnational connections and particularistic solidarities, to explore those stories of our past, those experiences at scales other than the nation, that have been forgotten, that have been obscured by the emphasis upon the centrality of the nation in daily life and in historiography.

A brief look at the context of the earliest American national histories helps to locate this exploration. The first histories of the people who settled British North America were not national histories, and neither were the first postrevolutionary histories. The social entities chronicled in the published histories of the colonial era were the town, the colony, or, in some instances, Protestant Christianity. The language of nation was not yet available. Even after the Revolution of 1776 and the Treaty of Paris that ended it in 1783, American histories were local and state histories, not national histories. The first national history was published in 1789, the year of the inauguration of the new and distinctly nationalist Constitution. It was the work of David Ramsay, a Charleston physician who had earlier, in 1785, written *The History of the Revolution of South Carolina*. That the American national state was created in the same year Ramsay published the first national history, *The History of the American Revolution* (1789), followed by Mercy Otis Warren's *History of the Rise, Progress, and Termination of the American Revolution* in 1805 in Boston, is not merely coincidental. Nations are, among other things, a collective agreement, partly coerced, to affirm a common history as the basis for a shared future. The near assimilation of history to national history over the course of the two centuries following the invention of the modern nation-state is one of the major themes of this volume.

The conceptual and practical limitations of the notion of bounded unity claimed by the nation-state and revealed in histories framed by the national subject is a second theme. If part of the argument that follows insists that professional history assimilated the ideology of the nation into its basic working premises, it is especially important to recognize earlier insights into these limitations and to build upon them to construct a more generous framing of American history. And this brings us to the historical reflections of Frederick Jackson Turner.

Turner's speculations about alternative ways of narrating American history, including his penetrating critique of the nation as the self-contained unit of historical narration, have been overshadowed by his brilliant and poetic evocation of the frontier as the defining narrative of American history. Turner is pertinent in another way as well: he reveals the importance of openly bringing the present into conversation with the past in the work of establishing interpretive strategies that will speak to the historian's present. As is widely recognized, he wrote his famous essay as the present was being transformed by the closing of the frontier and the development of industrial capitalism. Later, he suggested that the urbanization increasingly evident in the 1920s, the decade when the majority of Americans for the first time lived in cities and towns, invited an urban interpretation of American history. But before the famous frontier essay, his awareness of developments that we now call globalization prompted him to insist that the history of any nation be contextualized on an international, even global scale.

A century after Turner, we find ourselves in a strikingly similar situation. We are aware, too, of what seems to be a fundamental shift in the geography of our national life. We are intensely aware today of the extraterritorial aspects of contemporary national life. The inherited framing of American national history does not seem to fit or connect us to these transnational and global developments. Inevitably, contemporary historiography is being inflected by a new awareness of subnational, transnational, and global political, economic, social, and cultural processes. These circumstances invite, even demand, a reconsideration of the American past from a perspective less tightly bound to perceptions of the nation as the container of American history. One can no longer believe in the nation as hermetically sealed, territorially self-contained, or internally undifferentiated. Nor can we take the nation so unproblematically to be the natural or exclusive unit of historical analysis or, for that matter, as the principle of organization for history departments and graduate training.

Having invoked Turner, I want to explore his historical reflections in more detail. Perhaps surprisingly, he provides an important starting point for the reframing of American history that this book proposes. His was a richly complex and playful historical intelligence. If in his famous address of 1893, he moved the profession in the direction of nationalist insularity and contributed to the twentieth-century development of the notion of American exceptionalism, in other places, less attended to by later historians, he had quite different historiographical suggestions, including one that points quite directly to the agenda of this volume.

Turner's address "The Significance of the Frontier in American History," picking up on long-standing popular American myth, reframed the narrative of American history in a new and compelling way.[2] The first generation of professional historians of the United States, including Turner's mentor at Johns Hopkins, Herbert Baxter Adams, had located the narrative of American history in the Atlantic world, partly and notably outside of the boundaries of the American nation. Adams and his colleagues offered what was essentially a genetic history, one that drew upon another ethnocentric American myth. The seeds of American democracy, they presumed, had first germinated in the communal life of the primitive forests of Germany, then sprouted in the medieval villages of Anglo-Saxon England, and finally produced town-meeting democracy when planted in the rocky but somehow fruitful soil of New England.

Turner directly challenged this historiography. He moved the focal point of historiography away from the Atlantic world to the interior. "The true point of view in the history of this nation," he wrote, "is not the Atlantic coast, it is the Great West."[3] Commentary on Turner has focused on the theory of democratic evolution he associated with the frontier experience and on his contribution to the notion of American exceptionalism. The implication is that he understood American history to be self-contained; perhaps his famous address was an example of midwestern isolationism.

In fact, Turner, whom I would readily compare with Marc Bloch, was never as trapped in his rhetoric as many of his epigoni were. He broke the Eurocentric genetic chain, but he did not thereby intend to isolate American history, a point recently made by Ian Tyrrell.[4] Two years earlier, in an essay with an even more portentous title, "The Significance of History," he outlined a vision of history that Bloch would echo a generation later. "In history," Turner observed, "there are only artificial divisions," whether one is speaking temporally or geographically, for

> not only is it true that no country can be understood without taking account of all the past; it is also true that we cannot select a stretch of land and say we will limit our study to this land; for local history can only be understood in the light of the history of the world. . . . To know the history of contemporary Italy we must know the history of contemporary France, of contemporary Germany. Each acts on each. Ideas, commodities even, refuse the bounds of a nation. All are inextricably connected, so that each is needed to explain the others. This is true especially in the modern world with its complex commerce and means of intellectual connection.[5]

Charles Beard and W. E. B. Du Bois, the other great American historians working at the turn of the century, can be quoted in much the same way. Not only were American intellectuals aware of the closing of the frontier, they were beginning to grasp the global dimensions of modern life and thus of history. The literary scholar Thomas Peyser argues, in fact, that "global thinking permeated the literature of the realist period to an extent that has not been appreciated, and, for the most part, not even noticed."[6]

In our own present, when we have such an immediate sense of global transformation, I want to propose a rethinking of the narrative of American history, to move from Turner's more famous essay to the less famous one from which I have just quoted. Our moment is not unlike his moment; it is at least as protean as the one a century ago when Turner pondered on American circumstances and sought to describe a past that could more effectively engage the present.

For all of his prescience in understanding the interconnections and relations at the heart of any history, there is a telling omission in Turner's prescription for writing Italian history. The United States (and the Americas more generally) are not mentioned. But the Americas provide an essential component of Italian history. The creation of the Atlantic economy in the centuries following discovery of the New World by a Genoese navigator seeking the very old civilizations of the East displaced the Italian city-states—Venice was no longer the hinge of Europe, and Florence lost its position as the financial center of Europe.

In the 1890s, even as Turner wrote, agricultural developments in California impelled Italians into the Atlantic migration system, and had it not been for the explosive growth of the economy of Buenos Aires between 1890 and World War I, even more migrants from various parts of Italy would have arrived in New York, San Francisco, and other North American cities. To further elaborate on this point: massive international investment in Argentine railroads and other industries, mostly from Britain, but also from the United States, created extraordinarily rapid development and infrastructure construction, which produced a voracious market for unskilled labor. Without this movement of global capital, there would have been much less demand for labor in Buenos Aires, and the pattern of Italian immigration to the United States and elsewhere would have been different. It is important for our understanding of U.S. and Italian history to know that not all Italian immigrants came to the United States, or even to the Americas. In the 1890s, more Italians emigrated to France and Germany than to the United States.[7] And it is important to Italian as well as to American history that in going abroad Italy's peasants added to older village and regional identities the new one of Italian. On that basis, they became Italian Americans and simultaneously reinforced the developing Italian nationalism in the still new Italian republic. The experience of the peasants who migrated to France was different; they soon became French, just like contemporary French peasants who were being transformed by the cultural and bureaucratic policies of a centralizing state.[8] From this brief account, I trust that one can readily see that American history rather quickly gets bigger, more complicated, and more entangled in other histories.

My intention in stressing this disconnect on the part of Turner is to make an important point about American self-perceptions. In both academic and popular thought and in policy there is a tendency to remove the United States from the domain of the international. America is "here," and the international is "over there." If there is a practical aim in this enterprise of rethinking and deprovincializing the narrative of American history, it is to integrate the stories of American history with other, larger stories from which, with a kind of continental self-sufficiency, the United States has isolated itself.

My argument and that of this book is not for increasing the study of American foreign relations, although that is important. The point is that we must understand every dimension of American life as entangled in other histories. Other histories are implicated in American history, and the United States is implicated in other histories. This is not only true of this present age of globalization; it has been since the fifteenth century, when the world for the first time became self-consciously singular.

This means that American historians should be deeply involved in the current discussions about rethinking area studies. Such engagement is required to overcome the unhappy assumption that unites Americanists and area studies specialists. Both agree that "international" is everything that is not the United States. Without undoing this bifurcation that separates United States and the world, one has only the most distorted notion of the national history of the United States and very little historical foundation for understanding the contemporary relationship of the United States to transnational and global developments. We have yet to catch up with the writer in New York's *Journal of Commerce* who noted in 1898, an apt year for the comment, that "we are part of abroad."

For reasons of history, the history of our own profession, it is difficult for historians to make the move this volume advocates. The nation-state was from the start adopted by modern historiography as the natural unit of analysis, and the work of the historical profession was institutionalized as the study of past politics, a charter inscribed on the wall of Herbert Baxter Adams's famous Seminar Room at Johns Hopkins.

Well before Leopold von Ranke established the parameters of professional history, the nation had captured history. As early as the sixteenth century, with the emergence of secular history, the nation became the measure of development. Even Voltaire, who approached history as civilizational, could not help resorting to the French state of Louis XIV as "the implicit point of reference for his universal history."[9]

But it was in the nineteenth century that history, as a professional discipline, and the nation, as the new and dominant form of political subjectivity and power, established a tight connection that amounted to collaboration. With the founding of research universities in Europe and, in a more complicated way, in the United States, historians and humanities scholars produced national histories and certified national literatures and cultures, which in turn helped to sustain the project of making the modern nation-state.[10] Modern historiography, as Prasenjit Duara has observed, collaborated in enabling "the nation-state to define the framework of its self-understanding."[11]

Earlier uses of the nation in history had given it a broad significance as a carrier of something larger than itself: the collective progress of mankind. Ranke retained some allegiance to the notion of a universal history of progress, but his influence was otherwise. National histories became far more specific; the nation became the locus of differentiation and antagonism in a system of nations. When in this context the nation became the unit of politics and history, time within the international system became singular, and internal differences within the national territory were masked.[12] To the degree that European and American historians (and the public) were committed to evolutionary theories (and the commitment was considerable), place in time distinguished historical from nonhistorical societies. One could even say that this temporal difference was spatialized. Those peoples not organized in nations—referring mainly to colonies of European powers—were not only outside of the system of nations, they were outside of its understanding of "normal" time, or put differently, they were "backward," even though they were contemporary and entangled with the imperial powers.[13]

With these developments, the world was divided between history and anthropology: history taking those peoples organized into nations, with literatures and archives, leaving for anthropology all differently organized peoples, reduced to historical nonentities. The reframing of history being proposed here reflects in part the dissolution of that division between history and ethnology, both as method and as domain of study.

Professional history in the United States (and in Europe and Latin America) was institutionalized as a cultural investment in the work of modern nation-building. That work made resources available and gave the profession standing. As William McNeill has emphasized, history "got into the classroom. . . to make nations out of peasants, out of localities, out of human raw material that existed in the countries of Europe and in the not so very United States as well."[14]

The professional practice of history writing and teaching flourished as the handmaiden of nation-making; the nation provided both support and an appreciative audience. There was a problem in this arrangement, however. Only recently and because of the uncertain status of the nation-state has it been recognized that history as a professional discipline is part of its own substantive narrative and not at all sufficiently self-conscious about the implications of that circularity. Recent political and cultural changes have weakened the role of the nation and of national histories in the making of identities and in the management of socioeconomic activities, and this enables (and demands) more self-reflection than historians have heretofore given it.

In saying this, I do not mean to propose that historians became apologists for the modern state. In some sense, they were apologists for the nation as the proper instrument for the formation of historical subjectivity, but they were not thereby apologists for *their* particular nation, although, of course, we can all think of some historians who could be so charged. In fact, historians were often critics of the nation—hence the importance of the archive in the professional ideology of history. Empowered by the archive, historians could speak the truth to official power, as Beard did when he turned to treasury records to make his critique of the Supreme Court's sacralization of the Constitution in the Progressive Era. But now, after more than a century's duration, the marriage of the profession to the nation increasingly has the feel of a tie that binds.

History in Christian, Jewish, and Islamic cultures has always been linear, always beginning with a beginning. Both this linearity and the emphasis on origins has a cost. "All narrative history," François Furet argued, "is a succession of origin events."[15] Such histories are almost inevitably teleological, with a beginning and an ending (the present, or, sometimes, an envisioned future). The work of aligning the beginning and ending tends to screen much out, to narrow the history, to reduce the plenitude of stories. Deprovincializing the narrative of American history may require displacing the focus on origins and allowing a greater spatialization of historical narrative. We might attend to Herman Melville's description of the history he will tell in his resoundingly and probably intentionally unsuccessful novel, *Pierre, or, The Ambiguities* (1852): "This history goes forward and goes backward, as occasion calls. Nimble center, circumference elastic you must have."[16]

A history liberated from origins would, I think, historicize the axis of time itself, emphasizing structure, transformation, and relations (temporal and spatial). Attention to the relational aspects of historical phenomena is the key, and it differentiates this approach from most comparative history, which not only tends to reaffirm the nation as a natural category but, more important, seldom explores causal links between the two national experiences being compared.[17] One must explore interactions between social units of varying scales.

In seeking a respatialization of historical narrative in a way that will liberate us from the enclosure of the nation, it is important that we avoid imprisoning ourselves in another limiting conceptual box. Rather than shifting our focus from the nation to some other social/territorial unit, we would do better to imagine a spectrum of social scales, both larger and smaller than the nation and not excluding the nation. We must think of them not as inert points on a scalar axis, but as social worlds interacting with one another and thus providing multiple contexts for lives, institutions, and ideas.

In all of this, moreover, it is important to remember that one of the most persistent points of political contestation in American history has turned on precisely the question of what is "outside" and what is "inside," whether one is speaking of global traders, new media and popular culture, diasporic populations, peoples of particular class standing, or groups marked by distinctive cultural practices and heritages or by supposed racial phenotypes.

Our discipline is defined by time; perhaps, as a result, we do not question the historicity of time itself. In historicizing space, one inevitably historicizes time. To deprovincialize American history, we must learn to juggle the variables of time and space, to genuinely historicize both temporal and spatial relations.[18]

As the geographical terrain of history expands, time is pluralized. Indeed, if one looks closely, one discovers that there are different temporal rhythms both within the conventional boundary of the nation and beyond it. Our uncritical—and ahistorical—acceptance of the nation as a historical unit, the only historical unit, blinds us to these differences and relationships. We must take seriously the observation of Ernst Bloch: "Not all people exist in the same now. They do so externally, through the fact that they can be seen today. But they are thereby not yet living at the same time with each other."[19]

History thus becomes a complex weaving together of all coexisting histories.[20] For instance, with the creation of the Euro-Afro-American Atlantic world in the seventeenth and eighteenth centuries, a variety of histories— all with different narratives and temporal signifiers and significances— came into contact. It looked then—and does today to most historians— like a single system, but it was in fact a series of histories sharing space, relating to one another, often with causal consequences, but not assimilating one to the other.[21]

One sees this process and pattern in the first published narrative of an African enslaved in the newly constructed Atlantic world. Olaudah Equiano experienced not only loss of freedom but spatial and temporal change as he moved through the Atlantic world. He was taken forcibly from a particular place with a particular history, with its own scales of time and historical narratives; enslaved by Europeans whose lives were elaborations of other narratives with different temporal expectations; and he labored for ship captains and colonial planters. In all of these different locations, the temporal structure of life was distinct.[22] Or look at it from the European perspective: for them, time was European, or metropolitan, or Christian; Africans, at least in European eyes, were outside of those narratives and structures of time. The recent global millennium celebration, marked as it was by striking unities and diversities of timescales, provides a graphic example of the point I wish to make here.

Preparing ourselves for such a history demands that we explore more than we have the relations of time and space, and our relation to them, not only in the narratives we construct but also in our professional lives. If we historicize the nation, make it an object of inquiry instead of our professional platform, we may have to think more than we have about our audience, about who will pay the bill. (Historicizing our national platform is not unlike sawing off the branch upon which we are sitting.) We cannot be complacent. The extreme form of market values justified by the ideology of globalization frees individuals and governments not only from the obligation of addressing the consequences of unregulated capitalism but also from responsibility for sustaining culture and scholarship. We have, therefore, very practical reasons for trying to understand the dynamic of contemporary history.

While the aim here is to move beyond the uncritical acceptance of the nation as both the "natural" unit for historical study and the "natural audience" for historical work, this is not a plea for a postnational history. This volume is not intended as the obituary of national history; it argues instead for the value of "thickening" the history of the United States, making it both more complex and truer to lived experience and the historical record.

The result, I think, will be a richer understanding of the nation, with some sense of its importance in relation to other forms of social unity. To use an image that does not come naturally to me, it will clarify significance by sorting factors as in a multiple regression analysis. Or to provide a historical example, it opens up important questions too rarely pondered: Did foreign missionaries from the United States in the nineteenth century identify themselves (to themselves and to others) as Americans, as Anglo-American Christians, as Protestants, as heirs of the Puritans, or as the advance guard of civilization and modernity? A tight national narrative does not invite this sort of question, but once the frame is opened it is an obvious—and obviously important—question.

Can we imagine an American historical narrative that situates the United States more fully in its larger transnational and intercultural global context? Can such a narrative reveal more clearly than the histories we have at present the plenitude of stories, timescales, and geographies that constitute the American past? Can we historicize the nation itself in such a way that its historical career and its making and unmaking of identities, national and otherwise, can be better understood outside of itself, as part of a larger history than that of the bounded nation?

One important step in this direction is greater curiosity about the nation itself. A nation is grounded in an agreement, partly coerced, partly voluntary, to find significant unity in diverse personal memories and public historical narratives. Both as the foundation and as the product of that agreement, the nation is a field of social practices, all imbued with power of varying magnitudes and types, that are brought into some continuing relation, practically and imaginatively. Although it is true, as Renan pointed out, that the nation is a "daily plebiscite," once created, the nation has great powers for reproducing itself, for it has the power, partially, not completely, to shape future social practices and identities in the space it claims and seeks to delimit.[23]

The capacity of the nation to frame time and space is not inherent; it is a historical variable. Nor can the nation contain all the narratives that shape the subjectivities of those within its formal bounds, although in historically specific instances, it may well fairly claim to contain the more important ones. The task of historians is to look for the ties that bind a multiplicity of historical narratives to one another under the canopy of American history, even as they explore ways these histories connect the United States to histories outside of its bounds—sensitive in both instances of seams and fissures in the surface unity. The nation thus becomes a partially bounded historical entity imbricated in structures and processes that connect to every part of the world. Too fixed a notion of the nation will obscure all of these vital aspects of history and of historical understanding.

The historian needs to be a cosmopolitan. For that to happen, both historiography and the historian have to restore some sense of strangeness, of unfamiliarity, to American historical experience. American historiography has become too familiar, too technical and predictable. One aim of destabilizing the nation must be to defamiliarize the stories that make up American history, thus inviting a fresh curiosity that is not prompted by the ever more refined and increasingly technical analyses of long-established themes and questions.

The true cosmopolitan must cultivate a doubleness that allows both commitment and distance, an awareness at once of the possible distance of the self and of the possibility of dialogical knowledge of the other. Put differently, it is an error to think of the cosmopolitan as one who is comfortable in the world at large; rather, the cosmopolitan is always aware of the world's unfamiliarity, always slightly uncomfortable, even at home. The nation, its parts, and its surroundings thus become objects of inquiry, objects of a richer curiosity. In this spirit, Tzetvan Todorov has observed: "The man who holds his country sweet is only a raw beginner; the man for whom each country is as his own is already strong; but only the man for whom the whole world is a foreign country is perfect."[24]

The orientation to American history being proposed here has some obvious connections to a number of theoretical positions associated with the harder social sciences on the one side and cultural studies on the other, and it is important for us to both learn from those theories and seek to historicize the discussion of them. But this project, while informed by those theoretical positions, is not driven by them. The argument and method for this history converge in a commitment to be empirical. Historians, we are arguing, will be doing better history by being diligently empirical, accepting no artificial boundaries as they carefully follow the movement of people, capital, things, and knowledges across national and other boundaries. The aim is verisimilitude, no more, no less.

The task before such a new history is to notice the evidence of trans-nationalisms previously overlooked or filtered out by historians. For example, close examination of the Harlem press in the era of World War I reveals frequent discussion of and intense interest in Irish nationalism and the Easter Rebellion. An assumption that African-American intellectual life is bounded by Harlem, by the black community, or by the national borders of the United States is all too likely to define such discussions as extraneous, making for the all too common tendency to pass over such accounts. To do that is to shrink the territory occupied by black intellectuals, and it also misses a clue to a more complex history of the relationship between African Americans and the Irish in America.

If globalization powerfully shapes our own time and our sense of contemporary history, it is important to capture the imaginative space it offers for historical reflection. But it is important to remember, too, that the danger of recapture is real. It will do historiography no good to work free of the nation and its ideology only to embrace the ideology and process of globalization. Such a move promises new blindnesses, and there is, besides, the danger of complicity, conscious or not, in a triumphalism that justifies the current phase of capitalism.

Finally, in case there is any misunderstanding, this volume is not in any way a brief for writing global histories. The point is not to displace the monograph, only to thicken the layers of context it incorporates. Nor does this volume propose a dismissal of the nation as a concern, even a central concern, for historical analysis. The aim is to contextualize the nation.

This book originated in a series of four conferences, and the table of contents roughly reflects the sequence of issues that organized them. It begins with the question of the nation, moving to theoretical issues raised by questioning the nation as the sole and complete container of a national history, then providing examples of reinterpretations of major issues and themes in American history, and concluding with an examination (undertaken mainly by foreign historians of the United States) of the sociology of the professional practice of historians, identifying constraints on innovation, both unavoidable and voluntary.

Part 1, "Historicizing the Nation," begins with Prasenjit Duara's essay on the limits and distortions that can arise from framing histories too tightly as national narratives. Duara, whose historical work has been on modern

China, is concerned, to borrow a phrase from the title of one of his books, "to rescue history from the nation." History and the nation, he argues, historically mutually constituted each other, and the historian must stand outside of this process in order to obtain some perspective on the ways in which history makes national subjects and the ways in which the nation structures (he would say captures) historical thinking. The ideology of the nation-state threatens to enclose historiography in a way that in fact dehistoricizes the nation. By looking at the regional literature of the "borderlands" of the United States and of World War II Manchuria, Duara shows how complex the relationship between culture, place, politics, and nation is.

In the following essay, Akira Iriye begins on the terrain of the international and what he calls international history in order to insist that, paradoxically as it may seem, it is necessary to internationalize the study of international relations. He makes the important and increasingly influential point that while some social relations beyond a given nation are state-centered, many are not. Restricting the study of international relations to the relations of sovereign states misses a great deal of national, transnational, and international political, economic, and cultural history.

In an essay rich in both theory and description, Michael Geyer and Charles Bright, neither of whom is an Americanist and both of whom have written important essays on world and global history, theorize the global context and locate United States history in it. They explain that one must take care not to assimilate national history to the global, which is, in fact, not complete, universal, and totalizing. The task is to find historiographical space that treats the national and the global as separate processes but reveals, better than established narratives do, the manifold interactions between them and the imbrications of the one with the other. To illustrate their point, they focus on three historical configurations of American sovereignty. They elaborate the centrality of the production of a sovereign territory in the nineteenth century, the extension of the territory of production in the industrial era, and the partial deterritorialization of civil society since World War II. Referring consistently but carefully to what they call "off-shore America," which consists of both the imaginary and the practical, they establish the embeddedness of American history in contexts larger than itself and explore some of the implications of that historical condition not only for the United States but for other parts of the world.

The work of historicizing the nation invites closer examination of actual geographies of social practice and raises the issue of a pluralization of temporalities. Not only do historians tend to bound and homogenize space in their embrace of the nation as the container of history, but they also assume that time is singular. These issues are addressed in part 2, "New Historical Geographies and Temporalities."

Karen Kupperman shows that in early American history, the boundaries that we honor with the rubric "American history" were meaningless, and that in the territory now so labeled, there were groups speaking hundreds of languages, in hundreds of polities, mingling and contesting with one another. She reminds us, too, that Europe and Africa could be similarly described at the time. The Atlantic world was not yet organized by nation-state. In fact, she argues, the development of an Atlantic focus hastened national consolidations and national consciousness on both sides of the Atlantic. The nations of the Atlantic world were thus formed by and formed internationalism. Kupperman argues forcefully that one misses the dynamic of early American history if the colonies and settlements are assumed to be self-contained and self-sufficient, tied absolutely to their sponsoring colonial authorities. In showing such a terrain of complex interaction, she undermines the deeply embedded notion that the story of America is that of westering. More important, she would argue, were the many vectors of interaction that made the space that became the United States international from the beginning.

Robin D. G. Kelley recovers a vision of African-American history as an Atlantic story, not merely an American one. He argues that such a reframing of African-American history significantly remaps American history, not merely in the era of slavery but through its whole extent. American history is not only embedded in the world of the African diaspora, but Europe and the notion of the West were defined in part by their relations to Africa. The Atlantic world, Kelley argues, was the product of the historical interactions of the peoples of Europe, Africa, and the Americas, and many of the big questions have to do with the implications of that movement and the resulting contests and accommodations. Without overstating the capacity of a diasporic approach to American history generally, he shows how central the theme is to the American experience.

In a theoretically rich essay, Walter Johnson focuses on African-American history in its Atlantic context. But he probes a different implication of the geographical expansion of American history, showing that when one situates slavery in such a transnational, even global perspective, the historian must confront a pluralization of time. There are, by implication, many temporalities, many histories sharing the space of the Atlantic world. Although different participants in that world find themselves in common places, interacting with one another, that does not necessarily mean that they are temporally or narratively in the same place, and national narratives may in fact produce a convergence or even unity that distorts actual experience, in possibly significant ways. National histories generally do not question the structure of time. As a result, they often and silently privilege the temporal structure of modernity, a historical move so thick with political and moral implications that it ought not go unnoticed, as it tends to be. Johnson exposes this issue. At the same time, his essay opens up the unattended and profoundly important connection between time and space in historiography generally.

Ian Tyrrell suggests that American historiography is more deeply rooted in Europe than actual American experience has been, and that, as a result, most gestures in the direction of comparison, explicit or implicit, or transnational history have looked too exclusively toward Europe. While he recognizes the enrichment of context represented by recent formulations of the Atlantic world that include Africa and the southern part of the Americas, he points out other transnational patterns that point in the other direction, toward the Pacific. Building upon his own recent work in environmental history, which cannot be contained by the nation, he elaborates a model based on settler societies and staple economies for writing U.S. history that is calibrated to several scales, extending to the global.

The essays in parts 2 and 3 criticize traditional national narratives; explore theoretical issues of time, space, and narrativity; and propose directions out of the nation as container. But most obviously they are advocacy statements, urging a reframing and recontextualizing American history. The essays in part 3, "Opening the Frame," do the work being proposed. They are in intention exemplary. They examine large themes, issues, or periods through a wider lens, one fashioned by the advocacy and theoretical propositions of the first two parts. Here we see the rudiments of a new kind of history in operation.

So much immigration history has been written on the assumption that there were only two points on the compass, the point of origin and the port of New York (or some other American port), that we have too little sense of the *system(s)* of migration that in fact encompassed the globe. The capitalist quest for cheap labor (both free and unfree) combined with the pursuit of work (and freedom) by ordinary people sustained two Atlantic systems (one linked to Africa, one to Europe) and a Pacific one. There was also a systemic movement from the south to the north within the Americas. It is impossible to grasp the meaning of the immigrant experience in America outside of the framing provided by those systems and without comparing the reception and possibilities of different groups at their various destinations. These systems work at the global, regional, national, local, neighborhood, and even workplace levels, and all of these interact. It is not at all clear that the nation is the most important of these scales at all times. Often the most relevant factors structuring lives are nonstate and transnational ones, such as family economies and culture. Dirk Hoerder, in an extraordinarily rich and ambitious essay, sketches this larger history, which, without denying the nation reveals a history that could be called a peoples' history or, better, a history of peoples.

For Robert Wiebe, the issues of democracy, nationalism, and socialism are Atlantic-wide, not strictly national. He examines their careers in the United States comparatively and as part of a larger social history of the Atlantic world. Like Hoerder's study of migration, Wiebe frames an American topic in a context and a process larger than the nation. The result is a fresh interpretation not only of these global themes but of American democracy. In Wiebe's view, democracy, nationalism, and socialism are different ways of organizing a society's solidarities. As mechanisms of solidarity, they were made essential by massive demographic and social transformations (population increase, migrations, urbanization, etc.) first felt in the Atlantic world. Wiebe thus makes it possible to compare different national resolutions (comparative history) within a larger frame of experience that is eventually shared globally.

American Progressivism and the American welfare state are often seen as examples of American uniqueness or exceptionalism, and the greater part of the historiography treats their emergence as the result of local circumstances. Yet if one looks, as Daniel Rodgers does, at the agenda-setting general ideas about the crisis of industrial capitalism and unregulated urban development rather than looking at specific policy outcomes that tend to accent national distinctions, one sees an international conversation.[25] The United States was a participant in this conversation, offering important examples in the field of public education, mass production, and mass consumption. But the relationship was asymmetrical; the United States received more ideas than it gave to the Atlantic world of reform. In the nineteenth century, the United States had seemed to be at the cutting edge of history, revealing a democratic future for Europe and perhaps the world, as Tocqueville most famously proposed. In the age of social politics, however, the United States was, as Theodore Roosevelt observed, backward. To the confusion of many, the "Tortoise of Europe" had somehow "outdistanced the hare." But, of course, having "foreign experiment stations" was of great benefit to Progressive and, later, New Deal reformers. After 1945, the terms of the transatlantic (and increasingly global) conversation shifted, and the United States again claimed the mantle of modernity (as well as superior firepower).

Social politics in the Atlantic world in the past century has been complex: at once a common conversation and a set of diverse outcomes. Opening the frame, as Rodgers does, revises the usual understanding of the movement and appropriation of ideas ("influence"), a point with significant implications for the writing of intellectual history.

The second half of the twentieth century, when the United States was a global power, possessed of unprecedented power by the last decade of the century, might seem the easiest and most appropriate place to frame American history in global terms. In fact, it is more difficult; one must take care to avoid a simplistic whiggism and to ensure that those who lack American global power are not erased from history. One of the arguments of this volume is that the history of the United States has always been connected to the whole globe, but that since 1945 it has held a dominant position, a preponderance of power, in these relations. It requires a very subtle and sensitive history, and that is precisely what Marilyn Young provides in her essay, examining not only the American side of these connections but the impacts and responses—resistance, victimization, accommodation—at the receiving end of American power. The global history of the United States that she outlines is thus dynamic, dialogic, and morally focused.

Rob Kroes examines American cultural imperialism from, as he puts it, "the receiving end." He offers an appraisal of the capacity of the United States to project itself abroad, touching every nation on the globe. He recuperates the notion of American exceptionalism, but he makes it historically specific, examining the international collaboration that has constructed America as a global imaginative entity. The pervasiveness of this imaginative America makes the global position of the United States a "semiotic center," with all other nations in the position of being at least part-time receivers. Yet his carefully nuanced account makes an important additional point. If American cultural exports have been pervasive and powerful, they have not all been unmodified. Foreign consumers of imaginary and material objects of American origin have appropriated them in locally distinct, often surprising ways. Reception was situated, and the arrival of both the perturbations and opportunities presented by American commercial culture invited playfulness as often as simple consumption or resistance.

Having argued the case for reframing American history and having provided some successful examples, the volume concludes with more ambiguous statements. There are many aspects of historical practice that are worrisome, not simply in relation to reframing the narrative of American history, but in general. Still, there are distinctive questions or problems for those who would write a more transnational, relational, even global history of the United States. Interestingly, these more hesitant essays are all but one by foreign scholars. Their hesitation is not so much about the aspiration; rather, they doubt whether the inward-looking and self-referential aspects of American historiography can easily be overcome. The one American in part 4, David Hollinger, a self-consciously cosmopolitan historian, remains uncertain about just how far one should move from established professional practice and from the nation as the focus of history and contemporary life.

François Weil of France argues that we shall not be reading the obituary of national histories, American or otherwise, anytime soon. Indeed, he believes that to flourish, national and transnational histories need to be in a contrapuntal relation to each other. Still, he notes a strong parochialism in American historiography. This insularity, he argues, is structural, ideo-logical, and professional, not a general resistance to foreign historical con-cepts, and he notes that Americanists have been avid borrowers of specific methods from abroad. For him, the distinguishing quality of the American historical profession—and of U.S. Americanists in particular—is its scale, what he calls its "continentalism." This condition, a fortunate one in many respects, less happily encourages a sense of insular self-sufficiency or self-enclosure. Scale also facilitates a remarkable degree of specialization that cannot be matched or even easily followed by foreign colleagues. Together, self-referentiality and specialization deprive American history of foreign audiences. The unexpected result is that despite their quantity and mani-fest quality, American historical writings on U.S. history have had surpris-ingly little influence abroad.

Where Weil emphasizes continentalism and its consequences, Winfried Fluck, writing from Germany, examines the highly competitive character of American professional disciplines. As with Tocqueville's more general comments on American culture, Fluck notes the way competition and pu-tative equality promote the assertion of small differences to distinguish oneself, to mark one's own difference. The result for academic culture is a stress upon an originality that stresses its separation from, not argument with, different or adjacent interpretations. The consequent pattern of re-lentless redescription not only produces fragmentation but reduces con-text, treating it as a hindrance to originality, which in turn works against synthesis. But context and some level of commitment to the synthetic view are both essential to the historiographical revisionism proposed in this vol-ume. These qualities of American academic culture draw upon and affirm what Fluck calls "expressive individualism." It is this set of academic values, not substantive narratives of American history, that, according to Fluck, travel to academic cultures abroad, largely because of their modern and seemingly democratic promise of self-realization.

Ironically, then, if Fluck is correct, the increasingly global distribution of American academic culture may undermine the strong sense of contex-tualization central to the project of internationalizing the study of Ameri-can history. Yet there is another possibility: by so dramatically changing the terrain of American history and historiography, and by making it so unfa-miliar, the project might promote a new and invigorating curiosity, some-thing Fluck sees as having evaporated in the hothouse of American-style academic careerism.

Approaching the theme of internationalization as a "wary beneficiary of the new openness" to foreign scholarship and transnational perspectives, Ron Robin of Israel is uneasy with much of the ideology of what he calls a postnationalist perspective, evident in some versions of internationaliza-tion. The postnationalists seem to treat the nation as a thing more fixed and unified than it in fact is. Nor does this position attend to the temporal implications of the spatial reconfiguration it proposes. But more worrisome yet to Robin is a quality he ascribes to the postnationalist impulse: a refusal of all enclosure, not only the nation, but even the claims of professionalism. Turning from ideology to practice, he takes a quite different, but still skeptical look. He suggests that in fact most internationalism among Americanists is still driven by questions and concerns internal to U.S. history. His critique is not of the idea of internationalism but of elements of present ideology and practice that suggest, at least to him, a revolution manqué. In the end, however, he affirms a wider, more generous, and vibrant "borderless exchange of ideas and concepts."

In the essay that concludes the volume, David Hollinger urges caution in rethinking the nation and national histories. Endorsing a public role and responsibility for the historian in the politics of the nation, he urges what he calls a modest charter for a more cosmopolitan history. He reaffirms the danger of being used by the nation, but he warns that the ambition to escape the nation and the traditions of professional historiography has its own dangers. Worried about a tendency toward absolute dichotomies in some of the rhetoric surrounding new ways of writing history, Hollinger makes a careful argument for nation-centered histories *and* for strategies for recontextualizing the national focus, providing a variety of examples that historicize nation-making.

American historians of the United States, Hollinger notes, inevitably have an awkward relationship to their subject matter and to their fellow citizens, an awkwardness signaled, perhaps, by the cumbersomeness of the descriptive phrase that begins this sentence. That awkwardness, I would argue, may in fact be a heretofore unrealized asset. It contributes to the work of making American history strange again; it can be the prompt and object of a fresh curiosity. It makes us, or it can make us, more conscious of our narrative choices, more thoughtful in our definition of contexts, more aware of the continuing importance of the nation, even as we realize the historicity of the nation.

The death of the nation, like Mark Twain's, has been announced too soon. It is not about to disappear, and as long as the nation is granted the exclusive power to make citizens and protect their rights and to deploy legitimate violence, it must be a matter of continued and intense scrutiny. But it is not bounded by its own self-definition.

The agenda being offered here does not propose a postnational history, but rather an enriched national history, one that draws in and draws together more of the plenitude of narratives available to the historian who would try to make sense of the American past. If history is a discipline whose claims to knowledge consist in locating events, ideas, things, and persons in explanatory contexts, we must be more aggressive than we have been in following the extension of historical contexts spatially and temporally, at least insofar as they carry the promise of interpretive significance.

NOTES

1. Ernest Renan, "What Is a Nation?" in *Nation and Narration,* ed. Homi K. Bhabha (New York, 1990), 11.

2. On the foreground of Turner's essay, see Henry Nash Smith, *Virgin Land: The American West as Symbol and Myth* (Cambridge, Mass., 1950).

3. Frederick Jackson Turner, "The Significance of the Frontier in American History," in id., *Frontier and Section: Selected Essays* (Englewood Cliffs, N.J., 1961), 38.

4. Ian Tyrrell, "Making Nations / Making States: American Historians in the Context of Empire," *Journal of American History* 86 (1999): 1015–44.

5. Turner, "The Significance of History," in *Frontier and Section*, 20–21.

6. Thomas Peyser, *Utopia and Cosmopolis: Globalization in the Era of American Literary Realism* (Durham, N.C., 1998), x. See Charles A. Beard, *Readings in American Government and Politics* (New York, 1909), and, at least for this very early period, the dissertation of W. E. B. Du Bois, *The Suppression of the African Slave-Trade to the United States of America, 1638-1870* (New York, 1896), and his "Careers Open to College-Bred Negroes" (Commencement Address, Fisk University, June 1898), in *W. E. B. Du Bois: Writings* (New York, 1996), 827–41.

7. *Economist,* January 8, 2000, p. 83.

8. See Eugen Weber, *Peasants into Frenchmen: The Modernization of Rural France, 1870–1914* (Stanford, Calif., 1976).

9. François Furet, *In the Workshop of History,* trans. Jonathan Mandelbaum (Chicago, 1984), 69.

10. On the connection between the humanities and the nation, see Bill Readings, *The University in Ruins* (Cambridge, Mass., 1996), esp. 1–53. For some account of the role of the social sciences in this work, see Peter Taylor, "Embedded Statism and the Social Sciences: Opening Up to New Spaces," *Environment and Planning A* 28, 11 (1996):1917–28. See also Gulbenkian Commission on the Restructuring of the Social Sciences, *Open the Social Sciences* (Stanford, Calif., 1996).

11. Prasenjit Duara, "Historicizing National Identity, or, Who Images What, and When," in *Becoming National: A Reader,* ed. Geoff Eley and Ronald G. Suny (New York, 1996), 151.

12. See Tyrrell, "Making Nations / Making States," 1020–21.

13. For a particularly insightful and thoughtful historiographical and philosophical examination of European and colonial relations, see Dipesh Chakrabarty, *Provincializing Europe: Postcolonial Thought and Historical Difference* (Princeton, N.J., 2000), esp. 3–23.

14. Quoted in Joyce Appleby, "The Power of History," *American Historical Review* 103 (1998): 10.

15. Furet, *In the Workshop of History,* 55–56.

16. Herman Melville, *Pierre, or, The Ambiguities* (1852; New York, 1964), 79.

17. For two recent comparative histories that are *not* subject to his criticism, see James T. Campbell, *Songs of Zion: The African Methodist Episcopal Church in the United States and South Africa* (New York, 1995); and Ian Tyrrell, *True Gardens of the Gods: Californian-Australian Environmental Reform, 1860–1930* (Berkeley and Los Angeles, 1999). For an important essay on this issue, see Fred Cooper, "Race, Ideology, and the Perils of Comparative History," *American Historical Review* 101 (1996): 1122–38.

18. This echoes the call of Fernand Braudel in "History and the Social Sciences: The Long Term," in *The Varieties of History: From Voltaire to the Present,* ed. Fritz Stern (1956; rev. ed., New York, 1973), esp. 405–6.

19. Ernst Bloch, "Nonsynchronism and the Obligation to Its Dialectics," *New German Critique* 11 (1977): 22. I am taking this quotation for its descriptive power, for its recognition that beneath a seeming homogeneous surface, different temporalities may exist. This limited use separates the quotation from the specific argument about German history and capitalism in which it is embedded.

20. In a different context, Braudel made this point. Braudel, "History and the Social Sciences," 414.

21. See, e.g., Ira Berlin, *Many Thousands Gone: The First Two Centuries of Slavery in North America* (Cambridge, Mass., 1998); Peter Linebaugh and Marcus Rediker, *The Many-Headed Hydra: Sailors, Slaves, Commoners, and the Hidden History of the Revolutionary Atlantic* (Boston, 2000).

22. *The Classic Slave Narratives,* ed. Henry Louis Gates Jr. (New York, 1987), 1–182.

23. Renan, "What Is a Nation," 19.

24. Tzetvan Todorov, *La conquête de l'Amérique: La question de l'autre* (Paris, 1982), trans. Richard Howard as *The Conquest of America: The Question of the Other* (New York, 1984), 250. The history of this statement reveals something of the making of a cosmopolitan sensibility, which cannot be replicated, but it does suggest some of the continuing value of travel, something that should be much more encouraged for Americanists. Todorov, a Bulgarian living in Paris, took it from Edward Said, a Palestinian long a resident of New York, who took it from Eric Auerbach, a refugee German Jew living in Istanbul.

25. One should note that in a very important study of key progressive and social democratic intellectuals in Europe and America much the same point was made by James T. Kloppenberg, *Uncertain Victory: Social Democracy and Progressivism in European and American Thought, 1870–1920* (New York, 1986).

PART I

Historicizing the Nation

ONE

Transnationalism and the Challenge to National Histories

Prasenjit Duara

Speaking *grosso modo,* linear history was from the late nineteenth century until recently intimately identified with the nation in a process of mutual formation. Naturalizing the nation-state as the skin that contains the experience of the past has made history the major means of national identity formation. To be sure there have been many historians, such as Toynbee and Spengler, whose vision has risen above the nation. In the twentieth century, Marxists and historians of the *Annales* school, among others, have provided exceptions to this historiographical mode. But these historians have rarely attended to the myriad subtle ties between linear history and the nation-state, and thus they have often themselves slipped into the traps laid by national histories, discussed below.[1]

To be sure, historical knowledge is hardly alone in being dominated by the nation-state. Most humanistic and social scientific knowledge in the twentieth century has presupposed the nation-state's territorial representation of space as the horizon of its own understanding.[2] But history has had a special role in national pedagogies. It teaches a lesson that is somewhat invisible to both teacher and student. We do not learn the grammar or vocabulary of a discipline when we study history. Rather, because students learn dates, names, numbers, and stories, often by rote in much of the world, they are instilled with love, pride, shame, resentment, and even a desire for vengeance for the nation. The moral value of the national community is taken for granted in this pedagogy. As students, we learn no means to question what makes the nation the community that empirically defines history and political identity. Even less do we acquire the means to

Thanks are due to the conference participants for their valuable comments and especially to Thomas Bender for his help and confidence in my ability to speak to Americanists.

explore the time-space vectors that construct the nation as an object of inquiry.

Whatever our final opinions may be in regard to the relationship between nationalism and history, I believe that we have to recognize the dual function of historical pedagogy. Historical education not only teaches us about the past, it forms the learning subject in the ways in which it shapes understanding of the past. The challenge ahead of us is how to balance the identity-formation function of historical pedagogy with a critical understanding of that formation, or, in other words, to understand how historical education is also about the production of our moral and knowing selves.

A transnational, global system of nation-states shapes the nation form as the object of historical inquiry and establishes the terms upon which individual identity is formed. Historical narration constitutes a vector, which in a dictionary is defined as "a quantity that has magnitude, direction, and sense and that is commonly represented by a directed line segment whose length represents the magnitude and whose orientation in space [or time] represents the direction." The nation is seen as precisely such a quantity, moving forward in time. Conversely, traditional histories derive their meaning or sense by returning to a mythical past or transcendent ideal, such as the Kingdom of God.

The most basic model for historical linearity is an evolutionism in which the species is replaced by the nation, whether constituted by race, language, or culture. Historiography constitutes its object of inquiry as a bounded entity (like a species) that grows or should grow to some level to which a criterion of success is attached (whether this be competitive ability vis-à-vis other species, nationality, or simply self-consciousness). Just as there can be diversity and reversals in evolutionism, so too in modern history, the national species can regress, lose its unity, and receive "new blood" from elsewhere. Just as a species can find recessive genes, dormant organs, or unforeseen abilities, so historians find obscured traditions or repressed histories to show the unity or abilities of a people anew. What remains is the notion of a nationality as a unity or category, as in a species. Even multicultural histories reproduce essentially the same evolutionary narratives, identifying a subject of history that gradually gathers the self-consciousness that will enable it—be it gays or an ethnic group—to claim its rights.

To be sure, there is much complexity in the historiography of the early twentieth century, in China as elsewhere. Great historians like Gu Jiegang, Fu Sinian, and others saw that people were not only made, but also unmade in the course of history.[3] Pointing to breaks brought on by "barbarian invasions" and decentralized polities, they showed the implausibility of positing the continuous unity of a Chinese people. But in addressing the problem of rupture, their efforts were directed precisely at demonstrating the reestablishment of continuity, showing how the thread was retied.[4] The space-time vectors work inside their historiography to bound the nation as the natural historical object and to project the national history backward to eras that precede the nation. Territorial boundaries delimit a heterogeneous space, which is projected back in time as the homogeneous space of national sovereignty. Periodization schemes bring temporal coherence to this dubious spatial entity by linking disparate meanings across and within periods. Because the object of inquiry, the nation, was not constituted in this particular linear, evolutionary way, we may well inquire into why this evolving nation has dominated the framing of modern historiography.

Doubtless there are many factors, but a crucial one is that history becomes a principal means of claiming sovereignty in the emerging system of nation-states. Sometime by the late nineteenth century in Europe, and thenceforth in much of the rest of the world, a discourse of rights emerged, involving a three-way relationship between a people, a territory, and a history. This relationship became the means of creating a historical agent or (often juridical) subject capable of making claims to sovereign statehood. A "people" with a supposed self-consciousness of themselves as unified, developed a sovereign *right* to the territory they had allegedly originally or continuously occupied. Written histories represented this collectivity.

This historical subject is prefigured in Hegel's spirit evolving into self-consciousness. Without the record of history, there could be no self-consciousness, and without self-consciousness, no progress. While Hegel's spirit manifests itself over a variety of spaces and times, his teleology assumes its ultimate realization in the Prussian state. It is perhaps this realization of the nation and the national subject that has been distinctive to modern nations. This historical subject not only had the right to national sovereignty but also the right to conquer and colonize those who were not so organized into nations. Thus it is easy to see why colonizing nations might seek to identify their colonies as non-nations, and why those non-nations had to reconstitute themselves as nations to enter history and join the narrative of progress and modernity.

CHALLENGING HISTORICAL BOUNDARIES

Historical writing and the assumptions that underlie it are changing. Much historical writing today already defies the ideas of a stable and bound subject. The space-time boundaries of national historical production are being crossed in multiple ways. For instance, the idea of a revisionism that implies that there is a single (once and for all revisable) truth seems quite anachronistic in the face of the variety of stories written from different sites of domination or resistance, whether public or private. The situation resembles a jigsaw puzzle in which the outer frame is constantly changing and realigning. Moreover, the recognition of other modes of historiography, such as movies, fiction, or museum exhibitions, links historical understanding to other networks of knowledge, pushing the boundaries of the historical object still farther.

Some of the most adventurous historical writing in the past ten or so years has shown us the riches to be found by transgressing boundaries. Greg Dening's history of HMS *Bounty* is strategically located in the waters between eighteenth-century England and the Pacific islands it sought to dominate.[5] In the ship, we see an English microcosm of power, class, and opportunity. When its crew come into contact with native society, we witness the gradual disarrangement of this microcosm. Indeed, the Pacific reshapes England even as the imperial power dominates and domesticates the ocean and its islands and people. Dening's techniques are drawn from the theater, which performed the story of the *Bounty* innumerable times. It helps us to see how historians craft their stories and make moral judgments in the manner of playwrights and directors.

Although Robert Rosenstone's *Mirror in the Shrine* is in some ways a traditional biography of three Americans in Japan, it is uniquely adept at capturing the transformations of the self and the transvaluation of old narratives at the interface of two cultures, defined by two spaces.[6] Rosenstone employs the production techniques of the cinema to disclose the shaping power of different spaces. In Shahid Amin's "failure" to reconstruct a major event in the history of Indian nationalism—the 1922 riot in Chauri Chaura—Amin, a subaltern studies historian, reveals a different technology involved in the production of history: criminal legal process, both in and out of court.[7] Beyond showing how a judge and a peasant may register an event differently, Amin shows how the sources themselves construct an event very differently. Whether he is discussing the process of criminal law or the linguistic registers in which the event is recalled, Amin is extraordinarily sensitive to the dispersal of the meaning of an event over space and time. It is worth noting that even though each of these histories transgresses spatial and temporal boundaries, we are left with a richer history, not confusion.

In this spirit, I would like to explore the still deeper implications of these newer histories. Let us inquire into our very modes of making historical sense, namely, periodization, causation, and the historical postulate of space. These practices, I argue, are techniques, not merely of producing the national time-space, but of binding the self to that time-space—of producing identity. It is perhaps partly for this reason that despite the *practical* subversions of the national ideological project among historians, it has been extremely difficult to articulate an alternative paradigm.

Consider first how the theory of causation in scientific or positive histories works to secure the continuous nation and how the emergent view of causality complicates this continuity. Thus, for instance, it is now a commonplace that historical narratives are shaped by contemporary needs. Much recent work, including my own, has tried to show how national narratives respond to contemporary national imperatives. What this does is to reverse the flow of ordinary causal logic whereby a cause, anterior in time, produces an effect, later in time. Here a contemporary nation that "causes" the narrative posits itself as an effect of it.

This is brought out most dramatically in my recent research. The revolutionary nationalist Hu Hanmin was charged with the task of converting the overseas Chinese in southeast Asia to the revolutionary nationalist cause in the early twentieth century. Hu was disappointed by how many overseas Chinese in southeast Asia had lost their Chinese identity, and the extent to which those who remained Chinese were under the spell of Manchu customs. Indeed, the only way to identify them as Chinese was by the queues that they sported—a sign, of course, of submission to the Manchus in China. While Hu, on the one hand, decries their lack of a modern republican sensibility, he is thankful that the queue at least continues to identify them as Chinese. He then goes on to comment that he would have them cut off their queues after they had been made sufficiently Chinese![8] The passage symbolizes the complex transactions between sign and practice in historical process. It is the queue that enables the revolutionaries to attain their goal of establishing Chineseness; yet upon attaining that goal, they would efface this very cause and substitute it (its cutting, more precisely) as its effect. Might we not have been fooled by his account if he had not been so curiously explicit.

The problem of periodization is of still greater significance. One of the more subversive trends in the new historiography is the constant redefining of periods and dates or events that mark their beginnings (and by implication, the end). This is a virtual industry in most histories, but the various "modern" periods—whether 1840 and the Opium Wars in China, or 1789, or the Industrial Revolution—are particularly susceptible to being reevaluated or moved backward or forward in time. I believe that these movements ought to draw our attention to the philosophy of history that underlies any division of time. The absolute priority given to an organizing principle that reveals the truth of an era, or even one that "best explains" the historical materials and gives it its name, has to be understood, not simply in the context of that which has been left out, but in terms of the epistemology that produces the meaningful world. It is easy to see the philosophical bases of organizing principles such as the state or class in Hegelian or Marxist periodization schemes. Elsewhere, I have tried to show how the threefold division of early twentieth-century *national* histories into ancient, medieval, and modern well suited nationalist cosmology, which required both continuity and unity, as well as a modern future that broke with the past. The tripartite division allowed the historian to construct a continuous subject by connecting the modern period with the ancient (often by means of a "renaissance," which the great Chinese nationalist Liang Qichao once likened to a volcanic eruption from an ancient geological stratum buried under the present). At the same time, the historian could bypass the medieval and reject what was unsuitable to modernity as medieval accretions.[9]

Periodization is thus not simply a convenient way of organizing historical data; it is one of the most fundamental means of symbolizing historical time, and, consequently, of conferring meaning on individual identity. The gradual erosion of a date that symbolizes the birth or death of a period, such as 1776 or 1949, has radical implications. Say academic scholarship indicates that there are more fundamental long-term forces producing meanings quite different from individualism or freedom, or in the Chinese case, from socialism. Just as François Furet sought to demonstrate in the case of 1789 in the history of France, 1776 or 1949 might no longer be major milestones in this alternative periodization. When this knowledge penetrates public historical consciousness, the consequences for both individual identity and state sovereignty could be far-reaching. Something like this is going on in the People's Republic of China, which today perhaps best exemplifies a crisis of historical consciousness. Neither the Chinese state nor its people belong to the historical epoch in which they allegedly live. On the one hand, the regime is unable to publicly acknowledge the abandonment of socialist ideals, while on the other, the practices of everyday life reveal little trace of socialist values. The regime seems increasingly to fall back on nationalism—that relatively unacknowledged underpinning of twentieth-century socialism—as its only legitimating doctrine.

Our increasing awareness of what Paul Ricoeur called the symbolizing function of historical periods represents an expansion of historiographical possibilities. The lack of such awareness prevents us from considering alternative principles and strategies of periodization and thus continues to implicate historians who do history with a small "h" with the categories of a philosophy of history. A simple way to avoid the homogenizing function of periodization is for historians to reject the axiomatic conception of an era as an ontological condition and to think of it rather as a hegemonic principle. As such, what we usually think of as the "modern era" can be thought of as a certain pattern of time that seeks to dominate other temporalities. Although it is often the case, this relationship need not necessarily be agonistic; one can conceive of the coexistence of different kinds of time. Such a conception, which permits of multiple temporal lineages, can also diversify our sense of belonging.

Although we are still unable to name the emergent paradigm, a new historiography suggests that *boundedness and unicity are as socially constructed as domination and subject formation, and, especially, that each set shapes the other.* This development invites several questions: Why has this paradigm shift taken place now? What are the conditions of its emergence? What goals does it serve? After all, every historical explanation must seek to understand its own historicity in an effort to be consistent with its historicizing mission. The point in historicizing the self is not to achieve a complete transparency (and thus master the subject as object), but to recognize that the knowing subject may itself be shaped by a history that its own presumptions do not encompass.

One reason for the shift is that the nation-state itself bears a different relationship to global capitalism than it did in the first eighty years of the twentieth century, especially as seen in Europe. The very restructuring of large-scale political communities in response to the imperatives of global capitalism, as well as the rapid rise, fall, and reconstitution of nation-states after 1989, has denaturalized the nation form, or at least undermined its claim to be an evolving primordial essence. Other developments tied to advanced capitalism and loosely referred to as postmodernism—deterritorialization and the unleashing of the sign—have inclined us to attend to the *movement* of resources, peoples, and signs rather than to stable entities. At the same time, a proliferation of genres and "points of view," as well as forms of presentation, from the movies to Epcott Center and the *Enola Gay* exhibition, makes us more sensitive to what histories might hide.

If temporal, spatial, and discursive boundaries are to be defied, then do we not need some framing device to give meaning to our studies? There are no easy answers here, but I believe that the two sets outlined in the statement above are mutually entailed in their framing. Let me temporarily invoke the gestalt vocabulary of ground and figure. Structures of domination and control (problems of power and exploitation) can serve as the ground or provisional frame for understanding how temporal and spatial boundaries are constructed or sustained (e.g., personal versus public, modern versus premodern, national versus local); in turn, viewing spatiotemporal boundaries enables us to understand how they naturalize, reproduce, or constrain power, and their transformations (new periods, new types of boundaries) can alert us to changing structures of power. The important point here is not to see one as the naturally given frame for the other, but as enabling the other, both objectively and in our methodology. Unlike our initial metaphor of the ground/figure relationship, which is a static one, each framing yields a distinctive view of a *changing* field of power. Ideally, we should have an ever-opening history that reveals how the object of our study has been bounded and framed both subjectively and by objective powers that are also themselves partially produced by these framings.

SPACES OF HISTORY

The questioning of the space-time boundaries of the nation has already invited new modes of inquiry, particularly at the territorial borders of nation-states—in regions that are frequently both practically porous and ideologically charged. Spaces such as frontiers, borders, and "contact zones" represent relatively weak links in the ideological hegemony of nationalism and are hence often highly militarized or policed. The exploration of historical experiences in these regions does not simply reveal different histories, but also different ways of thinking about history and space. Geographers and analysts of space such as Henri Lefebvre have demonstrated that it is not simply a container. Powerful systems such as capitalism produce the kinds of space they require: abstract, exchangeable, and often deterritorialized space, which can serve as a factor of production as well as a commodity.[10] We too need to think of space not merely as a container of a history. A powerful history will produce its space, or at least, its spatial representation, and histories may efface contemporary territorial linkages, while joining separated territories, as much as spaces can divide and join histories.

Nowhere, perhaps, has the study of the national frontier dominated historiography as it has in the United States. While this frontier historiography tended, through such ideas as "manifest destiny," to moralize national expansionism even through much of the twentieth century, the last decades of that century witnessed a vigorous criticism of the frontier narrative. Students of American history are understandably much more familiar with this literature than am I, but I would like to draw upon a bit of it for comparative purposes. I shall elaborate a particular case of spatial representation from Manchuria—a contested borderland—in the early twentieth century. From 1932 to 1945, the Japanese puppet state of Manchukuo controlled the region, now simply called the northeast (*dongbei*) of China. I shall briefly compare my own approach to that of that of José David Saldívar and others who have explored the territorial and cultural borders between the United States and Latin America.[11]

Although my principal reason for making the comparison is to illumine methods to dismantle the givenness of national space, it will also help us challenge the uniqueness or exceptionalism that most nations claim for their histories. National histories often represent transnational and global developments as national processes. For example, nation-states frequently pursue the common goals of scientific modernity, adopt similar or related models to achieve these goals, encounter many of the same problems, and resort to similar solutions. Needless to say, their histories are not the same; distinctive histories emerge from the encounter between global models and preexisting and contingent formations. These formations are not necessarily national; they are often local or regional or transnational. Thus the historical event may well represent the encounter between the local and the global, but it may be portrayed as national.

The relevant historiographical space of the story I shall elaborate here is not the territorial nation but the transnational region—a certain East Asian region that is itself a changing space, for instance. In order to understand certain modern cultural and economic practices that constitute the urban experience, a map relating major East Asian cities such as Shanghai, Tokyo, Hong Kong, and Harbin, might be more relevant than a national map of China. Another regional network is formed by the lexicon of modernity. Thousands of specialized and common words, compounds, and phrases of classical Chinese provenance were given very different meanings in the modern discourses constructed in Japan. When they returned to China, this vocabulary seemed to establish a transparent relationship of the present to the Chinese past. In practice, this "lexical effect" actually inserted Chinese in a regional East Asian discourse of the modern. This may well have brought modern Chinese, Koreans, and Japanese—a temporal community—discursively closer to one another than, for instance, to peasants in their respective countries.

Similarly, Saldívar observes that many Chicano, Latin American, and African-American writers, such as Ntozake Shange, carve out territorial spaces that cut across national territories. Thus, Shange's Caribbean should be understood as a larger cultural and socioeconomic entity stretching from southern Virginia to eastern Brazil. For Shange, this extended Caribbean "is a historical and magical entity that can offer us a new way of imposing an imaginary coherence on the black experience of dispersal and fragmentation."[12]

One of the great ironies of modern nationalism is that it claims a primordial unity among its members—between the people and intellectuals, for example–even as nationalists are busy trying to remake the people in terms of the new and often alienating discourse. This unity is thus expressed less by any behavioral or practical demonstration than by the signs of the uniqueness and authenticity of the nation. The authenticity of the nation is among the more poorly understood aspects of nationalism. While, as we have seen, nations require and are driven by a linear history of progress, they also need to constitute a core of timeless authenticity.

The authentic refers to the true qualities, character, and values that cultures and nations seek to secure while they pursue the goals of modernity—or, in other words, while the nation lives in the linear time of flux and change as spectacle. The authentic then serves as the unchanging truth that provides identity in a world of change. The order of authenticity is politically important because it locates the source of authority in a society. It endows those who can speak for it with the power of cultural inviolability:

historically, we may speak of the Iranian revolutionaries, the Showa Restorationists, the Afghan Taliban, American paramilitarists, the antimodern spiritualist Gandhi, and the anti-Western Confucian essentialist Lee Kuan-yew as among those who have sought to speak for that authenticity. Internally, those who control it have the power to subordinate the individual to the collective in the name of that authenticity, and, externally, to provide an authoritative shield against charges made by other states or nations.[13]

The construction of national authenticity in East Asia draws upon circulating cultural resources within this transnational region, or at the very least, the region filters global processes. However, nationalist ideologies of authenticity and uniqueness deny or seek to obscure the external provenance–often traceable to enemy territory–of these resources. The authentic may be found in several areas: in the civilizational discourse of pan-Asianism; in the representation of woman, particularly "traditional" woman; in the ethnographic discourse of the "primitive" associated with modern territorial control of borders; and in the discourse of "locality" or native place (*xiangtu*) in a variety of academic, literary, and political practices. A fuller project, consonant with the gestalt dynamic or successive framings outlined above, might explore how a historical phenomenon or event—allegedly embodying the authentic—is produced in relation to wider forces (the structures of domination) and how it is instantiated as a local event or as lived experience (subject formation). Finally, it would show how the meaning of this instantiation is contested, appropriated, and *successively reframed* by different forces centered in different spatial orders so as to authenticate or naturalize such spaces as the nation, the empire, or the transnational region. Thus, by releasing the meaning of this event from a fixed relationship to the nation or any other single entity—both synchronically and diachronically—we can gain a fuller understanding of it in its varied relationships and gaps to different power centers.

In the modern state, the land and people of two kinds of spaces, both politically problematic for the nation, frequently appear to be invested with a certain authenticity: (1) the locality or the countryside, of which the native place is a special variation, and (2) the frontiers and peripheries of the bounded national territory, or the geobody. Both spaces are represented as timeless, or at least as belonging to a different temporality from the modern city, but, whereas the "primitive" in the periphery is frequently romanticized to represent a lost human *nature*, the peasants occupying the timeless heartlands often embody ancient civilizational values that the modern nation is in the process of losing. One of the interesting aspects of the Chinese native-place novel from Manchukuo that I examine is that in its own description of Manchuria as a repository of (threatened) heartland traditions, it itself displaces an earlier non-Chinese representation of the region as a frontier zone or borderland.

The supposedly ancient tie of the local people to the land and culture functioned within a discourse of identity and continuity that was in turn central to the doctrine of national sovereignty, because the peasants' timeless connection to the land itself authenticated the nation-state's right to the territory. If peasant primordiality was often constructed as a response to the problem of identity and sovereignty, the locality was also believed to be superstitious and backward, a drag on the progress of the nation, holding it back in a competitive capitalist world. The image of the peasants as the authentic representatives of Chinese culture in the republican period (1911–49) was as widespread as the opposite image of them as in need of reform, and often, most perplexingly, in the same writer or activist. Practically, this produced the problem of reforming the people of the locality without erasing the primordiality that they embodied. At its most fundamental level, the tension between the two images represented the problem of nations living in the linear, abstract time of capital: to progress in a competitive world while securing the terra firma—the problem of identity—within this vortex.

To pose the problem of the local in this way is to present it in its most baldly abstract and ahistorical mode, but I believe it is even more dangerous to miss this aspect. Besides, we can also often track the global impetus—in this case—through the set of discursive practices producing the authentic. Folklore, native-place writing, human geography, geopolitics, and ethnography were among the new global disciplinary knowledges of the first half of the twentieth century in China as elsewhere. They hovered over the same fault line dividing the locality, treated at once as primordial and as demanding transformation.

In China, two schools of opinion developed around the depiction of the native place or locality: one that sought to preserve or cherish its value in the face of capitalist urbanization and commodification, and one that accused the former of romanticizing the exploitation and misery of the countryside and strengthening the reactionary forces in the village and nation. But although Lu Xun, regarded by many as China's greatest modern writer, represented this latter critique, he was still repeatedly drawn to the native place as the source of the emotional identification of the writer and reader.[14] In Lu's writings, the local needs simultaneously to be both transformed and preserved; they recapitulate the tension within nationalism between modernizing and transformative forces consistent with global capitalism and the atavistic forces that saw the local as the object of identity. It is in these ways that we may see the transnational at the heart of the production of the national.

In Anglo-American cultures, the recurrent motif of the "pastoral" ideal represents a very similar, if older, complex; indeed, it may well be considered a stimulus for much American literary and philosophical writing. Leo

Marx's *The Machine in the Garden* (1964) is an exhaustive study of the pastoral as the trope of authenticity and virtue continually besieged by technology and history, tracking its history from Jefferson and the beginnings of industrialization to the post–World War II era. To be sure, Marx traces the complexity of what Raymond Williams has called the "structure of feeling" toward the pastoral. Thinkers such as Thoreau and Melville, like Lu Xun in China, recognized that nostalgia for an age of innocence might have nothing to do with what was "out there" and was more a matter of private and literary experience. At times, the views of Lu Xun—who spoke of "gathering dawn flowers at dusk"—appear to have been close to those of Melville. According to Marx, Melville recognized the problem of living "as in a musky meadow" when in truth one is "aboard a vessel that is plunging into darkness"—the problem of identity in uncharted linear time.[15]

The parallel with Marx's analysis also extends to a methodological issue; namely, that the pastoral thematic is most consistently explored in literature. Without directly venturing an answer to the question of why that may be so, let me suggest that literary analysis (whether by the writer or critic) has proved most useful in capturing the pastoral as a problem of spatial representation. Where historians are now turning to spatial analysis to pry open the time-space containers of history—and we shall see below how their innovations can lead to different ways of perceiving historical spaces—it is the literary field that discovered how writers as much as political forces have had to represent the spaces they sought to control. Mikhail Bakhtin's notion of chronotopes, for instance, has been most useful in this regard. A historical account will, of course, have to reach beyond the spatial representation to various practices, but the latter are by no means mere reflections or functions of the former.

Against this background, I have studied Liang Shanding's *Lüsede Gu* (Green Valley), a classic native-place novel set in Manchuria, which was written in 1942, at the height of Japanese censorship of Chinese writings in the puppet state.[16] In Bakhtin's terms, the novel deploys three chronotopes: that of the city, dominated by a destructive capital; that of the "green valley," in which a true but threatened moral community exists, despite a hierarchical relationship between simple peasants and paternalistic feudal patriarchs; and, finally, that of the primeval mountains and forests, whose cycles of natural regeneration since prehistory contain the truth and virtue of the universe. These truths are most closely followed by the secret brotherhoods who inhabit the forests, and, secondarily, by the peasants in the valley, to the extent that their lives also reproduce these same timeless cycles. The drama of the novel revolves precisely around the corrosion of their natural life by the incursions of urban capitalism through the railroad and the market. This same theme is implied or reproduced in countless contexts—whether they be rural reconstruction movements or ethno-graphic or geographical texts—not only in East Asia, but all over the world.

Lüsede Gu succeeds admirably in producing the local as an abiding source of value primarily because of the way in which its fundamental representational structures—the three chronotopes of the city, the primeval mountains and forests, and the green valley—clarify, even when they complicate, this source of value. Moreover, this representational scheme enables the author to reproduce a very powerful trope in Chinese popular culture, that of the "knight-errant" or Robin Hood tradition, which it places in the heart of the Manchurian landscape. This tradition had dominated Chinese popular literature and culture, and remarkably, the self-perceptions of secret societies, since the Ming era (1368–1644).

The novel draws inspiration from this popular cultural tradition to characterize "social bandits" as human embodiments of the natural and timeless authenticity of the primeval forests. In evoking this tradition, the author is able to infuse what is a global form and concern with a local meaning and power. By this I do not just mean that Liang Shanding merely cites or uses a traditional form for modern purposes. In recent historical writing, there is often a penchant for seeing the modern engagement with the past as duplicitous or suspect. Thus we talk about citation, or invention of tradition, or construction or imagination of the past. While modern historical actors do often deploy the past for modern purposes, we still live in societies—and, even more, study societies—that are not homogeneous; where different people do indeed inhabit different temporalities.

To assume that the past can only be understood in terms of our present is to deny this heterogeneity (or more precisely the power structure articulating these modes of time). Note how Shanding, in one of the most telling episodes of the novel, mobilizes the relationship between the two kinds of time. When a young heir to his family's property, Xiaobiao, decides all of a sudden to leave the valley to pursue his studies at a university, he addresses the disappointed young hired hands and tenants, who have developed a fondness for him. "The speech was full of such 'foreign,' temporal phrases such as 'historically speaking' and 'in the present stage,' and as Xiaobiao was uttering them, he saw the tenderness of the laborers toward him suddenly evaporate. He wondered if they suspected and hated these words; he hastened to conclude by saying that 'the land is our life; no matter who it is, to leave the land is to commit suicide.' "[17]

Although Liang Shanding may have romanticized the local as timeless and natural, he maintains the radical difference of a temporality that continues to circulate in society and invests it with immense critical power. There is no temporal suture here, no homogeneous time of the modern nation, whether Chinese or Japanese.[18] Linear time, according to Liang, is the time of capital, which is utterly destructive of community. The question of what he might have been trying to suggest by the novel during this period of foreign occupation is subject to different interpretations and, as we shall see, this undecidability is the source of the political significance of the novel. But for the moment, I want to continue with the literary comparison.

In *The Dialectics of Our America,* Saldívar demonstrates how the writer Rolando Hinojosa evokes spatial tropes to uncover a buried history in the Rio Grande valley. Saldívar embeds this study in a wider analysis of the Latin American tradition of the writer as an "organic intellectual" and the amazingly fertile literature associated with Gabriel García Marquez, Pablo Neruda, and others. These writers perceive the ways in which physically separated spaces and modes of time are joined together by systemic interdependencies and relationships of domination. They explore the hidden and mysterious connections between apparently unconnected regions in the United States or Europe and South America to show how these connections produce conflict and change in a remote community.[19]

Drawing upon this radical tradition that denaturalizes boundaries of space and time, politics and culture, Rolando Hinojosa writes about the mythical territory of Belken County, Texas, in his chronicle *Klail City Death Trip.* Hinojosa reconstructs a bloody history of two hundred years during which a traditional Hispanic society was transformed by world market changes. He reconstructs two distinct worlds—two chronotopes—in his narrative: a Mexican ranch society and an Anglo-American farm society.[20] The domination of farming over ranching and the consequent functional segregation of the races was a violent historical process, which continues to animate Chicano political and literary consciousness.

By seeking to recover an entire spatial formation buried under the national space represented by the triumphalist rhetoric of white supremacy and the heroism of the Texas Rangers, *Klail City Death Trip* functions not only as an alternative history but as an empowering one. By portraying two kinds of spaces opposed in their views of history, economic life, forms of knowledge and morality, and by employing materials from folklore, anthropology, history, bilingualism, and other linguistic resources, Hinojosa seeks to depict a deadly contest over the codes of representation in the Southwest. In this way, he seeks to produce historical subjecthood for a people suppressed and marginalized by another people's history.[21]

As Gabrielle Spiegel has suggested, the task of the literary critic is to deconstruct what has been constructed, whereas the historian is principally devoted to reconstruction. However, real-life spaces are often accessible principally through their dominant ideological representation by political powers, which frequently marginalize, suppress, or transform other histories. In this situation, the historian cannot but play the role of deconstructionist critic. But precisely because the representation of a space does not exhaust spatial practices, the historian is obliged to explore a variety of ways in which spaces and histories are articulated.

In a recent essay, the historians Jeremy Adelman and Stephen Aron have explored the transition from what they have called "contested borderlands" to national borders in several parts of the emerging United States, including the Greater Rio Grande Basin. In eighteenth century, the Basin, together with the Great Lakes and the Lower Missouri Valley, was a borderland of imperial rivalry and particularly fluid relations between Amerindians and European interlopers. By the nineteenth century, as empires were succeeded by nation-states and treaty-recognized boundaries, ethnic and social relations became more exclusive and hierarchical. Mutual adaptation, intermarriage, and the ability to secure favorable terms of exchange by Amerindians and métis, all conditions made possible by interimperial rivalry, gave way to a situation where the earlier inhabitants were excluded from the new conception of rights and citizenship and "began the long sojourn of survival within unrivaled politics."[22]

Adelman and Aron's essay reveals how a dramatically different type of historical society—with different conceptions of belonging and resource use—that existed a mere two centuries ago was obscured by the frontier myth of the nation. They show how a substantively different conception of the political space symbolized by territorial boundaries resulted in a transformation of spatial practices and of the fate of different people. The advent of a political space in which rights backed by state power, especially rights of property ownership, existed for citizens but not for others in the national territory, produced a situation where the earlier inhabitants were condemned to suffer the loss of political, social, and personal status.[23]

Following the lead of Lefebvre and others, I have tried to suggest how historical powers, especially the nation-state, have sought to reshape spaces in order that both the nature and extent of space conform to their needs or modes of control. Subaltern groups and organic intellectuals also recognize that the key to justice—if not to recovering their spaces and ways of life—is the contest over the codes for representing space. In these concluding paragraphs, I return to the green valley of Liang Shanding's *Lüsede Gu* to show that we need a historical understanding of a spatial representation—in this case, embodying the authenticity of the Manchurian landscape—in order to grasp how different regimes seek to produce the kind of spaces they can dominate. Different groups—both dominant and resistant—sought to control the meaning of the novel, so that it came to justify very different territories and polities. Thus the novel became a *historical* event in its reception by the Japanese, the Chinese communists, and contemporary Chinese critics from the region, all of whom sought to appropriate the meaning and resources of the native place. These appropriations reveal to us not only the power of the novel in producing local identity, but also how the local and local identity must be seen, not as a fixed part of the nation, but as process.

To be sure, the novel is involved in history even before its reception or appropriation. In writing a novel peopled almost exclusively by Chinese, the author was also respatializing Manchuria. Although Chinese agriculturalists had long lived in the southern parts of Manchuria, the Manchu emperors of the Qing dynasty (1644–1911) sought to ban Han Chinese migration to their ancestral homelands during much of their 250-year rule of China. For various reasons, they sought to preserve the frontier character of the region and a largely nonagricultural economy based on pasturelands and primeval forests, dominated by Mongols and various indigenous Tungusic peoples, of which the Manchus were one. When, in the later part of the nineteenth century, the Manchus faced imperialist encroachment in the region by Russia and Japan, the regime began to permit the settlement of Manchuria by Han agriculturalists, who during the last thirty years of Qing rule rapidly converted pasturelands and forests into a vast and productive agricultural economy. Needless to say, the rapid agrarianization of the economy began that other familiar process whereby the indigenous peoples who depended on the forests for their livelihood were mercilessly wiped out.[24]

The complexity of Liang Shanding's novel derives from his commitment to the Manchurian landscape. His quasi-mystical search for the fount of energy in a balance between agriculture and the primeval forest is pitted against the invasive forces of urban capitalism. What he obscures is the substitution of one set of actors for another. Indigenous ginseng gatherers, sable hunters, pearl fishers, mushroom growers, and gold miners frequently had their knowledge, means of livelihood, and women taken from them, and entire communities were reduced to bonded slaves by Han merchants and bandits. Yet the novel is strikingly silent about these people, and when there is reference to their shaman-centered cultures, they are chiefly depicted as malevolent forces. In their place, it is the Chinese bandit who is identified as the preserver of the secret power of the primeval forests. To be sure, the Chinese bandit in Manchuria was a legendary figure in his own right, a pioneer who had crossed the mountains and rivers to the remote corners of the Ussuri in search of the forest's wealth. It is by centering this figure that the novel seeks to inscribe the landscape as a Chinese one, although the sense in which it was Chinese was still open to contestation.

From the moment of its publication, most readings of the novel have located its ultimate significance outside the locality. This is even true of Liang Shanding's own reading of it in a postscript to its 1987 republication, written in light of his having suffered twenty-two years of incarceration (from 1957 to 1979), in part because the novel had been translated into Japanese.

Indeed, the salient features of Liang Shanding's life present us with the strongest evidence of the novel's historical reception. Born in 1914, he joined the anti-Japanese literary movement in Harbin after the Japanese occupation of Manchuria in 1931, together with his more famous and older colleagues Xiao Jun and Xiao Hong, and he continued writing until 1943, although most of the important members of this resistance movement had fled south to China proper by 1934. He wrote *Lüsede Gu* in 1942, and it was translated into Japanese the following year. While, as we shall see, the Manchukuo government did make use of the novel, it also censored passages in it that implicitly criticized the government's harsh taxation of country dwellers under the cover of Manchukuo political pieties. Liang Shanding was also harassed politically by the police after its publication and ultimately had to flee Manchuria for the Chinese interior in 1943. Subsequently, under the People's Republic, he was denounced in the anti-rightist campaign of 1957 as a traitor (*hanjian*) because of the Japanese translation and recognition of his work and condemned as a "rightist" to twenty-two years' hard labor.[25] He was rehabilitated in 1979, and *Lüsede Gu* was included in Reprints of Contemporary Chinese Literature, a series compiled by the Contemporary Literature Institute of the Academy of Social Sciences.[26]

The Japanese state's appropriation of the novel depended upon separating Liang Shanding's politics from his writing and also upon isolating two meanings of Chineseness. Despite his bona fide anti-Japanese politics (for which he was actively under surveillance and harassed), the fact that *Lüsede Gu* stresses the anticommunitarian nature of capitalism was usable in Japanese imperial rhetoric. Although Manchuria was actually dominated by Japanese capital, and Liang Shanding's critique was directed at capitalists of all nationalities, Japanese militarists could still use it identify capitalism as a Western curse. Second, if there was an alternative to the Chinese representation of Manchuria, it was the concurrent Japanese image of it as a vast frontier region whose culture, until recently, had been shaped by autochthonous peoples racially and linguistically closer to the Japanese than to the Chinese. Yet it was important for the Japanese to deal with the reality of the Chinese demographic dominance of Manchuria. The Manchukuo regime capitalized on the local color of the novel and, by means of literary education and sponsored debates, sought to link it with East Asiatic Confucian civilization. By emphasizing the traditional language of "loyalty" and "righteousness" (*zhongyi*), this reading of the novel affiliated it with an older, more encompassing conception of Chinese civilization, thereby bypassing the nation of China altogether.

The Maoist communists read the novel as deficient in both class and nationalist consciousness. According to Huang Wanhua, the peasants are depicted in the novel as feudal because they sided with the landlord against the anti-Japanese bandits of the *yiyongjun,* or resistance army.[27] The novel's translation into Japanese was also a sign that it was liked by the national enemy. Liang Shanding responded in 1987 with a postscript in which he depicts it as an anti-Japanese, nationalist novel written during the darkest period of Japanese rule in 1942. Pointing to its censorship and harassment by the Manchukuo authorities, he seeks to persuade the reader that the novel does deal with the oppression of the peasants, but as a work constrained by its time and circumstances, the peasants could not be shown to stand up for their rights, particularly because there was no Communist party there. In other words, he seeks to justify the absence of both nationalism and class-consciousness in the novel.

Liang Shanding's rehabilitation in 1979 and later probably had much to do with the efforts of the regional literary establishment in contemporary Manchuria, which has produced many pieces praising *Lüsede Gu,* not simply as the only great novel written in Manchuria under the Japanese occupation, but as a truly nationalist novel by a great son of the soil.[28] They make two arguments: that a native-place literature necessarily has to invoke the ancestral memory of a nation, and that it is necessary to read the nationalism of the novel between the lines, because of the oppressive censorship of the Japanese puppet government. Yet it seems to me that the novel as a local event does not quite live up to any of these readings. The Japanese had to select radically from the novel as well as keep its author's personal politics out of their appropriation of it. The communists could probably have found much more anticapitalism there if they had wanted to; and, most of all, the readings of the novel as a modern, anti-Japanese novel of the region miss out on its strongly antimodern pull toward an alternative, naturalistic model of authenticity. Indeed, in his 1987 postscript, writing in a world caught up in different forces, Liang Shanding, who emphasizes the class and nationalist character of the novel, himself seems to have forgotten the local meaning—the temporality that had resisted the linear time of capital—with which he had endowed it. Is there no way to restore the particular meaning of an event in its time, especially when its historical producers themselves reconceive it? Yet I am not sure whether the quest for the true meaning of the past is not made in terms of our present. Perhaps we can only recognize this meaning in its continuous dispersals by forces both large and small.

CONCLUSION

My discussion of the literature of the borderlands around the United States and China invites a rethinking of the way history is represented. In turn, that invites a reevaluation of the role of the historian and historiography, particularly in relation to the nation, whether lodged in formal academic institutions or located in less directly authorized and professionalized sites of historical production, such as in the domains of art or popular culture.

For me, personally, this reevaluation is necessary to counter the growing trend of ultranationalist, intolerant groups in many parts of the world, such as Japan and India, who are seeking to rewrite textbooks and otherwise seize control of the vast machinery of historical pedagogy established over the twentieth century. These battles are, of course, the most recent and dramatic contests in a global process whereby historical pedagogy became one of the most important means of creating individual identification with the nation and its morality. Although they are different from the early twentieth-century fascist movements, the homogenizing, exclusivist national tendencies of these historical rewritings are important reminders of the impact of the earlier movements on institutional knowledge.

I have tried to outline an agenda for an academic historiography more self-conscious of the political projects in which it is enmeshed as an institutional discipline. Understandably, there will be critics on both the left and the right who believe nationalism has had much good to offer, and that too great a self-consciousness will either weaken the weapon of collective self-consciousness against injustice (left) or lead to social incoherence (right). If nationalism has a claim to community based on rational grounds, there is no reason why it should be impossible to balance the identity-formation function of historical pedagogy with a critical understanding of that very formation. Certainly, as professionals, we are obliged to expose the myths and falsehoods that accompany so much ultranationalist historiography. But it is also important to attend to the reasons why ultranationalists find such fertile ground in history; or in other words, to the ways in which the object of historical inquiry is constituted by the space-time of the nation and those who would dominate it.

The last part of this essay in particular has considered three ways of writing history that enable us to elude the closure of boundaries. Spatially, it is necessary not merely to overlook different boundaries but also to see how modern territorial boundaries are illusory means of keeping histories apart. By now this is almost a banal point, but it is remarkable how little historiography crosses territorial boundaries. Exploring the modern idea of territoriality shows, furthermore, how a political space associated with the dominant discourse of a time authorizes and naturalizes a social order founded upon the erasure of the memory and representation of older spatial relationships.

Analysis of Liang Shanding's novel *Lüsede Gu* as *event* has presented an opportunity to probe, if not its true meaning, a different set of questions about an ever-opening history. Although in the most schematic way, I have tried to show that the manner in which the local is treated as authentic, even when it is formulated as irreducibly local, is related to the problem of temporality in the system of capitalist nation-states. Indeed, nostalgia for the pastoral emerges only when it is threatened by dissolution. The successive readings of the novel show how diverse political regimes controlling different spatial formations—imperialist, nationalist, and regional—sought to appropriate it and its author because it performed a nativist cathexis that could be elaborated as political loyalty. The various readings stressed those parts that fitted the cultural imaginary of these regimes: thus the Japanese stressed the Confucian civilizational elements embedded in the Chinese knight-errant tradition, whereas contemporary regional critics sought a balance between the "ancestral myths" of the region and its modernist politics. By locating the history of the novel across accepted periods—1911–49, 1932–45, 1949–78—and across territorial boundaries, we can see how, in less than fifty years, the local was able to authenticate entirely different and opposed polities.

Finally, disciplinary crossings are important not for their own sake, but because they enable us to see how a range of other modes of reconstructing the past—such as theater, law, cinema, and the novel—may inform and expand our grasp of the past. While the objective, evaluative, and causal model may continue to be most useful for the historian, the inescapably narrative structure of our apprehension of this past also obliges us to study those disciplines more sensitive to the political implications of spatial representations. Nations and other modern communities of identity rely powerfully upon symbols of authenticity that a causal analysis can illuminate only to a limited extent. Let us recall, after all, that a work of fiction lay at the heart of the historical process whereby the representation of Manchuria was pursued by so many political forces.

NOTES

1. Marxism supplies important insights into the ideological aspects of historiographical production, but the scientific paradigm of historical materialism, in which nationalism represents a false consciousness, makes it hard for Marxists to see how much of socialism is shaped by nationalism.

2. Peter J. Taylor, "Embedded Statism and the Social Sciences: Opening Up to New Spaces," *Environment and Planning A* 28, 11 (1996): 1917–28.

3. Fu Sinian was the author of many works and the first and longtime director of the highest government historical research entity in republican China, the History and Language Institute of Academica Sinica. As early as 1916, he criticized his compatriots for unreflectively accepting the Japanese periodization of Chinese history. Gu Jiegang, arguably the most brilliant historian during the republic, was the first to demonstrate—at considerable risk to himself—how much there was that was mythical in the Confucian narrative of early Chinese history. He also explored the non-Confucian traditions of the past to construct an alternative history. See Fu

Sinian, *The Complete Works of Fu Sinian* (Taipei, 1932); Gu Jiegang "Qin-Han tongyide youlai he zhanguoren duiyu shijiede xiangxiang" (The origins of Qin-Han unification and the image of the world during the warring states) (1926), reprinted in *Gushibian*, ed. Gu, 2.1: 1–10 (Beijing, 1930).

4. Prasenjit Duara, *Rescuing History from the Nation: Questioning Narratives of Modern China* (Chicago, 1995).

5. Greg Dening, *Mr. Bligh's Bad Language: Passion, Power and Theatre on the Bounty* (New York, 1992).

6. Robert A. Rosenstone, *Mirror in the Shrine: American Encounters with Meiji Japan* (Cambridge, Mass., 1988)

7. Shahid Amin, *Event, Metaphor, Memory: Chauri Chaura, 1922–1992* (Berkeley and Los Angeles, 1995)

8. Hu Hanmin, "Nanyang yu Zhongguo geming" (Nanyang and the Chinese revolution), in *Zhonghua minguo kaiguo wushinian wenxian*, 1.11, *Gemingzhi changdao yu fazhan*, 457–84; compiled by Zhonghua minguo kaiguo wushinian wenxian bianzhuan weiyuanhui. (Taipei, 1964), 475–77.

9. Duara, *Rescuing History*, 34

10. Henri Lefebvre, *The Production of Space*, trans. Donald Nicholson-Smith (Cambridge, Mass., 1991).

11. See José David Saldívar, *The Dialectics of Our America: Genealogy, Cultural Critique, and Literary History* (Durham, N.C., 1991).

12. Ibid., 104

13. Thus while the authentic embeds a legitimating function for regimes, as a transcendent source of authority, it performs a wider role. In many societies and situations, representations of the authentic are crucially important for individual identity formation. Not only do these representations–say of the self-sacrificing Japanese woman—become personal ideals, but the moral power that the transcendent authority confers upon individuals and groups may easily become politicized upon the perceived violation—dishonor, desacralization, defilement—of the authentic. For a fuller study of the authentic, see Prasenjit Duara, "The Regime of Authenticity: Timelessness, Gender and National History in Modern China," *History and Theory* 37 (October 1998).

14. Lu Xun, "Daoyan" (Introduction), *Xiaoshuo erji* (Second collection of fiction), ed. Lu Xun (Shanghai, 1935).

15. Leo Marx, *The Machine in the Garden: Technology and the Pastoral Ideal in America* (Oxford, 1964).

16. Liang Shanding, *Lüsede Gu* (Green Valley) (Shenyang, 1942; 1987 reprint).

17. Ibid., 75.

18. I am struck by the contrast between Shanding's use of the secret society traditions and Sun Yat-sen's use of them. Sun, too once viewed them as representing an authentic Chineseness, but in an effort to mobilize them to the republican cause, he narrated them as precocious modern revolutionaries committed to republicanism. However, the effort to paper over the radical difference did not work. Imagine the disgust of the revolutionaries when the secret societies celebrated the 1911 revolution in Ming dynasty imperial regalia! See Duara, *Rescuing History*, ch. 4. Obviously, neither the romanticization of the peasants as timeless nor the desire to deny their different temporality is satisfying. The challenge ahead of us is to grasp

the ways in which people inhabiting different temporalities may also periodically occupy the same temporal frame as those who describe them.

19. Saldívar, *Dialectics of Our America,* ch. 2

20. Rolando Hinojosa, *Korean Love Songs from Klail City Death Trip* (Berkeley, Calif., 1978).

21. Ibid., ch. 3

22. Jeremy Adelman and Stephen Aron, "From Borderlands to Borders: Empires, Nation-States, and the Peoples In Between in North American History," *American Historical Review* 104, 3 (1999): 840.

23. Ibid., 840

24. Owen Lattimore, *Manchuria: Cradle of Conflict* (New York, 1932; rev. ed., New York, 1975).

25. Hideki Okada "Manshu no kyodo bungei—Shan Ding 'Lusede gu' o jiku toshite" (Native place literature in Manchukuo—with reference to Shan Ding's "Green Valley"), *Nogusa* 44 (1989): 10–33.

26. Liang Shanding, *Lüsede Gu,* 235

27. Wenhua Huang, "Liang Shanding he tade 'Lüse de Gu'" (Liang Shanding and his Green Valley), *Dongbei wenxue yanjiu shiliao* (Harbin) 5 (1986): 11.

28. Lü Qinwen,"Dongbei lunxianqude wailai wenxue yu xiangtu wenxue" (Foreign and native-place literature in the literature of occupied northeast China), in *Zhongri zhanzheng yu wenxue,* ed. Yamada Keizo and Lü Yuanming (Changchun, 1992), 127–61. Sun Zhongtian. "Lusede gu yu xiangtu wenxue" (The Green Valley and native-place literature), in Feng Weijun et al., *Dongbei lunxian shidai wenxue* (Changchun, 1992), 224–35.

TWO

Internationalizing International History

Akira Iriye

That the study of the history of international relations must be internationalized may sound tautological. After all, international relations by definition deals with affairs among a plurality of nations; it would therefore make little sense to study the subject in the framework of just one nation. And yet a surprisingly large number of studies continue to have a uninational focus, seeing world affairs from the perspective of just one country. Many histories of the foreign policies of particular states fall into this category. They trace policy formations of one country by examining how its officials arrive at their decisions. Of necessity, such studies tend to be "uni-archival," in the sense that they use primary material from the archives and publications of the country being examined.[1]

Such uninationalism runs against the tradition of multi-archival work, a model held up by Otto von Ranke and other pioneers of diplomatic history. Ranke and his followers insisted that in studying external relations of nations—indeed, in examining the foreign policies of even one country—the available archives of all relevant states must be explored. This approach requires, of course, that the historian be equipped to handle several key languages. In reality, few scholars are capable of mastering more than a few foreign languages, so that even the most exemplary multi-archival histories will cite documents from only a small number of countries in the original. This may be justified when a historian is writing about international affairs in a period when they were dominated by a handful of European powers, such as the eighteenth and the nineteenth centuries; it may perhaps be enough, in that case, if the writer has read documents in English, French, and German, possibly with the addition of Spanish and Italian. (It may be noted, however, that even here, very few writers are capable of reading documents in Russian.) When international relations become more complex, with countries such as Japan and China playing increasingly important roles, or with Middle Eastern states becoming actors in world politics in their own right, linguistic Eurocentrism clearly has limitations, and in such instances those who can handle Chinese, Japanese, Arabic, and other non-European languages have come to the rescue, although few among such non-Europeanists have used more than a couple of European languages. Despite these problems, however, the ideal of multilingual, multi-archival work has been held up by some of the best historians of international affairs.[2]

The language problem, however, is only one factor inhibiting the internationalization of the study of international relations. Equally serious has been the tendency to focus on official decision-making, and therefore on those documents that show every twist and turn in the process through which public decisions are made. There is an understandable fascination with every new revelation, be it in the archives of the former Soviet Union or a hidden tape recorder in the White House. As historians seek to reconstruct decision-making processes, they have found it imperative to track down all possible evidence, even in unlikely places—except in the archives of other countries. Although superb and path-finding monographs exist that elucidate how a critical decision (to go to war, for instance) has been made, many others reproduce trivial details, merely recapitulating what one official has said, or has not said, to another on some insignificant issue. That may be of some antiquarian interest but hardly makes a major contribution to understanding international relations.[3]

The uninational focus of much work in international history would seem to have been reaffirmed by the recent tendency on the part of historians to try to delve more and more deeply into domestic sources of decision-making. Culture studies, gender studies, linguistics, and other fields have tended to affect the study of international affairs by compelling the student to pay close attention to the cultural and social trends that define a country's domestic power relations, which in turn are understood to produce its policies. An excellent example of this is Kristin Hoganson's *Fighting for American Manhood,* in which she seeks to demonstrate, quite successfully in my view, that self-consciousness about preserving national manliness was behind the rhetoric of war and empire in the late 1890s and the early years of the twentieth century. ("Statehood and Manhood" was the title of a speech Theodore Roosevelt gave in 1901.)[4] A study like this shows a connection between domestic and foreign affairs through the issue of gender relations. Somewhat different, but no less suggestive, is Frank Ninkovich's *Modernity and Power,* in which it is argued that a preoccupation with the possibility of global chaos accompanying modernization produced Wilsonian ideology (which Ninkovich calls "pessimistic internationalism" in his *The Wilsonian Century*) as the guiding principle of United States foreign policy.[5] And this ideology is in turn seen to be linked to developments within the nation, in particular the social changes brought about by such phenomena as rapid industrialization, massive immigration, and class tensions.

These are very valuable studies. However, precisely because they help us look more and more closely into the domestic sources of foreign affairs, they leave unaltered the uninational orientation of so much international relations history today. A fascination with conceptualizing national cultures in the frameworks of gender, ideology, and other factors has produced provocative studies of the roots of a country's foreign policy decision-making, but at the same time it cannot be denied that they have not prevented the study of international relations from remaining uninternationalized. Culture studies, discourse analysis, and the like have not encouraged a more global, comparative approach to international history. Indeed, some historians do not even believe in the possibility or desirability of global or comparative history, choosing instead to dwell upon the local scene, irrespective of what is happening elsewhere. The recent vogue for "synchronic history," the view that historians should assume no causal sequence among events, adds to such conceptual localism.[6]

If we are not to be satisfied with this state of affairs but to strive to internationalize the study of international relations, we may need to reconceptualize the field of international history itself. Defined as the history of international relations, the field privileges nations, or states, as the principal units of analysis. Even if we are to distinguish between nations and states, the former referring to people and their institutions, cultures, and the like that comprise national communities, and the latter primarily designating formal governmental and military establishments, we shall still be dealing with international (or interstate) affairs as traditionally conceptualized.[7] One might go beyond an examination of state-to-state relations, as traditional "diplomatic historians" have tended to do, and seek to understand international relations as involving society-to-society, culture-to-culture, even people-to-people, interactions. Excellent recent monographs suggest that this is one area where much fruitful work will be done and serve to broaden the field of international relations. For instance, Marc Gallicchio's *Black Internationalism* is a superb study of how African Americans have related to the countries of East Asia, while Mark Bradley's *Imagining Vietnam and America* makes a careful comparison of Vietnamese and American conceptions of history and of the world.[8] While formal diplomacy and war are mentioned, they are not the primary focus of these books' attention. Instead, they examine how individuals and groups from different countries related to one another. Nevertheless, it should be noted that these individuals and groups are still seen to be embedded in national units, and to that extent, international relations are understood as consisting of interactions among nations. The key assumption is that individuals, groups, and forces become meaningful subjects of study as members or constituents of national entities.

It seems plausible to argue, however, that not all behavior and activities in the world are produced by nationally defined actors. If individual Americans interact with individual Germans as representatives, conscious or unconscious, of their respective countries, that is one thing; such interaction can still be comprehended within the usual conception of international relations, although here we may be going much beyond government-to-government relations. Sometimes, however, individuals' or groups' nationality becomes less important than other categories that define them or their activities. If these Americans and Germans happen to be all female, their nationality may be of less relevance than their gender in accounting for the ways in which they interact with one another. More complex would be a situation where, in a particular setting in which Americans and Germans come together, the former consisted predominantly of men, and the latter of women. This was the case, for example, in the early phase of the occupation of Germany after World War II. Norman Naimark's landmark study of the Soviet occupation of Germany, *The Russians in Germany,* documents in great detail the consequences of the initial encounter between Soviet soldiers and German women.[9] The nationality of each group was, of course, of fundamental importance; the Soviet occupiers were quite conscious of this when they assaulted German women and viewed such acts as revenge for earlier German atrocities committed against the Soviet Union. At the same time, precisely because these acts of mutual sexual assault were so hideous, we may do well not to attribute them simply to the perpetrators' national identities. There were innumerable instances of rape by Soviet troops in liberated China (Manchuria), by Japanese forces in China proper, by U.S. soldiers in Germany, and so on, so that these stories may, at one level, have to be seen as aspects more of gender than of international relations.[10] This is not to deny the validity of a nation-focused analysis to account for the nature of a specific encounter between individuals of different backgrounds, but simply to caution against assuming that international relations are all about relations among governments, individuals, and groups as constituents of national communities.

Besides gender, individuals have many other identities. To continue with the example of Americans and Germans encountering each other, if they happen to be of the same religion, being Catholic or Jewish, for instance, this may sometimes be a more crucial factor in their relationship than either nationality or gender. If certain Americans and Germans are involved in student exchange programs, they may be seen as part of the larger phenomenon of international cultural relations. If these people are engaged in trade, global commercial affairs are the key framework, not relations between sovereign states. They may be reading the same book or listening to the same music thousands of miles apart but getting the same pleasure out of the experience, in which case they are part of transnational cultural consciousness. As a final example, Americans, Germans, and people from other countries organizing to protest against the death penalty or the killing of whales, say, are acting as concerned citizens of the world, regardless of which countries they come from.

In other words, individuals and groups of people from different parts of the world come into contact with one another, either directly or indirectly, in any number of ways, and to pigeonhole all instances of their interaction under the rubric of international relations is, therefore, a gross distortion. "Transnational affairs" may be a better term to describe many of these activities. Whereas "international" implies a relationship among nations, "transnational" suggests various types of interactions across national boundaries. Extraterritorial movements of individuals, goods, capital, and even ideas would seem to be less international than transnational phenomena.

"Transnational," however, still retains "national" as part of what it describes. To speak of movements across national boundaries is to continue to recognize the saliency of nations, whether or not their frontiers are being breached by individuals or cultures. May we not go a step further and speak of global relations, or even of human affairs? Neither term assumes that there have to be nations before we can examine certain "international" or "transnational" phenomena, such as migration, trade, tourism, technology, the environment, or human rights. Of course, nations and states do exist, so global or human relations may be a better alternative term to distinguish between worldwide and state-bound phenomena. Even in the United States, in many ways the clearest embodiment of the idea of the self-sufficient sovereign nation, officials and publicists have begun to speak of "human security" as an equally important object of foreign policy as national or international security. Unlike national or international security, human security—freedom from environmental hazards, from human rights abuses, from discrimination—is not specific to a nation. It concerns the whole of humankind and is thus a global issue. To study human and global issues, we need to get away not only from a uninational framework but also from the conventional international relations perspective and instead try to imagine a world community consisting of individuals, groups, their ideas, activities, and products interacting with one another in myriad ways.

Subjects of study for this reconceptualized international, that is, human or global, history, then, will not be foreign policies, national interests, or empires, but human migrations, economic exchanges, technological inventions and transfers, and cultural borrowing and transformation. Some of these topics have been studied closely by political scientists, economists, sociologists, and anthropologists. Recently, for instance, excellent examinations of global migration have been published.[11] Global movements of goods and capital have long been explored by economists and economic historians.[12] An increasing number of political scientists have been paying attention to the worldwide efforts to protect the natural environment or to promote other causes.[13] And several historians have written important studies of transatlantic cultural influences.[14] And yet historians of international relations have been rather slow to incorporate such studies into a systematic, novel synthesis or to construct an alternative international history on that basis.

In my own current work, I have been inspired by the work of political scientists and sociologists on international organizations, especially of the nongovernmental variety. Excellent studies of these organizations exist, and yet historians have not paid them the attention they deserve.[15] But I have felt that they provide a relatively easy way to reconceptualize international history, if for no other reason than that international organizations are by definition nonstate actors, so that to focus on them, rather than on sovereign states, is to begin to conceive of an alternative history of international relations. In particular, I am interested in the activities of international nongovernmental organizations, defined as those organizations that are not established through an agreement among governments and are nonprofit, nonreligious, and nonmilitary.[16]

It seems possible to write a history of international relations of the recent decades by chronicling the activities of these organizations, whose number has increased from about five hundred in 1945 to nearly thirty thousand fifty years later. In other words, whereas there were about ten times as many international nongovernmental organizations as sovereign states at the end of World War II, the ratio has increased more than tenfold. Not simply in number, but also in action, these organizations have demonstrated that not everything has to be related to the state in order to understand the nature of world affairs at a given moment in time. Particularly relevant to our discussion is that fact that these nonstate actors have dealt precisely with those transnational phenomena that are not within the purview of most work by historians of international relations: the resettlement of refugees, the protection of the natural environment, the problems of poverty and hunger in underdeveloped parts of the globe, and many others. Not sovereign states, but nongovernmental organizations (often in cooperation with intergovernmental organizations, another group of nonstate actors) have sought more energetically and effectively to cope with these global issues. A history of international relations as seen through the activities of nongovernmental organizations would, then, constitute a story of transnational cooperation, not of formal relations between states that are in a perpetual state of potential conflict, the usual model for the study of international history.

What will such a reconceptualized international history tell us? In examining nonstate actors and transnational phenomena, we may benefit from work by an increasing number of economists, political scientists, anthropologists, and others who have enshrined the theme of globalization as a key to understanding the contemporary world.[17] Historians need neither embrace the concept of globalization uncritically nor suppose that it is the only framework in which to understand international history. But they are uniquely equipped by training to historicize such a concept, if for no other reason than that globalization *is* a historical phenomenon. David Held and Anthony McGrew, two leading students of globalization, write that this term "refers to . . . entrenched and enduring patterns of world-wide interconnectedness . . . [and] suggests a growing magnitude or intensity of global flows such that states and societies become increasingly enmeshed in worldwide systems and networks of interaction."[18] Words like "become" and "increasingly" are part of the historical vocabulary, and so historians are in a good position to make a contribution to the literature. It would seem that they need to involve themselves more deeply than they have in the ongoing and often vociferous debate on the nature and direction of globalization, for if historians, especially of international affairs, cannot make a contribution in this area, these larger issues will continue to be argued ahistorically.

Learning something from the recent scholarship (mostly by nonhistorians) on globalization, and trying to incorporate some nonstate actors into a study of international relations, I have felt that it would be useful to postulate the simultaneous existence of two worlds, one consisting of sovereign states as they have actually developed over time, and the other a putative global community, a product of forces of globalization. Of course, in "reality" the two are not completely distinct, but at least conceptually, it seems helpful to imagine these two worlds, for only the former, the "real" world, has been an object of study traditionally, whereas the latter, the "imagined" world, has only recently begun to be taken seriously as an alternative framework for inquiry by historians. I would propose that the two worlds may be seen to have existed side by side for several centuries, and that to trace their changing relationship is a useful way of understanding the history of international (or transnational, global) relations.

For instance, may we not say that the tension between the two worlds became acute at the turn of the twentieth century, when the "imagined" world had become sufficiently strong to challenge the dominance of the "real" world? An increasing number of writers were paying attention to what they considered to be emerging transnational forces connecting distant parts of the world and making separate national existences less and less relevant. In 1906, J. A. Hobson called his readers' attention to the "influences which work upon the lives of all of us from distant parts of the world [creating] bonds of interest which band us together irrespective of the natural limits of the country to which we belong and in which we were born."[19] In 1914, H. G. Wells described the appearance of "a new kind of people, a floating population going about the world, uprooted, delocalised, and even, it may be, denationalised, with wide interests and wide views, developing, no doubt, customs and habits of its own, a morality of its own, a philosophy of its own."[20] And the editors of *La Vie Internationale,* the organ of the Office central des associations internationales, declared in the journal's first issue (1912) that the movement of ideas, events, and organizations had come to constitute "international life," penetrating all activities of people, who were no longer confined to their villages, provinces, or countries, and enveloping "the entire terrestrial globe."[21] What these writers were suggesting was the growth of a new world, consisting of transnational movements and trends, that was competing for influence with the existing world made up of sovereign states. This contest ended in 1914 in a temporary victory of the "real" world, as if to indicate that the forces of globalization were not powerful enough to alter the habits of the sovereign nations to pursue power and expand their respective interests. Worse, both the agencies and products of globalization were put to the service of the states as they fought a calamitous war against one another.

As a provocative recent book by Niall Ferguson, *The Pity of War,* makes clear, however, there was nothing inevitable about the triumph of the "real" over the "imagined" world.[22] Indeed, the Great War did much to destroy the former, whereas the imagined world community came back with renewed force in the wake of the war. I have traced one manifestation of it—what I have called "cultural internationalism"—in a recent study.[23] Histories of international relations during the 1920s and the 1930s are almost always written in the framework of "interwar" affairs, as if the two world wars were fixed pieces of furniture, and all that historians can do is merely to sweep everything under them. But that would ignore the real growth of the "imagined" world made up of international organizations and movements. The prewar ideas expressed by Hobson, Wells, and others were echoed in the "declaration of intellectual independence," a 1919 manifesto by European and American intellectuals including Romain Rolland, Hermann Hesse, and Benedetto Croce, who asserted that they would now honor only one truth, "free, without frontiers, without limits, without prejudice of race or caste."[24] The spirit of such internationalism provided the impetus for the creation of many international organizations during the two decades following the war. Over four hundred international nongovernmental organizations were registered with the League of Nations in

1929, and the number continued to grow in the following decade.[25] They were engaged in cultural exchange and humanitarian and other activities, sometimes in cooperation with the League and with sovereign states, but often on their own initiative. This story can never be understood in the "interwar" framework, for it belongs to the "imagined" world that did not anticipate another global catastrophe but was instead strengthening itself as a new international community.

That story, too, ended unhappily, in a global war out of which developed a horrific weapon that could wipe out human civilization. That, too, was globalization in the service of states, the "real" world preventing the "imagined" world from fulfilling its promise. But the picture in the second half of the twentieth century and after has been far more promising from the perspective of the latter world, and we shall need to go beyond such perspectives as "the Cold War," "the long peace," "a preponderance of power," and the like to understand the phenomenon.[26] These are valuable perspectives when dealing with postwar international affairs as traditionally understood, but we shall also need to pay closer attention to transnational developments since World War II, and in order to do so, we may find the interplay of the "real" and the "imagined" worlds a useful conceptual framework.

The relationship between the two worlds is far more than a contest between realism and idealism, the dichotomy often adopted by those who seek to understand aspects of international relations that do not easily fit into the realist paradigm. Such writers are still entrapped in the narrow framework of national decision-making studies, in which various forces operating upon officials and opinion-makers are analyzed. Whether or not we view their thought and behavior as having been realistic or idealistic or both, the key framework is still the nation. Only if we get away from such a framework will it become possible to examine how various transnational forces have combined to challenge the legitimacy of traditional geopolitics: how, in effect, global consciousness has sought to define a new world order as an alternative to the existing international system. In such a framework, the most important questions would be, not when the Cold War started or how it developed, but how transnational forces were enveloping all nations and how the process of globalization was hijacked by geopolitics. For it could be argued that globalization was the main theme in post-1945 international relations, not the Cold War. If so, the "imagined" world was the real world that was somehow subverted by the imagined Cold War. The third world war, after all, remains only in the imagination, while the forces of globalization steadily came to construct an international system that went beyond anything the great powers had ever imagined.

Some writers divide the history of post-1945 international relations into two periods, the Cold War and the post–Cold War eras, and are willing to concede that after the end of the Cold War, many new forces, including globalization, came to define the shape of the world. But that is still privileging an interpretation based on the traditional state-centered view and making it the determinant of chronology. A multinational perspective, however, might yield a different interpretation. It would characterize the immediate postwar years, not in terms of the origins of the Cold War, but as the time when forces of globalization and internationalism renewed themselves after they had been subverted by war. In the immediate aftermath of World War II, there was little more important than the establishment (or, in some instances, reestablishment) of international organizations, both governmental and nongovernmental. The United Nations and its affiliated agencies were only the tip of the iceberg. There were, according to one source of information, 81 intergovernmental organizations and nearly 800 international nongovernmental organizations in 1950, about twice as many as there had been ten years earlier. Many of them worked closely together. From its inception, the United Nations gave official recognition to some nongovernmental organizations, and a report published in January 1951 indicated that as many as 188 nongovernmental organizations had achieved affiliate status with one UN agency or another. Of this number, more than a third had been created during or after the war.[27] The number and activities of these and other organizations suggest a determination on the part of the people of the world to organize themselves outside the national apparatus for carrying out tasks that states were either unable or unwilling to perform.

What were these tasks? During the period between 1945 and the end of the 1950s, four areas of issues or concerns attracted their attention. First, international organizations were concerned with eliminating nuclear weapons, and, if this were not possible in the immediate future, at least restricting their testing and redirecting atomic energy to peaceful uses. While the UN Security Council tended to become an arena of great-power rivalry, the International Atomic Energy Agency was established, with the support both of the United States and the Soviet Union, in 1957, with a view to encouraging research on nuclear power as a source of energy. Private organizations like SANE (the Committee for a Sane Nuclear Policy), in the meantime, began a campaign for ending atomic tests. As the committee asserted, "The sovereignty of the human community comes before all others—before the sovereignty of groups, tribes, or nations."[28] Second, humanitarian relief, a traditional goal of many organizations, was stepped up in the aftermath of the unprecedentedly brutal war. Not only victims of the war-related destruction but also millions of "displaced" persons after the war, as well as those caught in the cross fire of colonial struggles and civil wars needed immediate assistance, and international organizations were there to help. The United Nations was extremely active, through agencies such as the International Refugee Organization (established in 1946), the UN International Children's Emergency Fund (1947), and the World Health Organization (1946). Especially notable at that time was the work of religiously affiliated organizations that were founded during or after the war for carrying out humanitarian projects, including the Church World Service, the Catholic Relief Services, and the World Jewish Congress.

Third, going a step beyond relief, efforts were begun to extend developmental assistance to newly independent countries. The United Nations anticipated the growing importance of economic development when it established the Economic and Social Council at its inception. Moreover, a Special United Nations Fund for Economic Development was created in 1951 and a Committee for Industrial Development in 1960. Private individuals, in the meantime, organized themselves into numerous groups to assist in the task. To cite just one example, a meeting of development specialists in Washington, D.C., led to the founding of the Society for International Development in 1957 in order to exchange information and train personnel in this increasingly important field.[29] And fourth, cultural internationalism was once again promoted vigorously through the UN Educational, Scientific, and Cultural Organization, as well as other organizations, many of them private. The founders of UNESCO viewed it as a continuation of the prewar efforts at intellectual communication across national boundaries, but after World War II, there was much greater emphasis now on education (through student and scholarly exchanges) and on cross-civilizational dialogue. (A ten-year project for "mutual appreciation of Eastern and Western cultural values" is a good example.)[30] UNESCO worked closely both with its branches ("commissions") in various countries and with nongovernmental organizations. Already toward the end of the 1940s, institutions such as the International Association for the Exchange of Students for Technical Experience and the International Federation of Musical Youth had been created.

To these four principal categories of organized activities, two new ones were added during the 1960s and the 1970s: the protection of human rights and the preservation of the natural environment. Although international organizations have been active in many other areas as well, these six (peace, humanitarian relief, developmental assistance, cultural exchange, human rights, and environmentalism) have been particularly notable, because sovereign states have not always been willing or able to devote their attention and resources to solving those problems.[31]

In many ways the 1960s was a pivotal era in international relations, in that efforts at organizing movements across national boundaries proceeded to such an extent that something like global consciousness emerged as a major force in the world arena. The history of that decade, like that of the 1950s, is usually seen in terms of the Cold War and such landmarks as the

Cuban missile crisis, the Vietnam War, and the split between the Soviet Union and the People's Republic of China. All these were, of course, important episodes in the Cold War, although some historians have argued that the Cold War defined as U.S.-Soviet confrontation changed its character, if it did not come to an abrupt halt, in the second half of the decade, when the two superpowers reached agreement on preventing the spread of nuclear weapons and when, simultaneously, a second cold war erupted between the USSR and the PRC. Interpretations vary as to whether the Vietnam War was waged as part of the global Cold War or as a more regionally specific Asian war. These conflicting viewpoints, however, are little more than a minor disagreement, because they are still taking the Cold War as the key theme of international relations during the 1960s. None of these interpretations tells us anything about other developments that were making a profound impact on the shape of the world. I would argue that the combined impact of these developments was nothing less than the transformation of international relations.

To begin with, during the 1960s, transnational movements rapidly expanded and added to global networks of interdependence. Many new nongovernmental organizations were created to provide humanitarian relief and developmental assistance, which cooperated with intergovernmental organizations and with newly independent states in promoting the well-being of local populations. While such assistance had been given by many organizations in the past, the 1960s was a landmark decade, in that these various programs tended to be promoted in the name of human rights. The concept of human rights had been an important part of the vocabulary of international relations since World War II, but in the 1960s, it came to be viewed as the very key to a peaceful world order. "The subjection of peoples to alien subjugation, domination and exploitation constitutes a denial of fundamental human rights . . . and is an impediment to the promotion of world peace and cooperation," the UN General Assembly declared in 1960. To "alien subjugation, domination and exploitation" were added discrimination based on "race, color or ethnic origin" (1963) and "discrimination against women" (1967), which all had to be eliminated, according to the United Nations, if a just international society were to be constructed. Such language suggests that something like a universal awareness was dawning upon people everywhere that there were such things as human rights and interests, as distinct from national rights and interests, and that their protection had to be the basic objective of international relations.

International affairs were becoming human affairs. Nowhere was this more graphically demonstrated than in the activities of newly established international nongovernmental organizations in such fields as human rights and environmental protection. Such organizations as Amnesty International and the World Wildlife Fund, both established in 1961, contributed immensely to creating a psychological environment in which the protection of "prisoners of conscience," of the victims of authoritarian regimes, and of animals threatened with extinction by indiscriminate hunting were no longer marginal activities but were at the core of world affairs, precisely because they broadened the perimeters of international relations. These relations would henceforth embrace incarcerated individuals and endangered species as much as sovereign states.

These trends continued into the 1970s and beyond, and have persisted to this day. From our perspective, the 1970s was particularly notable because of a phenomenal growth in the number of international nongovernmental organizations. According to the Union of International Associations, these organizations increased from 2,795 in 1972 to 12,686 by 1984, an unprecedented rate of growth.[32] How does one account for this? It seems possible to understand it in the framework of the growth of nonstate, nonterritorial actors in the world. It was during the 1970s that what Eric Hobsbawm calls a "transnational economy" developed, exemplified by the mushrooming of multinational business enterprises.[33] At another level, there was an impressive growth of civil society in many, if not all, parts of the globe, notably in eastern Europe, questioning the long-held hegemony of communist states. In nonsocialist countries, people's faith in their governments was beginning to decline, as Joseph Nye and others have pointed out.[34] At the same time, the ending of the Vietnam War and the tentative steps toward ending the Cold War itself, as seen in the U.S.-Chinese rapprochement and the détente between the United States and the USSR, were turning nations' attention more and more to nongeopolitical issues, including trade, international finance, energy, and human rights. Under these circumstances, it is not surprising that international organizations of all kinds came to play steadily expanding roles.

From this perspective, one needs to revise the geopolitically determined chronology of postwar international affairs that charts the history of the era in terms of the origins, intensification, and termination of the Cold War. If nonstate actors are factored into the equation, the steady process of globalization, rather than the rise and fall of bipolar superpower confrontation, emerges as the key phenomenon of recent history. The process has not been unidirectional, of course, and the emergence of a global community has been hindered not only by geopolitical conflicts but also by local loyalties, which in many cases have, if anything, grown stronger over the years. Nevertheless, paying close attention to transnational organizations and movements enables us to trace an alternative story of the world in recent decades.

If some such analysis is tenable, then not just the history of the past few decades but also of other decades and even centuries may be susceptible to a new, non-nation-centered approach. If what is at the heart of our historical inquiry is the human condition, then it makes sense to go beyond the nation or the state as the sole framework of analysis and deal with human affairs, human aspirations, human values, and human tragedies. States do play a role, but only a partial role in all of these. The task that challenges historians of international relations is to devise a new transnational perspective that takes into account both states and nonstate actors.

NOTES

1. There has been much discussion among historians of U.S. foreign relations about the merits of an "international" as opposed to a "national" approach. Works written in the "national" mode naturally tend to be unilingual and uni-archival.

2. Among the most impressive recent studies that are multi-archival are D. C. Watt, *How War Came: The Immediate Origins of the Second World War, 1938–1939* (New York, 1989); Paul W. Schroeder, *The Transformation of European Politics, 1763–1848* (New York, 1994); and Niall Ferguson, *The Pity of War* (London, 1998).

3. Among the exemplary decision-making studies published recently are Michael Schaller, *Altered States: The United States and Japan since the Occupation* (New York, 1997); and Campbell Craig, *Destroying the Village: Eisenhower and Thermonuclear War* (New York, 1998). But note that these studies do not simply trace decision-making processes but link them to perceptions and ideologies held by officials and opinion-leaders.

4. Kristin L. Hoganson, *Fighting for American Manhood: How Gender Politics Provoked the Spanish-American and Philippine-American Wars* (New Haven, Conn., 1998).

5. Frank Ninkovich, *Modernity and Power: A History of the Domino Theory in the Twentieth Century* (Chicago, 1994); id., *The Wilsonian Century: U.S. Foreign Policy since 1900* (Chicago, 1999).

6. There is a good discussion of "synchronic history" in André Gunder Frank, *ReOrient: Global Economy in the Asian Age* (Berkeley and Los Angeles, 1998).

7. The best recent treatment of the state and the nation in European history is Haugen Schulze, *States, Nations and Nationalism: From the Middle Ages to the Present* (Oxford, 1996).

8. Marc Gallicchio, *Black Internationalism in Asia: The African American Encounter with Japan and China* (Chapel Hill, N.C.: 2000); Mark Bradley, *Imagining Vietnam and America: The Making of Postcolonial Vietnam, 1919–1950* (Chapel Hill, N.C.: 2000).

9. Norman M. Naimark, *The Russians in Germany: A History of the Soviet Zone of Occupation, 1945–1949* (Cambridge, Mass.: 1995).

10. For an excellent recent study of American GI's encounters with German women and children after the war, see Petra Gödde's forthcoming volume, *GIs and Germans: Culture, Gender, and Foreign Relations, 1945–1949*.

11. See, e.g., Stephen Castles and Mark J. Miller, *The Age of Migration: International Population Movements in the Modern World* (1993; 2d ed., New York, 1998); and Peter Stalker, *Workers without Frontiers: The Impact of Globalization on International Migration* (Boulder, Colo., 2000).

12. An excellent recent example is Frank, *ReOrient.*

13. See *The Internationalization of Environmental Protection,* ed. Miranda A. Schreurs and Elizabeth C. Economy (Cambridge, 1997), and *Activists beyond Borders: Advocacy Networks in International Politics,* ed. Margaret E. Keck and Kathryn Sikkink (Ithaca, N.Y. 1998).

14. Richard Pells, *Not Like Us: How Europeans Have Loved, Hated, and Transformed American Culture since World War II* (New York, 1997); Daniel T. Rodgers, *Atlantic Crossings: Social Politics in a Progressive Age* (Cambridge, Mass., 1998).

15. Among the most valuable studies of international organizations are Harold K. Jacobson, *Networks of Interdependence: International Organizations and the Global Political System* (New York, 1984); *The Politics of Global Governance: International Organizations in an Interdependent World,* ed. Paul F. Diehl (Boulder, Colo., 1997); and *Constructing World Culture: International Nongovernmental Organizations since 1875,* ed. John Boli and George M. Thomas (Stanford, Calif., 1999).

16. There are various definitions of international non-governmental organizations, but I have used this narrow definition in my published work. See Akira Iriye, "A Century of NGOs," *Diplomatic History* 23, 3 (Summer 1999): 421–35. A further exploration of this subject will be found in my *Global Community: The Role of International Organizations in the Making of the Contemporary World* (forthcoming).

17. The best recent synthesis on globalization is David Held, Anthony McGrew, David Goldblatt, and Jonathan Perraton, *Global Transformations: Politics, Economics and Culture* (Stanford, Calif., 1999).

18. *The Global Transformations Reader: An Introduction to the Globalization Debate,* ed. David Held and Anthony McGrew (Malden, Mass., 2000), 3.

19. J. A. Hobson, "The Ethics of Internationalism," *International Journal of Ethics* 17, 1 (October 1906): 19, quoted in Hugh McNeal, "Imagining Globalization" (unpublished paper, 1999), 1.

20. H. G. Wells, *An Englishman Looks at the World* (London, 1914), 20.

21. *La Vie Internationale* 1 (1912): 5.

22. Ferguson, *Pity of War.*

23. Akira Iriye, *Cultural Internationalism and World Order* (Baltimore, 1997).

24. Quoted in ibid., 56.

25. Lyman Cromwell White, *The Structure of Private International Organizations* (Philadelphia, 1933), 11, 15.

26. Among the best accounts of international affairs since World War II in a traditional framework, see John Lewis Gaddis, *The United States and the Origins of the Cold War* (New York, 1972); Gaddis, *The Long Peace: Inquiries into the History of the Cold War* (New York, 1987); Gaddis, *We Now Know: Rethinking Cold War History* (New York, 1997); Melvyn Leffler, *A Preponderance of Power: National Security, the Truman Administration, and the Cold War* (Stanford, Calif., 1992).

27. Lyman Cromwell White, *International Non-Governmental Organizations: Their Purposes, Methods, and Accomplishments* (New Brunswick, N.J., 1951), 305–11.

28. Milton S. Katz, *Ban the Bomb: A History of SANE, the Committee for a Sane Nuclear Policy* (New York, 1987), 27.

29. Information obtained through http://sidint.org/about/40yearsI.html, August 1999.

30. See UNESCO, *Appraisal of the Major Project on Mutual Appreciation of Eastern and Western Cultural Values, 1957–1966* (Paris, 1968).

31. For a classification of activities by nongovernmental organizations, consult Lester M. Salaman and Helmut K. Anheier, *Defining the Nonprofit Sector: A Cross-National Analysis* (Manchester, 1997).

32. *International Organizations: Abbreviations and Addresses, 1984–1985,* ed. Union of International Associations (Munich, 1985), 508.

33. Eric Hobsbawm, *The Age of Extremes: A History of the World, 1914–1991* (New York, 1994), 277.

34. *Why People Don't Trust Government,* ed. Joseph S. Nye Jr., Philip D. Zelikow, and David C. King (Cambridge, Mass., 1997).

THREE

Where in the World Is America?

The History of the United States in the Global Age

Charles Bright and Michael Geyer

What could be more American than a move to reposition U.S.-American history in the path of world history—to frame a new historical imagination appropriate for a transnational polity in a global age that supersedes the frontier images devised for a largely agrarian nation or the images of the "arsenal of democracy" so suitable for an urban-industrial nation of ever growing abundance?[1] Rethinking this history in terms of where the world may now be going is entirely in keeping with powerful traditions in American historiography. There are no national histories known to us that so deliberately, and, some would say, recklessly, take the future as their horizon for thinking about the past. Indeed, it would not be unreasonable to suggest that much of the current unhappiness with the prevailing spirit of history writing in this country arises from the way the postwar boom of professional scholarship has effaced the grand narrative sweep of American historiography that once combined traces of religious promise, frontier mythology, and progressive reformism into thematic constructions that placed the "future" squarely at the center of readings of the past and made its putative arrival a confirmation of the special trajectory of American history.

A move toward globalizing U.S.-American history might place it in line with the future again, especially if globalization is defined as the Americanization of the world. But this tantalizing possibility is instantly countered by another, grimmer vision: the weight of the global narrative might over-

Our thanks to Thomas Bender, Ian Tyrrell, Geoff Eley, Gabrielle Hecht, Matthew Connelly, and Fred Cooper for their helpful and, at times, very critical readings of this essay as it developed, and to Andrew Oppenheimer and Geoffrey Klingsporn (University of Chicago) for their valuable research assistance.

whelm the history of the United States and dissolve it into timeless flows and multicultural interactions. Here surely is one source of the acute edginess that surrounds discussions of globalization: it seems to carry distinctly American inflections, yet it threatens the cherished uniqueness that has been held to define the category of the "American." On the one hand, the "world" complains of Americanization and MacDonaldization; on the other, Americans are not sure they want their global "identity" reduced to MacDonald's, Microsoft, pop culture, and cruise missiles. This mirrored construction in which the world, for better or worse, is Americanized, and quintessential things American dissolve in a vortex of globalization, frames the terms of engagement for journalists and pundits locked in presentist debates.[2] But it also sets a puzzle for rethinking the history of the United States of America in a global age, and this is a puzzle that we feel can only be solved historically.

The great attraction of a "globalizing" move for many American historians is the pressure it promises to put on the lingering notes of American exceptionalism, that bundle of self-satisfied and exclusionary conceits that not only stressed American uniqueness but sought to establish a timeless framework in which American history was exempted from the ordinary forces of history that trapped everyone else "in history."[3] To be sure, several decades of vigorous critique[4] have now muted the more robust expressions of this line, or replaced them, among professional historians, with the more modest claims of comparative history.[5] Comparative studies have delivered important insights in such areas as race, slavery, economic organizations, and urban and state formations. But there are manifest limitations to this approach, in that the issues studied comparatively tend to arise from questions important to American historiography—such as the frontier, slavery, immigration,—but rarely flow in the opposite direction, from the historiography of others—peasantries, regionalism, genocide, and so on—to shed light on neglected aspects of American history.[6] But the effort to put American history in its place, as part of a broader comparative history fosters a more reflexive history in which the American self is mirrored in the experience of others.[7]

The more substantial problem with the attempt to internationalize American history through comparative studies is that it treats countries or societies as discrete, free-standing entities, and it tends to take the nation as a presumptive and preexisting unit of containment at the center of the story.[8] Much of this effort has developed in opposition to what its detractors call the idea of nation as a "container." The chief appeal of a globalizing horizon for American history is that it displaces the putative centrality of the nation-state and reconfigures the terrain of the national narrative. Pressing against the self-defining predicates of the nation, breaching borders, and challenging the power of the nationalist state and its history to frame meanings and practices—all of this opens space to see the multiple levels on which historical processes work, many of these uneasily, if at all, contained within national frames, and to hear the multitude of voices, mostly not well-spoken or educated, that were silenced by the self-enclosed discourses of the nation. Recent work in the history of the colonial period,[9] the "black Atlantic,"[10] immigration,[11] and social movements[12] has made plain how leaky and porous the national(ist) vessel always was and still is. Repositioning American history in a transnational or global terrain challenges and potentially rewrites standard treatments.[13] It will certainly produce a more truthful or "realistic" history that finds its satisfaction in demolishing the powerful master narrative of national history, with its overtones of predestination, highlighting connectivity and flow, and making visible peoples and activities long deemed marginal to a nationalizing historiography.

Yet for all the promise of these developments, this is not, in our view, the vantage point from which to rethink U.S.-American history in a global age. If the "container nation" is not the vessel for engaging a wider history, then we must inquire into historical processes beyond the scope and surely beyond the control of the United States that have nevertheless shaped American history. Here the project must confront its own obstacles, not the least of which is the lack of agreement, or certainly of any theory, about what is entailed in the now fashionable use of the term "global." There is understandable resistance to the notion of globalization, especially in its more exuberant iterations, on the suspicion that it is but the latest formulation of a continuing "Westernization" or "Americanization" of the world.[14] This resistance is further underwritten by historians, particularly specialists in the early modern period, who see nothing especially new in the integration of the world. If so, talking of globalization will not put much pressure on the prevailing tropes of American (or any other) national historiography. Moreover, globalization is often treated as but another layer or shell added to the earlier containers of mainstream historiography that centered on regions and nations. Yet if we take the limits of national narratives seriously, "globalizing" U.S.-American history requires more than simply the addition of context or perspective to a self-contained and otherwise unchanged national history. Indeed any move out of the self-containment of national history writing demands a full-scale engagement with globalization and the problems of how to narrate its discrete history.

First and foremost, we must recognize that the history of globalization is not coeval with U.S.-American history, but a distinct story that nevertheless continually intersects with and implicates it. The challenge posed by globalization is to construct a history that imbricates the national and the particular in processes that at once make the world one *and* account for its particulars in historical time. This requires a double-edged historiography that writes U.S.-American history from within and out of a history of globalization. In doing this, no matter how powerful the critique of the national narrative or of the centrality of the national state that empowered that narrative, we cannot escape the nation or dissolve it into the ebb and flow of transnational processes or the timeless interplay of cultures and peoples. Both as an affair of the mind—an ideology, an imaginary, or a methodological concept—and as a manifest historical presence—as physical power—the nation-state has been, in its historical epoch, bent on bounding and capturing global forces in an effort to control them, and has thus continuously included/excluded and framed other processes in the production of U.S.-American history.

The history of globalization has always involved struggles to bound or contain global forces as part of particular efforts to escape, shape, or control the processes of global integration; for this reason, we cannot write American history from a global horizon without the nation-state. But by the same token, the history of the sovereign nation-state will not and cannot contain America. Not only have the boundaries of the nation-state never been precise or stable, but American civil society (understood here in the American sense, as having to do with private property, law, and family as much as the public sphere) has always been more than the United States—reaching, grasping, pushing beyond the territorial confines and evading control. Perhaps this is the condition of a society that, in constituting itself for self-government, embraced universal principles to achieve that end; of a society that, in constituting itself as a nation, exported the idea of the national imaginary to the world; of a society whose territorial expansion and economic growth was so rapid and so explosive as to leap over all prophylactic attempts by the state to contain or direct it. In idea and practice, America was always larger, more boundless than the United States, and in this respect always already a global nation.

Herein lies the paradox of U.S.-American history for a global age. Because the ties that bind "America" to the United States have been problematic throughout its history, because the labor of holding the nation together, and the contestation over the terms of that union, were so immense, U.S.-American history and its historians have been concerned with the nation to the exclusion of the world. They have made the United States into the exception against the world, precisely because the United States was so much part of the world. Yet because the making of this nation was so consistently driven by universalist principles, because "America" reached so persistently beyond the United States, the world has long been alert to, even obsessed with, what it calls "America." This paradox not only underwrites the peculiar, if familiar discrepancy between what Americans know and care to know about the world and the huge investment that the world has in knowing the United States and imagining America, but it establishes a vantage point from which to forge U.S.-American history in a global age. This is a history of both the deep and irremediable entanglement of the United States in the world, the unceasing effort to seek out the world and pull it in—people, territory, goods, knowledge—and the equally insistent efforts to put the world off and negotiate a separation that would define the nation, its territory and its culture from and over against the world.

GLOBALIZATION AND HISTORY

Discussions of globalization have passed the initial stage of speculation and awe; they are now producing hypotheses and narratives that are testable. As yet, however, there is no consensus about what globalization means or whether it is even a meaningful concept. Moreover, the dynamic areas of study—literary criticism,[15] cultural studies,[16] postcolonial and subaltern studies,[17] the new diplomatic history,[18] anthropological investigations of borderlands and migrations,[19] as well as international relations theory and comparative politics[20]—are working with assumptions and languages that are more or less incompatible. Yet it is plain that whatever globalization may be or become, it cannot be readily subsumed into the compartmentalized history and theory of nation-states or the systems they form, nor can it be made over into a transnational or postnational world-encompassing civil society.

It is now commonly held, thanks to the actual study of globalization, that the best way to approach it is as a process—or set of overlapping processes—in which the flows of peoples, ideas, and things accelerate and the networks of worldwide interconnectivity become ever denser, facilitated in part by the increasing speed of communication and ease of transportation. As a process, globalization stretches social activities across borders and extends them to encompass huge distances in real time; it increases the multiplicity of channels so that interconnectivity occurs at many levels and in many arenas simultaneously; it speeds up the velocity of transactions, collapsing the buffers of distance, and it heightens the sense of simultaneity. It makes every part of the world responsive to every other part, albeit very unevenly and in very different states of density.[21]

The "world" takes shape as a "global" whole through a bewildering matrix of intersecting grids—in communications, capital networks, exchanges of goods and services, cultural flows and mimicries, and military systems—whose discrete practices proliferate along channels of communication and transportation and pass through a series of relays and gates that coordinate and control interconnectivity.[22] Big, complex, and potentially everywhere though it is, globalization is neither totalizing nor universal nor unidirectional. One need not be concerned with the world as a whole in order to study the processes of interconnectivity that are integrating the globe, nor must we think that everything and everyone in the world is entangled in global networks. In key respects, globalization constitutes distinct spheres of interaction.

The actual process of globalization is, meanwhile, overturning certain settled expectations carried over from earlier paradigms of world history and world-systems theory.[23] Two of these expectations deserve brief mention, because they are hardwired assumptions commonly associated with globalization. One is the idea taken from modernization theory, that globalization leads to homogenization; the other is tied to older precepts of universalist world history and presumes that globalization will result in the formation of a global consciousness. Together, they lead the discussion of globalization in directions that bear little resemblance to lived experience and inhibit scholarship.

First, far from making the world a more homogeneous place, the effect of globalization is to redraw boundaries and lines of demarcation, not abolish them. Global networks bear down upon the world and intersect with one another, reworking social relations and cultural realms and producing new cleavages between rich and poor, men and women, young and old, educated and unskilled, ethnic and racial groups. The peoples of the world are pulled into processes of global interaction and emerge resegmented and transformed in their diversity. It makes no sense to conceive of this interaction as a clash between modern and traditional sectors, or between the principles of movement and stasis, as modernization and development theory would have it.[24] Everywhere, local worlds are being remade in tandem with global changes, unevenly, perhaps unwillingly, even unknowingly, but unrelentingly. This is happening, not as if by invasion from without, but rather through linkages and reworkings that come to ground in one place after another and are lived and articulated by people in the context of mundane struggles to reproduce basic social relations. Casual workers in a Haitian tennis ball factory, every bit as much as money managers on Wall Street, live in families, communities, locations, and languages that are not residuals of some premodern condition, but are being created and lived through their imbrication with the global. Global practices encode local contexts, but they are also remade by them. Difference is reproduced locally, not as an assertion of traditional meanings or practices, but as a product of engagements with the global processes of change that are played out in everyday life. The condition of globality, then, is at once a deepening of integration and a proliferation of difference.[25] A modern world of multiple modernities is taking shape.

By the same token, there is no indication that globalization is likely to produce a world free of want. Quite the contrary, the capacity of globalization to produce inequality is one of the key features of the process. Seemingly "soft" networks and flows have an extraordinary capacity to produce near-impenetrable channels, boundaries, and demarcations, which cross-cut the seemingly more rigid borders of states and fixed physical boundaries of geography. Enhanced connectivity sorts and segregates, and the fact that the whole world is, at least in principle, accessible to everyone else means that, in practice, the threshold of selection is high and exclusions are frequent. Corridors of wealth and connectivity girdle the earth next to great wastelands of poverty and isolation—not just out there in some "third" world, but next door in Detroit, Liverpool, or Los Angeles. Far from fostering a homogenization of the world, globalization has made the production of difference and inequality a much more proximate and intimate affair.[26]

Second, the process of demarcation in a seemingly "borderless world"[27] casts doubt on expectations that a unitary global consciousness will emerge with globalization. For one thing, it is quite possible, even common, for people to be caught up in the processes of globalization without seeing them—miners of uranium in Madagascar who have never heard of the atomic bomb and do not know, nor could be made to care, that we live in a nuclear age.[28] People who consume the labor of sweatshop workers may not want to be reminded of how, under what conditions, and by whom their clothes and shoes are produced.[29] Globalization takes shape through myriad overlapping channels and circuits, which certainly create connectivity, but a connectivity that often has the effect of lesser, not greater, awareness and concern. It is the nature of such highly developed divisions of labor that, by themselves, they do not produce community. Inasmuch as there is global discourse and global awareness, these are mostly functional collaborations, often framed in arcane language and codes that are impenetrable to outsiders. In the world of high-tech networking, there is a lot of deterritorialized boundary-making going on that interrupts, blocks, and secludes global conversations. Cosmopolitanism as the sense of being in and part of the world is not a direct effect of globalization.[30]

From within these processes, we can no longer purport to see the whole from a particular vantage point, that is, from any one region or place, because such putative centers are always already crisscrossed by other perspectives and implicated in other people's actions and imaginings. In a "preglobal," less mobile or interconnected world, imaginations of the world could proceed from home, from fixed and known horizons that anchored identity; in a world of transnational networks and information flows that remake localities and shape experience, it is no longer easy to imagine one's own position beyond or outside the conditions of the connected world. Even if people stay put (which is increasingly an option for the extraordinarily privileged and almost inevitable for the very poor), they no longer confront only their own heritage, their own values, norms, and artistry, but a multiplicity of concurrent and, as it were, lateral influences that blindside and confuse as much as they inform. The consequence is not unlike vertigo. The world is much better known, yet people have trouble finding themselves in it. Subjectivities become less fixed and more fluid as people assemble meanings and identity from everywhere (and nowhere).[31] In this way, cherished notions about culture—seen as the autonomous and indigenous production of norms and values, grounded in a unity of language and territoriality—have dissolved. Yet no general global culture or consciousness has emerged.[32]

Setting aside these inherited expectations about the nature and destination of globalization gives us a much clearer picture of the historicity of globalization. By interrupting the broad-gauged narrations—human progress, the rise and fall of empires, the development of capitalism—that informed the expectations now thwarted, we get a sharper purchase on the rupture or disjuncture that marks off a discrete history of globalization with a beginning and, undoubtedly, an end. These discrete processes cannot be captured in the long sweep of cultural and commercial interactions among settled civilizations that is the stuff of recent world histories, nor can they be written off the history of Europe as the diffusion of Western ways to and over everyone else. Rather, a history that focuses on the processes of globalization emerges from the histories of discrete regions and power centers as the density and velocity of interactions among them crushed the buffers of distance and time and made the production of autonomous histories increasingly impossible. The "world" became "global" as it lost the outer boundaries of physical distance, frontier exchanges, and liminal zones for nomads and pirates and became an interior space of interconnectivity.

Elsewhere, we have made a case for the middle decades of the nineteenth century as a rough point of departure for this history of globalization.[33] Between the 1840s and the 1880s, the earlier and continuing crises, and sometimes collapse, of old land-based and maritime empires in the Americas, along the Eurasian rim, and in the Pacific intersected with new forms of national politics and rapid developments in weapons and communications technology to rachet up the density and intensity of interactions among disparate regions of the world. The simultaneity of regional crises coupled with an intensification of interactions among regions hitherto distant and distinct produced a worldwide shifting of gears. The key to survival in this new environment was found in novel kinds of competitive self-mobilization—either in the form of nation-state-making projects, not all of them successful, that sought to carve out self-governing enclaves based on ethnic, linguistic, religious, or racial solidarities that could intensify the mobilization of resources and effort (Poland, Serbia, Italy, Germany, Egypt, Persia, Japan, Argentina, and the United States), or in the reformation of polyglot imperial systems, again not always successful, that appropriated new administrative and repressive techniques and deployed various forms of "official" nationalism[34] in an effort to shore up central authority (czarist Russia, British India, China, and the Ottoman and Hapsburg empires). The interaction among these parallel efforts of nation-making and empire-building and the densely competitive and now global environment in which they were played out lifted contacts between and among regions and power centers to a new plane of sustained interconnection that has never since been lost.

The history of globalization thus begins, not with the first transnational organization, nor with a cyclical surge of ongoing commerce and cultural exchange, but in the simultaneous and often quite febrile efforts of peoples and regimes, around the world *and* in real time, to secure and maintain control over autonomous destinies by means of a greater, more sustained engagement with all others. This gave sovereignty itself new meanings. It no longer lay in the body of the king or in some mystical *raison d'état* but in the delineation of sharp boundaries and the mobilization of people and resources within those borders for successful competition in global interactions. A fierce assertion of difference and, simultaneously, an urgent engagement in global competition posed old choices—to participate or to be dominated—in ways quite new to much of the world and now desperately relevant to all. Borrowing and copying from others in an effort to keep others at arm's length meant that an effort to separate out was the first evident sign of efforts to break into the processes of globalization. In these initial phases, global integration was carried on in the idiom of nationalism and nation-making, but increasingly the debate was framed, not over whether there should be global integration, but on what terms, by whose rules, and with what payoffs.

GLOBALIZATION AND U.S.-AMERICAN HISTORY

U.S.-American history anticipated and articulates the core dynamics of complicity and distance that came to characterize the history of globalization as it emerged in the course of the nineteenth century. One might even think of it as paradigmatic, in that, over time, it highlights two key features of globalization.

First, U.S.-American history is always already "everywhere else"—quite literally in the eye of the world and written into "other" modern histories— be it that of France, Japan, Brazil, or Liberia. It is part of the history of the world that produced it.[35] The existence of the United States of America was from the start predicated upon universalist principles that in both general and particular ways resonated around the world.[36] However read—as premodern or modern, liberal or republican—it was these Enlightenment principles that elevated a provincial backwater to global significance, placing it front and center in the histories not only of Europe but also of Haiti and the black Atlantic (of which America formed part as a slaving society). In setting out to make a reality of European ideas and ideals, the United States was not just a model or an influence upon others; it was part of their debates with themselves about their own political identity and national futures. Similarly, in Latin America, where the same principles were powerfully at work in the early nineteenth century, the United States was present, both as a fellow traveler in the debates over popular sovereignty and as a rival, or co-producing pioneer, in nation-making. Nor should we forget the more vernacular iterations of universalist principles that have punctuated American history: in the appeal to economic success and fabulous riches (legitimizing free market principles), the call to Christian redemption (building a new Jerusalem unencumbered by tradition and earthly subjugation), and the promise of global pacification (deploying both power and democratic ideology in the name of universal peace).

These ideas have reverberated everywhere. They were not simply projections of the American homeland, but continuing presences, both excesses and products of America beyond the United States. Hence, today people around the world think of America as the first democracy or, alternatively, as the land of MacDonald's. They trade and invest in U.S. dollars and appropriate the imagery of American movies and popular culture. They help shape an "offshore" America that is beyond the control of the United States, although of profit to it, and that, indeed, belongs to the world. This l'Amérique has never been merely an "image nation," to be watched, ogled at, and commented upon, but has always also been a physical presence— an expansive civil society that has continuously flourished beyond the territory and sovereignty of the United States, forming grids of action and interaction that both constituted the United States in a global space and entangled it in the history of globalization. American historians will need to excavate this buried history in writing American history for a global age. Although a more detailed history of this offshore America is urgently needed, we can, at this point, only evoke it and point to ways in which it has become ever more insistent and unavoidable in the late twentieth century.

The reason this offshore America remains so buried is that American history has long been written against it, as historians have sought to capture universalist principles and global practices for the national vessel and to remake offshore presences into manifestations of the "influence" or "effect" of the United States, otherwise conceived of as the distinct and relatively self-contained story of the "making of a nation."[37] For all that, however, we cannot take this nation for granted; nor should the role of universalist principles in its making lead us into searches for the roots or origins of an exceptional state. For although the American Revolution was fought in the name of universal principles and claims to citizenship, it is startling how little the making of the American nation conforms to the reigning paradigms of European nation-making: Americans were not strictly speaking an insurgent nationality formed in long struggles against an intransigent and oppressive imperial power (like the Irish, Czechs, Poles, Serbs, Italians, and Germans), and America was not simply the nationalist reimagining of ancient institutions within the framework of an established territorial state (like Britain, France, and the Netherlands).[38] The American nation was imagined neither as the renovation of an existing sovereign state nor as the articulation of insurgent claims from within such a sovereignty, but as a novel political formation, created through particularist compromise and appeals to universals, and imagined, as it were, after the fact.[39] Who were its citizens, if people, white and male, from almost everywhere and anywhere constituted the nation? What was its sovereign territory, if the borders were in motion and the state barely in control of a people pushing beyond them? What was the imagined community of the nation if its first principles were the rights of (all) mankind? How could a global nation be also, and at the same time, a sovereign nation?

Defining a particular against, but also in terms of, the universal meant that the history of the United States of America was always concerned with questions of sovereignty, with the efforts to define a people and territory fit for self-government. The constitution of self-government was both urgent and persistent, and the location, extent, and boundaries of the sovereignty of the United States—understood here, not in a legal sense, but as the outcome of contentious efforts to secure the conditions of life, liberty, and the pursuit of happiness—were always central to a U.S.-American nation, and, in our view, constitute the second challenge that the theory and practice of a history of globalization poses for the writing of American history. If, in cracking open the "container nation," we pose the question of the nature and extent of U.S. sovereignty, we do so not in order to disband the idea and practice of sovereignty but in order to raise the question of self-government and self-determination in a world that is not made in America. In this, American history is also paradigmatic in the history of globalization.

The dual challenge, then, is to write the history of the United States of America as simultaneously that of a sovereign and a global nation. The simple question we pose—where in the world is America?—may sound like a rhetorical ploy, but it is in fact the crux of the issue. In what follows, we sketch three moments or modes of American sovereignty in which the problem of constituting self-government entailed the renegotiation of inside and outside, of defining the United States of America against the world and placing it in the world. In its first iteration, answers to the question— where in the world is America?—were grounded in the production of territory, in the continuous and contentious efforts to bound, delineate, and possess a geographical space for republican self-government. This territorial nation was then overhauled, in a second iteration, by the consolidation of territories of production that drew in and revamped domestic spaces in a precocious effort to mobilize national resources and project power into an increasingly competitive global environment in which the industrial nation found its moorings and legitimacy. But while we treat these perhaps familiar themes of the territorial production of sovereignty extensively, we shall also have occasion to essay the offshore or "other" America along the way. For in the contemporary world, the question—where in the world is America?—has been reposed as the problem of preserving the capacity for self-government in the context of a globalization process that is read, by some, as the Americanization of the world and, by others, as the deterritorialization of U.S.-American sovereignty. At stake here is the present and future of the American project of forming a nation made of the world, but separate from it, and made within the world, but without being in control of it.

MAKING THE SOVEREIGN NATION: THE PRODUCTION OF TERRITORY / THE TERRITORIES OF PRODUCTION

For a half century after independence, U.S. sovereignty was grounded in the physical control of land. Territoriality guaranteed the new nation, providing security against European imperial powers and ensuring the prosperity of a growing population. From the Treaty of Paris through the Louisiana Purchase, the War of 1812, and the settlement of the Mississippi and Ohio valleys to the Monroe Doctrine, engrossing great swatches of the map and delineating precise boundaries was critical to carving out a republican space against the British, French, and Spanish empires. But territory also mattered for its concrete properties—not as something to be bargained back and forth as a token or trophy of diplomacy, but as a physical object to be imagined as space or potential and realized "under foot" in real property that was taken up, marked, owned, and rendered fruitful. The "strategic doctrine" that animated the authors of the Constitution proceeded from a vision of an American republic secured precisely by its capacity to expand into space and thereby to reproduce those conditions of civic and economic independence that guaranteed against tyranny. What began with Jefferson and Madison as an argument for liberty through equality of condition became by the time of Jackson an ideological insistence that the Republic needed to expand in order to remain dynamic and, more specifically to smother emerging strains between north and south over slavery. Within another generation, territorial expansion had become manifest destiny, and the favored story of the frontier as pioneer settlement and national self-actualization was already entering the historical lexicon, to be canonized by Frederick Jackson Turner at the century's end. Quite literally, the production of territory produced the sovereign nation.

Recent critiques of the national narrative of westward settlement have given the frontier a new lease on historiographical life by stressing its interactive nature, both as a natural resource for the world economy and as a multicultural zone of interaction and cohabitation.[40] But while the notion of borderlands makes visible those on the "outside" or "in between" and captures more complexity than the imagery of an advancing line of settlement, the effort to see the West as a zone of continuing cultural intermixing and social fluidity tends to mute the fundamental nature of the change that overtook the territorial hinterlands and its people during the nineteenth century.[41] The movement from borderless frontier to interactive borderlands to bordered nations in the space of half a century was a wrenching transformation, not only in U.S.-American history, but across the entire Western Hemisphere, and it signaled, we would argue, the inauguration of powerful new globalizing dynamics in the world beyond.

The slow-motion collapse of the British and Spanish empires in the Americas from the late eighteenth through the early nineteenth centuries undercut the geopolitics of the "middle ground" that had served as a buffer in the imperial game and had given space for indigenous people to shape the terms of their existence with some, limited autonomy.[42] Receding empires were replaced by a string of republics, large and small, across the whole hemisphere, north and south, which were engaged from the start in struggles to defend their sovereignty and stabilize their boundaries. At the heart of all these struggles was territoriality. Land was key to survival and self-definition.

Aside from the myriad sectional tensions and regional rebellions that undermined rickety states and strained the ligaments of constitutional structures, all these new nations faced the problem of how, as it were, to produce themselves. Clarifying and defending borders entailed complex diplomatic relations and frequent wars with neighbors, as well as efforts to fend off meddling European powers. There was no room here for liminal zones and borderlands, and everywhere in the hemisphere, the struggle to control territory involved state projects to erase the "mixed use" spaces of the hinterland and to subdue or eliminate indigenous peoples (a project completed in Argentina with the military occupation of the Pampas just as the final conquest of the plains Indians by the U.S. Army was under way). Moreover, engrossing land for production—especially to generate resources for fledgling national economies—created a general need to intensify the exploitation of the soil, concentrate and capitalize farming, deepen market connections for agricultural goods, establish infrastructures of communications and transportation, and displace squatters and indigenous peoples—in short, to reduce subsistence farming in favor of commercial agriculture. How land was handled, transferred to private hands, and rendered productive turned upon a range of issues that were, in turn, mapped onto the oppositions framing key political debates and conflicts across the hemisphere: between city and countryside, central power and regional autonomy, merchant and farm capital, free trade and protection, slave and free labor, autonomous and dependent paths of economic development, and so on. Issues of this kind divided regions and social groups throughout the Americas in this period, sparking political crises, breakaway movements, regional rebellions, and civil war.

Without question, this production of territory in the Western Hemisphere was a transnational, even global affair.[43] Earlier scholarship saw the process of conquering and populating the American hinterlands as the outer edge of an expanding capitalism restlessly reaching for new resources and organizing the production of raw materials, with European, especially British, capital and technology underwriting the construction of transportation and communication infrastructures. More recently, historians have focused on the flow of people, especially the mobilization of labor power across the Atlantic, both in the importation of African slaves and, after 1840, by the more voluntary mass migration of impoverished European peasants. The histories of the Atlantic economy and its diasporas underscore the fact that the Americas were embedded in a transoceanic ecumene bequeathed by the colonial era. Producing the nation—realizing territory as a viable foundation of sovereignty—depended on markets that could not be contained within national boundaries, and nation-making itself went forward as a transnational project, fueled by flows of people, resources, and information, by no means unidirectional, that were not then, nor can retrospectively be easily made over into, national subjectivities.

Yet a history of nation-making as a great settling of peoples in diaspora that drew in and deployed global energies must remain alert to the fact that with fluidity went foreclosure; the production of territory entailed a distinct narrowing and foreshortening of transnational connectivities. In the Atlantic world, the interplay of closure with flow steadily transformed an ecumene into an "inter-nation" system. The collapse of imperial structures disrupted the traffic in administration and policy across the Atlantic and interrupted the very networks of ideas and debates that had made the transatlantic revolutionary moment possible. The creole nationalism of the former colonies may have crossed the ocean, but it infused into Europe new ideologies of difference that reinforced distance. National distinction-making was underscored by diplomatic and military efforts to exclude European powers from the Americas. Moreover, the success of the transatlantic movement against the slave trade had the paradoxical effect of secluding Africa from the further peopling of the New World; indeed, the prohibition of the slave trade, one of the few internationally sanctioned human rights agreements of the nineteenth century, may be seen as presaging the new racial divisions of the world that would characterize the colonial segregation of the late nineteenth century in Asia and Africa. The breakup of empires also promoted a general recomposition of colonial trade, disrupting the triangular and intercolonial commerce that had knit the ecumene together and fostered the colorful limbo worlds of the sea. Especially in the production of grain and cotton, monocultural regimes emerged, binding primary suppliers to industrial (mainly British) markets in ways that promoted the simultaneous deepening and simplifying of trade across the Atlantic, at least until the 1860s.

Similar patterns of closure took shape between the new American republics on, as it were, the other side: in the interior of the Americas. By the 1830s and 1840s, the borderlands of the hinterland had gained a new status in the definition of sovereignty.[44] This was not just a question of "international" relations or an inability to tolerate ambiguity in the edge spaces between nations. It was also the way the borderlands impinged upon and disrupted the stability of national polities. In the U.S. case, this was precisely because the lines of settlement at the frontiers were never fixed or continuous, and a restless movement of people beyond the boundaries of the political nation continually generated crises at the center by posing and reposing the question of the territorial expansion of slavery. The compensatory efforts to forge political compromises over this issue all hemorrhaged in the borderlands, repeatedly threatening the Union with dissolution, renewing debate over questions of universal principles and citizenship, and driving home the lesson that the United States of America was not safe unless the proliferation of internal differences within civil society could be contained territorially or the world outside could be made a ready receptacle for the centripetal pressures that these differences generated. In this framework, the borderland zones of interaction were not just "in between" nations or a stage for rivalry between nations; they threatened to turn the outside in and unmake the nation.

The Mexican War was paradigmatic of this dynamic. The conflict between these two "United States"—which were, in the 1820s, of almost equal size and population[45]—was, like Chile's war with Peru and Bolivia or the war of the "triple alliance" of Brazil, Argentina, and Uruguay against Paraguay, a regional conflict in which European powers played very marginal roles, and it arose, like the others, out of borderland issues that were finally resolved by drawing a fixed international boundary. But the war was also about the extension of slavery. Texas was a problem "inside" the United States of America because it affected the political balance between slave and free states. The movement of American settlers into this territory and their subsequent movement for incorporation into the United States forced new and more elaborate compromises within the political nation as well as war with Mexico. Yet that war was ultimately more telling for what it did not do. The expansion into Mexican territory stopped short of colonial-type annexation. The decision of the Polk administration not to annex either all of Mexico or the area south of the Rio Grande to the 26th parallel, as some in the cabinet seriously urged, signaled a narrowing of the territorial definition of U.S. sovereignty: geopolitical security and the economic future would henceforth be grounded in a territoriality reserved for whites of northern European origin only, leaving little room for the administration, let alone assimilation, of colonial populations.[46] This more exclusive and racist definition of territoriality, and the fact that the Caribbean-Hispanic dimension of U.S. expansionism (especially the possibility of buying or seizing Cuba, so often broached by southern landowners as a solution to the future of slavery),[47] was not taken up in the decades before the Civil War, indicates that the United States was moving away from the kinds of colonialism based on hierarchical regimes and cross-racial compromises with local elites that, elsewhere in the world (especially in India) at this time, seemed promising options. As Anglo-Saxon racism began making the U.S. border, the result was regional conflicts with neighbors that had to do with separation and distance, not conquest. The North American republic was moving away from, not further into, the rest of the hemisphere.

It was this geopolitical turn, moreover, that transformed regional conflict into civil war. The Mexican conflict saw the first overt moves in the U.S. Congress to exclude blacks from American territoriality. Not only did the United States eschew colonial expansion toward the equator, but, with the Wilmot Proviso, even the most dedicated northern abolitionists made plain their determination to block the "menace of Negro immigration." The effort to place restrictions on the mobility of nonwhites anticipated, not only the national patterns of segregation that would take shape at the end of the century, but also a global pattern of the mid and late nineteenth century, in which whites were free to travel, migrate, colonize, and participate in markets and voting, while nonwhites were held in place, their movement regulated and constricted, their participation denied. But, just as important, this move to confine slavery to a southern "ghetto" indicated that the definition of territorial sovereignty was heading toward a break with the zone of slave and plantation agriculture that stretched from the Mason-Dixon line across the Caribbean to Brazil. This was a trajectory that would fracture the territorial foundations of the nation and precipitate civil war.

Yet the fact that this issue of slavery's future produced a political impasse within the United States also underscores the degree to which powerful currents of U.S. development were cutting against the increasingly dominant tendency in the Americas, including the southern United States toward subordinate incorporation, as primary producers, in a British-centered industrial order—a direction that seemed, at the time, a promising and profitable regional option. Indeed, seen from this perspective, we might just as well reverse the usual equation of who seceded from whom, and see a northern, increasingly industrial enclave breaking out of hemispheric and imperial formations toward a more egalitarian (although exclusively white and northern European) strategy of nation-building.

The Civil War formed a decisive hinge in the constitution of U.S. sovereignty. On the one hand, the war opened the final chapter in the production of a territorial nation. The Republican leadership of the 1860s was bent on waging a total war of destruction in order to preserve the Union. This renewed nation, forged in violence, was an egalitarian (white and male) democracy utterly committed to its own self-preservation and determined to enforce its territorial sovereignty to the point of unconditional surrender. This was played out, not only against southern rebels in the civil war, but against Indian nations in the plains wars that followed in the 1870s and 1880s. By eliminating slavery, in fact, the civil war made territorial consolidation "safe" for the nation. The fervent republicanism of the war effort, coupled with the new military capabilities of the nation, proceeded to impose on the peoples of the borderlands an implacable choice: reservations or extermination. The implicit decision not to tolerate diversity within U.S. borders left no room for indirect rule through protectorates with co-opted elites on the model of British India, and certainly not for the creation of a separate Amerindian state in the Union, any more than it could make space for the inclusion of former slaves in the nation. This was a democratic imperialism unique to the geopolitics of the mid nineteenth century, although perhaps not so unfamiliar to students of the twentieth: "democratic" in Tocqueville's sense of there being no limit to what could be done to luckless minorities so long as it did not adversely affect the interests of the majority, whose sovereignty was now firmly grounded in the territoriality of republican occupation.

Yet, at the same time, the war mobilization in the northern United States constituted a decisive move in the direction of an integral nation-state based on free labor and a full-throated industrialization. This was a new departure, in which U.S. sovereignty was rapidly and quite radically redefined; in the later decades of the nineteenth century, the conditions for ensuring life, liberty, and the pursuit of happiness came increasingly to depend on industrial output and projections of force rather than on the acquisition of territory. Here the lessons of war—self-conscious, state-led, and maximalist mobilization of human and natural resources in the production of power—were confirmed by the new terms of global competition and the intensification of national rivalries that took shape in the middle decades of the nineteenth century.

Infrastructure was key to these developments, both in the physical grids of transportation and connectivity that moved people and goods and in the principles of organization and logistics that maximized output. Already by the 1890s, as its steel mills were producing a high seas fleet, it was clear that the United States was capable of the kind of massive projections of force from its continental, industrial base that would make it the "arsenal of democracy" by the 1940s. The Spanish-American War may, indeed, have reflected the growing capacities of the U.S. state,[48] and the seizure of the Philippines might be construed (although we would not) as an extension of the expansionist momentum that had overrun the mainland into the Pacific world. But sea power in Alfred Thayer Mahan's conception was unequivocally infrastructural power, designed not to link the far-flung elements of a colonial empire but to establish the capacity to lift force over seas.[49] While it would have been reasonable to expect, say at the time of the Venezuelan crisis in 1895, that there would be more wars over empire, especially with Great Britain, U.S. power in the twentieth century was not to be grounded in the limitless acquisition and control of territory. The United States tangled with, but was not carried away by the "new imperialism." Rather sovereignty—as the guarantor of security and prosperity—was redefined around integrated territories of production, built on an infrastructure with global reach and capable of projecting force, commodities, and images.

In this, the United States was not alone. It was moving along a trajectory strikingly parallel to those of Germany and Japan in the late nineteenth century. All three were industrial newcomers, forged in the violence of the 1860s and part of the increasingly competitive global environment thereafter. They all engaged in concerted and self-conscious drives of industrial catch-up and aimed at autonomous development based on mass industrial consolidations behind high tariffs, a close nexus of productive forces and state power, and competing, but surprisingly complementary, ideologies of national self-discipline and mobilization. Although intensely nationalistic, they were engaged in a fundamentally transnational process, in which mass industrial sectors within nations, perched on narrow domestic bases, were tied to the world and one another in relations of exchange, competition, and reciprocal mimicry.

Their competitive engagement with one another was further complicated in the course of the twentieth century, as the efforts to transform old land-based empires into mass industrial societies brought Russia, and later China, into the struggles to define national sovereignty around the principles of industrial production, mass mobilization, and self-discipline. The alternative regimes that took shape, whether egalitarian or hierarchical, coerced or consensual, generated immense new power in global competition and thoroughly revamped national societies. They were in this respect quite distinct from, and often at odds with, colonial empires like those of

France and, especially, Great Britain, which were also rapidly elaborated in the late nineteenth century and consolidated in the early twentieth century as part of (national) responses to the newly generated competitive pressures; for the trajectories of colonialism were characterized precisely by their efforts to avoid the wrenching internal pressures of resource mobilization and self-discipline by exporting the pains of readjustment onto colonial subjects.

In deep competition with one another, these industrial rivals were also intensely aware of one another. For all of them, too, America beckoned as a paragon and model of modern ways. This was not merely a question of borrowings—from Taylorism to jazz and cocktails—but of imaginings. The Germans and Japanese imagined themselves doing in the twentieth century what they thought the Americans had done in the nineteenth: conquering a territorial hinterland that would serve as a source of food and resources, a controllable inland market, and a homeland for a growing population organized for maximum production. Remaking Eurasia and East Asia into the bases of hemispheric power capable of engaging in global projections and competition combined a potent nationalist imagination with reflections of an American reality. And while the genocidal brutality of the German and Japanese wars flowed along lines of long-standing prejudice, it fed on—and even sought legitimation in—the invidious comparison that had them settling their own hinterlands, purged of their savage inhabitants. In an analogous, but ultimately utterly distinct way (because it already had a hinterland and aimed at a regime of equality rather than racial hierarchy), Soviet Russia took "its" America as the goal and reward of crash industrialization; to mass-manufacture goods in pursuit of an egalitarian abundance was for a time, and in part, a justification of terror and ultimately the legitimation of the system that promised to bury capitalism.

None of these imaginings grew out of a close study or, for that matter, a duplication of American realities; this was the work of *l'Amérique* in the first half of the twentieth century. America was the supreme inspiration and ultimate enemy of its rivals—and the myriad ways in which they communed with and made purported copies of "their" America were never a deliberate export of the United States or under its control. That the United States was a model for the world, and that it managed to marshal its considerable assets to blunder through a passage that proved far more contested and, in the end, self-destructive, for the Germans, Japanese, and Russians, should not, however, blind us to the fact that, within the United States itself, the corporate industrial transformation was anything but easy or natural. The crisis-prone character of the early twentieth century was a global phenomenon that included the United States and made its history, in key respects, a version of others'.

The makeover of the United States was driven by a massive reorganization of peoples and spaces that, while it was happening, proved confusing, crisis-prone and violent. What came to be celebrated in the 1950s as the native expression of American genius and enterprise was no preordained movement. The formation of territories of production proceeded slowly and often hesitantly; while a corporate core of industrial concentration consolidated itself as the most potent sector of American civil society, it operated for a long time on relatively narrow platforms and was hardwired into an infrastructure of communication and transportation that covered the nation only gradually. Moreover, throughout the first half of the twentieth century, the industrial nation was widely perceived in the United States as undemocratic, un-American, and illegitimate. Indeed, it is our argument that as image and as reality, the industrial nation only established its domestic legitimacy as it became an "arsenal of democracy" for the world.

The internal story of this massive industrial transformation in United States is often told in national(ist) histories and needs no recounting here.[50] But we would emphasize two dimensions of the process that seem pertinent to locating it within a globalizing history. First, the new territories of production created by the concentration of industrial capacities and the reorganization of productive processes into regimes of mass production were never coeval with the territorial boundaries of the United States. Mass industrial production was perched on very narrow platforms within a territorial America that remained overwhelmingly agrarian until the 1940s. These territories of production were always more international than the rest of the national economy, and they were nestled in grids of power and connectivity—of electricity and telephone wires, railroads and highways, market and credit supply—that only gradually spread out and reorganized American territoriality.

As this process of corporate reordering went forward, moreover, it laid down new lines of inclusion and exclusion and generated new allocations of winners and losers.[51] Struggles over corporate consolidation thus had powerful spatial as well as cultural dimensions. These appear as conflicts at the core of the territories of production themselves: the restless experiments of management in organizing the factory floor and coordinating time and motion in space were met by equally determined efforts, whether organized or isolated, active or passive, to defend the spaces of workers' autonomy. The very terms used in these battles—"lockout," "sit-down," "open shop" and "closed shop," "walkout," and "picket"—signaled the territorial nature of industrial struggles.[52] There were also conflicts over urban spaces—parks, streets, neighborhoods—in which the ongoing work of segregation, in separating out immigrants, workers, blacks, and all "others," went hand in hand with the forging of new urban identities that centered on a modern, secular, and putatively American middle class.[53] And there were myriad conflicts between the industrial and agricultural sectors, the city and the countryside, that in mapping new allocations of success and failure across the hinterland turned small towns and whole regions into defensive redoubts of Jeffersonian, Protestant, and other "true" American values against the transformational intrusion of mass industrial practices.[54]

All of these conflicts were reproduced in the political arena as the consolidation of the territories of production fragmented old political solidarities and, in disrupting hallowed habits of civic and local autonomy, generated struggles over who controlled the process and its outcomes.[55] For over half a century, these political wars periodically paralyzed the state and acted as a powerful drag on the elaboration of a U.S. corporate order. Not only did variant voices of resistance and dissent have to be suppressed or co-opted,[56] but again and again, an "un-American"[57] ethno-nationalism that championed some vision of the nation as a container of differences and America as a melting pot had to be asserted (usually from the top down) against the actual multiplications of difference generated in the social upheaval and fragmentation that industrial integration produced.

The second point we would stress is that the corporate regime was stabilized domestically—that is, legitimized and naturalized as something quintessentially American and essential to security and prosperity—only when it became anchored externally in permanent projections of American power. Domestic resistance to the integrated concentrations of production was finally neutralized as the urban, industrial identity of the nation found its legitimacy in a global project. Notably, until World War II, there was little permanent in the exercise of U.S. corporate and military power abroad. The projection of naval force, the dispatch of troops overseas, the deployment of American capital, and the assertions of American leadership in forging international organizations or underwriting economic recovery retained a distinctly expeditionary quality.[58] It was transient and persistently impeded by a majority consensus that wanted nothing to do with foreign entanglements that ran counter to the seclusion of the territorial nation.

This view arose, not only from the continued rearguard opposition of an "older" territorial sovereign to the new industrial identity of the nation, but, paradoxically, from within the New Deal itself, whose priorities in the 1930s were focused on a program of national economic recovery and egalitarian social reform. The debate of the late 1930s over whether the sovereignty of a self-governing people was best secured by separation from, or intervention in, the world peaked, in fact, in a fierce collision between "left" and "right" visions of America's future, neither of which was especially well disposed to the corporate industrial order. It was not until World War II that an international way around this political impasse was discovered.

The salience of nationalist objections to American interventionism— which resonated in some quarters into the 1950s—was that global development did not require a permanent U.S. presence or even engagement. German and Japanese expansionism in the 1930s was thus read as regional conquest, rather than as projects to amass, in the new terms of global competition, the industrial muscles necessary for global projections of power.[59] In this respect, Pearl Harbor was both a revelation and a turning point that led, not only to a merciless war of revenge, but to the anxious, preemptive development of weapons of mass destruction. Yet there was still little about Soviet power, at least until the mid 1950s, that would gainsay the plausibility of the Taftite vision, based on the budget-cutting and anti-statist priorities of the Republican right, that had the United States pulling back to its continental base and hurling massive nuclear force against the Russians if they tried to use regional power in Europe against American interests.

What turned projections of American power into permanent outposts after World War II was the growing perception, from within the territories of production, that as the United States mobilized its industrial might to salvage democracy and restore prosperity in the world, it found legitimation abroad for the corporate order at home. This was the central lesson of the arsenal of democracy. In particular, the postwar recognition that the democratic conversion and rapid recovery of Germany and Japan was key both to containing the capacity of the Soviet Union to project power globally and to ensuring the legitimation and self-discipline of the corporate order domestically guided policy in the early Cold War. Notably, the Truman administration overcame congressional opposition to its long-term aid program for western Europe by couching it in terms of containing communism, which, Soviet intentions notwithstanding, deftly linked main street hatred of the New Deal, labor, blacks, and state regulation to permanent projections of American power overseas and thus, in turn, consolidated in the name of democracy and freedom the external legitimation of the corporate sector, while freeing it to pursue a program of domestic pacification and stabilization.[60] Whatever its plausibility as international politics, as a formula for domestic alignment, this was formidable: the salience of the image of an industrial nation defending democracy worldwide and developing it where it did not exist made the global arena into a powerful source of legitimacy for the territories of production and assured the remaking of the nation in the image of an industrial democracy.

In this way, the national project of industrial development acquired global buttresses. A particular kind of imperium took shape by the 1950s, anchored in the revived economies of Germany and Japan, with supporting players in Europe and Asia organized as suppliers or markets and disciplined by the terms of Cold War competition and the promise of upward mobility.[61] U.S. foreign aid and military assistance programs were designed to bolster world economic recovery and to cycle back in the form of demand and markets for domestic production. In this way, permanent projections of power underwrote domestic growth and were, in turn, anchored in a domestic political consensus. Expressed in terms of bipartisanship in foreign policy and the so-called labor pacts of postwar industrial relations, this internal resolution of conflict was actually grounded in a new definition of U.S. sovereignty. The implicit offer, made by Truman and renewed by Eisenhower, was that, as the federal government took full responsibility for guaranteeing the conditions of national security and economic growth, based on corporate industrial productivity and underwritten by a permanent projection of the U.S. dollar and military power into the world, everyone could be included who did not choose the "other" way of life.

The territories of production, buttressed by offshore extensions and protected by domestic pacification, were thus naturalized as the arsenal of democracy and bulwark of free-world enterprise. They *were* America, and indeed, quite literally made Americans: corporate tycoons metamorphosed into public servants doing what was good for both themselves and the nation; workers were Americanized, not as Henry Ford had imagined, but in the collective experiences of mass mobilization and domestic discipline, which, while not erasing cultural and linguistic affinities, created all-American consumers of abundance. And the message from the territories of production, now geared for maximum output, was that the manufacture of abundance could fulfill the American promise and stamp the American character every bit as much as the frontier had done.

RECOVERING THE GLOBAL NATION: SOVEREIGNTY IN A TRANSNATIONAL AGE

It is hard to say which is more striking, the imperious global reach of postwar U.S. power or the degree of self-containment that went with it. The prevailing historiography continues to narrate American foreign policy from the inside out and thus remains safely entrenched in an exceptionalist position that sees the United States as uniquely positioned in the postwar world to make it safe for the American way of life. Although strongly internationalist in tone, this literature expresses, rather than problematizes, the new definitions of sovereignty that emerged in the late nineteenth century and were consolidated in the wake of World War II. More important, by assuming the identity of state, nation, and civil society, it treats the problem of globalization either as the logical extension of U.S. projections of power overseas or as some new force that appears from over the horizon to entangle America—both of which miss the key trajectory of global development in the past thirty years toward the emergence of a transnational America.

It is this process, we would suggest, that created a crisis of American sovereignty at the end of the twentieth century. While it may seem perverse to suggest that a long cycle of sovereignty has come to an end, especially since the United States has just "won" the Cold War and purports to be a beacon of liberty and free markets for the world, the place of the United States of America in the world, and with it, its capacity for self-government, has been dramatically recalibrated over the past quarter century.

The turning point came neither in 1989 nor in 1945, but in between. The postwar American sovereign, built on the territories of production, had created vectors along which elements of the U.S. state and American civil society could move off into the world and benefit from the permanent projections of American power overseas. Multinational corporations could pursue portfolio investments and markets in the world of the 1950s and 1960s without losing their American character; primary production and resource extraction could be organized under the auspices of an American-centered regime of security; American military installations and personnel on permanent garrison abroad channeled U.S. dollars and cultural artifacts to the world; educational, entertainment, and training exchanges circulated American values, concepts, and practices, while the export of U.S. military know-how in the shape of equipment, tactics, and ideologies elaborated an international infrastructure of look-alike practices and outlooks framed in Cold War alignments. And, perhaps most dramatic, the entertainment industry created a new idiom of affluent leisure and popular desires, not least of which was the democratizing impulse that allowed people around the world to have desires and to have them gratified. The size, originality, and reach of this Cold War essay in global ordering should not be underestimated. What legitimized it, at least briefly, was its success in organizing a "free world" of stabilization and democracy that underwrote the tremendous economic boom of the 1950s and early 1960s. This in turn gave a powerful boost to patterns of integration on "our" side of the Cold War divide, which, for a time, the United States sought to control. The tools of control—military (the alliance systems and violence), economic (dollar aid and investments), political (the leverage and sanctions of a superpower), and ideological (the image of the United States as leader of the free world)—were tremendously powerful, and the ideological imaginary of the territories of production, with its emphasis on material progress and democracy, proved extraordinarily attractive. Needless to say, the point-blank counterpoise of the communist world made the domain of the territories of production seem more clear-cut than it actually was, but it was also the clarity of this Cold War alignment that brought to a close the protracted struggles over the nature of sovereignty in the mass industrial age and over the location of the American territories of production in the world.

But all of this is history. For it was not the continued projection of American power but its crisis in the late 1960s and early 1970s that marked a decisive turning point and opened avenues of decision and choice. In a moment of military defeat, when the Cold War domestic consensus cracked and the virtuous loops between world and nation that had anchored the territories of production and guaranteed U.S.-American sovereignty in the postwar era ruptured, an expanding civil society broke free and went global, and, in this rapid globalization, stretched and reshaped the definitions of sovereignty.[62] The crisis itself is familiar and quickly described: the incapacity of U.S. military power in Vietnam to subordinate the countryside to the priorities of an urban-industrial order; the domestic indiscipline that accompanied this failure and summed up (or revived) a long tradition of protest, "left" and "right," against the urban-industrial order; the inability of the United States, with OPEC, to control cheap energy sources or to prevent a worldwide recession and a general crisis of industrial production; and the rapid collapse of the Bretton Woods system, followed by the equally sudden collapse of the "imperial presidency" in Watergate—all tore at the sutures that had bound domestic prosperity to the global organization of power and allowed—or pushed—key currents of American civil society to develop outside the framework of the U.S.-American sovereign.

The singular importance of this crisis of power in the 1960s and 1970s was that important elements of civil society—of capital, business practice, law, culture, even religion—could no longer be contained within the political consensus of the nation and were set motion beyond the predicates of the Cold War regime of order. The agents of this movement were not missionaries of American promise and universal democracy, for this Wilsonian quest largely vanished in the wake of Vietnam and in the face of the neonationalism of the 1980s. To be sure, Wilsonian language found new iterations, especially in eastern Europe, Iberia, and Latin America in the movements against state oppression, whether communist or military-authoritarian, and these were soon taken up and theorized as the globalization of liberal democracy.[63] But the real work of promoting a globalization of civil society was carried on by individual and corporate raiders scouring the world for profitable investments or safe havens, by transnationalizing businesses seeking to maximize productivity by drawing resources and production from multiple (cheapening) sources and distributing output over a variety of markets, by the emergent monetary machinery that facilitated the coordination of capital movement, by agents of accelerated information and communications technology, and by the legions of lawyers and professionals who gave these transactions their distinct juridical and institutional form. It was here that American law, in the realms of property and contracts, as well as civil and human rights, began to serve local and global ends simultaneously.[64]

It was in the emergent debate over how to reap the advantages of "going global" without bursting the constraints and protections of self-government that conservatism found new voices in politics and religion and, as property became detached from production (as it had been unhooked from land a century before), the sovereignty of the territories of production, together with its politics, came unraveled.[65] The globalization of civil society was articulated, not in a new kind of political identity (as eastern European intellectuals soon discovered after 1989), but in new cultural proclivities and imaginings, which came to be represented most trivially in "fast food" but were in fact forging a new subjectivity—one that took freedom from constraint (be it political, social, or cultural) as the vital source of creativity and disruption and read from the possibilities thus created a whole series of contradictory admixtures of productive invention and burgeoning chaos.[66] Thus it seems to us that the best way of making sense of what has been happening in the past quarter century is to explore how a robust civil society, devoted to securing property and pursuing gain, cut itself loose from U.S. sovereignty and became incorporated into a global "trans-nation."

The fate of the U.S. dollar is perhaps a paradigmatic place to start. After being exported as a deliberate state strategy during the Cold War, it became a global currency during the 1970s, when the U.S. government stopped trying to regulate exchange rates and allowed the dollar to float in the global market. This produced an unplanned and largely uncontrolled generalization of the dollar as a medium of exchange, in the form of Eurodollars and petrodollars, for example, and generated secondary and tertiary monetary instruments that effectively placed the American currency beyond the purview or control of the nation-state. Indeed, the U.S. dollar became a globally accepted medium of exchange only as the ability of the U.S. government to control it collapsed.[67] This did not make it any less American. But the collapse of federal regulatory control, and the loss of face that went with it, brought forth a new transnational America with a global reach that skipped the territories of production and, while it may still be, or seem to be, American, it is no longer quite *of* the United States.[68]

Just as the dollar has been denationalized, so have business practices: the conventions, protocols, rituals, and forms of organization once thought typically American have transmogrified into globally recognized norms. American management practices, legal procedures, and institutional forms have been adopted or cloned worldwide, not to speak of the widespread use of English. While transnational corporations are rather overrated as world-encompassing operations, they are at the center of global struggles over access in the World Trade Organization and the North American Free Trade Association (NAFTA) and the development of transnational regulatory mechanisms. They have produced new patterns of transnational alliances, and global production networks operating through licensing and franchising have become ever more prominent.[69] These examples—

and others we might add in the realm of popular culture, consumption, and even crime—point to a vast process of privatization, a withdrawal of activities from the realm of politics and, indeed, from the realm of the public. Yet they have fostered, as a parallel development, an extraordinary proliferation of nongovernmental organizations and their almost immediate transnationalization both as networks of local organizations and in the form of global organizations.[70] Thus the globalization of American civil society and its incorporation into a transnational sphere can be heard in the discourses on rights, legal and human, which were long instruments of civil society in pursuit or defense of private interest, and in environmental debates, which have moved from conserving national resources to protecting the whole earth as habitat.[71] Some contend that the transnational advocacy networks that have emerged as extensions of principled, rights-oriented politics constitute new "global publics" that can counter both local oppression and the transnational reach of global operators.

We might multiply descriptions of such trajectories, but it is their consequences that require attention. For while the transformations of the past thirty years are usually described in terms of the sudden onset of globalization or as a process of readjustment in the face of "imperial overstretch"[72] and changing global conditions, what is strikingly novel, in our view, is the speed with which certain elements of American civil society have been incorporated into a "trans-nation" and become permanently distinct from the territorial nation. This has not dissolved the United States of America. Rather, the United States and its citizens have been powerful and experienced participants in this new formation. Nor do we argue that this transnationalism forms an all-embracing, gobal civil society, because, as we have seen, these new global practices, while no longer *of* the sovereign nation or its projections, are elaborated in corridors or channels of interconnectivity that remain segmented, preclusive, and often narrowly instrumental. Nevertheless, the expansion of American civil society beyond the territories of production, and its incorporation into the transnational realm, does make the hyphen in U.S.-America more a marker of separation and distance than of combination, and it leads us back to the central question: if America is now part of a globalizing "trans-nation," where in the world is America?

Much time and effort will be needed to disentangle this problem, to separate fact from fiction and test the usefulness of competing notions of globalization in bundling and grouping these webs of activity. It should be noted, moreover, that there is a quite sensible body of opinion—and this is not simply a reaction to overblown claims about globalization—that is skeptical, if not about the existence of this "trans-nation" or the degree of American involvement, then about its significance for the United States.[73] The pattern of recent wars and monetary crises points to the fact that the

United States remains a powerful, even dominant, force and can carry on its own. But the sheltering effect that comes with this superiority seems limited and precarious. Overall, the processes of globalization are now the matrix for articulating U.S.-America, and this has substantial consequences for the place of the United States as a self-governing nation in the world. Since the fact that America is part of the world is nothing new, we need to inquire more particularly into the consequences of this imbrication in the world in our time.

First, the question of national sovereignty is now being restated in dramatic new forms. For much of U.S. history, the solution to the question of sovereignty—of how a self-governing people can ensure its security and prosperity—was grounded in territoriality. This was pursued in the first instance through expansion and incorporation in the production of territory. Nation-making entailed a great settling of peoples in diaspora, bolstering the mythic themes of inclusion and equality, but it was also an exclusionary procedure in which choices were made about the character and composition of the occupants and in which expulsions, even exterminations, resulted that spawned new diasporas beyond and below the barriers erected against "others." This territorial nation became, in turn, a great territory of production and a paradigmatic model for the worldwide efforts to mobilize national resources and project power into a competitive global environment that have been characteristic of the history of globalization over the past century.

But now, while none of this is quite lost, American civil society, in order to reproduce itself, routinely partakes in networks that reach far beyond its territoriality. Because the sovereign nation can no longer ensure the conditions of security and prosperity that, in the twentieth century, were created by and within a territorial nation, it is no longer an effective riposte to the forces of globalization. The forces shaping the economic destiny of the United States are no longer contained in or effectively controlled by its politics. Neither is security. "[T]hreats to our security have no respect for boundaries" making it "clear that American security in the 21ˢᵗ Century will be determined by the success of our responses to forces that operate within as well as beyond our boundaries," says a Clinton administration national security study.[74] As the title of this document—"engagement and enlargement"—suggests, the security and prosperity of the United States depend on its being an active participant in the processes of globalization and in the formation of a "trans-nation" that is itself actively dissolving the boundaries between inside and outside. Paradoxically, the future of self-government depends on deeper engagement in the world, for sovereignty is increasingly grounded, not in territoriality, but in connectivity—in the ability to pull together and hold accountable the transnational sphere that cuts across territorial borders.

Second, *l'Amérique,* the offshore America that belongs to the world, has been vastly strengthened and amplified by the deterritorialization of civil society. Indeed, as more and more of America is appropriated by the world and detached from the regulatory practices and self-imaginings of the nation, and as more and more of the world is incorporated into this transnational sphere, America becomes, quite literally, part of everybody's business, and everyone gains fuller access to what they imagine to be America. This marks the old and continuing disjuncture between the location of America in the world and what America means to the world. But at the same time, it also creates a nexus that blurs the distinctions between the offshore *l'Amérique* and the territorial United States. The effects on law, human rights, and the environment, on the one hand, and on consumption, migration and the movement of money, on the other, are tangible.

The American presence in the world and the world's footholds in the United States enable people to assume and carry their transnationality around without entering the ambit of the accountability of nations. This condition also challenges territorial definitions of sovereignty. The constitution of sovereignty now depends on negotiating the shape, form, and scope of this "trans-nation" and devising means for its regulation and governance.[75] This cannot be done by a withdrawal into fortress America, any more than it can be done by appropriating the world to the United States in some bid for hegemony through "Americanization." Rather, self-governance in this "trans-nation," and the role of the United States in it, will have to be defined, articulated, and codified through furthering and deepening the practices of globalization. It might be added that this is a problem not just for the United States but for the world as a whole.

Third, the formation of this "trans-nation" has set off a vast, ramifying crisis within the United States. This is not just a question of rust belts or the restructuring of the domestic economy, traumatic as that may be; nor is it simply the penetration of the domestic economy by transnational forces, extensive though that may be. It is also a question of the integrity of the sovereign nation, of democratic government and its accountability. As American and global histories move together, efforts to maintain clear lines between inside and outside become acts of nostalgia, plaintive reassertions of isolationism and painful searches for core values and canons, vicious backlashes against alien "others" and stark refusals to pay for the United Nations, join nuclear test bans, or allow human rights law to have domestic jurisdiction. Sovereignty is no longer grounded in territoriality, and the territories of production are rapidly being evacuated. This does not mean the end of the (federal) state or some sudden implosion of its power, but it does mean, as many politicians and pundits in the United States have argued, from the meetings of the Trilateralists in the 1970s through the debates over NAFTA in the 1980s to the turmoil over the Asian banking crisis in the 1990s, that the sovereignty of the nation can only be secured through its own globalization. It is increasingly difficult for the state to deploy compensatory measures of stabilization and order without itself entering more deeply into global forms of organization and cooperation that bind and limit its options.

If this is taken to mean that the days of the people asserting their sovereignty as a nation against all others is past, or that the predicates of security and prosperity no longer lie within or under the control of the nation-state, a new globalizing definition of sovereignty makes sense. But this only begs the question: where in the world is America? How does a global nation retain the capacity for self-government. What is its territory, and who are its citizens? To whom are its public institutions responsible, and for what? These are essentially the same questions that confronted the founders in 1789, but from the opposite end: then, it was how a self-governing people could carve out a space of republican sovereignty without cutting off the world upon which the development of the United States depended; now, it is how a people whose security and well-being are imbricated in a global "trans-nation" can even imagine itself, let alone sustain its capacity for self-government and self-determination under conditions of globalization.

NOTES

1. The classic statements of these earlier imaginations are, of course, Frederick Jackson Turner, *The Frontier in American History* (New York, 1920), and David Morris Potter, *People of Plenty: Economic Abundance and the American Character*, Charles R. Walgreen Foundation lectures (Chicago, 1954).

2. Benjamin R. Barber, *Jihad vs. McWorld* (New York, 1995); Thomas L. Friedman, *The Lexus and the Olive Tree: Understanding Globalization* (New York, 2000).

3. The most recent exposition of this exemptionist line is in Francis Fukuyama's distinction between those "at the end of history" and those "trapped in history." See Francis Fukuyama, "The End of History," *National Interest*, no. 16 (1989): 3–18, and the fuller, more restrained statement in id., *The End of History and the Last Man* (New York, 1992).

4. For a useful recent review, see Ian Tyrell, "American Exceptionalism in an Age of International History," *American Historical Review* 96, 4 (1991): 1031–55; David Thelen, "Of Audiences, Borderlands, and Comparisons: Toward the Internationalization of American History," *Journal of American History* 79, 2 (1992): 432–62; and Daniel T. Rodgers, "Exceptionalism," in *Imagined Histories: American Historians Interpret the Past*, ed. Anthony Molho and Gordon S. Wood (Princeton, N.J., 1998).

5. George Fredrickson has been a leader in this. See George M. Fredrickson, *White Supremacy: A Comparative Study in American and South African History* (New York, 1981); *Black Liberation: A Comparative History of Black Ideologies in the United States and South Africa* (New York, 1995); *The Comparative Imagination: On the History of Racism,*

Nationalism, and Social Movements (Berkeley and Los Angeles, 1997); "Presidential Address—America's Diversity in Comparative Perspective," *Journal of American History* 85, 3 (1998): 859. Charles J. Halperin et al., "Comparative History in Theory and Practice: A Discussion" (in *AHR* forum), *American Historical Review* 87, 1 (1982): 123–43, is another early consideration of the subject.

6. Raymond Grew, "The Comparative Weakness of American History," *Journal of Interdisciplinary History* 16, 1 (1985): 87–101.

7. Perry Miller's famous preface to *Errand into the Wilderness* (Cambridge, Mass., 1956) included an impressive list of things "not studied"—social, economic, and political history; slavery; native Americans; non-Puritans—because they disturbed the "coherence" he sought. See Amy Kaplan, "Left Alone with America: The Absence of Empire in the Study of American History," in *Cultures of United States Imperialism*, ed. id. and Donald E. Pease (Durham, N.C., 1993), 3–21.

8. The most recent reaffirmation of American exceptionalism was built upon comparisons of the United States with Canada and Great Britain: see Seymour Martin Lipset, *American Exceptionalism: A Double-Edged Sword* (New York, 1996), which is little more than a rehash of his earlier statement in *The First New Nation: The United States in Historical and Comparative Perspective* (New York, 1963).

9. Jack P. Greene, *Interpreting Early America: Historiographical Essays* (Charlottesville, Va., 1996); and Alison Games, "History without Borders: Teaching American History in an Atlantic Context," *Indiana Magazine of History* 91, 2 (1995): 159–78.

10. Paul Gilroy, *The Black Atlantic: Modernity and Double Consciousness* (Cambridge, Mass., 1993); also Frederick Cooper, "Race, Ideology, and the Perils of Comparative History," *American Historical Review* 101, 4 (1996): 1122. On the intranational world of the sea, see Marcus Buford Rediker, *Between the Devil and the Deep Blue Sea: Merchant Seamen, Pirates, and the Anglo-American Maritime World, 1700–1750* (Cambridge, 1987); and Peter Linebaugh and Marcus Rediker, *The Many-Headed Hydra: Sailors, Slaves, Commoners, and the Hidden History of the Revolutionary Atlantic* (Boston, 2000)

11. James Barrett, "Americanization from the Bottom Up: Immigration and the Remaking of the Working Class in the United States, 1880–1930," *Journal of American History* 79, 3 (1992): 997–1020; James Barrett and David Roediger, "Inbetween Peoples: Race, Nationality, and the 'New Immigrant' Working Class," *Journal of American Ethnic History* 16, 3 (1997): 3–44; Kathleen Neils Conzen et al., "The Invention of Ethnicity: A Perspective from the USA," *Journal of American Ethnic History* 12, 1 (1992): 3–41; Mae Ngai, "The Architecture of Race in American Immigration Law: A Reexamination of the Immigration Act of 1924," *Journal of American History* 86, 1 (1999): 67–92. Much stimulating work has focused on U.S.-Mexican immigration: David Gutiérrez, *Walls and Mirrors: Mexican Americans, Mexican immigrants, and the Politics of Ethnicity* (Berkeley and Los Angeles, 1995); Matthew Frye Jacobson, *Whiteness of a Different Color: European Immigrants and the Alchemy of Race* (Cambridge, Mass., 1998); David Montejano, *Anglos and Mexicans in the Making of Texas, 1836–1986* (Austin, 1987); George J. Sanchez, *Becoming Mexican American: Ethnicity, Culture, and Identity in Chicano Los Angeles, 1900–1945* (New York, 1993). See also the special issue on "Rethinking History and the Nation-State: Mexico and the United States as a Case Study," *Journal of American History* 86, 2 (1999).

12. Ian R. Tyrell, *Woman's World / Woman's Empire: The Woman's Christian Tem-*

perance Union in International Perspective, 1880–1930 (Chapel Hill, N.C., 1991); Horace O. Russell, *The Missionary Outreach of the West Indian Church: Jamaican Baptist Missions to West Africa in the Nineteenth Century,* Research in Religion and Family, 3 (New York, 1999).

13. *Challenging Boundaries: Global Flows, Territorial Identities,* ed. Michael J. Shapiro and Hayward R. Alker (Minneapolis, 1996).

14. Theodore von Laue made this explicit in his early study on the Americanization of the world, *The World Revolution of Westernization: The Twentieth Century in Global Perspective* (New York, 1987).

15. *Cultures of United States Imperialism,* ed. Kaplan and Pease; Frederick Buell, "Nationalist Postnationalism: Globalist Discourse in Contemporary American Culture," *American Quarterly* 50, 3 (1998): 548–91; Lisa Lowe, *Immigrant Acts: On Asian American Cultural Politics* (Durham, N.C., 1996); José Eduardo Limón, *American Encounters: Greater Mexico, the United States, and the Erotics of Culture* (Boston, 1998).

16. Stuart Hall, *The Hard Road to Renewal: Thatcherism and the Crisis of the Left* (New York, 1988); *The Empire Strikes Back: Race and Racism in 70s Britain* (New York, 1992); *Nation and Narration,* ed. Homi K. Bhabha (New York, 1990); Edward W. Soja, *Postmodern Geographies: The Reassertion of Space in Critical Social Theory* (New York, 1989); Arjun Appadurai, *Modernity At Large: Cultural Dimensions of Globalization* (Minneapolis, 1996).

17. *Tensions of Empire: Colonial Cultures in a Bourgeois World,* ed. Frederick Cooper and Ann Laura Stoler (Berkeley and Los Angeles, 1997); *A Subaltern Studies Reader, 1986–1995,* ed. Ranajit Guha (Minneapolis, 1997); *Subaltern Studies: Writings on South Asian History and Society,* vol. 1, ed. Ranajit Guha (New York, 1982); *The Post-Colonial Studies Reader,* ed. Bill Ashcroft, Gareth Griffiths, and Helen Tiffin (New York, 1995).

18. See esp. Matthew Connelly, "The Algerian War for Independence: An International History" (Ph.D. diss., Yale University, 1997), and "Taking off the Cold War Lens: Visions of North-South Conflict during the Algerian War for Independence," *American Historical Review* 105, 3 (June 2000).

19. Roger Rouse, "Thinking through Transnationalism: Notes on the Cultural Politics of Class Relations in the Contemporary United States," *Public Culture* 7 (1995): 353–402; Jeremy Adelman and Stephen Aron, "From Borderlands to Borders: Empires, Nation-States, and the Peoples in Between in North American History," *American Historical Review* 104, 3 (1999): 814; Jeanne Chase, "Porous Boundaries and Shifting Borderlands: The American Experience in a New World Order," *Reviews in American History* 26, 1 (1998): 54; Oscar J. Martinez and David Lorey, "U.S.-Mexico Borderlands: Historical and Contemporary Perspectives," *Hispanic-American Historical Review* 77, 3 (1997): 491; Philip J. Ethington and George Sanchez, "Towards a 'Borderlands School' for American Urban Ethnic Studies?" *American Quarterly* 48, 2 (1996): 344; Robert R. Alvarez Jr., "The Mexican-US Border: The Making of an Anthropology of Borderlands," *Annual Review of Anthropology* 24 (1995): 447–70; Gary B. Nash, "The Hidden History of Mestizo America," *Journal of American History* 82, 3 (1995): 941–64.

20. David Held, *Global Transformations: Politics, Economics and Culture* (Stanford, Calif., 1999); James N. Rosenau, *Turbulence in World Politics: A Theory of Change and*

Continuity (Princeton, N.J.: 1990); James N. Rosenau, *Along the Domestic-Foreign Frontier: Exploring Governance in a Turbulent World,* Cambridge Studies in International Relations, 53 (New York, 1997); Saskia Sassen, *Losing Control? Sovereignty in an Age of Globalization* (New York, 1998).

21. Held, *Global Transformations,* has a very careful definition of the analytic dimensions of globalization.

22. Saskia Sassen, *The Global City: New York, London, Tokyo* (Princeton, N.J., 1991).

23. We have examined this reversal in greater detail in Michael Geyer and Charles Bright, "World History in a Global Age," *American Historical Review* 100, 4 (1995): 1034–60.

24. Fredrick Cooper and Randall M. Packard, *International Development and the Social Sciences: Essays on the History and Politics of Knowledge* (Berkeley and Los Angeles, 1997).

25. Charles Bright and Michael Geyer, "For a Unified History of the World in the Twentieth Century," *Radical History Review* 39 (1987): 69–91.

26. Richard Falk, *Predatory Globalization: A Critique* (Malden, Mass., 1999).

27. Ken'ichi Omae, *The Borderless World: Power and Strategy in the Interlinked Economy* (New York, 1990; rev. ed. 1999); note Omae's frustration with borders that stubbornly persist.

28. This example comes from the work of Gabrielle Hecht on the uranium industry and French colonies; see her *The Radiance of France: Nuclear Power and National Identity after World War II* (Cambridge, Mass., 1998).

29. United States Employment Standards Administration, *No Sweat—Shopping Clues for Consumers* (Washington, D.C., 1997); Andrew Ross, *No Sweat: Fashion, Free Trade, and the Rights of Garment Workers* (New York, 1997).

30. Ulf Hannerz, "Cosmopolitans and Locals in World Culture," in *Global Culture: Nationalism, Globalization and Modernity,* ed. Mike Featherstone (London, 1990), 237–52; Martha Nussbaum, *For Love of Country: Debating the Limits of Patriotism* (Boston, 1996); *Cosmopolitics: Thinking and Feeling beyond the Nation,* ed. Pheng Cheah and Bruce Robbins (Minneapolis, 1998).

31. Arjun Appadurai, *Modernity at Large: Cultural Dimensions of Globalization* (Minneapolis, 1996); and his "Sovereignty without Territoriality: Notes for a Postnational Geography," in *The Geography of Identity,* ed. Patricia Yaeger (Ann Arbor, Mich., 1996), 40–58.

32. It takes the labor of constituting a global political space or public in order to generate, if not consciousness, a global awareness and actionable global entity. See David Held, *Democracy and the Global Order: From the Modern State to Cosmopolitan Governance* (Stanford, Calif., 1995).

33. See Michael Geyer and Charles Bright, "Global Violence and Nationalizing Wars in Eurasia and America: The Geopolitics of War in the Mid-Nineteenth Century," *Comparative Studies in Society and History* 38, 4 (1996): 619–67, and id., "World History in a Global Age."

34. Benedict R. O. G. Anderson, *Imagined Communities: Reflections on the Origin and Spread of Nationalism* (London, 1983), ch. 6, defines this as stretching the skin of the nation over the polyglot body of the empire.

35. This was not, as some claim, solely because the United States was a very

powerful state, or empire. Noam Chomsky, *World Orders: Old and New* (New York, 1994).

36. David Brion Davis, *The Problem of Slavery in the Age of Revolution, 1770–1823* (Ithaca, N.Y., 1975); Robert Lloyd Kelley, *The Transatlantic Persuasion: The Liberal-Democratic Mind in the Age of Gladstone* (New York, 1969); Joyce Appleby, "America as a Model for the Radical French Reformers of 1789," *William and Mary Quarterly*, 3d ser., 28, 2 (1971): 267–86, reprinted in id., *Liberalism and Republicanism in the Historical Imagination* (Cambridge, Mass., 1992).

37. For a powerful example, see James W. Ceaser, *Reconstructing America: The Symbol of America in Modern Thought* (New Haven, Conn., 1997).

38. Geoff Eley and Ronald G. Suny, "Introduction: From the Moment of Social History to the Work of Cultural Representation," in *Becoming National: A Reader*, ed. id. (New York, 1996), 3–37.

39. See Geoff Eley, "Culture, Nation, Gender," in *Gendered Nations: Nationalisms in the Long Nineteenth Century: Europe and Beyond*, ed. Ida Blom, Karen Hagemann, and Catherine Hall (forthcoming). Standard texts on Europe include *The Formation of National States in Western Europe*, ed. Charles Tilly (Princeton, N.J., 1975); Tom Nairn, *The Break-up of Britain: Crisis and Neo-nationalism* (London, 1977); Ernest Gellner, *Nations and Nationalism* (Ithaca, N.Y., 1983). The literature on the American Revolution and the new republic is of course enormous. We follow Pauline Maier, *From Resistance to Revolution; Colonial Radicals and the Development of American Opposition to Britain, 1765–1776* (New York, 1972), and Gordon S. Wood, *The Radicalism of the American Revolution* (New York, 1992).

40. Most notably, William Cronon, *Nature's Metropolis: Chicago and the Great West* (New York, 1991); and Patricia Nelson Limerick, *The Legacy of Conquest: The Unbroken Past of the American West* (New York, 1987). A useful synthesis of the debate is Gregory H. Nobles, *American Frontiers: Cultural Encounters and Continental Conquest* (New York, 1997).

41. For a strong statement of these reservations, see Jeremy Adelman and Stephen Aron, "From Borderlands to Borders: Empires, Nation-States, and the Peoples in Between in North American History," *American Historical Review* 104, 3 (1999): 814–41.

42. Richard White, *The Middle Ground: Indians, Empires, and Republics in the Great Lakes Region, 1650–1815* (New York, 1991).

43. A stimulating survey from a geographer's perspective is D. W. Meinig, *The Shaping of America: A Geographical Perspective on 500 Years of History*, vol. 1: *Atlantic America, 1492–1800* (New Haven, Conn., 1986). Ultimately, however, this history needs to include the Pacific, not simply as an extension of European projects into a "middle ground" (see Eric R. Wolf, *Europe and the People without History* [Berkeley and Los Angeles, 1982, 1997]), but as extensions of the spheres of interaction and movement of goods in the Pacific ecumene. See, e.g., Marshall Sahlins, "Cosmologies of Capitalism: the Trans-Pacific Sector of 'the World System,'" *Proceedings of the British Academy* 84 (1988): 1–51.

44. On this shift, see, in particular, James E. Lewis, *The American Union and the Problem of Neighborhood: The United States and the Collapse of the Spanish Empire, 1783–1829* (Chapel Hill, N.C., 1998); Thomas M. Leonard, *United States–Latin American Relations, 1850–1903: Establishing a Relationship* (Tuscaloosa, Ala., 1999).

45. D. W. Meinig, *The Shaping of America: A Geographical Perspective on 500 Years of History*, vol. 2: *Continental America, 1800–1867* (New Haven, Conn., 1993), 128, notes that the territory of the United States of America totaled 1.8 million square miles, and that of the United States of Mexico, 1.7 million; there were 9.6 million people in the republic of the north and 6.5 million in the republic of the south.

46. Reginald Horsman, *Race and Manifest Destiny: The Origins of American Racial Anglo-Saxonism* (Cambridge, Mass., 1981); Alexander Saxton, *The Rise and Fall of the White Republic: Class Politics and Mass Culture in Nineteenth-century America* (New York, 1990).

47. Robert May, *The Southern Dream of a Caribbean Empire, 1854–1861* (Baton Rouge, La., 1973).

48. So argues Fareed Zakaria, *From Wealth to Power: The Unusual Origins of America's World Role* (Princeton, N.J., 1998). On the general subject, see Stephen Skowronek, *Building a New American State: The Expansion of National Administrative Capacities, 1877–1920* (New York, 1982).

49. On the debates over U.S. imperialism, see Walter LaFeber, *The New Empire; An Interpretation of American Expansion, 1860–1898* (Ithaca, N.Y., 1963); Akira Iriye, *From Nationalism to Internationalism: US Foreign Policy to 1914* (Boston, 1977); Gerald F. Linderman, *The Mirror of War: American Society and the Spanish-American War* (Ann Arbor, Mich., 1974). More recently, John Pettegrew, "'The Soldier's Faith': Turn-of-the-Century Memory of the Civil War and the Emergence of Modern American Nationalism," *Journal of Contemporary History* 31, 1 (1996): 49–73; Kristin L. Hoganson, *Fighting for American Manhood: How Gender Politics Provoked the Spanish-American and Philippine-American Wars* (New Haven, Conn., 1998); Cecilia Elizabeth O'Leary, *To Die For: The Paradox of American Patriotism* (Princeton, N.J., 1999).

50. Standard studies include Alfred Dupont Chandler, *The Visible Hand: The Managerial Revolution in American Business* (Cambridge, Mass., 1977); Alan Trachtenberg, *The Incorporation of America: Culture and Society in the Gilded Age* (New York, 1982); David F. Noble, *America by Design: Science, Technology, and the Rise of Corporate Capitalism* (New York, 1977); and, from a more sociological angle, Olivier Zunz, *Making America Corporate, 1870–1920* (Chicago, 1990).

51. See David E. Nye, *Consuming Power: A Social History of American Energies* (Cambridge, Mass., 1998).

52. Noble, *America by Design;* James Gilbert, *Designing the Industrial State: The Intellectual Pursuit of Collectivism in America, 1880–1940* (Chicago, 1972); Frederick W. Taylor, *The Principles of Scientific Management* (New York, 1947); Reinhard Bendix, *Work and Authority in Industry: Ideologies of Management in the Course of Industrialization* (New York, 1956); Robert Zieger, *American Workers, American Unions, 1920–1985* (Baltimore, 1986); David Montgomery, *Workers' Control in America: Studies in the History of Work, Technology, and Labor Struggles* (New York, 1979); Maurice Zeitlin, *How Mighty a Force? Studies of Workers Consciousness and Organization in the United States* (Los Angeles, 1983).

53. Eric H. Monkkonen, *America Becomes Urban: The Development of U.S. Cities and Towns, 1780–1980* (Berkeley and Los Angeles, 1988); James R. Barrett, *Work and Community in the Jungle* (Urbana, Ill., 1987); John J. Bukowczyk, "The Transformation of Working-Class Ethnicity: Corporate Control, Americanization and the Polish Immigrant Middle-Class in Bayonne, New Jersey, 1915–1925," *Labor History* 25, no.

1 (1984): 53–82; Olivier Zunz, *The Changing Face of Inequality: Urbanization, Industrial Development, and Immigrants in Detroit, 1880–1920* (Chicago, 1982); John Buenker, *Urban Liberalism and Progressive Reform* (New York, 1973); Daniel J. Walkowitz, *Worker City, Company Town : Iron and Cotton-Worker Protest in Troy and Cohoes, New York, 1855– 84* (Urbana, Ill., 1978).

54. Pete Daniel, *Breaking the Land: The Transformation of Cotton, Tobacco, and Rice Cultures since 1880* (Urbana, Ill., 1985); James Green, *Grass Roots Socialism: Radical Movements in the Southwest, 1895–1943* (Baton Rouge, La., 1978); Jack Kirby, *Rural Worlds Lost: The American South, 1920–1960* (Baton Rouge, La., 1987); George Marsden, *Fundamentalism in American Culture: The Shaping of Twentieth Century Evangelicalism, 1870–1925* (New York, 1980); William L. Bowers, *The Country Life Movement in America, 1900–1920* (Port Washington, N.Y., 1974).

55. Still one of the most stimulating treatments is Lawrence Goodwyn, *Democratic Promise: The Populist Moment in America* (New York, 1976). On provincial politics, we follow Michael E. McGerr, *The Decline of Popular Politics: The American North, 1865– 1928* (New York, 1986); and David Burner, *The Politics of Provincialism: The Democratic Party in Transition, 1918–1932* (New York, 1968). A valuable recent survey is Hal S. Barron, *Mixed Harvest: The Second Great Transformation in the Rural North, 1870–1930* (Chapel Hill, N.C., 1997).

56. See Alan Brinkley's treatment in his *Voices of Protest: Huey Long, Father Coughlin, and the Great Depression* (New York, 1982).

57. Following David A. Hollinger, *Postethnic America: Beyond Multiculturalism* (New York, 1995), 131–36.

58. Of a large literature, see Emily S. Rosenberg, *Spreading the American Dream: American Economic and Cultural Expansion, 1890–1945* (New York, 1982), and Frank Costigliola, *Awkward Dominion: American Political, Economic, and Cultural Relations with Europe, 1919–1933* (Ithaca, N.Y., 1984), esp. ch. 7.

59. Bruce M. Russett, *No Clear and Present Danger: A Skeptical View of the United States Entry into World War II* (New York, 1972).

60. On the formulation of Truman's Cold War policy, see Lloyd C. Gardner, Arthur Meier Schlesinger, and Hans Joachim Morgenthau, *The Origins of the Cold War* (Waltham, Mass., 1970); Melvyn P. Leffler, *A Preponderance of Power: National Security, the Truman Administration, and the Cold War* (Stanford, Calif., 1992); Melvyn P. Leffler and David S. Painter, *Origins of the Cold War: An International History* (New York, 1994); Carolyn Woods Eisenberg, *Drawing the Line: The American Decision to Divide Germany, 1944–1949* (New York, 1996); John Lewis Gaddis, *We Now Know: Rethinking Cold War History* (New York, 1997).

61. On Japan's recovery, see Bruce Cumings, *Parallax Visions: Making Sense of American-East Asian Relations at the end of the Century* (Durham, N.C., 1999). On Europe, see Geir Lundestad, *Empire by Invitation: The United States and European Integration, 1945–1997* (New York, 1998).

62. Generally on this crisis, see Peter Carroll, *It Seemed Like Nothing Happened: The Tragedy and Promise of America in the 1970s* (New York, 1982); Charles Morris, *A Time of Passion: America, 1960–1980* (New York, 1984); Andrew Hacker, *The End of the American Era* (New York, 1973).

63. Ralf Dahrendorf, *After 1989: Morals, Revolution and Civil Society;* (New York, 1997); John Keane, *Civil Society: Old Images, New Visions* (Stanford, Calif., 1998);

Michael Waltzer. *Towards a Global Civil Society* (Providence, R.I., 1995). See also the more cautious assessment of Jean Grugel, *Democracy without Borders: Transnationalization and Conditionality in New Democracies* (New York, 1999).

64. Louis Henkin, *The Age of Rights* (New York, 1990).

65. William C. Berman, *America's Right Turn: From Nixon to Clinton* (Baltimore, 1994); Godfrey Hodgson, *The World Turned Right Side Up: A History of the Conservative Ascendancy in America* (Boston, 1996).

66. *Global Modernities*, ed. Mike Featherstone, Scott Lash, and Roland Robertson (Thousand Oaks, Calif., 1995).

67. On this general development, among others, see Fred L. Block, *The Origins of International Economic Disorder: A Study of United States International Monetary Policy from World War II to the Present* (Berkeley and Los Angeles, 1977).

68. This is the message we take from Joseph S. Nye, *Bound to Lead: The Changing Nature of American Power* (New York, 1990).

69. The competing positions are captured by John Dunning, *The Globalization of Business* (London, 1993); Paul Q. Hirst and Grahame Thompson, *Globalization in Question: The International Economy and the Possibilities of Governance* (Cambridge and Oxford, 1996); Robert R. Reich, *The Work of Nations: Preparing Ourselves for Twenty-First-Century Capitalism* (New York, 1991).

70. Margaret E. Keck and Kathryn Sikkink, *Activists beyond Borders: Advocacy Networks in International Politics* (Ithaca, N.Y., 1998).

71. *The International Politics of the Environment: Actors, Interests, and Institutions*, ed. Andrew Hurrell and Benedict Kingsbury (New York, 1992).

72. Paul Kennedy, *The Rise and Fall of the Great Powers: Economic Change and Military Conflict from 1500 to 2000* (New York, 1987).

73. Paul Krugman, *Pop Internationalism* (Cambridge, Mass., 1996).

74. *A National Security Strategy of Engagement and Enlargement* (February 1996), http://www.usis.usemb.se/usis/1996strategy/ (downloaded July 13, 1998).

75. Friedrich Kratochwil, "Of Systems, Boundaries and Territoriality," *World Politics* 39, 1 (1986): 27–52; John Gerard Ruggie, "Territoriality and Beyond: Problematizing Modernity in International Relations," *International Organization* 47, 1 (1993): 139–47.

PART II

New Historical Geographies and Temporalities

FOUR

International at the Creation
Early Modern American History

Karen Ordahl Kupperman

History begins in the East and moves steadily westward over two centuries until it finally arrives at the Pacific coast. This is the foundational conception of American history, one that all Americans accept as self-evidently true and founded in the realities of the period of first contact and settlement. But this truism comes down to us more from the nineteenth century, when it was elaborated, than the seventeenth. This version of America's founding was cemented in place as the crisis of national identification grew. Daniel Webster, giving the first of the annual Forefathers' Day speeches in 1820, endorsed the nineteenth-century invention of the Pilgrims as the emblematic founders of America. Plymouth colony, he wrote, was "so peculiar in its causes and character, and has been followed and must still be followed by such consequences, as to give it a high claim to lasting commemoration. On these causes and consequences, more than on its immediately attendant circumstances, its importance, as an historical event, depends." Arguing that the Pilgrims came to America to establish purer religious worship, he portrayed their situation: "Everything was civilized but the physical world. Institutions, containing in substance all that ages had done for human government, were organized in a forest. Cultivated mind was to act on uncultivated nature."

Webster thus enunciated the central myth by which the history of early modern America has been written ever since: English colonists, motivated by religious ideology, entered an unchanging natural world and created in it a new, better version of Europe. Their only context was their relationship to England, and to later Puritan immigrants. Other colonists, even other English settlers, were seen as flawed in their motivation and were less authentic progenitors of America.

Webster went on to state the other great organizing principle of early

American history: civilization, even history itself, moved from east to west as the static native world gave way before the progress of English institutions. "Ere long, the sons of the Pilgrims will be on the shores of the Pacific. The imagination hardly keeps pace with the progress of population, improvement, and civilization."[1] As he predicted, history was about to arrive on the West Coast in the early nineteenth century. With only minor changes, we are still telling Webster's story.

The public, in company with many historians, assumes that the arrival of Puritans in New England was the "true" beginning of American history, a belief that has to do with myths of identity more than actual effect on the course of American development. Puritan settlers, described as devout and dedicated to community values, are esteemed appropriate progenitors of the American nation. Positing American origins in the emigration of England's "godly sort" appeals, James Muldoon observes, because our westward-moving history is itself a secularized version of "the biblical providential Five World Empires as well as the medieval *translatio imperii*. In this view the United States becomes the final stage of the providential plan, the final empire in the sequence of divinely ordained empires."[2]

John Adams proposed a secularized version of the *translatio imperii* in a letter written early in the French and Indian War. Adams mused on the emergence of great empires from small beginnings and argued that England, "the greatest nation upon the globe," was the successor to Rome. England had now spawned the seed of its successor: "Soon after the Reformation, a few people came over into this new world for conscience sake. Perhaps this apparently trivial incident may transfer the great seat of empire into America." Adams considered this outcome likely "if we can remove the turbulent Gallicks." Although the colonies sponsored by England contained a population gathered from many parts of Europe and Africa by 1755, Adams clung to the myth of purely English origins.[3]

This American history forces scholars and teachers into an exceptionalist position. By positing national origins in a particular subset of early modern English culture, it reinforces the notion of a special American trajectory. Moreover, it locates the engine of history in a purely English mode of enterprise. All others act against or with the main story or merely react to it. Efforts to write a more inclusive history are hamstrung by this framework. Whether the script is a tragedy or a comedy, and whether English colonists are portrayed as enlightened or rapacious, they are still the true actors. Only people in contact with them can be part of the story.[4]

This master narrative, created in a particular political environment, has outlived its usefulness and needs to be replaced.[5] Myths of time, space, and identity have conspired to create an origins story that renders our understanding of the entire colonial and early national period faulty and partial, and that has given us an origins story that is impoverished by seventeenth-century standards. We need to problematize our notions of when and where American history exists in the colonial period, and we must examine our assumptions about who is part of that history. Increasingly, as scholars have focused their attention on the many peoples and nations actually present and involved in the future United States in the early modern period, the old conception has been stretched unbearably, and teachers confronting the subject find it incoherent to the point of unteachability. Moreover, many historians who seek to offer a more comprehensive picture still retain the east-to-west movement of history, including other peoples and places only when the eastern thrust arrives among them. We need to construct a new master narrative on fresh principles that will allow us to tell a more realistic story without sacrificing coherence.

The new account of American history in the sixteenth and seventeenth centuries demonstrates that America was international before it became national. The unit of study is America, the future United States, and this space is acknowledged to exist, producing and experiencing history, throughout the period. And the motors for the generation of history are located throughout the Atlantic world and across the continent. Many nations and ethnic entities were involved in effecting history, and together they and their descendants come to make up the broad category of the American people.[6]

Many of the pitfalls of this enterprise lie in inherited terms and the assumptions embedded in them. It is symptomatic of the problem that we have no term by which to refer to the region that would become the United States. Geographic terms such as North America are not only inaccurate, but also, while appearing to represent a simple external reality, actually convey a complex set of values.[7] Equally value-laden are terms such as "nation" and "international," which are assumed anachronistically to apply to European polities and interactions but not to American and African forms.

We need to catch up with the early modern understandings. In ways that contemporary observers recognized, early modern polities all around the Atlantic paralleled one another more than they resemble the national forms that emerged in the nineteenth century. Europeans came from nascent nations still in the process of taking shape. As Charles Tilly remarks, "the Europe of 1500 included some five hundred more or less independent political units." Tilly's figure matches Alvin M. Josephy Jr.'s enumeration of American polities at that time.[8] The Mohegan sachem Uncas built and consolidated his domain through a series of dynastic marriages just as European monarchs did. Powhatan was reported to have inherited control of some peoples and to have conquered more than twenty additional subject groups in the Chesapeake, again like a European monarch. African kings and queens pursued similar courses. Throughout the Atlantic region, authority was achieved personally as much as through institutions.[9]

Reorientation toward the Atlantic accelerated the creation of nations and national consciousness on all shores; American history was therefore international before it was national. All the participants came from regions where boundaries were in negotiation and definitions were in process.[10] Their own identification was with their locality or with some larger, more amorphous entity; Anthony Parkhurst in Newfoundland, for example, wrote that he was a "Gentleman that commeth from Kent and Christendome."[11] On both sides of the Atlantic, the process of incorporating new products into traditional categories accelerated the course of national definition; Queen Elizabeth wore American pearls and a fine beaver hat as emblems of her greatness, just as Powhatan and Miantonomi sported badges of rank made of Venetian beads.[12]

Even before European colonization, nascent nations existed in North America, and the process of consolidation was dramatically intensified by the presence of Europeans. Europeans realized that they were dealing with highly organized American political formations, large and small, and some were aware that large-scale consolidations and movements had both preceded and accompanied the early years of transatlantic contact. Hernando de Soto led a group of Spanish adventurers on a 4,000-mile trek through the southeastern region as far west as the Mississippi River in the period 1539–43, and the chronicles of that trip describe the great chiefdoms they encountered. These, part of the system archaeologists have labeled Mississippian, were elaborate polities with hereditary aristocracies and chiefly lineages; great fortified cities indicate the expansive nature of the mightiest. Although the largest and most powerful among them, particularly the great city at Cahokia, had declined as the onset of Little Ice Age conditions made the region less hospitable for large-scale settlements, the Spanish were impressed by the extent and complexity of the chiefdoms they encountered.[13] Later French explorers were fascinated by the elaborate political system of the Natchez Indians to the south.[14]

In the Northeast, the powerful Iroquois League coalesced in the fifteenth century, creating the forms by means of which the League's members came, in the period of European contact and settlement, to play a key role between native groups and Europeans through the clientage relationships of the Covenant Chain. Other Iroquoians, such as the Hurons and Susquehannocks, also emerged as strong actors. As trade with Europeans expanded, Iroquoian influence spread, and the most adept of the French, Dutch, and English traders learned the forms of Iroquois diplomacy well.[15]

America was an international arena before Europeans even knew of its existence. Diplomacy and war were carried on between polities often over long distances and through elaborate forms, and the continent was tied together by long-distance trade lines. Pueblo-dwellers in the Rio Grande region consumed shells and coral from California and sold their dyed cotton, both woven and raw, and pottery throughout the Southwest. Obsidian for knives was another trade commodity, as was salt. Bison meat and hides came from the Plains Indians to the North.[16] Southern New England Indians used copper from Nova Scotia and the Great Lakes and shells from the South Atlantic and mid-Atlantic coasts. Natives around the Chesapeake Bay and the coastal Carolinas also possessed copper from the Lake Superior region. When European products began to appear in America, they were incorporated into these trade routes long before Europeans actually settled.[17]

Early trading relationships with Europeans were often forged through American initiative, and Indian chiefs and traders expected to use their own diplomatic protocols to control the terms of the trade. Jacques Cartier's ships moving along the coast of the Gaspé Peninsula in 1534 were approached by Indians "who set up a great clamour and made frequent signs to us to come on shore, holding up to us some skins on sticks."[18] For Cartier, this was a first encounter, but not for his Micmac hosts.

The Susquehannocks, a non-League Iroquoian chiefdom, offer an illuminating case study, as they made even more elaborate moves in order to secure a place in the just-forming European trade. These "great traders" were pivotal actors in the long-distance trade in Indian-produced commodities before colonization. As European goods increasingly entered the trade, and the Iroquois League came to play a leading role, the Susquehannocks moved three hundred kilometers south, from their home on the North Branch of the Susquehannah River to the northern reaches of Chesapeake Bay, in the middle years of the sixteenth century. Thus they were farther from the League Iroquois and closer to an independent source of trade goods. Novel urban architecture in the new location demonstrated the stakes involved in this level of trade; instead of the scattered small villages of their homeland, they built a single large fortified town.[19]

From this vantage point, the Susquehannocks sought trading partners. Captain John Smith, exploring the upper reaches of Chesapeake Bay shortly after Jamestown's founding in 1607, was approached by sixty Susquehannocks who offered to open trading connections. Before Smith met these towering Susquehannocks, he had been amazed to find European trade goods—"hatchets, knives, and peeces [guns] of yron, and brasse"— in the hands of Indians he knew as Tockwoghs. Upon learning that these things came to the Tockwoghs via the Susquehannocks, Smith expressed his desire to know them. The Susquehannocks then came to meet with Smith, bringing items of both American and European manufacture: "skins, Bowes, Arrows, Targets [shields], Beads, Swords, and tobacco pipes for presents."[20]

The Jamestown colonists were slow to take up this opportunity, so the Susquehannocks' first English trading partnership was with the adventurer

William Claiborne, who led a small triracial community of "Atlantic creoles" on Kent Island in Chesapeake Bay. Beginning early in the 1630s, Claiborne and his associates were able to plug themselves into the Susquehannocks' control of the beaver trade in the Chesapeake region and their trade connections, which spanned the eastern half of the continent. The Susquehannocks welcomed this relationship because it gave them access to European products independent of Iroquoian rivals to the north and their French connections.[21]

Europeans who gained American experience had no doubt that many Indians lived in polities that resembled emerging nations in Europe in important respects. Many early writers praised the authority of Indian rulers. John Smith and William Strachey, writing of the "Emperour" Powhatan, both described the awe inspired in them by his majesty; Strachey even asserted that he possessed the divinity of kingship.[22] When eyewitnesses referred to a leader as an emperor, they were using a technical term whose meaning their readers would have understood. An emperor was a ruler over other rulers who was beholden to no greater monarch. The English monarchy had adopted the closed imperial crown after Henry VIII dissolved his country's relationship with the pope, and only at that point did subjects begin to address the monarch as "Your Majesty"; "Your Grace" had been the normal mode before then. In New England, as in the Chesapeake region, writers such as William Wood and Roger Williams depicted great chiefs as ruling over "Viceroys."[23]

English accounts describe international law operating among Indian tribes. Roger Williams, for example, told what happened when a crime occurred "between Persons of diverse States." In that case, "the offended State sends for Justice."[24] The governor and council of Virginia debated an invitation to join a Powhatan punitive expedition against a tribe that had reportedly killed some Powhatan women, "Contrary to ye law of Nations."[25] Upon the marriage of Pocahontas and John Rolfe, the leader known as Powhatan gave the Virginia governor a chain of pearls for English ambassadors to wear so that he could be certain of the envoy's official status.[26]

The nationhood of Indian polities was acknowledged even more fundamentally in the system the Spanish instituted in Florida. There they recognized self-governing towns that made up the Republic of Indians separate from and paralleling the Republic of Spaniards, and these towns largely continued to operate according to their own ancient customs.[27]

Historians, governed by their own partial assumptions, have conspired to reduce the international character of early modern North America to a simplified national model, and this is true particularly of the history of the early colonies. Imperial historians have seen sixteenth- and seventeenth-century ventures as first steps in the creation of the great modern empires, and their treatment has been restricted to the ties and interaction between the parent country and its overseas colonies.[28] Among those who define themselves as American historians, the overwhelming majority narrow their treatment to England and its colonies, and, within that framework, virtually all early Americanists confine their attention to the creation and growth of one colony, or at most one colonial region, in relation to the parent country. The few who look at Dutch, French, or Spanish colonization similarly define their subject in terms of relationships between one European country and its colonies.

This tendency to examine the development of only one colony and to see that region in relation to its parent has to some extent been dictated by the literary sources. Richard Hakluyt, writing to promote the earliest English interest in American enterprise, propagated the "Black Legend" of Spanish cruelty and rapacity and implied utter incongruity between Spanish and English activities in America. William Bradford's and John Winthrop's classic histories of their colonies reinforced the conception of English exceptionalism. Their hostility to any people who ventured to the margins of their colonies or who crossed boundaries in their activities, even though those pursuits were absolutely essential to the success of the New England colonies, has been transmitted unquestioningly by many historians. The modern vogue of community studies, in which the community was the universe and leavers fell out of the study, further enhanced the xenophobia communicated by those sources.

As soon as the historian leaves these dominant sources and begins to look at the actual development of European colonies in America and of the range of native responses to the European presence, one becomes aware that the margins were crucial locations, and that all colonies were tied together by their mutual dependence. Moreover, whatever the official port books may have recorded, every colonial region was involved in trade throughout the Atlantic, and none would have survived without that trade. Commerce involved goods, often commodities produced by American Indians, but knowledge and technology were also widely traded. Whatever their sponsors might have thought, colonists necessarily acted in an international arena; without such open-ended willingness to trade widely, many more colonies would have failed.

Europeans became interested in North America's east coast in the sixteenth century. The most lucrative—and the most international—interest focused on the north, where large numbers of ships from England, Spain, Portugal, and France converged on the Newfoundland Banks every summer. American fish brought much-needed protein to Europe's burgeoning population and, especially as it was a summer-only activity and did not require the expensive support of a colony, fishing was a financially rewarding venture. This international community of fishermen rotated the position of admiral, effectively governor, among themselves every summer, offering a remarkable early instance of internationalism.[29]

French adventurers became involved in the fur trade in the St. Lawrence region as an Indian-initiated spin-off from the fishing, and their interest in the far north was cemented by its success. Farther south, both the Atlantic and Pacific coasts of North America had been explored and found to offer little to repay the massive costs of colonization. Thus the first and only continuing sixteenth-century European settlement in the future United States was San Agustín in Florida in the 1560s, placed there to protect the plate fleet as it exited the Caribbean on its annual trip from Havana to Seville. The Spanish decided to found a settlement after they had extinguished two small French colonies on the southern coast, and San Agustín, administered from Havana, was intended to be preemptive. Thus the European phase of American history begins with a Spanish colony in the far south and an international presence along the Atlantic northern coast. England's attempt to found a colony at Roanoke in the 1580s had ended in failure, as had the French colonies of Charlesfort and La Caroline and Juan de Oñate's expedition to establish a permanent Spanish presence in New Mexico.

At the beginning of the seventeenth century, France, Spain, and England all renewed their interest in North America, and the first decade saw the foundation of true American colonies: Jamestown in Virginia in 1607; Quebec on the St. Lawrence in 1608; and Santa Fe in New Mexico in 1610. As we study and teach American history, these ventures must be analyzed together. The renewed move to create presences in North America responded to changes in the Atlantic trades and in relationships on both sides of the Atlantic. All are part of American history, and it is anachronistic to allow later political distinctions to rule our view of the colonial period. The common course is to include Florida in American history only in the nineteenth century, after it had been conquered by the United States; if Florida is mentioned in discussions of an earlier period, it is only as a vacuum into which disorderly people were drawn. New Mexico and Texas enter American history in the 1840s, despite their priority in settlement, and California comes in even later—right on Daniel Webster's schedule.[30] The unexamined assumption is that to be Spanish is to be un-American.

We need a new organizing principle to replace the old westward-moving Anglo-Saxon model, with time rather than xenophobia as the central pole of the new early modern American history. Europeans began colonization focused on the territory of the future United States in the first decade of the seventeenth century, and this new level of overseas commitment led native political entities to begin to forge different relationships both among themselves and with the newcomers. The first two decades of the seventeenth century were a period of experimentation on all sides, and it was in the 1620s that the colonies began to grow. Plymouth, the first successful New England plantation, was founded at about the same time that Virginia, with tobacco in place as its crop, began to attract larger numbers of colonists. New Netherland was established simultaneously along the Hudson, first at Beverwijk and then at New Amsterdam, forming the first great nation-to-nation link with the Five Nations of the Iroquois League.[31]

Large-scale colonization was a phenomenon of the 1630s. The preceding decade had been one of economic hardship and severe Little Ice Age conditions in Europe. The beginning of the Thirty Years' War in 1618 and the growth of pressure on religious consciences led people to consider uprooting themselves for transplantation elsewhere. Meanwhile, the growth of trade in American products made transatlantic emigration seem more attractive. These factors in various combinations led promoters and venturers to greater efforts, and the small trickle of people willing to transplant became, especially in England, the flood of the great migration. English Puritans fearing future persecution founded Massachusetts Bay, while English Roman Catholics planted Maryland for the same reason. In both cases, established families and servants came to the colony along with their religious leaders, and founding communities centered around the Church. Large numbers also went to Virginia during this decade, and even more emigrated to the West Indies.

The 1630s also saw a new level of commitment in New Mexico, where married soldiers and their families came to settle down, and in La Florida. In both regions, cadres of priests fanned out, establishing missions over large areas. Thirty priests led by Fray Alonso de Benavides arrived in New Mexico in 1629, by which date there were already fifty churches and friaries there. In the Southeast, the missions spread through Florida and into present-day Georgia.[32] New Sweden was settled on Delaware Bay in 1638 as part of the burgeoning European interest in America and the trade possibilities presented by linkage with American international networks. Although Virginia had reluctantly been made a royal colony in 1625, none of the European colonies founded on America's east coast in the 1620s and 1630s was, strictly speaking, a national venture. All were planted by companies that, although they were chartered by their national governments, were controlled and financed by the corporations. All contained mixed populations.

The 1620s and 1630s also saw the beginnings of an African presence. These forced migrants came bearing their own national/ethnic identity and continued to think of themselves as members of their own national group. Early in 1620, thirty-two Africans, seventeen women and fifteen men, were recorded in a census of the Virginia plantations.[33] Recent research has demonstrated that the "20. and Odd Negroes" brought to Virginia in the summer of 1619 came directly from São Paulo de Loanda, the Portuguese capital in Angola, and shared a national/ethnic identity, which they carried forward into their American interactions. Other forced migrants from Angola came to the colony in the ensuing decade, and the records offer a striking piece of evidence confirming the ethnic/national identity they maintained. Anthony Johnson arrived in 1621, and he and his wife Mary, who arrived in 1622, earned their freedom and founded a large family. In 1677, their grandson John purchased a farm to which he gave the name "Angola."[34]

Africans also arrived in New Netherland in the 1620s, and the records offer the same kind of evidence of survival of national/ethnic identity among them. Many people of African descent incorporated Angola into their names, and these identifications were passed on from generation to generation. For example, Claes Emanuel, born in 1649, was the son of Emanuel van Angola and Phizithiaen D'Angool. Christyn van Angola stood godparent at his baptism. Claes married Lucretia Lovyse, daughter of Lovys Angola and Hilary Criolyo, who were married in 1660. In another instance in the 1660s, a free woman named Dorothe Angola, who had stood godparent to the child of Kleyn Anthony of Angola and his wife Louize in 1643 and had adopted the child, Anthony, when his parents died, moved to have him declared free so that he could inherit property. A free man named Domingo Angola filed a petition on behalf of the freedom of an enslaved young woman in the same period, and Jan Angola won a court suit against a Dutch servant. The many people who carried their Angolan identity in their names were joined by others; in 1646, a boy named Manuel Congo was the victim of rape by another slave. And in 1641, in a celebrated case of solidarity, nine Africans belonging to the Dutch West India Company jointly confessed to the murder of another, Jan Premero. Among the nine were Paolo d'Angola, Gracia Angola, and Simon Congo. These nine were given limited freedom and grants of land by the company in the 1640s, along with others including Pieter Santome, Anna van Angola, and Antony Congo. One of the men freed later married Isabel Kisana from Angola; another married Lucie d'Angola, daughter of Dorothy Angola. In addition to company manumissions, Bastiaen d'Angola was freed by his private owner. Other land grants went to Christoffel Santome and Assento Angola. In 1664, when the colony was under attack by the English, full freedom was granted to Ascento Angola, Christoffel Santome, Pieter Pietersz Criolie, Antony Antonysz Criolie, Salomon Pietersz Criolie, Jan Guinea, Lowies Guinea, and Bastiaen Pietersz.[35] People from Angola and Congo would have participated in a closely related cultural and linguistic heritage. In other parts of America, migrants from these regions, even though enslaved, formed national organizations.[36] French Louisiana, with its highly concentrated population from the Senegambia region of Africa, saw a remarkably coherent transatlantic national consciousness, especially as African methods were employed to cultivate the region's key crops.[37]

Old World people abroad and the native leaders and traders with whom they dealt were all engaged in intricate networks of relationships that involved essential interdependence. The entire Atlantic coast of North America and the West Indies were linked by trade, which cut across national lines, even international hostilities. Delineation of the intricacies of this trade takes us back to the Susquehannock case study. The Susquehannocks' partnership with William Claiborne's Kent Island group was disrupted when Charles I granted the northern Chesapeake region, including Kent Island, to Lord Baltimore for his colony of Maryland. Lord Baltimore attempted to divert the trade to his own employees, but the Susquehannocks rebuffed his advances. Instead, they approached the recently settled colony of New Sweden on Delaware Bay and offered a trade relationship.[38]

Throughout their partnership with the Swedes and Finns on Delaware Bay, the Susquehannocks made it clear that they were the senior partners. They refused to entertain any missionary activities: "And when we speak to them about God they pay no attention, but they will let it be understood that they are a free people, subject to no one, but do what they please."[39] Similarly, they made it clear that if they could not obtain high-quality trade goods reliably and in sufficient quantity from New Sweden, they would take their trade elsewhere. The Susquehannocks also oversaw New Sweden's relationship with their clients, the Algonquian-speaking Lenape Indians who lived near the colony.

Ensuring a reliable supply of trade goods was New Sweden's problem. Largely abandoned by the parent company in Sweden, the colonists found their salvation in becoming middlemen between English merchants from Hartford and New Haven in Connecticut and the Susquehannocks.[40] This trade and others like it also spelled salvation for the New England colonies, struck by economic hard times when the outbreak of civil war in England in the early 1640s ended the flow of migrants from England and the money they brought with them. New Englanders exported food to colonies in the Caribbean and the Chesapeake region, and increasingly entered into the Atlantic trades. New England's leaders recognized that the coastal trade was key to the colonies' survival, as the Winthrop family correspondence amply demonstrates.[41]

In the case of the Connecticut–New Sweden trade, the commodities were different. The merchants typically brought some corn to feed the colonists, but mainly their cargoes consisted of wampum produced by Indians who lived along the shores of Long Island Sound. Shells from the sound's shores made the most highly prized wampum; Delaware Bay did not produce the most desirable shells.[42] The Susquehannocks traded furs obtained from Indians far in the interior for the wampum, a product esteemed throughout

American communities for its spiritual value. Thus the New Sweden colony formed the nexus that facilitated a trade almost entirely in Indian-made commodities. Aware that the Indians wore badges and totems made of wampum, Governor Printz, who was called "Great Belly" by the Indians, fashioned himself into a personal advertisement for the trade connection. He had a suit specially made that was decorated all over with "their money, which was very artistic, threaded and worked with all kinds of animals, which came to a few thousand florins."[43] Long Island Sound wampum circulated throughout the region east of the Mississippi, just as felt hats made from American furs set new standards of elegance in Europe. National identifications meant little in America; these same Connecticut River merchants traded all along the coast and in the Caribbean, and the colonies thrived because of their activities. Isaac Allerton, a leading merchant in these trades, had residences in English New Haven and Dutch New Amsterdam simultaneously, and he held office in both jurisdictions, as well as in Plymouth colony.[44]

The very success of this trade drew the attention of other groups anxious to procure some of it for themselves. Merchants in Maryland to the south tried to detach part of the trade, and the Iroquois League to the north also worked to divert trade relationships their way. Both the New Netherland and New Haven colonies had claims to lands along Delaware Bay, which they pursued intermittently—even while New Haven merchants supported New Sweden with their trade. And the Delawares tried to free themselves of their clientage so as to forge an independent role.

Some international tensions escalated to full-scale war. The Susquehannocks were involved in a devastating war in the early 1650s with a nation to the west known as the Arrigahagas; the Swedes called them the Black Minquas, because they wore black badges. At the same time the first Anglo-Dutch War disrupted the coastal trade and New Sweden's trade system. New Netherland invaded and incorporated New Sweden, despite the early warning the Susquehannocks had given the Swedes of Dutch intentions. And the Susquehannocks took seriously their obligations to their clients in New Sweden. Peter Lindeström wrote that a force of over nine hundred Indians coordinated by the Susquehannocks then attacked New York "to exact revenge on our behalf." When they discovered Isaac Allerton at home in Manhattan, they "offered great insult" to him.[45] But, although the attack was devastating, neither the overthrow of New Sweden nor the changes in the trade could be reversed. Partly as a result of wars and partly because of epidemics, the Susquehannocks' power also diminished by the end of the century.

The lesson of the Susquehannock–New Sweden–Connecticut connection is not that it ended, but that it existed as an international nexus and involved networks of nations on both sides of the Atlantic. When it had ceased to exist, its place was taken by many other such relationships, which cut across national lines and ramified across the North American continent.

The later seventeenth century, of course, saw some consolidation along America's east coast. New Netherland was seized by the English during the second Anglo-Dutch War; thus New Sweden went from being Dutch to being English.[46] But in many ways America became more international. New Netherland had been a colony of mixed population from the beginning, and many settlers had emulated Isaac Allerton in moving down from New England; the change to English jurisdiction intensified that reality.[47] As slavery became the labor system of the southern colonies and England came to dominate the slave trade after 1670, huge numbers of people were imported from Africa; the majority were from the Bight of Biafra region. The population of Africans, as of Europeans, grew by natural increase, indicating that enslaved people had some opportunities to form families and pass on their own traditions, as exemplified in creole languages and musical traditions.[48] Angolans predominated in the South Carolina slave population, and John Thornton argues that the course of the Stono Rebellion in 1739 demonstrates the survival of Kongo military culture among them.[49] New York received several shipments of slaves, probably Muslims, from Madagascar in the later seventeenth century, and evidence that these maintained their allegiance to Islam occurs throughout the records.[50] National identities continued to define these populations.[51] New European colonists came from all over Britain and much of Europe. These settled together in groups and maintained their national identifications as earlier migrants had done.[52] Even those entities we call the English colonies were less English, judged by the composition of their populations, at the end of the seventeenth century, except perhaps for New England, which had ceased to be a promising target for migrants. But New England, even with its population of largely English and American Indian descent, was inextricably tied to international trade for its living.

A continental perspective is just as important at the end of the seventeenth century as at its beginning. Major changes were occurring with the entrenchment of elites in the longer-settled colonies, which experienced a wave of wars and rebellions. Leisler's Rebellion in New York can be seen as an international event, as the rebels, many of whom were Dutch, proclaimed the new English monarchs William and Mary with their Netherlands connection against James II, a monarch with Scottish roots. Allegiance to international Calvinism was at the heart of the rebels' organization, as was also the case in simultaneous rebellions in Massachusetts and Maryland. All were part of the Glorious Revolution, the transatlantic challenge to increasingly authoritarian Stuart administration.[53]

In Virginia, New England, and New Mexico, Indian resistance to European aggression, cultural and physical, led to devastating wars. The Pueblo

Revolt in 1680 responded both to a massive drought that seized the region and to the Franciscans' increasing pressure on them to give up their national religion. In the Indians' eyes, the two were intimately related.[54]

Bacon's Rebellion in Virginia reflected the spread of European settlement into an international arena. A major thoroughfare along the Appalachians had long linked great Indian nations in the Southeast—Creeks, Cherokees, and Catawbas—with the Iroquois League and the Susquehannocks. The highway saw both trade and war parties. Virginia settlers were disturbed by their proximity to these armed and powerful parties and demanded that the government in Williamsburg protect them. The circumstances in which the rebellion exploded involved Susquehannock parties caught up in a spiral of revenge attacks with the planters. Major Isaac Allerton, son of the merchant, was commissioned by Governor Sir William Berkeley along with Colonel John Washington to lead the militia against the Susquehannocks.[55]

Rather than visualizing early American history as the story of the slow westward spread of European settlements, historians might think of the interior of the continent as the international core. The great nations in the interior grew in power and extent as they absorbed refugees from the east, and new kinds of national consciousness began to emerge in the Ohio Valley.[56] The intricate negotiations between entities, European and Indian, in the region of the Great Lakes, the *pays d'en haut,* involved chains of policies and promises from Detroit to Albany to Montreal and beyond to London and Paris. The Iroquois League in partnership with New York formed the clientage relationships known as the Covenant Chain, and the League signed treaties of neutrality simultaneously at Montreal and Albany in 1701. At the same time, France sought to extend its control over the interior and establish links with the large Chickasaw and Choctaw nations with the establishment of Louisiana and Detroit. Certainly, policy-makers in Europe focused on this interior arena as they embarked on the series of imperial wars between France and England and their allies that began in 1689 and continued through to 1815. Alliances with Indian nations were central to the conduct of these wars in North America.[57] As the coastal colonies spread, they inevitably became involved in the international relationships that characterized the interior.

As we adopt the continental approach to the teaching and study of sixteenth- and seventeenth-century American history, the approach to later periods will also change in beneficial ways. One effect of our traditional misconception of the colonial period has been that the history of American Indians has always been considered a separate subject—even in courses on the nineteenth and twentieth centuries. The Bureau of Indian Affairs is within the Department of the Interior (having been moved from the War

Department), and this placement, reflecting the assumption that Indians belong to nature rather than politics, is echoed in our national histories.

A continental history will necessarily include all actors, and will thus reflect more clearly the actual concerns of people in the past, who did not think in the compartmentalized terms that we have imposed on their history. The first use by the U.S. government of its treaty powers under the Constitution was with the Creek Indians, and we see vividly today the consequences of the new government's definition of the Indians as members of nations. Indian affairs were intimately involved in political fights in the nineteenth century; for example, in the connection between the forced removal of Indians from the Southeast and the challenge posed by the Nullification Crisis early in the century. In the later part of the period, we can recover the links between campaigns to improve the lives of immigrants and slum-dwellers in the East and efforts to "reform" and "civilize" Indians in the West. Often these campaigns were formed and run by the same groups of reformers and were part of the same policy initiatives. We can also recover the degree to which America's relations with the world were shaped by the United States' conquest of the West and the policies that were formed as part of that campaign.[58]

Moreover, a continental story will acknowledge people in the West, Hispanic as well as Indian, as part of American history from the beginning. In modern times, all but the most obtuse have realized that the United States is a country of many nationalities and traditions, and that people of northern European extraction do not predominate in this population. It is time to recognize that such was also the case in the founding period.

NOTES

1. Daniel Webster, "First Settlement of New England: A Discourse Delivered at Plymouth, on the 22nd of December, 1820," in *Memoirs and Speeches on Various Occasions*, vol. 1 of *The Writings and Speeches of Daniel Webster* (18 vols., Boston and New York, 1903), 181–226.

2. James Muldoon, *Empire and Order: The Concept of Empire, 800–1800* (New York, 1999), 139–49, quotation from p. 140. On the Spanish empire as the successor of the Roman, see also Anthony Pagden, *Lords of All the World: Ideologies of Empire in Spain, Britain and France, c. 1500–c. 1800* (New Haven, Conn., 1995), ch. 2.

3. Adams to Nathan Webb, October 12, 1755, in *The Works of John Adams, Second President of the United States*, ed. Charles Francis Adams (10 vols., Boston, 1850–56), 1: 23–24.

4. For a compelling critique of this consensus, see Thomas Bender, "The Geography of Historical Memory and the Remaking of Public Culture," in *Towards a New American Nation? Redefinitions and Reconstruction*, ed. Anna Maria Martellone (Keele, U.K., 1995), 174–87.

5. Joyce Appleby describes American exceptionalism as an organizing principle in the early national period, and its costs in her presidential address to the Organization of American Historians, "Recovering America's Historic Diversity: Beyond Exceptionalism," *Journal of American History* 79 (1992): 419–31.

6. See Jack P. Greene, "Beyond Power: Paradigm Subversion and Reformulation and the Re-Creation of the Early Modern Atlantic World," in his *Interpreting Early America: Historiographical Essays* (Charlottesville, Va., 1996), 17–42.

7. Martin W. Lewis and Kären E. Wigen, *The Myth of Continents: A Critique of Metageography* (Berkeley and Los Angeles, 1997).

8. Charles Tilly, "Reflections on the History of European State-Making," in *The Formation of National States in Western Europe,* ed. id. (Princeton, N.J., 1975), 3–83, quotation from p. 15; Alvin M. Josephy Jr., *500 Nations: An Illustrated History of North American Indians* (New York, 1994). See also J. H. Elliott, "A Europe of Composite Monarchies," *Past and Present* 137 (1992): 48–71, and Muldoon, *Empire and Order,* 1–20 and passim.

9. On Uncas, see Eric S. Johnson, "Uncas and the Politics of Contact," in *Northeastern Indian Lives, 1632–1816,* ed. Robert S. Grumet (Amherst, Mass., 1996), 29–47. For Powhatan, see John Smith, *A Map of Virginia* (Oxford, 1612), in *The Complete Works of Captain John Smith,* ed. Philip L. Barbour (3 vols., Chapel Hill, N.C., 1986), 1: 173–74. On African political forms, see John A. Thornton, *Africa and Africans in the Making of the Atlantic World, 1400–1800* (2d ed., New York, 1998), and Gwendolyn Midlo Hall, *Africans in Colonial Louisiana: The Development of Afro-Creole Culture in the Eighteenth Century* (Baton Rouge, La., 1992), ch. 2.

10. Jane Ohlmeyer, "Seventeenth-Century Ireland and the New British and Atlantic Histories," in *The New British History in Atlantic Perspective* (forum), *American Historical Review* 104 (1999): 446–62, esp. 451.

11. Parkhurst to Richard Hakluyt the Elder, in *The Original Writings and Correspondence of the Two Richard Hakluyts,* ed. E. G. R. Taylor (London, 1935), 1: 131.

12. On the relationship of nation-building and overseas expansion, see David Armitage, "Greater Britain: A Useful Category of Historical Analysis," in *The New British History in Atlantic Perspective* (forum), *American Historical Review* 104 (1999): 427–45, esp. 428.

13. On the Mississippian chiefdoms, see Charles Hudson, *Knights of Spain, Warriors of the Sun: Hernando de Soto and the South's Ancient Chiefdoms* (Athens, Ga., 1997), esp. 28–30, 142–4, 169, 174, 228, 281, 308; Lynda Norene Shaffer, *Native Americans before 1492: The Moundbuilding Centers of the Eastern Woodlands* (Armonk, N.Y., 1992); and *The Forgotten Centuries: Indians and Europeans in the American South, 1521–1704,* ed. Charles Hudson and Carmen Chaves Tesser (Athens, Ga., 1994).

14. Daniel H. Usner Jr., "French-Natchez Borderlands in Colonial Louisiana," in *American Indians in the Lower Mississippi Valley: Social and Economic Histories* (Lincoln, Neb., 1998), 15–32.

15. Daniel K. Richter, *The Ordeal of the Longhouse: The People of the Iroquois League in the Era of European Colonization* (Chapel Hill, N.C., 1992); Daniel K. Richter and James H. Merrell, *Beyond the Covenant Chain: The Iroquois and Their Neighbors in Indian North America, 1600–1800* (Syracuse, N.Y., 1987); Richard White, *The Middle Ground: Indians, Empires, and Republics in the great Lakes Region, 1650–1815* (Cambridge,

1991); Dean R. Snow, "Dating the Emergence of the League of the Iroquois: A Reconsideration of the Documentary Evidence," in *A Beautiful and Fruitful Place: Selected Rensselaerswijck Seminar Papers,* ed. Nancy Anne McClure Zeller (Albany, N.Y., 1991), 139–46.

16. Carroll L. Riley, *Rio del Norte: People of the Upper Rio Grande from Earliest Times to the Pueblo Revolt* (Salt Lake City, 1995), 112–18.

17. Kathleen J. Bragdon, *Native People of Southern New England, 1500–1650* (Norman, Okla., 1996), 91–92; Jack Campisi, "Indian Governance," in *Encyclopedia of North American Colonies,* ed. Jacob Ernest Cooke et al. (3 vols., New York, 1993), 1: 453–55; John H. Moore, "Native American Economies," ibid., 726–27.

18. *The Voyages of Jacques Cartier,* ed. Ramsay Cook (Toronto, 1993), 20.

19. James W. Bradley, *Evolution of the Onondaga Iroquois: Accommodating Change, 1500–1655* (Syracuse, N.Y., 1987), 83, 90–99. See also Francis Jennings, "Glory, Death, and Transfiguration: The Susquehannock Indians in the Seventeenth Century," in *Proceedings of the American Philosophical Society* 112 (1968): 15–53. Johan Printz referred to them as "great traders"; see Amandus Johnson, trans. and ed., *The Instruction for Johan Printz, Governor of New Sweden* (Philadelphia, 1930), 132.

20. John Smith, *The Proceedings of the English Colony in Virginia* (Oxford, 1612), in *Complete Works,* ed. Barbour, 1: 148–50, 231; and *The Generall Historie of Virginia, New-England and the Summer Isles* (London, 1624), in ibid., 2: 106, 119.

21. J. Frederick Fausz, "Merging and Emerging Worlds: Anglo-Indian Interest Groups and the Development of the Seventeenth-Century Chesapeake," in *Colonial Chesapeake Society,* ed. Lois Green Carr, Philip Morgan, and Jean Russo (Chapel Hill, N.C., 1988), 47–91. On "Atlantic Creoles," see Ira Berlin, "From Creole to African: Atlantic Creoles and the Origins of African-American Society in Mainland North America," *William and Mary Quarterly,* 3d ser., 53 (1996): 251–88.

22. William Strachey, *The Historie of Travell into Virginia Britania* (1612), ed. Louis B. Wright and Virginia Freund (London, 1953), 60–61; John Smith, *A True Relation of such occurrences and accidents of noate as hath hapned in Virginia* (1608), in *Complete Works,* ed. Barbour, 1: 53.

23. William Wood, *New Englands Prospect* (London, 1634), 80; Williams, *A Key into the Language of America* (London, 1643), 141, 185 (misnumbered 132, 177). On the concept of empire, see Pagden, *Lords of All the World,* 12–19; David Armitage, "Literature and Empire," in *The Origins of Empire: British Overseas Enterprise to the Close of the Seventeenth Century,* ed. Nicholas Canny, vol. 1 of *The Oxford History of the British Empire,* William Roger Louis, gen. ed. (5 vols., Oxford, 1998), 99–123. For a fuller discussion of these issues, see Karen Ordahl Kupperman, *Indians and English: Facing Off in Early America* (Ithaca, N.Y., 2000), 91–97.

24. Williams, *Key into the Language of America* 76, 144 (misnumbered 136).

25. *Records of the Virginia Company of London,* ed. Susan Myra Kingsbury (4 vols., Washington, D.C., 1906–35), 3: 228.

26. Raphe Hamor, *A True Discourse of the Present Estate of Virginia* (London, 1615), 38–46.

27. Amy Bushnell, "Ruling 'the Republic of Indians' in Seventeenth-Century Florida," in *Powhatan's Mantle: Indians in the Colonial Southeast,* ed. Peter H. Wood, Gregory A. Waselkov, and M. Thomas Hatley (Lincoln, Neb., 1989), 134–50.

28. For an illuminating discussion of these issues, see David Armitage, *The Ideological Origins of the British Empire* (Cambridge, 2000).

29. Edward Hayes, "A report of the voyage and successe thereof, attempted in the yeere of our Lord 1583 by sir Humfrrey Gilbert knight," in *The Voyages and Colonising Enterprises of Sir Humphrey Gilbert*, ed. David B. Quinn (2 vols., London, 1940), 2: 400–401; see also 1: 85–87.

30. See the very interesting debate in James A. Hijiya, "Why the West Is Lost," *William and Mary Quarterly*, 3d ser., 51 (1994): 276–92, and replies in ibid., 717–54.

31. Richter, *Ordeal of the Longhouse;* Oliver A. Rink, *Holland on the Hudson: An Economic and Social History of Dutch New York* (Ithaca, N.Y., 1986), chs. 4–5; Donna Merwick, *Possessing Albany, 1630–1710: The Dutch and English Experiences* (Cambridge, 1990). On the 1620s, see Wim Klooster, "Winds of Change: Colonization, Commerce, and Consolidation in the Seventeenth-Century Atlantic World," *de Halve Maen* 70 (1997): 53–58.

32. On the Spanish civil/military and Franciscan commitment to both regions, see David J. Weber, *The Spanish Frontier in North America* (New Haven, Conn., 1992), ch. 3, esp. pp. 87–91, and ch. 4. On New Mexico, see Ramón Gutiérrez, *When Jesus Came, the Corn Mothers Went Away: Marriage, Sexuality, and Power in New Mexico, 1500–1846* (Stanford, Calif., 1991), ch. 3. On the Southeast, see Jerald T. Milanich, "Franciscan Missions and Native Peoples in Spanish Florida," in *The Forgotten Centuries: Indians and Europeans in the American South, 1521–1704,* ed. Charles Hudson and Carmen Chaves Tesser (Athens, Ga., 1994), 276–303; John E. Worth, "Late Spanish Military Expeditions in the Interior Southeast, 1597–1628," in ibid., 104–22. See also Michael Gannon, "The New Alliance of History and Archaeology in the Eastern Spanish Borderlands," *William and Mary Quarterly*, 3d ser., 49 (1992): 321–34.

33. "Coppie of the totall sums of the generall Muster of Virginia 1619," Ferrar Papers, Magdalene College, Cambridge. These papers are available on microfilm: *The Ferrar Papers, 1590–1790,* ed. David R. Ransome (14 reels, Wakefield, U.K.). The census is reel 1, 159. William Thorndale has argued on the basis of this census that thirty-two Africans were in Virginia before the arrival of the "20. and Odd Negroes," but Martha McCartney has recently demonstrated conclusively that the date is Old Style, so that the census was actually done in March 1620. See William Thorndale, "The Virginia Census of 1619," *Magazine of Virginia Genealogy* 33 (1995): 60–161; Martha W. McCartney, "An Early Virginia Census Reprised," *Quarterly Bulletin of the Archaeological Society of Virginia* 54 (1999): 178–96.

34. Engel Sluiter, "New Light on the '20. and Odd Negroes' Arriving in Virginia, August 1619," *William and Mary Quarterly*, 3d ser., 54 (1997): 395–98; John Thornton, "The African Experience of the '20. and Odd Negroes' Arriving in Virginia in 1619," ibid., 55 (1998): 421–34. On the Johnsons, see T. H. Breen and Stephen Innes, *"Myne Owne Ground": Race and Freedom on Virginia's Eastern Shore, 1640–1676* (New York, 1980), ch. 1.

35. Joyce D. Goodfriend, "Black Families in New Netherland," in *A Beautiful and Fruitful Place*, ed. Zeller, 147–55; Peter R. Christoph, "The Freedmen of New Amsterdam," in ibid., 157–70; Cynthia Van Zandt, "Negotiating Settlement: Colonialism, Cultural Exchange, and Conflict in Early Colonial Atlantic North America,

1580–1660" (Ph.D. diss., University of Connecticut, 1998), ch. 4, "Internal Threats to Colonial Authority: An African Community Challenges Nieuw Nederlandt."

36. Thornton, *Africa and Africans in the Making of the Atlantic World*, 62–63, 190–205; Johannes Menne Postma, *The Dutch in the Atlantic Slave Trade, 1600–1815* (Cambridge, 1990), ch. 3, esp. 56–61. On reading African names in America, see John Thornton, "Central African Names and African-American Naming Patterns," *William and Mary Quarterly*, 3d ser., 50 (1993): 727–42, and Hall, *Africans in Colonial Louisiana*, app. D.

37. Hall, *Africans in Colonial Louisiana*.

38. Fausz, "Merging and Emerging Worlds," 71–73.

39. Johnson, *Instruction for Johan Printz*, 153, 164.

40. On the Susquehannock–New Sweden–Connecticut connection, see Karen Ordahl Kupperman, "Scandinavian Colonists Confront the New World," in *New Sweden in America*, ed. Carol Hoffecker, Richard Waldron, Lorraine E. Williams, and Barbara E. Benson (Newark, Del., 1995), 89–111.

41. *Winthrop Papers* (5 vols., Boston, 1929–47).On the coastal trade, see John J. McCusker and Russell R. Menard, *The Economy of British America, 1607–1789* (Chapel Hill, N.C., 1985, 1991), and Bernard Bailyn, *The New England Merchants in the Seventeenth Century* (New York, 1964).

42. Lynn Ceci, "Native Wampum as a Peripheral Resource in the Seventeenth-Century World-System," in *The Pequots in Southern New England: The Fall and Rise of an American Indian Nation*, ed. Laurence M. Hauptman and James D. Wherry (Norman, Okla., 1990), 48–63.

43. Peter Lindeström, *Geographia Americae, with an Account of the Delaware Indians, Based on Surveys and Notes Made in 1654–1656*, trans. and ed. Amandus Johnson (Philadelphia, 1925), 129, 195–200, 207, 222.

44. Cynthia Van Zandt, "The Dutch Connection: Isaac Allerton and the Dynamics of English Cultural Anxiety in the *Gouden Eeuw*," in *Connecting Cultures: The Netherlands in Five Centuries of Transatlantic Exchange*, ed. Rosemarijn Hoefte and Johanna C. Kardux (Amsterdam, 1994), 57–82.

45. Lindeström, *Geographia Americae*, 235–6; Johan Rising, "Report of Governor Johan Rising, 1655," in *Narratives of Early Pennsylvania, West New Jersey, and Delaware, 1630–1707*, ed. Albert Cook Myers (1912; reprint, New York, 1967), 160, 170–76.

46. On the effect of the English takeover on Dutch consciousness seen through the experience of one official, see Donna Merwick, *Death of a Notary: Conquest and Change in Colonial New York* (Ithaca, N.Y., 1999).

47. Joyce D. Goodfriend, *Before the Melting Pot: Society and Culture in Colonial New York City, 1664–1730* (Princeton, N.J., 1992).

48. Robin Law and Kristin Mann, "West Africa in the Atlantic Community: The Case of the Slave Coast," *William and Mary Quarterly*, 3d ser., 56 (1999): 307–34; David Richardson, "The British Empire and the Atlantic Slave Trade, 1660–1807," in *The Eighteenth Century*, ed. P. J. Marshall, vol. 2 of *The Oxford History of the British Empire*, 440–64; Philip D. Morgan, "The Black Experience in the British Empire, 1680–1810," ibid., 465–86. On musical traditions, see Richard Cullen Rath, "African Music in Seventeenth-Century Jamaica: Cultural Transit and Transmission," *William and Mary Quarterly*, 3d ser., 50 (1993): 700–726.

49. Peter H. Wood, *Black Majority: Negroes in Colonial South Carolina from 1670 through the Stono Rebellion* (New York, 1974); John K. Thornton, "African Dimensions of the Stono Rebellion," *American Historical Review* 96 (1991): 1101–13.

50. Michael A. Gomez, "Muslims in New York" (paper presented to the Columbia Seminar in Early American History, February 8, 2000).

51. Michael Gomez, *Exchanging Our Country Marks: The Transformation of African Identities in the Colonial and Antebellum South* (Chapel Hill, N.C., 1998).

52. Richard R. Johnson, "Growth and Mastery: British North America, 1690–1748," in *Eighteenth Century,* ed. Marshall, 276–99.

53. Richard S. Dunn, "The Glorious Revolution and America," in *Origins of Empire,* ed. Canny, 445–66; David Voorhees, "The 'Fervent Zeale' of Jacob Leisler," *William and Mary Quarterly,* 3d ser., 51 (1994): 447–72.

54. Andrew L. Knaut, *The Pueblo Revolt of 1680: Conquest and Resistance in Seventeenth-Century New Mexico* (Norman, Okla., 1995), 61; see also Susan L. Swan, "Mexico in the Little Ice Age," *Journal of Interdisciplinary History* 11 (1981): 633–48.

55. Edmund S. Morgan, *American Slavery, American Freedom: The Ordeal of Colonial Virginia* (New York, 1975), 250–70. On the changing status of the eastern seaboard colonies, see Stephen Saunders Webb, *1676: The End of American Independence* (New York, 1984).

56. Gregory Evans Dowd, *A Spirited Resistance: The North American Indian Struggle for Unity, 1745–1815* (Baltimore, 1992).

57. Richard White, *The Middle Ground: Indians, Empires, and Republics in the Great Lakes Region, 1650–1815* (Cambridge, 1991), esp. ch. 3; Usner, *American Indians in the Lower Mississippi Valley;* Daniel K. Richter, "Native Peoples of North America and the Eighteenth-Century British Empire," in *Eighteenth Century,* ed. Marshall, 347–71. On the international context of these conflicts as well as of the earlier Anglo-Dutch wars, see Jonathan I. Israel, "The Emerging Empire: The Continental Perspective, 1650–1713," in *Origins of Empire,* ed. Canny, 422–44.

58. See, e.g., Walter L. Williams, "United States Indian Policy and the Debate over Philippine Annexation: Implications for the Origins of American Imperialism," *Journal of American History* 66 (1980): 810–31.

FIVE

How the West Was One
The African Diaspora and the Re-Mapping of U.S. History

Robin D. G. Kelley

What is the United States, if not a nation of overlapping diasporas? Perhaps this is the defining characteristic of the New World, if not the entire world—particularly in the age of modernity, when travel, discovery, settlement, and nation-building have been the order of the epoch. While historians have recognized and explored these overlapping diasporas, with roots in Europe, Asia, Africa, and Latin America, they tend to treat them as an assemblage of marginalized identities. Rarely has the concept of diaspora been employed as *the* central theme of American history.[1]

Part of the problem has been our conception of the United States as a discrete national entity, a social and political formation whose boundaries are clear, fixed, and traversed only in the most obvious ways (e.g., through immigration, international conflicts, movements of capital and labor, etc.). Our attachment as historians to nation-centered histories and our employment of categories such as "domestic" and "foreign" to frame historical processes and events limit our understanding of the international dimen-

I am deeply indebted to everyone who participated in the "internationalizing" seminars that met in New York City, Florence, Amsterdam, and Cambridge, England. I am especially grateful to Thomas Bender, who not only created the intellectual space to help me think about these issues, but understood better than I did the broader implications of what I was proposing. I have benefited immensely from the insights of Earl Lewis, George Lipsitz, Kwame Alford, David Thelen, Mauricio Tenorio, Alton Hornsby Jr., Marcellus Barksdale, and their wonderful students and colleagues at Morehouse College. I am also indebted to all who participated in the "Transcending Tradition" conference at the University of Pennsylvania, especially its distinguished organizers, Tukufu Zuberi and Farah Jasmine Griffin. Special thanks to Cedric J. Robinson, John Hope Franklin and the late John Henrik Clarke, without whom this essay could not have been written. Finally, I thank Tiffany Patterson; some of the ideas in this essay come out of my collaborations with Patterson, with whom I co-authored a longer piece about the African diaspora to appear in the *African Studies Review*.

sions of American history. Diaspora as an analytical concept enables us to move beyond such neat divisions. Diasporan subjects are transnational subjects: their thoughts, desires, allegiances, and even their bodies are between and betwixt nations. They represent a wide range of transnational political relationships and international connections that belie the idea that "domestic" struggles can be studied in isolation from world events.[2]

Most students engaged in the interdisciplinary fields of ethnic studies have long drawn on diaspora models to understand the U.S. experience. Black studies, Chicano/Chicana studies, Asian-American studies developed an implicit diasporic perspective growing out of the social movements of the late 1960s and 1970s. Whether they are speaking of borderlands, migrations, or diasporas, ethnic studies scholars examine the connection between place of "origin" and America. For people of African descent, "diaspora" has served as both a political term with which to emphasize the unifying experiences of African peoples dispersed by the slave trade, and an analytical term that enabled scholars to talk about black communities across national boundaries. Much of this scholarship examined the dispersal of people of African descent, their role in the transformation and creation of new cultures, institutions, and ideas outside of Africa, and the problems of building Pan-African movements across the globe. Although the black studies' conception of Africans and African descendants as one people (albeit diverse and complex, of course) has led to charges of essentialism, it is precisely this perspective of seeing black people in global terms that forced the field to be relentlessly international and comparative.[3]

Diaspora has recently returned to analytical prominence in both the humanities and social sciences, fueled in part by current debates about "globalization." Indeed, some of the latest efforts to develop a diaspora framework have profound implications, not only for our understanding of the black world, but for the way we write American history, if not the history of the modern West. The making of the African diaspora was as much the product of "the West" as it was of internal developments in Africa and the Americas. At the same time, racial capitalism, imperialism, and colonialism—the key forces responsible for creating the modern African diaspora—could not shape African culture(s) without altering Western culture.[4] The purpose of this essay, then, is to map out points of convergence where the study of the African diaspora might illuminate aspects of the encounter between Europe and the New World. At the same time, I want to draw attention to the ways in which specific formulations of the meaning of "diaspora" can also keep us from seeing the full-range of black transnational political, cultural, and intellectual links. I end with a few speculative remarks on how we might broaden our understanding of black identities and political movements by exploring other streams of internationalism that are not limited to the black world.

DEFINING "DIASPORA"

The term "diaspora" is essentially the Greek word for "dispersal," although its most common usage refers to the scattering of Jews throughout the world. For African Americans, however, the concept of diaspora and its particular meaning in New World black cultures has clear historical as well as biblical roots. Early activists, historians, and clergy frequently cited Psalm 68, verse 31, which prophesized that "Ethiopia shall soon stretch out her hands unto God." It has been used as a way of describing the black (world) condition and the source of liberation. This understanding of Ethiopia as the metaphor for a black worldwide movement against injustice, racism, and colonialism lay at the heart of the early historical scholarship on the role of African peoples in the making of the modern (and ancient) worlds.[5]

The metaphor proved especially powerful because African Americans practically had no "country" to speak of through most of the nineteenth century. Before the adoption of the Fourteenth Amendment, African Americans' citizenship status had not been legally established, and even a constitutional amendment was not enough to settle the matter. The implications of this condition for historical scholarship and national identity are enormous. While some black leaders insisted on their right to citizenship, others called on black people to leave the country and find a homeland of their own. African American leaders searched outside of the United States for political allies and often sought connections with North America's colonized people—the Native Americans.

Long after the ratification of the Fourteenth Amendment, the question of African-American citizenship had hardly been resolved, and emigrationist sentiment remained a central issue in black political discourse, rendering both issues critical topics for early historical investigation. Black Americans were not willing to relinquish their claims to citizenship; yet, they reached a point of profound pessimism and began to deeply question their allegiance to and identification with the United States. In his 1921 essay "Fifty Years of Negro Citizenship as Qualified by the United States Supreme Court" (reprinted and widely circulated three years later as a small booklet), the historian Carter G. Woodson does not mince words: "The citizenship of the Negro in this country is a fiction."[6]

Woodson's criticisms help explain black historians' early international perspective. Unlike the key figures in the U.S. historical profession, black historians tended to be critical of the nationalist, racist historiography of the era. In a measured but sharp critique of nationalism in the modern world, the historian Charles Wesley argued that imperialism was a natural outgrowth of nationalism. "Under the guidance of the national spirit," Wesley wrote, "imperialism made its way into Africa, Asia and the islands of the sea. The scramble for colonial empires was a distinct aspect of nationalism for the latter part of the nineteenth century. The glory of the nation seemed to be, in part, in its control of an overseas empire."[7]

Yet, for all their distrust of, or outright opposition to, U.S. nationalism, most of these early black historians were engaged in a different sort of nation-building project. Whether deliberately or not, they contributed to the formation of a collective identity, reconstructing a glorious African past to refute degrading representations of blackness and establish a firm cultural basis for a kind of "peoplehood." They identified with the larger black world in which New World Negroes were inheritors of African as well as European civilizations. To varying degrees, they were products of the same political imperatives that led to the formation of Pan-African, "Ethiopianist," and other black international movements. Thus, in assessing the political basis for black historians' peculiar internationalism, one might argue that it is a manifestation of a kind of "nationalism" or, rather, of a diasporic identity that might be best described as "imagined community."[8]

The term "African diaspora" in its contemporary usage emerges clearly in the 1950s and 1960s. It served in scholarly debates as both a political term emphasizing the unifying experiences of African peoples dispersed by the slave trade and an analytical term that enabled scholars to talk about black communities across national boundaries. Much of this scholarship examines the dispersal of people of African descent, their role in the transformation and creation of new cultures, institutions, and ideas outside of Africa, and the problems of building Pan-African movements across the globe.[9] A critical component of this work, as well as all diaspora studies, is the construction and reproduction of a diasporan consciousness. The main elements of such a consciousness (to varying degrees, of course) include a collective memory of dispersal from a homeland, a vision of that homeland, feelings of alienation, desire for return, and a continuing relationship and identity with the homeland.[10]

Although the analogies to studying nationalisms might seem obvious, we must remain cognizant of the distinct differences between nations, nation-states, and diasporas. First, the African diaspora is not a sovereign territory with established boundaries, although it is seen as "inherently limited" to people of African descent. Second, while there is no official language, there seems to be a consistent effort to locate a single culture with singular historical roots, no matter how mythical. Third, many members of this diaspora see themselves as an oppressed "nation" without a homeland, or they imagine Africa as home—either a place of return or a place from which they are permanently exiled.[11] They therefore understood their task as writing the "history of a race"—a people scattered by force and circumstances.

THE QUESTION OF AFRICA

One of the foundational questions central to African diaspora studies is to what degree are New World black people "African," and what does that mean? It's an old question, posed as early at the publication of Sir Harry Johnston's amateur anthropological writings in a prodigious and enigmatic book, *The Negro in the New World* (1910), and explored more systematically in the pioneering work of anthropologists such as Melville Herskovits and Lorenzo Turner. Indeed, it could be argued that anthropologists have been central to the first wave of diaspora studies during the interwar years. Scholars from all over the Western hemisphere, including Nina Rodrigues, Arthur Ramos, Mario de Andrade, Edison Carneiro, Roger Bastide, and Gonzalo Aguirre Beltran, made the case that some aspects of African culture survived the Middle Passage and continued to exist in the New World. Brazil, especially, became a focus for the scholarship on African survivals because of its large black population in Bahia and its brief history of repatriation of ex-slaves to Nigeria. The main point to bear in mind is that this group of anthropologists paved the way for a global/transnational approach to African and African-American studies precisely because they were interested in African retentions and the transformation of culture. During the 1940s, they attempted to create an international association, based in Mexico City, to coordinate research and discussion on the topic, and they published a journal called *Afroamerica,* which only yielded two issues.[12]

Based on these initial anthropological explorations, a new generation of scholars sought to prove that much of West and Central African culture survived in the Americas. Focusing on music, dance, religion, and even linguistic patterns, dozens of historians and anthropologists extended Herskovits's initial findings and discovered many examples of continuity and the persistence of cultural memory.[13] On the other hand, scholars such as Sidney Mintz and Richard Price revised the cultural retention models, placing greater emphasis on discontinuity. In a fairly early and provocative position paper, Mintz and Price described New World Afro-American culture as a process of syncretism shaped by the context of "culture contact." The creation of New World cultures involved a kind of creolization of many different West and Central African cultures. Arguing that no single African culture survived the Middle Passage intact, they suggest that the enslaved forged new institutions, religious practices, and kinship roles out of a common experience and understanding of the crises created by the transatlantic slave trade and the plantation complex. The Mintz and Price position does not rule out African retentions, but they reject claims of a singular African heritage and place greater emphasis on the emergence of new dynamic cultures.[14]

These debates have hardly died. Recent work, in fact, has found continuity by paying closer attention to specific ethnicities, religions, and cultural identities within Africa itself.[15] Michael Gomez's *Exchanging Our Country Marks* (1998) is distinctive in that it is an Africanist's interpretation of the making of the African diaspora. He carefully and painstakingly reconstructs African culture and social life *in time and space* in those regions directly affected by the trade. After following these groups across the Atlantic and showing the degree to which concentrations of specific African cultures remained intact, he then charts what he argues is a transformation from specific ethnic identities to an internal black conception of "race," or rather a collective identity that regards African-descended people as a common community. At no point does he suggest that this "community" became, in any way, monolithic or even "unified." On the contrary, he demonstrates how persistent differences by class and, to a lesser extent, gender, have roots in social relations indigenous to West and Central Africa. Within Africa, he identifies a series of units of organization, from village and clan relationships to linguistic groups, to entire "civilizations" with shared cultural practices and cosmologies and, in some cases, a lingua franca. People as diverse as the Wolof and Soninke actually share much in common because of their proximity to one another in the Senegambian region, their shared participation in common trade routes, and the fact that they were brought together by various imperial wars or larger imperial structures that dominated the region. In other words, many of our assumptions about diversity within African cultures ought to be rethought, particularly since scholars of African-American history sensitive to difference and diversity err in the other direction, treating each "ethnicity" as a discrete culture.[16]

The movement and transformation of cultures, however, was never a unidirectional process. As J. Lorand Matory demonstrates in a recent article on the origins of the Yoruba nation, the diaspora profoundly shaped, and even gave birth to, new cultures on the African continent. He found that some of the most basic elements of Yoruba culture did not derive from the hinterlands of Lagos, Nigeria, but from Brazil, Cuba, Jamaica, North America, the Virgin Islands, and Sierre Leone. Returnees of African descent who resettled in Lagos hailed from these regions, particularly Brazil. Indeed, these diasporan subjects proved critical to what became the "Lagos Renaissance" during the late nineteenth and early twentieth centuries, for this creolized elite played a key role in documenting, codifying, and ultimately canonizing Yoruba religious and cultural practices. As missionaries, priests, diviners, linguists, ethnographers, and travelers, this small but influential group (along with European missionaries and anthropologists) wrote books and articles that shaped Yoruba ethnicity and contributed to the spread of the Yoruba nation. Matory also challenges the anti-essentialist critics of African cultural nationalism who emphasize the direct parallels with the racialist ideas of nineteenth-century European nationalists. Emphasizing the diasporan connections to the Lagos Renaissance, he argues that African nationalism has deeper roots in African-American transnational politics than in Europe. In other words, the editors and readers of the *Lagos Times* were far more interested in the ideas of W. E. B. Du Bois and the black response to lynching than in the writings of Comte Joseph-Arthur de Gobineau (1816–82). Matory's larger point is crucial: Africa is neither a figment of New World imagination, frozen in time, nor the sole birthplace of modern African culture. Rather, he convincingly demonstrates that transnational politics "reshaped a diaspora and its homeland through their radically coeval dialogue."[17]

Whether we employ metaphors of survival, retention, exchange, transformation, acculturation, or dialogue, the remaking of African New World cultures has enormous implications, not just for the study of the African diaspora but for the Atlantic as a whole. We can ask similar questions and consider similar methodologies for studying the making of New World European and even Native American cultures/identities/ communities. The idea of a "European" culture or even "English" culture is often taken for granted and hardly ever problematized in the way that "African" is constantly understood as a social construction. For example, we might follow Nahum Chandler's lead and think of early New World Euro-Americans as possessing what Du Bois called "double-consciousness": say, English and American, with whiteness as a means of negotiating this double consciousness.[18] Or we might consider the "New World" as a source of Pan-Europeanism in the way that it became the source of Pan-Africanism. In other words, insights drawn from cultural studies of the African diaspora may offer new ways of understanding New World identity formations as sites of both exclusivity and inclusivity, deepening our understanding of race, nationality, and culture.[19]

The question of New World cultural formation has also been critical for the study of gender in New World African communities. For example, African historians have begun to ask questions such as, How much of the idea of women as culture bearers, embedded in Western thought, conflicts or resonates with ideas coming out of West and Central African societies? In much of Africa, spiritual access or power was not specifically gendered as male, so women priests and diviners were fairly common. In the Caribbean, one sees women practitioners of vodun, myalism, and obeah; yet, in the institutional black churches, there is a clear male-dominated gendered hierarchy. We might also consider the transfer of technology, especially in agriculture. In much of West and Central Africa, women were cultivators; yet Europeans assumed that men were both responsible and knowledgeable about cultivation—so how did Americans learn rice cultivation from Africans? Which Africans? Did the passage of this knowledge to men change power relationships? And when we look deeper at the gender division of labor under slavery, did women's participation in field work, hauling, lifting, and so on, free them of constraining notions of femininity, or was it consistent with their gendered work and lives in Africa?[20]

On the other hand, the "Africanity" question has recently been met with caution, if not outright hostility, by scholars concerned with essentialism and interested in locating hybridity and difference within black cultures. This is understandable; thinking of cultural change as a process of "destruction" or loss does more to obscure complexity than illuminate the processes of cultural formation. Furthermore, emphasis on similarities and cultural continuities not only tends to elide differences in black cultures (even within the same region or nation-state), but it does not take into account the similar historical conditions in which African people labored and created/re-created culture. Forced labor, racial oppression, colonial conditions, and capitalist exploitation were global processes that incorporated black people through empire-building. They were never uniform or fixed, but they did create systems that were at times tightly coordinated across oceans and national boundaries. This raises a number of questions. Were the so-called cultural survivals simply the most effective cultural baggage Africans throughout the world used in their struggle to survive? Or were they created by the very conditions under which they were forced to toil and reproduce? Are the anthropological studies from which many of these scholars draw their comparisons and parallels valid in view of the fact that they were made under colonial domination? Is Pan-Africanism simply the recognition that black people share the same timeless cultural values, as some nationalists would have us believe, or is it a manifestation of life under racism and imperialism?

Leading the critical assault against racial essentialism in the study of black culture is a group of Afro-British scholars, most notably Stuart Hall, Kobena Mercer, Hazel Carby, and Paul Gilroy. They are less concerned with African cultural retentions than with how New World black cultures are made differently within different empires. Much of their work focuses on the twentieth century, thus emphasizing the modern and postmodern processes by which cultures are constantly being remade and commodified under capitalism. Paying attention to the rich diversity within black diasporan communities, they paint a complex portrait of African-descended people fractured by class, gender, culture, and space. Taken as a whole, they have produced a sophisticated body of work that attempts to understand the sources and range of black identities and how they operate in political struggle.[21]

Paul Gilroy's *The Black Atlantic* has received the most attention because it functions as a kind of manifesto for new studies of diaspora. *The Black Atlantic* is a collection of essays on nineteenth and twentieth century intel-

lectual history that places slavery and race at the center of the Enlightenment and the dawning of modernity. Although he focuses exclusively on
African-American males (i.e., W. E. B. Du Bois, Frederick Douglass,
Richard Wright), by tracing their intellectual and cultural "routes and
roots," he is able to explain how diasporic connections can be made and
maintained through ideas and cultures that have little to do with Africa.
He builds on Du Bois's notion of "double-consciousness" to reveal how
black intellectuals' radical critique of Western culture and domination was
a product of their engagement with the West. Not only were these men
betwixt and between "Negro" and "American," but travel generated transnational identities between Europe and the United States. Gilroy's subtle
explorations of these men's lives and ideas also exposes the inescapable
hybridity of Western civilization—the dark secret that the most avid de-
fenders of the West refuse to acknowledge.[22]

Gilroy's most important intervention, however, might be his treatment
of popular/folk/vernacular cultures carried by the anonymous slaves and
their descendants. Focusing on music, he contributes to the hotly debated
question of whether we can talk about black cultures as "authentic" or not.
While insisting that black cultures are hybrid products of cultural exchange
and historical circumstances, Gilroy boldly returns to an older idea that
black music possesses a kind of spiritual transcendence and ineffability
whose essence remains somewhat constant over the centuries. He is not
reverting to some kind of essentialism, but he does position himself as an
"anti-anti-essentialist" who refuses to accept simple binaries. [23]

Gilroy has much to offer historians trying to make sense of nineteenth-
and twentieth-century America. Some will find his work at times ahistorical,
and his inattention to political economy, power, and the material conditions of slavery and racial oppression is jarring. But *The Black Atlantic* never
promised to be a history; rather, it ought to be read as a transatlantic philosophy of culture that draws insights from historical processes. In many
ways, it builds on another, lesser-known text by the political scientist Cedric
Robinson, *Black Marxism: The Making of the Black Radical Tradition.* Published
a decade before *The Black Atlantic,* Robinson's book is a work of history *and*
philosophy that pays attention to the political economy of slavery, feudalism, and capitalism. And whereas Gilroy limits his scope primarily to black
encounters with England and the United States (with detours to Germany,
France, and Israel), Robinson's ambitious project takes in half the globe,
from western and eastern Europe to the Caribbean, from Brazil to the
Middle East and the African continent.

Despite the title, *Black Marxism* is in part a history of the making of the
Atlantic world—not simply the African diaspora. Just when European labor
was being thrown off the land and herded into the newly formed industrial
order, Robinson argues, African labor was being drawn into the orbit of

the world system through the transatlantic slave trade. But political and economic interdependence did not translate into cultural assimilation. European civilization, whether in the shape of feudalism or of the nascent industrial order, simply did not penetrate African village culture. To understand the dialectic of African resistance to enslavement and exploitation, Robinson suggests, we need to look outside the orbit of capitalism, to West and Central African culture. The first African New World revolts were governed not by a critique of Western society but a total rejection of enslavement and racism as it was *experienced*. More intent on preserving a past than transforming Western society or overthrowing capitalism, Africans ran away, became outlyers, created Maroon settlements (often with indigenous people and renegade whites), or tried to find a way home, even if it meant death.

However, with the advent of formal colonialism and the incorporation of black labor into a more fully governed social structure, Robinson detects a more direct critique of the West and colonialism, a revolt set on transforming social relations and revolutionizing Western society rather than reproducing African social life. The contradictions of colonialism produced native bourgeoisies intimate with European life and thought, whose assigned task was to help rule. But their contradictory roles as victims of racial domination and tools of empire, as Western-educated elites who felt like aliens in the dominant society as well as among the masses, compelled some of these men and women to revolt, thus producing the radical black intelligentsia. Anticipating Gilroy's arguments about double consciousness as a source of an Afrodiasporic critique of the West, Robinson argues that black intellectuals' imbibing of Western civilization and their hybrid cultural lives had a radicalizing effect. But Robinson goes a step further: it was not simply a matter of confronting the limits of democracy under racial capitalism and colonialism. Rather, the renegades of the black intelligentsia were products of their confrontation with the uprisings of the black masses, whose access to bourgeois European culture was limited. For Robinson, then, the lower orders were still the motor of historical change; the actions and ideas of diasporan intellectuals can only be understood within a broader context of mass social movements and global political economy.

Finally, Robinson and Gilroy differ in another fundamental way that carries important implications for the study of the African diaspora. Gilroy's point, and one of his most important critical interventions, is to show the analytical limits of cultural nationalism and ethnic absolutism. He asserts that black people are products of the modern world with a unique historical legacy rooted in slavery and as much claim to the Western heritage as people of European descent. Gilroy sees no need to examine or consider continental Africa, emphasizing the Western roots of the African diaspora. Robinson, on the other hand, takes the same existential condition but comes to different conclusions: slavery did *not* define the black condition, because the enslaved were Africans *first*, with their own worldviews and ideas about life, death, community, property, and so on. And once we understand how Africans defined themselves collectively, then perhaps we can understand the persistence of nationalism and various forms of race consciousness (which has never been fully contained under the limited rubric of "nationalism"). *Black Marxism* is not so much interested in whether or not these collective forms of struggle and consciousness are "essentialist." Instead, Robinson wants to know where they came from and why they persist. Moreover, he is attempting to discover how these mass movements shaped the thinking and actions of the black middle strata, the most direct recipients of "civilization."

Both works agree that elite Europeans—the men of the Enlightenment—had no monopoly on the development of modernity. They view the modern world, and New World Atlantic societies in particular, as the product of numerous global encounters—through war, enslavement, cooperation and solidarity, intellectual and cultural exchanges, and so on—between Africans, Native Americans, and Europeans. Although Robinson examines the making of the English working class, the colonization of the Irish, and the myth of a unified "English" culture, neither book sets out to study all of the overlapping diasporas that have come to define the New World. A work that does—and does so brilliantly—is Peter Linebaugh and Marcus Rediker's *The Many-Headed Hydra: Sailors, Slaves, Commoners, and the Hidden History of the Revolutionary Atlantic*. It is an exemplar of transnational history, a model of how diaspora studies can be employed to construct a coherent, unified history of the Atlantic world. Building on the best traditions of "history from the bottom up," *The Many-Headed Hydra* is the story of the making of the modern working class—early capitalism's "hewers of wood and drawers of water." Born of dispossession—from the English countryside, the West African savannah, the North American forests—the Atlantic working classes were products of global revolutions in trade, industry, and colonization during the seventeenth and eighteenth centuries. Challenging the kind of nation-bound formulations of English working-class history developed in the pioneering work of E. P. Thompson and Eric Hobsbawm, Linebaugh and Rediker argue that the English working class can only be understood as a transatlantic, imperial working class—one that includes Africans, Native Americans, and other transplanted Europeans.[24]

As much as the colonizers and adventure capitalists tried to control and divide this multiracial gang of laborers, the hewers and drawers found ways to communicate, expressed their desire for liberty, envisioned a different sort of New World turned upside down. From Barbados to New York, Liverpool to the Guinea Coast, they revolted. And it is through revolts and conspiracies that Linbebaugh and Rediker are able to tell an international history of the formation of the United States. For it is in rebellion—whether in the form of an armed uprising or the formation of a Maroon village on the outskirts of the colonial settlement—that people from different parts of the world come together. The 1741 New York slave conspiracy, for example, turns out to be a critical event in Atlantic history, not just *American* history, or the history of Africans in the Americas. As the authors demonstrate, the conspiracy not only involved Irish and Native Americans, who identified as oppressed laborers and dreamers united in their hatred of "the whites," but its leaders included veterans of other revolts in the Western hemisphere. Some of the Africans had had experience organizing rebellions in the Caribbean and, for one reason or another, had been sold off to North America rather than executed.[25]

What most historians have understood as a local slave conspiracy, Linebaugh and Rediker reconceptualize as an example of working-class internationalism. Indeed, they have unearthed many other examples of workers' rebellions across the color line and the Atlantic Ocean, revealing how they shaped both the English and American revolutions. But finding such stories proved immensely difficult, because the laboring rebels were not the victors. The lack of sources documenting such movements, they remind us, is usually a by-product of suppression. The stories of revolt died with the rebels and were erased by the executioners: historical revision by way of the gallows, the rack, the guillotine. Nevertheless, the failure of these uprisings and conspiracies help us understand how the United States came into being as a "herrenvolk Republic" founded on capitalism, slavery, and the sanctity of private property. The outcome was hardly inevitable, nor was it some natural outgrowth of Western civilization. Rather, it was the product of a long and bloody struggle, from which a ruling class of white propertied men emerged victorious. In order to decapitate the "many-headed hydra," the new rulers sought to harden the color line and tighten the physical and ideological boundaries of the nation.

The Many-Headed Hydra, in short, reveals that American history is always international and diasporic history. At the very least, it is the story of how merchant and industrial capital, with its attendant maritime revolution, and the rise of the transatlantic slave trade, created a brand-new international working class and simultaneously gave birth to new, often suppressed, expressions of internationalism. In demolishing unilinear narratives that draw a line from, say, John Locke to the ideas of the American Revolution, Linebaugh and Rediker discover many competing ideas of liberty and freedom, derived from West and Central African religions, fugitive Maroon societies, various antinomian movements emerging out of Europe (the levelers, the diggers, the ranters), and other sources of Atlantic radicalism.

Likewise, Julius Scott's forthcoming book on New World black people in the age of the Haitian Revolution invokes the "sailing image" both literally and metaphorically to illustrate how networks of oral transmission and shared memory were the crucial dimensions of Afro-diasporic politics and identity. Black republicans not long out of Africa are its main characters, and they developed their own politically driven, relatively autonomous vision of an antislavery republicanism that in many ways was far more radical than anything being pursued in France or Philadelphia. Scott also demonstrates the level of ideological debate and international organization that existed among African Americans in the New World—a crucial element in the unfolding of the revolution. At the very least, Scott demonstrates how an Afro-diasporic approach can force us to rethink the history of the creation of New World republicanism, systems of communication in the eighteenth and early nineteenth centuries, the political and cultural autonomy of African people in the West, and the crucial role that black sailors played in the age of democratic revolutions.[26]

Scott's work more broadly echoes a tradition of scholarship that puts the end of modern slavery in global perspective. As W. E. B. Du Bois, C. L. R. James, Eugene Genovese, and more recently Eric Foner, Robin Blackburn, Rebecca Scott, Thomas Holt, and Frederick Cooper have demonstrated, the transition from chattel slavery to freedom was a global process, in which the struggle over the reconstruction of the labor force had enormous implications for capitalism, democracy, liberal thought, and racial ideology.[27] Over sixty years ago C. L. R. James's *The Black Jacobins* argued that the slaves themselves shaped debates in the French National Assembly on the meaning of freedom and liberty as a natural right. More than any doctrine or speech, the revolt of African slaves themselves put the question of freedom before Paris radicals. Michel-Rolph Trouillot's book *Silencing the Past* goes further, demonstrating that at the start of the nineteenth century, the Haitian Revolution not only represented the only truly universalist claim to freedom and liberty for all of humanity but proclaimed the right of slaves (and colonial subjects) to win that freedom by armed struggle— an idea that no Western "free" nation ever accepted, not even during much of the twentieth century.[28]

Taken together, these studies move beyond unitary narratives of displacement, domination, and nation-building that center on European expansion and the rise of "racial" capitalism. The rise of the transatlantic system not only helped forge the concept of Africa and create an "African" identity but proved central to the formation of a European/"white" identity in the New World. By seeing American history in a diaspora framework, the central role of African people in the making of the modern world becomes clear. Slave labor helped usher in the transition to capitalism; black struggles for freedom indisputably shaped discourses on democracy and the rise of republicanism; and cultures, ideas, and epistemologies taken from Africa or created in the New World have deeply influenced art, religion, politics, philosophy, and social relations in the West. Hence, just as Europe invented Africa and the New World, we cannot understand the invention of Europe and the New World without Africa and African people.

NOT OUT OF AFRICA: BLACK INTERNATIONALISM AND THE LIMITS OF DIASPORA

The concept of diaspora, as powerful as it is, falls short of illuminating all of the international dimensions and contexts of black identities. Too frequently we think of identities as cultural matters, when in fact some of the most dynamic (transnational) identities are created in the realm of politics, in the way people of African descent sought alliances and political *identifications* across oceans and national borders. We might follow Paul Gilroy's lead here and distinguish "identities" from "identifications"—the latter referring to the specific political choices people make in the context of struggle. Like identities, identifications are always contingent, transitory, and perhaps more than anything, strategic. By expanding the discussion from the question of black identity in the context of an African-centered notion of diaspora to black identifications—specifically questions of transnational political links and international solidarity—we open up new avenues for writing a world history from below.[29]

Consider the fact that black labor migrations (in slavery and freedom) were generally produced by many of the same needs of capital, the same empires, the same colonial labor policies, the same ideologies that forced so-called coolie labor from China and the Asian subcontinent to work on the plantations, mines, railroads of European empires and of the Americas. In fact, Pacific crossings and Asian migrations have profoundly influenced modern streams of African American nationalism, producing unique moments of black political identifications with pan-Asian movements. We can point to numerous examples of black solidarity with various Pan-Asian movements or specific national struggles, particularly during the eras of Japanese imperialism in the Pacific, after the success of the Chinese Revolution and the emergence of Maoism, and during the war in Vietnam.[30] One excellent example of work that begins to do this is Vijay Prashad's *The Karma of Brown Folk,* which documents a long history of black and Indian solidarity. Despite deliberate efforts on the part of the colonial and nationalist states to foster anti-Asian sentiment among blacks in the Caribbean and Africa, there were dramatic moments of solidarity. Radical black intellectuals like Du Bois recognized the racism suffered by Indians and promoted their struggle against British colonialism and South African racism.[31] On the other hand, Indians in India have occasionally found inspiration in radical movements in the African diaspora. For example, the black "untouchables" of India, known as the Dalits, developed an awareness of their

African ancestry and have linked their struggle against racism to the struggle of all black people. Some have even compared their experiences with those of American blacks and formed organizations modeled on the Black Panther Party.[32]

Knowing that many peoples were migrating from all over the world, especially as industrialization and revolutions uprooted millions of people from Europe to Asia, what were the political implications of these overlapping migrations? This is a particularly important question, for it illuminates the degree to which the "black" world can only be understood in the context of the larger world and vice versa. During the first two decades of the twentieth century, for example, the world was marked by massive migrations on a global scale, rapid industrialization, the building of the Panama canal, labor migration from Europe and Asia to North America, the Caribbean, and South Africa—these were developments that produced and were shaped by international wars, revolutions, famines, and violence. Indeed, this is precisely the context for international black movements such as Garveyism, the African Blood Brotherhood, the International League of Darker Peoples, and other black radical formations during the first part of the twentieth century. [33] With journals bearing such names as *The Negro World, The Crusader, New Dispensation,* and *The Messenger,* they covered uprisings and rebellions throughout the globe, never limiting their commentary to the black world. Immediately after World War I, the editor of *New Dispensation,* the black Harlem socialist Hubert H. Harrison, published a collection of his essays titled *When Africa Awakes: The "Inside Story" of the Stirrings and Strivings of the New Negro in the Western World.* Very much a product of wartime anti-imperialism, it was one of the most profound and widely read texts linking black concerns with international politics. In it he established the "colored world" as a majority of the global population, called on African Americans to support struggles not just in Africa but in India, Ireland, Egypt, the Philippines and other oppressed colonies under European domination.[34] Thus, while black liberation might have been the primary goal of these movements, they were also part of a long-standing dialogue with nationalists around the world.

My point here is that black internationalism does not always come out of Africa nor is it necessarily engaged with Pan-Africanism or other kinds of black-isms. Indeed, sometimes it lives through or is integrally tied to other kinds of international movements, such as socialism, communism, feminism, surrealism, and religion (e.g., Islam). Communist and socialist movements, for example, have long been harbingers of black internationalism and sources of radical Pan-Africanism that explicitly reaches out to all oppressed colonial subjects as well as to white workers. Although the relationships have not always been comfortable, the communist movement enabled new identifications with other oppressed peoples. Black people took up arms to defend the Spanish Republic in the late 1930s, traveled to Cuba and China in the 1960s, and made linkages with other radicals of the African diaspora in the most unlikely places—including the schools and streets of Moscow.[35]

Similarly, during the interwar period, a group of black intellectuals from the French-, Spanish-, and English-speaking world were drawn to surrealism for its militant anticolonialism and fascination with the unconscious, the spirit, desire, and magic. Aimé and Suzanne Césaire, the Afro-Chinese Cuban painter Wilfredo Lam, and René Menil, among others, would go on to play central roles in the formation of Négritude and the promotion of African culture in the diaspora through journals such as *Légitime Défense* and *Tropiques*. But they would also influence, if not fundamentally transform, surrealism itself, rather in the way radical black intellectuals significantly shaped the history of Western Marxism.[36] However, most of these encounters are seen in terms of how "Western" ideas have influenced black people as opposed to the other way around. The question we still need to grapple with is this: How have African-American struggles for freedom shaped other national or international movements beyond the United States?

One area where these questions have been taken up recently is in the history of the Civil Rights movement and its relationship to anticolonialism. Of course, scholars have always been aware of these linkages since Civil Rights activists themselves identified with the independence movements in Africa, Asia and the Caribbean. Recent books by Brenda Gayle Plummer, Penny Von Eschen, William Sales, Van Gosse, Timothy B. Tyson, Komozi Woodard, and others have gone even further, demonstrating just how fundamental Cold War politics and anticolonial movements were in shaping black domestic struggles for freedom. With Nazism barely in the grave, the horrors of European colonialism and U.S. racism came under closer scrutiny. Inspired by the anticolonial movements in Africa, Asia, and the Caribbean, African-American activists found allies in the newly independent nations, sometimes turning to the United Nations to criticize U.S. race relations as well as colonial policies abroad. Between 1946 and 1951, at least three Civil Rights groups submitted petitions to the United Nations on behalf of the entire black world to draw attention to the denial of human rights to African Americans in the United States. On the other side, several leaders of independence movements cited the civil disobedience campaigns in the United States as models for their own political mobilization.[37]

The impact of anticolonial movements and the growing "Third World" presence in the United Nations was felt not only by Civil Rights activists but by the federal government. Indeed, the enormous impact international politics played in promoting federal policies on race is the subject of a recent book by Azza Salama Layton, who documents the State Department's active support for desegregation, prompted in part by incidents involving diplomats and students from Asia, Africa, and the Caribbean who had suffered the indignities of Jim Crow—most frequently in the nation's capital. The State Department and the Justice Department filed briefs on behalf of plaintiffs in most of the major civil rights cases, from Shelly v. Kraemer (outlawing restrictive covenants) to Brown v. Board of Education. Desegregation was in the State Department's interests because UN delegates from India, Pakistan, and Burma, not to mention the Eastern-bloc countries, relentlessly criticized the United States for allowing Jim Crow to persist at home while claiming to be a beacon of democracy for the world. In their brief in support of Brown v. Board of Education, State Department officials minced no words when explaining the reason for their intervention: "The United States is trying to prove to the people of the world, of every nationality, race, and color, that a free democracy is the most civilized and most secure form of government. . . . The existence of discrimination against minority groups in the United States has had an adverse effect upon our relations with other countries."[38]

TOWARD A DIASPORIC APPROACH TO AMERICAN HISTORY

If we employed a diaspora framework to U.S. history, what would change? What might result? First, we would be compelled to write the kind of history that follows people back and forth across the physical borders of the United States, a history in which the boundaries are determined not by geopolitics but by people and their movements—physical and mental, real and imagined. Of course, this idea, although still undeveloped, is hardly new. A quarter century ago, Herbert Gutman suggested that immigrant workers drew on "cultural baggage" from their homelands in their struggle to survive and shape American industrialization. Another labor historian, John Laslett, built on Gutman's insights and developed a general theory of American working-class history based on "overlapping diasporas." In other words, the politics and cultures of immigrant workers tend to be bound up with the politics of their home country. Peter Kwong's *Chinatown, New York: Labor and Politics, 1930–1950,* for example, demonstrates how impossible it is to make sense of Chinese working-class politics in New York City without reference to the Chinese Revolution of 1949. Likewise, Mexican-American politics and labor struggles in the Southwest during the early twentieth century are incomprehensible without understanding the Mexican Revolution.[39]

Second, processes such as "creolization," which we associate with the early period of "contact," would become a primary subject of investigation for all periods of U.S. history. Indeed, we may discover that the most dynamic moments of creolization, cultural transformation, and hybridization—if we can use those terms—might have occurred as a result of post-1965 immigration. We might even begin to think of the United States as a "home" country out of which reformations of Old World cultures travel throughout the globe. The movement of American cultural forms, such as jazz in the mid to late twentieth century, might be studied not merely as another example of U.S. cultural imperialism but as an African American diaspora whose influence on Africa—the real and imagined place of black cultural "origins"—is itself profound. If we merely think of the impact of jazz and other black vernacular music as a return to the source, we miss the degree to which African American cultures are modern products of many overlapping diasporas. This way, the presence of Africa in America will not be limited to retentions during the period of early contact, but will be treated as a central question in the recasting of national history.

Finally, a diaspora framework ought to persuade scholars to revisit other intellectual traditions, other constructions of American history produced by so-called minority thinkers whose work consciously rejects the minority label. Here I am speaking of scholarship linked to social and political movements that have asserted global strength and significance through identification with a larger diasporic community. Whether independent activist/intellectuals or university-trained scholars, these scholars have much to teach us. Not only have they made marginalized groups visible, but their work has always started from the premises that history is global, and that in telling the stories of America, nothing is out of bounds.

NOTES

1. There are some outstanding exceptions, including Earl Lewis, "To Turn as on a Pivot: Writing African Americans into a History of Overlapping Diasporas," *American Historical Review* 100, 3 (June 1995): 765–87; John H. M. Laslett, *Challenging American Exceptionalism : "Overlapping Diasporas" as Model for Studying American Working Class Formation, 1810–1924* (Chicago, 1987); Donna R. Gabaccia, "Is Everywhere Nowhere? Nomads, Nations, and the Immigrant Paradigm of United States History," *Journal of American History* 86, 3 (December 1999): 115–34; Donna R. Gabaccia and Fraser M. Ottanelli, "Diaspora or International Proletariat? Italian Labor, Labor Migration, and the Making of Multiethnic States, 1815–1939," *Diaspora* 6 (Spring 1997): 51–84.

2. Obviously, this is changing, as evident from this very volume, as well as from recent issues of the *Journal of American History* and the *American Historical Review*. As Thomas Bender points out in his introduction, we have witnessed an explosion of transnational scholarship in American history, particularly in the areas of the Atlantic world, diaspora studies, environmental history, migration studies, intellectual history, and the history of political, social, and cultural movements.

3. See, e.g., Stuart Hall, "Cultural Identity and Diaspora," in *Identity: Community, Culture, Difference*, ed. John Rutheford (London, 1990), 222–37; Michael Hanchard,

"Identity, Meaning and the African-American," *Social Text* 8, 24 (1990): 31–42; Kobena Mercer, *Welcome to the Jungle: New Positions in Black Cultural Studies* (London, 1994); several essays in *Black Popular Culture*, ed. Gina Dent (Seattle, 1992); E. Frances White, "Africa on My Mind: Gender, Counter Discourse and African-American Nationalism," *Journal of Women's History* 2, 1 (Spring 1990): 73–97.

4. See Paul Gilroy, *The Black Atlantic: Modernity and Double Consciousness* (Cambridge, Mass., 1993); Peter Linebaugh, "All the Atlantic Mountains Shook," *Labour / Le Travailleur* 10 (Autumn 1982): 87–121; Cedric Robinson, *Black Marxism: The Making of the Black Radical Tradition* (Chapel Hill, N.C., 1983); and an excellent essay by Kim D. Butler, "What Is African Diaspora Study? An Epistemological Frontier" (forthcoming in *Diaspora*).

5. See George Shepperson, "African Diaspora: Concept and Context," and St. Clair Drake, "Diaspora Studies and Pan-Africanism," both in *Global Dimensions of the African Diaspora*, ed. Joseph E. Harris (Washington, D.C., 1982); for early examples of the Ethiopian analogy, see William Wells Brown, *The Rising Son; or the Antecedents and Advancement of the Colored Race* (Boston, 1876); Edward Wilmot Blyden, especially *Christianity, Islam and the Negro Race* (Edinburgh, 1967) and *Black Spokesman: Selected Published Writings of Edward Wilmot Blyden* (New York, 1971); Robert Benjamin Lewis, *Light and Truth: Collected from the Bible and Ancient and Modern History, Containing the Universal History of the Colored and Indian Race, from the Creation of the World to the Present Time* (Boston, 1844); J. E. Casely Hayford, *Ethiopia Unbound: Studies in Race Emancipation* (2d ed., London, 1969); Alexander Crummell, *Africa and America: Addresses and Discourses* (Springfield, Mass., 1891); Wilson J. Moses, *Alexander Crummell: A Study of Civilization and Discontent* (New York, 1989); Martin R. Delany, *The Condition, Elevation, Emigration, and Destiny of the Colored People of the United States* (reprint, New York, 1968); William Leo Hansberry, *Pillars of Ethiopian History*, ed. Joseph Harris, (Washington, D.C., 1974). See also William R. Scott, *The Sons of Sheba's Race: African-Americans and the Italo-Ethiopian War, 1935–1941* (Bloomington, Ind., 1993); Joseph E. Harris, *African-American Reactions to the War in Ethiopia, 1936–1941* (Baton Rouge, La., 1994); Wilson Jeremiah Moses, *Afrotopia: The Roots of African American Popular History* (New York, 1998); St. Clair Drake, *Black Folk Here and There: An Essay in History and Anthropology*, Afro-American Culture and Society, 7 (2 vols., Los Angeles, 1987–90), vol. 1; *Imagining Home: Class, Culture, and Nationalism in the African Diaspora*, ed. Sidney J. Lemelle and Robin D. G. Kelley (New York, 1994); Robert Weisbord, *Ebony Kinship: Africa, Africans, and the Afro-American* (Westport, Conn., 1973).

6. Carter G. Woodson, "'Fifty Years of Negro Citizenship as Qualified by the United States Supreme Court," *Journal of Negro History* 6, 1 (January 1921): 1. On the question of black citizenship, emigration, and political movements after the Fourteenth Amendment, see, e.g., Floyd Miller, *The Search for a Black Nationality: Black Emigration and Colonization, 1787–1863* (Urbana, Ill., 1975); Nell Irvin Painter, *Exodusters: Black Migration to Kansas after Reconstruction* (New York, 1977); Sterling Stuckey, *Slave Culture: Nationalist Theory and the Foundations of Black America* (New York, 1987); Hollis R. Lynch, *Edward Wilmot Blyden: Pan-Negro Patriot, 1832–1912* (London, 1964); William E. Bittle and Gilbert Geis, *The Longest Way Home: Chief Alfred C. Sam's Back-to-African Movement* (Detroit, 1964); Robert A. Hill, "Chief Alfred Sam and the African Movement," in *Pan-African Biography*, ed. Robert A. Hill, (Los

Angeles, 1987); Edwin S. Redkey, *Black Exodus: Black Nationalist and Back-to-Africa Movements, 1890–1910* (New Haven, Conn., 1969); V. P. Franklin, *Black Self-Determination: A Cultural History of African-American Resistance* (2d ed., Brooklyn, N.Y., 1992); Kevin Gaines, *Uplifting the Race: Black Leadership, Politics, and Culture in the Twentieth Century* (Chapel Hill, N.C., 1996).

7. Charles Wesley, "Three Basic Problems in Human Relations" (n.d., ca. 1950) reprinted in James L. Conyers Jr., *Charles H. Wesley: The Intellectual Tradition of a Black Historian* (New York, 1997), 191; see also L. D. Reddick, "A New Interpretation for Negro History," *Journal of Negro History* 22, 1 (January 1937): 18–19.

8. Benedict R. O'G. Anderson, *Imagined Communities: Reflections on the Origin and Spread of Nationalism* (1983; rev. ed., New York, 1991).

9. See George Shepperson, "African Diaspora: Concept and Context" and St. Clair Drake, "Diaspora Studies and Pan-Africanism," in *Global Dimensions of the African Diaspora,* ed. Joseph E. Harris (Washington, D.C., 1982); see, e.g., Robert B. Lewis's *Light and Truth: Collected from Bible and Ancient and Modern History* (Boston, 1844), William Wells Brown, *The Rising Son; or the Antecedents and Advancement of the Colored Race* (Boston, 1876), and, most important, the works of Edward Wilmot Blyden, especially *Christianity, Islam and the Negro Race* (Edinburgh, 1967) and *Black Spokesman: Selected Published Writings of Edward Wilmot Blyden* (New York, 1971). For more general works on the African diaspora, see *Out of One, Many Africas: Reconstructing the Study and Meaning of Africa,* ed. William G. Martin and Michael O. West (Urbana, Ill., 1999); Aubrey W. Bennett and G. L. Watson, eds., *Emerging Perspectives on the Black Diaspora* (Lanham, Md., 1989); Jacob Drachler, *Black Homeland / Black Diaspora: Cross Currents of the African Relationship* (Port Washington, N.Y., 1975); St. Clair Drake, *Black Folk Here and There,* vol. 2; W. E. B. Du Bois *The World and Africa: An Inquiry into the Part Which Africa Played in World History* (New York, 1947); *Studies in the African Diaspora: A Memorial to James R. Hooker (1929–1976),* ed. John P. Henderson and Harry A. Reed (Dover, Mass., 1989); *African Diaspora: Interpretive Essays,* ed. Martin L. Kilson and Robert I. Rotberg (Cambridge, Mass., 1976); Franklin Knight, *The African Dimension in Latin American Societies* (New York, 1974); *Imagining Home,* ed. Lemelle and Kelley; Vincent Thompson, *The Making of the African Diaspora in the Americas, 1441–1900* (White Plains, N.Y., 1987); Weisbord, *Ebony Kinship.*

10. William Safran, "Diasporas in Modern Societies: Myths of Homeland and Return," *Diaspora,* 1, 1 (1991): 83–84.

11. James Clifford, *Routes: Travel and Translation in the Late Twentieth Century* (Cambridge, Mass., 1997), 249–50, 251.

12. For an interesting and fairly comprehensive discussion of these scholars and the attempt to coordinate research on an international scale, see Melvile Herskovits, "The Present Status and Needs of Afroamerican Research," *Journal of Negro History* 36, 2 (April 1951): 123–47. Examples of this work include [Gonzalo] Aguirre Beltran, "Tribal Origins of Slaves in Mexico," *Journal of Negro History* 31 (1946): 269–352; Lorenzo Turner, "Some Contacts of Brazilian ex-Slaves with Nigeria, West Africa," *Journal of Negro History* 27 (1942): 55–67; E. Franklin Frazier, "The Negro in Bahia, Brazil," *American Sociological Review* 7 (1942): 465–78.

13. Melville J. Herskovits, *The Myth of the Negro Past* (Boston, 1941); id., *The New World Negro: Selected Papers in Afro-American Studies* (Bloomington, Ind.,

1966); *Africa's Ogun: Old World and New,* ed. Sandra T. Barnes (Bloomington, Ind., 1989); Leonard Barrett, *Soul-Force: African Heritage in Afro-American Religion* (Garden City, N.Y., 1974); Roger Bastide, *African Civilisations in the New World* (London, 1972); Roger Bastide, *The African Religions of Brazil: Toward a Sociology of the Interpretation of Civilisations* (Baltimore, 1978); George Brandon, *Santeria from Africa to the New World: The Dead Sell Memories* (Bloomington, Ind., 1993); Margaret Creel, "*A Peculiar People": Slave Religion and Community—Culture among the Gullahs* (New York, 1988); Joseph Holloway and Winifred Vass, *The African Heritage of American English* (Bloomington, Ind., 1993); Joseph Murphy, *Santeria: African Spirits in America* (Boston, 1988, 1992); Joseph Murphy, *Working the Spirit: Ceremonies of the African Diaspora* (Boston, 1994); Karen Fog Olwig. *Cultural Adaptation and resistance on St. John: Three Centuries of Afro-Caribbean Life* (Gainesville, Fla., 1985); Richard Price, *First Time: The Historical Vision of an Afro-American People* (Baltimore, 1983); Sterling Stuckey, *Slave Culture: Nationalist Theory and the Foundations of Black America* (New York, 1987); Jim Wafer, *The Taste of Blood: Spirit Possession in Brazilian Candomble* (Philadelphia, 1991).

14. Sidney Mintz and Richard Price, *The Birth of African American Culture: An Anthropological Perspective* (1976; Boston, 1992).

15. Robert Farris Thompson, *Flash of the Spirit: African and Afro-American Art and Philosophy* (New York, 1983); Michael Mullin, *Africa in America: Slave Acculturation and Resistance in the American South and the British Caribbean, 1736–1831* (Urbana, Ill., 1992); John Thornton, *Africa and the Africans in the Making of the Atlantic World, 1400–1680* (New York, 1992); Carolyn Fick, *The Making of Haiti: The Saint-Domingue Revolution from Below* (Knoxville, Tenn., 1990); João José Reis, *Slave Rebellion in Brazil: The Muslim Uprising of 1835 in Bahia,* trans. Arthur Brakel (Baltimore, 1993); Gwendolyn Midlo Hall, *Africans in Colonial Louisiana: The Development of Afro-Creole Culture in the Eighteenth Century* (Baton Rouge, La., 1992).

16. Michael Gomez, *Exchanging Our Country Marks: The Transformation of African Identities in the Colonial and Antebellum South* (Chapel Hill, N.C., 1998).

17. J. Lorand Matory, "The English Professors of Brazil: On the Diasporic Roots of the Yoruba Nation," *Comparative Studies in Society and History* 41, 1 (January 1999): 72–103, quotation from p. 98. Of course, there are many other examples of Afro-Diasporan expatriates shaping political movements on the African continent, some of the most obvious being the African-American missionaries and Garveyism. See, e.g., George Shepperson and Thomas Price, *Independent African: John Chilembwe and the Origins, Settings and Significance of the Nyasaland Native Rising of 1915* (Edinburgh, 1958); Alan Gregor Cobley, "'Far from Home': The Origins and Significance of the Afro-Caribbean Community in South Africa to 1930," *Journal of Southern African Studies* 18, 2 (1992): 349–70; Robert A. Hill and Gregory A. Pirio, "'Africa for the Africans': The Garvey Movement in South Africa, 1920–1940," in *The Politics of Race, Class, and Nationalism in Twentieth Century South Africa,* ed. Shula Marks and Stanley Trapido (London, 1987); Robin D. G. Kelley, "The Religious Odyssey of African Radicals: Notes on the Communist Party of South Africa, 1921–1934," *Radical History Review* 51 (1991): 5–24.

18. Nahum Chandler, "Force of the Double: W. E. B. Du Bois and the Question of African American Subjection" (MS).

19. There is a growing literature on whiteness and new ways of understanding European identities. Some are the best work includes, Alexander Saxton, *The Rise and Fall of the White Republic: Class Politics and Mass Culture in Nineteenth-Century America* (New York, 1990); David R. Roediger, *The Wages of Whiteness: Race and the Making of the American Working Class* (New York, 1991), and *Black on White: Black Writers on What It Means to be White*, ed. David R. Roediger (New York, 1998); Cheryl Harris, "Whiteness As Property," *Harvard Law Review* 106, no. 8 (June 1993): 1707–91; Grace Elizabeth Hale, *Making Whiteness: The Culture of Segregation in the South, 1890– 1940* (New York, 1998); Matthew Frye Jacobson, *Whiteness of a Different Color: European Immigrants and the Alchemy of Race* (Cambridge, Mass., 1998); George Lipsitz, *The Possessive Investment in Whiteness: How White People Profit from Identity Politics* (Philadelphia, 1998).

20. See especially Claire Robertson, "Africa into the Americas? Slavery and Women, the Family, and the Gender Division of Labor," in *More Than Chattel: Black Women in Slavery in the Americas*, ed. Darlene Clark Hine and Barry Gaspar (Bloomington, Ind., 1996), 3–42.

21. Paul Gilroy, *"There Ain't No Black in the Union Jack": The Cultural Politics of Race and Nation* (1987; new ed., Chicago, 1991), and *Black Atlantic;* Mercer, *Welcome to the Jungle;* Hazel Carby, *Race Men* (Cambridge, Mass., 1998) and *Cultures in Babylon: Black Britain and African America* (New York, 1999).

22. Gilroy, *Black Atlantic,*

23. Ibid.

24. Peter Linebaugh and Marcus Rediker, *The Many-Headed Hydra: Sailors, Slaves, Commoners, and the Hidden History of the Revolutionary Atlantic* (Boston, 2000); Marcus Rediker, *Between the Devil and the Deep Blue Sea: Merchant Seamen, Pirates, and the Anglo-American Maritime World, 1700–1750* (New York, 1987, 1993).

25. Linebaugh and Rediker, *Many-Headed Hydra*, 174–210.

26. Julius Sherrard Scott III, "The Common Wind: Currents of Afro-American Communications in the Era of the Haitian Revolution" (MS, forthcoming).

27. Robin Blackburn, *The Overthrow of Colonial Slavery, 1776–1848* (London, 1988); W. E. B. Du Bois, *Black Reconstruction in America, 1860–1880* (New York: 1935); Eric Foner, *Nothing but Freedom: Emancipation and Its Legacy* (Baton Rouge, La., 1983); Eugene Genovese, *From Rebellion to Revolution: Afro-American Slave Revolts in the Making of the Modern World* (Baton Rouge, La., 1974); Thomas Holt, *The Problem of Freedom: Race, Labor and Politics in Jamaica and Britain, 1832–1938* (Baltimore, 1992); Frederick Cooper, Thomas C. Holt, and Rebecca J. Scott, *Beyond Slavery: Explorations of Race, Labor, and Citizenship in Postemancipation Societies* (Chapel Hill, N.C., 2000); C. L. R. James, *The Black Jacobins: Toussaint L'Ouverture and the San Domingo Revolution* (1938; 2d rev. ed., New York, 1963).

28. See Michel-Rolph Trouillot, "An Unthinkable History: The Haitian Revolution as a Non-Event," in id., *Silencing the Past: Power and the Production of History* (Boston, 1995)

29. Gilroy, *Black Atlantic*, 276; James Clifford, "Diasporas," in *Routes: Travel and Translation in the Late Twentieth Century* (Cambridge, Mass., 1997), 268; see also Stuart Hall, "Subjects in History: Making Diasporic Identities," in *The House That Race Built*, ed. Wahneema Lubiano (New York, 1997), 289–99; Lisa Brock, "Ques-

tioning the Diaspora: Hegemony, Black Intellectuals and Doing International History from Below" *Issue: A Journal of Opinion* 24, 2 (1996): 10.

30. Ernest Allen Jr., "Religious Heterodoxy and Nationalist Tradition: The Continuing Evolution of the Nation of Islam," *Black Scholar* 26, 3–4 (Fall–Winter, 1996): 2–34; id., "Waiting for Tojo: The Pro-Japan Vigil of Black Missourians, 1932–1943," *Gateway Heritage* 16, 2 (1995): 38–55; id., "When Japan was 'Champion of the Darker Races': Sakota Takahashi and the Flowering of Black Messianic Nationalism," *Black Scholar* 24, 1 (Winter 1994): 23–46; Claude Clegg, *An Original Man: The Life and Times of Elijah Muhammad* (New York, 1997); Lipsitz, *Possessive Investment in Whiteness*, 184–210; Gerald Gill, "'Dissent, Discontent and Disinterest: Afro-American Opposition to the United States Wars of the Twentieth Century" (MS, 1988); Marc Gallicchio, *The African American Encounter with Japan and China* (Chapel Hill, N.C., 2000).

31. Vijay Prashad, *The Karma of Brown Folk*. (Minneapolis, 2000).

32. Ibid.; V. T. Rajshekar, *Dalit: The Black Untouchables of India* (Atlanta, 1995); *Untouchables: Voices of the Dalit Liberation Movement*, ed. Barbara R. Joshi (London, 1986).

33. See Wolfgang Abendroth, *A Short History of the European Working Class*, trans. Nicholas Jacobs and Brian Trench (New York, 1972), 69–76; Rod Bush, *We Are Not What We Seem: Black Nationalism and Class Struggle in the American Century* (New York, 1998), 83–112; Theodore Kornweibel, *No Crystal Stair: Black Life and the Messenger, 1917–1928* (Westport, Conn., 1975); Winston James, *Holding Aloft the Banner of Ethiopia: Caribbean Radicalism in Early Twentieth-Century America* (London, 1998); Mark Naison, *Communists in Harlem during the Depression* (Urbana, Ill., 1983), 3, 5–8, 17–18; Robert A. Hill, "The First England Years and After, 1912–1916," in *Marcus Garvey and the Vision of Africa*, ed. John Henrik Clarke (New York, 1974), 38–70; Tony Martin, *Race First* (Westport, Conn., 1976); 237–46; Robinson, *Black Marxism*, 296–301; David Samuels, "Five Afro-Caribbean Voices in American Culture, 1917–1929: Hubert H. Harrison, Wilfred A. Domingo, Richard B. Moore, Cyril Briggs and Claude McKay" (Ph.D. diss., University of Iowa, 1977); Theman Taylor, "Cyril Briggs and the African Blood Brotherhood: Effects of Communism on Black Nationalism, 1919–1935" (Ph.D. diss., University of California, Santa Barbara, 1981); Joe Doyle, "Striking for Ireland on the New York Docks," in *The New York Irish*, ed. Ronald Bayor and Timothy J. Meagher (Baltimore, 1996), 357–74.

34. Hubert Henry Harrison, *When Africa Awakes: The "Inside Story" of the Stirrings and Strivings of the New Negro in the Western World* (1920; Baltimore, 1997), 96–97, 103. See also Kevin Gaines, *Uplifting the Race*, 234–46; James, *Holding Aloft the Banner of Ethiopia*, 123–34; Robert Hill, "Racial and Radical: Cyril V. Briggs, the *Crusader* Magazine and the African Blood Brotherhood, 1918–1922," introduction to *The Crusader—Facsimile Editions* (New York, 1987 [reprint 1918–22]); and Jefferey Perry's forthcoming biography of Harrison.

35. Brock, "Questioning the Diaspora," 10; Allison Blakely, *Russia and the Negro: Blacks in Russian history and Thought* (Washington, D.C., 1986); Robin D. G. Kelley, "'This Ain't Ethiopia, but It'll Do': African Americans and the Spanish Civil War," in *Race Rebels: Culture Politics, and the Black Working Class* (New York, 1994); Robin D. G. Kelley, *Hammer and Hoe: Alabama Communists during the Great Depression* (Chapel

Hill, N.C., 1990); Robin D. G. Kelley, "The World the Diaspora Made: C. L. R. James and the Politics of History," in *Rethinking C. L. R. James*, ed. Grant Farred (New York, 1996), 103–30; Edward T. Wilson, *Russia and Black Africa before World War II* (New York, 1974); James R. Hooker, *Black Revolutionary: George Padmore's Path from Communism to Pan-Africanism* (New York, 1967); Introduction to Albert Nzula, I. I. Potekhin, and A. Z. Zusmanovich, *Forced Labour in Colonial Africa*, ed. Robin Cohen (London, 1979); *Between Race and Empire: African-Americans and Cubans Before the Cuban Revolution*, ed. Lisa Brock and Digna Castaneda Fuertes (Philadelphia, 1998); Kelley and Betsy Esch, "Black Like Mao: Red China and Black Revolution," *Souls* 1, 4 (Fall 1999): 6–41.

36. *André Breton: What is Surrealism? Selected Writings*, ed. Franklin Rosemont (New York, 1978), 37 and passim; "Murderous Humanitarianism," in *Negro: An Anthology*, ed. Nancy Cunard (London, 1934), reprinted in *Race Traitor (Special Issue—Surrealism: Revolution against Whiteness)* 9 (Summer 1998): 67–69; Max-Pol Fouchet, *Wilfredo Lam* (2d ed., Barcelona, 1989); Robin D. G. Kelley, "Introduction: A Poetics of Anti-Colonialism," in Aimé Césaire, *Discourse on Colonialism*, trans. Joan Pinkham (New York, 2000); Tyler Stovall, *Paris Noir: African Americans in the City of Light* (Boston, 1996); Brent Edwards, "Black Globality: The International Shape of Black Intellectual Culture" (Ph.D. diss., Columbia University, 1997); *Refusal of the Shadow: Surrealism and the Caribbean*, trans. Michael Richardson and Krzysztof Fijalkowski, ed. Michael Richardson (London, 1996); Cheikh Tidiane Sylla, "Surrealism and Black African Art," *Arsenal: Surrealist Subversion* 4 (Chicago, 1989): 128–29.

37. Brenda Gayle Plummer, *Rising Wind: Black Americans and U.S. Foreign Affairs, 1935–1960* (Chapel Hill, N.C., 1996); Penny von Eschen, *Race against Empire* (Ithaca, N.Y., 1997); Timothy B. Tyson's *Radio Free Dixie: Robert Williams and the Roots of Black Power* (Chapel Hill, N.C., 1999); Van Gosse, *Where the Boys Are: Cuba, Cold War America and the Making of a New Left* (London, 1993) and "Black Power and White America" (MS); Komozi Woodard, *A Nation within a Nation: Amiri Baraka (LeRoi Jones) and Black Power Politics* (Chapel Hill, N.C., 1998); Williams Sales Jr., *From Civil Rights to Black Liberation: Malcolm X and the Organization of Afro-American Unity* (Boston, 1994); Azza Salama Layton, *International Politics and Civil Rights Policies in the United States, 1941–1960* (Cambridge, 2000), 48–58.

38. Layton, *International Politics*, 112–16, quotation from p. 116.

39. Herbert Gutman, "Work, Culture, and Society in Industrializing America," in *Work, Culture, and Society in Industrializing America: Essays in American Working-Class and Social History* (1976): 3–78. See Peter Kwong, *Chinatown, New York: Labor and Politics, 1930–1950* (New York, 1979); *The Politics of Immigrant Workers: Labor Activism and Migration in the World Economy since 1830*, ed. Camille Guerin-Gonzales and Carl Strikwerda (New York, 1993). On Mexican-American workers and "home" country politics, one could go back to pioneering texts such as Rodolfo Acuña's *Occupied America: The Chicano's Struggle toward Liberation* (San Francisco, 1972), 4th rev. ed. titled *Occupied America: A History of Chicanos* (New York, 2000); John Hart, *Anarchism and the Mexican Working Class, 1860–1931* (Austin, Tex., 1978); Juan Gomez-Quinones essay "First Step: Chicano Labor Conflict and Organizing, 1900–1920," *Aztlan* 3 [1972]). For more recent examples, see George Sanchez, *Becoming Mexican-American* (New York, 1993); Camille Guerin-Gonzales, *Mexican Workers and American*

Dreams (New Brunswick, N.J., 1995); Emma Perez, "'Through Her Love and Sweetness': Women, Revolution, and Reform in Yucatan, 1910–1918" (Ph.D. diss., UCLA, 1988); Douglas Monroy, "Anarquismo y Comunismo: Mexican Radicalism and the Communist Party in Los Angeles during the 1930's," *Labor History* 24 (Winter 1983): 34–59; Mario T. Garcia, *Mexican-Americans: Leadership, Ideology, and Identity, 1930–1960* (New Haven, Conn., 1989); David Montejano, *Anglos and Mexicans in the Making of Texas, 1836–1986* (Austin, Tex., 1987).

SIX

Time and Revolution in African America

Temporality and the History of Atlantic Slavery

Walter Johnson

Let me begin with a famous misunderstanding. As he later recounted it, when Olaudah Equiano first saw the white slave traders who eventually carried him to the West Indies, he thought they were "bad spirits" who were going to eat him. Awaiting shipment across an ocean he had never heard of, Equiano, like many of the slaves carried away by the traders, made sense of an absurd situation with a narrative of supernatural power.[1] When he sat down to write his narrative, of course, Equiano knew better than to believe that the white men on the coast were "spirits." By that time he called himself Gustavus Vassa, and, having spent ten years in as a slave in the Americas and another twenty-three as a free man traveling throughout the world, Vassa could see what Equiano could not: that he was a descendent of the Lost Tribes of Israel, that his deliverance from heathenism marked him as a *"particular favorite of heaven,"* and that the events in his life were effects not of the evil intentions of African spirits but of the Christian God's "Providence."[2] Vassa resolved the collision of contending versions of cause and consequence in his own mind through a narrative of progressive enlightenment: he had learned that it had been God's Providence to steal him away from Africa and carry him to London where he could spread the gospel of antislavery.

Vassa's time travel reminds us that global historical processes are un-

My thanks to Mia Bay, Thomas Bender, Chris Brown, Elizabeth Esch, Ada Ferrer, Michael Gomez, Robin D. G. Kelley, Maria Grazia Lolla, Molly Nolan, Ulfried Reichardt, Jeffrey T. Sammons, Nikhil Pal Singh, Stephanie Smallwood, Sinclair Thomson, Henry Yu, and participants in the 1997 and 1998 NYU/OAH conferences on Internationalizing American History, the New Perspectives on the Slave Trade Conference at Rutgers University (November 21–22, 1997), and the Early American Seminar at Columbia University.

derstood through locally and historically specific narratives of time and history. And yet by invoking God's Providence, Vassa did not so much resolve the contention of these temporal narratives as superimpose one upon the other. Equiano's initial understanding of the situation of the coast was incorporated into the story of Vassa's eventual enlightenment. His African history was reframed according to the conventions of his European one.

Recent work in the humanities and social sciences has emphasized the darker side of the temporal conventions that have framed many Western histories of the rest of the world: their role in underwriting global and racial hierarchy. Concepts like primitiveness, backwardness, and underdevelopment rank areas and people of the world on a seemingly naturalized timeline—their "present" is our "past"—and reframe the grubby real-time politics of colonial domination and exploitation as part of an orderly natural process of evolution toward modernity. More than a fixed standard of measure by which the progress of other processes can be measured, time figures in these works as, in the words of Johannes Fabian, a culturally constructed "dimension of power."[3]

Seen in this light, Equiano's anachronistic account of the situation on the West Coast of Africa raises a host of questions about the history of Atlantic slavery: What were the historical and temporal narratives through which Africans and Europeans understood what was happening on the coast, in the slave ships, and in the slave markets of the Americas? How did these various understandings shape the historical process in which they were joined? In what cultural institutions were these ideas of time rooted, and through what practices were they sustained? What was the fate of African time in the Americas? What were the practical processes of temporal domination and resistance?

Taking time seriously suggests, at the very least, that the slave trade was not the same thing for Olaudah Equiano as it was for his captors. Most simply, this difference might be thought of spatially: "the slave trade" did not begin or end in the same place for European traders, American buyers, and African slaves. The African slave trade, after all, had an eastern branch stretching to Asia as well as a western one stretching to the Americas. Thus a historical account of the African experience of "the slave trade" necessarily has a different shape from an account of the European experience; indeed, properly speaking, "the slave trade" has not yet ended in some parts of Africa.[4] But even if we confine ourselves to the history of the Atlantic slave trade, the problem of boundaries persists. The journeys of the slaves who were shipped across the Atlantic Ocean often began in the interior of Africa, hundreds of miles from the coast where they eventually met the European slave traders, hundreds of miles away from where any European had ever been. Indeed, the First Passage was integral to the experience of those who eventually made the Middle Passage—to their understanding of what it was that was happening, their emotional condition going into the journey, and their ability to survive it.[5] And yet the First Passage is often elided from historians' accounts of "the slave trade," many of which focus solely on the Middle Passage, treating the trade as if it were something that began on the West Coast of Africa with sale to a European trader and ended in a port in the Americas with sale to a colonial slaveholder. In so doing, they have unwittingly embedded the historical perspective of a European slave trader—for it was only for the traders, not for the slaves or the buyers, that "the slave trade" happened only in the space between the coasts—in the way they have bounded their topics.[6]

The historical disjuncture marked by Equiano's version of the situation on the coast, however, was much deeper than a difference about beginnings and endings. It signals a fundamental difference between the versions of slavery that met in the Atlantic trade. To oversimplify: in Euro-America, slavery was, above all, a system of economic exploitation; in much of West Africa, slavery was, above all, a system of political domination. In the Americas, slaves were purchased in markets, held as legally alienable property, and put to work as laborers producing staple crops and some other goods, which were generally shipped to Europe in exchange for money and more goods.[7] In much of precolonial West Africa, slavery began with capture: a warrior who would otherwise have been killed was allowed to live on as a socially dead slave. Although most slaves in West Africa were agricultural laborers, many were employed as soldiers, state ministers, and diplomats, and even as governing placeholders for princes and kings. Some slaves owned slaves.[8] As such, West African slavery has often been described as a system of "institutionalized marginality," one among a set of intertwined social relations—kinship, fealty, clientage, and so on—by which one group of people held "wealth in people" in another. Some slaves, over time and generations, through marriage and connection, were able to move out of slavery and into another status.[9]

Equiano's confusion on the coast reminds us that two versions of slavery—"aristocratic slavery" and "merchant slavery" in Claude Meillassoux's formulation—met in the African trade. Those who entered the slave trade had been extracted from histories of enslavement and slavery that sometimes had very little to do with the Atlantic slave trade in the first instance. Rather, their story, as they understood it, was embedded in personal histories of isolation from protective kinship and patronage networks, in local histories of slave-producing ethnic conflicts, in political struggles, and wars that occurred hundreds of miles from the coast.[10]

This is not, however, to say that all African slavery was aristocratic slavery. The jagged boundary between aristocratic and merchant slavery, after all, often lay in the interior of the African continent—hundreds of miles beyond where any European had ever been. Many of the slaves who were eventually shipped across the Atlantic had been captured, transported to the coast, and sold by people who were themselves Africans. The frontier between the two types of slavery was patrolled by an African supervisory elite who presumably knew the difference between them and made their living by transmuting the one into the other. And just as the protocols of merchant slavery stretched well into the interior of Africa, those of aristocratic slavery could stretch well into the journey across the Atlantic. To describe the people they transported to the Americas, the ship captains and clerks of the French West India Company used the word *captif* rather than the more familiar *esclave*, a designation that apparently referred to the aristocratic slavery origins of those in the trade rather than their merchant slavery destinations.[11]

Corresponding to the different versions of slavery that met in the Atlantic trade were different ways of measuring the extent of slavery and marking its progress through time. The (aristocratic) slaveholding kings of precolonial Dahomey, for instance, represented their history as a story of continuous growth through military expansion and enslavement. Their history was measured in a yearly census—taken, historian Robin Law argues, as a means of "political propaganda . . . advertising the kingdom's successful growth"—and in mythical bags of pebbles kept in the castle that tracked the kingdom's expansion—one pebble per person—over time.[12] Other systems of aristocratic slavery had other measures. In precolonial equatorial Africa, Jane Guyer and Samuel M. Eno Belinga have argued, political power and historical progress were measured as wealth in knowledge rather than wealth in people. Rather than accumulating numbers of people, the leaders of kingdoms like that of the Kongo enhanced their power by acquiring, through capture or purchase, people with different types of knowledge.[13]

The African and European merchant slave traders with whom these kingdoms sometimes did business had still other ways of measuring the trade and imagining the history they were making: sacred time measured against an injunction to enslave non-Islamic outsiders or propelled by the "providence" of a Christian God; political history imagined as the conquest of monopoly rights along the African coast and market position in the Americas; market time imagined in macroeconomic cycles of depression and speculation; the microeconomic time of the slave trader, progress tracked across the pages of the ship's log, days defined by the weather and ship's speed, nights marked by the number of slaves who died in the hold—time reckoned in dead bodies and lost profits.[14]

For many of the slaves who were packed into the holds of the Atlantic slave ships, we can imagine still another set of temporal frames: those derived from local political histories of war and slave-raiding; a cultural cycle of social death and rebirth, the ethnic and political disorientation of capture and separation eventually giving way to new identifications with "shipmates" and "fictive kin"; a biographical culmination of lifetime fears of capture, kidnapping, or simply of falling through the cracks in the protections of patronage and kinship; the metaphysical horror of a "middle" passage journey that some must have thought would never end and others might only have recognized as a trip across the *kalunga,* the body of water that separated the world of the living from that of the dead—a flight from time measured in the gradual physical deterioration of the worldly body.[15] And so on: as many journeys on a single ship as there were ways to imagine the journey.

Each of the narratives of slavery described above represents a dimension of that confrontation, a way of being in time—a temporality—according to which historical actors made sense of what it was that was happening (God's Providence, the main chance, social death, etc.) and how they would respond at any given moment.[16] These temporalities were layered, intertwined, and mixed through the process of the slave trade, sometimes running concurrently, sometimes oppositionally, tangled together by a historical process that none of them alone sufficed to describe. None of this should be taken to suggest that societies are unified in their temporalities, still less that there was a simple division between a circular premodern African time and a linear modern European time.[17] Quite the contrary. Taking time seriously suggests that "the slave trade" was not a single thing that might be viewed from a European perspective and an African perspective (or a global perspective and a local perspective, or a systemic perspective and an individual perspective) and then summed up into a whole—the way one might walk around a physical object, measure every face, and create a three-dimensional diagram. Rather, like a web of unforeseen connections, the historical shape of the slave trade depended upon the point of entry. Time ran differently depending upon where you started the clock.

Lived history, I am suggesting, is produced out of the clash of contending temporalities. These temporalities, however, must be seen as being themselves historical. Rather than marking the difference between timeless cultural essences—African time and European time—they reflect the politically and historically embedded circuits through which they were transmitted. And because they were historically shaped and politically situated, it is not enough to simply set these temporalities side by side and split the difference. The history of time is one of continual contest: a history of arguments about history; of efforts to control events by controlling the terms of their description; of situated and sometimes violent acts of synchronization; of forcible reeducation, resistant appropriation, and everyday negotiation; of conflicts in which time itself was a dimension of contest.

As a way of illustrating the historical politics of time-making, I'd like to use the space I have left to consider briefly two aspects of the temporal

politics of American slavery: the temporal dimension of slaveholders' domination and the way that slave rebels tried to make history by imagining
themselves into time. As recent observers have noted, one of the many
things slaveholders thought they owned was their slaves' time; indeed, to
outline the temporal claims that slaveholders made upon their slaves is to
draw a multidimensional portrait of slavery itself. Slaveholders, of course,
defined the shape of the day. Whether it ran from sunup to sundown, it
was defined by the tasks that had to be done by its close or was measured
out in job-scaled clock time. Slavery's daily time was delineated by the master and often enforced by violence. Those who turned out late, quit early,
worked too slowly, came up short, or failed to wait deferentially while the
master attended to other things were cajoled, beaten, or starved into match-
ing the daily rhythms through which their owners measured progress.[18] As
well as quotidian time, slaveholders claimed calendar time as their own.
They decided which days would be work days and which days would be
holidays (or holy days); they enforced a cycle of planting, growing, and
harvesting timed around their crop cycles and commercial plans; they fractured their slaves' lives and communities with their own cycle of yearly hires
and calendar-termed financial obligations.[19] And slaveholders thought they
owned their slaves' biographical time: they recorded their slaves' birthdays
in accounts books that only they could see; they determined at what age
their slaves would be started into the fields or set to a trade, when their
slaves would be cajoled into reproduction, how many years they would be
allowed to nurse the children they had, and how old they would have to
be before retiring; they reproduced their own family legacies over time out
of the broken pieces of slave families and communities divided by sale and
estate settlement.[20] They infused their slaves' lives with their own time;
through the daily process of slave discipline, the foreign, the young, and
the resistant were forcibly inculcated with the nested temporal rhythms of
their enslavement.

As with any dimension of power, however, time could be turned back
upon its master. By working slowly, delaying conception, shamming sickness, or slipping off, slaves short-circuited their master's algorithms of temporal progress. By using the time at the end of the day to cultivate their
own plots, sell their produce, or visit their family members, slaves wedged
their own concerns into the interstices of their enslavement.[21] By naming
their children after the day of their birth (traditional among Gold Coast
slaves) or giving them the names of ancestors, they reconstituted fractured
links with their pasts and their families.[22] By adhering to the protocols of
living with ancestors present in time and space, obeying the demands of
moments that were themselves portentous of the success or failure of any
action undertaken, and observing the injunctions and respecting the power
of *obeah* men and conjurers, by finding time within the day to put down a

rug, face Mecca, and pray, or by keeping the Sabbath for the Christian God, they bent themselves to systems of temporal discipline outside their slavery.[23]

The temporal conflicts between slaves and slaveholders were resolved by a series of running compromises made at the scale of everyday life. Through acts of passive resistance like slowing down and of active defiance like running away, slaves were able to gain acceptance—sometimes explicit, sometimes tacit—of their right to use a portion of the day for visiting, worshipping, provisioning, or simply resting.[24] The boundaries of the possible, however, were hedged by slaveholders' willingness to enforce their own ideas of time through force. In fact, by attributing their slaves' failure to work as hard, as eagerly, or as long as they wanted to savagery, primitivism, and biological lassitude, slaveholders invested their own everyday politics of labor discipline with the force of natural history.[25] On the surface, at least, enslaved Africans were being dragged into their masters' history, forced into temporal frames of reference defined by slavery and race.

Occasionally, however, these everyday conflicts gave way to the broader, historical acts of resistance that historians have called slave revolts. These events have generally been explained according to one of two grand narratives of African-American history: the story of how black slavery was superseded by "freedom" or the story of how Africans became African Americans. The first narrative has emphasized the commonality of the oppressions visited upon enslaved people over the differences between them and treated events disparate in time and space—the Maroon wars in Jamaica (1690–1740; 1795–96) and Nat Turner's rebellion in Virginia (1831), for example—as similar phenomena, part, at bottom, of the same broad history of the attempt of enslaved people to gain their freedom.[26] The second narrative has framed the history of these events as part of a broader story of acculturation—the transformation of Africans into African Americans—and used the cultural content of New World slave revolts to measure the progress of this ongoing transformation at a series of stops along the way.[27] There is no doubt that both of these explanatory paradigms are instructive: there were, as I have argued above, certain material and ideological features common to merchant slavery that were shared by all of the Atlantic slave societies; and African populations in the New World *did* become African-American, a change that *was* reflected in their collective lives and their revolts.

And yet neither of these stories fully exhaust the historical content of the events they seek to explain. The set of explanations that emphasizes the similarities between slave rebels and their sequential struggle toward "freedom" has glossed over very real differences (over space and time) in the ideologies that defined the purposes of collective revolt, leaving a host of questions to go begging—if the Jamaican Maroon chieftan Cudjoe had met the Christian millenarian Nat Turner, what would they have said to each other? Would Cudjoe have tried to capture Turner and return him to his owner in order to protect his own community from slaveholders' reprisals? Would Turner have tried to convert Cudjoe or struck him down with all of the force of the Christian millenium? Nor, however, can the other set of (culturalist) accounts fully contain the complex history of these events. They cannot, for instance, explain either why New World slave rebels were almost exclusively male or why those conspirators were so often betrayed by their fellow slaves. They cannot, that is, explain why women or nonconspirators, who were presumably as African or African-American as their rebellious counterparts at any given moment in time, were not visible on the leading edge of what historians have taken to be their history.[28]

In fact, scarcely concealed in the contrasting outlines of these separate sets of explanations is a single story of progress: the metanarrative of racial liberalism—the story of black freedom and racial acculturation, of how black slaves became American citizens.[29] In treating slave revolts as a way to take the temperature of a historical process with a foreordained outcome, historians have often overlooked the way that the slaves themselves imagined the history that they were making—the arguments and politics, the historical process, through which they imagined themselves into time.[30] Historians, that is, have reworked the history of the rebels who were willing to risk their lives to escape from American history into a part of that history.

Excavating the internal politics of slave conspiracies from an archival record produced by slaveholders requires careful reading. The most detailed accounts we have of the way that slaves talked to one another about conspiracy and rebellion come from the records of the trials that followed the discovery of their plans: they are accounts shaped by slaveholders' fevered projections of their slaves' unfathomed purposes, by the terror of slaves whose lives depended upon the extent to which their confessions matched the expectations of their inquisitors, and by the torture riven so deeply into the archival record of Southern "justice." And yet, as anyone who has ever told a lie can tell you, the best way to make a story seem true is to build it out of pieces of the truth. Read against the grain, the conspiracy probes provide a sense of what slaves knew of the nature of slave conspiracies—where they happened, who was likely to be involved and what their plans would be, and, most important for our purposes here, what kinds of reasons slaves gave to one another as they argued about what they should do, to whom, and when. If we wish to understand the practical complexity and political philosophy of New World slave conspiracies, the trial records are our best source.[31]

The most elementary point that emerges from those records is that talk about subversive ideas and rebellious plans had to occur off the grid of everyday life: at the margins of a landscape defined by slavery and in the interstices of weeks, days, and even hours structured by slaveholders' demands. Plans for Gabriel's Revolt (1800) in Virginia, for example, were apparently discussed at riverside taverns on the James and at revival meetings and picnics in the countryside out of sight of white Richmond, and spread by mobile skilled slaves, men with abroad marriages that gave them an excuse to travel between plantations, and a network of enslaved rivermen. The Demerara Revolt (1823) in British Guyana was plotted at slave-led Sunday school meetings sponsored by the London Missionary Society, hushed encounters between slaves whose work took them to town, and in the large uncultivated spaces between plantations; news was spread through an interlocking set of connections between kin networks, mobile skilled and hired slaves, churchgoing slaves and, apparently, the colony's large population of Coramantee slaves.[32]

The discussions that traveled along this hybrid circuitry reflect the difficulty of the organizational task facing slave conspirators. Activating the existing circuitry of everyday life—family, community, and ethnicity—with the historical current of revolt was dangerous, and conspirators took a great deal of care to do it safely. In relating the shape of a conversation between two of the conspirators in Gabriel's Revolt, Douglas Egerton captures the tentative exchange of signs of dissatisfaction that could turn commiseration about the quotidian rigors of slavery into conspiracy. Egerton relates that the conversation in which Ben Woolfolk recruited King began with what must have been a commonplace discussion of King's dissatisfaction with the harsh discipline imposed by a new master. Woolfolk responded to King's comments with a series of non sequiturs that must have put King on the alert that something important was about to happen—"Are you a true man?" and "Can you keep an important secret?"—and when King didn't shirk from the direction the conversation was taking, Woolfolk escalated it to the point of conspiracy: "the Negroes are about to rise and fight the white people for our freedom"[33] In Denmark Vesey's Charleston (1822), the signal that subversive speech was about to begin seems to have been a question about "the news." Over and over again in the Vesey trial transcripts, the phrase "he asked me the news" is followed by accounts of the type of back-and-forth escalation that characterized the conversation between Ben Woolfolk and King. Other times, however, the ostensibly innocuous inquiry was shortly followed by answers that were not so much direct responses as attempts to end the conversation entirely: "I replied I don't know," or, "I said I could not answer," or, "I begged him to stop it," or, "I told him I did not understand such talk and stopped the conversation."[34] The signs that conspiratorial speech was beginning were apparently well known among Charleston slaves and viewed as being so explosive that some slaves wouldn't listen any further.

Indeed, the records of the trials that followed New World slave conspiracies are full of objections, of the arguments of slaves who tried to get the conspirators to slow down, leave off, or just leave them alone—of slaves who took a different view of the moment in time. Some were simply afraid to die: "I said I did not want death to take me yet and I quit him," remembered Patrick of a conversation with a man who tried to recruit him on the street. Some framed their objections in strictly pragmatic terms, saying they would join once it was apparent that the rebellion was going to succeed, but not before. Some felt bound by family obligations; asked if he would join Vesey's army, Bram responded, "I was so bound to my father that I could not go without his leave." Others clung to notions of justice and moral conduct that were a familiar feature of their everyday lives but were out of step with the plans of the conspirators. Acts that were axiomatic if you accepted Vesey's definition of the relation between master and slave as a state of "war," for instance, were murder if you did not. Many of those present at a meeting where Vesey outlined his plans remembered that, in the words of Jesse, "some said they thought that it was cruel to kill the ministers and the women and the children."[35] Still others remained divided from the rebels by local, historical, or traditional antagonisms: the Demerara revolt was apparently shot through with the suspicion that field slaves had of their enslaved drivers, that Creoles had of Africans, that the members of one chapel had of the members of another, and that many of those who revolted had of Muslims.

And, finally, there were those who were certain that the time just was not right. In Demerara, Daniel advised conspirators who approached him for help that they should wait for freedom rather than trying to seize it: if it was "a thing ordained by the Almighty," it would come in time. In the aftermath of Gabriel's Rebellion, Ben Woolfolk reported that he had advised his fellows to postpone their plans, because "I had heard that in the days of old, when the Israelites were in Servitude to King Pharoah, they were taken from him by the Power of God—and were carried away by Moses—God blessed them with an angel to go with him, but that I could see nothing of the kind in these days."[36] Framed as a matter of political organization, and viewed in light of the objections of reluctant slaves, the magnitude of the achievement of slave rebels in the New World is brought into sharper relief. Their task was nothing less than to compress the various scales of time running through the everyday life of slavery—the biographical, tribal, metaphysical, and other definitions of self and situation evident in the objections of these reluctant conspirators—into the focused immediacy of a single shared imperative.

Given the extraordinary complexity of the layered temporalities evident in the objections of nonconspirators, it took feats of extraordinary imagination (and sometimes intimidation) to synchronize slaves into a shared account of what was happening and what was to be done about it. Indeed, the shared accounts of time and history for which enslaved conspirators risked their lives and by which subsequent historians have measured their progress along the path from African to American were as much effects as they were causes of the process of revolt. When the Bambara leaders of the Natchez Uprising (1731) or the Kongolese warriors at Stono (1739) or the Coramantee rebels in Jamaica (1760), for example, prepared themselves for war through the sacred practices of their homelands, they were making an argument rather than proceeding according to a timeless cultural script known and readily accepted by all of their fellow slaves. As they drummed, danced, swore oaths, assigned ranks, and made plans to enslave rival groups, they were, through ritual practice at the scale of everyday life, giving a moment in time an identifiable historical shape: that of a war.[37] Not only that, they were doing so in a specifically male ritual idiom that underwrote the authority of male warriors to tell everybody else what to do. They were making a politically situated claim on the right to determine the proper correct collective response: this is a war and we are in charge.[38] New World slave rebels were making history by remaking time.

The history slave conspirators tried to make changed shape over time. In Haiti (1791–1804), Toussaint L'Ouverture joined his black followers to the revolution in the rights of man that was remaking the Atlantic world.[39] Gabriel in Virginia and Denmark Vesey in South Carolina imagined their own histories as continuation of the revolution begun in Haiti. Vesey, in fact, courted uncertain slaves by reading to them from the newspapers about the freedoms of Haitian blacks, advertising that he had written to the leaders of the black republic requesting military support, and promising that, in the words of two of the conspirators, "Santo Domingo and Africa will help us to get out liberty" by sending ships to carry them to Haiti, where "they would receive and protect them."[40] Effectively, Vesey was inviting his co-conspirators to join him in fighting their way out of the history of slavery and into that of a new Black Atlantic, or, as he put it, the "war" between the "blacks" and the "whites." In Southampton County, Virginia, Nat Turner followed a series of signs—marks on his own head and breast from the time of his birth, the voice of the Holy Spirit, drops of blood on the corn in the fields and hieroglyphs on the leaves in the woods, a crashing thunder in the sky in April of 1828, and a total eclipse of the sun in February of 1831—to the millennial recognition that "the time was fast approaching when the first should be last and the last should be first."[41] Rather than tracing out points along a foreordained path of historical development, these rebels were investing their everyday lives with temporal purpose—cracking moments open and giving them the shape of imperatives.[42]

In practice, none of these versions of cause and consequence had the simplicity of a pure form; the most successful of the nineteenth-century conspirators, at least, were those who could loosely gather a number of alternative accounts of what exactly it was that was happening into the common purpose of making whatever it was happen. Gabriel, whom the historian Douglas Egerton has identified as a "black Jacobin" seeking to pull Virginia into the history of black liberation that had begun in Haiti, was able to abide, if not himself articulate, other versions of the struggle. When challenged about his choice of the day upon which the slaves were to rise in arms, Gabriel turned to his brother, Martin, who settled the question in terms that were at once prophetic, pragmatic, and deeply personal: "There was this expression in the Bible—delay breeds danger . . . the soldiers were discharged, and the Arms all put away—there was no patrolling . . . and before he would any longer bear what he had borne he would turn out and fight with a stick." And when challenged again: "I read in my Bible where God says, if we will worship him, we should have peace in all our Lands, five of you shall conquer a hundred, and a hundred, a thousand of our enemies."[43]

Vesey, whose own ideology apparently synthesized the divided tribal legacies of South Carolina slaves into a revolutionary call for the liberation of a new historical subject, "the blacks," nevertheless organized some of his men into an "Ebo company" and a "Gullah company," the latter led by the conjurer "Gullah" Jack Pritchard.[44] Indeed, Vesey seems to have been remarkable for the number of temporal scales he could invoke in making the argument that the time for armed rising had come—or, even, in answering a single question. Among those who were present when Vesey was asked whether ministers, women, and children should be killed, there were slaves who recalled at least three versions of temporal scale of his response. "He then read in the Bible where God commanded, that all should be cut off, both men, women, and children, and said, he believed, it was no sin for us to do so, for the lord had commanded us to do it," remembered Rolla. "He thought it was for our safety not to spare one white skin alive, for this was the plan they pursued in St. Domingo," remembered Jesse. "Smart asked him if you were going to kill the women and children— Denmark answered what was the use of killing the louse and leaving the nit—Smart said, my God, what a sin—Vesey told Smart he had not a man's heart, told Smart that he was a friend to Buckra," read Smart Anderson's account of the meeting.[45]

Even Nat Turner was not above relying on the intricate complexities of psychological domination that characterized the daily life of slavery to help him clear the path for God's unfolding Providence—"Jack, I knew, was only a tool in the hands of Hark," he said of one of the slaves whom he entrusted with his plans.[46] Working their way up and down scales of time—metaphysical, political, local, psychological—the theorists of New World slave conspiracies were able to urge any number of historical agents—a tribal warrior, a Christian soldier, a liberal individual, a black man—to anneal themselves to the gathered strength of a single struggle.

When, in the aftermath of events, slaveholders tried to figure out what had caused the uprisings that had convulsed their societies, slaveholders restaged them as effects of their own agency rather than that of their slaves: *they* had allowed their slaves too much liberty (or not enough); *they* had given their slaves too much access to Christianity (or not enough); *they* had provided for too few patrols or allowed too many black seamen or poor whites or Frenchmen or missionaries or steam doctors or Yankee peddlers to come into contact with their slaves. They told themselves stories about what happened that emphasized their own agency and reworked the un-fathomed aspirations of their slaves, whether they were African, Jacobin, or millenarian, into a part of history as they recognized it—the ongoing history of New World slavery.[47] And, as I have argued, historians have often taken the slaveholders at their word and written these events into the history of American slavery as accounts of a labor force in arms. But look again and these conspiracies look like battle plans in a war for control of the New World, efforts to force Euro-Americans into another place in time: into the well-grooved tribal histories of African wars to determine who would be slave and who would be master; the history of the Black Atlantic that had begun in Haiti with the idea that freedom (rather than mastery) was the opposite of slavery; or the Christian millenarian history in which the first would be last and the last would be first. The term "slave revolt" is less a description of these events than the naming by one side—the winning side—of a bloody conflict characterized by the clash of alternative understandings of exactly what it was that was at stake in the Americas.

History, to paraphrase the historian Dipesh Chakrabarty, is a temporality backed by superior firepower.[48] Upon even the most casual observation, it is obvious that the promise of liberal equality that lies at the end of the progress narratives that frame so many American histories—the continual progress of "acculturation" and the succession of slavery by "freedom"—provides an inadequate account of the complexities and restricted possibilities of African-American life at the dawn of the twenty-first century. Indeed, outside the academy, these liberal metanarratives have been displaced by a set of historical counterpractices. The science fiction supernaturalism of Elijah Muhammad or the Afrocentric essentialism of Molefi Kete Asante, for example, contest the story of gradual acculturation that frames so many scholarly histories of the black experience. Similarly, popular histories that frame the slave trade as a single element of a ongoing *Maafa,* an African Holocaust, and emphasize its immediate psychological and emotional relevance to the contemporary black experience contest the redemptive linearity that frames the slavery-to-freedom narrative of American history. Finally, the call for reparations being made by historians like Sam Anderson emphasizes a counterhistory in which slavery cannot be said to have ended in 1865, but persists in African-American oppression, in the bitter fruit of its own unpaid debt, in the present day. In the words of the historian John Henrik Clarke: "The events which transpired five thousand years ago, five years ago, or five minutes ago, have determined what will happen five minutes from now, five years from now, or five thousand years from now. All history is a current event."[49] Seen in the light of the historian Robin D. G. Kelley's admonition that it is less important to debunk anti-historicist histories than it is to understand the source of their attraction for their adherents, these histories seem irruptive reminders of the possibilities suppressed by the forcible superimposition of European history that began with the slave trade.[50]

To say so is not to suggest we can step out of time and return to the lost temporalities of the past. It would, in any case, be a mistake wholly to abandon the liberal historical narratives that have supported what compensation African Americans have been able to exact for past wrongs. To emphasize that history-making itself is as an integral part of historical process is, however, to urge that scholarly history writing be punctuated by constant reminders of its own historicity, and of its complicity in events that it often purports to describe from a perspective of archimedean neutrality. At a time when there are estimated to be twenty-seven million slaves servicing the global economy, we do well to heed the warning that the meta-narrative of liberal individualism that has shaped so many of our existing histories might not be either linear of irreversible.[51]

NOTES

1. *The Interesting Narrative of the Life of Olaudah Equiano, or Gustavus Vassa, the African, Written by Himself: Authoritative Text, Contexts, Criticism*, ed. Robert J. Allison (New York: 1995), 53–54; see also the stories of Job Ben Solomon (p. 57) and Joseph Wright (p. 331) in *Africa Remembered: Narratives by West Africans from the Era of the Slave Trade*, ed. Philip D. Curtin (Madison: University of Wisconsin Press, 1967), "It was the Same as Pigs in a Sty: A Young African's Account of Life on a Slave Ship," in *Children of God's Fire: A Documentary History of Black Slavery in Brazil*, ed. Robert Conrad (Princeton, 1984), 39; John Thornton, *Africa and Africans in the Making of the Atlantic World, 1400–1680* (Cambridge, 1992), 161; Michael A. Gomez, *Exchanging Our Country Marks: The Transformation of African Identities in the Colonial and Antebellum South* (Chapel Hill, 1998), 160, where it is argued that fears of being made into oil and eaten were common among slaves in the trade; and Charles Piot, "Of Slaves and the Gift: Kabre Sale of Kin and the Era of the Slave Trade," *Journal of African History* 37 (1996): 38.

2. *Interesting Narrative of the Life of Olaudah Equiano*, 33, 44.

3. Johannes Fabian, *Time and the Other: How Anthropology Makes Its Object* (New York, 1983). See also Wai-Chee Dimock, *Empire for Liberty: Melville and the Poetics of Individualism* (Princeton: Princeton University Press, 1989), 17–20; Dipesh Chakrabarty, "Postcoloniality and the Artifice of History: Who Speaks for the Indian Past?" *Representations* 37 (1992): 1–26; Anne McClintock, *Imperial Leather: Race, Gender, and Sexuality in the Colonial Contest* (London, 1995); *Power of Development,* ed. Jonathan Crush (London, 1995); Reynaldo C. Ileto, "Outline of a Non-linear Emplotment in Philippine History," in *The Politics of Culture in the Shadow of Capital,* ed. Lisa Lowe and David Lloyd (Durham, 1997), 98–131; and Maria Josefina Saldana-Portillo, "Developmentalism's Irresistible Seduction—Rural Subjectivity under Sandanista Agricultural Policy," ibid., 132–72.

4. Patrick Manning, *Slavery and African Life: Occidental, Oriental, and African Slave Trades* (Cambridge, 1990). My thanks to Mia Bay for her pointed comments about contemporary slave trading.

5. See Joseph C. Miller, *The Way of Death: Merchant Capitalism and the Angolan Slave Trade, 1730–1830* (Madison, 1988). Miller makes the further point that mortality in the First Passage was tremendous and must be considered alongside exportation if the demographic impact of the slave trade in Africa is to be fully reckoned. See also Stephanie Ellen Smallwood, "Salt-Water Slaves: African Enslavement, Forced Migration, and Settlement in the Anglo-American World, 1660–1700" (Ph.D., diss., Duke University, 1999), 15–128.

6. See, e.g., James A. Rawley, *The Transatlantic Slave Trade: A History* (New York, 1981), and David W. Galenson, *Traders, Planters, and Slaves: Market Behavior in Early English America* (Cambridge, 1986). The unwitting prominence given to the slave traders' definition of the trade in these and many other accounts has to do with the fact that they limit themselves to treating it as an economic and demographic phenomenon, as well as with their reliance solely upon the records generated by the trade itself, an example of what the historian Michel-Rolph Trouillot has called "archival power," the material power that past actors have over their future through the records they create and keep. See Trouillot, *Silencing the Past: Power and the Production of History* (Boston: Beacon Press, 1995), 31–69.

7. Eric Williams, *Capitalism and Slavery* (Chapel Hill, 1944); Richard S. Dunn, *Sugar and Slaves: The Rise of the Planter Class in the English West Indies, 1624–1713* (New York, 1972); Elizabeth Fox-Genovese and Eugene D. Genovese, *Fruits of Merchant Capital: Slavery and Bourgeois Property in the Rise and Expansion of Capitalism* (New York, 1983).

8. Claude Meillassoux, *The Anthropology of Slavery: The Womb of Iron and Gold,* trans. Alide Dasnois (Chicago: University of Chicago Press, 1991). Meillassoux does not share the view of precolonial African slavery described in the following sentences.

9. Suzanne Miers and Igor Kopytoff, "African 'Slavery' as an Institution of Marginality," in *Slavery in Africa: Historical and Anthropological Perspectives,* ed. id. (Madison, 1977), 3–69; Jonathon Glassman, "The Bondsman's New Clothes: The Contradictory Consciousness of Slave Resistance on the Swahili Coast," *Journal of African History* 32 (1991): 277–312; Jane I. Guyer, "Wealth in People and Self-Realization in Equatorial Africa," *Man,* 28 (1993), 243–65; Jane I. Guyer, "Wealth in People,

Wealth in Things," *Journal of African History,* 36 (1995), 83–90; Jane I. Guyer and Samuel M. Eno Belinga, "Wealth in People as Wealth in Knowledge: Accumulation and Competition in Equatorial Africa," *Journal of African History* 36 (1995): 91–120; Piot, "Of Slaves and the Gift," 31–49.

10. See David Ross, "The Dahomean Middleman System, 1727–c. 1818," *Journal of African History* 28 (1987): 357–75; Robin Law, "Slave-raiders and Middlemen; Monopolists and Free Traders: The Supply of Slaves for the Atlantic Trade in Dahomey, c. 1715–1850, *Journal of African History* 30 (1989): 45–68; Miller, *Way of Death,* 40–49, 108–28; Meillassoux, *Anthropology of Slavery,* 237–323; and Steve Feierman, "Africa in History: The End of Universal Narratives" in *After Colonialism: Imperial Histories and Postcolonial Displacements,* ed. Gyan Prakash (Princeton, 1994), 40–65. From the other side of the Atlantic, see Ira Berlin, "From Creole to African: Atlantic Creoles and the Origins of African American Society in Mainland North America," *William and Mary Quarterly* 53 (1996): 251–88; Smallwood, "Salt-Water Slaves," 60–128.

11. Gwendolyn Midlo Hall, *Africans in Colonial Louisiana: The Development of Afro-Creole Culture in the Eighteenth-Century* (Baton Rouge: Louisiana State University Press, 1992), passim; see also Smallwood, "Salt-Water Slaves," 127.

12. Robin Law, "History and Legitimacy: Aspects of the Use of the Past in Precolonial Dahomey," *History in Africa* 15 (1988): 431–65; see also Ivor Wilkes, "On Mentally Mapping Greater Asante: A Study of Time and Motion," *Journal of African History* 33 (1992): 175–90.

13. Guyer and Belinga, "Wealth in People as Wealth in Knowledge," 108–19.

14. See Galenson, *Traders, Planters, and Slaves;* Miller, *Way of Death;* Ross, "Dahomean Middleman System"; Law, "Slave-Raiders and Middlemen"; on Islam as a "merchant ideology," see Meillassoux, *Anthropology of Slavery,* 243–48; on the slave trade as "providence," see "The Narrative of Samuel Ajayi Crowther," in *Africa Remembered,* ed. Curtin, 299.

15. See Orlando Patterson, *Slavery and Social Death, A Comparative Study* (Cambridge, 1982); T. C. McCaskie, "Time and the Calendar in Nineteenth-Century Asante: An Exploratory Essay," *History in Africa* 7 (1980): 179–200; Joseph K. Adjaye, "Time, the Calendar, and History among the Akan of Ghana," *Journal of Ethnic Studies* 15 (1987): 71–100; Richard Price, *First-Time: The Historical Vision of an Afro-American People* (Baltimore, 1983) and *Alabi's World* (Baltimore, 1990); Smallwood, "Salt-Water Slaves," 129–90; Gomez, *Exchanging Our Country Marks,* 147, 160.

16. On temporality, see Mikhail Bakhtin, "Forms of Time and Chronotopes in the Novel: Notes Toward a Historical Poetics," in *The Dialogic Imagination: Four Essays,* ed. Caryl Emerson and Michael Holquist (Austin, 1981), 84–258; Fernand Braudel, "Time, History, and the Social Sciences," in *The Varieties of History: From Voltaire to the Present,* ed. Fritz Stern (1956; rev. ed., New York: Vintage Books, 1973), 403–29; the essays in John Bender and David E. Wellerby, *Chronotypes: The Construction of Time* (Stanford, 1991), and *Remapping Memory: The Politics of Timespace,* ed. Jonathan Boyarin (Minneapolis, 1994). See also E. P. Thompson, "Time, Work-Discipline and Industrial Capitalism," *Past and Present* 38 (1967): 56–97; Jacques LeGoff, "Merchant's Time and Church's Time in the Middle Ages" and "Labor Time in the 'Crisis' of the Fourteenth Century: from Medieval Time to Modern Time," in his

Time, Work, and Culture in the Middle Ages, trans. Arthur Goldhammer (Chicago, 1980), 29–52; Michael O'Malley, *Keeping Watch: A History of American Time* (New York, 1990); Moishe Postone, *Time, Labor, and Social Domination: A Reinterpretation of Marx's Critical Theory* (Cambridge, 1993); Mark M. Smith, *Mastered by the Clock: Time, Slavery, and Freedom in the American South* (Chapel Hill, 1997); and Michael Hanchard, "Afro-Modernity: Temporality, Politics, and the African Diaspora," *Public Culture* 11 (1999): 245–68.

17. European markets, after all, inscribe time in cycles, as does the sacred time of Christianity—the cycle of death and rebirth yearly recapitulated through the ritual calendar. And there are plenty of example of linear time reckoning in "premodern" African history: work oriented around the accomplishment of specific tasks and the stone-accumulating censuses of the Dahomean kings being only the most obvious. See, generally, LeGoff, "Merchant's Time and Church's Time in the Middle Ages," 29–42; Akhil Gupta, "The Reincarnation of Souls and the Rebirth of Commodities: Representations of Time in 'East' and 'West,'" *Cultural Critique* 22 (1992): 187–211; see also Gyan Prakash, "Writing Post-Orientalist Histories of the Third World: Indian Historiography Is Good to Think," in *Colonialism and Culture,* ed. Nicholas B. Dirks (Ann Arbor, 1992), 353–88. For the idea that "Christianization introduced Africans to a sense of history moving linearly" (with which I am disagreeing), see Mullin, *Africa in America,* 275.

18. For time and "work-discipline" in American slavery, see Smith, *Mastered by the Clock,* esp. 93–128, and Philip D. Morgan, *Slave Counterpoint: Black Culture in the Eighteenth-Century Chesapeake and Lowcountry* (Chapel Hill, 1998), 172–94.

19. On crop and commercial calendars, see Morgan, *Slave Counterpoint,* 147–72, Emilia Viotti da Costa, *Crowns of Glory, Tears of Blood: The Demerara Slave Rebellion of 1823* (New York, 1994), 171, and Winthrop D. Jordan, *Tumult and Silence at Second Creek: An Inquiry into a Civil War Slave Conspiracy* (Baton Rouge, 1993), 39–45, 213–14; on hiring, see Charles B. Dew, *Master and Slave at Buffalo Forge* (New York, 1994), 67–70; on credit relations, see Richard Holcombe Kilbourne, Jr., *Debt, Investment, and Slaves: Credit Relations in East Feliciana Parish, Louisiana, 1825–1885* (Tuscaloosa, 1995), 49–74.

20. See Herbert G. Gutman, *The Black Family in Slavery and Freedom, 1750–1925* (New York, 1976); Deborah Gray White, *Ar'n't I a Woman? Female Slaves in the Plantation South* (New York, 1985), 91–118; da Costa, *Crowns of Glory, Tears of Blood,* 65–68, 117; Walter Johnson, *Soul by Soul: Life inside the Antebellum Slave Market* (Cambridge, 1999), 78–116.

21. Mechal Sobel, *The World They Made Together: Black and White Values in Eighteenth-Century Virginia* (Princeton, 1987), 15–67; White, *Ar'n't I a Woman?* 104–10; Morgan, *Slave Counterpoint,* 48–50, 153–55, 183–84, 191–93, 359–76; and da Costa, *Crowns of Glory, Tears of Blood,* 75–85, 115–18.

22. Adjaye, "Time, the Calendar, and History among the Akan of Ghana," 71–95; Smallwood, "Salt-Water Slaves," 317–19; Gutman, *Black Family in Slavery and Freedom,* 185–201.

23. Sobel, *The World They Made Together,* 171–229; Mullin, *Africa in America,* 175–84, 201–2; Gomez, *Exchanging Our Country Marks,* 2–3, 55–56, 59, 249, 283–90; da Costa, *Crowns of Glory, Tears of Blood,* 176–77, 271.

24. Ira Berlin, *Many Thousands Gone: The First Two Centuries of Slavery in North*

America (Cambridge, Mass.: Harvard University Press, Belknap Press, 1998), 2–6; da Costa, *Crowns of Glory, Tears of Blood,* 61–80.

25. See, e.g., Samuel Cartwright, "Diseases and Peculiarities of the Negro Race," *DeBow's Review* 11 (1851): 64–69, 212–13, 331–37; "Philosophy of the Negro Con-stitution," *New Orleans Medical and Surgical Journal* 9 (1852): 195–208, and "Eth-nology of the Negro of Prognathous Race," *New Orleans Medical and Surgical Journal* 15 (1858): 149–63. On the idea that ideas of historical alterity can develop out of everyday conflicts over time discipline, see Frederick Cooper, "Colonizing Time: Work Rhythms and Labor Conflict in Colonial Mombasa," in *Colonialism and Culture,* ed. Dirks, 209–45, and Keletso E. Atkins, *The Moon is Dead! Give Us Our Money! The Cultural Origins of an African Work Ethic, Natal, South Africa, 1843–1900* (London, 1993); Smith, *Mastered by the Clock,* 132.

26. See, e.g., Herbert Aptheker, *American Negro Slave Revolts* (1943; 6th ed., New York, 1996); Eugene D. Genovese, *From Rebellion to Revolution: Afro-American Slave Revolts in the Making of the New World* (Baton Rouge, 1979), and Michael Craton, *Testing the Chains: Resistance to Slavery in the British West Indies* (Ithaca, N.Y.: Cornell University Press, 1982). It may, at first glance, seem unfair to describe *From Rebellion to Revolution* as a book that emphasizes the commonality between enslaved people distant in place and time from one another over their cultural differences, since it is, in fact, a book that is framed around the contrast between African and African-American styles of revolt—or, more accurately, between "traditional" and "modern" styles of revolt. The book, however, is also framed by a strict teleology that labels "African" or "traditional" revolts as "reactionary impediments" to the "development of productive forces" (p. 82). Beneath the book's narrative of cultural transforma-tion lies the idea that those who laid down their lives in the New World, be they African or African-American, were, at bottom, slaves. The closer they came to that recognition, the further along the continuum of "progress" toward genuine self-realization Genovese locates them.

27. See, e.g., Mullin, *Africa in America,* and Douglas Egerton, *Gabriel's Rebellion: The Virginia Slave Conspiracies of 1800 and 1802* (Chapel Hill, 1993).

28. On these points, see James Sidbury, *Ploughshares into Swords: Race, Rebellion, and Identity in Gabriel's Virginia, 1730–1810* (Cambridge, 1997), 87–116.

29. Genovese is a complicated thinker and it may seem strange to describe his avowedly Marxist progress narrative as contributing, even unwittingly, to a "liberal" metanarrative. The point, however, is much less about Genovese's intention (or his politics) than it is about the capacity of an unarticulated set of assumptions about the course of history—a set of assumptions derived from a European history framed around the succession of modes of production, the development of the nation-state, and the emergence liberal notion of citizenship (hence the "progressive" character of slave revolts framed in the language of "the rights of man")—to organize a type of question historians ask and a type of question they ignore. For "liberal develop-mentalism" as a historical metanarrative immanent in the work of Marxist and other scholars, see Chakrabarty, "Postcoloniality and the Artifice of History."

30. The best account of a slave revolt as a process of political organization re-mains C. L. R. James, *The Black Jacobins: Toussaint L'Ouverture and the San Domingo Revolution* (1938; 2d rev. ed., New York: Vintage Books, 1963). Notable recent ex-amples, to my way of thinking, are Jordan, *Tumult and Silence at Second Creek,* da

Costa, *Crowns of Glory, Tears of Blood,* and Sidbury, *Ploughshares into Swords.* For the argument that I am making—that the realm of "politics" is where historical subjectivities are argued over and articulated—see Stuart Hall, "The Toad in the Garden: Thatcherism among the Theorists," in *Marxism and the Interpretation of Culture,* ed. Cary Nelson and Lawrence Grossberg (Urbana, 1988), 35–57.

31. On the inability of slaveholders (and subsequently historians) to imagine their slaves' motivations, see Trouillot, *Silencing the Past,* 70–107; on torture and testimony, see Elaine Scarry, *The Body in Pain: The Making and Unmaking of the World* (New York, 1985), and Saidiya V. Hartman, *Scenes of Subjection: Terror, Slavery, and Self-Making in Nineteenth-Century America* (New York, 1997); for examples of historians' effort to read terror-shaped sources against the grain, see Carlo Ginzburg, *The Cheese and the Worms: The Cosmos of a Sixteenth-Century Miller,* trans. John and Anne Tedeschi (Baltimore, 1980), and Jordan, *Tumult and Silence at Second Creek.*

32. Egerton, *Gabriel's Rebellion,* 29, 53–65, 119–23; Sidbury, *Ploughshares into Swords,* 61–70; da Costa, *Crowns of Glory, Tears of Blood,* 190–96.

33. Egerton, *Gabriel's Rebellion,* 56–57. For more on the conversational protocol of plotting a conspiracy, see Johnson, *Soul by Soul,* 71–76.

34. *An Official Report of the Trials of Sundry Negroes Charged with an Attempt to Raise an Insurrection in the State of South Carolina: Preceded by an Introduction and Narrative: And, in an Appendix, a Report of the Trials of Four White Persons on Indictments for Attempting to Excite the Slaves to Insurrection,* ed. Lionel H. Kennedy and Thomas Parker (Charleston: James R. Schenck, 1822), 45, 50, 62, 68. Those who testified that they had demurred at the first mention of "the news" had good reason to lie: their lives hung in the balance. But even if they were lying, the shared structure of their recountings—the conversational feint of asking about "the news," followed by the suggestion that the conversation be immediately terminated—seems to me to reflect what must have been a shared protocol for regulating the flow of seditious speech.

35. *Designs against Charleston: The Trial Record of the Denmark Vesey S←ve Conspiracy of 1822,* ed. Edward A. Pearson (Chapel Hill, 1999), 172, 195; *Official Report,* ed. Kennedy and Parker, 59, 68, 90. A similar boundary between acts of war and murder was invoked by Harry Haig, an active participant in the Vesey conspiracy, who had nevertheless refused an order from Jack Pritchard to poison his master's pump (*Official Report,* 79): "I refused to poison as I considered that murder and God would not pardon me 'twas not like fair fighting."

36. Da Costa, *Crowns of Glory, Tears of Blood,* 195, 186; Sidbury, *Ploughshares into Swords,* 76–77.

37. Hall, *Africans in Colonial Louisiana,* 97–118; John K. Thornton, "African Dimensions of the Stono Rebellion," *American Historical Review* 96 (October 1991): 1101–13; Mullin, *Africa in America,* 40–42. See also Sidbury, *Ploughshares into Swords,* 11.

38. On sex-specific societies, see Francesca Declich, "'Gendered Narratives,' History, and Identity: Two Centuries along the Juba River among the Zigula and Shambra," *History in Africa* 22 (1995): 93–122, and Gomez, *Exchanging Our Country Marks,* 94–102.

39. See James, *Black Jacobins.* It is interesting to note that James continually (see 108, 117, 125, 146, and 394) downplays evidence of "African" definitions of the rebellion in Haiti.

40. Genovese, *From Rebellion to Revolution,* 95; Sidbury, *Ploughshares into Swords,* 257–66; *Official Report,* ed. Kennedy and Parker, 28, 42, 59, 68 (quotations on 42 and 59). See also Julius S. Scott, "Afro-American Sailors and the International Communication Network: The Case of Newport Bowers," in *Jack Tar in History: Essays in Maritime History,* ed. Colin Howell and Richard J. Twomey (Fredericton, New Brunswick: Acadiensis Press, 1991), 11–36.

41. *The Confessions of Nat Turner and Related Documents,* ed. Kenneth S. Greenberg (Boston: Bedford Books of St. Martin's Press, 1996), 46–48.

42. Walter Benjamin puts it this way: "To articulate the past historically does not mean to recognize it 'the way it really was'. . . . It means to seize hold of a memory as it flashes up at a moment of danger. Historical materialism wishes to retain the image of the past which unexpectedly appears to [a] man singled out by history at a moment of danger." Walter Benjamin, "Theses on the Philosophy of History," in *Illuminations,* ed Hannah Arendt (New York: Schocken Books, 1968), 255.

43. Sidbury, *Ploughshares into Swords,* 76–77. Sidbury identifies the source for Martin's second statement as Leviticus 26:6–8.

44. For the racial ideology and tribal organization of the Vesey conspiracy, see Gomez, *Exchanging Our Country Marks,* 1–3.

45. *Official Report,* ed. Kennedy and Parker, 46, 59, 90.

46. *Confessions of Nat Turner,* ed. Greenberg, 48.

47. See Trouillot, *Silencing the Past,* 70–107.

48. Chakrabarty, "Postcoloniality and the Artifice of History," 20–21.

49. See Malcolm X, *The Autobiography of Malcolm X,* with Alex Haley (New York, 1965); Molefi Kete Asante, *The Afrocentric Idea* (Philadelphia, 1987); S. E. Anderson, *The Black Holocaust for Beginners* (New York: Writers and Readers Publishing, 1995); www.ncobra.com (website for National Coalition of Blacks for Reparations in America); www.maafa.org; www.swagga.com. I am grateful to the participants in the 1999 NYU/Faculty Resource Network seminar on United States History in International Perspective for thoughtful comments on issues of narrative and periodization in African-American history.

50. See Robin D. G. Kelley, "Looking B(l)ackward: 2097–1997," in his *Yo' Mama's Disfunktional! Fighting the Culture Wars in Urban America* (Boston: Beacon Press, 1997), 159–80.

51. The figure of twenty-seven million slaves is drawn from Kevin Bales, *Disposable People: New Slavery in the Global Economy* (Berkeley and Los Angeles: University of California Press, 1999), 8.

SEVEN

Beyond the View from Euro-America

Environment, Settler Societies, and the Internationalization of American History

Ian Tyrrell

American historiography was born in Europe, not America. It was Europeans who conceptualized the American continent as exceptional, and projected onto it all of their hopes and dysutopian fantasies.[1] Although American historiography became separated from Europe progressively from the late nineteenth century through to the 1940s, the European legacy remains strong in the notion of American difference, established, more often than not, by comparison with Europe. The call for a reorientation of American history toward transnational themes is as timely as the claims of Frederick Jackson Turner one hundred years ago on the frontier thesis, yet incomplete if it remains a view within Euro-America. The new transnational initiative proposes quite rightly to contextualize American development, to make the boundaries between local, regional, national, and transnational less rigid. It is understandable that the search for a more cosmopolitan American historiography should lead back to Europe, building upon obvious networks of comparative history and manifest evidence of transatlantic economic, demographic, intellectual, and environmental influences. To take that direction would not be enough.

Any plan to internationalize American history must draw on the histories of people from outside of Europe. Atlantic perspectives must be part of this maneuver, but they, too, are not enough. The importance of southern Africa and the African diasporas for the study of race relations in the United States is already well established.[2] These subjects are heavily researched, partly because they are contained within the Atlantic world and within the commerce of those European empires based especially upon the Atlantic region.[3] While it is important not to forget the wider concept of the Americas implied in any Atlantic perspective, it is equally vital to consider "new worlds" beyond the Americas that can open new questions about American history. These may concern matters currently central to historical debates, such as race and slavery, or other, more neglected topics, such as environmental history.[4]

SETTLER SOCIETIES

One way of widening the frame of reference involves looking at similar experiences to American development that occurred in the so-called "settler societies." These, mostly within the British empire, concerned large areas of the globe in lands where whites came to dominate and in some cases almost obliterated indigenous occupation. These societies shared (but to different degrees and in different combinations) a similar cultural inheritance, ideas of racial superiority, parliamentary traditions (for whites), capitalist markets, and the institutions of the common law.[5]

Parallels between these societies were well understood in the nineteenth century and much discussed by a range of public commentators. Comparisons of settlement colonies undertaken by J. A. Froude, Anthony Trollope, Sir George Dilke, Richard Jebb, J. R. Seeley, James Bryce, and others explored a range of similarities to—and differences between—the new lands and the "motherland." This genre frequently put the history of the United States in the larger context of British expansion. But the settlement society model was gradually dropped in the twentieth century as nationalism replaced shared imperial loyalties in the thinking of the leading historians of Canada, Australia, and other former British possessions. An evolutionary and comparative framework had influenced American colonial studies too, but, by the 1920s, American historians had rejected it as a model for postcolonial developments.[6] Revolution and republicanism had severed the imperial link and appeared to many historians to make the American case distinctive among settler societies.

To restore this wider context of European expansion and settlement processes would contribute greatly to the transnational agenda. It would involve comparative as well as transnational history, and conform to the strictures on comparative history set out long ago by that doyen of the *Annales* school, Marc Bloch. Comparative history was most likely to lead to fruitful explanations, Bloch stated, when it involved "a parallel study of societies that are at once neighbouring and contemporary, exercising a constant mutual influence, exposed through their development to the action of the same broad causes just because they are close and contemporaneous, and owing their existence in part at least to a common origin."[7] With the exception of geographic propinquity, a point diminished by improved communications in the late nineteenth and twentieth centuries, the settler societies fulfill these conditions. Differences of substance could, as Bloch argued, be better discerned within common patterns, and hypotheses more readily developed to explain observed differences than in cases that are radically unalike in the first place.

There are signs today in historiography of a revived interest in comparisons of this type, with calls for a reconsideration of what the nineteenth-century English historian J. R. Seeley called "Greater Britain."[8] But the limitations of the settler society model must be confronted.[9] Such an approach cannot provide an adequate alternative transnational framework unless it combines comparisons of settler societies with analysis of the systemic relationships between the "new worlds" and "old." These relationships were determined by the process of European, and particularly British, imperial expansion, and the economic relationships of trade and investment in a developing global economy that accompanied that process.

These transnational amendments are made essential by several cogent analytical and empirical objections to the settler society agenda. Postcolonial scholarship in the 1990s became critical of the "settler" formula as Eurocentric and oblivious to the realities of race and gender. These conquered territories were, the critique goes, always "settled," and the role of the indigenous in resisting Western penetration and challenging the colonialism of white settlers must be acknowledged.[10] Yet using the conceptual framework of settler societies need not deny imperial conquest, resistance, or the realities of race and gender (or class, for that matter). What the concept does stress is difference from those countries where extraction of wealth rather than a staking of a permanent claim to the land was a more prominent feature of colonialism.

Perhaps the best way to capture the complexities of the situation would be to acknowledge similarities and continuities with Patrick Wolfe's formulation in a study of the anthropological profession and its complicity in the making of the Australian nation, when he writes of "settler colonialism."[11] Such societies may have had more transformative effects through what Alfred Crosby calls the "demographic takeover" of indigenous peoples than occurred under classical imperialism. Settler societies represented a particularly complex and resilient form of European colonial expansion often not recognized as imperial conquest by its own agents precisely because they claimed to do more than extract wealth and then return to the metropolitan space.[12]

A settler society framework can be subtle and dialectical enough to incorporate the insights of postcolonialism. Taking the example of Australia, the work done on settler societies may be able to convey the *double identity* of European settlers as colonized and colonizer; as "new" land transformed by Europeans and derivative in many ways of European culture, and as a polity that has itself become a colonizer in its own country, as Wolfe stresses. Even the spread of American empire abroad has resonances with Australian and New Zealand roles in the South Pacific. Especially in Fiji, Samoa, and New Guinea, these have been imperial roles involving not only the formal attributes of imperial power but also the gender and racial hierarchies of power that typically reinforce and even express imperial/colonized power relations.[13]

A second and more serious problem with settler societies as models for any transnational agenda in American history is that they may not challenge the national framework of traditional comparative analysis. Under the sway of the latter, these societies have tended to be treated as self-contained, to be compared with one another. The work of Louis Hartz and other contributors to *The Founding of New Societies* (1964) fits this type of comparative history. Hartz used the opportunity to expand upon his theme of the United States as a unique "liberal society" and sought to validate the thesis he had put forward in *The Liberal Tradition in America* (1955) about the development of historical fragments of European political ideology and culture as part of a general theory of national development. The fragments, whether liberal, as in the American case, or radical Chartist, in the Australian, develop in a state of autonomy once spun off from their European origins. Comparisons of this type do not question the national unit or the characterization of the United States as a unique society, distinguished chiefly by its difference from Europe.[14]

The opposite extreme to this national comparative approach to the history of settlement societies is one in which all societies of settlement in the "new worlds" can be depicted as having common patterns that differ from those of the "old" world. The environmental historian Stephen Pyne's analysis of common trends in the use and control of fire by European settlers is an example. New fire regimes replaced the fire-stick farming of indigenous peoples, and settlers used fire in similar ways in a number of New World societies. Pyne's approach is superior to national comparisons, but assimilates American experience to that of other settler societies and homogenizes a European experience, in this case in environmental management, to be contrasted with New World experience.[15] The binary concept of Europe versus America, common in theories of American exceptionalism, is not entirely overcome by this approach; rather, the polarity is simply displaced, and the connections between old worlds and new are not explained.

What is needed is the linking of comparative analysis of settler societies with transnational contexts of imperial power and the expansion of global markets under capitalism. With this modification, settler society models can be useful for enriching American historiography. The result would not be to provide ready-made reinterpretation of American historiography but, rather, to open up new questions and challenge unthinking assumptions concerning unilinear and homogeneous national patterns. American history from this perspective looks different than it does from within, and from that of a purely European or Atlantic re-take on American events.

ENVIRONMENTAL HISTORY

Such assertions about the theories and methods of history need to be backed by concrete examples. Nowhere was the shared experience of European expansion more obvious than in the confrontation between settlement processes and the physical environments of "new" lands. This type of comparative and transnational history has not always been pursued in environmental analysis. Even though geographical influences rarely coincide with national boundaries, and transnational approaches appear to be a natural concomitant of environmental history, in this subfield, the boundaries between U.S. and other histories remain remarkably intact. It must first be conceded that when humans' interaction with their environment becomes the history of state policy, national boundaries must constitute one of the fundamental features of that history to be confronted. Yet the laws and policies of nation-states reflect only part of the interplay of forces that contributes to environmental history. American environmental history has inherited the traditions of American difference viewed in contrast with Europe, and has produced, as one Australian scholar has remarked, work that is "surprisingly nationalistic."[16] Great originality has been attributed to American development of national parks, wilderness ideas and ideals (including respectful studies of the iconic figure, John Muir), western conservation, and frontier themes.[17]

These topics have been analyzed critically, but often in a way isolated from developments elsewhere. As a key example, American historians have seen the conservation movement of the early twentieth century as a pragmatic response to conditions in the western part of the United States in the 1890s; or as the work of a political, business, and scientific elite associated with the Progressive Era of national reform. Either way, the conservation movement began in the United States and stemmed from American conditions. The prodigious research of Richard Grove, among others, has since provided non-American perspectives on this issue.[18] Grove shows that seventeenth- and eighteenth-century colonial experience in such places as Mauritius, St. Helena, and the Caribbean led to concern with deforestation and species extinction long before the American George Perkins Marsh published *Man and Nature* in 1864. Not only did the first American efforts at conservation postdate those in some other places; the United States also drew upon this international scholarship on environmental degradation, as Michel Girard has shown for Marsh's own intellectual development.[19]

This is not simply a question of what came first, or even of the flow of intellectual influence. It also affects the *content* of environmental thinking. In the American West there was much borrowing from foreign sources conceptualizing the environment in broader and more complex terms than the wilderness versus rational conservation perspective. From the international debates concerning the transformation of nature came ideas of environmental restoration, and what others call rectification, before the emergence of the modern American conservation movement around 1900.[20]

The failure to appreciate this international context highlights a narrow frame of reference in American history. Despite the valiant efforts of some to adopt global approaches, much American environmental scholarship has focused on, or been influenced by, concepts of wilderness, as in the evidence presented by Roderick Nash's *Wilderness and the American Mind* (1967). Europeans as well as Americans have contributed to this special focus. English commentators such as Peter Coates and D. J. S. Morris have, while differing in their interpretations, drawn upon this American tradition in a debate that attributed to American green politics an entirely different ethos from the European sensibility. These differences were said to be grounded in ideas of American exceptionalism and to have stemmed from the "crucible" of the frontier experience.[21]

Did no other nation have a sense of wilderness parallel to the one that touched the United States and that gave rise to the great national parks? Given that Australians (and South Africans) established a number of national parks during the late nineteenth and early twentieth centuries, including the second "national park" in the world in Australia (1878), on lines similar to those of Yellowstone and later Yosemite, assertions of American uniqueness are dubious. The Australian experience has not been as intensively studied as it ought to be, but from the available evidence, it appears to have paralleled the American example rather than derived from it.[22]

Underpinning wilderness ideas is the suggestion that American landscapes confronted by Europeans were unique. That is, because Europeans had turned "first nature" into manicured farms and fields, "America" was truly foreign to Europeans. Australian experience helps to put this set of perceptions into better perspective. Both European settlers in Australia and American visitors found the arid landscape and the flora and fauna to be truly unique. American trees—pines, oaks, and firs—were familiar to Europeans and could be assimilated to European ideas of beauty. Australian trees, the eucalypts, or gum trees, in particular, shed bark instead of leaves, and did not develop the riot of deciduous color that Americans and Europeans rejoiced to see across their autumn landscapes. Much of the Australian vegetation was scrub, rather than cathedral-like forest, and Australia's aridity did not help either. The twisted shapes of many eucalypts, such as the dwarf mallee varieties of the arid zone, added to the perception of the Australian environment as strange. European perceptions derived from Romanticism could accommodate redwoods, but not river red gum. Australia, not the United States, was profoundly foreign to Europeans in environmental terms. Americans, too, eventually found landscapes within their own expanding national ambit that deeply challenged their inherited environmental sensibilities, but this did not happen until they confronted the dry and often inhospitable Southwest, conquered from Mexico, where the land began to resemble that encountered in Australia.

But this uniqueness of Australia's "natural" environment has not been invested with the connotations of exceptionalism that have often greeted America's frontier and wilderness of abundance. It might be argued that it was not the American wilderness that was unique, relative to places in Europe, but the quantity of resources to be transformed. Europe had long since squandered its environmental largesse. Now it was America's turn. Australia, in comparison, proved to be poorer in terms of its ability to be fulfill these Euro-American fantasies about material abundance. Because of severe shortages of water and poorness of soil—measured in terms of the needs of European-style agriculture—much of Australia had more limited potential to be transformed into European-style gardens, farms, and parks. But all this places a very different construction upon the meaning and significance of wilderness in American culture, and upon an American exceptionalism grounded in material conditions.

American innovation in the national parks movement of the twentieth century is impressive, to be sure.[23] Yet the prominent and high valuation associated with American wilderness conservance begs the truly important questions posed by a wider frame of analysis. In fact, a number of the countries into which European settlement expanded developed this concept or showed themselves receptive to it, because the desire to preserve nature reflected, at bottom, a European confrontation with areas perceived as wilderness, yet inhabited by indigenous peoples. The Old World might no longer have much wilderness, but the process of European imperialism was integral to the construction of ideas of wilderness in the New World. A broader frame of reference will not merely recognize this fundamental irony but seek to establish the underlying patterns in environmental change. European ideas of conserving nature developed differently; in Britain, especially, the focus was on conserving the equilibrium that had been achieved over centuries in agrarian landscapes created by generations of farmers and graziers. The Nature Conservancy movement accepted cultural landscapes such as the preservation of hedgerows. National parks grew out of attempts to conserve and extend much altered landscapes, such as moors, rather than to preserve minimally altered wilderness zones as in parts of the United States and Australia. Though the Nature Conservancy strategy of purchasing private worn-out lands for rehabilitation was eventually introduced in the United States, this was not the main focus of conservation there. Not only does the role of peasants and subsistence farmers in the Old World need to be taken into account, but comparative histories are needed to incorporate indigenous peoples' management of the land.[24] The conservation strategies and roles of subsistence farmers and indigenous peoples have received less attention from American historians than have wilderness ideals. Isolating the significant American achievements in creating national parks presupposes that the path that needed to or realistically could be taken was toward wilderness preservation. There is enough criticism of wilderness as a constructed concept, especially from the point of view of its arrogance toward indigenous peoples, to explode this fundamental distinction that underpins the sense of American exceptionalism in environmental matters. Since environmental *management*, including the rectification and restoration of degraded landscapes, is crucial to environmental sustainability, it seems that we need to take this broader perspective on American efforts. Wilderness preservation may simply lead to a Disneyland of national parks in a sea of environmental decay.[25]

Questioning American claims to national distinctiveness through wilderness issues is not to downgrade American achievements. In fact, those achievements, for example in urban environmental action running back to the late nineteenth century, might be better acknowledged.[26] Rather, shifting the focus from uniqueness or originality would enable American historiography to better inform as well as draw upon international debates on environmental history. American environmental history, institutionally speaking, is currently not seen by leading European practitioners as having a "truly international outlook."[27] The pioneering contributions of many American environmental historians tend to be unfairly dismissed as too closely tied to American exceptionalist themes to be useful in the wider project of a transnational approach to environmental history.[28]

To make confident statements about American exceptionalism in this or any other area requires much more extensive research than hitherto undertaken into the histories of a range of other countries that have absorbed American influences, paralleled American innovations, and also perhaps even influenced American developments. Part of the problem of encouraging a transnational approach to American history lies in thin knowledge of American historians concerning the pasts of those other countries whose history might provide a fuller transnational context. To conceptualize American history better, U.S. Americanists need, paradoxically, to study the history of other countries more than they do, and possibly as much as they study their own national past.

This is not to say that Americans are ignorant of foreign histories. In fact, it has been cogently argued by some that America's colonial past has made U.S. historians more receptive than most to the study of foreign cultures. But the countries studied (traditionally those of western Europe) and the ways in which they are studied (as separate nations or regions) may promote consideration of the United States in isolation from wider intellectual, economic, and social currents. All this implies that internationalization of American history must *include,* rather than supersede, comparative history. Comparisons of parts of nations, and of particular movements and issues, is absolutely essential to an internationalizing project. Comparative history must be set within broader themes of transnational history, so as to demonstrate the contingent and ever-changing character of the nation.[29] One example illustrating the possibilities for such transnational comparisons is presented by the environmental connections between California and Australia.

THE VIEWPOINT OF THE PERIPHERY

The Australian colonies and nineteenth-century California were both frontier regions influenced by the process of settlement, but they also shared geographic distance from the main centers of capital and cultural influence. Both, I argue, were peripheral places.[30] Both places have their distinctive features, but their histories are part of larger movements to dominate native peoples on the edge of European expansion and to transform local environments through economic activity based on staple exports of primary products and the raw exploitation of natural resources. The approach I propose draws upon Australian and American historians' theories of economic peripheral status and social geographers' theories of cultural landscape that enable us to see how the confrontation of European peoples with new environments played out on the edge of empire.

We can reinterpret American history using the vantage point of peripheries, just as Frederick Jackson Turner utilized the role of its internal "peripheral" zone, the frontier, in domestic American development of the eighteenth and nineteenth centuries. The United States itself was once peripheral; part of a great empire, it has become an empire in its own right. Its mentality as a nation has been profoundly influenced, even forged, by this transition. Thus the United States must be seen in relation to its changing role within the world system of capitalism from periphery to metropolitan power, with all of the effects that the latter can have on other more marginal places.

The comparison and contextualization I am suggesting derives partly from the work of Immanuel Wallerstein and his disciples in the United States, which originated in Latin American dependency theory. The capitalist world economy is an important frame of reference for studies of the development of class relations and state developmental policies. Wallerstein's notion of a world system of capitalism is a powerful tool with which to assess "conventional comparative methods based on modernization's theory of relatively uniform and discrete national societies."[31] But the historical sociologist Phillip McMichael has noted that the crucial weakness of world-systems theory is its formalism: "Like formal comparison, it presumes a whole, an historical system 'whose future is inscribed in its conception.' " Or, to put the matter another way, "the unit of analysis is equated with the object of analysis. . . . By merging the concept of the world-system . . . with its empirical scope, the world-system perspective has no choice but to prefigure history."[32] McMichael's interest lies in the bearing of empirical cases upon the global framework of political economy, but his research project, which includes a major emphasis on Australia's social and economic development as a primary producing and exporting nation, also suggests that Latin American–derived models may not be enough to reveal the complexities of power relations between conquerors and conquered in the settler societies of the white, Anglo-American diasporas. Especially important is the need to realize that Europeans subjugated native peoples and other races on the periphery even where whites were simultaneously being controlled in some measure by the metropolis, either economically or politically.

Theories of staple export-driven economies, neglected in recent years, help to illuminate the problem of peripheral position. Staple theory is not the only example of how economic analysis can be used in the study of transnational history, to be sure. International capital flows, for example, can be charted to show how the trade cycles have operated transnationally, with great social as well as economic effects on employment, migration, and natural resource use.[33] But for peripheral societies, where the conquest of land and the extraction of raw materials were vitally important, staple theory allows us to deal with the unique relationship between colonies, their resources, and metropolitan centers, and to link this to the struggle of social classes over the course of economic development in peripheral zones.

Criticisms of staple theory come from economic historians, yet the theory's heuristic value can be rescued when treated not simply as an explanation in which the world economy operates as some exogenous force upon society; rather, social relations within the settler society need to be seen as part of the struggle to define the relationship between local and world economies. Class tensions and struggles have to be built into the analysis of staples by looking at the way in which social aspirations about the distribution of resources are shaped by and shape the focus on distant markets. Within any particular society, social classes have struggled over how to utilize their given environment to meet markets.[34] In both California and Australia, a prominent economic and social problem before 1900 was how to cater to the aspirations of the large numbers of people who came in the wake of the mining booms of the 1850s but who did not profit from gold; instead of accepting the domination of the land by capital-intensive mining and large-scale wheat, sheep, or cattle farming, social reformers dreamed of establishing a democratic, small-scale agriculture, centered on horticulture. The choice was not purely an economic one but an environmental one as well. Reflecting the settlers' European and eastern American aesthetic, horticulture involved the imposition of mixed or "garden" landscapes on parts of California and Australia.

In neither Australia nor California did the advocates of small-scale agriculture succeed, but circumstances enabled California to overcome its peripheral status and make fruit growing—operated eventually as a mass-production industry—a highly profitable and major part of California's long economic climb, beginning in the 1880s. The successes of one socioeconomic interest over another in this struggle over the course of economic development were determined partly by the available soil, water, forests, and other basic resources, but these environmental constraints did not operate in a vacuum. In California, transport and marketing opportunities, the influence of the railroads and other entrepreneurial interests, and eventual incorporation into the larger political economy of the American nation-state, with its vast internal market, allowed some basic environmental constraints to be overcome, at least in the short to medium term. In Australia, small-scale agriculture suffered from much greater distance from markets and lack of available entrepreneurial capital, as well as greater environmental obstacles posed for any group seeking to reproduce European styles of agriculture. Studying attempts of this sort to shape the relationship with external markets may explain how a vision of the reordering of the landscape succeeded in one settlement society but not in another.

THE SPACES OF TRANSNATIONAL HISTORY

These economic forces and cultural and social contests operate in and on particular places, and this process raises the issue of the precise spatial units of analysis within which American history might be situated. The idea of different spatial scales of human history, reminiscent of Fernand Braudel's levels of historical time in *The Mediterranean and the Mediterranean World in the Reign of Philip II,* has been advanced in relation to the environment by Richard White, who emphasizes the interaction of these levels—the spaces of history—with the relationships between them changing over time.[35] This fits well with the history of Australian and Californian contacts in the nineteenth century. Generally speaking, the problems of distance and European encounters with colonial environments created the space for innovation in environmental policy in peripheral zones of European capitalism. Frontier settlers were innovative in environmental policy because they were at the cutting edge of loss of environmental sustainability. Yet that space for regional autonomy did not last.

In the twentieth century, we witnessed a strengthening of nation-state powers, with environmental policy becoming more highly regulatory, centralized, and professionalized. Since the 1960s, however, we have seen the beginning of an international regime in environmental reform, with a series of UN conventions on the environment, such as the World Heritage Convention of 1972 and that on the Law of the Sea, which "finally came into effect" in 1994.[36] This transnational framework has produced a resurgence of international influences on environmental issues, but these have to take effect on and in different regions. International conventions do not override national interests, but provide sites for transnational organizations to lobby both international bodies and national governments for enforcement of conventions governments have signed. Thus it is important, as Richard White urges, to keep in view all of the levels on which environmental policy operates.

Global

At their broadest level, developments in California and Australia in the nineteenth century could be situated within a global context, commonly studied in the United States as "world history." Environmental history is an important part of the American movement to create a true world history, but even here the pull of Atlantic-focused work is strong, and it is difficult to feed back work by non-Americanists—for example, on Australian or British imperial environmental history—into these models. The idea of ecological imperialism, pioneered by Alfred Crosby, is a classic case of the application of an Atlantic model to explain global patterns, whereas consideration of the settlement societies on their own terms reveals more complex interactions between various new worlds. Crosby's interpretation of these ecological transformations as one-way and biologically deterministic looks different when we examine the cross-fertilization between Australia and South Africa, South America, New Zealand, and California.[37] These cases emphasize the need to temper the impulse toward global themes.

Globalization focuses on the world economy and economic integration of nation-states within its tentacles, yet these influences are often none too specific. In environmental history, some recent and contemporary problems are global, such as climate change and ozone damage, but the incidence even of large transnational influences such as acid rain has not been felt uniformly across hemispheres or regions. In economics, too, these global patterns have often been unevenly experienced. Flows of trade, people, and capital across the globe require rules to police markets, but these rules reflect the asymmetric power of the imperial centers of constantly shifting global systems. The nation-state is not withering away amid these global flows—certainly not in the case of the contemporary United States, which exercises disproportionate power in the setting of global rules but refuses in many cases to submit to conventions perceived as compromising its sovereignty and national interests. Because U.S. national actions are crucially important to global changes, it seems necessary to specify the links between national actions and events, on the one hand, and transnational processes, on the other. Such explanatory frameworks as staple economics and imperialism are useful in providing a historically grounded theory and may specify key changes in regional differences in position and environment.

Yet the long view on these changes is vital to understanding American history. The links between national and transnational influences must be shown in a historical way, since the changing trajectory of nation-state power rather than the legal position is at issue. The General Agreement on Tariffs and Trade (GATT) threatens aspects of U.S. environmental regulation today through the newly established World Trade Organization, as David Vogel shows.[38] Technology and tourism also threaten modern standards.[39] Conversely, the new international trade regime has changed the relationship between environmental lobbying groups and the state. For example, Greenpeace can use international public opinion to influence the policies of nation-states on climate change, oil spills, or the trade in endangered species.[40] How common was such action in the past? It is often forgotten that strong environmental regulation depends on a strong state, something the United States did not have in the nineteenth century. Proper national quarantine, for example, was not established until 1912, and before that time, environmental regulation of imported pests was minimal and chaotic, involving squabbling between the states and the federal government. Interest in international agreements for the protection of flora and fauna goes back to the first decade of the twentieth century and included American involvement.[41] Today, there is a focus on global instruments of cooperation, but most of these are of relatively recent origin. There is a long, underexplored history of efforts of particular lobbying groups to influence international policies over environmental diplomatic issues such as the protection of wildlife and the conservation of ocean fisheries since the Progressive Era. These have typically occurred in a regional setting, especially between the United States and Canada.[42]

Region

This raises the issue of transnational regional influences within American historiography. Regional perspectives, apart from that of the South, appear to be neglected because of the Euro-American and Atlantic bias in historical scholarship. Western American scholars still chafe at the inadequate incorporation of their regional specialization within American history, and trans-Pacific regional contacts, too, have partly been neglected in comparison with the Atlantic, because a majority of the American population (including African Americans) came across that ocean; but new economic development around the Pacific and large numbers of new immigrants to the United States from the region are now changing this. Yet if the recognition is new, the pattern can be traced back to nineteenth-century California and the impact of Asian immigration in the 1850s and 1860s. The 1996 La Trobe University Conference on the History of the Pacific Rim revealed many interesting parallels and connections between the United States and other societies around the Pacific. The work at the conference was much influenced by ideas of systemic international market forces, but the activities of regional social and political groupings were woven into the discussion as well.[43] Much of the interest in this work came from Americans specializing in economics and anthropology. "General" U.S. history made little contribution, because historians so often see the case of the United States, including California, as exclusive of other developments. Neither Pacific nor Atlantic systems of trade and migration should be neglected. Contacts between quite far-flung places, such as the societies around the Pacific, challenge American historians to broaden their focus.

The gold rushes of the second half of the nineteenth century provide evidence of these transnational exchanges. From California, people and goods flowed to the Klondike; from Australia to California and back; from Victoria to northern Queensland and to other parts of Australia; and from Chile and Peru to the southwestern United States.[44] The technology and customs of the miners crossed national boundaries and left traces both in the material culture and demographically, in the shape of ethnic diasporas, especially a Chinese diaspora. Americans imported their mining technology into Australia, along with mining personnel, including Herbert Hoover, who served for several years as an engineer on the Western Australian mining fields in the 1890s. American mining machinery, as well, had spin-off effects through its use for artesian bore (groundwater) pumps, which by the 1890s were vital to the cattle industry in the arid Australian Outback. Looking at American history from the vantage point of the Pacific would no doubt reveal other connections such as these.[45]

For the United States, Pacific connections involved, in many social processes, movements from west to east that, in the view of some, render irrelevant the teleology inherent in ideas of Manifest Destiny and a movement "west." Indeed, the very meaning of the American "West" is in question from this standpoint. Migration history is richly suggestive of a more complex process of interaction of cultures in North America from different regions of the western hemisphere and East Asia.[46] These migration patterns have been tied up with racism and war in the twentieth century. Discriminatory land-ownership, immigration, and citizenship laws, anchored in geopolitical anxieties, were widely canvassed and passed in the white settler societies of the Pacific Rim. Similar policies toward Chinese and Japanese settlers were adopted at about the same time in Australia, Canada, the United States, and New Zealand. The international diplomacy of this fear of Asia's "Yellow Peril" in the early twentieth century has been partly covered by historians, but the comparative history of the impacts of these policies on peoples and on the individual nation-states is only beginning to be understood.[47]

Border Crossings

As part of the wider study of regions such as the Pacific coast, specific cultural links between borderlands have received some recognition in American historiography in recent years,[48] but the focus has been on geographic contiguity, and again the perspective of the British settlement colonies is valuable in broadening this concept. Not just the interfaces between the United States and Mexico and Canada, but other kinds of border crossings need to be investigated. Settler societies such as those on the Pacific coast of the United States and Canada and in Australia and New Zealand, which underwent similar, although not identical, processes of colonization, shared ideas, technology, and personnel on a number of issues relevant to transforming the land. Transnational exchanges occurred in dealing with the deforestation that apparently resulted from the introduction of European livestock, especially of sheep in West Coast Meso-America and Australasia;[49] in irrigation technology concerning California, Australia, and British Columbia, where similar problems of aridity were faced and shared concepts of an Arcadian, garden landscape were developed; and in the biological control policies fashioned by Australia, New Zealand, and California in the 1880s and 1890s.[50]

NEW QUESTIONS

Study of borderland regions and transnational exchanges of these kinds is unlikely to change our understanding of the whole course of American historiography. What such study does do, however, is open up debate on the contingent development of national structures and sentiments. We are given pause in considering the idea of a unilinear course to American history. To pursue the environmental analogy, not only must we understand the various streams that have over time contributed to the mighty American river. We must investigate courses that have not been taken and assess the contribution of the streams that dried up. And at every step we must ask why. As Marc Bloch put it, there is no "greater danger in any branch of science than the temptation to think that everything happens 'quite naturally.' "[51]

Looking at the wider processes of colonial settlement may raise new questions about historical events and process previously interpreted from a purely internal American standpoint. The remainder of this essay explores three questions arising from the comparative and transnational history of Australia and California. The first concerns cross-national scientific movements that had environmental consequences. In many of the white settler societies, so-called acclimatization–the naturalization of alien species–took place in the wake of the gold rushes. The acclimatizers sought, often by deliberate policy, to exchange plants and animals so as to enrich New World environments with the products of the old, and vice versa. They have often been condemned for the introduction of exotics that became pests. The plague of European wild rabbits in twentieth-century Australia is the best-known example, but there are many others. Why has the introduction of alien flora and fauna received so little attention in U.S. historiography? Acclimatization between France and England, for example, has been the subject of comparative study, but this has not thus far extended to the United States.[52]

This is not to ask that old standby of American exceptionalism: why was the American experience radically different from the European? There was no *organized* naturalizing "movement" in the United States and, considered nationally, the patterns of activity were clearly different from those in Australia and New Zealand; familiar game animals were in abundance in North America, and so introductions for sporting purposes were not as significant an element in the transfer of species as in the case of Australasia.[53] Naturalization of flora was ubiquitous and more comparable. George Perkins Marsh was one of a number of prominent nineteenth-century conservationists who discussed acclimatization favorably, while the practical plant breeder Luther Burbank later combed the globe for new plants for his hybridization research in California. The importation of insects undertaken by the Californian State Board of Horticulture in the aid of biological control projects from 1888 to 1908 provides yet another example of the scope of planned exchanges.[54] Equally strikingly, the activities of the Bureau of Plant Industry under David Fairchild during the Progressive Era constitute a major, understudied topic in the area of ecological exchanges involving government policy.[55]

The reasons for such lacunae in American scholarship may be varied. But any answer would need to distinguish between different regions of the country. In California, there was much interest in the acclimatization movement because its international spread in the 1850s coincided with the American takeover of California. It was there that a range of practical acclimatizers sought strong international connections. Naturalized plants held out the promise of counteracting the destructive effects of mining on forests, steams, and agricultural land—problems as common in California as in Australia. Stimulated by the work of Marsh, the colonial Australian botanist Ferdinand von Mueller preached the gospel of afforestation to anyone who would listen. With improved and regular steamship communications across the Pacific between Sydney and San Francisco in the 1870s, Mueller's advice on the adaptation of plants in Mediterranean climates soon became well known in California. Mueller's labors on behalf of the eucalyptus genus contributed to the reforestation and afforestation of Californian landscapes. These plantings were intended to aid small-scale agriculture, and particularly horticulture, as a counterbalance, economically and environmentally, to destructive mining and pastoral impacts.[56]

There may be other examples of such conscious developments in cross-national science involving the United States. One might be the extent to which Americans experimented in the South with new productive and ornamental plants in the late eighteenth and early nineteenth centuries. Despite Thomas Jefferson's assertion that the "greatest service which can be rendered any country is, to add an useful plant to its culture,"[57] little has been done to trace the larger history of plant naturalization in America, apparently because it did not follow the same course as in Europe, where it was closely associated with government and with organized programs of scientific exchange.[58]

A second set of questions raised by the comparative history of environmental contacts and policies is that of the social and intellectual history of political economy and its neglected relationship to environmental thought. Attention to the history of other settler societies and to the impact of political and economic ideas of American origin abroad raises neglected questions as to the content of those American ideas. A prominent example concerns the work of Henry George, best known in the United States for *Progress and Poverty,* his extended and provocative commentary on the class conflicts of the Gilded Age and how to solve them. It must not be forgotten that George first worked out many of his ideas in California in an assessment of the relationship between land as a resource and political class struggle. George's ideas were taken up in terms of land politics more in Australia and New Zealand than in the United States. There has been a tendency, therefore, to forget just how much his political economy was concerned with environmental issues in the United States. George is seen as responding to class inequalities in industrializing society, and the environmental side of his thought concerning land tends to be forgotten. One might be able to look at other political economists and find a connection between land development on the periphery of European expansion, environmental thought, and radical social movements. We do know, for example, that in the 1880s and 1890s, farmers in the Middle West faced problems of drought and soil erosion as well as railroad discrimination. To what extent, then, were midwestern agrarian protests developing an environmental as well as an interest group or class critique of American society and its market economy?[59]

A third example is the role of the state. A pronounced tendency in American historiography has been to see the United States as a "weak" state political economy as opposed to the "strong" states of Europe. Comparison with the social democratic settler societies of Australia and New Zealand has seemed merely to confirm the exceptional status of the laissez-faire political economy of United States. But the histories of Australia and California in environmental policy in the nineteenth century show similar pragmatic patterns of use of state power combined with private innovation in each case. The choice of one over the other was not taken easily, and the variables dictating the combination are not what they are often thought to be.

The greater role played by the state in irrigation development and in other environmental policies in Australia should not, however, lead to ahistorical conclusions that contrast a laissez-faire and ideologically "liberal" America with a "socialist" Australia. The reality was always more complicated. One of the most striking aspects of environmental contacts between Australia and California from 1860 to 1900 was the interest in solutions derived from each other's experience. Greater Australian resort to government involvement in horticulture and irrigation after 1900 at the state level in Victoria, as opposed to California, reflected the failure of earlier, more hesitant strategies and private initiatives. Dictating the shift was a harsher natural environment relative to the demands of European-style agriculture, the lack of available capital, and the need for more cohesive and collective action to combat the advantages that competitors in other countries had in access to markets.[60] But the other side of the story was the considerable willingness of American westerners to resort to state power to alter their arid and harsh environments through irrigation. This story has been told in great detail by American historians, but rarely has the impact of Australian experiments in irrigation on these American cases been adequately assessed. That Elwood Mead, commissioner of irrigation in Washington, D.C., from 1925, brought experience to the job accumulated during eight years as state rivers and water supply commissioner in Victoria, Australia, is but one example of cross-fertilization and the use of Australian models to inspire state action in American irrigation policy.[61]

The patterns of state intervention in these roughly parallel cases of California and Australia seesawed over time. Ironically, it was in the United States, not Australia, that federal government intervention in environmental policy was greatest, once the Progressive Era and New Deal regulatory state had been created. Control of public land in the U.S. West, and hence major resource policy, was in federal hands, whereas in Australia, the states inherited control of the Australian equivalent, crown land, from the self-governing colonies at the time of federation. In Australia, fragmentation of environmental management persisted, and there was greater difficulty in developing major federal environmental initiatives such as those achieved in U.S. irrigation policy by the National Reclamation Act (1902), the Hoover Dam project of the 1920s and 1930s, and the even greater irrigation projects of post–World War II America.[62]

We can see from these brief examples how situating American history in the context of other societies that have undergone similar land transformations raises different questions. There is a need for American historians practicing outside the United States to take more account of work done on their subject in other countries, and European perspectives are not enough. Californian and other regional perspectives from the "new Western history" need to be—and are increasingly being—incorporated into mainstream American historiography, but viewing the history of the American West from comparative and transnational vantage points leads to the question of just how uniquely "western" that experience was. The Californian case illustrates the importance of Pacific connections in the further development of American historiography. Without Pacific perspectives—indeed, perspectives from every place touched by European expansion—the internationalization of U.S. history will reflect little more than Euro-American views.

NOTES

1. Dorothy Ross, *The Origins of American Social Science* (New York, 1991), 475; Jack Greene, *The Intellectual Construction of America: Exceptionalism and Identity from 1492 to 1800* (Chapel Hill, N.C., 1993), 1.

2. *Modern American Landscapes,* ed. Mick Gidley and Robert Lawson-Peebles, European Contributions to American Studies, 26 (Amsterdam, 1995); *Representing and Imagining America,* ed. Philip John Davies, European Papers in American History (Keele, U.K., 1996).

3. See esp. James T. Campbell, *Songs of Zion: The African Methodist Episcopal Church in the United States and South Africa* (New York, 1995); Frederick Cooper, "Race, Ideology, and the Perils of Comparative History," *American Historical Review* 101 (October 1996): 1122–38.

4. For example, on slavery, the convict labor widely imported into North America prior to 1776 seems, from the perspective of a convict colony such as Botany Bay was, unjustly neglected in American historiography as part of the range of labour used. Cf. A. Roger Ekirch, *Bound for America: The Transportation of British Convicts to the Colonies, 1718–1775* (Oxford, 1987), a book that partly fills the gap but raises as many questions as its analysis answers.

5. John C. Weaver, "Beyond the Fatal Shore: Pastoral Squatting and the Occupation of Australia, 1826 to 1852," *American Historical Review* 101 (October 1996): 980–1007.

6. Ian Tyrrell, "Making Nations, Making States: American Historians in the Context of Empire," *Journal of American History* 86 (December 1999): 1015–44.

7. Marc Bloch, "A Contribution towards a Comparative History of European Societies," in id., *Land and Law in Medieval Europe: Selected Papers by Marc Bloch,* trans. J. E. Anderson (London, 1967), 44–81.

8. See the *AHR Forum,* "The New British History in Atlantic Perspective," esp. David Armitage, "Greater Britain: A Useful Category of Historical Analysis?" *American Historical Review* 104 (April 1999): 427–45; and J. G. A. Pocock, "The New British History in Atlantic Perspective: An Antipodean Commentary," ibid., 490–500.

9. Louis Hartz, Kenneth D. McRae, et al., *The Founding of New Societies: Studies in the History of the United States, Latin America, South Africa, Canada, and Australia* (New York, 1964). For recent work, see, e.g., Weaver, "Beyond the Fatal Shore," 980–1007; Gary Cross, "Comparative Exceptionalism: Rethinking the Hartz Thesis in the Settler Societies of Nineteenth-Century United States and Australia," *Australasian Journal of American Studies* 14 (July 1995): 15–43; Aurora Bosch, "Why Is There No Labor Party in the United States? A Comparative New World Case Study: Australia and the U.S., 1783–1914," *Radical History Review,* no. 67 (1997): 35–78; Thomas R. Dunlap, "Australian Nature, European Culture: Anglo Settlers in Australia," *Environmental History Review* 17 (Spring 1993): 25–48.

10. Daiva Stasiulis and Nira Yuval-Davis, *Unsettling Settler Societies: Articulations of Gender, Race, Ethnicity and Class* (London, 1995); Phillip R. O'Neil, *Unsettling the Empire: Postcolonialism and the Troubled Identities of Settler Nations* (Ann Arbor, Mich., 1994); Donald Denoon, "Settler Capitalism Unsettled," *New Zealand Journal of History* 29 (October 1995): 129–41.

11. Patrick Wolfe, *Settler Colonialism and the Transformation of Anthropology: The Politics and Poetics of an Ethnographic Event* (New York, 1999).

12. Alfred Crosby, *Ecological Imperialism: The Biological Expansion of Europe* (New York, 1989).

13. Roger C. Thompson, *Australian Imperialism in the Pacific: The Expansionist Era, 1820–1920* (Carlton, Vic., 1980); Claudia Knapman, *White Women in Fiji, 1835–1930* (Sydney, 1986); Wolfe, *Settler Colonialism.*

14. Louis Hartz, *The Liberal Tradition in America: An Interpretation of American Political Thought since the Revolution* (New York, 1955); Hartz, McRae, et al., *Founding of New Societies.*

15. Stephen Pyne, "Frontiers of Fire," in *Ecology and Empire: Environmental History of Settler Societies,* ed. Tom Griffiths and Libby Robin (Melbourne, 1997), 19–34.

16. Tom Griffiths, "Introduction," to *Ecology and Empire,* ed. Griffiths and Robin, 10.

17. Alfred Runte, *National Parks: The American Experience* (New York, 1979), pp. xi, 1; Roderick Nash, *Wilderness and the American Mind* (1st ed., New Haven, Conn., 1967); in the revised 3d edition (1982), Nash added on a final chapter on international perspectives, but it does not sit well with the body of the text that precedes it. For examples of the continuing influence of American exceptionalism in assessing conservation policy, see Michael Kammen, "Culture and

the State in America," *Journal of American History* 83 (December 1996): 793, and Marcus Hall, "Restoring the Countryside: George Perkins Marsh and the Italian Land Ethic," *Environment and History* 4 (1998): 100. See also the critique of Muir studies, in Steven J. Holmes, *The Young John Muir: An Environmental Biography* (Madison, Wis., 1999), 54–58, 64–65, esp. concerning the Scottish inheritance and its influence on Muir.

18. Richard H. Grove, *Green Imperialism: Colonial Expansion, Tropical Edens, and the Origins of Environmentalism, 1600–1860* (Cambridge, 1995).

19. George P. Marsh, *Man and Nature, or, Physical Geography as Modified by Human Action* (New York, 1864); Michel F. Girard, "Conservation and the Gospel of Efficiency: Un modèle de gestion de l'environnement venu d'Europe?" *Histoire Sociale / Social History* 23 (May 1990): 63–80.

20. On rectification, see Alan Gilbert, "The State and Nature in Australia," *Australian Cultural History* 1 (1982): 9–28. Donald J. Pisani, "Forests and Conservation, 1865–1890," *Journal of American History* 72 (September 1985): 340–59, provided a path-breaking and superior survey of nineteenth-century American attitudes, but he too misses the strong transnational aspect to the movement. See also the perceptive remarks in Hall, "Restoring the Countryside," 91–103.

21. Nash, *Wilderness and the American Mind;* D. J. S. Morris, "'Help Keep the Peccadillo Alive': American Environmental Politics," *Journal of American Studies* 22 (December 1988): 447–55; Peter A. Coates, "'Support Your Right to Bear Arms (and Peccadillos)': The Higher Ground and Further Shores of American Environmentalism," *Journal of American Studies* 23 (December 1989): 439–46; D. J. S. Morris, "'Help Keep the Peccadillo Alive': American Environmental Politics: A Rejoinder," *Journal of American Studies* 23 (December 1989): 446.

22. Colin M. Hall, *Wasteland to World Heritage: Preserving Australia's Wilderness* (Carlton, Vic., 1992), 91–102, makes a start on what is a terribly neglected topic in Australian history.

23. Kammen, "Culture and the State in America," 793.

24. Stephen Pyne, "Frontiers of Fire," in *Ecology and Empire,* ed. Griffiths and Robin, 19–34; N. W. Moore, *The Bird of Time: The Science and Politics of Nature Conservation: A Personal Account* (Cambridge, 1987), pp. 69, 70–71, and ch. 6.

25. J. Baird Callicott, "Wilderness Values Revisited: The Sustainable Development Alternative," *Environmental Professional* 13 (1991): 236–45; William Cronon, "The Trouble with Wilderness; or, Getting Back to the Wrong Nature," *Environmental History* 1 (January 1996): 7–28, and the critiques of this argument that follow in the same issue.

26. Martin J. Melosi, "Environmental Justice, Political Agenda Setting, and the Myths of History," *Journal of Policy History* 12, 1 (2000): 53.

27. Franz-Josef Bruggemeier, "New Developments in Environmental History," in *Proceedings: Reports, Abstracts and Round Table Introductions, 19th International Congress of Historical Science, Oslo, 2000* (Oslo, 2000), 376.

28. See, e.g., Coates, "'Support Your Right to Bear Arms.'"

29. Ian Tyrrell, "American Exceptionalism in an Age of International History," *American Historical Review* 96 (October 1991): 1031–55; 1068–72.

30. Ian Tyrrell, "Peripheral Visions: Californian-Australian Environmental Contacts, c. 1850s–1910," *Journal of World History* 8 (September 1997): 275–302; id.,

True Gardens of the Gods: Californian-Australian Environmental Reform, 1860–1930 (Berkeley and Los Angeles, 1999).

31. Philip McMichael, "Incorporating Comparison within a World-Historical Perspective: An Alternative Comparative Method," *American Sociological Review* 55 (June 1990): 395.

32. McMichael, "Incorporating Comparison," 391.

33. J. T. R. Hughes, *American Economic History* (2d ed., Glenview, Ill., 1987), 298.

34. Philip McMichael, *Settlers and the Agrarian Question: Foundations of Capitalism in Colonial Australia* (New York, 1984), 38–39. A positive review of the value of staple theory for Australia can be found in W. A. Sinclair, *The Process of Economic Development in Australia* (Melbourne, 1976). See also Geoffrey Blainey, *The Tyranny of Distance: How Distance Shaped Australia's History* (Melbourne, 1966); Morton Rothstein, "West Coast Farmers and the Tyranny of Distance: Agriculture on the Fringes of the World Market," *Agricultural History* 49 (January 1975): 272–80; Morris W. Wills, "Sequential Frontiers: The Californian and Australian Experience," *Western Historical Quarterly* 9 (October 1978): 483–94; Douglass North, *Economic Growth of the United States, 1790–1860* (New York, 1966). For a summary of arguments against the North thesis, see Stanley Engerman and Robert E. Gallman, "U.S. Economic Growth, 1790–1860," *Research in Economic History* 8 (1983): 1–46.

35. Richard White, "Where Is America?" Paper presented to the New York University / Organization of American Historians' Conference on Internationalizing American History, La Pietra, Florence, July 1998; Fernand Braudel, *The Mediterranean and the Mediterranean World in the Age of Philip II,* trans. Siân Reynolds, 2 vols. (1972–73; reprint, Berkeley and Los Angeles, 1995).

36. Ann L. Hollick, *U.S. Foreign Policy and the Law of the Sea* (Princeton, N.J., 1981); Lorraine Elliott, *The Global Politics of the Environment* (New York, 1998), 29, 36.

37. Crosby, *Ecological Imperialism.*

38. David Vogel, "The Environment and International Trade," *Journal of Policy History* 12, 1 (2000): 72–100.

39. Elliott, *Global Politics of the Environment,* 213–14, touches on this, but see also the *Sydney Morning Herald,* May 24, 1997, 35.

40. Elliott, *Global Politics of the Environment,* 136; Vogel, "Environment and International Trade," 72–100.

41. For a brief sketch, see Nash, *Wilderness and the American Mind,* 3d ed., esp. 358–61; on the British Empire's role in the pioneer international agreements on the protection of fauna, see John M. MacKenzie, *The Empire of Nature: Hunting, Conservation, and British Imperialism* (Manchester, 1988), 211; see also Elliott, *Global Politics of the Environment,* 8, on the range of international agreements.

42. Elliott, *Global Politics of the Environment,* 8; Homer E. Gregory and Kathleen Barnes, *North Pacific Fisheries: With Special Reference to Alaska Salmon* (New York, 1939); William F. Thompson and Norman C. Freeman, "History of the Pacific Halibut Fishery," International Fisheries Commission, *Report no. 5* (Vancouver, 1930).

43. The work of this conference has been published as *Pacific Centuries: Pacific and Pacific Rim History since the Sixteenth Century,* ed. Dennis O. Flynn, Lionel Frost and A. J. H. Latham (London, 1999). See also my own, separately published contribution to the conference, "Peripheral Visions."

44. There is no adequate history of this subject. But for some indication of the possible scope, see Jay Monaghan, *Chile, Peru, and the California Gold Rush of 1849* (Berkeley and Los Angeles, 1973).

45. David Goodman, "Gold Fields / Golden Fields: The Language of Agrarianism and the Victorian Gold Rush," *Australian Historical Studies* 23 (April 1988): 21–41; and Goodman, *Gold Seeking: Victoria and California in the 1850s* (Sydney, 1994); for a valiant effort to incorporate the Pacific into world history, see Felipe Fernández-Armesto, *Millennium: A History of Our Last Thousand Years* (New York, 1995).

46. Ronald Takaki, *A Distant Mirror: A History of Multicultural America* (Boston, 1993); id., *Strangers from a Different Shore: A History of Asian Americans* (Boston, 1989; rev. ed. 1998).

47. Charles Price, *The Great White Walls are Built: Restrictive Immigration to North America and Australia, 1836–1888* (Canberra, 1974); see also Sean Brawley, *White Peril: Foreign Relations and Asian Migration to Australasia and North America, 1918–1978* (Sydney, 1995).

48. David Thelen, "Of Audiences, Borderlands, and Comparisons: Toward the Internationalization of American History," *Journal of American History* 79 (September 1992): 436–44; Gerald E. Poyo and Gilberto M. Hinojosa, "Spanish Texas and Borderlands Historiography in Transition: Implications for United States History," *Journal of American History* 75 (September 1988): 393–416.

49. Elinor Melville, *A Plague of Sheep: Environmental Consequences of the Conquest of Mexico* (Cambridge, 1994).

50. Tyrrell, *True Gardens*.

51. Bloch, "Contribution towards a Comparative History," 67. Bloch emphasizes that the role of comparative history was not to make "forced analogies"; rather, we must explore the "precise characteristics" of parallel processes that often produced different outcomes (58).

52. Warwick Anderson, "Climates of Opinion: Acclimatization in Nineteenth-Century France and England," *Victorian Studies* 35, 2 (1992): 135–57.

53. Thomas Dunlap, *Nature and the English Diaspora: Environment and History in the United States, Canada, Australia, and New Zealand* (New York, 1999), 52.

54. Tyrrell, *True Gardens*, ch. 9.

55. But see ibid., 19, 11; David G. Fairchild, *The World Was My Garden* (New York, 1938).

56. Edward Kynaston, *A Man on Edge: A Life of Baron Sir Ferdinand von Mueller* (London, 1981); Deidre Morris, "Baron Sir Ferdinand von Mueller," *Australian Dictionary of Biography*, 5: 308.

57. Quoted in Tyrrell, *True Gardens*, 23.

58. See, e.g., Lucile H. Brockway, *Science and Colonial Expansion: The Role of the British Royal Botanic Gardens* (New York, 1979); Michael A. Osborne, *Nature, the Exotic, and the Science of French Colonialism* (Bloomington, Ind., 1994).

59. Henry George, *Progress and Poverty: An Inquiry into the Cause of Industrial Depressions, and of Increase of Want with Increase of Wealth–The Remedy* (San Francisco, 1879). See, on this, the suggestive remarks in Timothy W. Luke, *Capitalism, Democracy, and Ecology: Departing from Marx* (Urbana, Ill., 1999). The best available American discussions of these issues are in John Thomas, *Alternative America: Edward Bel-*

lamy, Henry George, Henry Demarest Lloyd and the Adversary Tradition (Cambridge, Mass., 1987); and Charles Barker, "Henry George and the California Background of *Progress and Poverty,*" *California Historical Quarterly* 24 (June 1945): 97–115.

60. Louis Hartz, *The Liberal Tradition in America* (New York, 1955); Cross, "Comparative Exceptionalism"; Gilbert, "State and Nature in Australia," 9–28.

61. Joseph Powell, "Elwood Mead and California's State Colonies: An Episode in Australasian-American Contacts, 1915–1931," *Journal of the Royal Australian Historical Society* 67 (March 1982): 328–53.

62. For Australia, see Gilbert, "State and Nature in Australia"; Joseph Powell, *Environmental Management in Australia, 1788–1914* (Melbourne, 1976); for the extensive role of the state in the American west in irrigation policy, see Donald Worster, *Rivers of Empire: Water, Aridity and the Growth of the American West* (New York, 1985); Norris Hundley Jr., *The Great Thirst: Californians and Water, 1770s–1990s* (Berkeley and Los Angeles, 1992), 229–30; Marc Reisner, *Cadillac Desert: The American West and Its Disappearing Water* (New York, 1986). See also Kevin Starr, *Material Dreams: Southern California through the 1920s* (New York, 1990), 59–61.

PART III

Opening the Frame

EIGHT

From Euro- and Afro-Atlantic to Pacific Migration System

A Comparative Migration Approach to North American History

Dirk Hoerder

Men and women of many cultures actively created the societies of the Americas. Newcomers from three continents first established the Euro-Atlantic and Afro-Atlantic migration systems, then, in the 1570s, the early phase of a route across the Pacific to South America. After a century of Iberian migrations to Central and South America, northwest European migration to North America began. Eighteenth- and early nineteenth-century migration of Russians from Siberia, accompanied by Aleut fishermen, along the Pacific coast as far south as California remained quantitatively marginal.[1] African culture in the Americas was transferred from sub-Saharan Africa, shaped by the constraints of Euro-American planter societies, and influenced by free and bound migrants arriving from Asia. Inter-American migrations began at the end of the nineteenth century. Asian and European men worked on the same railroad lines or in the same mines, and women of many origins bought in the same stores or worked in the same industries. Children were of multiple origin. From Boston to Buenos Aires, immigrants from Europe relied on exchanges with indigenous peoples and on the labor and expertise of Africans.

"People, ideas, and institutions do not have clear national identities" David Thelen has observed. "Rather, people may translate and assemble pieces from different cultures. Instead of assuming that something was distinctively American, we might assume that elements of it began or ended

Parts of this essay are based on Dirk Hoerder, *Cultures in Contact: European and World Migrations, Eleventh Century to the 1990s* (forthcoming, Durham, N.C., 2002), and *Creating Societies: Immigrant Lives in Canada* (Montreal, 1999). My languages are limited to English, German, and French, but helpful colleagues made literature in other languages available to me. I am grateful to Donna Gabaccia and Christiane Harzig and the participants in the Project to Internationalize the Study of American History conference, July 1999, for comments.

somewhere else."[2] To illustrate the manifold cultural origins hidden behind received discourse, the seemingly well understood Boston Tea Party may serve as example. Boston implies New England and Englishmen—or English men?—and tea is an innocuous, nonintoxicating beverage. The cultural content and cast of actors were more complex. Colonial merchants refused to pay subsidies, disguised as politically imposed duties, to the British imperial core to rescue a London joint-stock company mismanaged by its directors. Bostonians' business and their waterfront jobs were part of the Euro-Afro-American Atlantic economies and included the transport and sale of African Africans and Caribbean Africans reduced by global white-black power relationships to bondage. "Party"-goers (rioters) disguised themselves as Amerindians, or, more exactly, according to their notions of what Amerindians looked like. They "doped" themselves with rum produced by African forced migrants in the Caribbean and destroyed tea produced by labor migrants in Asia. The property symbolized the British East India (South Asia) Company and the British (English, Scottish, Welsh) imperial government. The adoption of South Asian and Chinese tea-drinking customs by the colonists permitted women to take on a more active role than a boycott of Caribbean rum would have. The multiple-origin elements of the riot demonstrate the global interconnections of late colonial societies. Recent scholarship has demonstrated that historians can do better than reify nationhood and interpret all events and processes from that perspective.

To avoid one-way (or dead-end) interpretations, I seek in this chapter to put the United States and Canada in continental perspective. Rather than concentrating on the states and their territorial borders, I first discuss the interconnectedness of global, statewide, and family economies and cultures and point to the agency of migrants. Next, I outline the three trans-oceanic migration systems and the evolving continental zone of mobility and discuss the relationship between unfree and free migrations. A continental perspective reveals a shift of predominance from Latin America to the Euro-American North, which, I argue, can best be understood in terms of cultural regions, including bicultural ones in which hegemonic people interact with subaltern ones. Despite borderlines, people live and act in borderlands. Finally, after the 1960s, new migration systems and new attitudes to culture and color led to the emergence of multicultural societies. In developing this complex story, I reflect on historians' attitudes and paradigms welded to a Euro- or U.S.-centered perspective and leading to a view of history reflecting a New England or, in Canada, a British view of national history.

In public memory, the history of the people of the United States has been conceptualized in a mix of categories: free European immigrants, Negro slaves, and Oriental coolies. Historians socialized in the repositories of public memory, families, and schools reflected this terminology, as does the division between immigration history; history of slavery, or black history; and the history of Asian-Americans. Furthermore, the self-characterization of the United States as an "immigration country" veils refugee migrations of Amerindians, the mass flight of Loyalists/Tories during and after the American Revolution, seasonal migrations from northern Mexico, and internal and other migrations, as well as returns to Europe or Asia. Canadian historiography reflects the Anglo-French dualism, lumping together all other Europeans as immigrants and labeling Asians as Orientals. Canadians developed no Statue of Liberty myth, and in the United States the plaintive graffiti of Angel Island never entered public memory.[3] The history of the continent, and of the United States and Canada, began in many places.

AGENCY AND MIGRATION SYSTEMS: GLOBAL, STATEWIDE, FAMILY ECONOMIES AND CULTURES

Migrant men, women, and children actively structure their lives within ecological, societal, and economic constraints and unequal power relationships according to their cultural traditions and everyday practices, their identities. Individual agency, regional societies, transoceanic migration systems, and global power hierarchies and capital flows are reflected in gendered planning of their lives by men and women and may best be analyzed by life-course approaches combined with world systems approaches in regional settings.[4] Whatever migrants in the Americas chose to do or not to do involved a selection among multiple options and was influenced by childhood socialization in distant societies of origin, or, in the case of Amerindians, in pre- or postcontact societies.

A migration "system" connects two or more societies of regional, statewide, or continental extension, composed of multiple, hierarchically structured social groups of differing interests.[5] It involves clustered moves between a region of origin and a receiving region, continues over a period of time, and is distinct from nonclustered multidirectional moves. Migrants perceive, whether rightly or not, comparatively fewer constraints at the intended destination. With the exception of gold rush destinations, migrants did not expect unlimited opportunities, but preferred "unknown possibilities to known impossibilities," as Walter Nugent has phrased it. Returning migrants and sailors or letters informed men and women in the societies of origin about perceived achievements or failures, and the systems thus became self-regulating. Each and every change at either end of the migration trajectory, in intervening obstacles or inducements, influenced decisions. Thus "system" and "agency" condition each other.[6]

Agency is best analyzed in a three-tier model, the macro-level consisting of the global economy and whole societies, the meso-level of regional economies and cultures, and the micro-level of neighborhoods and families. Men and women are born into cultural traditions and as children are socialized into cultural practices and norms. Even if enslaved, migrants carry such cultural identities with them. They discarded restraining ones or, when bound, were forced to discard them. In contrast, they carried few material possessions, and survival demanded immediate labor for subsistence or, as in the case of the Pilgrim Fathers, Mothers, and their servants, food handouts (from the Wampanoag).

On the macro-level, world systems approaches cover patterns of capital transfers and power relationships between civilizations or specific states and societies. Studies of the emergence of the Atlantic World analyze the patterns of European financial investment in the Caribbean sugar or the U.S. cotton economy, each of which competed with sugar or cotton production elsewhere in the world. Since it was men (more often than women on this level) who made the decisions, developments should not be ascribed simply to Capital, Imperial Spain, or the British Empire. Migrants with few means experience such decisions and regimes as options or constraints, and they may have influenced colonial labor regimes by day-to-day resistance, if slaves; by strikes, if wage workers; or by struggles for land, if subsistence farmers.[7]

On the meso-level, potential migrants evaluate options and arrive at decisions in the context of regional societies, in which economic stagnation or growth and differential access to resources may diverge from statewide patterns, and in which specific cultures, often different from the hegemonic one, influence life options directly. Likewise, insertion in the new society takes place in particular regional circumstances of access to land or to particular labor market segments, or, for children, to regional education systems or family economies that involve child labor.

On the micro-level of individual and family human capital, the psychological propensity to migrate and ability to acquire social capital are actuated. Decisions are made in the context of family economies and in conjunction with kinship patterns and neighborhood relations, of information flows and regional job and income options. Economic needs and emotional relationships, as well as position in the sibling sequence and life cycle influence who departs, how departure is timed, and what material support, if any, is provided. Such decisions involve gender and intergenerational hierarchies.[8]

POPULATION COLLAPSE, TRANSOCEANIC MIGRATION, AND CONTINENTAL MOBILITY

Capital flows across the Atlantic and in the global colonial world; individual and family decisions by millions of free migrants; the shipment of countless slaves from Africa; and socioeconomic developments both in regions of origin and at destinations, all contributed to establishing the Euro-Atlantic, Afro-Atlantic, and Pacific migration systems. Contemporary European map-makers illustrated the (for them) New World with imagined beings, human and animal, fabled and monstrous, but in the northern part of the continent, they inserted a blank space between newcomers and residents. Thus whites seemed to explore, conquer, settle empty spaces. As regards the central and southern part, where contact was intense, European political philosophers debated whether the natives were human beings. Latin Christianity's canonical text asserted unequivocally that the gospel had been preached to *all* the peoples of the world. In the New World, however, this view collapsed, because Amerindians were judged morally, spiritually, and intellectually deficient.[9]

On the "new" continent, not yet named, the arrival of Europeans resulted in mortality and refugee migrations on an unprecedented scale. More destructive than the Europeans' superior weaponry were Eurasian pathogens and the imposition of allegedly superior Christian belief systems. In Central and South America, surviving members of indigenous elite families served as middlemen, interpreters, and wives, and were styled "caciques" or "princesses." Amerindians were drawn into the global fur trade, like Siberia's peoples, only in the seventeenth-century north.[10] Although the refugee-generating regime of the white intruders forced natives to retreat, rape, concubinage, and intermarriage with indigenous or black slave women set in motion a process of ethnogenesis.

In the sixteenth century, the Euro-Atlantic system connected southwestern Europe to Central and South America. In the seventeenth, it expanded to connect northwestern Europe to North America. Outside the Caribbean, with its plantation regimes, the separation of Mediterranean and transalpine Europe and of Latin and Anglo America kept migration flows distinct until the late nineteenth century. European indentured servants, if they had a choice, avoided the West Indies, however, because of high mortality rates and land prices. In the 1880s, the regions of origin came to include northern and eastern Europe and, selecting both Americas as destinations, Italian migrants as well as capitalists from much of Europe integrated the dual south and north Atlantic migration systems.[11]

The Afro-Atlantic system emerged out of early modern patterns of Mediterranean slavery. Unfree African men were among the conquistadors, and free "African Creole" merchants established transoceanic networks. On the macro-level, the slave system involved actors at both ends of the process and in the transition: sub-Saharan African practices of debt bondage; African warrior elites as captors and slave merchants; European merchants, captains, and crews during the Middle Passage; Euro-American merchants and slave owners in the plantation regimes. This system came to an end in the 1870s and 1880s, when new European migrants, especially from Italy and eastern Europe, provided both Americas with reservoirs of labor.[12]

In the Pacific system, in contrast, discontinuities prevailed. During a first phase from the 1570s to the early 1600s, free and enslaved Asian men came to New Spain's Pacific coast. In the next two centuries, while few migrants reached the continent, Hawaii became an important destination. During the second phase, from the mid nineteenth century to the 1880s or the 1930s in North and South America respectively, free, credit ticket, and contract labor migrants arrived. Another slowdown lasted until the repeal of exclusionist legislation in the 1940s. Large-scale free migrations, almost exclusively to the United States and Canada, recommenced in the mid 1960s (the third phase).[13]

While capital flows and Italian migrants had integrated the Atlantic system, the mid-nineteenth-century annexation of Mexico's north by the United States and U.S. investments in the Caribbean made the Anglo-Latin division of the continent permeable. Mexican men and women and, after the 1880s, Caribbean migrants headed north, and a Central American–Caribbean–North American migration region emerged and expanded in the first half of the twentieth century. After the mid twentieth century, separate regional migration systems directed men and women to Argentina and Venezuela; U.S. support for right-wing Central and South American regimes and perceived better options in the United States and Canada sent refugees, middle-class men and women, and workers northward. Information backflow made the migration system self-sustaining. In the 1990s, more than a century and a half after South American statesmen proposed a pan-American conference in 1826, Latin American migrants have achieved the integration of both Americas.[14]

Before 1939, about two million men and women came from Asia, about eleven million from Africa, and between fifty and sixty million from Europe. To the 1830s, more Africans than Europeans came to the Americas. Then, for a century and a half, European immigration dominated. In the 1970s, Latin American and Asian men and women formed the largest immigrant groups.

UNFREE AND FREE MIGRATIONS IN CONTINENTAL PERSPECTIVE

From the beginning of the arrival of European invaders, plantation entrepreneurs, and settlers, the crucial question of production and power, as well as of reproductive labor was, who was to be the laborer. Iberian hidalgos, like the motley crowd of English and other gentlemen in Virginia, despised physical labor. The former relegated it to North African Moriscos, the later to the English underclasses. European governing elites, planters, and farmers considered voluntary migration to the American colonies slow and labor too scarce. Bound labor was to provide a solution, with power relationships restricting the agency of common people. In a first step, Iberian and British gentry, as well as prospective plantation owners from other European states, instrumentalized the Church's concept of morally deficient natives to project their own dislike of labor onto the natives. For their own good, they were to be educated or, if unwilling to learn, forced to labor. Second, the lowly of European societies were to be induced to migrate as bound laborers. Third, Africa came to be considered a reservoir of labor, especially the societies of its western Atlantic littoral. Finally, Asian societies, southern China and British-ruled India in particular, were forced to supply workers. Power relationships resulted in class, eth-class, and race-class constructions and became constitutive elements of migration systems.

In the sixteenth-century Caribbean as well as in Central and South America, the colonizers' *encomienda* system, de facto slavery, tied indigenous families as labor units to haciendas or appropriated them to state officials or plantation owners. Under the *repartimiento* system, natives were forced to migrate to public works, mines, or plantations, and under the *mita* system, Amerindians were forced into long-distance labor migration to Peruvian mines.[15]

In Europe, where in the opinion of the powerful the lower orders should never be without master or mistress, unfree labor relations were traditionally imposed by the state. Contracts of indenture were the norm in England and became the norm in the American colonies. Contracts were enforceable— from the employer's side only—by state intervention, and thus even consensual labor was unfree for the duration of the contract.[16] In Virginia, which was intended to earn profits for investors immediately, the first migrant workers were to submit to military law and till the land collectively, and Massachusetts legislators attempted in 1641 to curtail the "excessive rates" demanded by laborers. European governments employed deportation as a punishment for criminals or as a means of getting rid of vagrants, orphans, and the destitute in general. Borderlines between poverty and criminality were kept fluid.[17] But in the colonies, medieval concepts such as that of the master-servant relationship could not be replicated. Both male and female laborers could migrate elsewhere or become independent farmers.[18]

Impoverished English, French, Dutch, and German migrants indentured themselves in order to emigrate. More bound than free European migrants reached the Americas before 1776: about three-fifths of all white migrants to British and Caribbean America were indentured workers for staple crop production or, later, skilled artisans in urban locations. Servants from the Germanies usually landed in Philadelphia and sought work among the region's German-speaking farmers and townspeople. The system was highly responsive to labor market demands, permitted postcontract independence, and made Pennsylvania, for example, the "best poor man's country."[19]

To prevent such self-determination, bondage for life was imposed on men and women from colonial societies in Asia in Latin America, and African so-called rights-in-persons and debt bondage were converted to chattel slavery. To avoid the Portuguese-controlled route to Asia around the Cape of Good Hope, the Spanish sent a fleet from Acapulco across the Pacific to the Philippines. In 1571, Manila became Spain's entrepôt for the transpacific "galleon trade." It supplied the upper classes of New Spain with luxury goods produced by Chinese craftsmen and was financed by silver dug from the Peruvian mines by forced migrant Amerindian labor. Chinese ship carpenters whose skills and technologies surpassed those of European artisans built the galleons in Manila and in Acapulco. From the 1570s to the 1590s, the Spanish transported several thousand enslaved native Filipinos, Chinese, and Japanese to Mexico and Peru. Merchants, artisans, and laboring men from the Indian Ocean trade emporia and the Chinese diaspora, departing from the Philippines, Portuguese Macao, and coastal towns of southern China, also migrated of their own free will. The population of Lima, Peru, of Asian origin amounted to 1.5 percent in 1600. With the decline of official Spanish shipments across the Pacific—and perhaps a rise in "smuggling," a type of private entrepreneurship—fewer migrants came. Since few women came, no lasting diasporas or ethnic enclaves emerged. Asian men were absorbed into South American societies through relationships with local women, and their descendents were identified as either Hispanic or Amerindian.[20]

For three centuries, the multidirectional trade in African slaves was the most important factor in the complex procedures of settlement on the western, American side of the Atlantic and an important factor of capital accumulation on its eastern, European side. "The economic model for enslavement is one of burglary, not of production. In economic terms, the value of the slave is not a real cost but an 'opportunity cost,' " according to Philip Curtin.[21] While Spain and Portugal used royal institutions to develop their colonial economies, the Dutch, French, and English states left colonization and administration to individual planters and governmentally chartered joint-stock companies. Officials and merchant financiers of the mid seventeenth century saw their future in producing specialized crops for European markets with permanently bound labor, creating what Franklin W. Knight calls "the Atlantic world of plantation agriculture, big business, international commerce, and slavery."[22]

The major societies of origin included the West African Wolof, Madinka, Yoruba, Songhai, and Hausa, and Bantu-speaking peoples from the Congo to Angola. Under Spanish control, a third of the imported slaves were to be women. In Portuguese Brazil, "those who came from the same African language group . . . often associated with one another under the label imposed by the slaveowners," Mieko Nishida notes. They sought to recreate common symbols and ways of everyday life. In contrast, the more heterogeneous slave populations of Spanish and British America tended to be absorbed into the generic African population.[23] According to Curtin, 3.8 million slaves were imported to the British, French, Dutch, and Danish Caribbean, 3.6 million to Brazil, 1.6 million to Spanish America, and 0.4 million to British North America. Other scholars have arrived at higher figures. The chronology of the slave trade reflects the expansion of plantation economies: 125,000 slaves came before 1600, 1.3 million in the next century, 6 million between 1701 and 1810, and another 1.9 million before 1870. In the Caribbean, only 0.6 million European voluntary and bound migrants joined the 3.8 million African forced migrants. But in 1800, only 2.1 million slaves lived in the region, as compared to 0.9 million Europeans, by Piet Emmer's calculation. While "seasoned" slaves were transported to North America, it was mortality that contributed to this outcome—slaves on sugar estates had a life expectancy of no more than six to eight years. This was the continent's second demographic catastrophe, after the collapse of the Amerindian populations.[24]

Because of their early annihilation there, the Amerindians contribution was weakest in the Caribbean, where that of people of African origin was conversely strongest. However, for three centuries, no slave population in the Caribbean was able to reproduce itself under the skewed male-female ratio and in view of the cost differential between raising and importing slaves. Planters preferred low-priced imported slaves to the cost of raising slave children. In early 1830s Jamaica, for example, to rear a slave girl or boy cost twice as much as importing a slave. Slaves, who formed families despite the sometimes violent interference of planters and slave drivers, often had to produce their own food on small plots of land and sew their own garments. This labor was matched by a concomitant increase in self-determination. Planters' and legislators' attempts to curtail or to interfere with self-provisioning and sale of surplus and with cultural and religious activities met with adamant opposition. Men and women resisted their exploitation by slow work and "sharp tongues," by self-organization and attempts to recreate their original cultures.[25]

Although Latin American societies evoke the image of Amerindian communities, in the mid seventeenth century, the population of Lima "was over half black. . . . Lima and Mexico City had in fact the largest concentrations of Blacks in the western hemisphere," Fredrick Bowser notes. Slaves worked on plantations and as miners and urban laborers. Creole master craftsmen and small entrepreneurs employed Africans who came with or acquired skills. Mine owners relied on experienced West African miners, who were permitted to sell gold dust on their own account and could purchase their freedom. In Brazil, whose economy was based on slave labor in the sugar plantations, the hinterland and the free Afro-Brazilian community made flight easy for acculturated slaves. Manumission followed color and gender lines: women were manumitted twice as often as men, and light-colored mulattoes more often than African-born blacks. Women with their partners created free communities, collected funds to liberate enslaved kin and friends, and migrated to cities because of better economic options. Free "persons of color," women in particular, dominated the small trade. British Caribbean planters, fearful of cultural interaction, refused to employ African Caribbean nurses for their children. The free population of mulatto or African lineage amounted to above 40 percent of the total population in Curaçao (1833) and Puerto Rico (1860), but to only 16 percent in Cuba (1860), and even less in Jamaica, Barbados, Saint Domingue (later Haiti), and Martinique. In Saint Domingue, where the male white planter aristocracy and free mulatto women formed unions, the mulatto population was able to establish itself as an independent economic and political factor.[26]

In North America, the history of Africans was different. First, the numbers imported directly from Africa were small, and most arrived after "seasoning" in the Caribbean in a second involuntary migration to yet another labor and race relations regime. Their share in the total U.S. population remained comparatively low: 18 percent (including 1.5 percent free) in 1790. Only in pre-1730s South Carolina did blacks form a majority. Second, slave marriages resulted in natural increase and a balanced sex ratio. Third, although the harsh paternalist and plantation-based slave owners did not work slaves to death, manumission was extremely infrequent. To regain agency, slaves fled to Spanish Florida, westward, or northward through the self-help network of the "underground railroad" to free states and to Canada. In contrast to Brazil, free communities, totaling some 320,000 in 1830, were too small, too poor, and too powerless to protect fugitives.[27] In Canada, an early free African community emerged in Halifax in the context of British Atlantic trade. Flight from the rebellious colonies brought black Loyalists and the slaves of white Loyalists to Canada after 1774. Jamaican Maroons came after 1796, but many of them emigrated to Sierra Leone. Self-liberated U.S. blacks settled in Ontario and Montreal. Among white Canadians, a discourse of protecting blacks from U.S. persecution developed.[28]Although cotton production was institutionally and economically the underpinning of Southern society, there were only about 380,000 slave owners out of a total white population of roughly 9 million in 1860 (about 4.25 percent). Of these, only 2,300 large planters (about .025 percent) owned more than 100 slaves. In this respect, Southern society resembled Belize more than it did, say, New York.

Both the admission of blacks to the United States and the nation's south-ward expansion were, to some degree, predicated on controlling the slaves. After the slave rebellion in Haiti, to contain talk of human rights and self-determination, some U.S. states prohibited both the importation of slaves from the West Indies and the entry of free blacks. The acquisition of Florida in 1819 was intended to prevent slaves from escaping to Maroon/Seminole communities. Blacks, both free and slave, also labored outside of the plantation economy, raising cattle in Texas, for example, being hired out to industrial establishments in Tennessee, and establishing small agricultural communities in the old Northwest. The end of the transatlantic slave trade increased internal trading and involuntary mobility, as it did later in Brazil. Retarding the establishment of self-determining black communities, the postbellum white South exerted brutal control over black lives through lynching, a combination of torture, auto-da-fé, and pogrom that had no equivalent in Latin American societies.[29]

Abolitionist impulses came from many parts of the European and African segments of the Atlantic economies, rather than originating in Britain as has often been argued. American Quakers demanded abolition in the 1770s, as did the Amis des Noirs in France after 1788, but most important, mulattoes and free blacks in the French colonies exerted pressure on the revolutionary National Assembly in Paris. The Haitian slaves' war for freedom changed the forum of debate from constitutional and human rights philosophy to front-page news. Slavery in French Caribbean possessions temporarily ended in 1794 and the slave trade in the British Empire in 1807.[30]

In the Americas, processes of ethnogenesis resulted in new mixed or creole peoples different from but as future-oriented as Crèvecoeur's "new man [and woman]."[31] Strict and visible control mechanisms left whites with the illusion of controlling the lives and cultures of blacks, whose spiritual and emotional aspects were invisible to them. The new sociopolitical regimes and peoples of the Americas developed within the exigencies of the new ecological contexts and economic and cultural constraints, amalgamating Amerindian, African, and European cultures.

MANY-CULTURED SOCIETIES
AND THE PREDOMINANCE OF THE NORTH

The long century from the independence of the thirteen British colonies in North America in 1776, via statehood of most Latin societies, to the abolition of slavery in Brazil in 1888 saw the establishment of new parameters for migration and acculturation as regards labor recruitment, political participation, and regional predominance. The shifting of Europe's economic center from the Iberian peninsula to the Netherlands and Great

Britain and the emerging economic role of new middle classes and capital accumulation favored the cultural and economic ascendancy of North America.

On the European side, the French Revolution and Napoleon's imperial expansion, 1789–1815, interrupted transatlantic migration and changed global power relationships. The reestablishment of European monarchies after 1815, with petty but haughty officials reaching down to the level of villages, as well as lack of land and the slow development of urban economies, led to transatlantic mass migrations, free within economic constraints. In the near-dormant Pacific migration system, the globally active British East India Company, reaching for the northwest coast of North America in the 1780s, copied Spanish reliance on Chinese labor and sent Chinese sailors and artisans to Vancouver Island. Within New Spain, men of Asian origin had migrated northward to California. Filipinos formed a colony in the eighteenth-century Mississippi river delta. On a trial basis, British planters organized shipments of Chinese contract laborers to the Caribbean in 1806 and 1810. Viewed from the African perspective, changes were slower. Britain, which had abolished slavery in its empire in 1834, began to press other states to follow its lead in order to equalize the cost of labor in the sugar-producing colonies. However, Cuba and Brazil did so only in the 1880s, and only then did the Atlantic slave trade end. In contrast, imperial economics initiated a major restructuring. When Britain abolished protective duties for sugar from the British West Indies in 1846, prices went tumbling and colonial wage levels collapsed in the financial crisis of 1847–48. Thus ended the "old order" plantation system and its labor regime in the Caribbean. The United States followed suit in the course of its bloody Civil War, 1861–65.

Wherever slavery was abolished, labor regimes had to be reconstructed. White planters tried to keep their black labor forces, for example, through state-mandated apprenticeship periods in Cuba and through refusal to grant forty acres and a mule to freed black families in the United States. Caribbean planters literally experimented with different types of human beings as replacement labor forces: semi-bondage of Afro-Caribbeans; free Afro-Caribbean workers; re-indenture of Africans freed from slave ships; the importation of blacks from the United States; encouragement of free migration from Africa; and the sale of Amerindian prisoners and peons with their wives by Yucatan hacendados for labor in Cuba. Turning to white workers in the 1840s, planters induced European governments to provide assisted passage, and Irish, English, French, Germans, Maltese, and Portuguese came before 1882. This collusion between capital and governments, often ascribed to the "capitalist system," may be traced to the power of planters in colonial legislatures and imperial administrations.[32]

Two major new migration systems finally came to provide free European and Asian contract labor. Only a decade after abolition of the first African slavery, the Asian "coolie system"—or "second slavery," as Hugh Tinker calls it—was in place. In the 1850s Caribbean, as in the United States of the 1870s, slavery-like labor codes and political constitutions intensified control over those whom Eric Wolf calls the "new laborers" and over disenfranchised nonwhite peoples.[33]

During the half-century of revolutions from 1776 to 1826, options in the Americas included white, black, and red models of political organization. African-American Maroon societies existed from Brazil to Florida. French support for the revolution in Haiti inspired by black slave and French republican concepts of human rights created more hopes for liberty than the French fleet ever gave U.S. revolutionaries. Amerindian polities had both encompassed empires and island societies, as well as the Iroquois Federation, the so-called Five Civilized Nations, and the peoples of the northwest Pacific coast. All of these red, brown, and black societies practiced some form of popular participation. Most also excluded specific groups, and some Amerindian and Maroon societies practiced slavery. Creole white societies in the Americas, like all others, denied rights to women, regardless of color and ethnicity, as well as to men defined as nonwhite. Caribbean Creole societies, however, had permitted women considerable economic and political influence. Military strength, power relationships, and concepts of the superiority of various shades of whiteness, rather than democratic theory and "the rights of English men," determined which models of political organization were adopted and which were annihilated. Seymour M. Lipset's concept of the United States as "the first new nation" reduces the many options available in the marketplace of political practice and theory in the Americas to a teleological one-way cultural transmission from England.[34]

In pursuit of homogeneity, hegemonic and usually relatively white elites in the racialized and culturally heterogeneous societies of the Americas institutionalized political systems copied from European concepts of nationhood. Life and language were made to follow middle-class cultural prescriptions; gatekeeper elites from Noah Webster (about 1800) to Brazilian reformers (about 1900) embarked on their *e pluribus unum* quests. The highly literate and economically increasingly strong United States advertised itself as the beacon of political inspiration. Cultural elites in the new societies fortified and expanded their own positions, but few or none of the "founding [and financially interested] fathers" understood the languages of the cultures around them.[35]

Interactions between Europeans and Amerindians in colonial North America have been widely studied, and several authors deal with the conversion of captured whites by Amerindian groups.[36] In the fur economy of the north, competing Amerindian peoples engaged in expansive and defensive migrations as well as warfare. Children of intercultural parentage entered the business as traders. Two distinct French and Scottish Métis societies emerged. French-Canadian *habitants,* who left the restrictive labor regime on the *seigneurs'* landholdings for self-determined lives in fur trading, married Amerindian women and formed the French-speaking Métis society of the Red River Valley (Manitoba). In the early 1870s, land speculators supported by troops of the recently established Dominion government of Canada not only aborted attempts to secure self-government but destroyed the society. Scottish traders of the Hudson's Bay Company and their Amerindian wives and "half-breed" children became the political elite of the colonies of British Columbia and Vancouver Island (1858). More powerful within the contexts of imperial rule and dominant language than the Red River Métis, these families became "white" and legitimate—a process resembling the whitening possible in flexible Latin American power relationships.[37]

Climate, comparatively thin settlement, and the high demand for labor made North America increasingly attractive to immigrants. In the 250 years before the 1880s, these "Second Peoples" created numerous regional cultures, including those of: (1) the French-speaking St. Lawrence valley (now Quebec), bicultural Acadia / Nova Scotia (now Canada's Maritime Provinces), and Puritan and later industrial New England; (2) the multiethnic Middle Atlantic states, including the Pennsylvania German enclave, whence nineteenth-century European immigrants set out to settle the prairies and mountains to the west; (3) the white-black South; (4) the Hispanic zone, from Florida via the Spanish/French enclave of New Orleans to the borderlands of Texas, the Mexican and Pueblo culture regions, and California; (5) the Euro-Asian contact zone along the Pacific coast from Los Angeles to Vancouver Island, with the distinctive Amerindian, or "First Peoples," cultures of the Pacific Northwest; and (6) the American-Canadian borderland, heavily settled by immigrants of German, Scandinavian, and Finnish origin west of the Great Lakes and by French Canadians in Michigan and, in particular, New England. Before 1924, the international borderline between the United States and Canada was an immigrant cultural belt. This perspective focuses on people and their everyday cultural practices, rather than on institutions and hegemonic "high" cultures or territorial borderlines established by the power relationships between states.[38]

By the mid nineteenth century, the territorial division of North America had been finalized. In the Oregon Treaty, Britain and the United States not only negotiated their boundary but also allocated Amerindian peoples as wards or subjects to either the United States or Canada. The Mexican War had moved the border across a quarter of a million people, expanding U.S. territory by a quarter and reducing Mexico's by more than a third. Toward the end of the nineteenth century, the shift from national to imperial mission in the agenda of U.S. capitalists and political leaders resulted in intervention in Cuba, Puerto Rico, and the Philippines. The free Chinese from the southern provinces and the diaspora who had migrated to Hawaii became part of U.S. imperial history when U.S. planters with capital migrated westward to Hawaii and had the islands annexed in 1898.[39] This new imperialism, combined with the earlier decline of Iberian Europe and the shift within the anglophone linguistic area from Great Britain to the United States, transferred intellectual hegemony to U.S. English-speaking gatekeeper elites and their political theories. Their constructions of the past became usable histories for the present—profitable to the English-speaking cultural group.

BICULTURAL REGIONS OF NORTH AMERICA

Historians attentive to the voices of the weak have added the world the slaves made to that of the slaveholders.[40] Above the status of bondage, other people in subaltern positions led their lives, made their history, and asserted their dignity against the blanket Anglo-American and Canadian readings of history: the world the French Canadians made and the world the Mexicanos made. Lastly, there is the world of the Amerindians: in the 125 years from 1763 to the 1880s, zones of native survival shrank under the onslaught of settlers, the U.S. Army, and treaties with Canada's government. Amerindians maintained a pueblo culture in Arizona / New Mexico, a prairie one in the Minnesota-Montana belt, and a coastal one in British Columbia. The Oklahoma settlements, stemming from deportations, are better classified as camps than as a locus of cultural fusion between different native peoples. The widely dispersed reservations remained without larger cultural impact but permitted survival. Only in the second half of the twentieth century did a new movement of resistance and self-affirmation and the new attitudes to human rights lead to reaffirmation of many peoples' cultures and values.

Three major bicultural regions emerged, French Canada and the Hispanic Southwest of the United States by conquest, and the slaveholding South through the importation of human beings. The juxtaposed multiple cultures of African and European origin in the South homogenized, the former because its heterogeneous origins prevented recovery of an African ethnicity, the latter because comparatively few nineteenth-century European migrants settled or gained political influence there. No sizable free black communities emerged to assume a mediating position. The powerful white and subaltern black cultures remained antagonistic, white child / black nanny relations, braided lives in the plantation economy, and separation from the democratic sector of the United States notwithstanding. Louisiana's culture, especially in New Orleans and the neighboring coastal regions, evidences European, Caribbean, Acadian French, and New Spanish cultural input to the present.

In the Northeast, the St. Lawrence valley French, the Acadian French, and the New England British lived in distinct societies, which repeatedly found themselves in conflict because of European imperial warfare. The bicultural area from northern Maine to Acadia (now Nova Scotia and New Brunswick) and Ile-Saint-Jean / Prince Edward Island was connected culturally to New France and commercially to New England. In the St. Lawrence valley (New France),[41] a mere 10,000 men and women had arrived by 1750, only one-seventh of them as free migrants.[42] France's imperial administrators retarded development by imposing old-regime social hierarchies, Catholic orthodoxy, and a colonial support economy. During the religious wars of the sixteenth and seventeenth centuries, when some 250,000 skilled Huguenots, many of whom possessed some capital, left France, they were refused permission to settle in French colonies. As a result almost every country in Europe and both British and Dutch colonies profited from their talents. The goal of keeping the French colonies Catholic was thus achieved at immense cost in loss of economic options, a loss borne by the colonists. In 1763, defeated in war by the British, France ceded unproductive New France to Britain in exchange for return of the revenue-producing plantation economies of Martinique, Guadeloupe, and St. Lucia under the Treaty of Paris, renouncing its societal-ideological project on the continent in favor of an economically more rewarding Caribbean one.

In the context of hegemonic and subaltern cultures, neither enterprising French-speaking fur traders nor immigrant French or deported Acadians in Louisiana could create self-governing societies of their own. After Acadia fell to Britain in 1713, the London government offset the Catholic French preponderance there by attracting Protestant settlers–some 2,500 British and another 1,500 from Hannover, Brunswick, and Switzerland– and deported about half to three-quarters of the 13,000 Acadians to Massachusetts and Louisiana in 1755. When many survivors migrated back over time, the distinct societies merged into a bicultural if hierarchical one.[43] Quebec, with its French culture, law, language, and Catholic religion, was, in contrast, granted separate status in 1774, becoming an island in the Puritan and Anglican English-speaking northeast. Rather than celebrating this autonomy, however, the *québécoise* elite enshrined the military defeat in 1759 in memory and made a shibboleth of their cultural integrity. In so doing, they established Quebec's claim to be the preeminent French society in the New World and marginalized other francophone American cultures, such as those of the Red River Métis and the Louisiana Cajuns. The position of French Canadians has been deeply influenced by demographic factors. First, unlike birthrates in other European nations, the French birthrate had stabilized, so that after the seventeenth century few people emigrated. Owing to this lack of French immigrants from Europe, French Canada became ever more distinct and distant from France. Secondly, the high birthrate promoted in French Canada by the Catholic Church led to internal population growth. In the 1760s, there were about 65,000 French speakers and a million English speakers in North America, but the American Revolution resulted in the migration of about 70,000 Loyalist refugees to Canada between 1774 and 1789, displacing proportionately more people than the French Revolution did. The United Empire Loyalists (or Tories, from the revolutionaries' viewpoint), who included Pennsylvania Germans, New York Dutch, free blacks, and African slaves, constructed themselves as a British ethno-political group. In New Brunswick and Quebec, these English-speaking newcomers, who had easier access to political resources than their long-resident French-speaking neighbors, established themselves as the dominant group. Among French Quebeckers, nineteenth-century population growth led to mass emigration. Since political and clerical elites opposed their departure, rather than taking advantage of fertile land in Ontario or, in the 1870s, in Manitoba, agricultural migrants settled marginal lands in Quebec or in Ontario's north and developed a discourse of loss and deprivation. Those who defied the elite's rhetoric, perhaps as many as a million, migrated to jobs in New England textile mills. The ultramontane, chauvinist Quebec clergy briefly expected a French Quebec–Maritimes–New England Catholic polity to emerge, but the migrants shared neither the *québécoise* culture of grievance nor the elite's chauvinism and took charge of their own lives. Although migration and cultural interaction left only historical memory in New England, there remained a bicultural Anglo-Acadian society in Nova Scotia, a bilingual New Brunswick, and a Quebec split over the choice between full participation in the English-speaking world, with possible loss of its francophone distinctiveness, and a past-oriented, separate enclave status.[44]

Hegemonic memory, which relegated early French settlers to a niche, has to be corrected as regards the Southwest, too. North America's colonial history began when, as early as 1598, 500 settlers from New Spain "established the first European settlement in the American West," a decade before the first permanent English settlement in the East, Jamestown. The bicultural belt from Texas to California, an Anglo-Hispanic borderland, emerged when Mexico became the destination of Texas-bound U.S. settlers and ranchers in the 1820s and of 100,000 California-bound gold rush migrants in the 1840s.[45] After the independence of Texas in 1836, the war of 1848, and the Gadsden Purchase in 1853 had stripped Mexico of these territories, some 75,000 Spanish-speaking Mexicans and 150,000 Amerindian men and women found themselves subject to the U.S. conquerors. The Amerindians, who had been citizens under Mexican law, lost that status under U.S. law. Hispanic Mexicans were promised but not given security of land titles. Only after English-speaking squatters and speculators had been satisfied did the "security of property" maxim take hold again. (The process resembles the dispossession of Amerindians earlier and Japanese-Americans later.) Upon the insistence of the Hispanic Californios, the California constitution of 1849 did not limit voting to whites and mandated bilingual publication of all state laws in Spanish and English. In subsequent decades, both Californios from the south of the state and Sonorans immigrated to northern California. Nuevo Mexicanos were pushed back after the coming of the railroads, and massive immigration of Anglo-Americans reduced Tejanos to 6 percent of the total population of Texas by 1860, when the cattle boom enticed in Mexican *vaqueros*. The bicultural period thus began with a process of subordination, but Hispanic culture was reinvigorated around 1900 by demand for and immigration of Mexican laborers.[46]

The migrations of the second half of the nineteenth century had only limited impact on the three bicultural regions and their position in the national narratives of the United States and Canada. Few French speakers emigrated from Europe; European immigrants entered the postslavery South only in small numbers; the Mexican-American territories, with the exception of Texas, did not lend themselves to quick agricultural or industrial development. As regards the fashioning of narratives, enslaved or subaltern and sometimes illiterate African Americans, Mexican Americans, and French Americans could not commit their versions to writing easily. The highly literate dissenting elites of the New England culture, in contrast, constructed their own historiography from the beginnings of their settlement, searching their souls for motivation and their success for signs of God's providence. Subsequent English speakers turned New England history into national U.S. history. Similarly, immigrant historians in Canada in the early twentieth century writing in their own languages were bypassed by their influential academic colleagues from the two self-styled "founding nations," who often could not read other languages. Early filiopietistic works on Irish and Scottish Canadians and interpretation of Canada as a staple-good-producing economy made accessible by the great Laurentian valley established hegemonic master narratives in the most literal sense.[47]

MULTIPLE MIGRATIONS, SHIFTING BORDERLANDS, AND PACIFIC CROSSINGS TO THE 1930S

The male-centered master narrative of European immigrants first conquering the wilderness in the East and then pushing the frontier and progress across the vast plains of the northern half of the continent is no more than a roughly hewn woodcut. It never captures the subtleties of the lives, minds, and histories of the subalterns, the servants. The immigrant and ethnic worlds need to be reinserted into the narrative. The image of a mobile society is not merely one of moving about geographically but also one of cultural conflict, interaction, and fusion. The deportations and refugee migrations of Amerindians, Acadians, Tories, and slaves were followed in the nineteenth century by complex, multidirectional internal migrations, both voluntary and coerced.

Migration decisions depended on the demand for and supply of labor and marriage partners, on abolition of slavery, on political regulation of labor and land, on investment and industrialization strategies. Westward migration of planters with their slaves toward the Mississippi and Gulf created a genuinely American-African culture and religion, as well as an even harsher plantation labor regime. Short-distance moves of New England women to textile mills from the 1820s to the 1840s involved accommodation to industrial ways of life and interaction with investors' interest in profits. Black slaves put to industrial work in the 1840s and 1850s interacted with free white laborers. Other moves include the population exchange in the Hispanic territories; the continent-wide spread of free European immigrant labor, with a male-female gender ratio of 60:40 up to 1917–24, including multiple, often eastward, city-bound, migrations; a small westward migration of black people from the South and of workers into northern cities from the 1910s on; and mobilization of women both during wartime manpower shortages and for clerical work in the 1920s. Low cotton prices in the 1930s pushed blacks and whites out of the rural South, just as the potato blight had evicted Irish peasants. Drought and the Depression forced families in the south central U.S. states and Saskatchewan to flee to California and British Columbia. In addition to the bicultural regions, city neighborhoods and small towns became cultural borderlands. Interactive cultures were disrupted by color lines, ethnic group boundaries, or exclusionist legal barriers. But people's migration strategies responded to economic and cultural options, and race ideology could neither prevent economic interaction, if hierarchically structured, nor smother migrants' projects for self-determined lives.[48]

The cultural-economic hierarchies in the three bicultural regions and the lack of investment and job creation led to massive out-migration. From the 1890s to the 1920s, between 300,000 and 400,000 or more French-Canadian men, women, and children migrated from the depressed Quebec economy and Catholic educational system to New England's textile mills. Considered cheap labor, they were labeled "the Chinese of the East," just as Italian labor migrants in Europe were called the "Chinese of Europe." Conversely, Chinese were labeled the "Jews of the Orient" in 1930s Southeast Asia. By such labels, gatekeepers compounded race and class position to segregate laborers wanted by capitalist entrepreneurs but unwanted by the hegemonic culture.[49] As regards the bicultural Southwest, the relationship of the United States to Mexico in some ways resembled that of Hohenzollern Prussia to Poland, one-third of which it had annexed in 1795. The German-Slavic and the Anglo-Hispanic borderlands served as reservoirs of temporary—not immigrant—workers.[50] "In the case of the Mexican, he is less desirable as a citizen than as a laborer," the Dillingham Commission declared in 1911. While "not easily assimilated, this is of no very great importance as long as most of them return to their native land." After 1917, Mexican *braceros* were recruited upon the insistence of California growers, the equivalent of German Junkers or Caribbean planters. In the 1920s, when half a million came, they could collect one-fifth of their seasonal pay only upon departure at the border. Nevertheless, increasing numbers of Mexicans also moved to northern industrial cities.[51] From the bicultural U.S. South, ex-slaves left for Kansas agriculture in the 1870s. Northern urban jobs attracted their children and grandchildren. When the transatlantic proletarian mass migration came to a sudden stop in 1914, the transcontinental "Great Migration" (1916–20) brought almost 10 percent of the 10.4 million black men and women northward (0.7 million) and westward (0.25 million), mainly into industrial jobs.[52] Their letters to kin in the South described the industrial cities in near-religious terms as a "promised land," calling to mind the Puritans' "Great Migration" and "City on a Hill" three centuries earlier.[53]

Parallel to these multiple internal moves, European, Asian, and Caribbean migrants arrived in transoceanic migrations. The culture of the Harlem Renaissance, for example, was part of the black Atlantic. U.S. investment in Caribbean economies encouraged migration, and some 35,600 Caribbean migrants arrived in the 1890s and 183,000 the 1900s. Havana cigar makers worked in Ybor City, Florida; New York's Caribbean colony numbered 100,000 in 1924; Toronto's Caribbean community was small but vibrant.[54] During the century before the 1930s, one-fifth of the European migrants bound for the Americas chose Latin America as destination. In this "proletarian mass migration," Italian harvest workers had commuted between Argentina and Europe since the 1880s, taking advantage of the inverted seasons. Music and dance styles, like the tango, emerged out of this fusion of cultures. In the 1920s, the door remained open for Europeans in Canada, where *raisons d'état* differed from those of the United States, and the government encouraged eastern European immigration, while capitalists recruited workers. The U.S.-Canadian border remained permeable. As *pays d'escale*—Bruno Ramirez's term—Canada became a country of stopover for migrants from Europe: 2.6 million moved to the United States from Canada between 1871 and 1930. In the opposite direction, Canada actively recruited settlers, excluding, however, black U.S.

citizens. Along the Pacific coast of the Americas and in the Caribbean region, labor forces were replenished by Asian men and women under contract.

Historians, engulfed in the discourses of their times, constructed a dichotomy between sojourning Asians and immigrant Europeans: the former clung to their secluded ways of life (e.g., in the congested opium dens of Chinatowns), the latter became Americans, if with a stopover in an ethnic enclave (or tilled the wide-open spaces of the prairies). However, one-third of the Europeans sojourned in the United States for a few years and then returned to Europe. In view of more constrained gender roles in the societies of origin, however, few women returned. As areas of origin shifted to southern and eastern Europe in the 1880s, and mass travel was organized in the ways of modern travel agencies, migrants could buy tickets to their final destination in their eastern European village of origin, with a prearranged transfer between train and ship and, if necessary, hostel accommodation.[55] As to the dynamism of developments in the United States, up to the early 1870s, immigrants received more capital from Europe (funds brought over, inheritances, gifts) than they remitted back to Europe. Their societies of origin had borne the cost of raising and educating them, and they left elderly parents behind to fend for themselves. Immigrants' dependency ratios were low. Undercapitalized agrarian regions in Europe, Asia, and Latin America thus subsidized the U.S. economy by bearing the social cost of raising children and caring for the elderly.[56]

Emigration from the United States is another aspect lost sight of under the hegemony of the immigration paradigm. Investor-planters migrated to Mexican Texas, independent Hawaii, and Spanish Cuba, each case involving annexations or creation of zones of influence. Black Americans and Canadians who moved back to Africa or were sent to Liberia and Sierra Leone included some 15,000 manumitted slaves and more than 1,000 Jamaican Maroons living in Halifax. A small "Back to Africa" movement emerged among African Americans in the 1920s. In consequence, Liberia was another zone of U.S. influence. Southerners fleeing the Civil War emigrated to Montreal in 1860–65, just as Americans escaping the Vietnam War moved to Canada and Sweden in the 1960s and 1970s. Outbound moves included the voluntary migrations of seasonal or multiannual workers to Asia, Europe, and the Caribbean, as well as the deportation ("repatriation" in official terminology) of Mexican *braceros* during the Depression. Under economic straits and social pressures, the 1930s were a period of involuntary departures.

In the early 1900s, Sikhs from British-ruled India came to Canada, many of whom moved on to bicultural California's fruit-growing regions to work, where some married women of Mexican origin. Half-pay officers came with their families from nonwhite British colonies and younger sons of the gentry from England—both stood out as high-handed and incapable of adjustment. African Canadians, often the descendants of refugees from U.S. slavery, left for jobs in U.S. industries in the 1920s.[57]

North American migrations were a variant of global patterns. The nineteenth-century agricultural frontiers of North and South America, which had succeeded the seventeenth- and eighteenth-century southeastern and eastern European ones, were in turn succeeded in the 1930s by a global northern belt of settlement from the Canadian Peace River District to Siberia and Manchuria. Westward migrations to the U.S. and Canadian prairies did not serve as a safety valve to defuse class conflict; rather—as in Europe—urbanization attracted the surplus rural population. Although more family farms were established in the early 1900s than ever before, "bonanza farms," or corporate latifundia, like plantations in the eighteenth-century Caribbean, displaced settler families. Manifold migrations crisscrossed North America: entrepreneurs moved to opportunities, as others did in Europe and Africa; traders headed for recently settled areas, connecting New York to New Mexico, for example, and Montreal to Regina. In mining and railroad work, laborers from three continents toiled alongside one another, ate in Chinese (and other) restaurants, bought in Jewish (and other) stores, and swore at American (and other) bosses.[58]

As to urban frontiers, 1850s Chicago was temporarily the western edge of the Atlantic migration system. It was founded—reportedly by the son of a black slave woman and a French nobleman—in 1803, a century after St. Petersburg (1703) and at a time when London counted two million inhabitants. Chicago's population grew to four million in less than a century. But cities across the world expanded. Budapest in Europe and Hong Kong in Asia, for example, also achieved phenomenal if less rapid growth. Chicago's demand for timber and firewood gave struggling immigrant farmers the opportunity to leave their families and to migrate to lumber camps in winter, just as European smallholders migrated to harvest work in summer. The need to supplement insufficient agricultural incomes by seasonal migration to wage work truncated families across the globe. Economic and emotional needs conflicted and had to be negotiated and, ideally, balanced. Tens of thousands of migrants returning from Chicago, St. Petersburg, or Budapest could relate stories of growth as well as of depressions and poverty to prospective migrants in their regions of origin. Urbanization in Budapest or New York, Americanization, Canadianization, or Germanization involved acculturation from the bottom up as well as institutional accommodation from the top down.[59]

In Asia, socioeconomic developments within the societies and outside interference from the colonizing powers mobilized laboring men and women, as well as settler families. While many settler families moved to Malaysia, Assam, and Manchuria, individuals and merchants first joined the

Southeast Asian Chinese diaspora and then became part of the second phase of the Pacific migration system. Free and, subsequently, indentured migrants came to North America; indentured and, later, free migrants to Latin America, mainly from China and India, as well as in smaller numbers from Japan, Korea, and the Pacific islands. Filipinos and (East) Indians came from societies connected to North America through the new United States and the old British Empire, and the Dutch imported 30,000 Javanese workers from their Asian to their Caribbean possessions. In Cuba and Peru, Chinese lived in de facto enslavement, with extreme mortality rates. The roughly 1.75 million migrants and bound workers who reached the Caribbean from 1811 to 1916, in addition to slaves, included 550,000 from India, of whom fewer than one-third returned. Counting multiple migrations, some 600,000 immigrants from the eastern rim of the Pacific arrived in the United States between 1850 and 1920; and the Canadian census of 1921 counted 45,000 Chinese and Japanese and 10,500 East Indians (i.e., South Asian British subjects).[60]

In North America—as in Australia—the arrival of free Chinese began with the gold rushes in California in 1848 and in British Columbia in 1858. Thereafter Chinese migrated to rural communities or to new gold strikes from the Fraser River to the Black Hills. In Latin America, free Asian communities had emerged by the 1870s, and second-time indentured migrants moved between the Caribbean islands' many labor markets. Time-expired South Asian, Teochiu, Hokkien, and Cantonese workers became peasant proprietors, combined small-scale agriculture with temporary plantation wage-labor, or seized opportunities in small trading. A newly affluent elite brought family members and brides from India or China, and the first East Indian Caribbeans had been elected to legislatures by the time the system of indenture formally ended in 1917. Immigration of California Chinese merchants reinvigorated communities in Trinidad and Havana. Acculturation into heterogeneous Euro-African-Amerindian Caribbean societies proceeded by a gradual change of language, intermarriage or liaison, and the emergence of a community of mixed ancestry.[61]

In North America, segregation was rigid. A network of free immigrants anchored both migrants who had got their tickets on credit, and so had to work off their fares, and contract laborers, who were bound for several years. Their legal position resembled that of eighteenth-century European indentured workers, but they performed gang labor, and when their contracts were up, they faced solitary lives as restaurant and laundry owners in small towns from Colorado to Ontario or in market gardening in California and British Columbia. Some moved to Louisiana's Gulf fisheries, others were hired by Southern planters to replace slaves after 1865, and still others traveled to eastern factories. While the Chinese community remained predominantly male, Japanese men, prevented from sojourning and rotating by exclusion, sent for women to form families.[62] Whites clashed over race ideologies and economic interests. Industry supported continued immigration; labor unions, cultural gatekeepers, and governments restricted entry. In 1908, the Canadian government sought to deport Sikhs who held British citizenship and had served in the imperial armed forces or police as "colonial auxiliaries." As legal immigrants, they worked as lumberjacks and agriculture laborers in British Columbia. The government in London prevented the Dominion from transporting them to British Honduras (Belize).[63] A Euro-Asian contact (and conflict) zone developed both along the western Pacific rim and in plantation societies further to the east.

Canadian immigrant life writings, the multi-ethnic experience of, for example, Chicago workers, and Mexican-Sikh and French-Amerindian marriages indicate less ethnic and racial antagonism in everyday life than is expressed in published discourse. Amerindians were distant, but upon contact helpful; blacks sometimes commanded respect; Chinese were sensitive and supportive. Groups marginalized by Anglo-Canadian gatekeepers, like the Jews and French, also seem to have evoked no negative stereotyping in these sources. On the other hand, prairie Canadians viewed Americans as horsethieves and whiskey smugglers, the English as generally arrogant and often incompetent. Bottom-up views thus differed widely both from the top-down discourse of hegemonic "national" spokespersons and from the boundary establishment of ethnic intellectuals in the press. Such published sources, rather than everyday lives, have, however, long informed historians' interpretations.[64]

In the Pacific migration region, power relationships curtailed agency and changed patterns drastically in the decades from the 1880s to the 1930s. A mere twenty years after Great Britain had imposed free emigration on the unwilling Chinese government in the 1860s, race ideologues from North America to Australia demanded exclusion of migrants from Asia, labeled as clannish because of their self-help organizations, as criminal because of British-induced opium smoking, and as inscrutable because host populations did not understand their languages. Literacy tests were imposed on Japanese when fewer Japanese immigrants arrived on the U.S. West Coast annually than poorly educated European immigrants on the East Coast *daily*. The gatekeepers closed the gates for migrants from Asia in the 1880s, and for southern and eastern Europeans regarded as "less than white" in 1924. The latter's shades of white made segregation difficult, but it could be imposed on black migrants from the South in industrial cities. However, in both Canada and the United States, the locally born children of Asian immigrants were citizens.[65] While U.S. and Canadian bureaucrats devised elaborate measures of exclusion, the Chinese developed equally elaborate means of conceiving "paper" children to create eligibility slots for immigration. Enterprising Japanese turned to Brazil and Peru as destinations, where immigration from Asia and access to citizenship was curtailed only during the Depression.[66] In Asia, growing national consciousness forced the British government abolish the coolie trade when India's support was needed in World War I. Under 1940s wartime imperatives, both the United States and Canada began to revise their racist attitudes.[67]

MULTICULTURAL SOCIETIES AND NEW MIGRATION SYSTEMS

After 1937, Japanese and German imperialist expansion ended the century-long traditions of emigration in Asia and Europe forever. After World War II, the Euro-Atlantic migration system briefly channeled displaced persons from war-devastated countries to both the United States and Canada. But in the 1960s, except for Italians and Portuguese, transatlantic migration slowed down, and a century after the Afro-Atlantic system ended, the Euro-Atlantic one tapered off. It was replaced by two continental south-to-north labor migration systems from the southern littoral of the Mediterranean and the Caribbean world to Europe north of the Alpine mountain range and North America respectively. Subsequently, North African migrants from the southern half of the Mediterranean world joined the northward movement, in particular to France and Spain. The European share of total immigration to North America fell from under half in the United States in 1960, and in Canada in the late 1970s, to less than a third in the United States in 1970, and in Canada in 1985–89. New multicultural societies emerged, and historians are now challenged to incorporate the pasts of the societies from which twentieth-century migrants came, and twenty-first-century migrants will come, into the national histories of the United States, Canada, and other countries.

Three factors influenced the shift in geographical origins and the decline of distinct cultural regions in the United States and Canada. First, merit-based admissions and the aspirations of well-trained young people resulted in a "brain drain" in emigrant societies across the world. Proposals for compensation to the countries of origin, put forward by the Geneva-based International Labour Organization, have come to naught in view of the opposition of worldwide power hierarchies.[68] The culturally expansionist U.S. agenda of restructuring education systems in several partially dependent states has accelerated this type of migration. U.S.-trained educators and returning exchange students introduced new concepts, teaching materials, and ideologies in an intended multiplier effect. In an unintended consequence, permanent migration to the United States or other Western countries has increased among the educated middle classes of countries with internal shortages of professionals.[69] Second, sexuality and gender form part not only of the public ideological constructions of nations but of private life projects. The wartime liberating role of U.S. forces and their subsequent imperial reach resulted in 6,000 Chinese women entering the United States as the wives of U.S. soldiers in 1945, and 48,000 Japanese, 16,000 Filipina, and 8,000 Korean women arrived between 1952 and 1962. As citizens, they could sponsor near relatives.[70] Third, U.S. support for right-wing noncommunist governments generated large-scale movements of refugees. Southeast Asian migration increased during and after the U.S. military intervention in Indochina. Latin American refugees left after coups and to escape *la violencia,* right-wing death-squad terror often sponsored by governments, armies, or political parties, and often tacitly or openly supported by successive U.S. governments. Three million or more people had been uprooted when the U.S. Refugee Act of 1980 granted them "temporary protected status." Immigrant communities emerged and migration networks became self-sustaining. In distinction to the United States, Canada has not been involved in refugee generation but has accommodated refugees from across the world. In the 1990s, it has participated in efforts to reduce refugee-generation by sponsoring the anti-land-mine treaty and supporting a world court to prosecute human rights violations.[71]

Men and women from Latin America and the Philippines have been admitted to the United States in large numbers as seasonal agricultural workers and, given the relatively well-paying jobs of many North American women, domestics and caregivers (both unskilled occupations by the definition of employers and immigration bureaucracies). Some five million Mexican workers were recruited for labor in the United States from 1942 to 1964, when the government—like that of nineteenth-century British India—broadly acceded to planters' and ranchers' demands for labor. When official recruitment ended, the relationship between workers and growers had been established, and migrants continued to come and to be hired, whether documented or undocumented. By the late 1970s and early 1980s, Mexico and the Caribbean had become the largest sources of legal immigrants to the United States. In Canada, French-speaking migrants from Haiti (as well as from civil-war-torn Lebanon) enlarged the francophone Quebec population, and special programs encouraged the immigration of women, first from among Europe's displaced persons, then from English-speaking Caribbean islands, as domestics and caregivers. These women, although bound to stay in their first job for a specified period of time, subsequently held immigrant status.[72] U.S. immigration legislation, in contrast, has always combined a restrictive official policy with a "back door" for cheap labor, Aristide Zolberg notes; in the words of Demetrios Papademetriou, "capital has always been clearly at the controls."[73]

Continentwide northbound labor and refugee migrations have combined the two Americas and the Caribbean into one migration region. To the degree that the migrations are consequences of U.S. global political and military interventions, they are comparable to the Europe-bound reverse colonial migrations of the 1960s and 1970s. From Asia outward, a third phase of the Pacific migration system developed with industrialization in Japan and South Korea, middle-class educational achievements in India, and lack of employment in several Southeast Asian societies. Migration by Pacific Islanders originates primarily from Hawaii, Guam, and Samoa. Because of independent migration strategies, family reunion clauses, and labor market demands, women have accounted for a slight majority of the immigrants since 1945.[74]

For many families, migration to North America is intentionally transnational, and middle-class, well-educated migrants enter all segments of the economy. Hong Kong, for example, may remain a family's economic base, while Canada and the United States provide passports and education for parts of the family. None of this is new: for centuries migrant families have kept a base and migrated afar, while children have been sent off for education and training. What is new is the amount of funds being transferred and the contribution to the economic integration of the Pacific world. Westbound transpacific migration and travel brought businessmen to Hong Kong, Singapore, Manila, and Japan, and millions of American, Australian, and other Western men were stationed in Asia in wartime. The fashionable "Pacific Rim" concept implies an "orientalist" view unless the Asian and Australian perspective, with the Americas as the rim, is incorporated.[75]

As long as the Atlantic was the core of the global political economy and of knowledge distribution, it was clear to the hegemonic gatekeepers where east and west were. But the ethno-cultural composition of the gatekeepers is also changing. Immigrants from Third World countries to Canada increased from 8 percent of the total in the early 1960s to 50 percent by 1975.[76] Critical voices have warned of the "browning" or "Asianization" of North America, but opinion polls show widespread acceptance of the development. Toronto's population changed to a non-European-origin majority in 2000. In the United States in 1990, 20 percent of the population was of a "race" other than European, and 9 percent were Hispanic "of all races." Whiteness both as power and as many-shaded color has been constructed and reconstructed for several centuries, and new options are tested daily. Racialization is loosing its hold over economic interests and minds—although according to Anthony Richmond, "global apartheid" persists because of investment patterns and terms of trade.[77]

From the perspective of the migration of peoples, the emergence of cultural regions in the Americas and within North America and related changes and disruptions have resulted in an increasing number of new interactions in individual lives, all ethnic boundaries, color bars, and gatekeeper exclusion policies notwithstanding. Since most of the post-1960s migrants stay in the cities of the United States and Canada, the distinctiveness of the bicultural regions has changed. In the United States, the Hispanic belt and black and white societies have been supplemented and eclipsed by ethnic urban enclaves and interaction across the country. California has become a tricultural Euro-Hispanic-Asian society. Only the French elites of the St. Lawrence valley have pursued a discourse of separation and cultural survival. North American societies are not experiencing a disuniting, as Arthur M. Schlesinger Jr. despaired a decade ago, echoed by similar statements in Canada. Rather, they are witnessing the final collapse of minority claims to hegemony, institutional privileges, and structural preferences. To old elite-centered literary and national-political versions of history, first, the working classes were added, then women were included, then nonwhite immigrants. The historiography of a population segment arrogating to itself the definition of nationhood is evolving into a complex and inclusive history of societies.

The new "master narrative" is a people's history of North America that replaces the segmented institutional, political, or elite cultural ones. Although some, among them native blacks in the United States and recent Caribbean newcomers of African origin in Canada, still need to be given more access to the center, this new narrative includes transcultural perspectives from origins across the globe to region of settlement after migration. It terminates the *pars pro toto* equation of gatekeeper elites, whether Boston Brahmins, Beltway pundits, or Ottawa British. Historians reflect the shift of the power of definition rather than a disintegration of national character dating from the U.S. Founding Fathers or the Canadian Founding Peoples. Early in the twentieth century, the Reverend James S. Woodsworth, a critic of the exclusionist master narrative, called his Methodist mission in the immigrant neighborhoods of Winnipeg, Canada, the "All People's Mission." All people's history is the agenda at the turn of the twenty-first century.[78] The implications are multiple:

1. This new narrative displaces the geographies, political boundaries, and institutions that framed traditional interpretations and deals with origins on many continents, with migration systems, social spaces, and bi- or many-cultured regions.
2. It illustrates the rich complexity of structures constantly being remade ("processural structures"), of multiple opportunities and choice, of the agency of men, women, and children, bounded by economic and, especially in the twentieth century, political constraints.
3. It reveals the connections of family and community formation, of communities and regions, as well as of the particular cultures: one single cultural origin, a mosaic of distinct but neighboring cultures, hybrid intermixture, practiced multicultural lives. Such interactions

have most often emerged and emerge in a complex combination of freedom and constraint. But even in intermixture under duress, the hegemonic has not smothered the weak; rather, new cultural practices have been created, children of many backgrounds have been born, and entwined lives have emerged.

4. The new narrative also incorporates gender, race, or color of skin, including whiteness, class or social status, and intergenerational continuity and conflict. In particular periods, the relative importance of these categories has changed. While race's impact on social relations has shown a remarkable continuity in the United States, it has always been less important in Canada, and it has changed remarkably in both countries since the 1980s. Gender, too, still is a salient maker of power hierarchies and cultural practices.

No distinctiveness, even if buttressed by a position of power, secured by suburban walled-in compound living, or enforced by ghetto-style segregation, isolates people from the whole of the society in which they act and from their immediate neighbors. All people's history is at the same time many distinct people's histories.

NOTES

1. Henry F. Dobyns, "Estimating Aboriginal American Population: An Appraisal of Techniques with a New Hemispheric Estimate," *Current Anthropology* 7 (1966), 395–449. Nicolás Sánchez-Albornóz, *The Population of Latin America: A History*, trans. W. A. R. Richardson (Berkeley and Los Angeles, 1974). *Cultivation and Culture: Labor and the Shaping of Slave Life in the Americas*, ed. Ira Berlin and Philip D. Morgan (Charlottesville, Va., 1993). F. A. Golder, *Russian Expansion on the Pacific, 1641–1850* (1914; reprint, New York, 1971); S. B. Okun, *The Russian-American Company*, ed. B. D. Grekov, trans. Carl Ginsburg (Cambridge, Mass., 1951). Donna Gabaccia, *From the Other Side: Women, Gender and Immigrant Life in the U.S., 1820–1990* (Bloomington, Ind., 1994); Ronald Takaki, *Strangers from a Different Shore: A History of Asian Americans* (Boston, 1989); Sucheng Chan, *Asian Americans: An Interpretative History* (Boston, 1991).

2. David Thelen, "Of Audiences, Borderlands, and Comparisons: Toward the Internationalization of American History," *Journal of American History* 79 (1992), 432–62, quotation from p. 436.

3. The Grosse Isle quarantine station below Quebec City and the role of Halifax as a port of arrival since the 1920s received attention in public memory only in the 1990s. See also Roger Daniels, "No Lamps Were Lit for Them: Angel Island and the Historiography of Asian American Immigration," *Journal of American Ethnic History* 17 (1997): 3–18.

4. See, e.g., *Theoretical Advances in Life Course Research*, ed. Walter R. Heinz (Weinheim, Germany, 1991, 1997), 9–22.

5. In the Amerindian case, trading systems connected different societies and economies to one another.

6. James H. Jackson Jr. and Leslie Page Moch, "Migration and the Social History of Modern Europe," in *European Migrants: Global and Local Perspectives,* ed. Dirk Hoerder and Moch (Boston, 1996), 52–69; Walter Nugent, *Crossings: The Great Transatlantic Migrations, 1870–1914* (Bloomington, Ind., 1992), 96. For other "systems approaches," see *International Migration Systems: A Global Approach,* ed. Mary M. Kritz, Lin L. Lim, and Hania Zlotnik (Oxford, 1992), 1–16; Robert J. Kleiner et al., "International Migration and Internal Migration: A Comprehensive Theoretical Approach," in *Migration across Time and Nations: Population Mobility in Historical Context,* ed. Ira Glazier and Luigi de Rosa (New York, 1986), 305–17; James T. Fawcett and Fred Arnold, "Explaining Diversity: Asian and Pacific Immigration Systems," in *Pacific Bridges: The New Immigration from Asia and the Pacific Islands,* ed. James T. Fawcett and Benjamin V. Cariño (Staten Island, N.Y., 1987), 453–73.

7. Janet L. Abu-Lughod, *Before European Hegemony: The World System* A.D. 1250–1350 (New York, 1989); Alan K. Smith, *Creating a World Economy: Merchant Capital, Colonialism, and World Trade, 1400–1825* (Boulder, Colo., 1991); Immanuel M. Wallerstein, *The Modern World-System* (3 vols., New York, 1974–88); *The World System: Five Hundred Years or Five Thousand?* ed. André G. Frank and Barry K. Gills (New York, 1993); Eric R. Wolf, *Europe and the People without History* (Berkeley and Los Angeles, 1982, 1997); Philip D. Curtin, *Cross-Cultural Trade in World History* (New York, 1984). Ralph Davis, *The Rise of the Atlantic Economies* (London, 1973, reprint, 1982). *The Politics of Immigrant Workers: Labor Activism and Migration in the World Economy since 1830,* ed. Camille Guerin-Gonzales and Carl Strikwerda (New York, 1993); Kusha Haraksingh, "Culture, Religion and Resistance among Indians in the Caribbean," in *Slavery in South West Indian Ocean,* ed. U. Bissoondoyal and S. B. C. Servansing (Moka, Mauritius, 1989), 223–37.

8. Louise A. Tilly and Joan W. Scott, *Women, Work and Family* (New York, 1978); Dirk Hoerder, "Migrants to Ethnics: Acculturation in a Societal Framework," in *European Migrants,* ed. Hoerder and Moch, 211–62. "Acculturation" implies a move of culturally formed persons, who change themselves, into a receiving society that adapts—if only to a very limited degree—to the newcomers. "Assimilation," in contrast, is understood as a surrender of premigration traits. "Integration" refers to help offered by receiving societies, and "insertion" to migrants' self-fitting into niches or enclaves.

9. Anthony Pagden, *European Encounters with the New World* (New Haven, Conn., 1993), and, *The Fall of Natural Man: The American Indian and the Origins of Comparative Ethnology* (Cambridge, 1982); *The Classical Tradition and the Americas,* ed. Wolfgang Haase and Reinhold Meyer (2 vols., Berlin, 1994), vol. 1: *European Images of the Americas and the Classical Tradition;* Helmut Reinicke, *Wilde Kälten 1492. Die Entdeckung Europas* (Frankfurt a./M., 1992); Tzvetan Todorov, *The Conquest of America: The Question of the Other,* trans. Richard Howard (Paris, 1982; New York, 1985).

10. Harold A. Innis, *The Fur Trade in Canada* (1930; reprint, Toronto, 1956); James Forsyth, *A History of the People of Siberia: Russia's North Asian Colony, 1581–1990* (Cambridge, 1992).

11. Nugent, *Crossings;* Dirk Hoerder, "Migration in the Atlantic Economies: Regional European Origins and Worldwide Expansion," in *European Migrants,* ed. Hoerder and Moch, 21–51. *Gli Italiani fuori d'Italia: Gli emigrati italiani nei movimenti operai dei paesi d'adozione, 1880–1940,* ed. Bruno Bezza (Milan, 1983); Donna Gabaccia, *Italy's Many Diasporas* (Seattle, 2000). Similarly, worldwide diasporas of Polish, Irish, Jewish, and Chinese laborers developed.

12. Ira Berlin, "From Creole to African: Atlantic Creoles and the Origins of African-American Society in Mainland North America," *William and Mary Quarterly* 53 (1996): 251–88; Herbert S. Klein, *The Middle Passage: Comparative Studies in the Atlantic Slave Trade* (Princeton, N.J., 1978); Patrick Manning, *Slavery and African Life: Occidental, Oriental and African Slave Trades* (Cambridge, 1990); *The African Diaspora: Interpretive Essays,* ed. Martin L. Kilson and Robert I. Rotberg (Cambridge, Mass., 1976); Joseph E. Harris, *Global Dimensions of the African Diaspora* (Washington, D.C., 1982); Paul Gilroy, *The Black Atlantic: Modernity and Double Consciousness* (Cambridge, Mass., 1993).

13. Hoerder, *Cultures in Contact,* chs. 8.4, 15, 19.5.

14. Lester D. Langley, *The Americas in the Age of Revolution, 1750–1850* (New Haven, Conn., 1996); Bonham C. Richardson, "Caribbean Migrations, 1838–1985," in *The Modern Caribbean,* ed. Franklin W. Knight and Colin A. Palmer (Chapel Hill, N.C., 1989), 203–28; Elizabeth M. Petras, *Jamaican Labor Migration: White Capital and Black Labor, 1850–1930* (Boulder, Colo.: 1988); Jorge Balán, "International Migration in Latin America: Trends and Consequences," in *International Migration Today,* ed. Reginald T. Appleyard and Charles Stahl (2 vols., Paris, 1988), 1: 210–63.

15. Silvio A. Zavala, *Los esclavos indios en nueva España* (Mexico, 1968); William L. Sherman, *Forced Native Labor in Sixteenth-Century Central America* (Lincoln, Neb., 1979); O. Nigel Bolland, "Colonization and Slavery in Central America," in *Unfree Labour in the Development of the Atlantic World,* ed. Paul E. Lovejoy and Nicholas Rogers (Ilford, U.K., 1994), 11–25; Thomas Gomez, *L'envers de l'eldorado: Economie coloniale et travail indigène dans la Colombie du XVIème siècle* (Toulouse, 1984).

16. Robert J. Steinfeld, *The Invention of Free Labor: The Employment Relation in English and American Law and Culture, 1350–1870* (Chapel Hill, N.C., 1991). David W. Galenson, "Labor Market Behavior in Colonial America: Servitude, Slavery, and Free Labor," in *Markets in History: Economic Studies of the Past,* ed. id. (Cambridge, 1990), 93–94; Paul Craven and Douglas Hay, "The Criminalization of 'Free' Labour: Master and Servant in Comparative Perspective," in *Unfree Labour,* ed. Lovejoy and Rogers, 71–101.

17. As late as the decades from the 1880s to the 1920s, British population planners attempted to get "surplus" people out of the country, including women with no prospect of marriage, men with wartime or other disabilities, children of the poor, and orphans.

18. Edmund S. Morgan, *American Slavery, American Freedom: The Ordeal of Colonial Virginia* (New York, 1975), 79–97, and Morgan, "The Labor Problem at Jamestown," *American Historical Review* 76 (1971): 595–611. Ruth Pike, *Penal Servitude in Early Modern Spain* (Madison, Wis., 1983); A. Roger Ekirch, *Bound for America: The Transportation of British Convicts to the Colonies, 1718–1775* (Oxford, 1987); *Representing*

Convicts: New Perspectives on Convict Forced LabourMigration, ed. Ian Duffield and James Bradley (Leicester, 1997).

19. The Portuguese and Spanish societies did not practice indentured servitude. In the English colonies, the system ended in the 1820s. Piet C. Emmer, "European Expansion and Migration: The European Colonial Past and Intercontinental Migration—An Overview," in *European Expansion and Migration: Essays on the Intercontinental Migration from Africa, Asia, and Europe,* ed. id. and Magnus Mörner (New York, 1992), 3; Abbot E. Smith, *Colonists in Bondage: White Servitude and Convict Labor in America, 1607–1776* (Chapel Hill, N.C., 1947), 336; David W. Galenson, *White Servitude in Colonial America: An Economic Analysis* (Cambridge, 1981); Farley Grubb, "The Incidence of Servitude in Trans-Atlantic Migration, 1771–1801," *Explorations in Economic History* 22 (1985): 316–39. A summary of research is provided in *Colonialism and Migration: Indentured Labour before and after Slavery,* ed. Piet C. Emmer (Dordrecht, 1986), 19–122.

20. William L. Schurz, *The Manila Galleon* (New York, 1959), 5–50; Charles F. Nunn, *Foreign Immigrants in Early Bourbon Mexico, 1700–1760* (Cambridge, 1979), 4; John M. Liu, "A Comparative View of Asian Immigration to the USA," in *The Cambridge Survey of World Migration,* ed. Robin Cohen (Cambridge, 1995), 253–59. Evelyn Hu-DeHart, "Latin America in Asia-Pacific Perspective," in *What Is in a Rim? Critical Perspectives on the Pacific Region Idea,* ed. Arif Dirlik (1993; 2d ed., Lanham, Md., 1998), 251–82.

21. Philip D. Curtin, *The Tropical Atlantic in the Age of the Slave Trade* (Washington, D.C., 1991), quotation from p. 13; Robert L. Stein, *The French Slave Trade in the Eighteenth Century: An Old Regime Business* (Madison, Wis., 1979), 3–6. Hugh Thomas, *The Slave Trade: The Story of the Atlantic Trade, 1440–1870* (New York, 1997); Robin Blackburn, *The Making of New World Slavery: From the Baroque to the Modern, 1942–1800* (London, 1987). David B. Davis, *The Problem of Slavery in Western Culture* (Ithaca, N.Y., 1966), and *The Problems of Slavery in the Age of Revolution, 1770–1823* (Ithaca, N.Y., 1975), remain the best comparative analyses.

22. David Watts, *The West Indies: Patterns of Development, Culture, and Environmental Change since 1492* (Cambridge, 1987), 44–53; Franklin W. Knight, *The Caribbean: The Genesis of a Fragmented Nationalism* (New York, 1978), 23–49, quotation from p. 49.

23. Nicolás Sánchez-Albornoz, "The Population of Spanish America," in *The Cambridge History of Latin America,* ed. Leslie Bethell (Cambridge, 1984), 2: 73; Maria L. Marcílio, "The Population of Colonial Brazil," in ibid., 2: 45–52; Katia M. de Queiros Mattoso, *To Be Slave in Brazil, 1550–1880* (4th ed., New Brunswick, N.J.: 1994), 12–69; Mieko Nishida, "Manumission and Ethnicity in Urban Slavery: Salvador, Brazil, 1808–1888," *Hispanic American Historical Review* 73 (1993), 361–91, quotation from p. 374.

24. Piet C. Emmer, "Immigration into the Caribbean: The Introduction of Chinese and East Indian Indentured Laborers between 1839–1917," in *European Expansion and Migration,* ed. id. and Mörner, 245–76, esp. 245–47. Philip D. Curtin, *The Atlantic Slave Trade: A Census* (Madison, Wis., 1969), 47–49, 119, 268, table 77; Robert E. Conrad, *World of Sorrow: The African Slave Trade to Brazil* (Baton Rouge, 1986), 34; Rolando Mellafe, *Negro Slavery in Latin America,* trans. J. W. S. Judge (Berkeley and Los Angeles, 1975), 73; Herbert S. Klein, *African Slavery in Latin*

America and the Caribbean (New York, 1986); Joseph E. Inikori and Stanley L. Engerman, *The Atlantic Slave Trade: Effects on Economies, Societies, and Peoples in Africa, the Americas, and Europe* (Durham, N.C., 1992), 83–84, 95; Fredrick P. Bowser, "Africans in Spanish American Colonial Society," in *Cambridge History of Latin America,* 2: 365.

25. Barbara Bush, *Slave Women in Caribbean Society, 1650–1838* (Bloomington, Ind., 1990), 1–50; Barry W. Higman, *Slave Populations of the British Caribbean, 1897–1834* (Baltimore, 1974); Richard B. Sheridan, "Slave Demography in the British West Indies and the Abolition of the Slave Trade," in *The Abolition of the Atlantic Slave Trade: Origins and Effects in Europe, Africa, and the Americas,* ed. David Eltis and James Walvin (Madison, Wis., 1981), 259–85; John Thornton, *Africa and Africans in the Making of the Atlantic World, 1400–1680* (Cambridge, 1992), 167–68. In the mentality of mobility-restricting clauses imposed on Europe's lower classes, one English governor called free Afro-Americans "unappropriated people." Jerome S. Handler, *The Unappropriated People: Freedmen in the Slave Society in Barbados* (Baltimore, 1974).

26. Bowser, "Africans in Spanish American Colonial Society," quotation from p. 367; id., *The African Slave in Colonial Peru, 1524–1650* (Stanford, Calif., 1974), 5–103; Ana Maria Barros dos Santos, "Quilombos: Sklavenaufstände im Brasilien des 17. Jahrhunderts," in *Amerikaner wider Willen: Beiträge zur Sklaverei in Lateinamerika und ihren Folgen,* ed. Rüdiger Zoller (Frankfurt a./M., 1994), 161–73; A. J. R. Russell-Wood, *Black Man in Slavery and Freedom in Colonial Brazil* (New York, 1982), 105–25; Jürgen Hell, *Sklavenmanufaktur und Sklavenemanzipation in Brasilien, 1500–1588* (Berlin, 1986), 108–26; Frank Tannenbaum, *Slave and Citizen: The Negro in the Americas* (New York, 1946), 43ff., 97–98; Nishida, "Manumission and Ethnicity," 374–86; R. K. Kent, "African Revolt in Bahia: 15–24 January 1835," *Journ. Soc. Hist.* 3 (1969–70), 334–56.

27. John Hope Franklin, *From Slavery to Freedom: A History of Negro Americans* (1947; 3d rev. ed., New York, 1967), 60–70, provided a repeatedly updated valuable synthesis early. On black community and family formation, see E. Genovese, H. G. Gutman, and G. Rawick among others. Peter Wood, *Black Majority: Negroes in Colonial South Carolina from 1670 through the Stono Rebellion* [1739] (New York, 1974); Philip D. Curtin, "The Tropical Atlantic in the Age of Slave Trade," in *Islamic and European Expansion: The Forging of a Global Order,* ed. Michael Adas (Philadelphia, 1993), 165–97; Elizabeth Fox-Genovese, *Within the Plantation Household: Black and White Women of the Old South* (Chapel Hill, N.C., 1988); Herbert G. Gutman, *The Black Family in Slavery and Freedom, 1750–1925* (New York, 1976); Jacqueline Jones, *Labor of Love, Labor of Sorrow: Black Women, Work, and the Family from Slavery to the Present* (New York, 1985); Lawrence W. Levine, *Black Culture and Black Consciousness: Afro-American Folk Thought from Slavery to Freedom* (New York, 1977); *More than Chattel: Black Women and Slavery in the Americas,* ed. David Barry Gaspar and Darlene Clark Hine (Bloomington, Ind., 1996).

28. Robin W. Winks, *The Blacks in Canada: A History* (New Haven, Conn., 1971).

29. Jerome S. Handler, "Slave Revolts and Conspiracies in Seventeenth-Century Barbados," *Nieuwe West-Indische Gids* (Utrecht) 65, 1–2 (1982): 5–42; Herbert Aptheker, *American Negro Slave Revolts* (1943; 2d ed., New York, 1969); Alice H. Bauer and Raymond A. Bauer, "Day to Day Resistance to Slavery," *Journ. Negro Hist.* 27

(1942), 388–419; Eugene D. Genovese, *From Rebellion to Revolution. Afro-American Slave Revolts in the Making of the New World* (Baton Rouge, La., 1979); O. Nigel Bolland, "Colonization and Slavery in Central America," in *Unfree Labour,* ed. Lovejoy and Rogers, 11–25, esp. 20.

30. Alfred N. Hunt, *Haiti's Influence on Antebellum America* (Baton Rouge, La., 1988); Daniel F. Littlefield, *Africans and Seminoles: from Removal to Emancipation* (Westport, Conn., 1977); David Eltis, *Economic Growth and the Ending of the Transatlantic Slave Trade* (New York, 1987); Martin A. Klein, "Slavery, the International Labour Market and the Emancipation of Slaves in the Nineteenth Century," in *Unfree Labour,* ed. Lovejoy and Rogers, 197–220; Michèle Duchet, "Reactions to the Problem of the Slave Trade: An Historical and Ideological Study," in UNESCO, *The African Slave Trade from the Fifteenth to Nineteenth Century* (Paris, 1979), 31–54; Seymour Drescher, "The Ending of the Slave Trade and the Evolution of European Scientific Racism," in *African Slavery in Latin America and the Caribbean,* ed. Herbert S. Klein (New York, 1986); Joseph E. Inikori and Stanley L. Engerman, *The Atlantic Slave Trade: Effects on Economies, Societies, and Peoples in Africa, the Americas, and Europe* (Durham, N.C., 1992); Robin Blackburn, *The Overthrow of Colonial Slavery* (London, 1988).

31. J. Hector St. John de Crèvecoeur, *Letters from an American Farmer* (1782).

32. Walton Look Lai, *Indentured Labor, Caribbean Sugar: Chinese and Indian Migrants to the British West Indies, 1838–1918* (Baltimore, 1993), 1–18; Keith O. Laurence, *Immigration into the West Indies in the Nineteenth Century* (Barbados, 1971); David Eltis, "The Traffic in Slaves between the British West Indian Colonies, 1807–1833," *Econ. Hist. Rev.* 25 (1972), 55–64; *Between Slavery and Free Labor: The Spanish-Speaking Caribbean in the Nineteenth Century,* ed. Manuel M. Fraginals, Frank M. Pons, and Stanley L. Engerman (Baltimore, 1985).

33. Hugh Tinker, *A New System of Slavery: The Export of Indian Labour Overseas, 1830–1920* (London, 1974); Wolf, *People without History.*

34. The extensive literature on Maroon/Cimarrón communities has received little attention among historians of nation-building in the Americas. The classic collection is *Maroon Societies: Rebel Slave Communities in the Americas,* ed. Richard Price (Baltimore, 1979). See also *Out of the House of Bondage: Runaways, Resistance and Marronage in Africa and the New World,* ed. Gad Heuman (London, 1985); *Maroon Heritage: Archaeological, Ethnographic and Historical Perspectives,* ed. E. Kofi Agorsah (Kingston, 1994); Pedro D. Chapeaux, "Cimarrones Urbanos," *Revista de la Biblioteca Nacional* José Martí 2 (1969), 145–64; Gabriel Debien, "Le Marronage aux Antilles françaises au XVIIIe siècle," *Caribbean Stud.* 6 (1966), 3–44; Mavis C. Campbell, "The Maroons of Jamaica: Imperium in Imperio?" *Pan-African Journ.* 6 (1973), 45–55. Seymour M. Lipset, *The First New Nation: The United States in Historical and Comparative Perspective* (New York, 1963).

35. On nation-building and formation of national consciousness, see Benedict Anderson, *Imagined Communities: Reflections on the Origin and Spread of Nationalism* (London 1983); *The Invention of Tradition,* ed. Eric J. Hobsbawn and Terence Ranger (Cambridge, 1983); Miroslav Hroch, *Social Preconditions of National Revival in Europe* (Cambridge, 1985); Dirk Hoerder, and Inge Blank, "Ethnic and National Consciousness from the Enlightenment to the 1880s," in *Roots of the Transplanted,* ed. Hoerder et al. (2 vols., New York, 1994), 1: 37–110; Tania R. de Luca, "Ethnic

Progress and Civilization: Challengers to the Nation [in Brazil]" (paper given at the European Social Science History Conference, Amsterdam, March 1998).

36. Gary B. Nash, *Red, White, and Black: The Peoples of Early America* (Englewood Cliffs, N.J., 1974); *La résistance indienne aux États-Unis: XVIe–XXe siècle*, ed. Élise Marienstras (Paris, 1980), 41–102. Annette Rosenstiel, *Red and White: Indian Views of the White Man, 1492–1982* (New York, 1983); J. Norman Heard, *White into Red: A Study of the Assimilation of White Persons Captured by Indians* (Metuchen, N.J., 1973); *The Indian and the White Man*, ed. Wilcomb E. Washburn (Garden City, N.Y., 1964); James W. Covington, *The Seminoles of Florida* (Gainesville, Fla., 1993).

37. D. N. Sprague, *Canada and the Métis, 1869–1885* (Waterloo, 1988); Jennifer S. H. Brown, *Strangers in Blood: Fur Trade Company Families in Indian Country* (Vancouver, 1980); *The New People: Being and Becoming Métis in North America*, ed. Jennifer S. H. Brown (Vancouver, 1985); Sylvia Van Kirk, *"Many Tender Ties": Women in Fur Trade Society in Western Canada, 1670–1870* (Winnipeg, 1980), and *Towards a Feminist Perspective in Native History* (Toronto, 1987); Adele Perry, *On the Edge of Empire: Gender, Race, and the Making of British Columbia, 1849–1871* (Toronto, 2001).

38. The three cultures along the Atlantic coast, francophone, mercantile, and slave are discussed in Marc Egnal, *Divergent Paths: How Culture and Institutions Have Shaped North America* (Oxford, 1996). See also Joel Garreau, *The Nine Nations of North America* (Boston, 1981).

39. Clarence E. Glick, *Sojourners and Settlers. Chinese Migrants in Hawaii* (Honolulu, 1980); John M. Liu, "Race, Ethnicity, and the Sugar Plantation System: Asian Labor in Hawaii, 1850 to 1900," in *Labor Immigration under Capitalism: Asian Workers in the United States before World War II*, ed. Lucie Cheng and Edna Bonacich (Berkeley and Los Angeles, 1984), 186–209, and Liu, "Comparative View," 253–59; Ronald Takaki, *Pau Hana: Plantation Life and Labor in Hawaii, 1835–1920* (Honolulu, 1983).

40. Eugene D. Genovese, *The World the Slaveholders Made: Two Essays in Interpretation* (New York, 1969), and *Roll, Jordan, Roll. The World the Slaves Made* (1972; reprint, New York, 1976); Gilberto Freyre, *The Masters and the Slaves: A Study in the Development of Brazilian Civilization*, trans. Samuel Putnam (2d ed., New York, 1986); Zoller, *Amerikaner wider Willen*, 175–202, 203–30. Vincent Bakpetu Thompson, *The Making of the African Diaspora in the Americas, 1441–1900* (New York, 1987).

41. The territorial extension of modern Quebec is of relatively recent definition and includes both almost exclusively anglophone areas and Native American territories.

42. Frédéric Mauro, "French Indentured Servants for America, 1500–1800," in *Colonialism and Migration*, ed. Emmer 83–104; Peter Moogk, "Manon's Fellow Exiles: Emigration from France to North America before 1763," in *Europeans on the Move: Studies on European Migration, 1500–1800*, ed. Nicholas Canny (Oxford, 1994), 244–45; Leslie Choquette, *Frenchmen into Peasants: Modernity and Tradition in the Peopling of French Canada* (Cambridge, Mass., 1997).

43. *Les Acadiens des Maritimes: Études thématiques*, ed. Jean Daigle (1980), trans. as *The Acadians of the Maritimes: Thematic Studies* (Moncton, N.B., 1982) ; C. A. Brasseaux, *The Founding of New Acadia: The Beginnings of Acadian Life in Louisiana, 1765–1803* (Baton Rouge, La., 1987); *The Northeastern Borderlands: Four Centuries of Inter-*

action, ed. Victor Konrad, James Herlan, and Stephen Hornsby (Fredericton, N.B., 1989).

44. Jean-Pierre Poussou, "Les mouvements migratoires en France et à partir de la France de la fin du XVe siècle au début du XIXe siècle: Approches pour une synthèse," *Annales de démographie historique,* 1970, 11–78; François Weil, *Les Franco-Américains, 1860–1980* (Paris, 1989); Hubert Charbonneau et al., *Naissance d'une population: Les Français établis au Canada au XVIIe siècle* (Paris, 1987); Bruno Ramirez, *On the Move: French-Canadian and Italian Migrants in the North Atlantic Economy, 1860– 1914* (Toronto, 1991), published in French under the title *Par monts et par vaux: Migrants canadiens-français et italiens dans l'économie nord-atlantique, 1860–1914* (Quebec, 1991). Jean R. Burnet with Howard Palmer, *"Coming Canadians": An Introduction to a History of Canada's Peoples* (Toronto, 1988), 15–19; Donald Greer, *The Incidence of Emigration during the French Revolution* (Cambridge, 1951).

45. The early settlers quelled the resident Acoma Pueblo people's opposition (which they styled "rebellion") by cutting off the right feet of 24 captive warriors. The gold rush migrants included some 8,000 Mexicans from Sonora and 5,000 Chileans and Peruvians. *New York Times,* 3 May 1998, 19. See also Evelyn Hu-DeHart, "Nativism and the New World Order" (MS, Duke University, 1995).

46. Matt S. Meier and Feliciano Rivera, *Mexican Americans / American Mexicans: From Conquistadors to Chicanos* (1993), 103–58.

47. Dirk Hoerder, "Ethnic Studies in Canada from the 1880s to 1962: A Historiographical Perspective and Critique," *Canadian Ethnic Studies* 26, 1 (1994): 1– 18.

48. Thomas Dublin, *Women at Work: The Transformation of Work and Community in Lowell, Mass., 1826–1860* (New York, 1979); Robert S. Starobin, *Industrial Slavery in the Old South* (New York, 1970); Charles B. Dew, "Black Ironworkers and the Slave Insurrection Panic of 1856," *Journal of Southern History* 41 (1975): 321–38; Fred A. Shannon, "A Post-Mortem on the Labor-Safety-Valve Theory" (1945), reprinted in *Turner and the Sociology of the Frontier,* ed. Richard Hofstadter and Seymour M. Lipset (New York, 1968), 172–86.

49. Massachusetts Bureau of the Statistics of Labor, *Twelfth Annual Report, 1881,* 469–70; Marcus L. Hansen with John B. Brebner, *The Mingling of the Canadian and American Peoples* (New Haven, Conn., 1940); R. W. Coats and M. C. MacLean, *The American-Born in Canada* (Toronto, 1943); Donna Gabaccia, "The 'Yellow Peril' and the 'Chinese of Europe': Global Perspectives on Race and Labor, 1815–1930," in *Migrations, Migration History, History: Old Paradigms and New Perspectives,* ed. Jan Lucassen and Leo Lucassen (Bern, 1997), 177–96; *The First Franco-Americans: New England Life Histories from the Federal Writers' Project, 1938–1939,* ed. C. Stewart Doty (Orono, Me., 1985); Jacques Rouillard, *Ah les Etats! Les travailleurs canadiens-français dans l'industrie textile de la Nouvelle-Angleterre d'après le témoignage des derniers migrants* (Montreal, 1985).

50. The cross-border migrations along the 49th parallel and the Rio Grande led a U.S. scholar of population movements to speculate whether they "would result in the transfer of a considerable portion of the territory of the United States to Mexico and Canada," as had happened after the plebiscites in the borderlands of the shrinking German empire in 1918. Maurice R. Davie, *World Immigration with Special Refer-*

ence to the United States (New York, 1936), 208–22, quoting Niles Carpenter, *Immigrants and Their Children, 1920,* Census Monographs, 7 (Washington, D.C., 1927), 129.

51. Meier and Rivera, *Mexican Americans,* 115–33; Abraham Hoffman, "Stimulus to Repatriation: The 1931 Federal Deportation Drive and the Los Angeles Mexican Community," *Pacific Hist. Rev.* 42 (1973): 205–19; Juan Gómez-Quiñones, "The First Steps: Chicano Labor Conflict and Organizing 1900–1920," *Aztlan* 3, 1 (1973): 13–50; Kitty Calavita, "Mexican Immigration to the USA: The Contradictions of Border Control," in *Cambridge Survey,* ed. Cohen, 236–44, citing Dillingham Commission, p. 236. Ulrich Herbert, *A History of Foreign Labor in Germany, 1880–1980* (German orig. 1986; Ann Arbor, 1990), 46–81.

52. The preceding westward migration has been analyzed by William L. Katz, *The Black West* (Garden City, N.Y., 1971); Kenneth W. Porter, *The Negro on the American Frontier* (New York, 1971); W. Sherman Savage, *Blacks in the West* (to 1890) (Westport, Conn., 1976).

53. Daniel M. Johnson and Rex R. Campbell, *Black Migration in America: A Social Demographic History* (Durham, N.C., 1981), provide a concise survey. Nell I. Painter, *Exodusters: Black Migration to Kansas after Reconstruction* (rev. ed., Lawrence, Kans., 1986); Spencer R. Crew, *Field to Factory: Afro-American Migration, 1915–1940* (Washington, D.C., 1987); Florette Henri, *Black Migration: Movement North, 1900–1920* (Garden City, N.Y., 1975); Carole Marks, Farewell—*We're Good and Gone: The Great Black Migration* (Bloomington, Ind., 1989); *The Great Migration in Historical Perspective. New Dimensions of Race, Class, and Gender,* ed. Joe W. Trotter Jr. (Bloomington, Ind., 1991); Nicholas Lemann, *The Promised Land: The Great Black Migration and How It Changed America* (New York, 1991), continues the story from 1940 to 1970, when five million black men, women, and children left a rural South still lacking democratic institutions as well as jobs.

54. Bonham C. Richardson, *The Caribbean and the Wider World: 1492–1992. A Regional Geography* (Cambridge, 1992), 132–42; Elizabeth M. Petras, *Jamaican Labor Migration: White Capital and Black Labor, 1850–1930* (Boulder, Colo., 1988); Alan B. Simmons and Jean Pierre Guengnat, "Caribbean Exodus and the World System," in *International Migration Systems,* ed. Kritz et al., 94–114. For subsequent migrations, see *International Migration in Latin America,* special issue ed. Mary M. Kritz and Douglas T. Gurak, *Intl. Migration Rev.* 13 (New York, 1979); Aristide Zolberg and Robert C. Smith, *Migration Systems in Comparative Perspective: An Analysis of the Inter-American Migration System with Comparative Reference to the Mediterranean European System* (Washington, D.C., 1996). Harold Troper, *Only Farmers Need Apply: Official Canadian Government Encouragement of Immigration from the United States, 1896–1911* (Toronto, 1972).

55. Dirk Hoerder, "Immigration and the Working Class: The Remigration Factor," *Intern. Labor and Working Class Hist.* 21 (1982), 28–41; Mark Wyman, *Round-Trip to America: The Immigrants Return to Europe, 1880–1930* (Ithaca, N.Y., 1993); Arno Armgort, *Bremen–Bremerhaven–New York* (Bremen, 1992); *Fame, Fortune and Sweet Liberty: The Great European Emigration,* ed. Dirk Hoerder and Diethelm Knauf, trans. Thomas Kozak (Bremen, 1992).

56. *International Migrations,* ed. Walter F. Willcox, Imre Ferenczi, et al. (2 vols.,

New York, 1929–31); *Historical Statistics of the United States* (2 vols., Washington, D.C., 1976), series U 183.

57. Edwin S. Redkey, *Black Exodus: Black Nationalist and Back-to-Africa Movements, 1890–1910* (New Haven, Conn., 1969); Dan Hill, "The Blacks in Toronto," in *Gathering Place. Peoples and Neighbourhoods of Toronto, 1834–1945*, ed. Robert F. Harney (Toronto, 1985), 75–105; Rodolfo Acuña, *Occupied America. A History of Chicanos* (2d ed., New York, 1981), 123–54; *Hitting Home: The Great Depression in Town and Country*, ed. Bernard Sternsher (Chicago, 1970).

58. Isaiah Bowman, *The Pioneer Fringe* (New York, 1991); *Pioneer Settlement: Cooperative Studies*, ed. W. L. G. Joerg (New York, 1932); *Jews of the American West*, eds. Moses Rischin and John Livingston (Detroit, 1991). Ray A. Billington, *The American Frontier Thesis: Attack and Defense* (Washington, D.C., 1958; reprint, 1971); John Bodnar, *The Transplanted: A History of Immigrants in Urban America* (Bloomington, Ind., 1985); Roger Daniels, *Coming to America: A History of Immigration and Ethnicity in American Life* (New York, 1990); Gabaccia, *From the Other Side.*

59. *Peasant Maids, City Women. From the European Countryside to Chicago*, ed. Christiane Harzig (Ithaca, N.Y., 1997); James R. Grossmann, *Land of Hope: Chicago, Black Southerners, and the Great Migration* (Chicago, 1989); Dirk Hoerder, "Migrants to Ethnics," 211–62; James R. Barrett, "Americanization from the Bottom Up: Immigration and the Remaking of the Working Class in the United States, 1880–1930," *Journ. Am. Hist.* 79 (1992), 997–1020; Catherine Collomp and Marianne Debouzy, "European Migrants and the U.S. Labor Movement 1880s-1920s," in *Roots of the Transplanted*, ed. Hoerder et al., 2: 339–81; Donald Avery and Bruno Ramirez, "European Immigrant Workers in Canada: Ethnicity, Militancy and State Repression," in ibid., 2: 411–40; Donald H. Avery, *Reluctant Host: Canada's Response to Immigrant Workers, 1896–1994* (Toronto, 1995); John Bodnar, *Workers' World: Kinship, Community and Protest in an Industrial Society, 1900–1940* (Baltimore, 1982).

60. Piet C. Emmer, "Immigration into the Caribbean: The Introduction of Chinese and East Indian Indentured Laborers between 1839–1917," in *European Expansion and Migration*, ed. id. and Magnus Mörner, 245–76, esp. 245–47; Basdeo Mangru, *Benevolent Neutrality: Indian Government Policy and Labour Migration to British Guiana, 1854–1884* (London, 1987), 13, passim; Bruno Lasker, *Filipino Immigration to Continental United States and to Hawaii* (Chicago, 1931); John S. Furnivall, *Netherlands East Indies: A Study of a Plural Society* (Cambridge, 1944); *The Cuba Commission Report: A Hidden History of the Chinese in Cuba*, ed. Denise Helly (Baltimore, 1993), 3–34; Duvon C. Corbitt, *A Study of the Chinese in Cuba, 1847–1947* (Wilmore, Ky., 1975); Evelyn Hu-DeHart, "Chinese Labour in Cuba in the Nineteenth Century: Free Labour or Slavery?" *Slavery and Abolition* 14, 1 (1993): 67–86; Philip D. Curtin, "Migration in the Tropical World," in *Immigration Reconsidered: History, Sociology, and Politics*, ed. Virginia Yans-McLaughlin (New York, 1990), 21–36, esp. 32.

61. Judy Yung, *Unbound Feet: A Social History of Chinese Women in San Francisco* (Berkeley and Los Angeles, 1995); *Chinese on the American Frontier*, ed. Arif Dirlik (Lanham, Md., 1997); Lai, *Indentured Labor*, 19–49, 52–153, 188–64; Judith Weller, *The East Indian Indenture in Trinidad* (Rio Piedras, P.R., 1968).

62. David Northrup, *Indentured Labor in the Age of Imperialism, 1834–1922* (Cambridge, 1995), 7; Gunther Barth, *Bitter Strength: A History of Chinese in the United States, 1850–1870* (Cambridge, Mass., 1964), 117–20; Alexander P. Saxton, *The Indispen-*

sable Enemy: Labor and the Anti-Chinese Movement in California (Berkeley and Los Angeles, 1971, 1995); James W. Loewen, *The Mississippi Chinese: Between Black and White* (1971; 2d. ed., Prospect Heights, Ill., 1988); Shih-Shan Henry Tsai, *The Chinese Experience in America* (Bloomington, Ind., 1986); Peter S. Li, *The Chinese in Canada* (Toronto, 1988), 11–40; Harry H. L. Kitano, "Japanese," in *Harvard Encyclopedia of American Ethnic Groups*, ed. Stephan Thernstrom, Ann Orlov, and Oscar Handlin (Cambridge, Mass., 1980), 561–71; W. Peter Ward, *The Japanese in Canada* (Ottawa, 1982); Ken Adachi, *The Enemy That Never Was: A History of the Japanese Canadians* (Toronto, 1976), 133–56.

63. Hugh Johnston, *The Voyage of the "Komagata Maru": The Sikh Challenge to Canada's Colour Bar* (Vancouver, 1989); Norman Buchignani, Doreen M. Indra, and Ram Srivastva, *Continuous Journey: A Social History of South Asians in Canada* (Toronto, 1985), 12–70; *The Sikh Diaspora: Migration and Experience Beyond Punjab*, ed. N. Gerald Barrier and Verne A. Dusenbery (Delhi, 1989); Karen I. Leonard, *Making Ethnic Choices: California's Punjabi Mexican Americans* (Philadelphia, 1992).

64. Hoerder, *Creating Societies*, ch. 13.

65. Roy L. Garis, *Immigration Restriction* (New York, 1927); John Higham, *Strangers in the Land: Patterns of American Nativism 1860–1925* (New Brunswick, N.J., 1955); Robert C. Brown, "Full Partnership in the Fortunes and in the Future of the Nation," *Nationalism and Ethnic Politics* (Fall 1995), 9–25; Neville Bennett, "Japanese Emigration Policy, 1880–1941," in *Asians in Australia: the Dynamics of Migration and Settlement*, ed. Christine Inglis et al. (Singapore, 1992), 32; Howard Palmer, *Patterns of Prejudice: A History of Nativism in Alberta* (Toronto, 1982), 17–60.

66. C. Harvey Gardiner, *The Japanese and Peru, 1873–1973* (Albuquerque, 1975), 22–41; Donald Hastings, "Japanese Emigration and Assimilation in Brazil," *Intl. Migr. Rev.* 3.2 (1969), 32–53.

67. India provided 1.2 million men as soldiers and laborers to the British war effort, and about 100,000 Chinese coolies labored in northern France. Hugh Tinker, *Separate and Unequal: India and the Indians in the British Commonwealth, 1920–1950* (London, 1976); Paul Bailey, *Chinese Labour on the Western Front* (Leicester, 1999); Sean Brawley, *White Peril: Foreign Relations and Asian Immigration to Australasia and North America, 1919–78* (Sydney, 1995).

68. The U.S. act still treated the Eastern and Western hemispheres differently. Hania Zlotnik, "Policies and Migration Trends in the North American System," in *International Migration, Refugee Flows and Human Rights in North America: The Impact of Free Trade and Restructuring*, ed. Alan B. Simmons (New York, 1996), 81–103. George J. Borjas and Richard B. Freeman, *Immigration and the Work Force: Economic Consequences for the United States and Source Areas* (Chicago, 1992).

69. Liu, "Comparative View," 253–59; John M. Liu, Paul M. Ong, Carolyn Rosenstein, "Dual Chain Migration: Post-1965 Filipino Immigration to the United States," *Intl. Migration Rev.* 25 (1991): 487–515.

70. Michael C. Thornton, "The Quiet Immigration: Foreign Spouses of U.S. Citizens, 1945–1985," in *Racially Mixed People in America*, ed. Maria P. P. Root (Newbury Park, Calif., 1992), 64–76.

71. Studies quoted in Alan B. Simmons, Sergio Diaz-Briquets, and Aprodicio A. Laguian, *Social Change and Internal Migration: A Review of Research Findings from Africa, Asia, and Latin America* (Ottawa, 1977), 80–81; Elizabeth G. Ferris, *The Central Amer-*

ican Refugees (New York, 1987); UNHCR, *The State of the World's Refugees, 1995: In Search of Solutions* (Oxford, 1995), 50–51, 72, 150–51; Aristide Zolberg, Astri Suhrke, and Sergio Aguayo, *Escape from Violence. Conflict and Refugee Crisis in the Developing World* (Oxford, 1989), 180–224; Naomi F. Zucker and Norman L. Zucker, "US Admission Policies towards Cuban and Haitian Migrants," in *Cambridge Survey,* ed. Cohen, 447–51; Doris M. Meissner, "Political Asylum, Sanctuary and Humanitarian Policy," in *The Moral Nation: Humanitarianism and U.S. Foreign Policy Today,* ed. Bruce Nichols and Gil Loescher (Notre Dame, Ind., 1989), 123–43.

72. *Maid in the Market: Women's Paid Domestic Labour,* ed. Wenona Giles and Sedef Arat-Koç (Halifax, 1994); Christiane Harzig, "'The Movement of 100 Girls:' 1950s Canadian Immigration Policy and the Market for Domestic Labour," *Zeitschrift für Kanada-Studien* 36 (1999): 131–46.

73. Aristide Zolberg, "The Main Gate and the Back Door: The Politics of American Immigration Policy, 1950–76" (paper presented at the Council on Foreign Relations, Washington, D.C., April 1978); Demetrios G. Papademetriou, "International Migration in North America and Western Europe: Trends and Consequences," in *International Migration Today,* ed. Appleyard and Stahl, 1: 311–79, quotation from p. 320; U.S. President's Commission on Migratory Labor, *Report on Migratory Labor in Agriculture* (Washington, D.C., 1951); *International Migration,* ed. Simmons, esp. Kathryn Kopinak, "Household, Gender and Migration in Mexican Maquiladoras: The Case of Nogales," 214–28.

74. Elliott R. Barkan, *Asian and Pacific Islander Migration to the United States. A Model of New Global Patterns* (Westport, Conn., 1992); Cathy A. Small, *Voyages: From Tongan Villages to American Suburbs* (Ithaca, N.Y., 1997); Appleyard, "International Migration in Asia and the Pacific," in *International Migration Today,* ed. Appleyard and Stahl, 1: 126; Bill Ong Hing, *Making and Remaking Asian America Through Immigration Policy, 1850–1990* (Stanford, Calif., 1993), 17–42, 79–138; John Salt, "Highly Skilled International Migrants, Careers and International Labour Markets," *Geoforum* 19 (1988), 387–99; Donna Gabaccia, "Women of the Mass Migrations: From Minority to Majority, 1820–1930," in *European Migrants,* ed. Hoerder and Moch, 90–111; Monica Boyd, "Female Migrant Labor in North America: Trends and Issues for the 1990s," in *International Migration,* ed. Simmons, 193–213, and "Immigrant Women in Canada," in *International Migration: The Female Experience,* ed. Rita J. Simon and Caroline B. Brettell (Totowa, N.J., 1986), 45–61.

75. See the essays by Arif Dirlik, Alexander Woodside, Bruce Cumings, and Donald M. Nonini in *What Is in a Rim? Critical Perspectives,* ed. Dirlik, 3–96.

76. Leon F. Bouvier and Anthony J. Agresta, "The Future Asian Population of the United States," in *Pacific Bridges,* ed. Fawcett and Cariño, 285–301; Ronald Skeldon, "East Asian Migration and the Changing World Order," in *Population Migration and the Changing World Order,* W. T. S. Gould and A. M. Findlay (Chichester, U.K., 1994), 173–93; Anthony H. Richmond, *Post-War Immigrants in Canada* (Toronto, 1967), and Richmond and Lawrence Lam, "Migration to Canada in the Post-War Period," in *Cambridge Survey,* ed. Cohen, 263–70; D. Chuenyan Lai, "Emigration to Canada: Its Dimensions and Impact on Hong Kong," in *Migration and the Transformation of Cultures,* ed. Jean Burnet et al. (Toronto, 1992), 241–52; C. Michael Lanphier, *A Study of Third World Immigrants* (Ottawa, 1979).

77. G. Reginald Daniel, "Beyond Black and White: The New Multiracial Con-

sciousness," in *Racially Mixed People,* ed. Root, 333–41; essays by Roderick J. Harrison and Claudette E. Bennett, William H. Frey, Barry R. Chiswick, and Teresa A. Sullivan in *State of the Union: America in the 1990s,* ed. Reynolds Farley (2 vols., New York, 1995), 2: 141–336; Richard D. Alba, *Ethnic Identity: The Transformation of White America* (New Haven, Conn., 1990); Mary C. Waters, *Ethnic Options: Choosing Identities in America* (Berkeley and Los Angeles, 1987); Sharon M. Lee, "Racial Classification in the U.S. Census: 1890–1990," *Ethnic and Racial Studies* 16, 1 (January 1993): 75–94; Angus Reid Group, *Multiculturalism and Citizenship: National Attitude Survey, 1991* (Ottawa, 1991); Jeffrey G. Reitz and Raymond Breton, *The Illusion of Difference: Realities of Ethnicity in Canada and the United States* (Toronto, 1994); Report to the Toronto City Council, June 1998; Philip L. Martin, "Trade and Migration: The Case of NAFTA," *Asian and Pacific Migration Journal* 2 (1993): 329–67; *American Mixed Race: The Culture of Microdiversity,* ed. Naomi Zack (Lanham, Md., 1995); Anthony H. Richmond, *Global Apartheid: Refugees, Racism, and the New World Order* (Toronto, 1994).

78. Arthur M. Schlesinger Jr., *The Disuniting of America: Reflections on a Multicultural Society* (New York, 1991); James S. Woodsworth, *Strangers within Our Gates, or Coming Canadians* (Winnipeg, 1909; reprint of 2d ed., Toronto, 1972).

NINE

Framing U.S. History
Democracy, Nationalism, and Socialism

Robert Wiebe

What follows, it scarcely need be said, is no more than the sketch of how we might situate the history of the United States in a transoceanic context. Just as obviously, it is a choice among many possible frameworks, one that spotlights some people and some subjects as it shades others. It gives preference to Europe and North America over the rest of the world, the free over the enslaved, and men over women. If it incorporates eighteenth-century history as a running start, it ignores the seventeenth. As compensation, it allows us to think about the Western world's three most powerful modern movements as interactive aspects of a common transoceanic process. During the nineteenth and twentieth centuries, no substantial group living between the western boundaries of Russia and the United States escaped their influence; in the twentieth century, no substantial group anywhere in the world could avoid the repercussions.

After centuries of erratic ups and downs, Europe's population doubled between the mid eighteenth and late nineteenth centuries. As William McNeill has explained it, Europe's disease pool stabilized, protecting the young in particular against epidemic disaster, and its food resources diversified, increasing caloric intakes and thereby enabling more people to survive on the same land. Nevertheless, population pressures continued to mount, with the overflows pouring out of swollen villages in search of work, often to live and die in the cities. Then, in a second phase of the demo-

For their thoughtful comments, I am grateful to those who attended the La Pietra Conference of July 1999, especially François Weil; to participants in the History Seminar of May 2000 at the John F. Kennedy Institute of the Freie Universität, Berlin, especially Michael Kimmage; and to members of the Cambridge History Seminar, above all Tony Badger, the soul of patience, who heard one too many versions of this work in progress.

graphic transformation, sanitized water and improved sewage systems significantly lessened urban death rates in the nineteenth century. As city populations soared, consolidated farms with seasonal labor fed them, sending even more villagers on the move. Now the inertia of European society kept people in motion, not in place.

Even if, as Charles Tilly claims, "the *pace* of migration changed much less than its *character*," the consequences were revolutionary.[1] Instead of swinging out year after year to work and return, work and return, increasing numbers kept going. Millions of villagers transformed themselves into city dwellers. Others—about 65,000,000 between 1800 and 1914—crossed the Atlantic. Millions who thought they would return never did, but many others who thought they would never return did. Once cheap transportation allowed it, smaller numbers shuttled back and forth. At the peaks of migration between 1870 and 1914, the effect was "one of a swarming or churning of people back and forth across the Atlantic."[2]

While population pressures drove some people out of their communities, others left willingly enough in search of opportunities. Nothing persuasive argues that those old societies of quasi-serfdom and hovering catastrophe were somehow more natural (Pierre Nora) or more humane (Louis Dumont) than the ones to follow, or that migration produced massive anomie. Working people always had hard lives. In fact, what stood out was a remarkable adaptability, especially among families.

As more and more matters central to community life fell beyond local control, families took increasing authority upon themselves. What David Sabean has said of the Neckarhausen peasantry of the early nineteenth century applies equally in the Irish countryside and the Russian ghettoes: "[A]s a large part of the village became dependent on wages [from outside sources], kinship became more rather than less important."[3] Especially in migration, chains of kin were indispensable, relaying news, job prospects, and remittances back and forth along the lines of movement.

In new settings, people with ties to the same locality or region stood in as relatives, uniting kin with adopted kin in a cultural weave that highlighted the similarities among chance acquaintances. It did not require much of a stretch for migrants to join the adoptive kin around them with fictive kin around those adoptive kin in widening circles where cultural similarities created the sense of being a single people. History did its part, verifying a common ancestry and sanctifying soil that the sacrifice of those ancestors had made the heritage of all succeeding generations. In reinforcing fashion, people who assigned a unique meaning to one set of customs could now distinguish members from outsiders and look to insiders with a certain familiarity, a feeling of kinship that mingled a special understanding with at least a greater hope of mutual trust.

These fictive kin composites were nations, and nationalism expressed the desire within a nation to establish its own government on the land that it claimed as peculiarly its own. A nation was not like an extended family; it was an extended family, culturally constructed—as all kin systems were—in response to the challenges of migration. Seen in this light, nations and nationalism solved a crucial problem that migration posed. Indeed, they spun a circle: extended kin sustained migration, migration underwrote nations, and nationalism glorified the grand fictive family.

The same broad transformation also generated socialism and democracy. As populations ballooned, more people had to go farther in order to find work, and when they did, they more often received wages in return. Goods made by wage earners undercut those made by local artisans and cottagers, forcing more people out to find wage work. Urban pressures to produce more food more cheaply turned more peasant farmers into wage earners. Although migrants overseas sometimes found a reprieve in agricultural communities of their own, nothing eased the pace in Europe, where more people continued to crowd their working lives into the same spaces.

As local cultures of work, revolving around land, household, and artisanal skills, disintegrated, standards of living did not necessarily fall: some people did better, some worse. Winners and losers alike, however, increasingly lost control over the terms of their labor, widening the gap between what they did today and what they could plan for the future and sending more and more of them in search of an elusive security. The more they moved from job to job, the more their work resembled an impersonal game, rigged against them. Increasing numbers of wage earners saw themselves being used by others in ways and toward ends about which they had no say, a class set apart by the nature of their work in a hostile system.

Class replaced an outworn local identity with a portable one ready for the new working world. Wherever wage earners went, they found others in similar situations, people on the loose whose livelihood depended on twists and turns beyond their control. Especially for those who saw no way out of the working class, socialism went directly and dramatically to the heart of the matter: it promised an entirely new system built around principles of fairness. Socialism, in other words, was a system of work for workers, with as much protection against the hazards of chance as the nineteenth century was able to provide.

Local public life, ascribing rights and responsibilities in a hierarchy of familiars, also unraveled under the pulls of migration. People's standing rarely moved with them; a society of strangers required new rules, and citizenship—a single common identity to replace myriad local ones—supplied the formal solution. Nevertheless, a uniform cover for people on the move evolved slowly and unevenly. Because those of highest prestige were the least likely to migrate, the emerging modern state continued to draw its resources through traditional hierarchies as long as it could, and well into the nineteenth century, the inertia of vested rights kept the meaning of citizenship entangled in a mesh of property, status, birthplace, and local jurisdiction. Even states otherwise quite responsive to change accommodated to these tradition-laden complications, as the special provisions for localism, customary privilege, and favored forms of property in the British Poor Laws and the constitutions of the United States and Prussia demonstrated.

Although it took time to work out the effects, the drastic changes accompanying the French Revolution and the Napoleonic Empire channeled Europe's development in the direction of uniform state citizenship. Wherever those regimes held sway, they destroyed the legal basis for a tiered, decentralized conduct of state affairs. Patching up the Humpty-Dumpty of the ancien régime after the collapse of the empire might have turned out better if the relentless flows of population had not eroded every effort. After Napoleon, it no longer made sense to hire armies from Europe's flotsam and jetsam: the state's own young men were the soldiers of the future. Yet more and more of them were on the move: neither local quotas nor British press gangs were a reliable answer. The solution lay in creating a single pool of male citizens, available wherever and however often they moved within the state. Much the same applied to the problem of taxing a mobile population, too elusive a target for tax farmers and local grandees but manageable enough on a statewide basis.

Systematizing citizenship did not popularize it. At first it offered little more than a right to a place—initially perhaps in a locality, eventually throughout a state. For that right to live somewhere under the state's laws, citizens had to accept the state's right to levy taxes, extract labor, and exact services. It was a bad bargain: these streamlined new regimes took more out of people's hides than the cumbrous old ones. But citizenship also marked the path into an open public life where participation affirmed a person's humanity: liberty, equality, fraternity, as the eloquent, if gendered, revolutionary slogan expressed it. It was this thrilling expectation that democracy promised to fulfill. People who ruled themselves could guarantee the justice of their own government.

In sum, three sequences mapped out solutions to the problems that mass migration created. One ran from family life to ethnicity to nationalism, one from working life to class to socialism, and one from public life to citizenship to democracy. Each, that is, gave priority to one of the three critical issues that community breakdown raised. All three were complicated processes: it was a long, winding road from families under stress to nationalism, from job grievances to socialism, and from overtaxed townsmen to democracy. Of course, not all expressions of ethnicity were nationalistic, not all class schemes socialistic, and not all forms of citizenship democratic. Nevertheless, in the nineteenth century, other variations increasingly orbited these dynamic centers.

Democracy, socialism, and nationalism were holistic visions: We the People; Working People; My People. Each purported to be a total solution. Nationalism, with its own version of political self-determination, also envisaged an economy of trust among kindred folk. Socialism, itself a kind of comradely kinship, also pictured honest governance emerging naturally out of economic justice. As democracy promised to free citizens for their own pursuits, it doubled, under a loose cover of civic wholeness, as a vision of economic opportunity and family autonomy. Each of the three carried within it the radical potential of a new equality—at the ballot box, among laboring comrades, in a conclave of kin—and the engine in each case was migration. "Modern society is not mobile because it is egalitarian," in Ernest Gellner's neat summary; "it is egalitarian because it is mobile."[4] All three affirmed both the personal worth and collective power of their members: new individual identities provided new means for concerted action. In each area, action itself was a triumph. The experience of asserting rights generated rights. Each of the three addressed pressing needs by grandly enlarging the scope within which they could be met and by turning the very elements of crisis in civic, work, and family life into solutions. Atomization became freedom. Alienation became strength. Strangers became kin. As the three of them were rendering old social arrangements obsolete, each claimed to be preserving the best of the past: the spirit of the town meeting, the personal connection between workers and tools, the mutual assistance of family life. In fact, each cultivated a fantasy of edenic roots: the myth of the social contract, the innocence of the honest worker, the urconnectedness of the first kin.

Each had distinctive weaknesses and strengths. Socialism, the most abstract in its reasoning, dealt most effectively with survival issues like food, shelter, and health. Democracy, with the thinnest provisions for mutual support, compensated by best expressing individual aspirations. Nationalism, the least articulated, issued the most open invitation to membership: no citizens' rights to win, no class loyalty to prove. Kinship, the claim went, explained itself. In the nationalist fold, there were no orphans, no bastards, no families without heirs. Yet necessarily the three movements interacted. Who could say where the disruption of civic life ended and the redefinition of work life began, or where needs at work separated from needs in the family? Sometimes these interweavings led to cooperation. Labor movements often powered drives for a democratic franchise, and many democrats championed working people's welfare. Threats to the nation rallied democrats and socialists alike. At critical moments, however, each readily dispensed with the other two. Neither the nation's autonomy nor the socialists' collective ownership could survive democracy's uncertain outcomes; democracy, by the same token, had no stake in either of those causes.

The crucial partner in this trio's development was the modern state, which came bristling and snorting out of the seventeenth century. Long before Randolph Bourne's famous barb, war proved to be the health of the state, and those best geared for war—first Britain, then Napoleonic France, then Germany—served as Europe's models for modernity. Early on, the modern state recognized the advantage of turning the loyalties that migration was generating to its own purposes. Patriotism, increasingly cultivated as state policy, was its counter to the attachments of nationalism, democracy, and socialism. At first, democracy, socialism, and nationalism alike, visualizing their connections laterally rather than hierarchically, associated the modern state with autocracy and repression, and the state for its part outlawed their movements as subversive. Not only was each of them a wild card, capable of popular surges beyond the state's control; at the radical end of the spectrum, each wished the state away: nationalism through a general will, socialism through a classless order, democracy through a self-regulating liberty.

At heart, however, these movements made no sense without the state. Democracy presupposed the existence of a state, nationalism aspired to the equivalent of one, and even socialism, ostensibly boundless, accommodated to the state's jurisdiction by competing for its power. At the same time, the state was their natural predator. It set out to overwhelm democracy's suspicion of arbitrary power with a glorification of one country right or wrong; to replace nationalism's mutual assistance among kin with patriotism's rituals of duty and obedience; and to sacrifice the class needs of working people to the state's preoccupation with production and warfare. None of the three could live with the state, none could live without it: that was the contradiction inherent in the new order.

As European states centralized and bureaucratized after 1870, the trio of movements mimicked them. Optimistic and diffuse, nationalism in the time of Mazzini, democracy in the time of Chartism, and socialism in the time of Saint-Simon still dreamed of spontaneous successes and experimental futures. Around the turn of the century, deepening political animosities and heightening cultural barriers hardened all three. The nationalism of Michael Collins, the democracy of Beatrice Webb, and the socialism of Leon Trotsky were harsh and hierarchical, burdened both by ideologies and by various racial and religious antipathies. All three movements relied more and more on organized violence and as a result depended more and more on state sponsorship. States acquired labels: nationalist Japan, socialist Sweden, democratic Czechoslovakia. Eventually, the trio of movements, rattling the cages of an overextended state system, seemed to divide the globe: Third World nationalism, a socialist empire spanning Europe and Asia, a democratic alliance in the West. Winner take all, metatheorists predicted.

As swollen populations disrupted customary ways in Europe, the consequences spread across the Atlantic with the migrants themselves. The story of the tens of millions who made that journey was not a matter of uprooting and transplanting, metaphors that superimposed the state, with its official statistics of emigration and immigration, on the actual experience of migration. Movement within Europe both preceded and paralleled transatlantic migration. Ports of entry along the North American coast were less likely to be destinations than cities of embarkation in a continuing journey, one with stops but no natural end. Stopping points for one generation's journey were often starting points for the next. Urbanization, then suburbanization, were integral to the process.

The migration-driven needs to reconceive kin connections, work relationships, and civic roles made themselves felt early along North America's Atlantic coast, where substantial numbers of white migrants were already pushing east to west and north to south during the eighteenth century. What was happening in America was part and parcel of Western society's re-creative process. Wherever they had been born, people moving through American territory found themselves in the midst of an ongoing experiment in remaking identities, one in which mobility, the source of their problems, had to be turned into solutions as well.

Bracketing for a moment the slaughter of indigenous people that cleared the way, America was a remarkably pristine site for these transforming experiences. Very little of what had to be undone originated in America, where the challenge for whites in the eighteenth and nineteenth centuries was less to redesign than to create a social order. No country in the world was more inviting to mobile white people. For them, land was cheap, agriculture varied, and short-term labor usually in demand. Whatever else modernization meant in the United States, it translated into a passion for accessible long-distance transportation. High rates of white literacy facilitated communication among these mobile people; the speed with which protocapitalist and capitalist economies took hold in agricultural as well as commercial and industrial sectors was an index to their multiplying connections across both the continent and the ocean. In all kinds of settings, trying something new seemed normal.

Within the context of a common transatlantic process, two interrelated characteristics set their stamp on the American side of the story: a skeletal government and a diffuse society. In nineteenth-century Europe, hovering states forced each of the trio into defensive, resisting postures. Nationalists, socialists, and democrats alike ducked their police and dreamed of ways to capture their armies. Big states, in turn, glowered at one another as they fattened in preparation for more wars. Modern states, Anthony Giddens reminds us, "only exist in systemic relations with other [modern states] . . . 'International relations' is coeval with [these states'] origins."[5] In the United States, by contrast, government resources were stretched thin across a continental domain that, by the early nineteenth century, no other state could threaten. Loyalties diversified into the voluntary associations that Tocqueville and his followers have exalted, among levels of government, and along myriad channels of cultural identification. Without the discipline of danger, these attachments could remain vague and open, a crazy-quilt of possibilities. On the eve of Secession, white people's decisions in the upper South were a study in agony and outrage at the unaccustomed necessity of making an exclusive commitment.

In nineteenth-century Europe, the more the trio of movements appealed to the same people in the same places, the more they threatened to eliminate one another. In nineteenth-century America, on the contrary, the three movements to a striking degree lived apart. Its society without a core left room for a good many socialist experiments and nationalist assertions that neither intruded on one another's space nor involved themselves with the government—which in any case rarely gave more than a token response. When socialists and nationalists competed for the same constituents, they clashed in quite limited settings. Social democracy was equally a local phenomenon.

This scattering of people and power affected each in the trio quite differently. America's diffusion played havoc with socialism. The most clearly articulated and least flexible of the three, it took advantage of dispersed white settlements in the first half of the nineteenth century to lay out what Arthur Bestor Jr. has called "patent-office models of the good society," communities designed to resolve basic issues of work and justice in ways that, the founders anticipated, would attract ever wider circles of converts.[6] Unwilling or unable to float their ideas on the currents of migration, these various test cases relied on people coming to them. As a result, community socialism atrophied. Although industrial socialists did adapt their causes to a mobile society, they in turn functioned most effectively with large concentrations of workers, not with the geographic dispersal of enterprises that characterized the United States during most of the nineteenth century. Moreover, America's heavy dependence on laborers, rather than on artisans or skilled operatives, further diminished the prospects for socialist organization, which almost never started from the bottom up.[7] Above all, the general assumption among white men that they could control their own working lives—perhaps the most revolutionary change in early nineteenth-century America—crippled movements that asked those same men to think of themselves as pawns in some vast game.

In one sense, a mixed migrating population had even more devastating effects on nationalism, a way of thinking that America's diversity made irrelevant. The closest approximation to a dominant ethnic group had no ready means of distinguishing itself from its English parent and in any case lived cheek by jowl with people cultivating a wider and wider variety of competing loyalties. No powerful enemy except possibly Britain itself hovered close enough for long enough to force a new collective identity. Nor did a generalized American Protestantism ever transcend the many denominations and sects into which it splintered. What was left? A thin history on occupied land and an official language that increasing numbers of migrants considered optional did not qualify as any kind of nationalism.

But what killed American nationalism allowed nationalism in America to thrive. Although nationalism's sacred places might be on the far side of an ocean, the connections that bound people into common movements ran back and forth across the water: feelings of kinship moved friction-free with a mobile population. As nationalism heated and hardened toward the end of the nineteenth century, those passions simultaneously spread among migrants with European backgrounds and drew strength from them. Nationalism, arising out of migration, prospered from it. The swallowing of local and regional loyalties inside national identities occurred among fictive kin at about the same time and same rate on both sides of the ocean. Early in the twentieth century, as more and more expressions of ethnicity worldwide turned into state-seeking nationalism, America continued to provide an impressive number of these movements with a second home.

The biggest winner in this diffuse American setting, however, was democracy. In Europe, migration encouraged states to articulate their boundaries and elaborate their rules; in America, these stayed soft and porous: citizenship was easy to get, easy to transport. With minimum fuss, whites could take it anywhere in the country. Although the Revolution and its crucial documents were democratic only in American mythology, they did bring a surge of popular involvement and a sharp rise in assumptions about civic participation. Here myth anticipates reality. The more white people moved, the less a locally rooted status counted; the more leveled they were, the more easily they moved through one another's communities. Elections reaffirmed white men's equality; legislatures kept citizenship readily available; and governments generally left citizens to their own devices.

Around this swirl of activities, democracy drew a line: inside lay America, outside something else. If migrants took ethnic and class identities wherever they went, the meaning of citizenship more or less stopped at the border. What accompanied citizenship—a common civic life—enabled whites to identify one another as American. America turned its distinctive claim to democracy into a source of cohesion. Critics who moaned that citizenship in the United States had been given away for a pittance, with voting cheapened even further by the participation of resident aliens, missed the crucial point: civic connectedness was the only connectedness. Those who distributed the benefits had as much at stake as those who received them.

Democracy's cover hung loosely over American society. Providing a sense of connectedness across such a variety of white people required more than a little calculated vagueness, a common civic enterprise "expressed in values and symbols that were accessible to all ethnic groups, so that in embracing an American identity no one [was] required to give up [a] pre-existing cultural identity."[8] If in some situations, nationalism took on the coloration of democracy, democracy never functioned as a surrogate family. Naturalized citizens became civic equals, not everybody else's cousins. Uncle Sam was no one's relative. In fact, democracy (like class) seemed at times to be giving unencumbered, single men pride of place. What Elaine Spitz has said of contemporary affairs applies equally well to the nineteenth century: majoritarian politics served American society "by recognizing its diversity [and] enabling its multiple parts to achieve some overall direction."[9] Moreover, a loose tether did not mean a weak attachment. Nothing in the record of the nineteenth century indicates that the intensity of white men's loyalties to American democracy suffered in comparison with those binding people anywhere to a class or a nationalist alternative.[10]

There have been other ways of talking about an American identity, of course. Equating America with opportunity was a common one in the nineteenth century. When publicists called the United States a classless society, they were not denying its inequalities, even its deeply rooted ones, so much as claiming that no superimposed barriers blocked individual ambition. Exemplary Americans were simply doers, that argument went. In a similar vein, some old-time conservatives and new arrivals alike touted good honest labor as sufficient to qualify one as an American. By turning a commitment to action into a cultural theme, other commentators here and abroad located the meaning of America in what was to come: its future rather than its past, its destiny rather than its history. Goethe and Whitman were only the most famous of these. *Where* Americans enacted their history rather than precisely *who* was enacting it offered still another vision of unity. What ancestry could not provide, in other words, place did. If the Sons and Daughters of the American Revolution verged on self-parody, Frederick Jackson Turner's frontier thesis expressed values central to his culture: America's distinctiveness could only have arisen out of American soil. Echoing John Quincy Adams and Thomas Jefferson before him, Turner chose to make the formidable North American continent a source of unity, but the oceans adjacent to it, so much easier to navigate, sources of separation.

These several ways of construing an American identity pointed to happenings in the United States without establishing how they connected the people who lived there. Except at an impossibly high level of abstraction, nothing in the pursuit of material opportunities or the dream of a better future or the conquest of a continent reinforced feelings of an American commonality. In all these cases, people just did things. Since World War II, the still-thriving enterprise of seeking the key to a national culture has continued to suffer from the same limitations as its nineteenth century precursors. Asking us to stand with them outside the historical process, interpreters from David Potter and Daniel Boorstin to Richard Slotkin and Christopher Lasch have hypothesized about what gave American culture *its* coherence but not about what gave people sharing that culture *their* feelings of cohesion.

The one serious competitor to civic connectedness as a source of cohesion is race. Indeed, whatever unity civic life has generated in the United States may be merely a study in whiteness. The term "American democracy" rarely suggests that democracy suffused America, only that there was democracy in America, a democracy restricted above all by perceptions of color. To that end, racist laws, racist language, and racist violence reinforced one another until the second half of the twentieth century. Before then, African Americans, along with Asian Americans, Native Americans, and Latins in America, had to pick their place of residence carefully in order to enjoy some of the rights of citizens. As compelling as any evidence, the repeated attempts over the past four decades to replace America's white democracy with something more inclusive have managed to widen divisions without raising prospects of a new unity.

White racism suggests the possibility that the United States did, after all, draw on sources of cohesion comparable to those in nationalism. Miscegenation statutes, hysteria about impending rape, and even residential segregation reveal how ideas about family and kinship merged with racism in ways that resemble nationalist exclusions. Denying newcomers and other suspect groups certification as white, even when skin color was scarcely at issue—"That Jew expected me to treat him like a white man"—can be interpreted as further buffering of America's racial boundaries.

Nevertheless, boundaries do not a nation make. Although an ethnic identity requires a distinction between members and outsiders, that distinction does not create an ethnic identity. Here as elsewhere, the question devolves into what, if anything, united the whites inside these race borders. Whiteness itself contained almost no glue: in the jargon of our time, race in America created a *them* without creating an *us*. In fact, occasional efforts to compress America's heterogeneous whites into a single people with a single culture merely sharpened their differences. Moreover, white commitment to those color boundaries varied considerably with time and place. Because democracy, unlike nationalism and socialism, could incorporate a greater and greater diversity of people without reconstructing itself, those who came through the holes in the racial walls usually found places in the motley of American life. Jews who were "not really white" in one context set Hollywood standards in another. For their all-out assault on the color line, blacks mobilized resources at least as much inside the white walls as outside them.

In any case, white racism in America was almost always a variation on white racism in the Western world as a whole. Although centuries of encounters did produce a special record of racially motivated violence in North America, the values defining those battles moved along the chains of transatlantic migration. Only black slavery in its final decades clearly set the United States apart. Soon after the Civil War, the same assumptions about black savagery and white dominance were once again reverberating across the Atlantic, with the record of white savagery even more horrific in Europe's colonies than in the United States. On both sides of the ocean, racism peaked early in the 1940s, then declined sharply, only to rise again at the end of the century. That is to say, it has almost always been a story with a transatlantic curve.

By World War I, democracy, nationalism, and socialism dominated public agendas throughout the Western world. The timing of these movements' arrival and the nature of their interactions gave each of these Western sites a distinctive stamp. It mattered profoundly that American democracy rose to prominence early in a small-government society, and that before World War I, transatlantic nationalism faced almost no resistance from that government. The ability of its many variants to occupy separate social, cultural, and political spaces meant that nothing stopped fervent but dispersed nationalists from being fervent but dispersed democrats too. For similar reasons, industrial socialism, which in the Western world grew along with a menacing government, mounted its major challenge late in the United States, and as a consequence found itself the odd movement out, with both democracy and nationalism long since entrenched.

The common risk in interpreting American history is to make democracy, however flawed and truncated, normative. When did it appear? Who qualified to participate? Whom did it hurt? How did it change? What influence did it have abroad? Used in this fashion, democratic standards have many applications. They illuminate stories of dismal failure just as well as ones of shining triumph. But explaining everything in light of those standards transforms them into the universal context and strips democracy of a context of its own. Democracy in America was a way of reckoning with certain deep but by no means all-encompassing social challenges. It did not blanket the land. Before the 1860s, slavery was no more an anomaly in the land of democracy than democracy was an anomaly in the land of slavery. Democracy's meaning derived from its relations with two other ways of reckoning with social transformation, nationalism and socialism; together, they comprised a trio of transoceanic movements, with influence flowing in every direction. Sometimes, as in the case of nineteenth-century democracy, America modeled a cause for people living elsewhere. Sometimes, as in the case of industrial socialism, only regular infusions from abroad sustained an American presence. Sometimes, as in the case of transoceanic nationalism, it was impossible to tell—and essentially irrelevant—whether migrants to America or residents in a homeland made the larger contribution.

As brilliantly as Louis Hartz explored the subject of America's place in the Western world, the United States has not been, as he would have it, an arrested spin-off of European history. The special characteristics of American history represent not a separation from the rest of the world but a particular kind of immersion in it, not a way of distinguishing the United States from other countries but a way of distinguishing it among them.

The brief, intense conflict among socialism, democracy, and nationalism during World War I prefigured major changes across the board. First of all, at a halting and then a breathtaking rate, America's modestly endowed, federated state system was transformed into the world's largest concentration of power. This process accelerated hierarchical, antipopulist trends that had been affecting all three movements since the beginning of the century and that, along with the pacesetting big state, arrived in America at full force around midcentury. By then, the state enveloped democracy. In Woodrow Wilson's day, American democracy—at least rhetorically—still rose out of the public and shaped the government; after midcentury—at least rhetorically—the state itself was the democracy. The Constitution, once suspect in populist eyes, became this democracy's sacred text. Like leaders in other big twentieth-century nations, America's leaders now promised to meet all the basic needs that had traditionally been associated with socialism and nationalism. Because states worldwide were wrapping themselves in the mantle of the three great movements, it was not out of line for the biggest among them to claim platonic status: the USA on one side as quintessential democracy, the USSR on the other as quintessential socialism.

In this scheme of monoliths, nationalism belonged to what people in the West called the Third World. Nothing about America's big state prepared it to deal with that global challenge. Its own proxy for nationalism was a democracy screwed tightly into a constitutional structure. Historically, the United States accommodated to transoceanic nationalism only as long as its battles were fought elsewhere, and then not in territory, such as the Philippine Islands, that the U.S. government set out to rule. Domestically transoceanic nationalism fell under the rubric of ethnicity—a backward scheme of values, many commentators thought, but generally benign. When ethnic groups went at each other's throats in a struggle to shape their own states, it seemed pure irrationality—"tribalism," American publicists disdainfully labeled it, in an interesting parallel to the popular term for indigenous peoples who had long since lost control over their own sacred land. Americans lived peacefully with pluralism, went the customary wisdom: why couldn't other people? For policymakers who equated the world's health with the stability of its state system, no movement—nationalist, socialist, or democratic—had a right to be disruptive. At the end of the century, there was even nostalgia for those recently dismantled authoritarian structures that at least had known how to keep people in their place.

During the 1990s, it was common in America to encapsulate the end of the Cold War this way: democracy had defeated socialism, only to be plagued by a more elusive and less tractable nationalism. Whatever its deficiencies, this approach has the considerable virtue of asking us to look at big events in the light of forces that operate at the heart of modern Western history and profoundly affect the rest of the world.

NOTES

1. Charles Tilly, "Migration in Modern European History," in *Human Migration: Patterns and Policies,* ed. William H. McNeill and Ruth S. Adams (Bloomington, Ind., 1978), 57. Emphasis in original. William McNeill and Charles Tilly are major influences in my thinking on population and migration.

2. Walter T. K. Nugent, *Crossings: The Great Transatlantic Migrations, 1870–1914* (Bloomington, Ind., 1992), 3.

3. David Warren Sabean, *Property, Production, and Family in Neckarhausen, 1700–1870* (New York, 1990), 37.

4. Ernest Gellner, *Nations and Nationalism* (Ithaca, N.Y., 1983), 24–25.

5. Anthony Giddens, *The Nation-State and Violence* (Berkeley and Los Angeles, 1985), 4.

6. Arthur E. Bestor Jr., "Patent-Office Models of the Good Society: Some Relationships between Social Reform and Westward Expansion," *American Historical Review* 58 (April 1953): 505–26.

7. On the predominance of unskilled labor, I am borrowing from Gavin Wright's unpublished paper "The Origins and Economic Significance of Free Labor in America" (February 1996).

8. David Miller, *On Nationality* (New York, 1995), 141.

9. Elaine Spitz, *Majority Rule* (Chatham, N.J., 1984), 214.

10. Some scholars call the kind of public life I discuss here "civic nationalism." But why ask one term, "nationalism," to cover realms of activity as different as an ethnic group's drive for statehood and an electorate's participation in the governing process? Each has its own origins, its own characteristics, and its own history. Common sense and sound analysis both argue for separate terms to designate separate patterns of behavior.

TEN

An Age of Social Politics

Daniel T. Rodgers

The age of social politics was the fourth great phase in the history of the relationship between Europe and the emergent United States. The first was an age of outpost settlements, highly diverse, thinly connected both to their European metropoles and to one another, subsisting in rough military and economic parity with the Native American populations of the continent. The second, running roughly from the last quarter of the seventeenth century to the last quarter of the eighteenth, was an age of commercial Atlantic empires, binding the Euro-American settlements to their imperial centers (and, far beyond that, to the Amerindian peoples of the great Mississippi trading basin, to the slave coast of Africa, and to the sugar and slave islands of the West Indies) in ever-denser webs of trade in extractive resources and commercial goods, in human labor, and in manners and ideas. The third great phase, beginning with the political eruptions on both sides of the Atlantic of the 1770s and 1780s and continuing through the American Civil War, was a century-long age of revolutionary nation-building. The most recent phase, extending from World War II through our own time has been the age of the world hegemony of the United States. Between these last two great phases in the relationship between the United States and Europe, from the late nineteenth century through the mid 1940s, lies what we may call, in shorthand, an age of social politics. The resulting

This essay represents, in part, an extension of the arguments of and, in part, a condensation of one of the narrative threads in my *Atlantic Crossings: Social Politics in a Progressive Age* (Cambridge, Mass., 1998). For much fuller documentation and historiographical discussion, readers are referred there and to the wide-ranging critical symposium, by Harry M. Marks, Victoria de Grazia, David Hammack, Seth Koven, Sonya Michel, and Pierre-Yves Saunier, H-Net Reviews in the Humanities and Social Sciences (http://h-net.msu.edu), 1999.

schema is a primitive one, but, for all its skeletal character, perhaps not without its advantages.

Seen in this frame, one cannot but be struck by how tightly both popular and historiographical conceptions of the European-American relationship have fastened on the third of these phases, the age of revolutionary nation-building, as the essential, normative one. In contrast, the international dynamics of the age that followed have been shuffled off to the margins of national memory. The great texts of American national character, whose phrases the rhetoricians of American patriotism still mine in our own day, cluster in the century after 1770: Crèvecoeur's paean to the "new man" being smelted down in America from older European materials, Tocqueville's reflections on the world promise and world dangers of American democracy, Lincoln's evocation of America as the last, best hope of earth. Such a sense of world-historical importance may be critical to every nation-state formation project, but certainly the Americans took to it with unabashed passion. Within two generations of independence, the margin dwellers of the seventeenth century and the provincials of the eighteenth century had reimagined themselves as vaulted into history's very forefront—model nation to the world, thorn in the side of Europe's old and decadent monarchies, torchbearer of progress itself.[1]

What above all gave late eighteenth- and early nineteenth-century Americans their sense of world-historical centrality was their revolutionary reconfiguration of the mechanics of legally and politically constituted power. How could monarchical sovereignty be permanently overthrown and political power be so channeled and distributed as to preclude either its recentralization in the hands of new elites or its dissolution in an anarchic series of redivisions? What legal-constitutional rights did persons, associations, and majorities in a republic possess? How far could citizenship and suffrage be safely extended, and who was to barred, by design, from the inner circle of republican liberties?

These were pressing questions everywhere the eighteenth- and nineteenth-century movements of revolutionary nationalism gathered force. The Americans' importance on the world stage in the century after 1770 did not derive from their answering all of them well. Some, like the legal constitution of slavery within a white, male democracy, they answered so badly that their nation-state project barely survived its unfolding consequences. Nonetheless, the flaws and instabilities of their revolutionary republic notwithstanding, the Americans were among the very first to reformulate the terms of legal-constitutional politics on antimonarchical lines and to invent a lasting mechanics of modern popular governance. Even their imperfect success carried powerful subversive force throughout late eighteenth- and nineteenth-century Europe. Radicals like Paine and Priestley, liberals like Bright and Cobden, democratic nationalists like Mazzini, even mid nineteenth-century Marxian socialists could all imagine the political destiny of Europe as "anticipated" in the United States.[2]

By the end of the century, however, the terms of politics were shifting rapidly under the Atlantic-wide transformation in the scale and organization of capital. The new loci of power—trusts and cartels, regions of massed industrial concentration and explosive industrial conflict, megalopolis and *Millionenstadt*—were different from those that had existed before and less clearly addressed by the constitutional mechanics of the earlier age. The same was true of the era's new forms of exploitation. To many of the radicals and reformers who had once looked confidently to the promise of legal-constitutional democracy, the formal categories of politics began to seem brittle and ineffective. Even the new nation-states, their borders forged in war and revolution, proved porous and exposed to the transformative effects and quicksilver movements of industrial capital. The problems of the age, one began to hear with increasing force on both sides of the Atlantic, were economic and social—the "labor problem," the "social question," the crisis in class relations, the suddenly expanding field (as Britain's Joseph Chamberlain was calling it by the 1880s) of "social politics."[3]

The new language of politics constructed around the idea of the "social" did not extinguish the old. As long as liberty or suffrage remained tightly restricted, as they did along gender, class, and ethno-racial lines throughout Europe and the United States, as long as parliaments remained toothless and political authority arbitrary and distant, the questions of the revolutionary age continued to bear heavy weight. Through the 1870s they still formed the core axis of party politics from Berlin to Washington, D.C.[4] But sometimes emerging out of the terms of the older democratic and republican arguments, at other times in competition with them, one begins to see the formulation of new categories of politics and power.

Like most emerging fields, the field of the "social" possessed no clear or stable boundaries. Welfare capitalists, social imperialists, and social and racial hygienists all worked within its newly sociologized categories. Its terms formed a well from which social Darwinists could draw as freely as reform socialists, Catholic social conservatives as readily as Protestant social gospelers. Still, if there was a leading thread in the tangle of issues opening out from the new primacy of economic and social relations, it was the thread of capitalist transformation. To find ways to curb or to direct the ferocious energies of industrial capitalism, to insulate pieces of social life from the commodifying pressures of the age, to encourage new forms of social solidarity to counter the fragmenting forces of labor-capital conflict, and to design forms of public compensation where the injuries of the capitalist transformation cut most deeply—these constituted the core terms of the new social politics. They did not monopolize the terrain of the "social," but for an era they dominated its center.

What is much more rarely noted of these shifts in the field of politics is the extent to which they destabilized the pattern in the relationship between the United States and Europe. From a commercially peripheral, agriculturally based, capital- and goods-importing nation, the United States vaulted almost overnight into the role of the world's foremost engine of capitalist social and economic production. By the end of the century, the fruits of globally mobile labor and newly consolidated capital had begun to pour back into Europe in an "invasion" of American-made manufactured goods—and, soon, manufactured culture. But if this was a triumph in the race for world economic supremacy, it was a deeply ambiguous one for both the Europeans and the Americans who had begun to be drawn to the field of the social question. The Americans' very success in dismantling the formal monopolies of state power and privilege left them weak in resources to steer or contain the revolutions in capital, labor, and markets. Inadequate state structures and aggressively dynamic capital, unprecedented material production and permanent labor conflict, a politics trapped in money corruption and ineffectual, lawyers' formalisms—if these were the legacies of eighteenth-century radicalism, they carried costs that its Paines and Franklins had not fully entered on their ledger books.

For all these reasons, in many of the late nineteenth-century radical and progressive circles where the political promise of American democracy had once been celebrated, one cannot miss its new deflation. Sidney and Beatrice Webb, as eager as Fabians before them to see the United States for themselves in 1898, found themselves appalled at their hosts' "infantile" faith in constitutional mechanics, so patently inadequate, they thought, to the social problems engulfing them—and so patently unlike the practical social radicalism they thought they saw at work in Australia, New Zealand, and at home. Marxian socialists had already written off the United States as a land of unbridled monopoly capitalism and corruption. Even a moderate reformer like Toynbee Hall's Samuel Barnett, traveling through the United States in 1890–91, thought he saw a filthy and barely governed society, its cities lorded over by the mansions of its new plutocrats, even its vaunted Yosemite Valley swarming with swindlers, a nation pervaded by racial antagonisms and impending "class war," to which the vast majority of its inhabitants, trapped in "this incessant mutual admiration society habit of mind," seemed utterly indifferent.[5]

Americans traveling in the opposite direction were not so quick to accept the exhaustion of their politics or the eclipse of the world-historical mission of the United States. Through the letters and diaries of turn-of-the-century American observers of Europe runs the republican citizen's shock of butt-

ing up against the continental European state apparatus—its monarchical
pomp, its titled land monopolies, its swarms of officials, the parades of
soldiers "that pranced and caroled through the Brandenburg Gate," as
W. E. B. Du Bois remembered Berlin in the 1890s, "and brought the world
to a sudden salute before William, by the Grace of God." Samuel Gompers,
returning to the England of his boyhood in 1909, thought there was nothing for an up-to-date American to learn from Europe. "The Old World is
not our world. Its social problems, its economic philosophies, its current
political questions are not linked up with America. . . . In the procession
[of nations], America is the first."[6]

In monarchical Europe, the political promise of the United States could
still carry force, as the crowds that mobbed Woodrow Wilson's arrival in
Europe in 1919 so dramatically showed. Immigrants, hoping to ride the
cresting wave of world capitalism, voted with their feet by the millions for
the Americas. But to an ever-growing number of European progressives
and radicals, the model nation in the West slowly slid into irrelevance. The
fixation of American politics on legal-constitutional rights and formally
constituted power seemed one-sided, economically and socially naïve, ar-
chaic—as H. G. Wells put it, "pure eighteenth century."[7]

Even as European progressives and radicals dampened their admiration for
the United States, they set a new transnational social politics in motion
within industrializing Europe. Wherever the transformative force of industrial capitalism touched, a common family of intellectual and political responses began to be seen.

An essential part of the transnational work of agitation and publicization
was carried by the new associations of the working class, both laborist and
socialist, whose explosive international growth was one of the fundamental
events of the age. Their role was crucial in the transformation of politics,
both in framing critical parts of the social-political agenda and in deploying
the threat of class conflict that so often swung middle-class and elite reformers into action. The people the industrial capitalist transformation set
in motion—migrants and immigrants whose traveling social cultures were
to be found throughout all the industrial regions of Europe as well as the
United States—did another critical part of the nation-crossing work. [8] But
it was in the nature of politics in pre–World War I Europe, where the formal
monopolies of political power were far from dismantled, that workers' associations were rarely close to the levers of state power.

It was in this regard that bourgeois and university-based reformers carried a weight in the formation of the new social politics so far beyond what
their numbers might suggest. Liberals who found their traditional inheritance too individualistic to deal effectively with privately and economically

constituted power, middle-class figures whose consciences had been touched by social Protestantism or social Catholicism, women working at the radical edges of charity endeavor or the new institutions of women's solidarity, and social scientists grown skeptical of the mechanical abstractions of classical economics, all played key roles in the articulation of the social. The imagination of the bourgeois reformers was piecemeal, empirically rooted, and unsystematic, but in the genesis and diffusion of the policies and information that were to become the new politics' common ground, their work was indispensable.[9]

Among their central constructions was an array of new pan-European institutions of social-political discussion and exchange. The Paris expositions of 1889 and 1900 were key sites in this project; the Congrès international des accidents du travail (later the International Congress on Social Insurance), the Association internationale pour la protection légale des travailleurs, the Congrès international des habitations à bon marché, and the Congrès international des oeuvres et institutions féminines were all born there, spinning out of the expositions' new sections on "social economy." Nor were these small endeavors: 1,639 persons are listed in the register of the International Congress on Public Assistance and Private Charity that met in Paris in 1900; over 2,000 attended the International Housing Congress in Vienna in 1910.

Beyond the social-political congresses, there spread a web of institutions of pan-European policy exchange. Public and privately sponsored international inspection visits multiplied to try to take the measure of German high-tariff protectionism, social insurance, or city planning, British model cities and methods of collective bargaining, Danish cooperative creameries, or Italian credit banks. Other connections flowed through experts with accumulated knowledge of other nations' social policy such as Lujo Brentano, the leading German expert on British-style industrial relations in the Verein für Sozialpolitik, or William Dawson, author of more than a dozen books on German social policy, who laid some of the key statistical groundwork for the British National Insurance Act. On the eve of World War I, Paris, Berlin, and Frankfurt all boasted social museums devoted to the diffusion of international social political endeavors. Even in a second-tier city like Lyon, as Pierre-Yves Saunier has shown, municipal authorities assiduously gathered in, from across the European nations, models and information on urban health and welfare.[10]

The alliances that first propelled this work into the parliaments were uneasy, diverse, and shifting, but they quickly learned to use imitation and emulation to their advantage. By the 1870s, English forms of workplace regulation had begun to be taken up in France, Germany, and elsewhere; the movement for international labor standards treaties, the first of them focused on women's labor protection statutes, dates from the early 1890s.

Over the next four decades, sometimes in defiance of nation-state rivalries, sometimes fueled by them, the international pace of borrowings of this sort accelerated. Danish old age pensions were imported (via New Zealand) to Britain, British industrial liability codes to France, French-modeled public subsidies to mutual assistance and insurance associations to Denmark, Holland, and Scandinavia, even as more radical French social progressives envied German-style compulsory state insurance. Among the noisiest and most aggressive of these transnational appropriations was the National Insurance Act that brought public health insurance to Britain in 1911, cheered on by David Lloyd George, less than three years before World War I, as outstripping Germany at its own social-political game—a compliment the Germans returned by appropriating British-style public unemployment insurance for themselves in 1927.

In these contests over the new terrain of social politics, the old party systems bent and reformed. On the left, labor and socialist parties grew in strength—although not until the 1930s in Scandinavia, and not until the 1940s elsewhere in Europe, did they gain a serious, lasting hold on power. Everywhere, new political configurations emerged out of the older, bourgeois, liberal and democratic-radical parties: the "new liberals" in Britain, the "new radicals" in post-1890 France, German social progressives trying to wedge their way between the socialists on the left and the captains of land and industry on the right—and, not the least, the progressives in the United States.

It is this last recognition of the close cousinhood of the American progressives to their counterparts in Europe that catches the U.S. historian up short. We are used to thinking of the Progressive period as an age of internal self-scrutiny and domestic social and political realignments, propelled by a distinctively eruptive mix of monopolist consolidation, immigrant labor exploitation, and urban misgovernment, and publicized by media eager to fork up the muck and chaos beneath the ordinary crust of social and economic relations for a new American middle class to see. But it would be as accurate to say that for a critical number of American progressives, it was in London and Berlin that they began to sense the shifting power relations of the age, to learn the new vocabularies of society and the state, and to acquire the stock of borrowed and practically tested experience that was to be essential to their own variation on the social political movements abroad. They, too, took their place in the international networks of progressive exchange.

Some of these Americans turned up as early as the 1870s in the universities of imperial Germany, where they heard the giants of the German economics faculties explode the syllogisms of classical economic liberalism; they, in turn, were to send a generation of American students to learn the fundamentals of empirical and institutional economics in a foreign land

and a foreign tongue. Other Americans went on private missions, like Jane Addams's to Toynbee Hall, or Randolph Bourne's to the centers of German municipal science on the eve of World War I, or, still later, Lewis Mumford's Guggenheim-funded immersion in what still remained of Weimar social utopianism in the early 1930s. Others were sent on journalistic missions, like Charles Edward Russell, dispatched around the globe by *Everybody's Magazine* in 1905 to bring back reports on the world's "soldiers of the common good." By the eve of World War I, one could travel to Europe, often in conjunction with the meetings of one of the major international social-political associations, on a specially packaged "sociological tour," with stops at Europe's model cities and its most up-to-date examples of social welfare provision.

Organizations competed on the new terrain of transnational social politics. The international women's movement was a major conduit for the spread of women's health and welfare initiatives.[11] The socialist parties ran an ambitious international circuit of speakers. The American Federation of Labor organized its own independent delegations of inspection and fraternal exchange. Business associations learned to play the game of comparative social politics; when interest in city-owned gas, electric, and streetcar systems mushroomed in 1905–6, the National Civic Federation dispatched a highly publicized commission of experts to Britain to try resolve the question through a comparison of public and private utility costs and services. The new philanthropic institutions of the age—Rockefeller, Carnegie, and Russell Sage—were active and innovative players in the field. State and federal governments quickly became major players as well, through endeavors ranging from the quiet fact-gathering work of Bureau of Labor investigators to the mammoth, some 120-person Commission on Agricultural Cooperation and Rural Credit in Europe, which trooped across Italy, Germany, Denmark, and England in the summer of 1913 to prepare the way for the Federal Farm Loan Act.

World War I shocked and reshaped this system, but from the American point of view, it did not shatter it. The war brought socialist revolution to Europe; it also brought American capital, manufacturing techniques, and consumer goods to Europe in unprecedented quantities. But even in this newly polarized terrain, the international associations quickly reformed, assisted now by the new International Labor Organization in Geneva. Within months, the social-political inspection commissions had resumed. Even the sociological tour packagers were back in business again by the late 1920s.

In some ways, all these earnest, generally well-educated, often well-placed Americans hunting for policies and ideas in what the *Arena*'s editor called "our foreign experiment stations abroad" were not radically different from elite Americans before them who had immersed themselves in the art and culture of Europe on a season's "grand tour." But what struck the new travelers was not Europe's otherness but its uncanny familiarity. From the Ruhr to western Pennsylvania, London to New York, Berlin to Chicago, they sensed common social and economic transformations at work that made the "social question" the same from one end of the Atlantic world to the other. In this region of common force, they felt common affinities. When the British Labourite Ramsay MacDonald was elected to Parliament in the early twentieth century, Lillian Wald of New York City's Henry Street Settlement wrote in congratulation that she felt as if it had been a victory for "our party." The Kansas progressive William Allen White put the same sentiment in more radical terms: "We were parts, one of another, in the United States and in Europe. Something was welding us into one social and economic whole with local political variations. It was Stubbs in Kansas, Jaurès in Paris, the Social Democrats in Germany, the Socialists in Belgium, . . . fighting a common cause."[12]

This transformation in imagined space entailed, finally, a transformation in imagined time. Far from the centers of social-political production, many of the progressive Americans who made their way into the networks of Atlantic progressive exchange found themselves unexpectedly cast back into the role of provincials—latecomers scrambling for place in a procession of nations they had once imagined they led. The theme of backwardness runs as a striking motif through their writings. "Among the most belated of nations," Theodore Roosevelt called the United States in 1908 in his message recommending European-style workmen's compensation legislation to Americans. A "backward" and "lagging" nation, others termed it, "more and more a camp follower among the great peoples of the earth."[13]

"We are no longer the sole guardians of the Ark of the Covenant," Walter Weyl opened his *The New Democracy* in 1912. "Europe does not learn at our feet the facile lessons of democracy. . . . Foreign observers describe our institutions with a galling lack of enthusiasm." He added: "To-day the tables are turned. America no longer teaches democracy to an expectant world, but herself goes to school to Europe and Australia. . . . Our students of political and industrial democracy repair to the antipodes, to England, Belgium, France, to semi-feudal Germany. . . . Why has the tortoise Europe outdistanced the hare?"[14]

Ambivalence competed with envy in judgments like these. None of the American scavengers for ideas and institutions in London, Glasgow, Paris, or Berlin were ready to swallow whole what they found there. The close, crowded warrens of the old city cores, the wooden-clogged peasant women working the fields, the plumed and marching soldiers, all weighed on the consciousness of American social tourists in Europe, and with each came a reflexive reassertion of American patriotism. But the social-historical point remains: at the high point of the Atlantic progressive connection, between the 1890s and the end of the 1930s, a critical reservoir of ideas, proposals, and experience for progressive Americans lay overseas in the "advanced" nations of Europe.

Nothing more clearly illuminates the strength of the Atlantic progressive connection than an inventory of the legislation that moved through it from Europe to the United States. Workmen's liability and workmen's compensation legislation, women's labor protection statutes, workplace safety regulation, minimum wage legislation, and systems of labor disputes mediation were all conscious reworkings in the United States of European policy precedents. So were public forests, federal farm loans, and rural farm cooperatives; zoning and land-use planning; publicly owned city utilities and public housing for the poor and the working class; public baths and public milk stations for mothers and children; social insurance against the economic risks of sickness, unemployment, and old age; vocational education for working-class youths; and "pensions" for the morally blameless poor.

Nor were these quiet, veiled borrowings. Turn-of-the-century Chicago urban progressives fought their fight for municipal streetcar ownership with headlines blazoning the success of Glasgow's example. Florence Kelley's Committee on Congestion of Population campaigned for stricter land-use regulation in the city of New York with traveling exhibits of the best urban land-market controls Europe could offer. The National Consumers' League's briefs for shorter women's working hours legislation drew their "sociological" evidence and legislative precedents from around the globe. The American Association for Labor Legislation, the most important Progressive-era lobby for workers' health and social insurance provisions, made its politics unabashedly out of its expert knowledge of European precedents.

In the aftermath of World War I, when their German models suddenly turned suspect and double-edged, many American progressives retreated to less overt importation strategies. The New Dealers were more circumspect about their European borrowings than the prewar progressives—but all the more so because their projects were so full of them. The New Dealers gave progressive politics a consciously American stamp in a symbolic language that was regionalist and nationalist. As one of the few instances of progressive political breakthrough anywhere in the depression-mired 1930s, the New Deal had a riveting impact on Europe. But its legislative record is full of reworked ingredients, gathered in from a generation of progressive policy scavenging across the Atlantic world. The National Recovery Administration was a revival of the structures of economic management employed during World War I, forged, in turn, out of very close observation of the economies of the European belligerents during 1914–17. The National Employment System Act was an explicit adaptation of the British labor exchange legislation of 1909. The Social Security Act of 1935 was a highly conscious borrowing from German and British precedents, drafted by committees stocked with experts on European social insurance experience. The Wagner public housing act of 1937 was built explicitly on British municipal housing precedents; the American housing experts' manifesto of 1934, outlining most of the housing act's terms, had been largely drafted by Raymond Unwin, the grand old man of the British housing and town planning movement. The National Labor Relations Act drew its beginnings from Australian, British, and Canadian labor disputes precedents. The Agricultural Department and the Resettlement Administration were full of admirers of British planned cities, Danish folk schools, and Irish farm cooperatives—not least among them Agriculture Secretary Henry Wallace himself, who had made a young man's pilgrimage to Dublin in 1912 to see the Irish agricultural revival in action. Even in this most "American" of political moments, the nation-state turns out to be a startlingly porous container.

Now clearly there is an artifice to such a formulation. There was no "Europe" in the age of social politics, only a set of quite distinct, rival European polities, full of their own foreign reworkings and appropriations, their own calculations of lag and progress, and their own deep rivalries in technique and social strategies. In every nation within these systems of exchange, cosmopolitan progressives competed with those whose political inspiration was more tightly bounded by local or national policy traditions and who looked with deep distrust on foreign precedents. Social radicals in pre–World War I France, envious of aspects of German social policy, faced as intense a nationalist resistance as their American counterparts confronted in the United States. Great power rivalry strained all the international social reform associations, even before the Nazis broke them apart into warring geopolitical camps.

"Exchange," too, is a metaphor. The Atlantic progressive connection was not a simple device for the transmission of inert ideas but a field of social-intellectual politics. Perception, misperception, translation, transformation, co-optation, preemption, and contestation were all intrinsic to it. No policy idea could be plucked cleanly from one context to another. Some came burdened with extensive baggage: models of empire and imperial administration, strong gender assumptions, or "modern" notions of race and eugenic improvement, all of which were under intense discussion in these same nations, often within the same circles. Other policy ideas, by contrast, could not be prized from their settings at all.

Within these processes, the flow of influence was never unidirectional. American systems of public education attracted keen interest in progressive

Europe. Children's playgrounds were an American invention, important enough in the eyes of American progressives for American social workers to import them into war-devastated France. The London County Council parks committee of the 1890s drew its plans for a greener London with a conscious eye on the bold, new urban park developments in Chicago and New York. Continental European women suffragists often looked with envy on the power that their American sisters could mobilize; British feminists worked hard to import American precedents in mothers' "pension" legis-lation.[15] In the 1920s, Fordism was a major force and powerful lure for Europeans—not the least, as Molly Nolan has shown, for European labor unionists, who saw in Fordism's high wages, rationalized techniques, and mass consumer goods production a potential escape from capitalism's in-ner, Ricardian contradictions.[16] Roosevelt's New Deal attracted eager atten-tion in progressive Europe. In France, Léon Blum modeled much of the rhetoric of his Popular Front government in 1936–37 on the New Deal; David Lloyd George mounted his bid to revive the British Liberal Party in the same terms. From imported movies to American-style chewing gum, the impress of American consumer culture on twentieth-century Europe was continuous and profound.

We must, then, imagine American progressives within a highly complex web of international institutions and influences at a moment when the primacy of the "social" lowered many bars to the movement of policies and proposals across all national boundaries. Traffic within this system was never unidirectional. Still, within this frame, the asymmetry of the flows to and from the United States between the 1890s and the 1940s is striking. Lay the public policies Europeans took from the United States in this pe-riod against those that traveled from Europe to America; compare the sharp but intermittent interest of European progressives in the United States, even in the Fordist 1920s, against the sustained American interest in Europe; add up the itineraries and steamship receipts of the Atlantic's sociological travelers, and the contrast is pronounced.

Social politics in the United States in the Progressive and New Deal years was not simply a contemporaneous product of the transformations in eco-nomic and social relations at work throughout the capitalist world econ-omy. It was not essentially a domestic phenomenon merely augmented by European influences. It was a phenomenon simultaneously rooted in do-mestic *and* international contexts, constituted within the era's new systems of social-political transit, imitation, and exchange.

How have historians contrived to miss the event, to cabin the Progressive and New Deal years within a frame much more insular than contemporaries themselves would have recognized?[17] If the project of internationalizing the history of the United States is to have a chance of success, this is a critical question to raise—although not, of course, simple to answer. Two key elements, however, are worth pulling into relief. The first is an excessively simplified (and unconsciously nationalized) understanding of the processes of politics. The second is an excessively powerful (and unconsciously static) vocabulary of national historical comparison.

Processes first. Follow the trail of interests, Charles Beard instructed students of history and politics; it was—and remains—good advice. Interest group analysis focuses attention not on the ideational aspects of politics, with their ambiguous fluidity, but on precise legislative outcomes. Administrative and legislative details are the currency with which legislative coalitions are made, logs are rolled, favors paid, and key constituencies rewarded. Because the configuration of interests is differently structured in each polity, because popular political pressures are differently organized (and by the same token differently muted and demobilized), because the historical legacies of the political parties, the linkages between parties, constituencies, and governance, and the constitutional frames in which they operate differ significantly between the nation-states, a focus limited to outcomes and interests unconsciously magnifies national differences.

Let a common impulse come to bear on different party and legislative systems, and even small differences in structure will produce large differences in result. The interwar British response to the national and international agitation over the paucity of decent, cheap, working-class housing, through directly built, tax-financed, municipal construction, differed strikingly from the interwar German response, which funneled extensive public credits through cooperative and limited-dividend housing associations, many of them tightly linked to the labor movement. And both differed sharply once again from the best that New York City housing reformers in the 1920s could achieve: tax subsidies to low-cost builders, the most active of which were deep-pocketed commercial life insurance companies. Even more precise policy appropriations entailed, by necessity, a vast amount of modification and reformulation, as the transit of the social insurance project from Bismarckian Germany in the 1880s to Britain in 1911, and from there into the U.S. Social Security Act of 1935 so clearly showed.

But the processes of politics are broader than the final acts of legislative bargaining where difference proliferates. A critical part of the necessary work of politics occurs in its prelegislative phases. It is here, to adopt Nancy Fraser's terms, that "needs" escape the realm of the "private" (or the fated and inevitable) and are elbowed successfully into the sphere of public, political contestation. Or, conversely, where needs, failing to make the leap into the "political," fall back again, inert and reprivatized. Social movements play a major role in politicizing needs. But a second, equally critical element is the connection of need to an imagined political solution—or, better yet, to an already working device or readily modified one. The successful meeting of social need and imaginable public solution is the intellectual precursor to legislation, and it has dynamics as critical to the political process as the end games of interest and party maneuver. It is also the field of politics most porous to materials from beyond the nation's borders.[18]

This, then, was the core work of the international networks of social-political debate and exchange—to augment the agendas to which legislators had to respond, to publicize a world of imaginable solutions to otherwise muted and fatalism-enmired need. Moments of political impasse, when the existing stock of ideas and proposals ran out or ran up against massive fiscal or institutional obstacles, often gave the figures in these networks their political opportunity. It was in these circumstances, as E. P. Hennock has shown, that David Lloyd George reversed the long-standing British dismissal of German-style social insurance ("utterly alien to the tradition of this country," the government's spokesman had called it 1908), and, with the help of Winston Churchill at the Board of Trade, brought the social insurance principle to Britain in 1911.[19] German-style urban zoning came to New York City in the context of a deadlocked argument over transportation, population crowding, and merchant-manufacturer conflict over property uses along Fifth Avenue. Glasgow's city-owned streetcar system caught the imagination of Chicago progressives when the customary processes of city politics were stalled in monopoly and corruption. The Depression in itself constituted an impasse of this sort writ large, when the conventional economic wisdom gave out and the political influence of the business institutions most closely attached to it was temporarily weakened in result. It was at these moments that the international social political networks accrued special power, that they were able to sweep another nation's policy measure across the parochial and nationalist resistance that, in normal times, hedged round the agenda of domestic politics. In such contexts. the quality of being ready-made and experience-tested became a prized asset.

Failed importations, of course, strewed both sides of the Atlantic as thickly as successes. However intricately crisscrossed the early twentieth century was with social-political ambitions and agendas, not everything slipped easily across nation-state borders. Transformation and hybridization were built into the very core of the process; and so were failure and defeat. It is precisely the commonality of issues across these tightly interconnected nations that makes the analysis of the points of failure analytically significant.

But here social policy comparativists have brought not too little but too much explanatory power to bear. Overdetermination is the rule. Let a historical event follow a differential course in two different polities and in retrospect *everything* seems stacked in favor of difference: ideologies and political cultures, class and racial/ethnic divisions, interest group configurations and mass political pressures, state and party structures, policy traditions and path-dependent histories. Let it be asked why the deep and active ferment over social politics did not reproduce in the United States the "welfare state" we mistakenly take to have been, all along, in embryo in Europe, and the conventional answer brings them all to bear: the absence of sufficient working-class pressure on the structures of politics in the United States, the counterlure of high wages and a culture of mass consumption, the rigidities of a two-party system and tight constitutional adjudication, the absence of sufficient need, the presence of an anti-statist ideology so powerful as to block need from its own consciousness, and so forth. The exceptionalist hand is seemingly so full of trumps and face cards as to all but foreclose the game before the argument has even begun.

But the case for the stark difference between United States and European social politics in this period is, in fact, riddled with self-serving assumptions. One is a crude and falsely anticipatory understanding of other nations' politics. Nations that came very late to modern social politics—Sweden is a key example—are all too commonly credited with long-term progressive traditions they did not possess; weak labor coalition governments—interwar Britain's is a classic case—are credited with a strength they never had; deep intra-European differences in economic and social policy are conjured away; the battlefields of ideology are flattened out into highly stereotyped national value systems; the radical, temporal shifts in constituted powers and political values that Bruce Ackerman calls "constitutional moments" are all but effaced.[20] The stories historians tell about the nations at the center of their attention are subtle and time-dependent; other polities can be treated, in contrast, with a striking indifference to history and contingency. The "why no socialism in America" question, predicated on an ahistorical, if not altogether fantastical, image of Europe, was one of many cases in point.[21]

The second limitation of the exceptionalist line of argument is that too many of the explanatory cards in its hand are structural; too few pay serious attention to time and sequence. Even the subtlest and most historical of the comparative politics schools, that constructed by Theda Skocpol and her students, does not fully transcend the problem.[22] Timing not only, as they have shown, creates certain policy traditions, administratively and intellectually institutionalized grooves and patterns that resist sudden change; it continuously changes the field of intellectual and political possibilities.

Hazards of all sorts frustrated the importation of social policy projects into the late nineteenth- and early twentieth-century United States. With each new measure, the task of social policy formation began again. Intellectual discovery and reinvention, elite and popular mobilization, coalition formation, passage through the processes of legislative logrolling, trial in the courts—at each of these stages the project could unravel.

Sometimes the distinctive organization of law in the United States—the "practically cast-iron Constitution," as the British planner Thomas Adams called it 1911—got in the way. [23] The courts' role in skewing most forms of pre–New Deal labor standards legislation toward protection for "dependent" women and children is a critical case in point; the reconstruction of zoning in the United States as a boon for suburban land developers is another. Yet it would be a myth to imagine that the law's special considerations for property and gender did not bear down hard on social politics everywhere through formal and informal constitutional structures less familiar to American historians.[24] Sometimes ideological considerations intervened—although it is even more illusory to imagine that bourgeois commitments to liberal individualism and property consciousness were peculiar to the United States or even peculiarly salient there. Differences in state capacity sometimes played a role in the failure of an imported policy measure; so did differently configured party structures, and, still more often, differently configured arrays of interests—although none of these was fixed or incapable of sudden disruption.

But within all these structural considerations, timing and sequence mattered as well. Sometimes the work of timing was precise and happenstantial. The progressive-labor campaign for public health insurance of 1915–19, launched just when compulsory health insurance's German origins made the project most vulnerable, was a case in point. The municipal ownership campaign, which fed quickly in Britain on the capture of gas and water profits, arrived in the United States when streetcar monopolies had moved to the fore, and they proved a much more difficult challenge for politics. But timing had more pervasive consequences as well. The "lag" that so embarrassed American progressives was not an idle metaphor. Lagging nations accrue certain advantages; the costs of experiment and mistake may have already been paid off by earlier experimenters, the choices may be clearer, the techniques packaged and refined. But latecomers accrue costs as well. The ideological and institutional space into which the reformers hope to move will almost certainly be more crowded still with claimants, if not preempted outright by players too strong to move.

Take in this regard, the most embarrassing of the American progressives' failures: their failure to bring to the United States a version of the broadly based systems of public health insurance which had become widespread in Europe by the late 1920s. Differential need not does not hold the answer. Where the line between poverty and wage work was so often paper-thin, the threat of income loss through accident and sickness was an acute point of working-class distress through all the industrial nations. It was the political and institutional contexts that were less stable. In the 1880s, when Bismarck sought to preempt the issue of industrial wage workers' health and safety and seize credit for social protectionism for the emperor and the state, he had a relatively open field in which to work. The German labor movement was weak. The socialists had been outlawed. German doctors were not strongly organized professionally; most were accustomed to contract work for one or another of the empire's thousands of voluntary mutual assistance societies. Commercial insurance companies in Germany were still in their infancy. Liberals in the Reichstag objected intensely to the principle of state compulsion. But the mutual assistance societies, which the social insurance legislation promised to absorb largely intact into the system, did not. Nor at the outset did the doctors or the commercial insurance societies put up powerful institutional resistance to it. By the time the doctors' restlessness peaked in the early twentieth century, the system, now expanded outward well beyond the classes of wage earners originally covered, had set down deep institutional roots in the German population.

When the British "new liberals" brought German-style tax-financed and state-mandated health insurance to Britain in 1908–1911, the terrain was no longer the same. The labor movement possessed much more political influence and organizational freedom than in 1880s Germany. Like labor organizations elsewhere, it had no liking for the wage taxes that were fundamental to the social insurance project. But already in delicate and complicated alliance with Liberal, middle-class progressives over labor bargaining rights, state assistance to the elderly poor, and unemployment relief, the unions did not throw their weight against it. The physicians were much better organized in 1910s Britain than in 1880s Germany. The leading, nationally organized British Friendly Societies, although undermined by actuarial miscalculations, were significantly more powerful than the local mutual assistance societies of Bismarck's Germany. Finally, the commercial insurance companies in 1910s Britain now formed a major economic interest, their sales force peddling penny death and burial policies in every working-class neighborhood. On this field, Lloyd George launched the Liberal Party's campaign for public health insurance with a raft of German data, an eagerness to trump the claims of the tariff-protectionist Conservatives as the true friend of the British working class, and a readiness to co-opt where he could not persuade. The Friendly Societies, once they had secured themselves a place in the administration of benefits, came nervously aboard. The doctors, having cut themselves into the local administration of health services, and the commercial insurance companies, having obtained a key place in its distribution, withdrew their opposition.

When all these precedents came to a head in the United States in 1915–19, the field was yet differently configured and some of the players still better organized. Like labor movements elsewhere, the American labor organizations were ambivalent about wage-tax financing of health insurance; at the top, the AFL chieftains, who had fallen out sharply with middle-class progressives over appointments to some of the key new social policy commissions, were strenuously opposed. The mutual assistance associations were numerous but politically weak, splintered along uncrossable lines of race, religion, and ethnicity. The doctors, with little experience in contract work, were deeply committed to entrepreneurial medicine. The commercial insurance companies, offshoots of their British progenitors, were even more firmly entrenched in the United States and determined to resist public competition in the insurance market, even through forms of insurance they did not yet think it profitable to offer. In this crowded field of players, the doctors' organizations and insurance companies were able to resist, fiercely and successfully, public inroads into their terrain.

American progressives tried again in the 1930s, this time with the advantage of the crisis in policy habits and convictions precipitated by the Depression. Knowing what they wanted, Roosevelt and his labor secretary loaded the Committee on Economic Security with experts on European models of social insurance. The Milbank Memorial Fund, sponsor of a recent, massive world survey of public health endeavors, loaned the government its staff experts on health and sickness insurance. The labor unions were less strongly opposed than before; the insurance companies were on the ropes. But the American Medical Association, determined not to be outmaneuvered, voted to oppose health insurance even before the drafters had completed their work. Fearful that the old-age and unemployment insurance sections of the committee's work would fall victim to the controversy, Roosevelt shelved the health insurance section and sent the social security bill to Congress without it. In the 1940s when the Truman administration and the CIO unions tried to pick up the cause once more, the growth of employment-based, commercial health insurance made the project even harder than before. And it was to be harder still when the Clinton administration, this time dissociating itself from virtually every foreign precedent, tried again a half century later.

Differences, in short, need not be the structural, virtually timeless contrasts American historians have used so often, borrowed from Louis Hartz or Tocqueville or elsewhere. The systems of cross-national transmission also served as constantly shifting sorting machines, allowing some measures through, blocking others, and creating still more in hybrid form from the intrusion of a foreign precedent into the field of domestic politics. The networks of social political information and mobilization did not make social politics in any of the nation-states of the early twentieth century the same. What they did was to press onto the political agendas of the nation-states a new set of problems, a common family of needs, and a heightened urgency about them. Still more, they stocked those nations with an array of policy ideas and measures far greater than any of them could have generated on its own. For the latecomers to this system, the Americans of the Progressive and New Deal years, this last was formative.

The systems of international social-political exchange set in motion in the late nineteenth century did not evaporate in the crises of the mid twentieth; but their character changed and, still more, the place of the United States within them. Within Europe itself, they were never stronger than in the half century after World War II. Around the economic and social offices of the United Nations and the new agencies of European economic integration burgeoned powerful new institutions of transnational social-politics. The systematic "welfare states" of present-day Europe, most of them constructed in the 1950s, are among their most important achievements. Americans were not distant from these events. American labor organizations' international ties grew, if anything, stronger in the postwar years, fostered by the Reutherite CIO's connections with European social democracy. American proconsuls helped restore the institutions of public social provision and insurance that the Nazis had cashiered in Germany. But deeply as Americans were involved in the construction of these postwar institutions, they no longer played the part in domestic American politics that they had played before.

If the pattern was different, it was, above all, because the post-1945 patterns of global economic and political hegemony were so dramatically changed. The second "suicide" of Europe, as some observers called the extended crisis of 1933–45, shattered the economies of the nations that had dominated the nineteenth century and, at the same stroke, enriched the United States beyond any relative earlier measure. The rough equality of condition, the sense of comparable economic forces and vulnerabilities so essential to construction of the social-political networks of the early twentieth century, evaporated in the years of the Marshall Plan, European rationing and food shortages, and gifts of hand-me-down American stockings. When capitalism regained its feet in Europe, in a revived "social market" relationship with state and society, it was now to play a junior role to the giant postwar American economy—as a field for investment and export, not one of serious political-economic rivalry.

The yawning postwar imbalances in economic power were exacerbated by the emerging Cold War. Nothing more radically internationalized the reach of American politics than the new world rivalry with the Soviet Union, and nothing more radically contributed to its insularity. If it was a consequence of the Cold War to send Americans more deeply into the world than ever before, as administrators, scholars, proconsuls, cultural mediators, military commanders, and economic aid distributors, with their fingers in every nation's political pot, the very weight of the Americans' hegemonic world responsibility made it harder to admit that that there was anything to be learned from the world abroad—or to imagine that it was politically advantageous to appear to think so. Where admission of domestic imperfection carried new global dangers, the old terms of relationship became unsustainable. The metaphors of "lag" and "backwardness" melted away in the postwar reconfiguration of power. In a world that now demanded to be led, American statesmen talked about the awesome "burden of greatness" that lay on the Americans' shoulders.[25] Historians wrote about American "exceptionalism."

A portent of these changed times had appeared even before the outcome of the war was clear, with the publication of the Beveridge Plan in Britain in 1942. Of all the social policy manifestos of the postwar era, none matched Beveridge's in its transnational influence or its electrifying impact. Beveridge's plan to "abolish want" was discussed in every corner of Britain, from radical union gatherings to staid churchmen's conferences; copies were distributed to the troops and clandestinely circulated across the Nazi-occupied Continent. The first attempt to bring the piecemeal social politics of the prewar age into comprehensive design, the Beveridge Report set the model for welfare state developments across the world.[26]

But in the American progressive journals that had once been such eager conduits for European social policy news, that at the end of the previous war had spread Sidney Webb's "Labour and the New Social Order" boldly across their pages, a new tone of superiority intruded. The *Nation* all but ignored Beveridge's document. The *New Republic* quickly concluded that there was nothing in it for progressive Americans. The Beveridge Report's guarantee of universal minimum provisions of income and health services, American progressives objected, was not the foundation for a truly "revolutionary" social policy. That policy needed to focus on employment. Henry Wallace repeated the *New Republic*'s point: static and defeatist, the Beveridge Plan had no fundamental relevance for a "dynamic" growth economy like that of the United States. The issue ran deeper than Beveridge's failure to focus on the business cycle, which he soon made up for in 1945 in *Full Employment in a Free Society,* one of the central Keynesian texts of the age.[27] American progressives had looked at the most widely influential blueprint for postwar European social politics and seen no room of their own in it.

The inward turn in American social politics after 1945 did not spell the end of progressive ambitions in the United States. Full-employment liberalism was an important progressive project in its own right. From the 1940s through the early 1970s, American progressives filled far more legislative pages than their prewar mentors had ever written, expanding the categories of social politics across new dimensions of race, gender, and environment, even bringing a form of piecemeal public health insurance to those old enough or poor enough to fall into its categories. But though postwar American progressives often knew a good deal about foreign analogues and connections, they did not often talk about them as freely as before. At the end of the 1970s, when the tide shifted back toward the proponents of the automatic, guiding hand of markets (the "Washington consensus," as Europeans call it), the center of the neoliberal global network of policy consultants, world bankers, international businessmen, and intellectuals was now unabashedly the United States.[28]

Like all endings, the end of the era in which social politics agitated the Atlantic nations in tightly related languages, envies, organizations, and endeavors was blurred and complex. For scholars and scientists, businessmen and investors, even for certain kinds of policy experts, the boundaries of the nation-states have never been weaker than in the present age. In the era of U.S. hegemony, American history now *is* international history by the very weight of its world force and presence. But foreign models after 1945 no longer played the major public role in American politics they had played before. Flurries of interest in Japanese corporate management, Swedish labor market policies, Canadian health insurance, British urban enterprise zones, and "third way" convergence may agitate the headlines, but they have left behind no inventory of legislation as dense as that which marked the age of social politics. The referents of American politics are now more insular, and its worries and dissatisfactions are more self-absorbed. After 1945, there were to be no more American presidents who would risk talking, as even so nationalist a figure as Theodore Roosevelt had done, of the United States as "among the most belated of nations" in the procession of the world.

NOTES

1. Daniel T. Rodgers, "Exceptionalism," in *Imagined Histories: American Historians Interpret the Past*, ed. Anthony Molho and Gordon S. Wood (Princeton, N.J., 1998).

2. David P. Crook, *American Democracy in English Politics, 1815–1850* (Oxford, 1965); R. Laurence Moore, *European Socialists and the American Promised Land* (New York, 1970); C. Vann Woodward, *The Old World's New World* (New York, 1991).

3. Sanford Elwitt, *The Third Republic Defended: Bourgeois Reform in France, 1880–1914* (Baton Rouge, La., 1986); *Laboratoires du nouveau siècle: La nébuleuse réformatrice et ses réseaux en France, 1880–1914*, ed. Christian Topalov (Paris, 1999); *Weder Kommunismus noch Kapitalismus: Bürgerliche Sozialreform in Deutschland vom Vormärz bis zur Ära Adenauer*, ed. Rüdiger vom Bruch (Munich, 1985); Laurence Goldman, "The Social Science Association, 1857–1886: A Context for Mid-Victorian Liberalism," *English Historical Review* 101 (1986): 131.

4. Robert Kelley, *The Transatlantic Persuasion: The Liberal-Democratic Mind in the Age of Gladstone* (New York, 1969).

5. *Beatrice Webb's American Diary, 1898*, ed. David A. Shannon (Madison, Wis., 1931); Henry Pelling, *America and the British Left: From Bright to Bevan* (New York,

1957); Samuel Barnett, Diary of a round-the-world tour, 1890–91, Samuel Barnett Papers, Greater London Record Office and History Library.

6. W. E. B. Du Bois, "Germany, 1894–1916," W. E. B. Du Bois Papers (microfilm ed.), University of Massachusetts at Amherst Library; Samuel Gompers, *Labor in Europe and America* (New York, 1910), 286–87.

7. H. G. Wells, *The Future in America: A Search after Realities* (New York, 1906), 74.

8. Albert S. Lindemann, *A History of European Socialism* (New Haven, Conn., 1983); Donna R. Gabaccia, "Is Everywhere Nowhere? Nomads, Nations, and the Immigrant Paradigm," *Journal of American History* 86 (1999): 1115–34; Marcel von der Linden, "Transnationalizing American Labor History," ibid. 86 (1999): 1078–92; John H. M. Laslett, *Colliers across the Sea: A Comparative Study of Class Formation in Scotland and the American Midwest, 1830–1924* (Urbana, Ill., 2000).

9. James T. Kloppenberg, *Uncertain Victory: Social Democracy and Progressivism in European and American Thought, 1870–1920* (New York, 1986).

10. Pierre-Yves Saunier, "Changing the City: Urban International Information in the Lyon Municipality, 1900–1940," *Planning Perspectives* 14 (1999): 19–48.

11. Leila J. Rupp, *Worlds of Women: The Making of an International Women's Movement* (Princeton, N.J., 1997); Ellen Carol DuBois, "Woman Suffrage around the World: Three Phases of Suffragist Internationalism," in *Suffrage and Beyond: International Feminist Perspectives,* ed. Caroline Daley and Melanie Nolan (New York, 1994); *Protecting Women: Labor Legislation in Europe, the United States, and Australia, 1880–1920,* ed. Ulla Wikander, Alice Kessler-Harris, and Jane Lewis (Urbana, Ill., 1995); *Mothers of a New World: Maternalist Politics and the Origins of Welfare States,* ed. Seth Koven and Sonya Michel (New York, 1993).

12. Benjamin O. Flower, *Progressive Men, Women, and Movements of the Past Twenty-Five Years* (Boston, 1914); Kenneth McNaught, "American Progressives and the Great Society," *Journal of American History* 53 (1966): 512; William Allen White, *The Autobiography of William Allen White* (New York, 1946), 410.

13. *The Works of Theodore Roosevelt,* memorial edition (New York, 1923–26), 17: 591; "The Government as Landlord," *Arena* 33 (1905): 325.

14. Walter Weyl, *The New Democracy: An Essay on Certain Political and Economic Tendencies in the United States* (New York, 1912), 2, 20.

15. *Social Justice Feminists in the United States and Germany: A Dialogue in Documents, 1885–1933,* ed. Kathryn Kish Sklar, Anja Schüler, and Susan Strasser (Ithaca, N.Y.: 1998); Susan Pedersen, *Family, Dependence, and the Origins of the Welfare State: Britain and France, 1914–1945* (New York, 1993).

16. Mary Nolan, *Visions of Modernity: American Business and the Modernization of Germany* (New York, 1994); Victoria de Grazia, "Changing Consumption Regimes in Europe, 1930–1970: Comparative Perspectives on the Distribution Problem," in *Getting and Spending: European and American Consumer Societies in the Twentieth Century,* ed. Susan Strasser, Charles McGovern, and Matthias Judt (New York, 1998).

17. For exceptions, see Benjamin R. Beede, "Foreign Influences on American Progressivism," *Historian* 45 (1983): 529–49; Kenneth O. Morgan, "The Future at Work: Anglo-American Progressivism, 1890–1917," in *Contrast and Connection: Bicentennial Essays in Anglo-American History,* ed. H. C. Allen and Roger Thompson (Athens, Ohio, 1976); and Melvyn Stokes, "American Progressives and the Euro-

pean Left," *Journal of American Studies* 17 (1983): 5–28. The point about the insularity of the study of social politics could equally be raised, of course, of European history for this period. Among the useful correctives: Allan Mitchell, *The Divided Path: The German Influence on Social Reform in France after 1870* (Chapel Hill, N.C., 1991); Stefan Berger, *The British Labour Party and the German Social Democrats, 1900–1931* (Oxford, 1994); Tony Freyer, *Regulating Big Business: Antitrust in Great Britain and America, 1880–1990* (New York, 1992); *The Emergence of the Welfare State in Britain and Germany, 1850–1950*, ed. W. J. Mommsen (London, 1981); Hugh Heclo, *Modern Social Politics in Britain and Sweden: From Relief to Income Maintenance* (New Haven, Conn., 1974).

18. Nancy Fraser, "Struggle Over Needs: Outline of a Socialist-Feminist Critical Theory of Late-Capitalist Political Culture," in *Women, the State, and Welfare,* ed. Linda Gordon (Madison, Wis., 1990). See also John W. Kingdon, *Agendas, Alternatives, and Public Policies* (Boston, 1984); David Brian Robertson and Jerold L. Waltman, "The Politics of Policy Borrowing," in *Something Borrowed, Something Learned? The Transatlantic Market in Education and Training Reform,* ed. David Finegold, Laurel McFarland, and William Richardson (Washington, D.C., 1993); Richard Rose, *Lesson-Drawing in Public Policy: A Guide to Learning across Time and Space* (Chatham, N.J., 1993).

19. E. P. Hennock, *British Social Reform and German Precedents: The Case of Social Insurance, 1880–1914* (Oxford, 1987).

20. Bruce Ackerman, *We the People,* vol 1.: *Foundations* (Cambridge, Mass., 1991). On persisting intra-European differences in social policy, see Gøsta Esping-Andersen, *The Three Worlds of Welfare Capitalism* (Princeton, N.J., 1990).

21. For corrective reframings: *Working-Class Formation: Nineteenth-Century Patterns in Western Europe and the United States,* ed. Ira Katznelson and Aristide R. Zolberg (Princeton, N.J., 1986); Gary Marks, *Unions in Politics: Britain, Germany, and the United States in the Nineteenth and Early Twentieth Centuries* (Princeton, N.J., 1989); Ross McKibbin, "Why Was There No Marxism in Great Britain?" *English Historical Review* 99 (1984): 297–331. The more recently posed inquiry, "Why no social citizenship in America?" unmarred by gender and racial inequalities, threatens to fall into the same polarities. See in this regard, Alice Kessler-Harris' otherwise acute and critical discussion of the limits of New Deal social policy: "In the Nation's Image: The Gendered Limits of Social Citizenship in the Depression Era," *Journal of American History* 86 (1999): 1251–79.

22. Theda Skocpol, *Protecting Soldiers and Mothers: The Political Origins of Social Policy in the United States* (Cambridge, Mass., 1992); Margaret Weir and Theda Skocpol, "State Structures and the Possibilities for 'Keynesian' Responses to the Great Depression in Sweden, Britain, and the United States," in *Bringing the State Back In,* ed. Peter B. Evans, Dietrich Rueschemeyer, and Theda Skocpol (New York, 1985).

23. Thomas Adams, "Garden Cities and Town Planning in America," *Garden Cities and Town Planning,* n.s., 1 (August 1911): 168.

24. *Gender and Class in Modern Europe,* ed. Laura L. Frader and Sonya O. Rose (Ithaca, N.Y.: 1996); *Gender and the Politics of Social Reform in France, 1870–1914,* ed. Elinor A. Accampo, Rachel G. Fuchs, and Mary Lynn Stewart (Baltimore, 1995); David Crew, *Germans on Welfare: From Weimar to Hitler* (New York, 1998).

25. *The Papers of Adlai E. Stevenson,* vol. 5: *Visit to Asia, the Middle East, and Europe,*

March–August 1953, ed. Walter Johnson (Boston, 1974), 488–89.

26. José Harris, *William Beveridge: A Biography* (Oxford, 1977).

27. Max Lerner, "Charter for a New America," *New Republic* 108 (1943): 369; Henry A. Wallace, "Jobs for All," *New Republic* 112 (1945): 139; William A. Beveridge, *Full Employment in a Free Society* (New York, 1945).

28. See, e.g., Yves Dezelay and Bryant Garth, "Le 'Washington Consensus': Contribution à une sociologie de l'hégemonie du néoliberalisme," *Actes de la recherche en sciences sociales* 121–22 (March 1998): 3–22; H. W. Arthurs, "Where Have You Gone, John R. Commons, Now That We Need You So?" *Comparative Labor Law and Policy Journal* 21 (2001).

ELEVEN

The Age of Global Power

Marilyn B. Young

The interesting task of this volume is to develop a way of thinking about and writing the history of the United States that avoids the customary practice of American historians, especially in the post–World War II period, of transforming the commonsense notion of different national histories into a conviction that the United States is unique. "Of the controlling themes in contemporary United States history writing," Daniel Rogers observes in a recent essay, "none were pressed more urgently upon professional historians by the surrounding culture than a desire not merely for difference but for a particularity beyond all other nations' particularities: a yearning for proof of its own uniqueness so deep that it tied every other nation's history in fetters."[1] Other nations might be enchained by universal laws of history, but the United States was the Ptolemaic center of the world, around which they all revolved. Oddly, this conviction was accompanied by another, equally firm one: that the U.S. effort to "create some order out of the chaos of the world," as Dean Acheson put it, was simply a response to the "Soviet menace."[2] The United States was thus at once powerful and passive. The flurry of postwar plans, doctrines, interventions, alliances, and wars were reactions to external aggression (flexibly understood to include "internal subversion").

The combination of the three—America as exceptional, powerful, and passive—has yielded policies and interpretations that are intellectually tautological and politically solipsistic. The United States has not been an aggressor, because, by definition, it does not commit aggression. The hostility of others to the United States cannot, again by definition, be a response to American actions, because the United States does not invite hostility but only reacts to it. What the United States claims it intends, rather than what it does, should persuade any fair-minded observer of the righteousness of its policies.

There is a double Archimedean dilemma involved in the effort to think about U.S. history outside of its own terms. Where can the historian stand in order to lever the history of the United States off its assumed centrality? Policy-makers and, in large measure, the American public, live deeply inside an exceptionalist ideology that has retroactively shaped the material world the historians interpret. Most analyses begin with the injunction that it is necessary to understand and convey to readers the worldview of the policy-makers before engaging in an analysis of the choices they have made. "You must remember what it was like in the 1940s [or 1950s, or 1960s] . . . ," historians of U.S. foreign policy chide those among them who seem to be treating the United States too critically. The result is often a rendering of U.S. history that reproduces U.S. ideology. But the second part of the dilemma may be the more difficult. It arises from the fact that for the past fifty years, the United States has been the most powerful country in the world. Europe, Asia, Latin America, and Africa might serve as reasonable ground on which to rest one's lever, were it not that, since at least 1945, each of these continents, one way and another, has had little choice but to engage the centrality of American power.

Obviously, I do not mean that the United States totally dominated all aspects of the daily lives of the world's population, nor that it always and everywhere imposed its will. People around the world have found reasons enough of their own to engage in civil and other wars, with the result that the United States has sometimes had to conclude that domination over half a country was better than none. But in its impact on global culture, economics, military hardware, and international diplomacy, no other power or coalition of powers comes close to the United States. This is especially the case since the collapse of the Soviet Union, but I would argue it has been true for much longer. To write the history of the United States in the world from outside its claims to a limitless horizon means to take the country as simply one nation among others. This is true and also not true. So the problem is not only how to think about the United States without reinstating its own centered sense of itself but how to do this without ignoring the success it has had in achieving, in Melvyn Leffler's words, a "preponderance of power," a centralizing power, in the world.

Another way to describe the problem is in terms of the inability of many Americans to envision other countries *as* countries in their own right. Thus the United States is able to operate without awareness of the way in which even minor exercises of U.S. power affect the lives of others; sometimes without even remembering that anything happened at all. Fundamentally, other countries simply do not have much purchase on the American imagination. Here is an example: the result of an American-engineered over-throw of the government of Cheddi Jagan in Guyana in 1963 reduced that country to a state of unprecedented poverty and corruption. America's man in Guyana, Forbes Burnham, ruled the country through "force and fraud," accumulating over $2 billion in foreign debt, the equivalent of five times its GDP; interest payments consumed 80 percent of Guyana's revenue and 50 percent of its foreign earnings. Thirty years later, in 1992, after the country's first free elections in the three decades, Cheddi Jagan was re-turned to office, and shortly thereafter President Clinton nominated one of the architects of the Kennedy administration's plot to overthrow Jagan as ambassador to Georgetown. The nomination was withdrawn when the Guyanese protested, and, in a move toward damage control that only drew more attention, U.S. government records of Kennedy's policy toward Guy-ana, which were scheduled to be released, instead were sealed. Apparently, neither Clinton nor any of his senior advisers remembered the plot; if they did, the nomination was a deliberate insult, but this seems less likely than that they simply forgot. "Maybe President Clinton doesn't know our his-tory," Cheddi Jagan remarked, "but the people who advise him should at least know their own history."[3] John Lewis Gaddis, the preeminent historian of American foreign relations, does know U.S. history and includes the incident in his recent book on the Cold War, but he is no more interested than Clinton in the history of Guyana. "Bill Clinton," he writes, "had been a precocious teenager . . . and could not have been expected to know. But the fact that none of his senior advisers remembered the crisis . . . suggests how much has changed since the days when Americans saw dominoes lined up, ready for toppling, all over the 'third world.'" Guyana makes its ap-pearance in Gaddis's book solely as an example of the shift in Washington's perceptions since the United States won the Cold War.[4] For the historian, as for Washington, Guyana does not really exist.

H. W. Brands's history of the Cold War, *The Devil We Knew*, begins by locating America in an international context. The United States is neither a city on a hill nor, as in some versions of revisionist history, an evil empire; rather, the Cold War was "simply the management of national interests in a world of competing powers." Yet as a metaphor that launched military Keynesianism, erased domestic divisions of class and race in the service of a homogeneous anticommunist cause, and turned complex issues into sim-ple choices, the Cold War had the power to create a hermetic virtual reality of Manichean divisions and savage "limited" wars. Brands understands the self-intoxicating nature of Cold War ideology: "Americans recognized the utter peril that arming the world on an unprecedented scale was placing them in. They felt the economic burden of maintaining the most powerful and expensive military establishment in human history. Recognizing the peril and feeling the burden, they naturally came to believe that it was all necessary." Although Brands seems to want to normalize U.S. history, he cannot concede that, apart from its power, it was a nation like any other. Americans, he writes, "have from the beginning of their national existence demonstrated an incurable desire to make the world a better place."

Had he written that Americans "have from the beginning of their national existence believed themselves to have demonstrated, or were told they had demonstrated, an incurable desire to make the world a better place," the reader might have looked forward to an analysis of this curious phenomenon. But Brands says something different: "In 1945, nearly all Americans and probably a majority of interested foreigners had looked on the United States as a beacon shining the way to a better future for humanity, one in which ideals mattered more than tanks. During the next forty years, American leaders succeeded in convincing many Americans and all but a few foreigners that the United States could be counted on to act pretty much as great powers always have." This "incurable desire to make the world a better place" also defines the United States for Loren Baritz: America, he writes, "must be for freedom, for dignity, for genuine democracy, or it is not America." Baritz concludes that "it was not America in Vietnam." Who was it then?[5] The problem may be that the United States was itself in Vietnam; and that the belief in America as a shining beacon was the spark that lit and kept burning the fire of the Cold War.

Diplomatic historians are aware of the irony of writing about U.S. engagement with other nations as if it were a monologue. We are instructed to learn other languages, to use foreign archives, to write not just bilaterally but multilaterally. But to do this without at the same time addressing the consistency with which other countries have remained insubstantial to U.S. policy-makers and their public distorts the record beyond the redress of polygottal achievement. As the United States made war against Korea, for example, Dean Acheson insisted that the war wasn't a "Korean war on either side" but rather "the global strategy of global purpose on both sides."[6] Countries were counters in a zero sum game, reversing Kant's categorical imperative. Not only were these countries not taken as ends, they mattered only insofar as they figured in America's calculation of its own economic or political interest. When China was "lost," Korea became important for entirely extrinsic reasons. It was not, Senator Henry Cabot Lodge pointed out, "much good, but it's ours."[7] Or, for an example closer to the present, we can contemplate Secretary of State Madeleine Albright's acknowledgment to an interviewer asking about the deaths of an estimated half a million Iraqi children due to American-imposed sanctions that it was a "hard choice," but "we think the price is worth it."[8]

American power is thus compounded by a conviction that the world at large is isomorphic with its own needs and ambitions, or should be. In November 1965, Secretary of Defense Robert McNamara warned President

Johnson that the Chinese were attempting to construct a coalition in Asia. If they succeeded, McNamara was certain the president would agree, this would constitute a "straightforward security threat." But there was another more important thought that the secretary wished to share with Johnson: "namely, that we have our view of the way the U.S. should be moving and of the need for the majority of the rest of the world to be moving in the same direction if we are to achieve our national objectives." "Our ends cannot be achieved," McNamara went on, "and our leadership role cannot be played if some powerful and virulent nation—whether Germany, Japan, Russia or China—is allowed to organize their part of the world according to a philosophy contrary to our own."[9] It would take no great effort to accumulate a collection of Favorite American Imperial Quotes: Henry Kissinger, who did not see "why we need stand by and watch [Chile] go communist due to the irresponsibility of its own government"; John J. McCloy on the right of the United States "to have our cake and eat it too," operating independently in South America while retaining the right to "intervene promptly in Europe"; Acheson's promise to "help people who believe the way we do, to continue to live the way they want to live."[10] The combination of nationalism and universalism these statements reflect may characterize all imperial states, but the point I want to stress is that during much of this century the United States has had the power to act on the basis of its imperial self-image. This makes it difficult for the historian attempting to de-center the history of U.S. foreign relations, not to speak of the people on whom its power is visited.

The work of John Lewis Gaddis is an example of how the past fifty years look if one takes America at its own word. Unlike earlier mainstream historians, Gaddis does not hesitate to name America imperial. However, he believes that the American empire, in contrast to others, was built without either "imperial consciousness or design." The long-standing tradition of the United States was anti-imperial, at least outside the Western hemisphere, despite "departures" like the Spanish-American War. After World War II, empire was, like greatness on Malvolio, thrust upon the United States by Europeans who found Stalin's approach to imperial management unattractive and so invited a protective American overlordship. On the whole, the American empire has been a good one, perhaps even—as the Founding Fathers themselves intended—an empire for liberty. "The Americans," Gaddis concludes, "constructed a new kind of empire—a democratic empire—for the simple reason that they were, by habit and history, democratic in their politics."[11] Gaddis has recently rediscovered the role of ideology in Soviet policy. He now argues that the Cold War was visited upon a reluctant American-led free world by the romantic, paranoid, revolutionary visions of Josef Stalin. The United States, by contrast, operated outside of ideology.[12]

Gaddis does address various U.S. policy excesses. He labels the U.S. intervention in Guatemala in 1954, for example, a "massive overreaction to a minor irritant." On the impact of that overreaction, which led to a civil war lasting four decades in which some 200,000 people died at the hands of the U.S.-supported right-wing government, Gaddis has only a brief comment, which releases the United States from any responsibility for the consequences of its actions. "[The intervention] did little to alter the course of events inside Guatemala," he writes, "where Arbenz's regime had made so many enemies among the landowners and the military that it probably would not have lasted long in any event."[13] Since the intervention "probably" did not alter the miserable course of Guatemalan history, any consideration of that history need not detain us, nor enter into an understanding of Cold War American history.[14] It is certainly possible that the Arbenz regime would have fallen without U.S. encouragement; it is however certain that it *was* overturned with considerable U.S. help, with such consequences as we know.

Gaddis offers his assertion that the United States lacked "imperial consciousness" as an empirical description of the American way of empire. A brief but comprehensive review of twentieth-century U.S. foreign policy by Walter LaFeber reaches a different conclusion. U.S. policy, LaFeber argues, demanded a world "safe and assessable for the American economic system." Rather than a commitment to a "democratic empire," he finds, policies "shaped by the desire to create democratic systems in foreign lands formed the exception rather than the rule. . . . When explicitly pro-democratic policies were advanced, the cost involved was usually perceived to be slight. When the cost promised to be high . . . the push stopped."[15] But no one in the Kennedy administration questioned Cheddi Jagan's legitimacy. He had been elected three times before Kennedy ordered his overthrow; but, as "some sort of Marxist," Arthur Schlesinger Jr. pointed out, the question was "whether he was recoverable for democracy." He displayed "deep procommunist emotion" and the United States could not afford a "quasi-communist regime on the mainland of Latin America."[16]

Gaddis's "democratic empire" is obviously more gratifying to Americans than the one described by LaFeber; it is what politicians tell the country about itself, what high school teachers teach, what students believe. And it lies at the heart of the difficulty involved in any effort to rewrite the national story. For a conviction that an American empire, as opposed to those established by other nations, is democratic, that American interests are consonant with the last, best hopes of all mankind, occludes both the fact of U.S. power and the effect of its exercise. The syllogism is simple: all nations deserve freedom and democracy; the United States embodies both, and its policies, despite some excesses, seek to bestow them on others. Such an ambition, in the absence of military and economic power, would be impossible; but the ambition renders the power itself innocent, harmless, essentially invisible to itself.

I want now to discuss the disparity between the impact of U.S. power on the world and the soft impact of the world on the United States at the point where the impact is hardest and therefore possibly clearest: when international relations turn violent, in moments of armed U.S. intervention.

One likely place to start an exploration of the remarkable power of the nationalist narrative to cushion and mute that impact is the Spanish-American war. Indeed, calling it the Spanish-American war made Cuba, where it took place, and its long struggle for independence, invisible. As Louis A. Pérez Jr. has pointed out, "It is not simply that the historiography has failed to represent the presence of Cubans as relevant to outcomes; it has not even noticed their absence."[17]

Lasting a bare 100 days, with only 379 combat dead and 1,600 wounded on the U.S. side, and an astonishing yield of new possessions (from the Caribbean to Southeast Asia), the war of 1898 was the first limited war in American history. Recent analyses by literary critics and cultural historians have stressed two aspects of the conflict: the way it served to unify the nation and the role it played in reestablishing structures of racial and gender hierarchy in a period of increasing instability. Amy Kaplan understands the war as a "nostalgic recuperation of the heroism of an earlier generation and . . . a purgative final battle, healing the wounds and divisiveness of internecine war while completing the goals of national reunification."[18] Gail Bederman, among others, concentrates on the linking of manliness, race, and imperialism by politicians like Theodore Roosevelt.[19] And Anders Stephanson, in his meditation on the concept of Manifest Destiny, writes of the "all-pervasive" concept of race and the way in which the new racial laws enacted by state legislatures in the 1890s against blacks "found a logical connection to the need to keep subject aliens abroad in their proper place."[20]

Such efforts to recast standard American historical accounts by rejecting a focus on the state or on state-to-state relations, however, run the danger of being themselves as reflexive as the histories they mean to displace. Writing from a Caribbean perspective, the historian Ada Ferrar observes that in these analyses, the areas that came under U.S. rule are present "only as sites where American anxieties and desires unfold."[21]

In a recent essay, Pérez carefully disassembles the ideology that governed U.S.-Cuban relations from the 1898 to 1959. He analyzes first the "debt of gratitude" Americans believed Cubans had incurred for their liberation from Spain and then the necessity Cubans have felt to contest the American representation of the war of 1898. "The revolution of 1959," he writes, "canceled the debt."[22] On the Cuban side, perhaps, but current U.S. policy toward Cuba derives, at least in part, from a persistent U.S. conviction of

Cuban "ingratitude." The difference between Cuban and American representations of 1898 is that the United States has the power to harm those who insist on their own.

The war against Spain, understood as a crusade for Cuban liberation, did not raise many questions about American national identity. But the general public found it more difficult to assimilate the brutality of the campaign against Filipino insurgents than it did the easy victory over Spain. The United States sent 126,500 soldiers to the Philippines, of whom 4,234 died. Michael Hunt has calculated that this was "perhaps the highest ratio for any U.S. war." Not surprisingly, Filipinos suffered greater losses: 20,000 war dead and possibly as many as one-tenth of the population dead as a result of famine and disease between 1899 and 1903.[23] Despite efforts at military censorship, press reports of U.S. atrocities appeared early and plagued the military throughout the war. Journalists and politicians who had fully supported the war against Spain as the fulfillment of an American emancipatory mission turned sharply against the administration when it became clear that the annexation of the Philippines could be achieved only by force of arms. By 1901, reports of the widespread rape and murder of Filipino noncombatants and the systematic torture and summary execution of prisoners of war forced a congressional investigation of army tactics. Chaired by a reluctant Henry Cabot Lodge and stacked with war-friendly witnesses, the investigation ran parallel with two courts-martial revealing shocking details of the ongoing war of extermination against the insurgents on the island of Samar.

Even the jingo press seemed embarrassed. At Balangiga, in October 1901, Brigadier General Jacob Smith, who had learned how to fight "savages" at Wounded Knee, had ordered his troops to kill every Filipino male over the age of ten and turn Samar into a "howling wilderness." Smith was not the only military figure to draw on the experience of the Plains wars. "The country won't be pacified," one returning soldier told the press, "until the niggers are killed off like the Indians."[24] The war was doubly domesticated; and, as with Indians and rebellious African Americans, the real victims were the soldiers, not the Filipinos. What were the soldiers to do, one editorial pointed out, "try moral persuasion on the infuriated bolomen who were massacring our soldiers daily?" Within months, Smith had been forgiven by the mainstream press; the anti-imperialists were being accused of treason, and editorial writers deplored those who had maligned our "brave soldiers" in their fight against "the savages and cannibals over there."[25]

The *New York Times* set out the dilemma: "A choice of cruelties is the best that has been offered in the Philippines. It is not so certain that we at home can afford to shudder at the 'water cure' unless we disdain the whole job. The army has obeyed orders. It was sent to subdue the Filipinos. Having the devil to fight, it has sometimes used fire."[26]

Theodore Roosevelt shrank from neither fire nor water. The water cure (in which prisoners were persuaded to talk by force-feeding them water and then pounding on their swollen stomachs), he reassured a friend, was just "an old Filipino method of mild torture. Nobody was seriously damaged, whereas the Filipinos had inflicted incredible tortures on our people."[27] Many Americans took refuge in such rationalizations and were relieved when Roosevelt announced victory on July 4, 1902, although fighting would continue for many years thereafter. On Roosevelt's orders, Secretary of War Elihu Root congratulated the army for having fought a "humane war" against a "treacherous foe." Root praised the army for having abided by the rules of war in a situation where it was "impossible to distinguish friend from foe." In a peroration resonant with familiar colonial tropes (peaceful natives intimidated into opposing the colonial power), Root concluded: "Utilizing the lessons of the Indian wars, [the Army] has relentlessly followed the guerrilla bands to their fastness in the mountains and jungles and crushed them. . . . It has added honor to the flag which it defended."[28]

In retrospect, the rapidity with which disturbing accounts of American military behavior in the Philippines were erased is a little surprising. Efforts by the anti-imperialist press to gather and publish antiwar sentiments from returning soldiers had mixed results. Although a majority of officers and men criticized the war, they were unanimously opposed to withdrawal short of total victory. Even those against annexation insisted that the United States had first to beat the Filipinos "into submission." The historian Stuart Creighton Miller found the sentiments of Corporal Moses Smith typical: "Now I don't believe that there is a soldier or American but believes the Filipinos must be whipped thoroughly. After that we can give them their independence under an American protectorate."[29] Returning veterans, when they spoke in public at all, defended army tactics as necessary in a guerrilla war. The only sustained protest by veterans was over their loss of benefits, since the conflict in the Philippines was classified as an insurrection rather than a war. Efforts to draft these aging veterans into the movement against the war in Vietnam consistently stumbled over their imperturbable patriotism.[30]

Miller, contemplating the difference between the response to the Vietnam and the Philippine wars, has argued that the popularity of imperialist expansion at the turn of the century defused any lasting opposition to the means by which empire was acquired. Indeed, many anti-imperialists shared both the imperialists' patriotism and their racism. Some anti-imperialists saw a U.S. empire as a deviation from the righteous path of the Founding Fathers, but imperialists argued that it was expansion that really fulfilled the original vision.

Those who sent the U.S. Army to the Philippines, the men who fought there, and most of the historians who have written about it since were also protected from disturbing memories of the actual conduct of the war by their conviction that American intentions had been good. Even Miller, while setting out the horrors of the war, concludes that in the Philippines, as later in Vietnam, Americans were motivated "in part by good intentions to elevate or aid the victims, and not simply to conquer and exploit them."[31] Henry Adams expressed a similar sentiment, though with some irony:

> I turn green in bed at midnight if I think of the horrors of a year's warfare in the Philippines; . . . we must slaughter a million or two foolish Malays in order to give them the comforts of flannel petticoats and electric railways. . . . We all dread and abominate the war, but cannot escape it. We must protect Manila and the foreign interests, which, in trying to protect the natives from Spain, we were as obliged to assume responsibility for.[32]

William Vaughn Moody's poem "On a Soldier Fallen in the Philippines" is less confident. Laurels and flags will have to be heaped on the dead soldier so that he will "doubt not nor misgive," the reasons for his death. For the dead soldier must be protected from recognizing what was the case: the terrible possibility that his "bullet's scream went wide of its island mark" and struck instead "the heart of his darling land where she stumbled and sinned in the dark."[33] This sympathetic silence reassured the public that the purposes for which it had sanctioned a war were not vitiated by its brutalities.

A good illustration of how a shield of righteousness could protect even dissident Americans against loss of their Ptolemaic certainties is John Dos Passos's novel *1919,* which savagely indicts the society that produced the industrialists, militarists, and politicians Dos Passos deemed responsible, not just for World War I, but for the imperialist Spanish-American War that had preceded it. Peopled by both fictional and historical characters, *1919* fuses the two realms in a culminating vision of the burial of the Unknown Soldier, a figure who, by definition, has no history. The author denies him even a meaningful annihilation: he died simply because "the shell had his number on it." John Doe dies messily as well as meaninglessly: the "blood ran into the ground, the brains oozed out of the cracked skull and were licked up by the trenchrats, the belly swelled and raised a generation of bluebottle flies." Once dead, the Unknown Soldier is taken home in a flag-draped coffin to "God's country," where he suffers an ironic and multiple commemoration: medals of all nations are pinned to "where his chest ought to have been" and everyone brings flowers. "Woodrow Wilson brought a bouquet of poppies."[34] The relentless list of medals, the hypocrisy of diplomats, generals, admirals and politicians, the ghoulish concluding image of Wilson with a bouquet of poppies crescendo to a furious rejection of war.

Yet the ferocity of *1919*'s conclusion is also patriotic in its assumption that genuine honor could have been gathered, as well as a meaningful death. For Dos Passos never loosens his embrace of the idea of America, which he enshrines in a vision of its common people. Richard Poirier has observed that most American writers critical of the United States "are rather madly in love" with the country. "There is perhaps no other literature quite so patriotic because none is so damning of the failure of the country to live up to its dreams and expectations."[35]

Mobilization for war has never been easy or automatic, as both Woodrow Wilson and Franklin Delano Roosevelt discovered, although once launched, the memory of prior resistance yielded to a stronger need to make supportable what had seemed in prospect and briefly in retrospect, insupportable. In this respect, America is not exceptional, of course. The literature of World War I, in Europe as well as in the United States, snatched the attractions of war from even the most realistic representations of its irrationality, inhumanity, and sheer craziness. World War II recruits joined up to fight inspired by blurred, self-serving memories of World War I veterans and the contradictory messages of postwar literature and cinema. British and American soldiers who fought in World War II, Paul Fussell has written, "couldn't help noticing the extra dimension of drama added to their experiences by their memories of the films about the Great War." Thus, the parapets of the no-man's-land of World War I appear, geographically most out of place, in Norman Mailer's *The Naked and the Dead*.[36] Subsequently, virtually every American who spoke or wrote of his experience in Vietnam did so in the language of the World War II movie imagery he brought with him to Saigon.

But construing World War II as an American crusade, a process that began during the war and has continued to the present day, does speak to American exceptionalism. Most Americans imagine their country to have won the war more or less on its own. Few know anything at all about the role played by the Soviet Union. Just how strenuous an effort was involved in the creation of America's self-image is evident in the work of the most popular U.S. World War II correspondent, Ernie Pyle. In his daily columns (published in three volumes during the war itself), James Tobin writes, Pyle constructed a "mythical hero, the long-suffering G.I. who triumphed over death through dogged perseverance" and by his unquestioning commitment to the Four Freedoms. The myth gave readers "the sense that they were seeing a hard-bitten portrait of war as it really was, yet also a sense that life was affirmed and went on in the midst of death."[37] Many correspondents contributed to this myth, which Hollywood then standardized. In a 1958 collection of his war journalism, John Steinbeck insisted that everything he reported had really happened. The reporters weren't liars; it is "in the things not mentioned that the untruth lies." They were not reported only in part because of military censorship. Mostly it was because "there was this huge and gassy thing called the War Effort." Judgments about what should be omitted were largely a matter for the correspondent himself to decide, and he carried "the rule book in his head and even invented restrictions for himself in the interest of the War Effort." The rules were simple: first, cowardice did not exist in the U.S. Army and "of all the brave men the private in the infantry was the bravest and the noblest." This was necessary because given the danger and the stupidity of what was asked of them, privates had to "be reassured that these things . . . were actually necessary and wise, and that he was a hero for doing them." Second, there were no "cruel or ambitious or ignorant commanders"; third, none of the five million young men in the military had any interest whatsoever in sex. It wasn't just that reporters went along with the War Effort, Steinbeck remembered, it was that "we abetted it. Gradually it became a part of all of us that the truth about anything was automatically secret and that to trifle with it was to interfere with the War Effort." Central to self-censorship was the correspondents' sense of responsibility to their readers at home. "The general feeling was that unless the home front was carefully protected from the whole account of what war was like, it might panic."[38]

At a certain point, Pyle came dangerously close to forgetting the rules, and rather than risk that, he left the Italian campaign before it was over, explaining to his readers that he had been "too close to the war for too long. . . . I had come to despise and be revolted by war clear out of any logical proportion. I couldn't find the Four Freedoms among the dead men." He feared that his disgust and war weariness would lead him to "begin writing unconscious distortions and unwarranted pessimisms," that he was unable any longer to see "the little things that you at home want to know about the soldiers." In his strained effort to explain himself, Pyle almost reported a war he knew he shouldn't report, revealing what the public had no wish to read about and military authorities would certainly have censored. Between the lines, the dead bury the cause for which they were supposed to have died, the cause Americans at home continued to see as justification for their deaths. Rather than write this suppressed and dangerous story, Pyle decided to stop reporting altogether, until he was able to write as he knew he should.[39]

Two years later, in an unpublished column found on his body after his death, Pyle explained why the news of victory in Europe left him feeling not elated but only relieved. All he finally remembered of the war, he wrote, were "dead men by mass production . . . in one country after another—month after month and year after year. Dead men in winter. Dead men in summer. Dead men in such familiar promiscuity that they become monotonous. Dead men in such monstrous infinity that you come almost to hate them."[40]

Because correspondents made every effort to follow the rules, to keep their revulsion within "logical proportions," the real war in Europe and the Pacific went largely unreported, known only to the men who fought it. Peace came with a final atrocity, the nuclear bombing of Hiroshima and Nagasaki. When the troops came home, it was to a hero's welcome and a home front moved by its own sense of self-sacrifice, justice, and power. Paul Fussell and Gerald Linderman, among many other accounts of World War II, make it clear that troops in the field fought in order to survive and for one another.[41] But these veterans of World War II, like their predecessors, surrendered their war to the one civilians told them they had fought.

The consciousness of America's destructive power, illuminated by the atomic bombs with which the war ended, was obscured by the fear the mobilization of the population for the Cold War engendered. Almost immediately the United States assumed the familiar stance in which it was more threatened than threatening.[42] The Cold War enshrined World War II as the "good war," a sacred icon of national virtue, even as World War II served to explain and justify the Cold War. America was at the center of them both: then, the pursuit of world justice; now, the focus of the Soviet threat. Russian communists replaced German Nazis; Red China replaced fascist Japan. Every effort was made to convince Americans that the Cold War was a real war, and when public faith in the need for tripling the defense budget wavered, the news that the North Koreans had crossed the 38th parallel invigorated it.

The absence of domestic consciousness of U.S. actions abroad is apparent in the ignorance of the great majority of Americans that the United States had been actively intervening in Korea from 1945 to the outbreak of war.[43] North Korean actions seemed gratuitous, inexplicable except as a preemptive move on the part of the Soviet Union against the United States. So powerful was the rhetoric of the Cold War and its Manichean division that the antiwar movement of the 1960s initially criticized the Vietnam War because it seemed to lack the morality and logic of the Korean conflict. Yet for five years, the U.S. government had helped the government of Syngman Rhee suppress a popular left-wing nationalist movement; armed and trained the South Korean army and police forces; arranged for a U.N.-supervised election establishing a separate government in the south; and turned a blind eye to South Korean violations of the 38th parallel.

Despite brutal tactics, high casualties, and public doubt about war aims, or possibly because of them, the public seems largely to have screened out the war.[44] Its savagery was, on occasion, however, reported in considerable detail.[45] And at least one senator, Edwin Johnson of Colorado, insisted that the United States had unwisely intervened in a civil war and should seek an immediate cease-fire. The "only tangible result" of the war, Senator Johnson insisted, had been the "indescribable misery which has been heaped upon the Korean people."[46] Public approval, which had been high in June 1950, reversed itself after Chinese entry into the war in January 1951: 66 percent of Americans polled were in favor of withdrawal, and 49 percent now thought the intervention should never have taken place.[47] But the impression of those fighting the war was that it had simply been forgotten. "It would be easier to take if people back home were helping," Harry Brubaker complains in James A. Michener's 1953 novella, *The Bridges at Toko-Ri*. "But in Denver nobody even knew there was a war except my wife." "If any war that our country ever engaged in could have been called a forgotten war," General Matthew Ridgway complained bitterly, "this was it."[48]

Certainly, that has been true until very recently. Samuel Hynes Jr., the author of a recent book entitled *Soldier's Tale: Bearing Witness to Modern War*, says, quite simply, "I have nothing to say . . . about the war in Korea, a war that came and went without glory, and left no mark on American imaginations—though nearly as many Americans died there as in Vietnam."[49] Given the literary legacy of the Vietnam War, W. D. Ehrhart, a poet and Vietnam veteran, decided that Korea must have left some traces, and a determined search eventually uncovered a small body of work, most of it written long after the war was over. "The Vietnam war," Ehrhart wrote in an introduction to an anthology of six poets, "seems to have been a catalyst for most of these poets, releasing pent-up feelings that had perhaps been held in check by the personal and cultural stoicism bequeathed to them by their generational older brothers."[50] When he asked the poets themselves why Korea had been passed by so lightly, several answered in terms of the war's "lack [of] nobility," of it having been a "non-war," "futile," "bloody, a dirty uncompromising conflict with few positive images." These factors called upon to explain the silence surrounding Korea, however, are the same as those generally adduced to explain the volubility of Vietnam veterans.

The Korean War did occasion some soul-searching in its aftermath, but it was focused almost entirely on the behavior of American prisoners of war while in Chinese captivity. Had they collaborated with the enemy? To what degree? Why did so many die, so few try to escape? What had happened to the young manhood of America? Some rather odd answers were offered. Betty Friedan, in her influential book *The Feminine Mystique*, thought the prisoners were "models of a new kind of American"—"apathetic, dependent, infantile, purposeless," the children of women "who lived within the limits of the feminine mystique."[51]

The focus on the individual failure of prisoners discouraged questions as to whether their behavior was connected to the particular war they were asked to fight. It was a war, the novelist William Styron wrote, in 1963, in which the "issues were fuzzy and ambiguous, if not fraudulent, a war that could not possibly be 'won,' a senseless conflict so unpopular that even the most sanguinary politician or war lover shrank from inciting people to a patriotic zeal, a war without slogans or ballads or heroes."[52]

For a time, it seemed that, with the Vietnam-American War, the American national story, whose plot casts the United States as defensive in a treacherous world, had at last come to an end. Everyone knows how the Vietnam War hastened the unraveling of America's sacred history, already under way as a result of the Civil Rights movement. And yet even this war has not entirely escaped the force field of American solipsism. At the conclusion of Oliver Stone's movie *Platoon* the hero muses that the United States had not fought the enemy but itself in Vietnam. Most of the movies about the war, except those that fantasize a surrogate victory, such as the Rambo series, offer a similar analysis. The moviemakers would seem to agree with Richard Nixon: only Americans can defeat America. With the exception of the occasional female victim who stands metaphorically for Vietnam as a whole, film versions of the war, like many of the memoirs and histories, lack Vietnamese. Most accounts of the war begin with the statement that it was the most divisive war in U.S. history, save only the Civil War. But the Vietnam-American War was a civil war in Vietnam, not in the United States.

A recent experiment in writing the history of the Vietnam-American War from both the U.S. and the Vietnamese sides was intended to break the bell jar. Its failure finally to do is as interesting as its limited success. Over a period of four years, a group of American historians and officials met with their Vietnamese counterparts. Robert S. McNamara was the moving force. Convinced the war was the result of "mutual misperception, misunderstanding, and misjudgement by leaders in Washington and Hanoi," McNamara was anxious both to explain the United States to the Vietnamese and to get them to admit their responsibility. *"If each side had known the truth about the other's reality, might the outcome have been less tragic?"* he asks with italicized intensity.[53] Responsibility for the tragedy of the Vietnam War, McNamara argues, was shared; the blood guilt of 3.8 million Vietnamese and 58,000 Americans must be mutually carried. Vietnam's failure lay in its inability to understand, and disarm, the American Cold War "mindset." The United States was not, the Americans repeatedly insisted, an imperialist country; it did not want to dominate Vietnam; it had gone to the aid of a threatened ally. But the American Cold War mind-set that McNamara patiently explained to the Vietnamese sounds impervious to outside reasoning. Why could not the Vietnamese, during the Geneva Convention or earlier, have explained to the Americans that they were not tools of the Russians and the Chinese, one American official demanded. But we did, the Vietnamese responded, and you would not listen. But, the same official persisted, what was it "that made you think [in the 1950s] that the United

States was your enemy? Was it propaganda from the Soviets and the Chinese? Was it Dulles?"[54]

The Vietnamese reminded the Americans of their aid to the French during the first Indochina war, and the Americans responded that, after all, French requests for American intervention at the time of Dien Bien Phu had been rejected, and, in any case, aid to France had had to do with the situation in Europe, not Vietnam. As Colonel Herbert Schandler put it:

> [T]he United States was taking a *world* view of all these issues. The Iron Curtain was falling all across Europe. This was shocking. We had fought a bloody war in Europe, and had won, only to have half of Europe reconquered by a totalitarian system. . . . Communism, we felt, had to be stopped. The Iron Curtain then fell in Asia in 1954 with the armistice in Korea and with the Geneva Accords. . . . Sometimes it looked to us [as though] we were on the losing side of history.

And Chester Cooper, who attended the Geneva Convention as a representative of the CIA, explained that the United States had not been Vietnam's enemy at the time and that Vietnamese policy decisions based on fear of U.S. intervention had been misguided:

> Yes, of course, eventually we became enemies. . . . But I am telling you as authoritatively [*sic*], as a member of the U.S. government at the time we are talking about, and as one who dealt every day with these issues, that you were wrong in your assessment *then*, in the mid-1950s. Wrong, wrong, wrong! We had made no such decision to intervene. But . . . because you *assumed* that we were hostile, and were seeking to destroy you, then you did things, you made statements, that appeared to us to confirm the views of people like John Foster Dulles that *you* were our mortal enemy.

Luu Doan Huyhn conceded that perhaps America had not been ready to intervene at that precise moment in time. "But really," he went on,

> your bullets are killers of our people. We see that this is America's gift to Vietnam—allowing the French to kill our people. This is the most convincing evidence we have of America's loyalties. . . . So how can we conclude you are not our enemy? . . . we understand all your arguments about U.S. interests and the French and so on. We believe Mr. Chester Cooper when he says that he did not consider Vietnam an enemy. But please try to understand me when I say: *Blood speaks with a terrible voice!*[55]

There was a similar exchange over the Diem regime. Cooper thought "it's fair to say we wished [Diem] well" but denied that there had been a U.S. military presence in Vietnam at that time. The Vietnamese refrained from correcting him but pointed out that Diem's security forces had been trained in the United States. "Now Mr. Chester Cooper says that the orders to kill our people in 1955 did not come from Washington. Okay. But how could we know this? He was your guy, and he was killing our people. You see, blood again—blood speaks loudly when you are the one who is bleeding."[56]

The conclusions McNamara drew from these discussions with the Vietnamese stress mutuality of misperception. "Hanoi," he writes,

> in effect projected onto the United States a kind of colonial mode of operation not significantly different from the French. . . . However, unlike the French, the Americans were ambivalent about their global role and were not colonialists in the way that the French could be characterized. Had Hanoi understood this—had it achieved a more empathetic understanding of American fears and motivations—it could have appealed to a strong set of American motives emphasizing self-determination and anti-colonialism. But Hanoi did *not* understand this.[57]

Of the disparity of power between the two countries, of the difference between bullets and "statements," McNamara has nothing to say. Nor do any of the participants reflect on the fact that had America not lost the war, had Vietnam been divided as was Korea, the discussion itself would never have taken place. It is intolerable to McNamara to assume responsibility for the Vietnam War. The fault lies not only in "missed opportunities for peace" on both sides but with the Vietnamese failure to understand that the United States, as an aspect of its essential character, is for self-determination—appearances to the contrary not withstanding. America's overwhelming power vis-à-vis Vietnam disappears in this formulation and the abiding conviction of American dedication to universal values remains, untouched by history.

In the forlorn last days of America's occupation of Saigon, an American reporter pressed a reluctant diplomat for the "lessons of the war." " 'They will be whatever makes us think well of ourselves,' " he replied, " 'so that our sleep will be untroubled.' "[58] In seeking to ensure the national repose, the United States is hardly unique. To help their countrymen sleep better, historians and politicians have often transformed past unpleasantness into something palatable, and calls to rethink national history are more often calls for nationalist revival than self-criticism. It is especially important that the history of foreign wars, which might pose a serious challenge to somnolence, be domesticated, so that neither the country's self-image nor its capacity to make war in the future is too severely damaged. Anders Stephanson has argued that the history of the country has until recently moved between two poles in its relation to the rest of the world: the first "was to unfold into an exemplary state *separate* from the corrupt and fallen world, letting others emulate as best they can." The second approach, usually identified with Woodrow Wilson, "was to push the world along by means of regenerative *intervention.*"[59]

In both modes, the central, indeed the singular, referent is American. The self-aggrandizement of the truly powerful, the fact of U.S. power combined with the solipsism of the majority of America's inhabitants, have shaped the history of the past fifty years and more. Efforts to internationalize America's history, to diversify and multiply its culture, need to keep in mind the reality of American hegemony and its dominant, self-absorbed culture. Of course that hegemony is continuously challenged, both at home and abroad; of course, the United States is not exceptional, only exceptionally powerful. De-centering America in one's head is a good thing. But it does not of itself create a world free of its overwhelming military and economic power, and it is crucial to remember the difference or the effort to de-center American history will run the danger of obscuring what it means to illuminate.

NOTES

1. Daniel T. Rogers, "Exceptionalism," in *Imagined Histories: American Historians Interpret the Past,* ed. Anthony Molho and Gordon S. Wood (Princeton, N.J., 1998), 21.

2. Quoted in obituary of Dean Acheson, *Time Magazine,* October 25, 1971, 20. I am grateful to Lloyd Gardner for the reference.

3. Tim Weiner, *New York Times,* October 30, 1994, 10.

4. John Lewis Gaddis, *We Now Know: Rethinking Cold War History* (New York, 1997), 186.

5. H. W. Brands, *The Devil We Knew: Americans and the Cold War* (New York, 1993), 225, 228; Loren Baritz, *Backfire: A History of How American Culture Led Us into Vietnam and Made Us Fight the Way We Did* (New York, 1985), 341.

6. Bruce Cumings, *The Origins of the Korean War,* vol. 2: *The Roaring of the Cataract, 1947–1959* (Princeton, N.J., 1990) 628

7. Quoted in Lloyd Gardner, "Do We Learn from History?" (MS), 7.

8. Quoted in Noam Chomsky, "Crisis in the Balkans," *Z Magazine,* May 1999, 43.

9. Quoted in Lloyd Gardner, "From the American Archives," *Diplomatic History* 22, 2 (Spring 1998): 335.

10. Kissinger quoted in Thomas J. McCormick, *America's Half-Century: United States Foreign Policy in the Cold War* (Baltimore, 1989), 186; McCloy quoted in Gabriel Kolko, *The Politics of War: The World and U.S. Foreign Policy, 1943–1945* (New York, 1968), 470–71; Acheson quoted in William Appleman Williams, *America Confronts a Revolutionary World, 1776–1976* (New York, 1976) 171–72; Kissinger is quoted in John Prados, *Presidents' Secret Wars: CIA and Pentagon Covert Operations since World War II* (New York, 1986), 317.

11. Gaddis, *We Now Know,* 39, 289, acknowledges that this beneficient empire held sway primarily in Europe and Japan. About Latin America, the Middle East, and Southeast Asia, he is more circumspect, even agnostic. In these areas, invitations

were periodically extended and withdrawn to both the United States and its imperial rival, the Soviet Union. "Whether the Russians or the Americans responded more brutally—or more humanely—it is difficult to say: as always the 'third world' defies easy generalizations" (286).

12. See Melvyn Leffler, "The Cold War: What Do 'We Now Know'?" *American Historical Review* 104, 2 (April 1999): 501–24.

13. Gaddis, *We Now Know*, 178.

14. Ibid., 178.

15. Walter LaFeber, "The Tension between Democracy and Capitalism during the American Century," *Diplomatic History* 23, 2 (Spring 1999): 284.

16. Arthur M. Schlesinger Jr., *A Thousand Days: John F. Kennedy in the White House* (Boston, 1965), 774, 778. The British, still the colonial power at the time, urged Kennedy to support Jagan, declaring that his rival, Forbes Burnham, was an "opportunist, racist and demagogue intent only on personal power." But Kennedy had been deeply disturbed after a conversation in which Jagan expressed admiration for Paul Sweezy and the *Monthly Review*. "I have the feeling," Kennedy told Schlesinger, "that in a couple of years he will find ways to suspend constitutional provisions and will cut his opposition off at the knees." To avert this disaster, Kennedy leaned on the British to suspend the constitution and delay independence until Jagan was safely out of the way (778, 776, 777).

17. Louis A. Pérez Jr., *The War of 1898: The United States and Cuba in History and Historiography* (Chapel Hill, N.C., 1998), 109. See esp. ch. 4.

18. Amy Kaplan, "Black and Blue on San Juan Hill," in *Cultures of United States Imperialism*, ed. id. and Donald E. Pease (Durham, N.C., 1993), 219.

19. Gail Bederman, *Manliness and Civilization: A Cultural History of Gender and Race in the United States, 1880–1917* (Chicago: 1995), ch. 5, passim.

20. Anders Stephanson, *Manifest Destiny: American Expansion and the Empire of Right* (New York, 1995), 90.

21. Ada Ferrer, *Insurgent Cuba: Race, Nation, and Revolution, 1868–1898* (Chapel Hill, N.C., 1999), introduction.

22. Louis A. Pérez Jr., "Incurring a Debt of Gratitude: 1898 and the Moral Sources of United States Hegemony in Cuba," *American Historical Review* 104, 2 (April 1999): 398.

23. Michael J. Hunt, "East Asia in Henry Luce's 'American Century,'" *Diplomatic History* 23, 2 (Spring 1999): 324.

24. Stuart Creighton Miller, *"Benevolent" Assimilation: The American Conquest of the Philippines, 1899–1903* (New Haven, Conn., 1982), 219, 220, 222; id., "The American Soldier and the Conquest of the Philippines," in *Reappraising an Empire: New Perspectives on Philippine-American History*, ed. Peter W. Stanley (Cambridge, Mass., 1984), 20. The Filipinos would not be the last insurgents to find themselves redefined as American Indians. Soldiers in both the Korean and the Vietnam wars referred to the country outside their bases as Indian country. In one much-praised Korean war novel, Thomas Anderson's *Your Own Beloved Sons . . .* (New York, 1956), for example, a sergeant standing guard invokes older, equally heroic moments: he has the feeling of "being watched by *something* out in front of his position. . . . Perhaps, a hundred years before, another man much like him had stood thus, watching the night over the American continent while behind his back, in the center of the

circle of closely parked wagons, his woman and children, and the women and children of other men, slept together on the ground thus encircled and captured from the unknown" (8).

25. Miller, *"Benevolent" Assimilation,* 246.

26. Ibid., 247.

27. Ibid., 235.

28. Ibid., 254.

29. Miller, "American Soldier and the Conquest of the Philippines," 19.

30. But in 1971 a veteran of the Samar campaign felt moved to tell the press that the massacre at My Lai was hardly unique: his own mission had involved a fishing village. "We snuck through the grass as high as a man's head until both platoons had flanked them. We opened fire and killed all but one. They were unarmed." Quoted in Miller, *"Benevolent" Assimilation,* 267. For views of veterans on Vietnam, see 272–73.

31. Ibid., 269

32. Quoted in Marilyn B. Young, *The Rhetoric of Empire: American China Policy 1895–1901* (Cambridge, Mass.: 1968), 270.

33. Quoted, in Miller, *"Benevolent" Assimilation,* 275–76.

34. John Dos Passos, *1919* (1932; New York, 1969), 466–67.

35. Richard Poirier, *Norman Mailer* (New York, 1972), 27.

36. Paul Fussell, *The Great War and Modern Memory* (New York, 1977), 221, 320; Norman Mailer, *The Naked and the Dead* (New York, 1948).

37. James Tobin, *Ernie Pyle's War: America's Eyewitness to World War II* (New York, 1997), 143.

38. John Steinbeck, *Once There Was a War* (New York, 1958), xiii, xi, xii, xiii, xvii

39. *Ernie's War: The Best of Ernie Pyle's World War II Dispatches,* ed. David Nichols (New York, 1986), 166, 167.

40. Ibid., 419.

41. See, Paul Fussell, *Wartime: Understanding and Behavior in the Second World War* (New York, 1989), and Gerald Linderman, *The World within War: America's Combat Experience in World War II* (New York, 1997).

42. Tom Engelhardt, *The End of Victory Culture: Cold War America and the Disillusioning of a Generation* (New York, 1995).

43. Walter Sullivan, reporting for the *New York Times* from December 1949 to April 1950 was an exception. His predecessor, Richard Johnston, arrived in Korea on board the ship carrying Lt. Gen. John Hodge, and he shared Hodge's perspective and identified with Hodge's mission.

44. Arne Axelsson attributes this attitude to public distaste for limited war: "The widespread disenchantment with the strategy used in Korea was . . . expressed as a refusal to consider this war relevant to America and Americans." Arne Axelsson, *Restrained Response: American Novels of the Cold War and Korea, 1945–1962* (Westport, Conn., 1990), 62.

45. See, e.g., John Osborne, "The Ugly War," *Time,* August 21, 1950, 20–22.

46. *Congressional Record,* May 17, 1951, 5424.

47. Rosemary Foot, *The Wrong War: American Policy and the Dimensions of the Korean Conflict, 1950–1953* (Ithaca, N.Y., 1985), 107.

48. James A. Michener, *The Bridges at Toko-Ri* (New York, 1953), 35. Ridgway is

quoted in Axelsson, *Restrained Response,* 62. This was also the theme of most of the forty novels Axelsson surveys.

49. Samuel J. Hynes Jr., *Soldier's Tale: Bearing Witness to Modern War* (New York, 1997), xiii.

50. W. D. Ehrhart, "Soldier-Poets of the Korean War," *War, Literature and the Arts* 9, 2 (Fall/Winter 1997): 8. Much of the publication on Korea, as well as two TV documentaries about it, are explicitly the product of the Vietnam War. Callum McDonald's book title is a succinct expression of this: *Korea: The War before Vietnam* (New York, 1986).

51. Betty Friedan, *The Feminine Mystique* (New York, 1963), 275.

52. William Styron, "The Long March," in *This Quiet Dust and Other Writings* (New York, 1993), 334.

53. Robert S. McNamara, *Argument without End* (New York, 1999), 6

54. Ibid., 83–84.

55. Ibid., 82, 85, 87.

56. Ibid., 94.

57. Ibid., 379.

58. Quoted in Ward Just, "The American Blues," in *The Other Side of Heaven: Postwar Fiction by Vietnamese and American Writers,* ed. Wayne Karlin, Le Minh Khue, and Truong Vu (New York, 1995), 7.

59. Stephanson, *Manifest Destiny,* xii (emphasis in original).

TWELVE

American Empire and Cultural Imperialism

A View from the Receiving End

Rob Kroes

The internationalization of American studies can mean various things. The phrase pops up in various contexts. There used to be broad agreement that the object of American studies was the history, society, and culture of the geopolitical entity that we know as the United States, commonly referred to by both its own citizens and outsiders as America. As recent trends in American studies make clear, however, the object of study needs to be internationalized, and so do scholarly approaches to it. A further goal of internationalization appears to be greater interaction among the worldwide constituency of American studies scholars.

Internationalizing the object of study means redefining it, taking it out of its nation-state frame of perception and interpretation, if not away from the national emphasis in the narratives that it has spawned. Even when taken to exceptionalist extremes, the nation-state perspective always implies a tacit comparative dimension. America can only be conceived of as an exception if one assumes the existence of a rule to which the rest of the world is subject. Yet precisely because it is deemed exceptional, the story has to be told separately, in relative insulation from the forces of history at work elsewhere. If the implicit comparative dimension adds a touch of irony to the exceptionalist view, there is further irony in the fact that non-Americans have contributed strongly to the exceptionalist reading of America's historical experience.

Now, increasingly, the need is felt to see America as presenting specific historical configurations of forces that affect the United States as much as other parts of the world. Histories of slavery and the slave trade, of migration and diasporic communities, of the settlement of the Western hemisphere, of industrialization and urbanization and the social movements that attended these massive transformations, and studies of class, race, and gender all squarely place the United States within a transnational and comparative perspective. Relatively straightforward as this program for research may appear, it has become clear recently that two clashing paradigms are vying for the meaningful recasting of the study of the United States.

One—let us call it the Thelen approach—aims at exploding the very context of the nation-state as the central structuring element in historical narratives. As David Thelen puts it in the introduction to a special issue of the *Journal of American History* devoted entirely to transnational perspectives on United States history: "Since it seemed increasingly strange that history had centered its concern with time and place on the nation-state, we wanted to design a special issue that would interrogate, not assume, the centrality of the nation-state as the organizing theme for American history. We wanted to explore how people and ideas and institutions and cultures moved above, below, through, and around, as well as within, the nation-state, to investigate how well national borders contained or explained how people experienced history."[1] The second direction in which to take the project of internationalizing the study of the United States—let us call this the Daniel Rodgers paradigm—is one that sees the United States as just another nation among nations, without any messianic destiny or exceptionalist aspirations. It is an approach that, unlike the Thelen paradigm, reemphasizes the nation-state character of the United States, and proposes to present a non- (or post-)exceptionalist history of the country, as one whose history is contingent upon larger historical forces and connected to the impact of and response to those forces in other nation-states.[2]

I would suggest that there is a third way to internationalize the study of the United States, one that ironically reintroduces an exceptionalist element. If, in much recent work, the United States as an object of study has lost its national boundedness, this has also been the result of scholarly approaches that look at America as *inherently* an international phenomenon. Studies of the way in which the country has projected itself as a force affecting the lives of many people across the globe, in the course of what became known as the American Century, are inherently international. They explore the ways in which America's power, political, military, economic, and cultural, is experienced and made sense of elsewhere. Many Americas arose in the process, as so many constructions in the minds of people elsewhere trying to make sense of the forces that have changed their lives. If those forces today are often subsumed under the catch-all term "globalization," the problem for research is to try and discern the American agency affecting them. Globalization and Americanization are not identical, although they are intertwined. In addition to American agency, though, there are the further and crucial questions of mediation and reception, questions to do with the manifold ways in which people at the receiving end recontextualize American culture as it reaches them. There is a freedom involved in cultural reception that may make us aware of the agency implied in the process of reception. If America as an imaginary entity results from a cultural construction going on all over the globe, that America (or those Americas) in particular constitute what I have called the inherently international object of study for American studies scholars. The exceptionalist moment in this approach lies in the structural imbalance between America's position as a semiotic center relegating *all* other nation-states to the position of receivers.

American scholars have hitherto dominated American studies, and this third way of internationalizing the field may expand the agenda of U.S. historiography by removing it from their exclusive control. The collective gaze of scholars on the periphery has for too long centered on America. Scholars studying America from abroad have for too long taken their cues from the U.S. center, where their work has remained relatively obscure. As a result, too, that work has been little noticed by fellow scholars elsewhere on the periphery. Many recent attempts to internationalize American studies have aimed precisely at bringing scholars from the various margins together, trying to create a sense of community among them and arousing an awareness of shared concerns and research interests that does not naturally arise at the center.

In the following, by way of a case study, I propose to explore a number of research questions that are inherently international but all relate to America as a central force in our present-day world. The forces of globalization have allowed America to project itself more forcefully across the world than any other contemporary nation. In the process, it has planted the many emblems of its worldwide presence across the globe, emblems that may evoke cultural resistance or serve as carriers of American culture. My focus is on forms of American commercial culture, particularly advertising.

CULTURAL IMPERIALISM AND THE FREEDOM OF RECEPTION

Students of Americanization are in general agreement as regards the semantic transformations that attend the dissemination of American cultural messages across the world. Depending on their precise angle and perspective, some rather tend to emphasize in their explorations the cultural strategies and auspices behind the transmission of American culture. Whether they study Buffalo Bill's Wild West Show when it traveled in Europe, Hollywood movies, or World Fairs, to name just a few carriers of American culture, their focus is on the motifs and organizing views that the producers were trying to convey, rather than on the analysis of what the spectators and visitors did with the messages they were exposed to. All such cultural productions taken as representations of organizing worldviews do tend to lead researchers to focus on senders rather than receivers of messages. Yet such a focus hardly ever leads these researchers to look at the process of reception as merely one of passive imbibing. Whatever the words (such as "hybridization" and "creolization") one uses to describe what happens at the point of reception, current views agree on a freedom of reception, a freedom to resemanticize and recontextualize meaningful messages reaching audiences across national and cultural borders. Much creativity and inventiveness goes into the process of reception, much joy and exhilaration springs from it. Yet making *this* the whole story would be as fallacious as a focus centered solely on the schemes and designs of the senders of messages. Whatever their precise angle, researchers have come to agree on the need to preserve a balance in their approach to the problems of Americanization.

Furthermore, some researchers have tended to conceive of Americanization as a process tied to early American economic expansionism, or, more recently, to an emerging global economy structured by the organizing logic of corporate capitalism, still very much proceeding under American auspices. The main area in which Robert Rydell, for example, sees Americanization at work is in the "commodification of culture which colonizes the leisure time of people worldwide." World's Fairs and other transmitters of America's commercial culture conjure up a "veritable 'dream world' of mass consumption, a simulation through spectacle of the good life afforded by the technological advances associated with modernization."[3] He goes on to contrast this simulacrum of the good life with the ravages wrought by corporate capitalism in many parts of the globe. He explicitly wants to keep the concept of Americanization in our critical lexicon as a useful reminder of what American economic expansionism has meant in terms of advancing the interests of American corporate culture overseas.

I am not so sure whether this is the right tack. Rydell seems unduly to read the autonomous rise of global corporate capitalism as due to American agency. It is a common fallacy in much of the critique of Americanization to blame America for trends and developments that would have occurred anyway, even in the absence of America. From Marx, via Hobson and Lenin, all the way to the work of the Frankfurt School, there is a long line of critical analysis of capitalism and imperialism, highlighting its inner expansionist logic. Surely, in the previous century, much of this expansion has proceeded under American auspices, receiving an American imprint, in much the same way that a century before, the imprint was British. The imprint has often confused critics into arguing that the havoc wreaked by an overarching process of modernization, ranging from the impact of capitalism to processes of democratization of the political arena or the rise of a culture of consumption, were truly the dismal effects of America upon their various countries. From this perspective, the critique of Americanization is too broad, exaggerating America's role in areas where, in fact, it was caught up in historic transformations much the way other countries were.

From a different perspective, though, this view of Americanization is too narrow. It ignores those vast areas where America, as a construct, an image, a fantasma, has played a role in the intellectual and cultural lives of people outside its national borders. There is a repertoire of fantasies about America that even predates its discovery. Ever since, the repertoire has been fed in numerous ways, through many media of transmission. Americans and non-Americans have all contributed to this collective endeavor, making sense of the new country and its evolving culture. Especially in the century that has just ended, America has become ever more present in the minds of non-Americans, as a point of reference, a yardstick, a counterpoint. In intellectual reflections on the courses and destinies of other countries and cultures, America became part of a process of triangulation, serving as a model for rejection or emulation and providing views of the future, whether seen in a negative or a positive light. America has become a *tertium comparationis* in culture wars elsewhere, centering on control of the discourse concerning national identity and the national culture. Typically, when America has been rejected by one party in such contests, the other has seen it as a liberating alternative. Writing the history of such receptions of America is as much part of American studies as of the historiography of countries other than the United States. It also should form part of a larger reflection upon processes summarily described as Americanization.

Undeniably, though, in the course of this allegedly "American Century," America has assumed a centrality that one might rightly call imperial. Like Rome in the days of the Roman Empire, it has become the center of webs of control and communication that span the world. Its cultural products reach the far corners of the world, communicating American ways and views to people elsewhere, while America itself remains relatively unaware of cultural products originating outside its national borders. If, for such reasons, we might call America's reach imperial, it is so in a number of ways. It is imperial in the economic sphere, in the political sphere, and in the cultural sphere, and if it were still possible to use the term in a relatively neutral way, describing a factual configuration rather than the outcome of concerted effort and motive, one might speak of economic, political, and cultural American imperialism. Trying to accommodate themselves to their diminished role and place in the world, European countries have at times opted to resist particular forms of America's imperial presence. In the 1960s, France, perhaps the most telling case, fended off political imperialism by ordering NATO out of the country, while Jean-Jacques Servan-Schreiber's best-selling book *Le défi américain* warned against America's economic imperialism;[4] later, the French government even briefly considered preventing the film *Jurassic Park* (1993) from being released in France, seeing it as a case of American cultural imperialism and a threat to French cultural identity.

Yet, suggestive as the terms are of neat partition and distinction, the three forms of imperialism in fact overlap to a large extent. Political imperialism promotes economic imperialism. As the new political hegemon of the Western world, the United States was, for example, able to restructure trading relations through the Marshall Plan, which guaranteed access to European markets for American products, including American cultural exports, such as Hollywood movies. Economic imperialism thus translated into cultural imperialism. Conversely, American products, from cars to movies, from clothing styles to kitchen apparel, all actively doubled as agents of American cultural diplomacy, representing the good life American-style. Thus, trade translated back into political imperialism. And so on, in endless feedback loops.

In my own work of recent years, I have chosen to focus on the cultural dimension of all these various forms of the American imperial presence. American culture, seen as a configuration of ways and means that Americans use for expressing their collective sense of themselves—their Americanness—is mediated through every form of American presence abroad. From the high rhetoric of its political ideals to the golden glow of McDonald's arches, from Bruce Springsteen to the Marlboro Man, American culture washes across the globe. It does so mostly in disentangled bits and pieces, for others to recognize, pick up, and rearrange into a setting expressive of their own individual identities, or identities they share with peer groups. Thus, teenagers may adorn their bedrooms with the iconic faces of Hollywood or rock music stars in order to provide themselves with a private place for reverie and games of identification, but they are also engaged in a construction of private worlds that they share with countless others. In the process, they recontextualize and resemanticize American culture to make it function within expressive settings entirely of their own making.

Rydell cites the English journalist W. T. Stead (1849–1912), who called Americanization "the trend of the Twentieth Century," seeing it mostly as the worldwide dissemination of material goods produced by American technical and entrepreneurial prowess. It would be for later observers to look at these consumer goods as cultural signifiers as well, as carriers of an American way of life. An early example of an observer of the American scene with precisely this ability to read cultural significance into the products of a technical civilization was the Dutch historian Johan Huizinga. In his collection of travel observations, published after his only trip to the United States in 1926, he showed an uncanny awareness of the recycling of the

American Dream into strategies of commercial persuasion, linking a fictitious world of self-fulfillment—a world where every dream would come true—to goods sold in the market. High-minded aesthete though he was, forever longing for the lost world of late medieval Europe, he could walk the streets of the great American cities with an eye for the doubling of American reality into a seductive simulacrum. He was inquisitive enough to ask the right questions, questions that still echo in current research into the reception of mass culture in general, and of commercial exhortations in particular. He wondered what the effect of the constant barrage of commercial constructions of the good life would be on ordinary people. "The public constantly sees a model of refinement far beyond its purse, ken and heart. Does it imitate this? Does it adapt itself to this?" Apposite questions indeed. Huizinga was aware of the problem of reception of the virtual worlds constantly spewed forth by a relentless commercial mass culture. More generally, in these musings, he touched on the problem of the effect that media of cultural transmission, like film and advertising, would have on audiences not just in America but elsewhere as well.[5] In these more general terms, the problem then becomes one of how non-American audiences read fantasy worlds that American imaginations have produced and that show all the characteristics of the American way so vehemently indicted by European critics.

In what follows, I propose to explore some approaches to how American mass culture in the post–World War II period may have affected European cultures that were more than ever before within America's imperial sway. My focus is on advertising, seen as a peculiar blend of economic and cultural imperialism.

ADVERTISING: THE COMMODIFICATION OF AMERICAN ICONS

A nation that stops representing itself in images stops being a nation. It is doomed to lead a derivative life, vicariously enjoying worlds of imagery and imagination imported from abroad. Or so France's President François Mitterrand is reported to have mused. In a mood of cultural protectionism, against the backdrop of a seemingly unstoppable conquest of Europe's cultural space by American images, Mitterrand's France called for—but failed to get—a clause exempting cultural goods from the free-trade logic of GATT. The episode, in the final negotiating stages of the Uruguay Round, is reminiscent of earlier defensive ploys by France in the face of the threat of Americanization. There is the story, as told by more than one author,[6] of the fight that France chose to pick to keep Coca-Cola out of the country. Coca-Cola became the symbol of everything that a certain intellectual discourse in Europe had always rejected in America, as the country that had succeeded in mass-marketing bad taste. If there was much to be envied in America as a model of modernity, it offered an example that France should be following selectively and on its own terms—under strict "parental guidance," so to speak. Yet the example as set by America was tempting, precisely because it undercut parental authority and cultural guardianship, promising the instant gratification of desire rather than its sublimation, consumption rather than consummation. Coca-Cola was the item that the French chose to symbolize this pernicious pleasure principle in the global transmission of American mass culture. The soft drink, in this French campaign, was turned into an icon of an alleged American strategy of cultural imperialism. It also gave the strategy a name: Coca-Colonization.

More recently, an ad for another soft-drink, Seven Up, illustrated the seductive semiotics that underlies so many of the messages that reach us from across the Atlantic Ocean. It did this without drawing on the repertoire of American icons. There was no Marlboro Man roaming the open spaces of the American West, no Castle Rock, no Statue of Liberty. Instead, it introduced a streetwise little brat, a cartoon character by the name of Fido Dido (If I do, they do?). Few among the European audiences watching the commercial would have been aware of its American auspices. As it happened, however, the cartoon character was American, and so was the commercial itself. Yet, to all intents and purposes, it could have been produced by any advertising agency anywhere. The only clearly American referent in the commercial was the product it tried to promote, a soft drink that saw its market share slipping and felt in need of a new image.

In the first installment of what turned out to be a little series of narrations centering on Fido Dido, we see him meeting the hand of his maker. Briefly, it may seem like a lighter, cartoon version of the scene in the Sistine Chapel where a drowsy Adam, touching fingers with God, is brought to life. But Fido Dido's meeting is of a different kind. His confrontation is with parental authority, with the commanding hand of social propriety. The hand of the maker, "in living color," holds a pencil and gets ready to retouch Fido Dido. First, his unkempt hair gets neatly combed and partitioned. Fido Dido indignantly shakes his hair back into its previous state. The pencil continues the attack and dresses Fido Dido in jacket and tie. It moves on to the object in Fido Dido's right hand, also in full color, as real as the hand and pencil: the can of Seven Up. The pencil tries to erase it, but the can is beyond such manipulation. Fido Dido meanwhile has moved toward full rebellion. Jacket and tie have already been thrown off; a well-aimed kick hits the pencil. Its tip breaks and hangs limply—a fitting symbol of parental impotence. Victoriously, Fido Dido walks off the screen. In final retaliation, his yo-yo now hits the pencil. The broken point falls off. His victory prize is a taste of the elixir of freedom: cool, sparkling Seven Up. The semiotics all merge into one message: a simple soft drink has been turned into a symbol of freedom. Much as the product, like the cartoon character and the ad itself, may be American, the message is understood internationally.

We may see in this one example the end stage of a process of internationalization and generalization—decontextualization, if one wishes—of a sales pitch that was developed in America and, in its earlier stages, relied on much more explicit American iconography. The Marlboro Man has been mentioned as a contemporary case of strong American symbolism— the West as open space, a realm of freedom—used to connect the sense of freedom, of being one's own man, to a simple item of merchandise like a cigarette. Yet the Marlboro Man is only a recent version of the commodification of American symbols of freedom that as a process has gone on for over a century. America as empty space, the epic America of the frontier, America as a mythical West, had been turned into a symbol of freedom long before the consumer revolution. The West as a beckoning yonder had kept alive the dream, in far-away corners of Europe, of a life lived in freedom and independence. As the promise of a new world and a new era, it could vie with contemporary utopian views offered by Marxism or similar emancipation movements. Posters, produced for shipping lines, emigration societies, and land development agencies contributed their imagery to the continuing construction of America as the very site of freedom and space. To many, such imagery must have represented the promise of freedom and escape offered by America.

If such is the central appeal of "America" as an image, we need not be surprised at the craving for material that could visualize the image. Chromolithographs, photographs, and stereographs, with their suggestion of three-dimensionality, all tried to still this hunger. They allowed people to move beyond the limited horizons of their daily lives and to enter into an imaginary space, a fantasy world. They offered reality and illusion at the same time.

Nor need we be surprised that such pictures were soon turned into advertising tools. When images of the West, or, rather, of America as one huge space, could trigger fantasies of fulfillment and liberty, common merchandise might hope to benefit from an association with such images. Today, everyone is familiar with the West as "Marlboro Country," with the successful marriage of a cigarette brand with the Marlboro Man. But as early as a century ago, advertisements tried to bring about this union. A colorful 1860 poster advertises the Washoe Brand of the Christian and Lee Tobacco Company of Richmond, Virginia. No tobacco leaf, cigar, or pipe in sight. What we do see are images of the West—Western horsemen, far horizons—grouped around a medallion that shows us a picture of the goddess Columbia draped in the American flag, an eagle, a globe with the Western hemisphere turned forward, and a pot brimming with gold coins. The West appears as a vision of plenty. Another poster, from the same period, advertises Westward Ho Smoking Tobacco. Its very name ties the tobacco to the beckoning call of the West. Yet the producer, G. W. Langhorne and Co., of Lynchburg, Virginia, did not leave it at that. The poster shows us an allegorical female figure, a version of Columbia with stark Indian features, feathers in her hair, her extended hand holding forth a calumet, her body, save her breasts, wrapped in the Stars and Stripes. This is not Europa abducted by Jupiter, this is America, impetuously galloping forth on elk-back: "Westward Ho!" indeed.

Apparently, well before the roaring twenties, commerce had appropriated the allegorical repertoire of the American dream. The images that now flooded across the country through techniques of mechanical reproduction could be endlessly rearranged to render new symbolic messages. The West as a realm of the imagination could connect with the world of trite consumption goods such as tobacco or cigarettes. Advertising developed into an art of symbolic alchemy that has continued to retain its potency. The symbolic connection that advertisers sought to establish hinged on the concept of "freedom." This linking of evocative images of American freedom and space tended to work best with leisure goods, such as cigarettes, beer, a car or a motorbike, a pair of blue jeans. Consumption, leisure time, and "freedom" thus became inextricably interwoven. And even today "America" can be counted on to trigger an association with freedom. The iconography of America has become international. Italian jeans manufacturers now advertise their wares in Germany on posters depicting Monument Valley. The German cigarette brand West mounted an international advertising campaign whose central metaphors revolve around the American West. The Dutch non-alcoholic beer Stender used the imaginary West of American road movies for its television commercials, including brief encounters at gas stations in an empty West, an exchange of glances between the sexes, the half-inviting, half-ironic sizing up, the beginning of erotic tension. The release of tension occurs, surprisingly, when he or she, in gleaming black leather, irrespective of gender, in the true macho style of the West, flips the top of a bottle of Stender and takes off again on a shiny motorbike into the empty distance.

America's national symbols and myths have been translated into an international iconographic language, a visual lingua franca. They have been turned into free-floating signifiers, internationally understood, free for everyone to use. Yet it is only a replay, on an international scale, of what had previously occurred in the United States. Given the characteristic American bent for disassembling whatever presents itself as an organically coherent whole, only to reassemble it differently, this American leadership role need not surprise us. In their production of commercial messages, this same cultural bent has been at work, removing symbols from their historical context and rearranging them into novel configurations. The appropriate metaphor may be that of Lego construction, which uses the individual pieces as just so many "empty signifiers," combining them into ever-changing meaningful structures. Commerce and advertising are but one area where we can see these rituals of cultural transformation at work. For, indeed, consumption goods as well can freely change their meaning, appearing in ever-changing configurations, furnishing a realm of virtual reality, turning into simulacra at the hands of the wizards of advertising. They become true phantasms, set free by the human imagination.

No bastion of conventional order is immune to this erosive freedom. In the area of advertising, as well as in other areas of cultural production, we can discern a moving American frontier, affecting an ever-increasing number of social conventions with its "deconstructing" logic. Recent shifts in this frontier have affected the established constructions of gender, rearranging at will reigning views of what constitutes the typically male and female, the masculine and feminine. "Gender-bending" is the word that American English has invented to describe this process. Pop culture heroes like Michael Jackson, Grace Jones, and Madonna project invented personae that are strangely androgynous. Hollywood is busy bending gender in films like *Alien II,* where the enemy computer is called Mother and the heroine copes as if she were a man. Commercials like those for Stender also play on the repertoire of accepted gender definitions. The best recent example is a television commercial for Levi's 501. A chocolate-skinned young woman, invitingly dressed, her midriff bare, is shown taking a New York cab. While the driver is ogling her in his rearview mirror, his lips moving a toothpick back and forth, suggestively, as if engaged in a mating ritual, she coolly adds a few final touches to her makeup. But then the tables are turned. What gives the driver a start and brings his cab to a full stop, is the sound of an electric razor and the sight of his passenger shaving. The last shot is of the passenger walking away, the victor in another battle of the sexes, the Levi's as snug and inviting as ever. As the text reminds us, in case we didn't know already: "Cut for Men since 1850." Thus, in all these cases, an entire new area has opened up for fantasies of freedom to roam.

There may be a cultural "deep structure" underlying such developments that is characteristically American, but my point is that the appeal of such cultural *bricolage* is international. Even in the absence of clearly American markers, as in the case of our Fido Dido commercial, the underlying logic of recombination, tying "freedom" to a soft drink, is American. The appeal, though, is worldwide. In that sense, we have all become Americanized. We have grown accustomed to a specific American mode of cultural production, or rather to the ways in which American culture reproduces itself through endless variation and recombination. Not only have we cracked

American cultural codes and can read them flawlessly, we have also appropriated those codes. They have become part of our collective imaginary
repertoire.

One illustration will make an additional point. In the spring of 1994,
on walls all over Italy, there were posters displaying a scene taken from the
history of the conquest of the West. We see a covered wagon in what is
clearly a Western landscape, dry and desolate. A few men gather together
in front of the wagon. The scene is one of relative relaxation. Clearly, the
day's work has been done. The poster's color is sepia, suggesting a reprint
of an old photograph. Its text tells us: *Vendiamo un' autentica leggenda*—We
sell an authentic legend. This is clearly a variation on Coca-Cola's claim to
be "the real thing," but the viewer is left wondering what the authentic
legend might be. Is it the Levi's blue jeans? The answer must be yes. Is it
the American West? Again, the answer is yes. A commodity, a piece of
merchandise as down-to-earth as a pair of workingman's trousers, has become a myth, while the West as a myth has become commodified. And
Levi's, as the poster honestly tells us, sells it. Yet there is more to this poster.
There is an ironic *sous-entendu,* an implied wink to the audience. After all,
the audience has long since got the message. They *know* that Levi's is a
myth and they *know* what the myth represents. It represents more than the
West, it represents their own collective memory of growing up in a Europe
filled with American ingredients. Generation upon generation of Europeans, growing up after the war, can all tell their own story of a mythical
America as they constructed it, drawing on American advertisements,
songs, films, and so on. Ironically, these collective memories—these imagined Americas where people actually spent part of their past growing up—
are now being commodified: to all those who on the basis of Jack Kerouac
and a pop song remember Route 66 without ever having crossed the Atlantic, a Dutch travel agency now offers nostalgic trips down that highway.
The road may no longer be the same, but it reoccurs as a replica of itself,
a simulacrum in the great Disney tradition.

The point is clear: generation after generation of Europeans have grown
up constructing meaningful worlds that they shared with their peers and
that drew crucially on American ingredients. Mythical "Americas" have become part and parcel of the collective memory of Europeans. This takes us
back to Mitterrand's musings. It seems as if he fell victim to a misreading
of the way the collective memory of Europeans was built in the postwar
period. Why, indeed, must a collective memory be a matter of, as Mitterrand has it, a country depicting itself in images? Why not admit that the
collective memories of national populations are crucially a matter of the
appropriation and digestion of foreign influences? One ignores these only
at peril of centrally imposing definitions of what constitutes the nation.
And in fact many of the arguments in favor of the cultural exemption

clause, protecting national cultural identities, seem to betray this narrow paternalist view of the nation and its identity.

Commercial messages have been only one of the transmission belts of American culture abroad. Modern media of mass reproduction and mass distribution, like film, photography, the press, radio, television, and sound recordings, have filled the semiotic space of people everywhere with messages made in America. Americans themselves, through their physical presence abroad, in the form of expatriate colonies, of armies, of businessmen, have equally contributed to the worldwide dissemination of their culture. Yet commercial messages, in the way they transmit American culture, are a particular case. They are not simply neutral carriers, conveying American culture for others to consume and enjoy; they give a particular twist to whatever ingredients of the American imagination they use. A recent illustration of this process can be seen in a commercial message broadcast by CNN, the worldwide cable news network, and paid for by the Advertising Council in London. In what is in fact an advertisement for advertising, the point is made that without advertising, we all would be worse off, getting less information through the media, whether the press or the electronic media. Advertising is presented as a necessary prop for the continued existence of a well-informed public in a functioning democracy. The little civics lesson offered by this commercial ends with the slogan: "Advertising—The Right to Choose."

This blending of the rationale of capitalism and democratic theory is not new. It is reminiscent of what happened in the early 1940s in America. Then, on the eve of America's participation in World War II, President Franklin Delano Roosevelt made his powerful contribution to American public discourse in his "Four Freedoms Speech," a rallying cry in which he called on his countrymen to fulfill an American world mission as he saw it. In all likelihood, he had picked up the Four Freedoms as a rhetorical figure in the public domain. The Four Freedoms, as a group of four statues erected along the main concourse of the New York World Fair of 1939–40, had already left their imprint on the millions of visitors to the fair. Working on his final draft of the State of the Union Address, Roosevelt briefly toyed with the idea of Five Freedoms, but clearly he did not want to move away from the popular foursome at the Fair. If he wished his words to reverberate among the larger public, he needed to draw on a popular repertoire that was already established. The link with political views among the larger public was further reinforced through Norman Rockwell's series of four oil paintings, made after Roosevelt's speech, each representing one of the four freedoms. Using his appeal as an artist who had succeeded in rendering a romantic, small-town view of life cherished by millions of Americans, he managed to give the same endearing touch to Roosevelt's message. Through the mass distribution of reproductions, Rockwell's paintings of the Four Freedoms facilitated the translation and transfer of Roosevelt's high-minded call to a mass audience.

If this is an illustration of American political culture as an element of American mass culture, of political rhetoric as it emanates from the public domain and returns to it, it was unaffected by the rationale of business. If anything had to be sold at all, it was a matter of political ideas; if a sales pitch was needed at all, it was a matter of public suasion, explaining the world to the larger democratic public and calling upon it to take appropriate action. Yet it was not long before Roosevelt's Four Freedoms would be joined by a Fifth, in an advertisement by the Hoover Vacuum Cleaner Company in a 1944 issue of the *Saturday Evening Post*. It was an illustrated ad in the style of Norman Rockwell. We recognize the setting, the faces are familiar. An old woman, a middle-aged man, and a young girl—"people from the neighborhood." They look upward toward a beam of light; providence, if not the good provider, is smiling upon them. In their arms they hold an abundance of packages, all of them gift-wrapped. This is Norman Rockwell country. With a difference, though: Rockwell's mythical small-town people, carriers of democratic virtue, now appear in the guise of Americans as consumers. Three years after Roosevelt decided that there were four, not five, freedoms, the Hoover advertisement reminded Americans that "the Fifth Freedom is Freedom of Choice." If America had joined the struggle to safeguard democratic values, this implied safeguarding the freedom of choice. By a simple semantic sleight of hand, the (con)text of the advertisement shifted the meaning of freedom of choice: the "signified" was no longer the realm of politics, but the freedom of choice of the citizen in his role as consumer. Thus spheres of freedom smoothly shaded into one another.

And they still do. The Hoover Company may have chosen to use language popular at the time, and to speak of a Freedom. The CNN message is cast in the language of rights, reminding us of our Right to Choose (again playing on the political ring that the phrase currently has). In both cases, what we see happening is the commodification of political discourse. The language of political ideals, of rights and freedoms, is being highjacked in order to dress purposeful commercial action in stolen clothes. Whether dressed as a freedom or a right, a commodifying logic appears in pure form, unconnected to any particular product. Yet it is a logic we have met before in particular cases, which tied the promise of freedom to cigarettes or soft drinks. It is a logic that commodifies, and pedestrianizes, political ideals by putting them in the service of commercial salesmanship. In that sense, we seem to have struck upon just another instance of the vulgarizing impact of American culture, corroborating a point made by so many European critics of American mass culture.

Yet this is not the whole story. The very slogans chosen by sales departments, affirming our "Freedom of Choice," or our "Right to Choose," are semantically unstable and may well convey a message different from that which the salesmen had in mind. A word like "choice," when it is left unspecified, sits uneasily astride the divide between the political and the economic spheres. "Freedom of Choice" in particular may well read as the "Choice of Freedom," a simple inversion that may put political ideas into the heads of an audience addressed as consumers. Paradoxically, then, advertising stratagems cooked up by commercial sponsors may well have the effect of a civics lesson, if not of a subversive and anti-authoritarian call. Precisely there, it seems, lie the secrets of the appeal that so many American commercial messages have had, domestically as well as abroad. Exploring frontiers of freedom, of children rebelling against parental authority, of sexual freedom, of freedom in matters of taste and in styles of behavior, American consumer goods have been instruments of political and cultural education, if not of emancipation. Generation upon generation of youngsters growing up in a variety of settings in Europe, west *and* east of the Iron Curtain, have vicariously enjoyed the pleasures of cultural alternatives conjured up in commercial vignettes. Simple items like a pair of blue jeans, Coca-Cola, or a brand of cigarette, thus acquired an added value that helped these younger generations to give expression to an identity all their own. They have been using American cultural language and have made American cultural codes their own. To that extent, they have become Americanized. To the extent, though, that they have "done their own thing," while drawing on American cultural repertoires, "Americanization" is no longer the proper word for describing what has gone on. If anything, those at the receiving end of American mass culture have adapted it to make it serve their own ends. They have woven it into a cultural language whose grammar, syntax, and semantics—metaphorically speaking— are recognizable in French, Italian, or Czech too. All that the recipients have done is make new statements in that language.

There are more instances of such recontextualization. Surrounded as we are by jingles, posters, neon signs, and billboards, all trying to convey their commercial exhortations, we all at one point or another ironically recycle their repertoires; we quote slogans while bending their meaning; we mimic voices and faces familiar from radio and television. We weave them into our conversations precisely because they are shared repertoires. Used in this way, two things happen. International repertoires become national, in the sense that they are given a particular twist in conversation, acquiring their new meanings only in particular national and linguistic settings. Secondly, commercial messages stop being commercial. A decommodification takes place, in the sense that the point of the conversation is no longer a piece of merchandise or a specific economic transaction. In this ironic recycling of our commercial culture, we become its masters rather than its slaves.

Many things have happened along the way since American mass culture started traveling abroad. American icons may have become the staple of a visual lingua franca that is understood anywhere in the world, yet their use can no longer be dictated solely from America.

For one thing, as we have seen, it is clear that European commercials made for European products may draw on semiotic repertoires initially developed in and transmitted from America. Yet, in a creolizing freedom not unlike America's modularizing cast of mind, Europeans in their turn now freely rearrange and recombine the bits and pieces of American culture. They care little about authenticity. T-shirts produced in Europe are as likely to say "New York Lions" as they are "New York Giants."[7] What is more, American brand names, as free-floating signifiers, may even be decommodified and turned into carriers of a message that is no longer commercial at all. Admittedly, the T-shirts, leather jackets, and baseball caps sporting the hallowed names of Harley Davidson, Nike, or Coca-Cola still have to be bought. Yet what one pays is the price of admission into a world of symbols shared by an international youth culture. Boys or girls with the name "Coca-Cola" on their T-shirts are not unpaid peddlers of American merchandise. Quite the contrary. They have transcended such trite connotations and restored American icons to their pure semiotic state of messages of pleasure and freedom. Within this global youth culture, the icons youngsters carry are like the symbol of the fish that early Christians drew in the sand as a code of recognition. They are the members of a new International, geared to a postmodern world of consumerism rather than an early modern one centered on values of production.

There are many ironies here. What is often held against the emerging international mass or pop culture is precisely its international, if not cosmopolitan, character. Clearly, this a case of double standards. At the level of high culture, most clearly in its modernist phase, there has always been the dream of transcending the local, the provincial, the national, or, in social terms, transgressing the narrow bounds of the bourgeois world and entering a realm that is nothing if not international: the transcendence lies in being truly "European," or "cosmopolitan." But clearly what is good at the level of high culture is seen as a threat when a similar process of internationalization occurs at the level of mass culture. Then, all of a sudden, the defense is not in terms of high versus low, as one might have expected, but in terms of national cultures and national identities imperiled by an emerging international mass culture. There is a further irony in this construction of the conflict inasmuch as it contrasts an emerging global culture seen as homogenizing to national cultures seen as havens of cultural diversity. In the real world, of course, things are different. There may be a hierarchy of taste cultures, yet it is not a matter of higher taste cultures being the more national in orientation. It seems to be the case that this hierarchy of taste cultures is itself transnational, and that there are indeed international audiences who at the high end all appreciate Beethoven and Bartók but at the low end all fancy Madonna or Prince. Yet in a replay of much older elitist tirades against low culture, advocates of high art see only endless diversity where their own taste is concerned, and sheer vulgar homogeneity at the level of mass culture. They have no sense of the variety of tastes and styles, of endless change and renewal in mass culture, simply because it all occurs far beyond their ken.

Allow me one final observation. From the point of view of American mass culture traveling abroad, in many cases the exploration of cultural frontiers is taken to more radical lengths than anything one might see in America. Whereas sexual joy and freedom are merely hinted at in American commercials, where Coca-Cola at best holds the promise of more intimate intercourse in its vignettes of rapturous boys and girls on the beach or in boats floating down rivers, European posters and TV commercials are often more explicit. There is a brooding, erotic Italian poster of a macho guy, bare-chested, standing astride a scantily clad, sexually aroused young woman crouched between his legs. She wears a crown reminiscent of the Statue of Liberty, and there is an American flag. The commercial is for the one piece of clothing on the man's body, his jeans. Similarly, in the Netherlands, in a poster and TV campaign sponsored by the government, inviting (in small print) people to become organ donors and to wear a donor codicil, we see a young couple making love, both naked, she sitting on his lap, curving backward in rapture. The text, in large print, reads: "Give your heart a new lease on life." Pasted across the country, on railway platforms, on bus shelters, the poster must have made visiting Americans bashfully turn their heads away. To them the campaign would not appear as the outcome of a process of Americanization taken a few daring steps further. Nor for that matter would another poster campaign, again sponsored by the Dutch government, on behalf of safe sex. Graphically, for everyone to see, couples are shown taking showers together or engaged in similar forms of foreplay. Shocking stuff indeed, but nor is this all. Yet another frontier is being explored, if not crossed: in addition to hetero couples, gay couples are shown.

Admittedly, these poster campaigns no longer convey commercial messages, although in fact the Dutch government, in order to get its messages across, has adopted advertising techniques and in fact uses advertising bill-boards, rented, one assumes, at the going market rate. In a sense, we have come full circle. Where the Hoover Company advertisement drew on republican language to claim the freedom of the advertiser, we now see advertising space being reclaimed for statements pro bono publico. If democracy is a marketplace, it has become inseparable from the economic market. It is in fact one indivisible and noisy place, with cries and calls vying for the public's attention, echoing back and forth. The perfect illustration of this was being pasted all across the Netherlands in January 1995. A huge poster produced by a Dutch advertising agency solely for the Dutch market advertised the Levi's 508, yet playfully drew on American political language for its commercial message. What the poster showed was the lower part of a half-nude male torso, covered from the waist down by a pair of jeans. Intertextuality abounded. The poster was reminiscent of famous album covers such as the Rolling Stones' *Sticky Fingers,* designed by Andy Warhol, or the Bruce Springsteen album *Born in the USA.* But there is more. Playing on the classic version of the Four Freedoms, the poster rephrased them as follows: freedom of expression, freedom of thought, freedom of choice, and—Levi's 508—freedom of movement. The third freedom, as we have seen, already makes the transition from the political to the commercial; the fourth, political though it may sound, is meant to convey the greater room for movement provided by the baggier cut of the 508. The picture illustrates the point by showing the unmistakable bulge of a male member in full erection, casually touched by the hand of its owner. Clearly, the semiotics of American commercial strategies have been taken to lengths, so to speak, that are inconceivable in America. America may have been less embarrassed in exploring the continuities between the political and the commercial; Europe later on may have been more daring in its pursuit of happiness, graphically advertising it all across Europe's public space.[8]

For, indeed, as European examples from the political and the economic marketplace serve to illustrate, the logic of a choice of freedom knows no bounds, once set free from controlling American standards of taste and decency. As is a lingua franca's wont, it moves in a realm of free creolization, where the controlling authority of a mother culture no longer holds. Americanization, then, should be the story of an American cultural language traveling and of other people acquiring that language. What they actually say in it is a different story altogether.

NOTES

1. David Thelen, "The Nation and Beyond: Transnational Perspectives on United States History," *Journal of American History* 86, 3 (December 1999): 965–76, quotation from p. 967.

2. Daniel Rodgers, "Exceptionalism," in *Imagined Histories: American Historians Interpret the Past,* ed. A. Molho and Gordon S. Wood (Princeton, N.J., 1998), 21–41.

3. E.g., Robert Rydell in a contribution to the 1998 Lisbon conference of the European Association for American Studies: see R. W. Rydell, "The Americanization of the World and the Spectacle of the American Exhibits at the 1900 Paris Universal Exposition," in *Ceremonies and Spectacles: Performing American Culture,* ed. T. Alves, T. Cid, and H. Ickstadt (Amsterdam, 2000), 93–101; quotation from p. 99.

4. Jean-Jacques Servan-Schreiber, *Le défi américain* (Paris, 1967), trans. Ronald Steel under the title *The American Challenge* (New York, 1968).

5. Rydell, "Americanization of the World." W. T. Stead, *The Americanisation of the World, or The Trend of the Twentieth Century* (London, 1902). Stead was among the many who went down with the *Titanic.* J. H. Huizinga, *Amerika levend en denkend: Losse opmerkingen* (Haarlem, 1927).

6. See R. Kuisel, *Seducing the French: The Dilemma of Americanization* (Berkeley and Los Angeles, 1993); M. Pendergrast, *For God, Country and Coca-Cola: The Unauthorized History of the Great American Soft Drink and the Company That Makes It* (London, 1993)

7. As pointed out by Elizabeth Neuffer, "US Pop Culture in Europe," *Boston Sunday Globe,* October 9, 1994, 22.

8. In this connection it is of interest to note that the campaign for the Levi's 508 was produced by a Dutch advertising agency solely for the Dutch market. The video for the 501 that I referred to earlier was made by a British agency for the European market.

PART IV

The Constraints of Practice

THIRTEEN

Do American Historical Narratives Travel?

François Weil

At the 1983 meeting of the American Historical Association, a panel discussion on "American History Today: Parochial or Cosmopolitan?" provided Raymond Grew, then editor of *Comparative Studies in Society and History,* with an opportunity to discuss what he called "the comparative
weakness of American history." Arguing that there seems "to be some resistance to or inhibition against comparative approaches in the way that
American history is conceived and practiced," Grew wondered "why the
historiography of the United States has not had a greater impact on the
historical discipline generally," noting:

> It is likely that more historians have studied the history of the United States
> than the history of any other society in the record of mankind. Battalions of
> historians have marched across and finely mapped a field limited to little
> more than three centuries and have explored its depths with spade work that
> constitutes saturation sapping. Despite this favorable ratio of scholars to object
> of study, the conquests made do not seem more remarkable than those ac-
> complished by smaller companies covering the larger terrain of other socie-
> ties. Historians of the United States cannot be said to have had a greater
> impact on the general understanding of society or on the way in which history
> is written than have historians of France; they have not contributed more to
> standards of research than historians of Germany, nor achieved greater nar-
> rative power or topical breadth than historians of England; they have not been
> more effective than historians of the ancient world in showing how to inte-
> grate the study of society and culture, nor made more striking discoveries of
> previously overlooked historical sources than ancient or medieval historians;
> their work has not had greater impact on the other social sciences than studies
> by historians of Asia, the Near East, or Africa.[1]

In short, American historiography does not travel well, and despite its quality, quantity, and sophistication, it has had relatively little impact on other historiographies. This is not because it lacks originality. On the contrary, much research in the field exhibits the paradigmatic dimension that Thomas Kuhn deemed essential for a conceptual revolution and its potential exportation.[2] Nor is American history impervious to outside influences, either geographical or methodological. Some of its best work in the past few decades has in fact been informed by notions or concepts borrowed from foreign scholarship—ranging from European historical demography and the influence of *Annales* historians in the case of colonial and religious history to E. P. Thompson and *Past & Present* in the case of social and labor history. Since the 1960s, too, American historiography has also interacted with the social sciences, as demonstrated by the impact of sociology and modernization theory in the 1950s and 1960s, cultural anthropology in the 1970s and 1980s, and, more recently, even linguistics.[3]

The limited influence of American historiography abroad is ironic, given the American academic context. After all, according to Grew, "however parochial a people we Americans may be, our history departments are surely not. In no other nation are there so many historians teaching and doing significant research on the history of other societies and eras. And that work takes place in a system of universities remarkable for the range and depth of their faculties in all the disciplines related to history and for the richness of their libraries."[4]

And yet, for all the embarrassment of riches that apparently characterizes American academe, American historiography exerts a remarkably small influence outside of the country itself. In proportion to their number, relatively few American specialists in U.S. history are known and read by non-Americanists throughout the world. The proportion of books on American history translated into foreign languages is low. More strikingly, whereas American historians often travel abroad to lecture or participate in conferences, few American historiographical debates have a direct impact on other historiographies. Apparently, ideas travel less easily than scholars do.

Granted, there are some significant exceptions to this situation. In the 1970s and 1980s, the "new" economic history influenced many foreign scholars in Europe, Latin America, and Australasia. Jan Pomorski of Poland, Maurice Levy-Leboyer and Jean Heffer of France, György Ránki of Hungary, and Jaime García-Lombardero and Francisco Bustelo of Spain, among others, served as go-betweens and helped spread cliometric methodologies abroad.[5] Similarly, in the 1980s and 1990s, the type of organizational business history made famous by Alfred D. Chandler's prize-winning analysis of the growth of large-scale corporations in the United States, *The Visible Hand,* transformed the way business history was conceptualized in Japan and western Europe.[6]

But the "new economic history" actually developed in departments of economics, and most of the Chandlerian "new business history" sprang up in schools of business and management. "New histories" that developed within history departments, by contrast, have had less significant impact on foreign scholarship. The "new intellectual history" that developed since the 1970s certainly demonstrated its curiosity and attention vis-à-vis the rest of the world. Writing "from the American province," as one of the leading American practitioners of the field put it, intellectual historians study ideas that cross borders as easily as the people who travel with them. Recent works on the history of such intellectual projects as Progressivism, for instance, demonstrate the importance of understanding the international conversations that nurtured transatlantic progressive impulses. And yet, despite its subtlety and cosmopolitanism, American intellectual history has seldom influenced other historiographies. To return to the case of Progressivism, major books like James Kloppenberg's comparison of progressive ideas in Europe and the United States and Daniel Rodgers's analysis of the various "Atlantic crossings" that fed into American Progressivism have had little impact yet upon other historiographies.[7]

Likewise, the narratives of U.S. social and cultural history—perhaps the two fields anchored in history departments that have experienced the greatest growth in the past four decades—have for the most part not been exported. One significant exception is the "new labor history" that has developed since the 1960s. For one thing, the new labor history grew from the start in an international context, thanks to the extraordinary influence of British Marxist historians, such as Eric Hobsbawn, Raymond Williams, and, above all, E. P. Thompson, on American labor history. During the 1970s and the 1980s, labor historians established several international intellectual clearinghouses, which provided many opportunities for contacts between American and non-American labor historians. One such was the international research network created in January 1975 in Paris by the historian Georges Haupt, a specialist in the history of the Second International who was teaching at the École des hautes études en sciences sociales. Haupt knew American labor historians, partly through his own work, partly because he had been a visiting professor at the University of Wisconsin, and he had an extraordinary talent for stimulating international discussions. Between January 1975 and June 1977, he organized or helped organize eight round tables at the Maison des sciences de l'Homme in Paris, as well as in Pittsburgh, London, and Constance. These gatherings brought together, among others, the British scholars Eric Hobsbawn and E. P. Thompson, the Americans Leopold Haimson, David Montgomery, and Charles and Louise Tilly, and Pierre Bourdieu, Marianne Debouzy, Patrick Fridenson, and Michelle Perrot of France, in addition to Haupt himself.[8] Other strategic places included conferences organized in Italy and

Germany. These and other initiatives helped sustain transatlantic networks of labor historians and labor history periodicals—*Labor History* and *International Labor and Working Class History* in the United States, *Labour / Le Travailleur* in Canada, *Le Mouvement Social* in France, *Movimento operaio e socialista* in Italy, and *Geschichte und Gesellschaft* and *Archiv für Sozialgeschichte* in Germany.[9]

And yet direct impact of American labor historians on other historiographies is hard to pinpoint, aside from that of the late Herbert Gutman and of David Montgomery. Before Gutman's death in 1985, his work was widely known and admired outside of the United States. His book *Work, Culture, and Society in Industrializing America* was translated into Italian in 1979, and he visited Italian universities several times between 1977 and 1985. Yet the historian Bruno Cartosio considers that since the Italian "debate about the new social history, which had been tied to workers' self-activity in previous years, had fallen into a state of lethargy" by the early 1980s, "Gutman's work did not have the role and importance it was expected to have." Gutman also spent a year in France in the early 1980s as occupant of the French-American Foundation Chair in American Civilization established at the École des hautes études en sciences sociales.[10] As for Montgomery, two of his books, *Workers' Control* and *Citizen Worker,* have been translated into Spanish, and several of his articles have appeared in translation in major journals around the world. More important, Montgomery has had an impact not only on foreign Americanists but also on French, Italian, and German labor historiography.[11]

Gutman and Montgomery are, however, exceptions. Most American new labor historians are far less known outside of the United States, particularly among non-Americanists. They are also more accurate examples of the generally limited impact of American historiography abroad. Consider the following comparison between books that won the prestigious Frederick Jackson Turner Award and books by twelve former presidents of the Organization of American Historians. Since its creation in 1959 to distinguish "an author's first book on some significant phase of American history," thirty-nine books have received the coveted Turner prize. Only three of these, however—Sean Wilentz's *Chants Democratic* (1985), David Montejano's *Anglos and Mexicans in the Making of Texas* (1988), and George Chauncey's *Gay New York* (1995)—have been or are being translated abroad.[12]

In contrast, quite a few books by former OAH presidents have been translated abroad. Spanish-language readers have access to works by David Brion Davis, Michael Kammen, Gerda Lerner, David Montgomery, and Gary Nash. Books by William Chafe, John Higham, Kammen, and Lerner have appeared in Japanese. One finds French translations of Chafe and Kammen, and German translations of Davis and Lerner. Eric Foner's work is accessible in Chinese. So is Chafe's. Books by Davis, Foner, and Montgomery exist in Italian, while Davis and Foner's have been translated into Portuguese. As for Kammen, he may also be read in Arabic, Burmese, Indonesian, and Korean.[13]

These various examples demonstrate that *some* American historiography *does* indeed travel abroad. Lest one fall prey to undue optimism, however, we should note that these transfers operate according to rather strict thematic and economic rules. Thematically, there is an interest abroad in slavery (Davis, Foner, Nash), labor (Montgomery), feminism and women (Lerner, Chafe), and some aspects of the social and cultural fabric of U.S. history (Higham, Kammen). Economically, the books that are translated must be viable. With the exception of three Frederick Jackson Turner Award winners, this excludes monographs. Therefore, to find its way outside of the United States, innovative, path-breaking scholarship has to wait for the consecration provided by mid-career interpretative synthesis—the celebrated second, or third, or fourth book—as demonstrated by books by former OAH presidents that are influential abroad. Moreover, until the mid 1990s the diffusion of American historiography abroad greatly benefited from a program of translation funded by the United States Information Agency (USIA). Unfortunately, this innovative program was terminated in the mid 1990s as a result of political and budgetary decisions at the USIA. Therefore, foreign publishers now must limit their translations to either textbooks or works of synthesis and interpretation that occupy a middling position between monographs and textbooks.[14]

This assessment of the difficulty in exporting American history would not be complete without the expected recognition that *importation* to the United States from abroad of American historiography is no easier. Ron Robin, a professor of American history at the University of Haifa, notes that "we who study the American past from abroad are professionally marginal. With few exceptions, most scholars of the American past would be hard pressed to name more than one book on American history written by an international scholar."[15] In 1988, Robert H. Walker, a former senior editor of *American Studies International* and a professor at George Washington University, remarked that there were "legions of American specialists producing important work around the world" and regretted that "not all Americans seem aware of this transformation." He added: "Although we should know well what it means to be treated like colonies (especially in intellectual and cultural matters), many members of the academy and the bureaucracy still act as though the study of America outside the U.S. were but a pale reflection of the genuine article."[16] The publication in 1986 of an issue of *Reviews in American History* devoted to American History abroad and important efforts by the Organization of American Historians (OAH) and the *Journal of American History* (*JAH*) since the early 1990s have increased the exposure of foreign scholars and diminished casual indifference, dismissal, or patronizing of scholarship from abroad. Under the impulse of the *JAH*'s editor, David Thelen, the OAH has instituted a foreign-language book prize and a foreign-language article prize. The *JAH* has created a network of foreign contributing editors whose task it is to develop and keep open channels of communication between scholarship in their countries and in the United States. It also routinely publishes reviews of books published abroad.[17]

Notwithstanding these and other similar efforts, there are so many apparent obstacles to both exporting and importing American historiography that the issue requires further consideration. No simple explanation or remedy is available, but I want to argue here that: (1) these impediments have to do with the kind of American history that is being written and the way it is produced within a national framework; (2) they are related to the manner in which the American historical profession is organized; and (3) they raise questions not only about exportation of American history from the United States but also about its importation from the United States into various countries around the globe.

OF PARACHUTISTS AND TRUFFLE HUNTERS:
NEW HISTORIES, THE NATION, AND THE OUTSIDE WORLD

Until the 1970s, the narrative of American history was avowedly nation-bounded and nation-centered. In terms of content, the object of U.S. historiography was the history of the nation; as members of a profession, American historians of the United States were partaking in the process and grand narrative of nation-building. "Why are not American historians the principal interpreters of America to Europe," the British historian Frank Thistlethwaite wondered four decades ago. "Because the tradition of American historical writing has been shaped by historians whose unquestioned purpose has been to explain America to Americans," he answered. The first president of the American Historical Association, Cornell University's President Andrew White, asserted in 1884 that "all history must be rewritten from an American point of view"—a nationalizing view that contributed to the marginalization of local history.[18] That is not surprising, and rather unexceptional. As Benedict Anderson remarks: "Awareness of being imbedded in secular, serial time, with all its implications of continuity, yet of 'forgetting' the experience of continuity—product of the ruptures of the late eighteenth century—engenders the need for a narrative of 'identity.' "[19]

In many countries, this "narrative of identity" took the form of history in the nineteenth century. As James J. Sheehan notes, "everywhere in nineteenth-century Europe, the political triumph of the nation over the life of the present helped to ensure its conceptual triumph over the study of the past." The five volumes of Heinrich von Treitschke's *Deutsche Geschichte im neunzehnten Jahrhundert,* which he began publishing in 1879, soon became one of the flagships of the *kleindeutsch* historiographical tradition.[20] Indeed, the national framework remained long dominant in German historiographical debates. "Although German historians these days seem to disagree about almost everything," Sheehan notes, "the one thing most of them accept is the historiographical legitimacy of the settlement of 1871."[21]

The marriage of the historical profession to the nation-state is also quite visible elsewhere in Europe, from Ireland to Poland and from Sw erland to Portugal.[22] In France, following the eloquent example of the romantic historian Jules Michelet, successive generations of professional historians offered an exceptionalist, organicist reading of French national history and elaborated a Republican history of the Republic.[23] Outside of Europe, national historiographies developed throughout the Americas, linking "national identities and national projects" within historical writing. This was clearly the case in nineteenth-century Latin American historiography. It was also apparent in Canada, where late nineteenth-century English Canadian historians and many of their twentieth-century successors saw "history as an indispensable index of a maturing nationality," focusing accordingly on what one of them, Arthur Lower, called the transition from *Colony to Nation.*[24]

Indeed, recent debates in Quebec even suggest that there is no need for an *actual* nation-state in order for a national historiography to develop—the *desire* for a nation-state is enough. Until the so-called Quiet Revolution of the 1960s, the framework of Quebec historiography was openly nationalist. Beginning with François-Xavier Garneau in the nineteenth century and Abbé Lionel Groulx in the early twentieth, French Canadian historians developed a model that asserted Quebec's distinctiveness and emphasized the survival of French Canadian cultural values.[25]

Since the 1960s, these various national narratives have come under heavy fire. In the United States and elsewhere in the world, some scholars followed various intellectual strategies aimed at "rescuing history from the nation," in Prasenjit Duara's apt phrase.[26] One such strategy, almost universally adopted, undertook the task of contextualizing and historicizing these narratives. To demonstrate their constructed nature was to show that they were not a given, but the product of a certain historical time and space. In France, for instance, historians began to rewrite French history along more constructionist lines. They attempted to include immigration in the national narrative, for instance, or to delineate the process of elaboration of a narrative they used to take for granted—thus allowing for a better understanding of the various sociocultural processes of stratification and sedimentation at work in French history.[27] Other critics underlined the parochialism of national histories and called instead for a radical denationalization of historiography that would expand the practitioners' focus *beyond* the national framework and lead them to develop comparative, transnational, international, and world histories[28].

Most American historians, however, followed yet a third strategy, one that aimed at undermining the national narrative from within by reducing their research focus. The impressive success of the "new social" and "new cultural" histories was linked to the profession's attraction for pluralistic identities—a trend some feared was fragmenting American history.[29] This phenomenon was hardly unique to the United States. North of the 49th parallel, for instance, the Toronto historians Ramsay Cook and J. M. S. Careless, among others, submitted the formerly dominant nation-building approach to Canadian history to a severe critique and called for more pluralism in scholarship. And many historians around the world, not only in the United States, would have agreed with what the Australian historian Graeme Davidson had to say about the evolution of Australian history: "Historians, with one or two illustrious exceptions, no longer see themselves as the interpreters of national character or purpose. If they champion a cause it is more likely to be that of a class, a party, an ethnic or racial group, a locality or a gender rather than that of the nation as a whole."[30]

Pluralist history, however, did not so much cause the national frame of historiography to disappear as lead historians to ignore it to a considerable extent by renouncing the ambitions and pitfalls of writing a national narrative. To borrow Emmanuel Le Roy Ladurie's metaphor, historians abandoned the position of the parachutist and adopted that of the truffle hunter. As Lawrence Stone describes it:

> [T]he former looks down from a great height. He sees very clearly the contours of the landscape, the rivers, the forests, and the mountains, but he is too far away to detect individual trees or rocks or small streams, much less the dense undergrowth on the ground. The latter has his nose deep in the dirt, snuffling out rare truffles (in this case manuscript data) lying underneath the soil. From the latter's vantage point he can see nothing of the broad features of the landscape, but he can pick out many of the individual items that compose it.[31]

Indeed, specialization brought about a much better understanding of the complexity, contradictions, and wealth of American history. At the same time, however, the new paradigm created one unforeseen consequence. Pre-1960 American history had always experienced a reasonable degree of exportation, clothed as it was in the mantel of a discourse about the nation. Under the prodding of Vittorio de Caprariis, classic American historians such as Francis Parkman, Frederick Jackson Turner, and J. Franklin Jameson had been translated into Italian in the 1950s and early 1960s. So were contemporary scholars like Samuel Eliot Morison, Richard Hofstadter, and Arthur Schlesinger Jr.[32] Likewise, German, Spanish, or French readers can read translations of books by Schlesinger, Hofstadter, Turner, and Daniel Boorstin. By contrast, "new histories" made the exportation of American history more complicated—truffle hunters are more interested in digging in their favorite spots than in publicizing them around the world. Interestingly, a similar phenomenon occurred in the field of American studies. There, too, "a powerful body of work investigating concepts of social difference in relation to representation and social power" has developed over the past three decades. Yet, as Jane C. Desmond and Virginia R. Dominguez convincingly argue, "there is a tendency in these critiques to limit discussion of cultural diversity and multiculturalism to issues affecting populations living within the United States"—resulting in what they appropriately call an "inward looking orientation."[33]

How to develop a renewed interest for an outward-looking orientation without losing sight of the sense of complexity brought about by the new historians is certainly one of the most daunting challenges faced by the profession. It probably involves reconnecting to or reinventing a national narrative that fully embraces diversity. In itself, such an endeavor would not be contradictory with other current efforts to develop comparative, transnational, or world histories. As John Higham points out, "neither a transnational nor a national history can properly flourish without the balance-weight of the other."[34]

CONTINENTALISM AND ITS VICISSITUDES: SELF-SUFFICIENCY AND SMUGGLED NARRATIVES

American history's professional and organizational structure is a second factor that discourages exportation. The number of American historians of the United States always strikes foreign Americanists. Whereas there are a few hundred African, European, Latin American, or Australasian historians of the United States, there are thousands and thousands of American historians in the United States, thousands and thousands of graduate students, of Ph.D. dissertations, books, and journal articles. Everywhere else in the world, U.S. history is artisanal or protoindustrial at best—"sparsely populated" in the words of the Dutch historian Rob Kroes. As Maurizio Vaudagna of Italy emphasizes, in Europe, historians of the United States "are but a tiny fraction of the historical fraternity. The five full professors and ten associate professors who specialize in United States history in Italy are but an example of how small the community of American historians is in each European nation."[35] By contrast, in the United States, American historiography is a mass-production branch within the great American academic economy.

Size and scale effects may not always be apparent to insiders, but they are to outsiders. In a thoughtful musing on "some theoretical aspects of writing history at a distance," the American-born, Australian-resident historian and anthropologist Donna Merwick contrasts "the attendance of two Americanists, one a U.S. resident and the other an Outsider, at the American Historical Association convention":

> [T]o the resident scholar, it means the casual, yearly engagement with colleagues about history. During the three days of post-Christmas meetings much goes on, but attention is to content. At the sessions, in corridor exchanges, in conversations at bars, coffee "shoppes" and seventh-floor suites, preoccupation is with the substance of the event—the many historical issues, the profession's future direction. The meaning of what is going on asks no scrutiny of the distinction between the convention's appearances and its substance, between form and content.

On the other hand, Merwick suggests, "for the Outsider the convention is an occasion that demands such analysis. To the stranger, it is a midwinter ritual, a ceremonial occurrence, an annual display of performances that separate from substance and give meaning. It is a *collage* of rites, a series of actualizations from which she inevitably makes appropriations out of her cultural system overseas. Adrift from her own structures, she discovers meaning where she may, looking to the textual quality of the spoken presentations and of the convention itself. When the meetings are over and the plastic nameplate discarded, the insiders return to the teaching and research routine from which the late December days were a suspension, but which gave them meaning. They return to constructing the metaphors that will make sense of one or other aspect of a culture shared with colleagues and students. The Outsider has no share in that process, returning to social realities of which the insider knows nothing."[36]

Of course, professionalization is neither a uniquely American phenomenon nor limited in the United States to specialists in American history. In its American format, it is more generally an attribute of academic history as it is being practiced in the United States, and a result of a century-long evolution. There is a crucial difference, however, between the Americanists and the non-Americanists in history departments. To a considerable extent, American Americanists may easily operate according to a model of internal demand on an unrivaled continental scale. Self-sufficiency appears normal, because it results from size and scale effects of an extent unique to U.S. historiography.

This phenomenon, which I propose to call continentalism, frames the contours of the various processes of intellectual legitimization at work within the profession. "In-house" training, for instance, is the usual norm for graduate students in American history. Graduate programs place little or no emphasis on the acquisition of linguistic skills—admittedly a long-standing nightmare for most graduate students, and later a subject of self-derogatory jokes for many American historians. Consider the following statement, excerpted from the Ph.D. program summary in a large research university somewhere in the United States: "Knowledge of one language other than English is required of students in United States history; for all other students, the requirement is two languages. The purpose of this requirement—in addition to the relevance it may have to primary research—is to minimize scholarly provincialism and facilitate exposure to historical literature in languages other than English." While it exhibits a commendable eagerness to avoid "scholarly provincialism," this requirement does not avoid contradiction in distinguishing between the less cosmopolitan Americanists and the more cosmopolitan "other students."

Likewise, few graduate programs in American history consider the possibility of students spending a year abroad in a foreign graduate program in American history, or simply emphasize the possibility that there may be scholarship worthy of even brief consideration outside of the United States. The only exceptions are usually students specializing in fields that are international or relational almost by definition, such as migration (but not necessarily ethnic) history or diplomatic history.

Continentalism operates no less powerfully for scholarly journals or academic books. Unless they are invited to contribute to a foreign journal, American historians usually do not read periodicals or books on American history published outside of the United States. Language is obviously an issue here, but it is probably not the most determining factor. Nor is the alleged provincialism with which American historians sometimes flagellate themselves. More important is the structure of professional recognition and legitimization. There are implicit and explicit rules to an American historian's career, and until now an international perspective has never been one of them. Since competition is extreme in the market-oriented American academic world, there is hardly any room or need for outsiders.

Very different are the consequences of professionalization à l'américaine for American scholars who do not specialize in U.S. history. They benefit from the large-scale organizational capacity the profession exhibits, but they do have to take into account non-American specialists of their chosen field of research—if only those of the country or region they study. Clearly, American specialists in the history of Brazil, Germany, or Japan could not afford to ignore Brazilian, German, or Japanese scholars working in the same field without demonstrating a regrettable lack of professional standards. Scholarly journals illustrate this trend: footnotes and book reviews in the various American journals that focus on the histories of other countries display a remarkable awareness of and critical engagement with "native" scholarship.[37]

Indeed, these American historians have established so many links with the historians of the countries they study that they may well hinder the exportation of American historical narratives in yet another, admittedly unexpected way. It seems that many of the questions, problems, or methodologies that underlie the narratives of U.S. history at any given time actually lead American historians specializing in the history of the rest of the world to raise similar interrogations about their own subject. In so doing, they "smuggle" abroad these questions or problems while rendering the transfer of the original American narrative useless.

Consider the example of mobility studies, a pet subject of the new social history of the 1960s and 1970s. Very little of these works or the debates they sparked directly influenced scholarship outside of the United States. American Europeanists, on the other hand, did export the themes and methodologies of mobility studies through their own research on various European countries. In the case of Germany, for instance, Hartmut Kaelble explained in 1978 that the study of social mobility long "remained an underdeveloped field of research, especially in comparison with the United States and her wealth of urban studies." American historians of Germany like David Crew and Frederick Marquardt played an important role in stimulating works focusing on the German case. German historians like Kaelble himself and Jürgen Kocka developed important comparisons between the United States and Germany. Conspicuously absent from these discussions were American specialists in the field of social mobility in the United States.[38]

More surprisingly, perhaps, many American historians who specialize in women's or gender history outside of the United States play an important role in the transfer of the categories and themes of American women's history. They do so because of the extraordinary development of the history of women and gender in American universities over the past three decades. As a result, however, works by American specialists on the subject of European, Asian, Latin American, and African women are better known outside of the United States than those by American Americanists. Also, the *content* of American women's and gender history has little impact outside of the United States. There are undoubtedly exceptions to this pattern. Gerda Lerner's work, for instance, is particularly well known and influential in Germany, where most of her books have been translated. However, few Americanists enjoy an influence comparable to that of the Europeanists Joan Scott or Louise Tilly, for instance.[39]

This particular situation is obviously related to the more general situation of the historical profession in the United States and results from American historians' diversity of interests, sophistication, and professional development. It is indeed ironical that the non-Americanists among American historians may mobilize enough scientific and professional resources to influence foreign scholarship, but that the Americanists among them usually fail to do so.

CRITICAL INTERNATIONALISM
AND THE CONCEPTUALIZATION OF AMERICAN HISTORY

The sorry lack or slowness of international mobility displayed by American history also raises questions about its reception in or importation into various countries around the world. There, as in the United States, the situation of specialists in American history should be considered separately from that of non-Americanists.

As I have previously argued, aside from the infrequent importation of questions and methodologies, non-Americanists are usually quite indifferent to U.S. history. They often operate within their own national framework and may sometimes display unmistakable signs of their own parochialism. In Australia, according to Donna Merwick, "the Americanist is odd-man-out to fellow-historians and students, the majority of whom do Australian history or have a firm European orientation. The Americanist's taste in, say, colonial England—let alone New Netherland—is not particularly shared; discourse on that subject (if one persists in it) soon shades into soliloquy."[40] Similar reactions everywhere around the world testify to the modest interest in U.S. history exhibited by most non-Americanists.

The situation of foreign Americanists is quite different. Certainly, they lack the national framework that pervades U.S. historiography. Nor do they generally enjoy the organizational and structural benefits of "made-in-the-U.S.A." American history. But more important, the type of reception American history receives among foreign Americanists results from these scholars' postures vis-à-vis U.S. history. They have a choice between three possible attitudes or stands, which may either succeed one another or co-exist, albeit with tensions.

What often characterizes the first attitude is indifference to American historiography. Many foreign scholars busy themselves writing textbooks and focus on teaching general surveys, generally avoiding any specialized research or scientific interaction with fellow historians from the United States. Their indifference to historiographical developments does not facilitate the transfer of American historical narratives, even though these scholars' position is clearly one of intellectual dependency.

In 1958, an American historian of France, the late David H. Pinkney, offered one of the best and most sophisticated analyses of this posture. According to what has come to be known as the "Pinkney thesis" (its author called it "the dilemma of the American Historian of Modern France"), American historians of France should not attempt "to beat the French at their own game" and should concentrate not on massive research works but "on works of synthesis and interpretation."[41] Needless to say, by 1991, Pinkney himself acknowledged that the field of French history in the United States had changed so much that it was high time "to bury the Pinkney thesis." No foreign historian of the United States has ever attached his or her name to this attitude—one that long prevailed among foreign Americanists and may well have a future because it answers to the needs of many teaching-oriented academic institutions.

A second attitude for foreign Americanists is one of scholarly assimilation. This is the scientist posture best described in Tony Badger's 1992 "Confessions of a British Americanist," published in the *Journal of American History:* "I, like my contemporaries, set out on my Ph.D. determined to make my work indistinguishable from that of an American graduate student. I planned to work on domestic American history, not on Anglo-American themes; I aimed to make my research as thoroughly grounded in the archives as the most conscientious American dissertation; my ultimate ambition was to be published in the States and to have my work reviewed and assessed according to the highest standards of the American historical profession." Indeed, Badger liked to think of himself as "a historian who happened to be British but who was working on a theme in domestic American history in the context of a clearly defined American historiographical problem."[42]

Like Badger, many foreign scholars have attempted and sometimes succeeded in "going native," in "becoming Americans" by getting rid of their colonial dependency, emulating and seeking to equate with their American counterparts. Scholars like Willi Paul Adams of Germany, Christopher Clark of England, Rhys Isaac and Ian Tyrrell of Australia, Alessandra Lorini and Ferdinando Fasce of Italy, Rob Kroes of the Netherlands, Ron Robin of Israel, and Reinhold Wagnleitner of Austria have all produced major books, published by American academic publishers, that have received well-deserved consideration from their American-based peers.[43] Foreign graduate students in American history at various institutions throughout the world are now trained in a way that, it may be hoped, will make them as knowledgeable in their field as their American-based counterparts. "Studying like in the United States," Jessica Gienow-Hecht argues, is one of the goals of a pilot project of week-long intensive seminars in American history recently developed at the Center for United States Studies of the Martin-Luther-University Halle-Wittenberg in Lutherstadt Wittenberg, Germany.[44]

Several recent European books exemplify this trend. Ester Fano's *Una e divisibile: Tendenze attuali della storiografia statunitense* (One and divisible: Current tendencies of U.S. historiography), Jean Heffer et al.'s *Chantiers d'histoire américaine* (Workshops of American History), a collection published in 1994, and Claude Fohlen et al.'s *Canada et États-Unis depuis 1770*

(Canada and the United States since 1770) all attempt to provide readers (mostly graduate students and colleagues) with analytical accounts of the evolution of most major fields of American history.[45]

In his review of *Chantiers d'histoire américaine* for the *Journal of American History,* James Henretta noted that "the essays in the volume vary in quality" but "are completely up-to-date in their scholarship, asking the same questions and citing the same books and articles as similar essays published in the United States." He went on to ask:

> Should we celebrate this mastery of the idiom of American scholarship by these French scholars, nearly all of whom hold academic positions in French universities? Or should we lament the increasing homogeneity of scholarly discourse? In making themselves experts in American history, the authors have imbibed the terms of reference and the intellectual assumptions of their American colleagues. The major difference is their relative detachment from the passions of American historiographical debates, which enables them to assess the strengths and the weaknesses of the contending arguments.[46]

Of course, such evaluation was music to the ears of the twenty-or-so contributors to the volume under review. Apparently, they had at least partially managed to become American historians, calling to mind Tony Badger's conclusion that he remained "unrepentant" in his "original aim to eschew a distinctive British voice and concentrate, albeit unavailingly, on becoming just a good historian of the United States who happens to work in Britain."[47]

Such an approach, of course, aims at fully integrating the values and categories of American historiography. At the same time, in yet another way, it prevents American historical narratives from traveling abroad, for without distance, there is no possible travel. It also shuts out any possibility that a non-American historian of the United States might have something original to say about American history. "Perhaps to downplay one's British identity in a desire to achieve credibility as an American historian is to sacrifice the opportunity to make a substantial contribution to American historiography," Tony Badger remarks. "Are British historians simply to be anonymous clones of worthy but conventional professional American historians?"[48]

More conducive to travels and transfers is a third posture, which may be called historiographical intervention. It is based on the idea that foreign scholars need to rethink their geographical, cultural, political, and intellectual distance from American historiography, offer explicit accounts of their intellectual posture within their own national historiographical context, and put this distance to good use in their research into U.S. history.

This third posture presents a double challenge to foreign historians. In order to engage American historiography on its own terms, they must achieve a command of American historiographical issues equal to that of their American counterparts. In other words, they cannot escape the moment of historiographical assimilation that I have previously described. But they also need to construct their distance vis-à-vis their research object by explicitly accounting for their own intellectual posture, their relationship to their graduate training or to their own national traditions and processes of intellectual legitimization and professional validation. European scholars, for instance, would do well to ponder Rob Kroes's sound advice:

> Whatever the precise academic and institutional history of the field, however, it can be argued that Europe has known a history of intellectual reflection on the United States that allows one to speak of a European American Studies tradition, with its canon of great names, from Tocqueville to Sombart, from Bryce to Huizinga, from Myrdall to Pavese. It is in fact a tradition older than the one which in the United States emerged as the American Studies movement and which, after the war, became a model for many American Studies programs elsewhere to follow. Clearly, any program for a European approach to American studies should start from this recognition. European students of American history, society and culture should be trained in an awareness of these longer lines of European reflection on America, on its "Otherness" offering cultural counterpoints to Europe as well as on its similarities and parallels. Only then can the American Studies movement in the United States be seen as serving different existential needs, answering different questions of national identity, than the European reflection on America.[49]

Perhaps migration history offers adequate metaphors for this process. Historians of migrations have long been attentive to invisible but quite real migratory paths and chains. It is a similar image I have in mind. Historical narratives cannot travel under the influence of "push" or "pull" forces. What they need is identifiable, active paths of intellectual exchange through which historiography can be reconceptualized. Migration history offers the obvious example of a field where this kind of interaction has taken place over the past three decades. Among many others, historians such as Frank Thistlethwaite of Britain, Dirk Hoerder of Germany, and Bruno Ramirez of Canada and other places have actively contributed to a major reappraisal of the international context of transatlantic, transpacific, or trans-American migration movements.[50] Historiographical chains imitate and reproduce migratory chains.

But meaningful international conversations of this kind need not be limited to those fields that are relational almost by definition. There is nothing that prevents comparable dialogues in most fields of domestic American history, including social and political history, and so forth. In some countries, unlike in the United States, economic and social history form a single field. There is little doubt that the categories used by these economic and social historians significantly differ from those used by their American colleagues, and could contribute to recasting these fields.

Donna Merwick has best described this third posture in anthropological terms. "We who write about Americans from overseas are the 'professional stranger' to them as he [Malinowski] was to the Pacific islanders. We are, like him, men and women at a distance." Outsiders, in other words—a position that puts one, as Merwick points out, "in double jeopardy: Outsider to the mainstream historical discourse" of one's homeland, and also "Outsider to the 'natives' and those historians blessed to reside permanently among them."[51] Yet the position of outsider is not without its merits, its ironies, or its subversive possibilities.

CODA: TOWARD THE END OF "WE-NESS"?

About twenty years ago, the French historian François Furet took his readers to "the workshop of history." The metaphor is a useful one for reflecting upon the question of historiographical self-enclosure. American historiography operates according to a certain set of guiding principles. American Americanists use certain types of tools to write historical narratives, and they operate in a market-oriented, highly competitive, continental context that does not favor exportation. These principles, tools, and modes of operation may not be entirely peculiar to U.S. historiography. What is specific, however, is the scale and scope effect brought about by continentalism.

In another sense, delineating the patterns that help us understand why so little of American historiography travels abroad suggests that the current situation is not a fatal outcome. One may well imagine that foreign Americanists will demonstrate their own artisanal talents and use their own tools to demonstrate the know-how they have accumulated during their apprenticeship. It is also likely that American Americanists will develop renewed perspectives on their history's national dimension and, at the same time, continue to explore much-needed comparative, transnational and international paths. Bringing "we-ness" to an end, in fact, will not depend on either American or foreign Americanists alone, but rather on the development of a more demanding interaction between them.

The internationalization of American history, if it is to succeed, cannot remain what it is now—largely a top-down movement driven by a relatively small group of cosmopolitan academics. The teaching of U.S. history will need to change. The survey will continue to exist, but it must adapt. It must partake in the process of decentering and relativizing the weight of national history. It should emphasize the constructed nature of maps, borders, cultures, and social relations. The profession may also have to evolve. This is probably the most difficult aspect of the whole issue, because the stakes

here are not purely intellectual. Without undue naïveté, one can nevertheless imagine the advent of changes, both from within and from without,
and probably more easily so in professional organizations than in history
departments. There is less at stake in enlarging the scope of professional
conferences or in including foreign-based colleagues on panels and committees than in redesigning the intricate and often delicate intellectual,
political, and social architecture of American academic entities. Obviously,
such professional implications are quite different for American and foreign-based historians. Foreign-based students who are taught U.S. history
learn the history of the Other, not their national history; their conception
of the center is different from that of their American-based counterparts.

Internationalization also works both ways. It should be seen neither as
only what non-American-based historians bring to their colleagues in the
United States nor as only what those relatively rare American historians
who are interested in historiographical exports offer their foreign counterparts. Networks, information flows, flexibility, and multilateral exchanges are the key ideas.

This should reassure all those who may be wary of any attempts by American Americanists to behave in an imperialist mode. It just cannot work.
Consider the attempts by American scholars and the U.S. government to
develop programs in American studies throughout Europe in the 1950s
and 1960s. As Richard Pells and other scholars suggest, most European
scholars simply did not behave as Americans expected. They did not rally
around the ambitious projects of U.S.-defined American studies (then a
holistic conceptualization of American civilization particularly attentive to
myths and symbols). Rather, they embarked upon developing new forms
of Europeanized American studies, which varied from one country to another but shared a common distance vis-à-vis the original product. Any
observer of the field of American studies today, both inside and outside of
the United States, could draw similar conclusions.[52]

Finally, the intellectual benefits of internationalization are not a given,
and are not even certain. They are based on the clarification of the various
conceptual circles through which scholars coming from different, often
mixed traditions operate. A call for internationalization is therefore a call
for self-reflexivity.

NOTES

1. Raymond Grew, "The Comparative Weakness of American History," *Journal of
Interdisciplinary History* 16 (Summer 1985): 87. Thomas Bender formulated the
problem in similar terms when he asked me to think about these issues, saying: "The
question is whether there is a kind of 'we-ness' in the framing of American historiography that makes it difficult for American history to travel."

2. See Thomas S. Kuhn, *The Structure of Scientific Revolutions* (1962; 3d ed., Chicago, 1996).

3. On the evolution of American historiography, see John Higham, *History: Professional Scholarship in America* (Baltimore, 1986); *The Past before Us: Contemporary Historical Writing in the United States,* ed. Michael G. Kammen (Ithaca, N.Y.: 1980); *The New American History,* ed. Eric Foner (Philadelphia, 1997), and *Imagined Histories: American Historians Interpret the Past,* ed. Anthony Molho and Gordon S. Wood (Princeton, N.J., 1998). On American historiography's complicated relation to the social sciences, see Edward N. Saveth, *American History and the Social Sciences* (New York, 1964); Dorothy Ross, *The Origins of American Social Science* (New York, 1991); id., "The New and Newer Histories: Social Theory and Historiography in an American Key," *Rethinking History* 1 (1997): 125–50; and *The Historic Turn in the Human Sciences,* ed. Terrence J. McDonald, (Ann Arbor, Mich., 1996).

4. Grew, "Comparative Weakness of American History," 89.

5. Maurice Lévy-Leboyer, "La 'New Economic History,'" *Annales: Economies, Sociétés, Civilisations* 24 (September–October 1969): 1035–69; Francisco Bustelo, "La 'Nueva Historia Economica': Revision Critica," *Moneda y Credito* 125 (1973): 37–56; Jaime García-Lombardero, "La 'Nueva Historia Economica': Consideraciones teoricas y de metodo," *Moneda y Credito* 125 (1973): 3–35; Jean Heffer, "Une histoire scientifique: La nouvelle histoire économique," *Annales: Economies, Sociétés, Civilisations* 32 (July–August 1977): 824–42; *La nouvelle histoire économique: Exposés de méthodologie,* ed. Jean Heffer (Paris, 1977); György Ránki, "Az uj gazdasa tortenet amerikai iskolaja," *Magyar tudomány* 22 (1977): 164–72; Jan Pomorski, *Paradygmat "New Economic History": Studium 2 teorii rozwoju nauki historycznej* (Lublin, 1985); Andrzej Zybertowicz, "New Economic History," *Storia della storiografia* 13 (1988): 128–31; id., "The American New Economic History and Its Significance for the Methodological Reconstruction of Historiography," *Studia Historiae Oeconomicae* 20 (1993): 39–51. See also, for Argentina, Gustavo Marques, "Historia y ciencia," *Ciclos* 4 (1994): 231–39.

6. Alfred D. Chandler Jr., *The Visible Hand: The Managerial Revolution in American Business* (Cambridge, Mass., 1977). See also, e.g., *Managerial Hierarchies: Comparative Perspectives on the Rise of the Modern Industrial Enterprise,* ed. Chandler and Herman Daems (Cambridge, Mass., 1980); *Scale and Scope: The Dynamics of Industrial Capitalism* (Cambridge, Mass., 1990), ed. Chandler and Takashi Hikino; and Chandler, Franco Amatori, and Takashi Hikino, *Big Business and the Wealth of Nations* (New York, 1997).

7. David A. Hollinger, *In the American Province: Studies in the History and Historiography of Ideas* (Bloomington, Ind., 1985); James T. Kloppenberg, *Uncertain Victory: Social Democracy and Progressivism in European and American Thought, 1870–1920* (New York, 1986); Daniel T. Rodgers, *Atlantic Crossings: Social Politics in a Progressive Age* (Cambridge, Mass., 1998). On the importance of conceptualizing Progressivism in an international context, see also Rodgers's insightful "In Search of Progressivism," *Reviews in American History* 10 (1982): 113–32.

8. For these round tables, see Michelle Perrot, "Les tables rondes de la MSH," *Mouvement Social* 111 (April–June 1980): 34–36. I am grateful to Patrick Fridenson for suggesting this source. This issue of *Le Mouvement Social,* dedicated to Georges Haupt (1928–78) contains many articles about Haupt's international impact.

Haupt's books include *Socialism and the Great War: The Collapse of the Second International* (Oxford, 1972) and *Aspects of International Socialism, 1871–1914: Essays* (New York, 1986).

9. See, e.g., *Le Mouvement Social* 102 (January–March 1978), *Ouvriers des États-Unis,* special issue on American labor history, ed. Marianne Debouzy, with articles by James R. Green, Herbert Gutman, and David Montgomery, among others.

10. Bruno Cartosio, "Herbert Gutman in Italy: History and Politics," *Labor History* 29 (1988): 356–62. See, however, Susanna Delfino, "Potere e cultura: I temi centrali della storiografia de Herbert G. Gutman," *Movimento operaio e socialista* 12 (1989): 137–44, for a more optimistic assessment of Gutman's influence in Italy. In French, see Herbert G. Gutman, "La politique ouvrière de l'entreprise américaine de 'l'Âge du Clinquant': Le cas de la Standard Oil Company," *Mouvement Social* 102 (January–March 1978): 67–99.

11. The best assessments of the influence of American labor history in Italy are Ferdinando Fasce, "American Labor History, 1973–1983: Italian Perspectives," *Reviews in American History* 14 (1986): 597–613; id., "La New Labor History de David Montgomery: Un seminario e un libro," *Movimento operaio socialista* 9 (1988): 79–79. See also Mariveccia Salvati, "Cultura operaia a disciplina industriale: Ipotesi per un confronto tra correnti storiografiche," *Movimento operaio e socialista* 1 (1980): 5–17. For another example of historiographical influence, see the review of Daniel T. Rodgers's *The Work Ethic in Industrial America, 1850–1920* (Chicago, 1978) by Pietro Bairati, "L'etica del lavoro," *Rivista storica italiana* 92 (1980): 164–75. For an example of Montgomery's influence in Germany, see Thomas Welskipp, "Arbeitsplatz, Staat und Arbeiteraktivismus: David Montgomery's 'Fall of the House of Labor' als Neue Synthese Amerikanischer Arbeitergeschichte," *Geschichte und Gesellschaft* 18 (1992): 94–106. Montgomery's books have not been translated into French, although the Maison des sciences de l'Homme co-published *The Fall of the House of Labor: The Workplace, the State, and American Labor Activism, 1865–1925* with Cambridge University Press in 1987. His articles in French journals include "Quels standards? Les ouvriers et la réorganisation de la production aux États-Unis (1900–1920)," *Mouvement Social* 102 (January–March 1978): 101–27; and "Labor and the Republic in Industrial America, 1860–1920," *Mouvement Social* 111 (April–June 1980): 201–15. For an example of Gutman and Montgomery's influence on French Americanists, see *In the Shadow of the Statue of Liberty: Immigrants, Workers, and Citizens in the American Republic, 1880–1920,* ed. Marianne Debouzy (Urbana, Ill., 1992).

12. Sean Wilentz, *Chants Democratic: New York City and the Rise of the American Working Class, 1788–1850* (New York, 1984), Japanese trans., Tokyo, 1995; David Montejano, *Anglos and Mexicans in the Making of Texas, 1836–1986* (Austin, Tex., 1987), Spanish trans., Mexico, D.F., 1991; George Chauncey, *Gay New York: Gender, Urban Culture, and the Makings of the Gay Male World, 1890–1940* (New York, 1994), French trans., Paris, forthcoming. The Frederick Jackson Turner Award was not awarded in 1960, 1963, 1964, 1968, 1975, and 1976. Two books were chosen in 1985 and 2000. I thank Laura Young Bost (University of Texas Press), Ariane DePree (Stanford University Press), Dan Dixon (University of California Press), Ted Gerney, Cordelia Hamilton, and Frank Smith (Cambridge University Press), Peter Ginna (Oxford University Press), Aubrey L. Hicks (Cornell University Press), Norah

Piehl (University of Illinois Press), Rebecca Thurgur (Yale University Press), Jennifer Webster-Burnham (University of Chicago Press), Vicky Wells and Laura Gribbin (University of North Carolina Press), and Craig Wilkie (University of Kentucky Press) for answering my queries about translations of American history books abroad.

13. William Henry Chafe's *The American Woman: Her Changing Social, Economic, and Political Roles, 1920–1970* (New York, 1972) has been translated into Chinese, French, and Japanese (personal communication to the author, November 22, 2000). David Brion Davis, *The Problem of Slavery in Western Culture* (Ithaca, N.Y., 1966), Italian trans., Turin, 1971; Spanish trans., Bogota, 1996; Portuguese trans., Rio de Janeiro, 2000; id., *Revolutions: Reflections on American Equality and Foreign Liberations* (Cambridge, Mass., 1990), German trans., Berlin, 1993. Eric Foner, *Nothing but Freedom: Emancipation and Its Legacy* (Baton Rouge, La., 1983), Portuguese trans., Rio de Janeiro, 1988; id., *The Story of American Freedom* (New York, 1998), Italian trans., Rome, 2000; Chinese trans., Beijing, forthcoming. John Higham, *Send These to Me: Immigrants in Urban America* (Baltimore, 1984), Japanese trans., Tokyo, 1994. Michael G. Kammen, *People of Paradox: An Inquiry Concerning the Origins of American Civilization* (New York, 1972), has been translated at least into Burmese, French, Indonesian, Japanese, Korean, and Spanish; id., *A Machine That Would Go of Itself: The Constitution in American Culture* (New York, 1986), has been translated into Arabic and Korean (personal communication to the author, November 23, 2000). *Black Women in White America: A Documentary History,* ed. Gerda Lerner (New York, 1972), French trans., Paris, 1975; Gerda Lerner, *The Creation of Patriarchy* (New York, 1986), German trans., Frankfurt a./M., 1991; Spanish trans., Barcelona, 1990; Japanese trans., Tokyo, 1996; id., *The Creation of Feminist Consciousness: From the Middle Ages to Eighteen-Seventy* (New York, 1993), German trans., Frankfurt a./M., 1993; id., *The Majority Finds Its Past: Placing Women in History* (New York, 1979), German trans., Frankfurt a./M., 1995. David Montgomery, *Workers' Control in America: Studies in the History of Work, Technology, and Labor Struggles* (New York, 1979), Italian trans., Turin, 1980; Spanish trans., Madrid, 1985; id., *Citizen Worker: The Experience of Workers in the United States with Democracy and the Free Market during the Nineteenth Century* (New York, 1993), Spanish trans., Mexico, D.F., 1997. Gary B. Nash, *Red, White, and Black: The Peoples of Early America* (Englewood Cliffs, N.J.: 1974), Spanish trans., (1989); *Struggle and Survival in Colonial America,* ed. David G. Sweet and Gary B. Nash (Berkeley and Los Angeles, 1981), Spanish trans., (Mexico D.F., 1987). I am deeply indebted to the following past presidents of the OAH for answering my query: Joyce Appleby, Allan Bogue, William Chafe, David Brion Davis, Eric Foner, George Fredrickson, John Higham, Michael Kammen, Stanley Katz, Gerda Lerner, David Montgomery, and Gary B. Nash.

14. On the role of USIA, see Tiziano Bonazzi, "American History: The View from Italy," *Reviews in American History* 14 (1986): 523–41, who notes that the American Cultural Services in Italy helped the Bologna publisher Il Mulino translate U.S. history into Italian as early as the 1950s. American Cultural Services in France played a similar role through their in-house publishing house, Nouveaux Horizons. In one of their last actions before their budget was slashed, Nouveaux Horizons financed the translation into French of Sara Evans's *Born for Liberty: A History of American Women* (New York, 1989), French trans., Paris, 1993, and bought several thousand

copies of the book to be given away by American diplomats in French-speaking countries, particularly in Africa.

15. Ron Robin, "The Outsider as Marginal Scholar: Reflections on the Past, the Foreign and Comparative Studies in American History," *American Studies International* 31 (April 1993): 118.

16. Robert H. Walker, "The Internationalization of American Studies," *American Studies International* 26 (April 1988): 68, 69.

17. See in particular David Thelen's introductory articles "Of Audiences, Borderlands, and Comparisons: Toward the Internationalization of American History," *Journal of American History* 79 (September 1992): 432–62; "Rethinking History and the Nation-State: Mexico and the United States," ibid. 86 (September 1999): 439–52; and "The Nation and Beyond: Transnational Perspectives on United States History," ibid. 86 (December 1999): 965–75.

18. Frank Thistlethwaite, "Reflections on Boorstin's America," *Journal of Modern History* 32 (December 1960): 371; Andrew White, quoted in David Thelen, "Making History and Making the United States," *Journal of American Studies* 32 (1998): 385. On the links between history and the nation in the United States, see also David D. Van Tassel, *Recording America's Past: An Interpretation of the Development of Historical Studies in America, 1607–1884* (Chicago, 1960); Higham, *History;* H. G. Jones, *Historical Consciousness in the Early Republic: The Origins of State Historical Societies, Museums, and Collections, 1791–1861* (Chapel Hill, N.C., 1995); and Peter Novick, *That Noble Dream: The "Objectivity Question" and the American Historical Profession* (New York, 1988).

19. Benedict R. O'G. Anderson, *Imagined Communities: Reflections on the Origin and Spread of Nationalism* (1983; rev. ed., New York, 1991), 205. See also Reinhart Koselleck, *Le futur passé: Contribution à la sémantique des temps historiques* (Paris, 1990).

20. James J. Sheehan, "What is German History? Reflections on the Role of the Nation in German History and Historiography," *Journal of Modern History* 53 (March 1981): 3. See Heinrich von Treitschke, *Deutsche Geschichte im neunzehnten Jahrhundert* (Leipzig, 1879–95). On this historiographical tradition, see also G. P. Gooch, *History and Historians in the Nineteenth Century* (Boston, 1959) and Georg Iggers, *The German Conception of History* (Middletown, Conn., 1968).

21. Sheehan, "What is German History?" 3. On the problem of a national history, see Ernst Nolte, "Zur Konzeption der Nationalgeschichte heute," *Historische Zeitschrift* 202 (1966): 603–21; Stefan Berger, *The Search for Normality: National Identity and Historical Consciousness in Germany since 1800* (Providence, R.I., 1997).

22. On Ireland, see Donald MacCartney, "The Writing of History in Ireland, 1809–30," *Irish Historical Studies* 10 (September 1957): 347–62; on Poland, Marta Herling, "Storiografia e questione nazionale in Polonia fra otto e novecento," *Storia della storiografia* 20 (1991): 29–46; on Portugal, Sergio Campos Martos, "Historiographie et nationalisme au Portugal au 19e siècle," ibid. 32 (1997): 61–70; on Switzerland, Peter Stadler, "L'historiographie suisse vers 1900," ibid. 8 (1985): 116–22.

23. See Pierre Nora and Lawrence D. Kritzman, *Realms of Memory: Rethinking the French Past* (New York, 1996); Charles-Olivier Carbonnell, *Histoire et historiens: Une mutation idéologique des historiens français (1865–1885)* (Toulouse, 1976); Francois Hartog, *Le XIXe siècle et l'histoire: Le cas Fustel de Coulanges* (Paris, 1988). See also

Lionel Gossman, "Augustin Thierry and Liberal Historiography," *History and Theory* 15 (1976): 1–83; Madeleine Rebérioux, "Histoire, historiens et dreyfusisme," *Revue historique* 255 (1976): 407–32; Antoine Prost, "Charles Seignobos revisité," *Vingtième siècle: Revue d'histoire* 43 (July 1994): 100–118; Gérard Noiriel, *Sur la "crise" de l'histoire* (Paris, 1996); and Christophe Charle, *Paris fin de siècle: Culture et politique* (Paris, 1998). I am indebted to Christophe Prochasson for guiding me through this historiography.

24. Carl Berger, *The Writing of Canadian History. Aspects of English-Canadian Historical Writing since 1900,* 2d ed. (Toronto, 1986), 2; Arthur R. M. Lower, *Colony to Nation: A History of Canada* (Toronto, 1949). On Latin America, see, e.g., E. Bradford Burns, "Ideology in Nineteenth-Century American Historiography," *Hispanic American Historical Review* 58 (1978): 409–31, and Nikita Harwich Vallenilla, "National Identities and National Projects: Spanish American Historiography in the Nineteenth and Twentieth Centuries," *Storia della storiografia* 19 (1991): 147–56.

25. Ronald Rudin, "Revisionism and the Search for a Normal Society: A Critique of Recent Quebec Historical Writing," *Canadian Historical Review* 73 (March 1992): 30–61; id., *Making History in Twentieth-Century Quebec* (Toronto, 1997). Jean-Marie Fecteau, "Between Scientific Enquiry and the Search for a Nation: Quebec Historiography as Seen by Ronald Rudin," *Canadian Historical Review* 80 (December 1999): 641–66; Rudin, "On Difference and National Identity in Quebec Historical Writing: A Response to Jean-Marie Fecteau," ibid. 80 (December 1999): 666–76. See also Jocelyn Letourneau, "The Current Great Narrative of Quebecois Identity," *South Atlantic Quarterly* 94 (1995): 1039–53, and Matteo Sanfilippo, "Storia, nazione ed etnia nella piu recente produzione sul Canada francese," *Studi emigrazione* 33 (1996): 461–72.

26. Prasenjit Duara, *Rescuing History from the Nation: Questioning Narratives of Modern China* (Chicago, 1995).

27. See, e.g., *Histoire de la France,* ed. André Burguière and Jacques Revel (4 vols., Paris, 1989).

28. See Ian Tyrrell, "American Exceptionalism in an Age of International History," *American Historical Review* 96 (October 1991): 1031–55.

29. For various assessments of the "new histories" of the 1970s and 1980s, see Higham, *History; Past before Us,* ed. Kammen; *New American History,* ed. Foner. Participants in the debate on fragmentation include Bernard Bailyn, "The Challenge of Modern Historiography," *American Historical Review* 87 (February 1982): 1–24; Thomas Bender, "Wholes and Parts: The Need for Synthesis in American History," *Journal of American History* 73, (June 1986): 120–36; David Thelen, "A Round Table: Synthesis in American History," ibid. 74 (June 1987): 107–22; Allan Megill, "Fragmentation and the Future of American Historiography," *American Historical Review* 96 (June 1991): 693–98; and John Higham, "The Future of American History," *Journal of American History* 80 (March 1994): 1289–1309.

30. See Ramsay Cook, *Canada and the French-Canadian Question* (Toronto, 1966); id., *Canada, Quebec, and the Uses of Nationalism* (Toronto, 1986); J. M. S. Careless, "'Limited Identities' in Canada," *Canadian Historical Review* 50 (March 1969): 1–10; Berger, *Writing of Canadian History,* 259–65; Graeme Davidson, "Slicing Australian History: Reflections on the Bicentennial History Project," *New Zealand Journal of History* 16 (April 1982): 4.

31. Lawrence Stone, "The Revolution over the Revolution," *New York Review of Books* 39 (June 11, 1992): 51–52.

32. Bonazzi, "American History: The View from Italy," 527.

33. Jane C. Desmond and Virginia R. Dominguez, "Resituating American Studies in a Critical Internationalism," *American Quarterly* 48 (1996): 475–90.

34. Higham, "Future of American History," 1303.

35. Maurizio Vaudagna, "The American Historian in Continental Europe: An Italian Perspective," *Journal of American History* 79 (September 1992): 532.

36. Donna Merwick, "'Being There': Some Theoretical Aspects of Writing History at a Distance," *Reviews in American History* 14 (1986): 497.

37. For one example among many, see *French Historical Studies* (1958–).

38. See Hartmut Kaelble, "Social Mobility in Germany, 1900–1960," *Journal of Modern History* 50 (September 1978): 439–61; Kaelble, *Historische Mobilitätsforschung: Westeuropa und USA im 19. und 20. Jahrhundert* (Darmstadt, 1978), trans. Ingrid Noakes under the title *Historical Research on Social Mobility: Western Europe and the USA in the Nineteenth and Twentieth Centuries* (New York, 1981). David Crew, "Definitions of Modernity: Social Mobility in a German Town, 1880–1901," *Journal of Social History* 7 (1973): 51–74; Frederick D. Marquardt, "Sozialer Aufstieg, sozialer Abstieg und die Entstehung der Berliner Arbeiterklasse, 1806–1818," *Geschichte und Gesellschaft* 1 (1975); Jürgen Kocka, *Angestellte zwischen Faschismus und Demokratie: Zur politischen sozialgeschichte der Angestellten: USA 1890–1940 im internationalen Vergleich* (Göttingen, 1977), trans. Maura Kealey under the title *White Collar Workers in America, 1890-1940 : A Social-Political History in International Perspective* (Beverly Hills, Calif., 1980).

39. Articles by Joan Scott or Louise Tilly that influenced European historiography include Joan W. Scott, "Gender: A Useful Category of Historical Analysis," *American Historical Review* 91 (1986): 1053–75; id., "Les verriers de Carmaux, 1856–1895," *Mouvement Social* 76 (1971): 67–93; id., "Social History and the History of Socialism: French Socialist Municipalities in the 1890's," ibid. 111 (1980): 145–53; id., "'Ouvrière, mot impie, sordide . . . ': Le discours de l'économie politique française sur les ouvrières (1840–1860)," *Actes de la Recherche en Sciences Sociales* 83 (1990): 2–15; Louise A. Tilly, "Structure de l'emploi, travail des femmes et changement démographique dans deux villes industrielles: Anzin et Roubaix, 1872–1906," *Mouvement Social,* 105 (1978): 33–55; Louise A. Tilly and Miriam Cohen, "La famiglia ha una storia?" *Passato e presente* 2 (1982): 105–45. For one recent illustration of historiographical transfer, see Clare Crowston, "Le travail féminin en France, vu par l'historiographie américaine," *Revue d'Histoire Moderne et Contemporaine* 45 (1998): 837–53.

40. Merwick, "'Being There,'" 493. On the local situation of foreign Americanists, see in particular the precious inventory assembled in *Guide to the Study of United States History outside the U.S., 1945–1980,* ed. Lewis Hanke (White Plains, N.Y., 1985), the various articles in *Journal of American History,* special issue, 79 (September 1992): 432–542, and Willi Paul Adams, Wolfgang J. Helbich, and Maurizio Vaudagna, "Germany: Maurizio Vaudagna Interviews Willi Paul Adams and Wolfgang J. Helbich," *Storia nordamericana* 7 (1990): 121–36; Bonazzi, "American History: The View from Italy," 523–41; id., "American Studies in Italy," *American Studies International* 15 (1976): 35–44; id., "Trends in Italian Historical Research into North American

History, 1945–1983," *Storia nordamericana* 1 (1984): 5–21; Marianne Debouzy, "American History in France," *Reviews in American History* 14 (1986): 542–56; id., "Regards français sur les États-Unis: De l'observation à l'histoire," *Revue Française d'Études Américaines* 7 (1982): 41–50; Claude Fohlen, "Les débuts de l'histoire américaine en France," *Revue Française d'Études Américaines* 7 (1982): 27–40; Fohlen, "American History Abroad: France," *OAH Newsletter* 18 (1990): 3, 23; Robert Kelley, "The Study of American History Abroad," *Reviews in American History* 15 (1987): 140–51; Alexander S. Manykin and Maurizio Vaudagna, "The Soviet Union: Maurizio Vaudagna Interviews Alexander S. Manykin," *Storia nordamericana* 7 (1990): 155–65; Michal Rozbicki and Maurizio Vaudagna, "Poland: Maurizio Vaudagna Interviews Michal Rozbicki," *Storia nordamericana* 7 (1990): 137–53.

41. David H. Pinkney, "The Dilemma of the American Historian of Modern France," *French Historical Studies* 1 (1958): 11–25; id., "The Dilemma of the American Historian of Modern France Reconsidered," *French Historical Studies* 9 (1975): 170–81; id., "Time to Bury the Pinkney Thesis?" *French Historical Studies* 17 (Spring 1991): 219–23. See also id., "American Historians on the European Past," *American Historical Review* 86 (1981): 1–20; Thomas J. Schaeper, "French History as Written on Both Sides of the Atlantic: A Comparative Analysis," *French Historical Studies* 17 (1991): 233–48; Jeremy D. Popkin, "'Made in U.S.A.': Les historiens français d'outre-Atlantique et leur histoire," *Revue d'histoire moderne et contemporaine* 40 (1993): 303–20; and Richard F. Kuisel, "American Historians in Search of France: Perceptions and Misperceptions," *French Historical Studies* 19 (1995): 307–19.

42. Tony Badger, "Confessions of a British Americanist," *Journal of American History* 79 (September 1992): 516, 517.

43. Christopher Clark, *The Roots of Rural Capitalism: Western Massachusetts, 1780–1860* (Ithaca, N.Y.: 1990); Rob Kroes, *If You've Seen One, You've Seen the Mall: Europeans and American Mass Culture* (Urbana, Ill., 1996); Rhys Isaac, *The Transformation of Virginia, 1740–1790* (Chapel Hill, N.C., 1982); Alessandra Lorini, *Rituals of Race: American Public Culture and the Search for Racial Democracy* (Charlottesville, Va., 1999); Ron T. Robin, *Enclaves of America: The Rhetoric of American Political Architecture Abroad, 1900–1965* (Princeton, N.J., 1992); Ian R. Tyrrell, *Sobering Up: From Temperance to Prohibition in Antebellum America, 1800–1860* (Westport, Conn., 1979); id., *The Absent Marx: Class Analysis and Liberal History in Twentieth-Century America* (Westport, Conn., 1986) ; id., *Woman's World / Woman's Empire: The Woman's Christian Temperance Union in International Perspective, 1800–1930* (Chapel Hill, N.C., 1991); id., *True Gardens of the Gods: Californian-Australian Environmental Reform, 1860–1930* (Berkeley and Los Angeles, 1999); Reinhold Wagnleitner, *Coca-Colonization and the Cold War: The Cultural Mission of the United States in Austria after the Second World War* (Chapel Hill, N.C., 1994); *Here, There, and Everywhere: The Foreign Politics of American Popular Culture*, ed. Reinhold Wagnleitner and Elaine Tyler May (Hanover, N.H., 2000).

44. Jessica C. E. Gienow-Hecht, "U.S. History as a Model: Studying Like in the United States," *Perspectives: American Historical Association Newsletter* 36 (1998): 34–37.

45. *Una e divisibile: Tendenze attuali della storiografia statunitense*, ed. Ester Fano (Florence, 1991); *Chantiers d'histoire américaine*, ed. Jean Heffer and François Weil (Paris, 1994); Claude Fohlen, Jean Heffer, and François Weil, *Canada et États-Unis depuis 1770* (Paris, 1997).

46. James A. Henretta, "The Triumph of the Academy: French Style," *Journal of American History* 82 (September 1995): 641.

47. Badger, "Confessions," 523.

48. Ibid., 519–20.

49. Rob Kroes, "Studying America in Europe: Four Vignettes and a Program," *Journal of American Culture* 20 (Winter 1997): 63–71.

50. See Frank Thistlethwaite, "Migration from Europe Overseas in the Nineteenth and Twentieth Centuries" (1960), in *A Century of European Migrations, 1830– 1930,* ed. Rudolph J. Vecoli and Suzanne Sinke (Urbana, Ill., 1991); *Labor Migration in the Atlantic Economies: The European and North American Working Classes during the Period of Industrialization,* ed. Dirk Hoerder (Westport, Conn., 1985); *European Migrants: Global and Local Perspectives,* ed. Dirk Hoerder and Leslie Page Moch (Boston, 1996); Bruno Ramirez, *On the Move: French-Canadian and Italian Migrants in the North Atlantic Economy, 1860–1914* (Toronto, 1991).

51. Merwick, "'Being There,'" 488.

52. Richard H. Pells, *Not Like Us: How Europeans Have Loved, Hated, And Transformed American Culture since World War II* (New York, 1997); *Exporting America: Essays on American Studies Abroad,* ed. Richard P. Horwitz (Westport, Conn., 1993); Richard P. Horwitz, "The Politics of International American Studies," *American Studies International* 31 (April 1993): 89–116; *The Fulbright Experience, 1946–1986: Encounters and Transformations,* ed. Arthur Power Dudden and Russell R. Dynes (New Brunswick, N.J., 1987). On the history of American Studies, see Gene Wise, "'Paradigm Dramas' in American Studies: A Cultural and Institutional History of the Movement," *American Quarterly* 31 (Summer 1979): 293–337; Allen F. Davis, "The Politics of American Studies," ibid. 42 (September 1990): 353–74. On the problem of self-enclosure in American Studies, see Karen J. Winkler, "Scholars Chide American Studies for Ignoring the Rest of the World," *Chronicle of Higher Education,* November 13, 1985; Carl Bode, "American Studies: Guilt for Being Provincial," ibid., December 11, 1985. On the development of American Studies outside of the United States, the best source is the journal *American Studies International.* See also "Forum: American Studies in Europe," ed. Maurizio Vaudagna, *Storia nordamericana* 7 (1990): 117– 78; and *American Studies Abroad: Contribution in American Studies,* ed. Robert H. Walker (Westport, Conn., 1975).

FOURTEEN

The Modernity of America and the Practice of Scholarship

Winfried Fluck

The humanities have been decisively reshaped by their transformation into a competitive profession. This transformation is, at present, most advanced in the United States, where growing professionalization encourages a race for new and "original" insights, which compete for visibility. The result is an academic culture of constant redescription, which, in turn, leads to a growing fragmentation of knowledge. While the volume of scholarship increases steadily, the volume of available knowledge is thus constantly reduced. Ironically enough, however, scholars in the humanities have little interest in working against this trend, because they are profiting from it in two significant ways. First, professionally, the increasing fragmentation and decontextualization of knowledge provides the individual scholar with a golden opportunity for individual distinction, because decontextualization is a useful precondition for offering new and apparently original readings.[1] Second, culturally, the practice of scholarship in the humanities that has become dominant, especially in the United States, opens up entirely new possibilities for an expressive individualism that bases its claims to recognition on the notion of "difference." The current cultural radicalism in the humanities, which defines itself in contrast to an earlier form of political radicalism, can be seen as manifestation of this expressive individualism.[2]

Advanced stages of professionalization and individualization thus reinforce each other, which explains why the American model is spreading and taking hold in other parts of the world. The "Americanization" of the humanities, which is only one of innumerable areas in which the American model is gaining dominance as a world standard, is thus not an effect of cultural imperialism but of a promise of new possibilities of self-empowerment and self-fashioning. The worldwide triumph of the American model is therefore almost effortless (and criticism of it is largely hypocritical, inasmuch as the cultural Left does not acknowledge its own contribution to this development and the stakes it has in it). If one wants to change this development, then a reconsideration of the current institutional conditions of the production of knowledge in the humanities and their ties to certain cultural formations is overdue.

In a way, the development of the humanities in the period after World War II is a success story. On the institutional level, the number of professional positions created in colleges and universities all over the world is remarkable. As a consequence, humanistic knowledge is spread more widely than in the past, and more of it is available to us nowadays than in the past. At the same time, this successful institutional expansion has intensified an ever-increasing proliferation and fragmentation of knowledge.[3] Paradoxically, this development threatens to undermine the very promise that underlies the success story of the humanities: the promise of meaning.[4] The case is most obvious in literature and arts departments. If there are twenty different theoretical approaches to the interpretation of *Huckleberry Finn* and more than a thousand interpretations of the book, all defining themselves against one another, and thus differing from other readings as a matter of principle, it is no longer even possible to establish relations among them in order to sort out their respective strengths and weaknesses. The hermeneutic rule of entering into a dialogue with other positions and aiming at an integration of insights is replaced by a race for readings that are original in the sense of differing from other positions by setting up strong counterclaims.[5] But, in a somewhat lesser form, the problem plagues other disciplines of the humanities as well. The proliferation of ever more detailed studies of historical material or ever more specialized discussions of philosophical problems has increased fragmentation to a point where knowledge becomes a matter of willful choice.[6]

A paradoxical professional logic that transforms an indispensable strategy of critical insight and interpretive correction into a source of fragmentation and potential disorientation is at work here. In principle, a plurality of interpretive approaches helps give us a critical perspective on an object, thus correcting for the apparently inescapable dialectic of blindness and insight that characterizes all interpretations of world and text. Once plurality becomes endless proliferation, however, the initial gain threatens to become a loss.[7] Because we are overwhelmed by a flood of new approaches and interpretive claims, scholarly work begins to lose its power of correction and functions instead as mere displacement.[8] There are simply too many different claims to assess their validity or to establish meaningful connections between them in order to put them into perspective. The full impact of this constantly increasing proliferation of meaning-making is demonstrated by the fact that even those with a critical perspective on the competitive or disruptive nature of the present social and academic system cannot help but contribute to this process, because they have to work within the same institutional framework. Under present conditions, the institutionalized mode of production of knowledge has therefore gained priority over any ideological position in determining the function and effects of work in the humanities. The political Left and Right are equally affected by it. One could argue, for example, that the recent revisionism in American studies has provided a fundamental and long-needed change in perspective. But once this perspective is established, it becomes part of the same formation of knowledge production that characterizes the scholarship it replaces.[9] Another race for professional distinction through difference begins. But the more interpretations we get, the greater the dispersal of meaning, because all of these interpretations must, by definition, correct prior interpretations in order to justify their existence. What started out as a heroic effort to undermine false generalizations thus leads to an endless flow of new claims, which ultimately begins to undermine any basis for a claim to representativeness on the part of the knowledge produced.

No particular approach or position is to blame for this situation, because it is produced by historical developments that go beyond the impact of any particular position. My argument should thus not be confused with the conservative criticism of the alleged fragmentation of canons or values brought about by the recent revisionism in American studies. Actually, I think that the impact of these developments on the idea of the canon is often exaggerated, because, inevitably, these movements merely replace older canons with a new set of preferred and canonized material, to which scholars return again and again. Thus, in discussions in which challenges to existing canons of cultural or historical material are blamed for fragmentation, the term "fragmentation" is often used as code for value conflicts or political disagreements.

The fragmentation of knowledge I am talking about here was going on before such recent revisions and has gone on after them, and it is not tied in any causal and unique way to any of them. It has epistemological, social, and institutional reasons. Its origin lies in historicism and its insistence that sense-making and interpretation are historical acts; consequently, each period, generation, and group will feel the need to offer its own interpretation of a phenomenon. This tendency has been accelerated, in fact, institutionalized as a professional practice, by professionalization and the emergence of an academic culture of knowledge production. Gradually, but especially after the explosion of higher education after World War II, this professionalization has begun to change the function of cultural and historical reinterpretation and has inverted the priorities. While professionalization originally had the purpose of providing interpretation with a solid institutional and methodological base, it has now tied reinterpretation to professional advancement. This means that, while in the past each generation or group had its reason for reinterpretation, now each scholar has. This reinterpretation, in turn, must be defined by disagreement and difference, for otherwise it would not meet professional criteria for qualification. A feminist scholar cannot simply publish an essay in which she praises another feminist's interpretation of the cult of domesticity. There has to be, at least to a certain extent, a revision, disagreement, or contradiction in order to justify her intervention professionally.[10] Historicism may thus authorize reinterpretation, but professionalization institutionalizes disagreement and difference as professional necessity. The result is a breathtaking proliferation of work, whether "conservative" or "progressive,"[11] that undermines (and delegitimizes) all interpretations in similar ways, because, in a professional culture of institutionalized difference, a text can no longer be taken as representative of anything but the author's professional position.[12]

Quantity is not the only or the major problem of the current proliferation of meaning-production, however. Even if one had the time, energy, and institutional capacity to sort out the strengths and weaknesses of the diverse approaches and innumerable interpretations and aim at an integration of the knowledge produced by these various approaches, there would no longer be any point in doing so, because these interpretations are generated by the professional need to be different, so that a metatheoretical comment on their adequacy or inadequacy or an unsolicited integration would be considered "policing." Such a metatheoretical position would be inconceivable anyhow, however, because it would have to be based on the premise that it is possible to evaluate interpretive truth-claims, which would have no consensual basis after the demise of the "grand narratives." Methodological discussions thus nowadays proceed in exactly the opposite way, namely, seeking to unmask theoretical or methodological claims to interpretive adequateness as disguised power games. The only consensus remaining seems to be a broadly defined antifoundationalism, which is strong in subverting arguments for general criteria on which claims for interpretive adequateness could be based but weak in suggesting possible alternatives, unless one wants to accept the neopragmatist advice to do what one does anyway as such an alternative.

The current antifoundationalism reflects the changing institutional and social conditions of a profession that has gone from being a self-appointed guardian of cultural and social values to being a white-collar profession with its own pressures for professional distinction.[13] The basic social problem of democracy, already diagnosed perceptively by Tocqueville, namely, that of distinguishing oneself from the mass of others, repeats itself on the professional level and creates an escalating logic of "strong" (over)statements, which serve the purpose of standing out from the rest.

The more professionals in the humanities, the greater the need for difference and distinction. Thus, an endless spiral is set in motion: the more scholarly work exists, the greater the need for difference and interpretive disagreement in order to distinguish oneself. The greater the disagreement, the greater the fragmentation. The greater the fragmentation, the greater the need—and room!—for new interpretations. Inevitably, however, these new interpretations come at a price that carries a counterproductive logic of its own. For the more interpretations we get, the greater the need to devalue individual interpretations, and thus, in turn, the greater the need to stand out by forceful overstatement.

For a while, the solution to this proliferation of meaning production seemed to be an increase in theoretical and methodological reflection. Theory was defined as the intellectual discipline of reflecting systematically about the premises and methodological problems of interpretation. By now, however, theory has been transformed from a systematic philosophical discipline into another area of professional empowerment. In its current use and application, theory has not solved the crisis of orientation in the humanities. On the contrary, it has deepened the crisis, not only by becoming useful "symbolic capital" in the professional race for distinction, but also by feeding and accelerating that race in entirely new and unforeseen ways. The special usefulness of theory for this purpose lies in two aspects. To start with, theory can function as a shortcut, because it permits the description and characterization of an interpretive object without long, extended study. This extended study can be avoided because theory, as a rule and for good reasons, aims at general statements (often of a sweeping nature), so that explanatory claims tie the interpretation of cultural material to historical laws, social conditions, human faculties, linguistic or cultural mechanisms of inclusion and exclusion, and so forth. In the appropriation of theory by a new generation of scholars, it has begun to change in nature, however: it, too, becomes a form of symbolic capital that is judged not by its capacity for clarifying and justifying underlying premises but by its strong claims potential.[14]

This explains two striking facts about the present theory boom in the humanities. On the one hand, it has been observed that almost none of the thinkers who have influenced critical theory in the humanities recently really fare well in their original disciplines, where their theories and statements are considered to be too sweeping and undifferentiated—which is, on the other hand, exactly the basis for their appropriation by other disciplines. The fact that the exchange value of theory as symbolic capital dominates its current application also explains the fact that many European theories developed over years of patient scholarly work were imported wholesale into the new American market for theory and used up in rapid succession, so that, by now, American scholarship seems to have run out of imports. The reason for this mode of appropriation is that theory has become another instrument in the white-collar race for difference. Nobody has actually refuted the approaches or thinkers that are quickly discarded. They cease to play a role in theoretical discussions, not because they have been disproven, but because they are no longer on the cutting edge of professional distinction.

However, the most striking aspect of recent developments in the humanities is not their theoretical but their radical nature. The dominant approaches of the past fifteen years, ranging from poststructuralism and deconstruction, new historicism and cultural materialism to the various versions of race, class, and gender studies, may be widely different in many of their arguments, premises, and procedures. What unites them is a new form of radicalism, which, in contrast to older forms of political radicalism, I would like to call cultural radicalism, because the central source of political domination is no longer attributed to the level of political institutions and economic structures but to culture.[15] The origin of this paradigm shift in the definition of power lies in the student movement of the late 1960s. In response to the puzzling and irritating fact that the "oppressed" did not form coalitions with the students, and following the lead, above all, of Herbert Marcuse, a critique of the capitalist system based on instances of political repression was replaced by the idea of "structural" or "systemic" power,[16] that is, by a redefinition of power as exerted not by agents or institutions of the state but by the system's cunning ways of constituting "subjects" or ascribing "identities" through cultural forms. Thus, recent critical theories in the humanities, different as they may be in many respects, nevertheless have one basic premise in common (and are amazingly predictable in this one respect): they all take as their point of departure the assumption that there is an all-pervasive, underlying systemic element that constitutes the system's power in an invisible yet highly effective way. The names given to this systemic effect change; they have included "the prison-house of language," "ideology redefined as semiotic system," "the reality effect," "the ideological state apparatus," "the cinematic apparatus," "the symbolic order," "discursive regime," "logocentrism," "patriarchy," "whiteness," and "Western thought."[17] But the basic claim is always the same: the invisible power effect of the systemic structure derives from the fact that it determines meaning, and the perception of the world before the individual is even aware of it, by constituting the linguistic and cultural patterns through which we make sense of the world.

This redefinition of power has led to a constant pressure to outradicalize others.[18] If power resides in hitherto unacknowledged aspects of language, discourse, or the symbolic order, then there is literally no limit to ever new and more radical discoveries of power effects. And if it is power that determines cultural meaning, then the major question must be the possibility or impossibility of opposition. "Opposition," however, also changes in nature. In view of the shrewd containment of all resistance by discursive regimes, the only way out lies in radical otherness or difference. Thus, the development of cultural radicalism has taken a characteristic course: from neo-Marxism with its critique of the market (which still implies the possibility of resistance) to Foucauldian neohistoricism (which unmasks this form of resistance as really a hidden form of complicity) to race, class, and gender studies (which revive the possibility of resistance by locating it in "difference"). Actually, the current umbrella concept "race, class, and gender" is a misnomer, because the category of "class" cannot constitute radical difference. Consequently, class analysis no longer constitutes a genuine theoretical option for the new cultural radicalism, while, sexual preference, on the other hand, constitutes elementary, unbridgeable difference and has therefore moved to the center of revisionist approaches.

By resting all hope of resistance on the category of difference, another theoretical problem is created, however, because a term for denoting unbridgeable otherness is used as the basis for a broadly defined group-identity that does not account for the possibility of difference within this group. Hence, a constant movement or "sliding" in the use of the category "difference" can be observed: in order to make the concept politically meaningful, it must be used as a comprehensive category of distinction and must be equated with a particular gender, ethnic or racial group, or form of sexual preference. Such redefinition of difference as, for example, racial or engendered identity runs the danger, however, of reessentializing identity and works against the very idea of difference. The problem arises from the fact that a category taken from linguistic and semiotic analysis, where it describes an uncontrollable dissemination of meaning, is employed to justify claims for social recognition. In the first context, it is an antirepresentational term, used to deconstruct a belief in the possibility of representation; in the second, the idea of representation is not only revived but becomes the central criterion for judging and classifying cultural texts.[19]

Arguments within race, class, and gender studies constantly oscillate between the two options and arrest them almost at will wherever needed. In accordance with the professional culture of performance, difference is used as a means of self-definition and of self-empowerment. This, in fact, is the thrust and net result of the current cultural radicalism in the humanities. Since "power" is redefined as an effect of systemic structures that are virtually everywhere, the term is no longer a category of political analysis but a word for all possible barriers to the self. And since the self is, in principle, constituted by systemic effects or is seen, at best, as the site of conflicting systemic effects, it can only be defined through difference, so that the claim or assertion of difference becomes the supreme form of self-empowerment.[20]

The far-reaching radicalization of the humanities in the United States has been an entirely unforeseen and highly surprising development from a European point of view. More specifically, there were two surprises. For once, radicalism reemerged in the United States after it had just turned dogmatic in Europe and thereby discredited itself completely. One of the recurring arguments of conservatives during the heyday of the student movement in France, Germany, and other European countries was the charge of ideologization, which was considered a typically European weakness and regularly contrasted with Anglo-Saxon "common sense." As it turned out, however, "common sense" was no match for radicalization. Why? And why was there no consideration of the negative experiences in Europe? The explanation, I think, lies in the fact that this new-wave American radicalization is not what it appears (and often claims) to be, namely, a critical theory with political goals and a political theory. Although it is constantly pointed out that not only the private but literally every aspect of social life is political, there is no systematic reflection on the structures or procedures through which the claims of difference or "the other" could become political reality. One reason surely is that the realization of one claim inevitably runs the danger of violating the claims of somebody else. Such "violations" can only be justified on the basis of a set of normative ideas, but normative ideas violate difference, as the various forms of poststructuralist and neopragmatist antifoundationalism point out again and again. There was nothing to be learned, then, from European political radicalism, because the new form of cultural radicalism has entirely different goals: it pursues a politics of self-empowerment, and its analyses thus need no longer be based on Marxist or other social theories that attempt to describe the relation between various groups and members of the political system as a whole. Instead, radicalism can focus on the systemic barriers to self-empowerment, while, politically speaking, it remains a form of interest group politics or an untheorized form of radical egalitarianism. The problem, then, is not that the humanities have been instrumentalized by politics, as conservatives have it. As cultural radicalism rightly claims, there is no way around politics. The interesting theoretical problem is that they have been appropriated by what, in following the lead of Robert Bellah, I would like to call the politics of expressive individualism.[21]

The important point to grasp here is that expressive individualism is not a narcissistic deformation but the successful end-product of a central project in the humanities. It does not reflect the humanities' crisis but rather their success. Self-empowerment through cultural difference is not a pathological distortion of the true goals and function of the humanities but a modern manifestation of a promise of self-empowerment in which the humanities have played a crucial role since their inception. The intellectual justification and support of individual development and self-assertion is a major element of what we call modernity (in the sense of *Neuzeit*). Crucial "breakthroughs" in Western intellectual development that stand at the center of the humanities, such as the philosophical "discovery" of the subject, the idea of the Enlightenment, the doctrine of individual rights, the modern understanding of the aesthetic as a nonmimetic mode of experience, and the "reinvention" of art as a fictive realm to transgress the boundaries of existing worlds have all contributed to this process of individualization and provided it with both intellectual tools and moral justification.[22] My claim is that, contrary to its self-perception, the current cultural radicalism does not stand in opposition to this process but merely represents a new, radicalized stage of it.

The process of individualization in Western societies can be divided into two major stages, as suggested by Bellah and his co-authors in their study *Habits of the Heart*, where a distinction is made between economic or utilitarian individualism and expressive individualism. Disregarding the nostalgic communitarian context of their argument, I find these terms heuristically useful in drawing attention to two different manifestations of individualism in the modern age, which, in going beyond Bellah, can best be distinguished by reference to two different sources of self-definition and self-esteem. In the traditional form of economic individualism, as analyzed by Max Weber and numerous others after him, self-esteem is derived primarily from economic success and social recognition. In order to obtain these, the individual has to go through an often long and painful act of deferred gratification and self-denial. Analogous to the act of saving, the goal is to accumulate a stock of capital, in both economic and social terms, which will eventually yield its profits in the form of increased social approval and a rise in the social hierarchy. The prototypical narrative genres of this economic individualism are the autobiographical success story, but also the bildungsroman or the story of female education, such as, for example, the domestic novel. They are teleological in conception, their basic narrative pattern is that of a rise or fall, their recurring emotional dramas are the experience of injustice and the withholding of just rewards, but also, possibly, a final moment of triumphant retribution; their ideal is the formation of a character that is strong enough to survive this long ordeal of social apprenticeship.

In contrast, the culture of expressive individualism is not primarily concerned with a rise of the individual to social respectability or its (tragic or melodramatic) failure, but with the search for self-realization. Its major issues are no longer economic success or the promise of social recognition, but the assertion of cultural difference, that is, the ability of the individual to assert his or her own uniqueness and otherness against the powers of cultural convention and encroaching disciplinary regimes. If development and growth are key concepts in economic individualism, difference is the key concept in expressive individualism.[23] This change in the main sources of self-esteem is the logical outcome of an ever-intensified process of individualization and, along with it, increasingly radical forms of cultural dehierarchization. In this process, the individual has to assert his or her self-worth in opposition to those forces that stand in its way. Initially, these were obvious sources of inequality such as caste, class, or patriarchy. With the increasing democratization of Western societies—in itself a result of individualization—these sources of inequality have been undermined in authority, and have, in fact, often been dissolved or weakened decisively. Inequality remains, but it can no longer be as easily attributed to social structures.[24] Hence the search for new "systemic effects" of inequality, and hence an increased importance of self-fashioning by means of cultural difference.

If the source of power is cultural, however, then culture must also serve as the source of counterdefinition and the search for self-realization must become the search for alternate cultural options. It is therefore culture that takes the place of the economy as the major model for self-realization, self-assertion, and self-fashioning, because the realm of culture provides something like an archive or storehouse of different models of self-definition. In contrast to the realm of the economy, where self-discipline and a strong "identity" are the most desirable qualities, culture offers an almost inexhaustible supply of options for role-taking and imaginary self-empowerment. Ironically, it is nowadays not a ritual of consent that absorbs "the radical energies of history," as Sacvan Bercovitch has it,[25] but a new stage of individual self-empowerment, articulated most forcefully by cultural radicalism, that redefines political engagement or professional activities as a cultural option of self-definition, and thus as one possibility of role-taking among many.

As a form of expressive individualism, radicalism changes its function. Instead of providing an ideological base for political analysis, it becomes an intellectual instrument for the pursuit of difference. This explains its most striking feature: its focus on, if not obsession with, the question of oppositionalism. The striking fact that cultural radicalism's interest in art and history seems almost entirely absorbed by the problem of whether their objects of study were truly oppositional or not is closely linked with the question of cultural difference: "Opposition is the best way to assert cultural difference, for it is opposition that allows difference to emerge most clearly and pointedly."[26] Thus, cultural radicalism can nowadays be regarded as one of the supreme manifestations of expressive individualism in the realm of the humanities. Although it sees itself as a political turn in cultural or historical studies, it really represents, at a closer look, another turn of the screw in the cultural history of individualization. This individualism needs radical dehierarchization to eliminate cultural restrictions on self-empowerment, but it also needs the cultural construction of difference to escape from the consequences of radical equality. In this sense, cultural radicalism does not provide an alternative to individualism, but a more radicalized version of individualization, not a critique of individualism by "politics" but a critique based on the politics of expressive individualism.

My point, then, is that it is the transition from economic to expressive individualism that stands at the center of recent developments in the humanities.[27] The effects of this development have been ambiguous. By turning intellectual and scholarly work into imaginary role-taking, the attractiveness of the humanities for the individual has increased, while their importance and social relevance have decreased.[28] The more important and useful the humanities become for the individual in search of imaginary self-empowerment, the more irrelevant insights or claims to representativeness become for society. It is, thus, the expressive reconfiguration of individualism that I see as the driving force in the current development of the humanities. As long as cultural radicalism uses the category of the political to give authority to its own claims of self-definition, this aspect is effectively obscured. In this version, the political is opposed to individualism, because individualism is regarded as a typical manifestation of capitalism. Actually, however, individualism is a product of modernity, whose idea of self-development also provides a base for cultural radicalism, although the extension of the possibilities of the individual is no longer seen in terms of "growth," but in terms of an increased space for "performance."[29]

To talk about individualism is thus not to pass moral judgment on "selfishness." Tocqueville already noted that individualism is not to be confused with egotism or selfishness. Individualism is a social attitude that also attracts those who would distance themselves strongly not only from egotism but from cultural radicalism. To give but one example from my own professional background: in its redefinition of literary meaning as (partly) the result of an actualization through the reader, reception theory has given a theoretical boost to individualization within the humanities—as has modernism in general. The reason for this was not "selfishness," but quite the opposite, namely, an antitotalitarian impulse that sought to strengthen the individual through the perspectivizing potential of its own reading experience, always basing this liberating move, however, on the interpretive truth claims of hermeneutic theory. This, in fact, is a recurring event in the history of modernity. Its interventions on behalf of the individual are almost always based on the expectation of a new consensus of liberated individuals who are finally able to realize their true human potential. But it never turns out that way. Individualism gladly welcomes the new opening but soon disregards the norms and values that served as its justification.

My analysis seems in many respects to tie into what must be considered the most penetrating recent analysis of the state of the humanities, John Guillory's *Cultural Capital*, which draws on Pierre Bourdieu's theory of symbolic capital. For Guillory, the crisis of the humanities reflects the fact that, as a form of creating capital, the humanities have become increasingly obsolete in a society in which technobureaucratic values dominate. Basically, Guillory attributes the crisis of the humanities to the emergence of a professional-managerial class in the university that "no longer requires the cultural capital of the old bourgeoisie": "The decline of the humanities was never the result of newer noncanonical courses or texts, but of a large-scale 'capital flight' in the domain of culture."[30] The turn toward theory in the humanities thus "has the oblique purpose of signifying a rapprochement with the technobureaucratic constraints upon intellectual labor." But if "the career of the college professor is increasingly structured as a mimesis of the bureaucratic career,"[31] why are intellectuals all over the world, and especially young people (often, and increasingly so, from marginalized groups) submitting themselves to this regime in the first place and in ever-growing numbers, despite an often bleak professional outlook? The bureaucratization of higher learning along the lines of greater economic efficiency is indeed a crucial aspect of recent developments in the humanities. However, the deterioration of working conditions connected with it is obviously not yet strong enough to offset promises of self-definition and self-empowerment that have increased with recent developments in most disciplines within the humanities. On the contrary, cultural radicalism has provided a profession once associated with the dust of archives with the allure of an avant-garde existence in postmodern times. As a consequence, what we are witnessing today is not, or not primarily, a redefinition of the humanities on the basis of the needs and values of a new "professional-managerial class" with its "technobureaucratic constraints" but a redefinition of the humanities in terms of the needs of expressive individualism.

In Guillory's Marxist view, class analysis remains the best way to comprehend the crisis of the humanities. Since it is the function of the humanities to produce cultural capital, any crisis must signal a social and economic realignment. A new "class" needs new cultural capital. This arguments perpetuates a view in which economic structures shape culture. It may be, however, that the cultural realm has turned into a sphere that is, increas-

ingly, contradicting (not opposing) dominant economic and social structures (and thereby creating problems for them): while the economic
sphere may indeed be governed by technobureaucratic values, the cultural
realm is nourishing forms of imaginary self-empowerment that contribute
to a growing individualization of society—and, for that matter, to a potential subversion of technocratic values. Contrary to what Guillory claims, the
distinction offered by cultural material nowadays is no longer "based on
inequality of access to cultural goods"[32] but on its performative and expressive potential for representing "difference." Guillory is right in claiming that the humanities, despite their own official self-image as a disinter-
ested search for meaning and aesthetic value, are seriously affected and
transformed by professionalization. But the main pressures—and possibilities—that these professional structures exert do not tend to technobureaucratic streamlining but, on the contrary, to a proliferation of individual
expression and self-definition. Guillory's theory of modernization as a relentless extension of technobureaucratic values to all areas of cultural
meaning-production tells, at best, one side of the story, the organizational
one. However, the work currently being done in the humanities is not
simply homologous with the organizational pressures under which it is produced. On the contrary, if anything, it stands in opposition to such pressures and provides a whole array of arguments for the critique of systemic
effects.

If one looks at the general development of work in the humanities since
1970, one unmistakable tendency stands out: what drives this development
is neither a growing adaptation to technocratic values nor simply a drive
for professional newness per se.[33] To be sure, there is a constant and constantly growing professional pressure for newness, but this race for newness
stands in the service of an ever-increasing process of individualization. To
give an example, let me briefly trace some crucial stages of this development in my own field, that of American studies. In doing this, I shall focus
on a central question in the interpretation of cultural and historical material, that of the representativeness of one's material. For, clearly, the usefulness of a historical study or cultural analysis will depend on the insight
this material can provide beyond itself. To interpret a cockfight in Bali is
only of interest if the interpretation goes beyond the mere physicality of
the act and manages to bring forth some helpful insights into the culture
or society under study.

Debates in American studies have therefore, from the start, focused on
the question of what objects and categories are best suited to provide insights into American society and culture that can be considered representative. In the beginning, American studies answered the question by following the traditions of intellectual and literary history and based its
interpretations of "the American experience" on the assumption that spe-

cial artistic and intellectual achievements provide a kind of condensed insight into its inner nature. Scholars such as Perry Miller and F. O. Matthiessen concentrated on high culture because they looked for "profound" expressions of a given period in American history. In this approach, key documents in the history of ideas and works of art embody the highest potential of American civilization. The main objection to this view came from sociological studies of American culture and, more specifically, of popular culture and the media. American studies was criticized for linking a claim of representativeness with material that did not appear to speak for a large number of Americans. The answer to this challenge was provided by the categories of myth and symbol, through which individual texts could be described as manifestations of a widely shared cultural pattern and yet, at the same time, could also be interpreted as significant expressions of subjective experience (cf. Henry Nash Smith's definition of myth as "an intellectual construction that fuses concept and emotion into an image").[34]

The claims of the myth and symbol school in American studies were undermined in the 1970s by the new social history, which questioned the representativeness of the kind of American myths analyzed in books like Henry Nash Smith's *Virgin Land*[35] and replaced it with a more complex model of different social groups that stand in changing and varying relations to society's dominant myths. At the same time, the claims of the myth and symbol school were also undermined from within by a politicization of the study of patterns of thought, in which American myths were redefined as disguised, and therefore especially effective, forms of ideological control.[36] After these challenges from the outside and inside, it was no longer possible to regard a myth as an expression of *the* American experience. On the contrary, one had to assume a countertradition that was not yet fully incorporated and that had to be unearthed from underneath the official self-definitions of American culture. In this revisionist form of American studies, what were "truly" representative were the cultural manifestations of oppressed groups and oppositional movements.

One such movement was the women's movement. However, no sooner had its perspective, together with that of other groups, begun to influence and shape work in American studies than it was, in turn, criticized for its unwarranted generalizations and unacknowledged essentialism. One point of this charge of "essentialism" is that an identity construction as "woman," based exclusively on the fact of sexual difference, is not considered adequate for capturing the whole range of female experience. Instead, it imprisons women in a fiction of sexual identity. To work against this discursive trap, the category of gender was introduced in order to emphasize the cultural constructedness of sexual identities. Identity is thus discursively ascribed and not determined by biology, but even such "liberation" from biological fate still traps the female individual in a binary scheme. Feminist scholars may disagree on what constitutes female identity, but they still assume that there is such a thing, and that it can be represented in the double sense of the word. Hence, the next move in feminist debates leads to the idea of "performed gender," in which gender is part of an open, mobile staging of identity and any claim to group representativeness is thus radically dissolved. Consequently, to analyze a text or person in terms of the performance of gender can, in the final analysis, no longer provide any insight beyond itself, for no two performances are alike. The individual has liberated herself from the iron grip of group identities, but this achievement can only illustrate her own potential. In this, it ironically comes close to the single creative performance of the work of art from which early American studies set out—with the one essential difference that the performing individual herself has now become the work of art. The radical claims to individuality originally reserved for special artistic achievements have been democratized.

In Perry Miller's intellectual history, women—the Anne Hutchinsons and Anne Bradstreets aside—do not have a voice of their own. The clerical elite speaks for them. In principle, the same applies to the myth and symbol school, although there is the hint of something like an indirect representation, since the relevant works express deeper needs of all members of society. A myth is no longer restricted to an elite. In the new social history and in feminist studies, this "universalism" is finally discarded and women gain a voice of their own—but only insofar as their fate is representative of that of women in general. A domestic novel, for example, can merit interpretation as an example of the ideological limits or subversive possibilities of the cult of domesticity. The subsequent development in feminist scholarship, however, is characterized by ever-intensifying debates about how representative such material really is as an expression of female experience. Black women do not feel represented; lesbians seek to retreat from a biological definition or from a mere male-female binarism. Inevitably, in each case, different historical or cultural material is considered representative. Consequently, the development in American studies has had an unmistakable trajectory: general claims have been undermined by more and more detailed and differentiated studies of particular groups, which, in turn, are then questioned for their unexamined "universalist" or "essentialist" assumptions. In this sense, historical or cultural studies will never run out of work, for they can always point out that prior work on the subject is still based on unwarranted generalizations. Ultimately, the individual can only represent her- or himself.[37]

The analysis I have offered so far seems to follow a familiar pattern, that of the European discussing American developments in terms of excess or deformation. The word that stands at the center of this type of analysis is "Americanization." And indeed, I have followed the pattern by characterizing the development I have analyzed as the "Americanization of knowledge." However, as I indicated earlier, in the context of my analysis, the term "Americanization" is not used to evoke insinuations of imperialism but to refer to a trend of modernity that for a number of reasons has emerged most clearly and strongly in the United States, so that "America" has come to signify this promise of modernity. But this trend is also becoming dominant in other parts of the world, including most European countries, even though the humanities in those countries have a long and venerable tradition of their own. This raises the interesting question why the American practice of scholarship in the humanities is becoming dominant.

Cultural imperialism would be an easy answer. To be sure, with influential international institutions like the Salzburg Seminar, the Rockefeller Center at Bellagio, and the Wilson Center, not to forget the drawing power of America's elite universities, Americans have developed powerful and effective instruments of cultural politics in the humanities. After a beginning inspired by humanistic ideals of personal growth, many of these institutions have left their early idealist phase behind and have turned into active centers for the recruitment and training of an international political and cultural elite.[38] And yet, so far, these institutions have had little influence on the directions disciplines in the humanities have taken. Even American studies, with its obvious political usefulness for a Cold War agenda, eventually, and in entirely unexpected ways, developed ideas highly critical of American exceptionalism. The truth of the matter is that official or semi-official American cultural politics have remained haphazard, inconsistent, and underfunded and have not been instrumental in shaping current intellectual agendas in the humanities. Nevertheless, the gradual Americanization of knowledge production, and, more specifically, of the humanities seems to spread almost effortlessly.

One obvious conclusion is that the process of "Americanization" does not need additional political or institutional support. Whether the developments I have described are likely to transcend their American context is no longer an open question. By and large, it has already been decided. What the cultural imperialism paradigm does not grasp in its focus on national interests, whether political or economic, is that the nation is itself part of a larger historical context, that of modernity. The reason why the United States is not in need of imperialist politics in the traditional sense of the word is that American society is realizing certain tendencies of modernity more radically than other countries. In fact, one might argue that it is not Europe that poses the norm for the historical development of modernity, to which the United States is exceptional, but the other way round. In making this case, Tocqueville is more helpful than other well-established theoreticians of modernity.[39] In contrast to thinkers like Weber and Habermas, Tocqueville does not put reason or the iron grip of rationality at the center of his understanding of modernity, but democracy—a democracy defined as a way of life in which the elimination of the institutionalized hierarchies of aristocratic society creates the specifically "modern" drama of a restless individual in incessant search of recognition and self-esteem. Central aspects of modernity, such as the disenchantment of the world, the loss of traditional authority, and increased mobility, intensify the need for new sources of self-esteem.

Marshall Berman has put these developments in the larger context of the culture of modernity. In his book on cultural modernity, with the fitting title *All That Is Solid Melts into Air,* taken from Karl Marx, Berman focuses on the promise of individual self-realization established by the culture of modernity and, linked with it, the unlimited dynamic of self-development unleashed by modernity. Modernity introduces a promise of individual self-realization and self-development that provides the drive for distinction and recognition, diagnosed by Tocqueville, with its own logic of acceleration. A restless individualism, as Berman calls it, throws all culture into a constant flux. All sources of authorization or self-legitimation are subject to constant change. As a consequence, this restless individualism constantly seeks a form of recognition that will provide distinction from the mass of others.

As Tocqueville has pointed out, democracy complicates and intensifies this search. Because the link to a chain of family tradition, characteristic of aristocratic societies, is broken, and a person's worth is no longer automatically established by her or his social position, the individual becomes responsible for establishing his or her own worth in the eyes of others. This task, however, is complicated by the fact that under the premise of equality, everyone else pursues the same task, so that the challenge is to find a way of distinguishing oneself from all the others. Tocqueville, in fact, attributes the strong elements of performance in American culture—the striking persistence of a theatrical or, as he puts it, "bombastic" style of communication that draws attention to itself—to this challenge. The developments in the humanities I have described can be seen as a manifestation of the same tendency, albeit one that Tocqueville could not possibly have anticipated.

As mass democracies spread on a global scale, conditions begin to resemble those that Tocqueville already observed in the United States. The future global system will look "Americanized" in the sense that it will bear the marks of the American model. There won't be much coercion in order to achieve this. At present, for example, as a result of European unification, a far-ranging Americanization of European universities is under way. The professional mode of knowledge production institutionalized in the United States will become the common transnational practice of scholarship. The result will not be homogenization, however, but an increase in diversity, not because more nations enter the global dialogue but because the new global standard is one that, as I have argued, has an insatiable hunger for diversity—not primarily for political, moral, or cultural reasons but for professional ones. Thus, institutionally, an internationalizing of American history is to be expected, but the effects on American historians will still be negligible, because they will hardly take note of that new diversity, for a few simple reasons: (1) there is little professional distinction to be gained from it in the American academic world; (2) the networking effect is not substantial enough; and (3) the numbers are against it. In view of the increasing proliferation of scholarship, American historians will have their hands full in keeping up with the American scene; the great size of the U.S. history profession, its "continentalism," makes American humanities largely self-sufficient.

Similarly, unless there is an attempt to take the current institutional conditions of knowledge production into consideration, the—well-intentioned and long-overdue—project of establishing a "transnational" point of view in the writing of American history will encounter the same structural problems that I have outlined above: either this extension is based on a specific theory or view of why such a contextualization is necessary, in which case it will become another new approach among others, or it will not be based on the authority of a single "grand theory," in which case it will open up undreamt-of new possibilities of going in all directions, and will thereby only add another dimension to the already-existing tidal wave of studies. We end where we began. As I have tried to argue, in the present situation, all questions of disciplinary development have to take into account the current direction of professionalization, because this institutional base determines the practice of scholarship more decisively than any ideological commitment. On the contrary, such ideological commitments have been co-opted as new options of self-fashioning in the advanced culture of professionalism that has emerged at American universities. If we want to work toward change in the humanities, a rigorous self-examination of the conditions that shape the direction and function of current scholarship has to be the starting point. Unless these conditions are changed, all well-intended disciplinary reorientations are bound to fall prey to the same institutional logic.

NOTES

1. The four C's of interpretive integration—comparison, connection, contextualization, and categorization—are therefore going out of fashion.

2. For an elaboration of this point, see pp. 350–54, below.

3. My own approach to the question under debate is through the field of American studies from which most of the following examples are taken. However, I think

that my argument can be applied to the humanities in general, including the discipline of history.

4. In his report on Conference II of the Project on Internationalizing the Study of American History, Thomas Bender reminds us of this goal when he speaks of history as "a contextualizing discipline, a discipline whose claims to knowledge consists in locating events, ideas, and persons in explanatory contexts" (4).

5. Methodologically, this rejection of comparison and connection has another welcome advantage: because questions of integration and contextualization are not addressed, claims about single objects of study can function metonymically, that is, they come to stand for a larger whole without ever having to justify this implication.

6. In his introduction to a recent volume of essays, Martin Jay traces the consequence of this development to its logical end:

> Is it possible, let me ask in conclusion, to soar above these essays and provide a sovereign overview of the argumentative pattern they reveal? Can we find a figure in this bewildering carpet of attempts to explore the multiple contexts of visuality. . . . In short, we have a welter of competing interpretations of the meaning and implications of vision and visuality. Choosing among them, moreover, is no easy task, as it is not clear what would count as evidence for or against one or the other. Evidence, after all, is a word derived from the Latin *videre*, which suggests it may be based on a visual metaphor whose innocence can no longer be assumed. As is the case with Lacan's suggestive, if not always fully coherent, theories, on which so many of these essays depend, a certain leap of faith is required before one account can be accepted as superior to another. ("Vision in Context: Reflections and Refractions," in *Vision in Context: Historical and Contemporary Perspectives on Sight,* ed. Teresa Brennan and Martin Jay [New York, 1996], 9–11)

7. The same could be said of specialization. As a research strategy, specialization is indispensable and an important source of insight. As an institutionalized mode of dealing with knowledge, the gain may become a loss when the sheer number of observations or interpretations can no longer be integrated and quantity minimizes the meaningfulness of knowledge. On this point, see my essay on "The Americanization of Literary Studies," *American Studies International* 28 (1990): 9–22. In the (European) institute in which I teach, we recently had a particularly shocking illustration of the degree of specialization at American universities when we asked a well-known American guest professor to teach a survey course on American history to first-year students, in order to provide them with a perspective from abroad, and then got the following reply: "As to the survey course, covering all of American history from beginning to end does pose a serious problem for me—probably a typically American problem, given how specialized we are in U.S. universities. I have never in my entire career taught the first half of American history (until 1865), and haven't taught the late nineteenth century in thirty years. Nor am I familiar with Boyer's textbook. Nor, except when I'm on or chairing search committees (as I am at the moment), do I have even the vaguest idea of what's been written on, say, Puritanism, the Revolution, or the coming of the Civil War."

8. On this point, cf. David Bordwell: "[I]t is just that, in American institutions of higher education, intellectual disputes among competing premises and methods tend to be avoided simply by adding the 'new approach' onto existing structures." *Making Meaning: Inference and Rhetoric in the Interpretation of Cinema* (Cambridge, Mass., 1989), 96.

9. See, e.g., Cornel West's comments on the situation of black intellectuals: "Black intellectuals are affected by the same processes as other American intellectuals, such as the professionalization and specialization of knowledge, the bureaucratization of the academy, the proliferation of arcane jargon in the various disciplines, and the marginalization of humanistic studies." West, *Race Matters* (New York, 1994), 62.

10. This does not mean, of course, that a claim for representativeness cannot be made, but as the history of recent critical approaches demonstrates, such a claim will not survive for long and will immediately become the target of another critical intervention.

11. The recent revisionism in the humanities has further intensified this process but only in consequent application of historicist premises.

12. Again, there is, in my view, no escape from this development, because one cannot ignore the postmodern and poststructuralist critique of the arbitrariness of each act of centering. This, in fact, provides an important theoretical justification for professional developments such as the new social history, cultural studies, or race, class, and gender studies, because the less we can privilege certain texts or interpretations as representative sources of insight, the more we need to extend the scope of our material. However, the more we extend our scope, the more we accelerate the process of diffusion and proliferation. This problem cannot be solved by taking back the claim of representativeness to a privileged subculture or to one's favorite dissenting voice, because, inevitably, the process of diffusion will renew and repeat itself on this level for the institutional reasons described.

13. I have called this development the "Americanization" of the humanities in a different context. By "Americanization" I mean an advanced stage of professionalization developed most clearly and strongly in the United States but setting new standards for scholarship in the humanities all over the world. Again, one should emphasize that this professional structure characterizes and shapes work of the Left and the Right with equal force. For a more extended discussion of some of the consequences, cf. my essay on "The Americanization of Literary Studies."

14. Cf. David Bordwell: "In an institution that favors novelty, the stakes constantly rise. The critical exemplars get mastered, and for all their merits, they come to seem obvious. They must be surpassed." *Making Meaning*, 246.

15. For a more detailed analysis, see my essay on "Literature, Liberalism, and the Current Cultural Radicalism," in *Why Literature Matters*, ed. Rüdiger Ahrens and Laurenz Volkmann (Heidelberg, 1996), 211–34. In the following analysis, my purpose is not to discredit this new form of radicalism, which has opened up important new perspectives, but to understand the logic of its choices.

16. The German student movement called this systemic effect *strukturelle Gewalt*, which not only expresses the central idea of a form of power that does not manifest itself through an agent or somebody's action (= the usefulness of the idea of structure) but also describes this "invisible" exertion of power through structure as a form of coercion or violence (*Gewalt*).

17. It would be fascinating indeed to compare these categories as different versions of the idea of systemic effect: their range of explanation, their implied definition of the system, their definition of what can constitute resistance, and so on.

18. Again, my goal here is to describe the inner logic of a development and the

problems it creates. The redefinition of power as all-pervasive systemic effect provides valuable insights into the manifestation of power effects in seemingly "natural" or "innocent" aspects of social life. But it also creates the problem of where to locate power and how to specify its social and political consequences. On this point, see the excellent analysis of Wolfram Schmidgen, "The Principle of Negative Identity and the Crisis of Relationality in Contemporary Literary Criticism," *REAL — Yearbook of Research in English and American Literature* 11 (1995): 371–404.

19. In his book *Cultural Capital,* John Guillory speaks of "a confusion between representation in the political sense—the relation of a representative to a constituency—and representation in the rather different sense of the relation between an image and what the image represents." *Cultural Capital: The Problem of Literary Canon Formation* (Chicago, 1993), viii. I think it is more adequate, however, to speak not of a confusion but of a conflation.

20. This cultural self-empowerment is not to be equated with "real" social or political empowerment (although it may have such consequences—witness, for example, the impact of feminism on American society). The term is understood here as an imaginary construct and refers to the possibility of imagining and fashioning oneself as different—stronger, weaker, nonwhite, etc.—and thereby as distinct and exempt from an all-pervasive systemic effect.

21. Robert N. Bellah et al., *Habits of the Heart: Individualism and Commitment in American Life* (Berkeley and Los Angeles, 1985). Although I do not see a ready alternative, I am aware of the difficulties the term "expressive individualism" poses. One is the communitarian bias in Bellah's use of the term "individualism." As the following paragraph is to show, I do not share this view.

22. I am deliberately using the term "individual" here, and I am using it in the Tocquevillian sense of the smallest social unit. In this sense, "individual" is not to be confused with "individualist," "individualistic," or an ideology of individualism defined by claims of personal freedom or autonomy. It is also not to be confused and conflated with philosophical conceptualizations of the individual as "subject" or "self." Deconstructing the category of the subject does not affect the use of the term "individual" as a sociological category, because it only deconstructs a particular philosophical interpretation given to that social unit. The fact that the concept of the subject may be an illusion of Western thought and that, consequently, there are no (unified) subjects, does not mean that there are no individuals. Every scholar in the profession acts as such an individual, no matter what his or her status of self-definition as a subject (illusionary unity, correctly decentered, or happily performative) may be said to be. That such a retreat from the category of the "subject" might be of use for philosophy as well, is pointed out by John Smith, who notes:

> Over the past several years, however, a change has been taking place. The focus in the human sciences has been shifting from denunciations or affirmations of the subject to a "reconstruction" of the individual in a way that avoids the nostalgia for an undeconstructed self. These new efforts do not strive for a return to or of the (repressed) subject. Rather, they work through the crisis of subjectivity toward a new definition.

In this context, subject and individual are defined in the following way:

> The "subject" I shall relegate to a philosophical paradigm culminating in Descartes. That paradigm attempts to define "self-consciousness," which I take to be a fact, mistakenly in terms of self-reflection. Moreover, that paradigm tends to limit notions of

selfhood to self-conscious subjectivity. I shall argue, in good measure following Manfred Frank's lead, that the concept of the "individual" is more fruitful for our self-understanding. It allows us to shift attention away from the (historically) limited views of subjectivity and self-reflection without abandoning ontologically, politically, epistemologically, and semiotically necessary notions of particularity (resistance to the universal) and interpretation (dialectic between individual and universal). In short, we can abandon the subject but need the individual to arrive at richer conceptions of meaning, self, consciousness, and action. (John Smith, "The *Transcendance* of the Individual," *Diacritics* 19 [1989]: 82)

23. In many of these cases, the poststructuralist notion of *différance* provides a major inspiration but the conceptualizations of difference go far beyond poststructuralist versions. In historical terms, poststructuralism (including deconstruction) provides only one manifestation of this search for difference and is thus part of a larger trend of cultural and intellectual history. One reason for the growing historical importance of the need to be different can be inferred from Tocqueville's observation that democratic societies take away symbolic distinctions. By doing so, they settle the individual with the task of making up for this loss. In economic individualism, the possibilities for doing this are still limited in comparison to expressive individualism, where the resources of culture have moved to the forefront.

24. This statement requires qualification: it only describes a tendency, of course, not a fully achieved reality. Class differences continue to exist in the United States and other Western countries, but they no longer play an important social or cultural role for the middle class, including the white-collar worlds of art and scholarship.

25. Sacvan Bercovitch, *The Office of "The Scarlet Letter"* (Baltimore, 1991), 90.

26. Winfried Fluck, "Cultures of Criticism: *Moby-Dick,* Expressive Individualism, and the New Historicism," *REAL — Yearbook of Research in English and American Literature* 11 (1995): 222–23.

27. Obviously, these two forms are not neatly separated in their actual historical appearance. There are mixed forms and many forms of coexistence. Benjamin Franklin, whom Bellah mentions as exemplary representative of economic individualism, is also a master of self-fashioning. But this talent is still instrumentalized for, and subordinated to, the goal of a social rise to material success and social respectability. On the whole, it seems warranted to say, that (a) the social role of expressive individualism has dramatically increased since its first breakthrough in the Romantic period; (b) this development was propelled decisively by the growing authority of art and other forms of cultural self-expression, but, especially, by the increased possibilities of imaginary self-empowerment offered through fiction; and (c) this gradually emerging expressive individualism has found a whole new range of options in the era of postindustrialism and postmodernism with its new "postmaterialist" values of self-realization and radical self-determination. While the Romantic period and the experimental culture of modernism can be seen as avant-garde movements of expressive individualism, the postmodern period has witnessed the broad "democratization" of their cultural insistence on the right (and need) to be different.

28. This development was already noted with regret by, among others, Herbert Gutman in his essay "The Missing Synthesis: Whatever Happened to History?" *The*

Nation (November 21, 1981): 553–54, and Thomas Bender in "Wholes and Parts: The Need for Synthesis in American History," *Journal of American History* 73 (1986): 120–36.

29. An excellent discussion of the ambiguities of modernity, which could provide a useful basis for a reconsideration of the contribution the humanities have made to modernity and the process of modernization, is provided by John Tomlinson in *Cultural Imperialism* (Baltimore, 1991), ch. 5, in which he draws on the work of Marshall Berman, *All That Is Solid Melts into Air: The Experience of Modernity* (New York, 1982), and Cornelius Castoriadis, *L'institution imaginaire de la société* (Paris: Seuil, 1975), trans. by Kathleen Blamey under the title *The Imaginary Institution of Society* (Cambridge, Mass., 1987). Tomlinson, who considers modernity as the "fate" of all cultures within the global capitalist market (which are "condemned to modernity" [141]), also argues against the conflation of the concept of modernity with concepts like modernization and so-called modernization theory, which has prevented recent cultural criticism, including the new revisionism in the humanities, from seriously considering the concept of modernity as an analytical frame: "The problem for cultural analysis is that the modernisation theorists have tarred all theories of cultural modernity with their brush and so there has been a reluctance amongst radical theorists, until quite recently, to speak of development and modernity in the same breath" (144). Recently, the concept of modernity seems to have fallen prey to the postmodern critique of "grand narratives," because it has been equated with a naïve story of emancipation. However, most theories of modernity, in contrast to modernization theories, express a deep ambivalence about the impact of modernity and, consequently, trace a paradoxical logic of gains and losses. For Berman, for example, it is not the literature of Enlightenment that provides the key sources for his analysis of the culture of modernity, but, as the title of his book suggests, Karl Marx and his analysis of modernity, especially in the *Communist Manifesto*.

30. Guillory, *Cultural Capital*, 45.

31. Ibid., 253.

32. Ibid., 339.

33. For a succinct evocation of the role of "newness" in the writing of American history, see the beginning of Thomas Bender's essay "Wholes and Parts": "The American cant of newness, so pervasive in the general culture, is all the more remarkable for its capacity to penetrate even specialized professional discourses. What a succession of 'new' histories populate the profession's recent past: the new economic history, the new labor history, the new social history, the new urban history, the new political history, and other greater or lesser 'news' too numerous to list" (120).

34. Henry Nash Smith, *Virgin Land: The American West as Symbol and Myth* (Cambridge, Mass., 1950), vii.

35. Cf., e.g., Laurence Veysey's exemplary critique of the "lack of precision" in *Virgin Land*, which is, at a closer look, really a doubt about the representativeness of Smith's material: "Another classic instance of this lack of precision is found in Henry Nash Smith's *Virgin Land*, where for long stretches we are not sure whether given thought patterns are being attributed to all Americans, to Westerners, to Easterners thinking about the West (as Smith insisted was the case in a letter to

me many years ago), or, what is more believable, to second-rate novelists and poets."
Veysey, "Intellectual History and the New Social History," in *New Directions in American Intellectual History*, ed. John Higham and Paul K. Conkin (Baltimore, 1979), 21.

36. See the argument of Richard Slotkin in his influential study *Regeneration through Violence: The Mythology of the American Frontier, 1600–1860* (Middletown, Conn., 1973), which traces modern America's problems in Vietnam and elsewhere to the mythic belief in a regeneration through violence.

37. In his summary of a lecture by Jacques Revel, Thomas Bender's Report on Conference III of the Project of Internationalizing the Study of American History (1999), provides a neat formulation for this trend: "History is no longer the grand tradition, the reign of Louis XIV but rather 20 million Frenchmen in the era of Louis XIV."

38. Where the American government has become involved in cultural policies, as, for example, in the cultural centers established in postwar Germany, the so-called *Amerikahäuser*, a similar development can be observed.

39. Alexis de Tocqueville, *Democracy in America* (1835–39; Garden City, N.Y., 1969). I am referring specifically to the second volume. There is a tendency in the current revisionism to dismiss Tocqueville in passing, with no actual discussion, because of the well-known fact that his sources of information were mostly conservative. However, the perceptiveness of Tocqueville's analysis vastly exceeds the conservatism of his informants, because he is not primarily interested in democracy as a moral ideal but as a whole way of life, that is, as a cultural practice that affects and transforms all spheres of life.

FIFTEEN

The Exhaustion of Enclosures

A Critique of Internationalization

Ron Robin

This essay seeks to delineate the theoretical and practical significance of the internationalization movement within the American historical guild. It is written from the perspective of a wary beneficiary of this new openness who feels that the impulse is welcome but that its impact on the international scholar of the American past is disappointing. My critique is based on generalizations that flatten the range and varieties of philosophies contained in the current debate. Not all advocates of internationalization fit snugly into my compartmentalized analysis. Nevertheless, the literature in leading journals as a whole points toward these generalizations.

The most visible aspect of the internationalization movement is the fostering of dialogue between U.S. and international scholars of American culture and history. Over the course of the past few years, the major journals of American culture and history have solicited non-American contributions and dedicated considerable space to international perspectives and comparative inquiries. The *Journal of American History* (*JAH*), the flagship publication of the Organization of American Historians (OAH) has been an enthusiastic leader in this field. The creation of a foreign scholars editorial advisory board is clearly intended to encourage contributions from foreign participants. Attentive to the language barriers affecting scholarship outside of the anglophone world, the OAH offers prizes and awards for works on American history written in foreign languages. In 1999 alone the *JAH* published three lengthy forums on internationalization. The impressive number of articles published in the *JAH* and other journals provide sufficient material for an assessment of the culture and politics of internationalization, as well as of its ramifications for the non-American scholar.

The internationalization paradigm is driven by a pervasive disenchantment with enclosures. Internationalization denies a clear frontier between "us" and "them." It questions the validity of boundaries, whether political geographical, disciplinary, or cultural. The discrediting of overarching enclosures, Sacvan Bercovich has observed, is not dominated by any one discipline. "Multi-culturalists deny the claims of Americanness; social historians have turned consensus into a term of derision; literary critics speak of American literature, if at all, in the plural, as diversity of traditions, audiences, even languages," while traditional "contrasts between the Old World and the New have been 'subverted' through such meta-geographical categories as 'empire' and 'patriarchy.' "[1]

As far as history is concerned, internationalization is driven by the impulse to discover alternatives to the much-maligned enclosure of the nation-state and the embattled paradigm of American uniqueness. There are, of course, notable exceptions to this rule. Michael Kammen argues that notwithstanding homilies about national similarities, a wide range of empirical studies suggest that coherent patterns of development that differ from those observed in other countries can be seen in many aspects of the political and economic evolution of the United States.[2] Thomas Bender approaches the national unit as a useful, if not indispensable, device for "making the parts find their relation to the whole."[3] In the context of the vast majority of recent publications, however, these scholars are exceptions to the rule.

For the most part, internationalists argue that the conflating of history with the nation-state has distorted or even eradicated alternative ways of organizing historical knowledge. Thus, internationalization offers challenges and opportunities for American historians, who have frequently been condemned as intellectual isolationists for their single-minded concentration on unique aspects of the American nation-state. Language barriers, political circumstances, and geographical happenstance, as well as a tinge of self-absorption, have, according to this critique, isolated American scholars both physically and intellectually. Interaction with other modes of writing history thus opens up new trajectories, and a broad discourse with non-American scholars of the U.S. past is of cardinal importance. Viewing the American past from the periphery, rather than the center, promises to provide glimpses of hitherto hidden vistas. Differences that seem sharp, distinctive, and stable from within lose their uniqueness when dissected from without.

In political terms, internationalization seeks to decolonize the axiomatic assumptions of American culture and history. Advocates call for a reevaluation of assumptions, organizational concepts, and theories in reaction to accusations that American historiography's conceptual framework may have been as much a tool of hegemonic designs as a form of dispassionate intellectual inquiry. Certainly, much of this impulse has been salutary insofar as it stimulates self-reflection about methods, categories, and themes among historians of the United States. But there is also a danger of simplistic caricatures of the nation and an ahistorical understanding of nationalism and nation-making.

INTERNATIONALIZATION PAST AND PRESENT

The call for international or comparative perspectives is, of course, nothing new. Ever since the professionalization of American historiography in the late nineteenth century, comparative history has been a major and constant theme. Students of slavery and the frontier, in particular, have produced numerous impressive comparative perspectives.[4] But early efforts of internationalization differ from the current internationalization impulse in several ways. To begin with, much of past comparative scholarship assumed some sort of American exceptionalism. From Frederick Jackson Turner's frontier thesis through David Potter's *People of Plenty* (1954), American historians compared the United Sates and other countries in order to underscore the unique qualities of the American nation. C. Van Woodward, one of the most insistent promoters of comparative American history, explained that the point of departure of most post–World War II comparisons was the outsider's concept of the special status of the United States. Writing in 1968, he explained that foreign people, whose lives had been affected by the post–World War II Pax Americana, "want to know first of all how the American experience relates to their own—what, from their point of view is the *relevance* of American history."[5] The occasional effort to draw transcendental theoretical significance from the American past, such as David Potter's provocative use of comparative history to underscore the American Civil War as a powerful conflation of liberalism and nationalism, remained the exception to the rule.[6] The comparative scholar was fatally attracted to exceptionalism.

The classic comparative paradigm also privileged the national framework. Nation-states, national character, and so on served as central themes. Underlying even the most sophisticated comparative histories, Ian Tyrell notes, lay a compulsive reliance on "national units of analysis." Thus, he observes, slavery in the United States is "compared to slavery in Brazil or to serfdom in Russia," while other analytical frameworks—such as region, class, or gender—were reformulated to fit into nation-based comparisons. "The research design in comparative history is narrowly conceived to test purely national differences rather than convey a more varied sense of the elements that make up the diversity of the historical experience."[7]

With a few notable exceptions, the new wave of internationalists dismiss the notion of American uniqueness, are wary of national narratives, and criticize their guild for its privileging of national enclosures. They approach the very concept of national histories as misleading, intellectually limiting and politically suspect. According to David Thelen, historians invented the national narrative to persuade people to interpret the past within a restrictive political framework. Quoting from Prasenjit Duara's provocative analysis of the historiography of modern China, he argues that it is time to "rescue history from the nation."[8]

The new internationalists may be divided roughly into two main groups: postnationalists and transnationalists. The postnationalist first and foremost seeks the fragmentation of the nation-state in order to empower the hidden voices of the past. The nation, Gary Gerstle argues, is a coercive "structure of power." Its privileged analytical status limits "the array of identities" for understanding the past. Gerstle and others chastise American historiography for inattention and neglect of alternative social, cultural, and political forms of historical change. Multiculturalism as well as the competing frameworks of race and gender all suffer from the unquestioning acceptance of the nation-state as the main and sometimes exclusive analytical framework. Outside of the national framework, a plethora of identities and boundaries compete and complement the national framework. The unquestioning acceptance of the collective fiction of the all-encompassing national community turns historians into complicit collaborators in "the nasty work that building a national community entails."[9]

The postnationalist impulse of fragmentation is derived from a certain hopelessness vis-à-vis large-scale social change and justice. The nation is approached as a monolithic power structure that defines and restricts identity and personal agency. The implication is that the naturalized nation-state is not only artificial; it is, as well, impervious to change. Thus, the postnationalist seeks alternative, private spaces outside of or hidden from the national framework. Having given up hope of autonomy and agency under the discursive regime of nationhood, the postnationalists withdraw to the margins and borderlands.

In contrast to the fragmentation of the postnationalists, the transnationalist critics of nation-centered American history seek alternative large, global conceptual frameworks. A typical example would be the pervasive trend among immigration historians to recontextualize the old story of immigration and assimilation. The "new" immigration historians actively avoid the national paradigm. Instead of concentrating on national enclosures, Donna Gabbaccia notes, immigration historians now move toward discussions of "migration and geographical mobility," in which the American immigration experience is but "one pole in a multivalent analysis of global economies, linkages of Old and New Worlds" and forms of identities "in a variety of settings, not all of which conform to the rigid and often arbitrary borders" of the nation-state.[10]

THEORY AND INTERNATIONALIZATION

Both transnationalists and postnationalists are united in their promotion of theory over narrative. Theory provides a path out of stifling nation-oriented narratives. When historical developments are viewed through the prism of abstract concepts, the nation-state loses its misleadingly authoritative aura. Theory, Donna Gabaccia argues, enables us "to query the tyranny of the national in the discipline of history."[11]

Transnationalist studies of trade patterns, the spread of technological innovations, and the interaction of civilizations—the logic of systems—replace the simplistic mechanism of cause and effect. Contrary to previous generations of comparative historians who use the model of diffusion and dominance, the transnationalists "decline to divide variables into the independent and dependent." Rather than focusing on culture as "an identifiable social unit," transnationalists rely, instead, "on adjectival forms, speaking of process rather than product; they analyze cultural production and cultural change rather than cultures or cultural traits." Rather than diffusion of culture from a dominant center to a receptive periphery, they envision the emergence of cultural products as always ephemeral and multidirectional.[12]

Contrary to this focus on sweeping global patterns, the postnationalists seek fragmentation and deconstruction. The theories offered for advancing the postnationalist cause are on the cutting edge of American academia. David Thelen, for example, has singled out theories linked to "recent explorations of Mexican-American borderlands and queer theory and practice."[13] The common link between the notion of queer theory and borderlands may be found in what Michel Foucault characterized as "discursive regimes." In its broadest sense, queer theory exposes how a web of discursive regimes governing social customs and moral and linguistic conventions restrains personal freedom and identities. Just as labels such as "homosexuality" and "heterosexuality" control and constrain our expression of self through erotic desires, so presumably the discursive regime of national identity regulates personal freedom and limits the types of identity we might choose for ourselves. Moreover, in promoting the dissolving of sex roles and stable identities, queer theory highlights the indelible connections between sexual oppression, economic inequality, and political domination.

The nation, according to queer theorists, is produced in manner not unlike the imposition of gendered identities. The nation, like gender, is a ritualistic, synthetic creation affirmed, legitimized and "naturalized" by symbols and ceremonies. Affirmations of nationhood—the singing of the national anthem at sports events, the symbolic clashes of nations in international athletic competitions, the pervasive presence of national monuments and nation-centered public holidays, to say nothing of national histories—transform the discursive framework of nationhood into an unquestioned facet of everyday life.[14] In a similar manner, the queer theorist Judith Butler argues, gender is constructed not "by a founding act" but by a regulated pattern or repetition. Much like national identity, gender identity becomes an essentialist, uncontested reality through the pervasive spread of gender norms by mass culture and through the authority of science and religion.[15]

The concept of borderlands, while not as exotic and as provocative as queer theory, identifies a space in which the hierarchies of center and margin, inclusion and exclusion, are replaced by a ceaseless exchange of meanings and identities that challenge any overarching trope. Based on studies of the Mexican-American frontier, the advocates of the borderlands concept argue that a border region is neither a cultural "break" nor a political barrier separating two national entities. When freed from the blinders of national history, the border represents "a zone of pulsion, exchanges, interactions and 'free'-flow."[16] Within the physical space of borders, as well as the philosophical borderlands of cultural studies, seemingly stable identities are deterritorialized and renegotiated. Here, in the borderlands, a liberating confusion of identities challenges the superimposed boundaries of culture class and region, as well as gender and nation.

American postnationalists have sought, in particular, to transcend the regulating powers of national tropes in the borderlands of personal experience. This, indeed, is the theme of Roy Rozenzweig's and David Thelen's investigation of the private production of history by ordinary citizens. Based on interviews with 1,453 informants from all walks of life, they reported on a past quite different from the nation-centered histories of textbooks and classrooms. The informants, and by implication, ordinary Americans in general, "reject[ed] nation-centered accounts they were forced to memorize and regurgitate in school." Instead, they presented a "familial and intimate past," in which great events were personalized in "patterns, narratives that allow them to make sense of the past." [17] By identifying with the nation, Rozenzweig and Thelen argue, professional history may cut itself off from such stories.

The key obstacle to decentering the nation and uncovering these personal pasts is, we are informed, professionalization. The mobilization of professional credentials, critics argue, is not an intellectual issue but a political effort to delegitimize competing paradigms. According to this view, the professionalization of history has paralleled "the centralized drive of businessmen to create and control national markets. Beginning in the late nineteenth century, and until recently, "the professionalizers tried to overwhelm competitors," to "dismiss subnational or transnational visions of experience," and "turn the focus of history from local pride to national identity."[18]

In a rather startling leap, it is argued or asserted that removing history from the authority of professional guilds and its transferal to other sites goes hand-in-glove with internationalization. The acceptance of "patterns of popular history making" and the internationalization of the parochial guild of American historians promises to replace nation-centered narratives of American exceptionalism with the more relevant questions of how "texts and products and institutions were embraced, shaped, rejected, and reshaped" by ordinary people espousing subnational identities. While professional historians have been obsessively engaged in propping up the questionable authority of the nation-state, "the world's people were making their own fundamental historical developments." Thus, a central task of the postnationalist (and postprofessional?) American historian is to abandon the role of complicit collaborator in nationalist projects and, instead, redeem, reconstruct, and produce alternatives to "nation-centered" perspectives.[19]

THE LIMITS OF INTERNATIONALIZATION

The new internationalism raises a series of thorny problems, the most obvious being the insistent flogging of American exceptionalism, a long-dead conceptual horse. Internationalists define American exceptionalism as a timeless stigma to be assigned to American historians of all generations. American exceptionalism, Michael McGerr reminds us, is commonly defined as the chauvinistic and unfounded belief in American divergence from common trajectories of historical development. Exceptionalists assume "that this divergence is unchanging" and presumably endorse axiomatic assumptions regarding American superiority and unparalleled greatness. Although previous practitioners of comparative history may have been driven by this narrow definition of exceptionalism, McGerr argues, it would be hard to find any contemporary historians who accept such definitions nowadays. Not all who find developments within the United States to be different are necessarily claiming exceptionalism or American superiority. In fact, contemporary "American historians typically invoke 'exceptionalism' when they want to attack, not defend, the idea of national uniqueness, or greatness."[20]

The critique of nation-centered history is, as well, afflicted by simplistic definitions. Attacks on nation-oriented historiography erroneously assume that its advocates are ensnared by a frozen concept of the nation-state. In actual fact, the nation is, and has always been, the most mobile of concepts.

The very existence of the nation, Ernest Renan observed in a classic 1885 essay "is a daily plebiscite."[21]To the degree that the nation is a discursive regime, it surely is an elusive one, ever changing and redefining itself.

By contrast, the new internationalists tend to approach the nation as an enduring cultural construction, unchanging over historical time. In actual fact, nation-centered histories accept the United States, not as a frozen collective fiction, but as a slippery, mutant concept that incorporates, reacts to, and acknowledges communal loyalties and multiple identities. Rather than imposing a restrictive discursive regime, the nation is continuously reinterpreted, reinvented, and reimagined in response to changes in identity, group identities, and international trends. Contrary to the charges of critics, the continuing renegotiating of the meaning of nation assumes an active, broad-based participation in defining its meaning. Changing notions of gender, ethnicity, and belonging in general all affect the meaning of "nation." Such an approach calls into question the internationalist critique's point of departure.[22]

The internationalists' neglect of temporal divisions is another significant fault in this vision of new conceptual horizons. The abandoning of nationally derived spatial divisions is rarely accompanied by a rethinking of rigid and intellectually indefensible chronological divisions. Internationalist historians tend to skirt the issue of periodization—their main field of expertise—preferring, instead, to focus on anthropological and geographical issues. The theories offered by advocates of internationalization are almost exclusively critical of the notion of *spatial* boundaries. However, conventional American-centered periodization is infrequently and only reluctantly discussed. Periodization, Jerry Bentley reminds us, "involves much more than the simple discovery of self-evident turning points in the past; it depends on prior decisions about the issues and processes that are most important for the shaping of human societies" and, by definition, calls into question "the coherence of conventionally recognized periods."[23]

The periodization privileged by American advocates of internationalization is still decidedly ethnocentric, thereby limiting much of the effort to address alternative frameworks. Moreover, American historians favor a mostly anthropocentric framework, while some of the most important turning points in human history result from the destruction or rearrangement of biological boundary lines, rather than, or in addition to, social or political boundaries.[24] The limits and demarcations of time still accepted by most internationalists suggest that the call for decentering history is still very much tied to an American agenda and has not entailed "a reevaluation of time spaces."[25]

The internationalist condemnation of professionalization as a political act of gatekeeping raises serious problems as well. This cavalier dismissal of standards as politically informed, rather than intellectually legitimate, reached a crisis state in 1991, when the OAH accepted a call for papers from the Institute of Historical Review, an organization dedicated to Holocaust denial. Despite the protestations of the OAH's president, Joyce Appleby, who opposed the request on the grounds that it repudiated the professional standards and "values that bring us together as members of the OAH," the executive board accepted the advertisement. First Amendment rights were the ostensible reason for publishing the ad. Yet far more intriguing than this curious recourse to the Constitution was the board's stubborn unwillingness to offer professional guidelines for separating history from pseudohistory. Driven by an adamant desire to encourage the submission of historical perspectives "representing all points of view"—not only those of professional practitioners, but among the public at large—the executive board declined censorship even of obviously fraudulent scholarship. The outrage of OAH members offended by the relinquishing of professional standards and the moral implications of the board's decision led to the eventual acceptance of Joyce Appleby's position, as well as a public repudiation of Holocaust denial. However, in an after-the-fact explanation, the board continued to disclaim a mandate to invoke professional standards in deciding on the legitimacy of any interpretation of the past. Decisions on legitimacy, even in so obvious a case as the fraudulent scholarship of Holocaust deniers, were, the board argued, the exclusive province of the general public.[26]

In actual fact, and contrary to the attack on standards and espousal of pluralism, the postnationalist strain of internationalization is not the antithesis of constraining professionalization but, rather, its grandest result. In the past, professionalization may have led to the elimination of competing paradigms. However, its most enduring contemporary legacy is quite the opposite. The historiographical landscape is cluttered with enclaves of hyperspecialization and a deluge of perspectives that, Thomas Bender argues, have destroyed any notion of synthesis, "leaving only many disconnected pasts." The intensification of specialization and professionalization has encouraged "American historians to identify socially and intellectually with restricted subgroups rather than with the American field or the discipline as a whole." This model, whatever its advantages in opening up new conceptual horizons, has created a void. Such "centrifugal scholarship legitimates everything and equalizes everything." The threat is, of course, that "the past will look like the university, a conglomeration of equally important and unrelated fields." Bender hopes for, but does not forecast a new and more complex synthesis arising from this mode of centrifugal scholarship. Growing interest in "the interior of subculture," he argues, has produced an irreducible particularity that obscures the shared elements of a given common culture, national or otherwise.[27]

INTERNATIONALIZATION AND THE FOREIGN SCHOLAR

The advantages of internationalization for foreign scholars are obvious. Ostensibly, the internationalization impulse provides a variety of opportunities for foreign scholars. The *JAH,* the leading promoter of internationalization, lists close to 100 international contributing editors and offers impressive array of articles written for and by foreign scholars.

David Thelen explains this influx of outside perspectives with an economic metaphor. "Of the $10,000 an American consumer paid General Motors for a new Pontiac Le Mans, $3,000 went to South Korea for routine labor and assembly, $2,150 to Japan, Taiwan, and Singapore for components; $750 to Germany for styling and design engineering; $250 to Britain for advertising and marketing; and $50 to Ireland and Barbados for data processing."[28] Quoting Robert Reich, Thelen predicts that ultimately there will be no national products or national industries.

The analogy with the mass production of history is quite clear. Here, too, the nationally assembled artifact seems quaintly antiquarian. In a world where national scholars receive their education somewhere else, and ideas flow through the borderless Internet, the idea of national intellectual product appears to be parochial, if not reactionary. The future belongs to the postnational scholar and the transnational journal.

Nevertheless, I propose that that internationalization as a strategy for drawing foreign scholars into a dialogue with American scholars is, at best, a revolution manqué. A cursory glance at the *JAH* and other journals of American history and culture reveals that there are almost no foreign parts in the American knowledge machine. The long roll call of "international contributing editors" listed in every issue of the *JAH* does little to compensate for the absence of foreign members from the *JAH'*s "real" editorial board. With the exception of the occasional Canadian, the OAH has no foreign elected officials either.

The engagement of international scholars in the making of the U.S. past is also thematically limited. To be sure, as Jane Desmond and Virginia Dominguez note, we have witnessed an "extensive acknowledgment of the intertwined histories of Latin America and the United States." They caution, however, that that such enterprises are usually "limited to analyses of the migration of people from Latin America to the United States, the historical contests over the U.S. border, the theorization of cultural borderlands, and the development of a Hispanic population in the United States." Rarely are Latin American scholars "acknowledged to have something to say about U.S. history or contemporary U.S. culture except with regard to these issues and then only in terms of internally generated U.S. paradigms of cultural difference."[29]

The predominance of comparative studies linking South Africa and the

United States is another revealing example of the limited engagement of foreign scholars in the production of American scholarship. Second only to inquiries into the U.S.–Latin American nexus, the South African connection is prominent in all major journals. Most of the South African contributions focus, predictably, on racial topics and analogies.

The resonance of South African voices and the focus on white institutional racism reveals a central weakness of the internationalist paradigm: the tendency to seek obvious and well-worn comparisons rather than complex new perspectives. As both the Latin American and the South African examples suggest, most internationalist scholarship rests either upon a national link, as in immigration, or on comparative studies of racism and other aspects of social injustice, associated in one way or another with a domestic American agenda. Such historical comparisons of institutional inhumanity lend themselves to comparisons because they are deceivingly universal. The well-documented incidents of European injustice in different parts of the world encourage facile comparisons between societies that were, and still are, fundamentally different. Moreover, the exclusive focus on Western modes of oppression seems to suggest that similar patterns in non-Western surroundings are not worthy of attention.

In the final analysis, foreign scholars engage the attention of Americans only if they adhere to an American-generated agenda. Such unreflecting internationalism, the cultural critic Benjamin Lee notes, merely worsens the professions' nearsightedness, because it views the world as an extension of American concerns. The agenda of internationalism invariably emanates from the United States and by default places the foreign scholar in a supporting role. The universalization of an American agenda solidifies and amplifies "deficiencies that already exist with our [American] understandings of other cultures."[30] Most of the foreign scholarship presented in U.S. journals for American consumption merely validates or "reproduces the paradigms of U.S. scholarship while sketching similarities and differences."[31]

There was a time when American historians looked abroad only to confirm the incomparability of the nation's history. The pendulum has now swung in a radically different direction. The American historical profession is now concerned with transcending the nation-state and identifying similar, comparable historical trajectories in different chronological and geographical circumstances. These new conceptual vistas are still quite restrictive, because they have not moved beyond well-worn American-generated concerns. Typically, American historians engage foreign scholars on subjects such as the role of "Le Melting-Pot" in France, "Frontier Myths" in America and Israel, the "McDonaldization" of other parts of the world, or the manner in which racism in South Africa resembles the American pattern.[32] We foreign scholars are thus relegated to the task of sanctioning the sometimes narrow topical agenda of U.S. scholarship. It remains to be seen whether such restrictive scholarship will move beyond this one-way conduit, eventually dissolving and evolving into a multidirectional, borderless exchange of ideas and concepts.

Finally, the validity of internationalization and its critique of enclosures and exceptionalism is not the real issue. Whether internationalization is, indeed, a conceptually superior paradigm is almost beside the point. Its immediate importance lies in its epistemological authority, its power to impose an understanding of the American historical experience and regulate the role of the scholarly "other." Having been endorsed as the most accessible port of entry to the inner sanctum of the American historical guild for international scholars, there is a very real danger that it will cause all other approaches to lose their attractiveness. This act of exclusion— whether intentional or not, whether recognized or not—reaffirms rather than challenges the parochialism of American historiography and the inequalities in the international academic system.

NOTES

1. Sacvan Bercovitch, review of *American Chameleon: Individualism in Trans-National Context*, ed. Richard O. Curry and Lawrence B. Goodheart (Kent, Ohio, 1991), and *Is America Different? A New Look at American Exceptionalism*, ed. Byron E. Shafer (New York, 1991), *American Political Science Review* 87 (December 1993): 1017.

2. Michael Kammen, "The Problem of American Exceptionalism: a Reconsideration," *American Quarterly* 45 (March 1993): 1–43.

3. Thomas Bender, "Wholes and Parts: The Need for Synthesis in American History," *Journal of American History* 73 (June 1986): 122.

4. For good illustrations of comparative perspectives, see Peter Kolchin, "Comparing American History," *Reviews in American History* 10 (December 1982): 64–81; Kammen, "Problem of American Exceptionalism"; Carl Guarneri, *America Compared: American History in International Perspective* (2 vols.; New York, 1997).

5. David M. Potter, *People of Plenty: Economic Abundance and the American Character* (Chicago, 1954). *A Comparative Approach to American Slavery*, ed. C. Van Woodward (Washington, D.C., 1968), vii–ix, 3. For an excellent review of this collection of essays, produced for the Voice of America, see Carl Guarneri, "Reconsidering C. Van Woodward's *The Comparative Approach to American History*," *Reviews in American History*, 23 (September 1995): 552–63.

6. David Potter, "Civil War," in Woodward, *A Comparative Approach*, 147–58.

7. Ian Tyrell, "American Exceptionalism in an Age of International History," *American Historical Review* 96 (October 1991): 1031–56.

8. David Thelen, "Making History and Making the United States," *Journal of American Studies* 32 (1988): 373–97; Prasenjit Duara, *Rescuing History from the Nation: Questioning Narratives of Modern China* (Chicago, 1995).

9. Gary Gerstle, "Liberty, Coercion, and the Making of Americans," *Journal of American History* 84 (September 1997): 527.

10. Donna Gabaccia, "Liberty, Coercion, and the Making of Immigration Historians," *Journal of American History* 84 (September 1997): 574.

11. Donna Gabaccia, "Is Everywhere Nowhere? Nomads, Nations, and the Immgirant Paradigm of American History?" *JAH* 86 (December 1999): 1115–34.

12. Patrick Manning, "The Problem of Interactions in World History," *American Historical Review* 101 (June 1996): 776.

13. Thelen, "Making History and Making the United States," 391.

14. Joanne Sharp, "Gendered Nationhood: a Feminist Engagement with National Identity," in *Bodyspace: Destabilizing Geographies of Gender and Sexuality,* ed. Nancy Duncan (London, 1996), 97–108.

15. Judith Butler, *Gender Trouble: Feminism and the Subversion of Identity* (New York, 1990), 145.

16. David Avalos, John Welchman, "Response to the Philosophical Brothel," in *Rethinking Borders,* ed. John Welchman (Minneapolis, 1996), 188.

17. Roy Rosenzweig and David Thelen, *The Presence of the Past: Popular Uses of History in American Life* (New York, 1998), 12–13.

18. Thelen, "Making History and Making the United States," 385.

19. Ibid., 377–78.

20. Ibid. See also Kammen, "The Problem of American Exceptionalism: A Reconsideration," for a provocative defense of American uniqueness.

21. Ernest Renan, "What Is a Nation?" in *Nation and Narration,* ed. Homi Bhabha (London, 1990), 19.

22. This more complex definition of the nation is the theme of Bender, "Wholes and Parts," as well as the important study by David Hollinger, *Postethnic America: Beyond Multiculturalism* (New York, 1995).

23. Jerry Bentley, "Cross-Cultural Interaction and Periodization in World History," *American Historical Review* 101, 3 (June 1996), 749. See also Peter Stearns, "Periodization in World History Teaching: Identifying the Big Changes," *History Teacher* 20 (1987): 561–80; William Green, "Periodization in European and World History," *Journal of World History* 3 (1992): 13–52; William Green, "Periodizing World History," *History and Theory* 34 (1995): 99–111.

24. Albert Crosby, *The Columbian Exchange: Biological and Cultural Consequences of 1492* (Westport, Conn., 1973); Albert Crosby, *Ecological Imperialism: The Biological Expansion of Europe, 900–1900* (New York, 1986).

25. Patrick Manning, "The Problem of Interactions in World History," *American Historical Review* 101 (June 1996): 771.

26. Joyce Appelby, letter to the editor, *OAH Newsletter,* November 1991, 4; David Thelen, Mary Frances Berry, Dan Carter, Cullom Davis, Sara Evans, Linda Gordon, Lawrence Levi, Mary Ryan, letter to the editor, ibid., February 1992, 5.

27. Thomas Bender, "The New History: Then and Now," *Reviews in American History* 12 (December 1984): 612–22. See also Bender's "Whole and Parts."

28. David Thelen, "Toward the Internationalization of American History," *Journal of American History* 79 (September 1992): 437.

29. Jane Desmond and Virginia Dominguez, "Resituating American Studies in a Critical Internationalism," *American Quarterly* 48, 3 (1996): 476.

30. Benjamin Lee, "Critical Internationalism," *Public Culture* 7 (1995): 559–92.

31. Desmond and Dominguez, "Resituating American Studies."

32. See, e.g., Nancy Green, "Le Melting-Pot: Made in America, Produced in France," *JAH* 86 (December 1999): 1188–1208; S. Ilan Troen, "Frontier Myths and Their Applications in America and Israel: A Transnational Perspective," ibid., 1209–30; George Ritzer and Elizabeth Malone, "Globalization Theory: Lessons from the Exportation of McDonaldization and the New Means of Consumption," *American Studies* 41 (Summer–Fall 2000): 97–118; Greg Cuthbertson, "Racial Attraction: Tracing the Historical Alliance between South Africa and the United States," *JAH* 81 (December 1994): 1123–36.

SIXTEEN

The Historian's Use
of the United States and Vice Versa

David A. Hollinger

Nations can easily turn historians into tools. When David Potter etched this point into the collective mind of historians in 1962, he assumed that nations, for better or for worse, would remain the central subject of historians. Potter paused at the start of "The Historian's Use of Nationalism and Vice Versa" to find it a bit odd that he and his colleagues could really suppose that "the 2,500,000,000 people of the world would fall naturally into a series of national groups." But he went on swiftly and confidently to conclude that nations were *it*. That even a historian as skeptical as Potter could do this reveals the width of the gap between his historiographical era and ours.[1] Some four decades later, we routinely take the view that nations are only one of many central subjects. We have extensive subnational and transnational monographic literatures. We are preoccupied with the contingent, constructed character of nations. We are awash in "postnational" speculation that nation-states are on their way out. Furthermore, we easily understand a growing suspicion of nation-centered history as anachronistic at best and reactionary at worst. And we are more convinced than ever of the wisdom of Potter's caution against our being "used" by nations, even as we decide when and when not to apply the label "nation" to a given solidarity.

What are the prospects for national narrative today in the case of the United States? Where do historians of this particular nation now stand in relation to Potter's dilemma?

Conversations over the years with Willi Paul Adams, Ferdinando Fasce, Winfried Fluck, Ron Robin, and François Weil have influenced my thinking about the internationalization of American history, and I also thank Thomas Bender, James T. Kloppenberg, and the publisher's anonymous readers for their comments on a draft of this paper.

One obvious course of action is to focus less on the nation and more on its constituent parts, and on the transnational networks of which any nation is a node. With regard to the United States, we might argue, in Potter's terms, that in view of our sharp awareness of transnational and subnational experience, historians have less use for the United States than they once did. And the less use historians have for the United States, the less danger there is, presumably, that the United States will "use" historians. Hence an attractive escape from Potter's dilemma is to escape the nation, to "rescue history from the nation," as Prasenjit Duara has phrased this program in relation to the historiography of modern China.[2]

Yet nations are not the only formations that threaten to turn historians into tools. Nonnational and antinational movements and solidarities can do the same. In dealing with them, we may find ourselves without even the modest measure of control over our own instrumentality that we gain from our increasingly acute suspicion of the nation. By virtue of their presumed innocence, nonnational solidarities may be able to use us more easily than nations can. Potter specified for nations what is actually a generic problem for the historian in relation to any solidarity that holds moral resonance for historians or for their audiences.

The solidarities we call nations do, moreover, retain a justified hold on a substantial amount of our attention. Even if we accept Charles Maier's formulation of the 1970s as the end of a distinctive historical epoch of nation-centered human striving, it will not do to project onto the past the particular dispersion of power that Maier and others see as characteristic of the last quarter of the twentieth century.[3] Even should it be determined that the national community of the United States figures smaller in the lives of many of its citizens and inhabitants than it once did, that determination would provide no basis for a less nation-centered history of the United States during the years prior to this putative transformation. However likely or desirable we may judge a more transnational or postnational future to be, the national past remains no less formidable. Hence contemporary speculation about the replacement of the world of nations by a world of something-elses is of heuristic value at best to historians concerned with the people who have lived in the United States.

If there is any one nation in the contemporary world the history of which, *as a nation,* requires telling now, it is the one that displays the most successful nationalist project in all of modern history.[4] Despite the failure of some history faculties around the world to register this insight, the United States is of world-historical significance. What marks the national project of the United States as "successful" is not its virtue—although it would be disingenuous of me to deny that I personally believe that the United States does have many virtues—but certain simple, uncontested facts. Two-and-one-quarter centuries after its founding and 135 years after its Civil War, the United States is the most powerful nation-state in the world and the only twenty-first century power that operates under a constitution written in the eighteenth century. Its significance is measured by its sheer longevity, its influence in the world arena, and its absorption of a variety of peoples through immigration, conquest, and enslavement and emancipation. The formidable presence of the United States in the world has been achieved at notorious costs, including, as we historians have become quite skilled at demonstrating, the systematic mistreatment of people on the basis of color, language, and religion. One may lament the success of the United States, or at least the evils by which that success has been achieved. One may instead rejoice in what support the United States provides for whatever ideals one may hold. Or, one may be morally indifferent to it. And one can explain it in a number of different ways. But no matter how one judges the national project of the United States morally, and now matter how one explains it historically, the national project of the United States is part of the primal stuff of history to be engaged.

Thus historians do still have real use for the United States. And vice versa: the United States can no doubt use historians, and in ways that threaten their autonomy and their loyalty to the truth. Potter's dilemma persists.

But this dilemma now presents itself in a specific historiographical context that invites clarification. Among the winds of doctrine that have swept through the ranks of professional historians of the United States during the 1990s, two have been especially bracing. One pushes historians to speak to a nonprofessional public. The other pushes historians to interpret American history in truly global perspective. The first promises to affect the terms on which the United States might turn historians into tools. The second promises to affect the terms on which historians might achieve maximum independence.

Historians should work harder at being public intellectuals, we are told. Historians within the orbit of the Organization of American Historians are constantly calling upon one another to stop talking simply to ourselves. Rather, we should, in this popular version of our calling, write more "crossover" books, engage more fully with the teaching of history in secondary and even elementary schools, coordinate our activities as research scholars with those of museum curators and public historians, challenge the sometimes benighted priorities of the History Channel, and generally integrate our work as historians more fully with our responsibilities to the public, above all, the public of the United States. These concerns have generated a multitude of initiatives, including closer official connections with public historians and the participation of academic historians in the National History Standards.

Yet historians are also told to stop thinking about the United States in the parochial terms of American citizenship. Historians encourage one another to adopt a global perspective on what goes on within the United States. Many of the same historians who support the OAH's outreach to the American public also support the "internationalization" of the field. In this internationalist view, we are to see the functions of the American national solidarity in the sweep of *Weltgeschichte,* and write history framed by the human species, and even with the earth itself in mind. Our history will be a lot better, we tell ourselves, if we liberate ourselves from a preoccupation with the role our work plays in the public life of the United States. This move toward the global is substantially strengthened by the surveillance of U.S.-based historians by a world community of historians finally taking a more active interest in U.S. history. After all, the particularistic tendencies and patriotic biases of German historians of German history, of Italian historians of Italian history, and of Japanese historians of Japanese history have all been scrutinized and significantly corrected by an international community of historians, in which leading roles have been played by U.S.-based specialists in the histories of those other nations. Are not historians within Germany, Italy, Japan, and a number of other nations less thoroughly "used" by their nations as a result of an international community of historians? Is it not an enormous boon to more fully warranted interpretations of the history of the United States, then, to have a genuinely international scholarly community engaged with the study of that history? The strength of this international community makes it less likely that the United States will turn historians into mere instruments. This incorporation of U.S.-based historians of the United States into a genuinely global community of scholars may help emancipate "American history," at long last, from its role as a historical theology for the civil religion of the United States.

But what then of the responsibilities of historians to a public smaller than the species? If the arguments for a global perspective are so compelling, what becomes of the distinctly American public to which we try to speak? Where does the intensified professionalism of a more global historiography meet the intensified obligation to get beyond professionalism to engage the civic culture of one's nation? Should historians determined to interpret the United States in global perspective renounce altogether any engagement with the destiny of that nation's political community? Should U.S.-based historians of the United States orient themselves to the American public any differently than Australian-, Brazilian-, French-, or Russian-based historians of the United States, and if so, on the basis of what theory? Is the record of historians who have sought to build, sustain, or diminish national consciousness in the United States so negative in all its variations that the whole enterprise of solidarity building and critical revision should be left to nonhistorians? To what extent does the mere act of writing national narrative implicate a historian in the national project, regardless of his or her intentions?

To make these questions explicit and to call attention to their importance is more to my purpose here than providing a series of convincing answers. A book published in the year 2002 entitled *Rethinking American History in a Global Age* might well end with this list of questions.

But I do want to engage Potter's dilemma in the context of these questions. Within globally oriented scholarship, I believe, there is still substantial room for national narrative that speaks to the American public, and that even has among its several purposes the critical maintenance of the United States considered as a political solidarity. In so arguing, I take collegial issue with a widely discussed essay on some of these questions, David Thelen's "Making History and Making the United States." Thelen and I are allies in the movements for internationalization and for greater public engagement by historians. Yet this particular essay of 1998 invites a critical response here for several reasons. It displays the very difficulty my reading of Potter warns against: in focusing so much on the dangers of the nation, we risk falling into the uncritical embrace of something else: in Thelen's case, formations that are not national and not professional. The piece was published in a European venue that is especially vital in the internationalization of the study of the history of the United States, the *Journal of American Studies*. "Making History and Making the United States" deals more systematically with the relevant issues than do Thelen's other, more episodic writings, some of which are closer to my own views. I cite some of these below by way of indicating the common ground within which my disagreements with Thelen are situated.

The critique of nation-centered scholarship Thelen offers in "Making History and Making the United States" concentrates heavily on the *motives* of historians over the course of two centuries. Of special concern are the "professionals" of the late nineteenth century who, like the businessmen of that epoch, were eager "to create and control national markets." Thelen reminds us that nationally minded historians have been actors in the process by which the people of the United States have come to think of themselves as a nation and have achieved a certain measure of loyalty to national political institutions.[5] But even if one were to accept without caveat Thelen's account of the motives of historians of the past, it does not follow that today's historians who place a priority on national history are of a political piece with those of fifty, a hundred, or a hundred and fifty years ago. Thelen leaves the impression that these scholars of our own time are uncritical inheritors and perpetuators of a narrow nationalistic tradition.

In fact, to study the nation is not necessarily to be an ideological nationalist. National narrative is now being practiced with great skill by a host of contemporaries who can be construed as American nationalists only if our understanding of "nationalist" is considerably more commodious than that assumed by Thelen's account of our historiographical ancestors. Eric Foner's *The Story of American Freedom* is a widely appreciated example.[6] Linda Kerber's *No Constitutional Right to Be Ladies: Women and the Obligations of Citizenship* should serve as a reminder of the importance of constitutional history, and of the role of state power in affecting the lives of individuals.[7] Another prize-winning volume that resoundingly vindicates national narrative is Rogers Smith's *Civic Ideals: Conflicting Visions of Citizenship in U.S. History,* which shows, in Smith's words, how "lawmakers pervasively and unapologetically structured U.S. citizenship in terms of illiberal and undemocratic racial, ethnic, and gender hierarchies, for reasons rooted in basic, enduring imperatives of political life."[8] The *Oxford History of the United States,* perhaps our era's most conspicuous endeavor in the production of national narrative, now includes distinguished volumes by Robert Middlekauff, James McPherson, David Kennedy, and James Patterson.[9] If Thelen wishes to find fault with the motives of nation-centered historians, let him address these contemporaries.

Thelen's critique of nation-centered history is caught up in a larger complaint. He finds professional historians insufficiently responsive to public taste. Thelen urges scholars to spend less time talking about the nation and more time talking about "the ways that individuals make and remake their larger circumstances and cultures and institutions." He reminds us that many people consider "the past of their own families to be more important than the past of the nation." Largely on the basis of evidence that the public believes this, he calls for "a new kind of history" focusing more on individuals and their families. This new history would be "one in which people can be participants, not spectators, and can use the past to explore their agency as human beings." Thelen complains that historians, by "focusing on conflicts and changes in the larger circumstances, institutions, and cultures," tend to "emphasize that individuals and families are shaped by these larger categories—which are largely about power."[10]

Well, historians do tend to make a lot of power. And for good reason. Historians have traditionally felt a responsibility to tell the truth about the dispersion and consequences of power. Looking away from the nation, and toward subnational and transnational aspects of the experience of inhabitants of the United States, may entail a withdrawal from this responsibility. Power turns out to be real concern of Thelen's, but more by way of influencing its future deployment than by clarifying its past structure and operation. A design of his program for a less nation-centered history is the empowering of some people and the disempowering of other people. "Interrogating nation-centeredness leads to interrogation of the authority of those who have promoted national perspectives," he tells us in relation to an extended commentary on nationalist sentiments in the development of

American historiography from David Ramsey to today's "liberal national-ists."

Thelen wants to make nonhistorians into active "participants" in the writing of history and to emphasize their own "agency" in the history that gets written.[11] Noble as this apparently democratic and egalitarian aspira-tion may be, the aspiration invokes and begs questions about agency that historians routinely ask. Debates over what role individuals and groups and inherited structures and contingent conditions play in determining a given outcome are standard business for historians. Social historians have for a number of decades now been exploring the agency of subnational and transnational elements of American society. Biography, too, is a well-established mode of historical study. Indeed, attention to social groups and families and individuals reached a point of such saturation in history and the social sciences generally by the end of the 1980s that a chorus of voices asked to "bring the state back in."

Thelen implies that focusing on the agency of individuals and families is a good thing for historians to do regardless of just how much or how little force such agency might be shown to have in any given situation. He is much affected by the feelings of the public as revealed in "a random telephone survey of 1,400 Americans" that Thelen and a colleague con-ducted in 1994. Thelen here justifies the historiographical diminution of the American nation largely on the grounds that this diminution will pro-vide a more user-friendly history to those parts of the public whose talk about history Thelen describes sympathetically in the following account of his interviewees:

> They talked about needs, ambitions, dreams, love, and fears, and they re-flected on the past to learn about how to treat other individuals and how to make a difference in the course of their lives. They used terms like pride, shame, guilt, commitment, and trust. Their narratives were about aspiration, tragedy, and irony that have often been better presented by poets and nov-elists than historians because they are about human dilemmas that transcend time and place.[12]

This gushing appreciation for the language of everyperson invites a sus-picion that historians will become tools of untutored public opinion. Pop-ular memory and critical history have their own claims, as Michael Kammen and Kerwin Klein have argued convincingly.[13] If Robert Paxton had been respectful of popular memory in France, and of the stories each family wanted to tell of its heroic role in the resistance to Nazism, the world would be considerably less cognizant than it now is of French participation in the destruction of France's own Jewish population under the Vichy regime. The story people wanted to hear was one of dogged subversion of Nazism. Paxton's defiance of those desires was crucial to his now acclaimed achievement.[14] It would never do, of course, to suppose that only professional historians have the ability to see evil and the courage to address it, nor would it do even to suppose that most history writing by professionals is distinguished by these virtues. But studies of World War II provide an excellent example of how the obligations of professional integrity can conflict with the pressures to give the public the kind of history it wants.

Most of the people Thelen and his colleague, Roy Rosenzweig, interviewed described the history they had studied in school as "boring," and this Thelen hopes to change. But a national history more skillfully conceived and executed might well be as relevant to this goal as might a history less national in scope. National history sometimes does include events that involve ambitions, fears, pride, shame, and tragedy, and indeed all of the generic human experiences Thelen lists. The exceedingly popular, nationally oriented books of Stephen Ambrose and David McCullough certainly display these generic aspects of human striving, as do the frequent presentations these two historians make on television. Many of the programs on cable TV's History Channel, a mainstay of national narrative, present the American past in terms that exactly fit the sensibility Thelen attributes to an American public poorly served by academic historians.

But one need not look beyond academic historical writing to find prominent examples of national history that include the generic experiences that most interest the public, and that meet the most demanding of professional standards. One compelling recent instance is David M. Kennedy's *Freedom from Fear: The American People in Depression and War, 1929–1945*, which deserves attention here because it is located on the historiographical spectrum about as far away as it is possible to get from the historiographical future envisaged by "Making History and Making the United States." Kennedy's contribution to the *Oxford History of the United States* is largely about presidents and generals. *Freedom from Fear* concentrates on affairs of state and on aspects of society, culture, and economy that impinge on how those affairs are resolved. This book also shows that a global perspective and a national narrative are not incompatible. The point is to determine when and how to bring the subnational and supranational histories into the national narrative. And this conception of the challenge, let me hasten to point out, is largely accepted by Thelen himself in some of his more recent writing in the *Journal of American History*.[15]

Kennedy's accounts of the suffering experienced during the Depression and of the horrors experienced in warfare convey a sense that every life counted, but he never implies that each exercised equal influence over the course of events. He reminds us of the sergeant who improvised the "hedgehog" that enabled tanks to better penetrate the defenses of Normandy, but he has the good sense to do so in a footnote. Kennedy does not allow his readers the fantasy that the representation of the personal experience of soldiers can be a substitute for analysis of the course of a military engagement. One can appreciate what both an excellent commercial film like *The Thin Red Line* and a scholarly book like *Freedom from Fear* tell us about Guadalcanal without expecting either to perform the tasks of the other. The relative agency of Franklin Roosevelt and Douglas McArthur and the other principals amid the webs of circumstance and the contingencies of experience is a major theme of *Freedom from Fear.*

But no feature of Kennedy's treatment of *The American People in Depression and War* is more relevant to developing a perspective alternative to Thelen's than is Kennedy's studied refusal to yield to public memory. His account of World War II is written against a popular narrative of a "good" and "just" war "waged by a peaceful people aroused by anger only after intolerable provocation, a war stoically endured by those and home and fought in faraway places by brave and wholesome young men and dedicated women standing behind them on the production lines." Kennedy's own narrative challenges the reading public to confront what historians know better than the public does. Kennedy's own summary paragraph is worth quoting here, despite its length, because it so cogently brings together themes of this book that mark it as a synthesis of a generation of professional scholarship, and displays a global perspective that Kennedy shows can inform a distinctly national story. National narrative informed by transnational values and embedded in a world-historical perspective is indeed possible, and in an idiom popular enough to win, as Kennedy's book now has, a Pulitzer Prize. In the passage I quote, Kennedy, without denying the aspects of the war that the public remembers as good and just, is describing aspects of the war that the American people largely ignored or suppressed, but that they might have reflected upon in 1945 had they truly understood their situation and possessed the moral courage to face it:

> They might have reflected with some discomfort on how slowly they had awakened to the menace of Hitlerism in the isolationist 1930s; on how callously they had barred the door to those seeking to flee from Hitler's Europe; on how heedlessly they had provoked Japan into a probably avoidable war in a region where few American interests were at stake; on how they had largely fought with America's money and machines and with Russia's men, had fought in Europe only late in the day, against a foe mortally weakened by three years of brutal warfare in the east, had fought in the Pacific with a bestiality they did not care to admit; on how they had profaned their constitution by interning tens of thousands of citizens largely because of their race; on how they had denied most black Americans a chance to fight for their country; on how they had sullied their nation's moral standards with terror bombing in the closing months of the war; on how their leaders' stubborn

insistence on unconditional surrender had led to the incineration of hundreds of thousands of already defeated Japanese, first by fire raids, then by nuclear blast; on how poorly Franklin Roosevelt had prepared for the postwar era, how foolishly he had banked on goodwill and personal charm to compose the conflicting interests of nations, how little he had taken his countrymen into his confidence, even misled them, about the nature of the peace that was to come; on how they had abandoned the reforming agenda of the New Deal years to chase in wartime after the sirens of consumerism; on how they alone among warring peoples had prospered, emerging unscathed at home while 405,339 American soldiers, sailors, marines, and airmen had died. These men were dignified in death by their service, but they represented proportionately fewer military casualties than in any other major belligerent country. Beyond the war's dead and wounded and their families, few Americans had been touched by the staggering sacrifices and unspeakable anguish that the war had visited upon millions of other people around the globe.[16]

Freedom from Fear is an imposing, enthralling work of national history even though it does not cover everything of historical significance that took place within, or surrounding, the United States between 1929 and 1945. It contains next to no intellectual history, very little religious history, and not much about the arts, popular or elite. Reinhold Niebuhr is not mentioned; nor is Margaret Mead, William Faulkner, or Benny Goodman.

Even within Kennedy's justifiable focus on affairs of state, one can imagine a yet more international focus. Daniel T. Rodgers's *Atlantic Crossings: Social Politics in a Progressive Age* convincingly details a transatlantic intellectual and organization matrix that informed the making of government domestic policy through the 1930s. It was the war, indeed, that sharply diminished this international policy discourse just as, paradoxically, the United States became more politically involved beyond its borders: having supposed that they had "saved the world," Rodgers remarks of Americans of the 1940s, they had trouble imagining that they still had "much to learn from it."[17] But if only Rodgers's Americans had understood the war and the world of 1945 the way Kennedy now reconstructs them, Americans might not have been so arrogant, and so unwilling to continue to learn from the western European tradition of social democracy.

That tradition is among the chief subjects of another book that deserves attention in any consideration of fate and promise of nation-centered history. In *Uncertain Victory: Social Democracy and Progressivism in European and American Thought, 1870–1920,* James T. Kloppenberg challenges American exceptionalist assumptions with regard to pragmatism and progressivism, while taking careful account of the distinctive contexts of the four national cultures in which his cast of characters developed their ideas. This 1986 book interprets as closely related—and indeed as structurally connected— many of the chief developments in modern philosophy and political argumentation in four nations of the North Atlantic West, France, Germany, the United Kingdom, and the United States.[18] *Uncertain Victory* can serve to remind us that transnational history is being vigorously researched and written in terms that complement and enrich, rather than necessarily undermine, national narratives.

Intellectual history, the subfield to which Kloppenberg's widely appreciated book was contributed, would seem to be an ideal place to look for alternatives to an excessively nation-focused scholarship. Intellectual historians have long been attentive to what Thelen describes in passing as the "transnational circulations" of "religion or art or ideas" that parallel the "story of how capitalism and its agents" cross "national borders."[19] Thelen might have turned, for example, to several prominent books of the decade of the 1970s that addressed American thought in the context of exactly such transnational circulations, among them Henry F. May's *The Enlightenment in America*, Bruce Kuklick's *The Rise of American Philosophy*, Daniel W. Howe's collection on *Victorian America*, and James R. Moore's *The Post-Darwinian Controversies*.[20] While social historians of that decade made their greatest contributions by exploring a variety of local settings within the United States, creating a substantial "subnational" historiography of groups within American society, intellectual historians were practicing an increasingly transnational scholarship.

There are other, equally obvious fields in which to look for strong international emphases. Historians of diplomacy and historians of religion have long maintained an international frame of reference. Most surprising of all, Thelen does not turn to historians of science, perhaps the supreme exemplars of the study of things American in the specific contexts of international communities. The ways in which the international endeavor of science takes particular forms within particular national cultures has been a concern of historians of science for a full century, ever since the publication in 1904 of J. T. Merz's classic discussion of national styles of science in the first volume of his *A History of European Thought in the Nineteenth Century*.[21]

What might a nation-centered scholarship that speaks both to a global community of professional historians and to citizens of the United States look like? The examples I have provided above, especially Kennedy's *Freedom from Fear*, may be a sufficient answer to this question. But I want to push the question further, without implying that we should be searching for a single formula. Historians can be expected to disagree among themselves on exactly how the narrative of the nation should be constructed, and even on what the story should primarily be about. Yet widespread appreciation for, if not agreement upon, certain senses of the matter may not be so elusive.

It cannot be repeated often enough that the United States is both a *site* for history and a *player* in history. We can take it for granted that historians need to attend to aspects of history that simply happen "on site" in the United States, as well as aspects of history that are constituted by the United States. But just what do we take the latter to be? Being clear about this may better enable national narrative to flourish without getting in the way of other kinds of history dealing with things that take place in the American site, and vice versa. What is the history of the United States—as opposed to a history of things that happen within it—a history *of*? Answers to this question are implicit in narratives centered on the slavery question, on the frontier, and on the elaboration in America of English institutions. Each of these classic narratives of the United States was a product of its own times. We should not suppose that any narrative we develop will be anything other than a product of ours.

A defensible focus for a national narrative in our own time, I believe, is the notion of *a national solidarity committed—but often failing—to incorporate individuals from a great variety of communities of descent, on equal but not homogeneous terms, into a society with democratic aspirations inherited largely from England.*[22] There is much more to the United States than this. But if one tries to sum up in a single sentence what a national narrative might narrate, this sentence has a number of promising features.

The United States is, indeed, a national solidarity of the kind described. To place emphasis on this fact can serve to reinforce the liberal and cosmopolitan elements of the national self-image without denying the parts of American history that are not liberal and not cosmopolitan. A narrative of this solidarity would have plenty of opportunities to detail the dispersion and consequences of power. It could address episodes in which the nation was a liberating force, a formation that could be called upon to overturn injustices perpetuated by local, regional, and state segments of the nation. But so, too, could such a narrative attend to the episodes of the opposite kind. A national narrative of the sort I envisage here is consistent with, and could easily incorporate many of the contributions to transnational history published in the *Journal of American History*'s two special issues of September and December 1999, edited by Thelen.[23]

This modest "charter" for national narrative expresses the vital idea that people can be politically equal without being culturally identical, yet it does not suggest that history has enacted this ideal. It acknowledges the individualistic focus of the American polity; individuals, not groups, are incorporated into the nation. Yet the opportunity is there to tell the story of how the boundaries of national solidarity came into being, how and when they were challenged and sometimes changed, and by whom. How has the United States drawn and redrawn its social borders to accommodate, repel, or subjugate this or that group, in defiance of its egalitarian and individualistic self-image? How have groups been defined, and by whom? How has racism and the struggle against it proceeded in a sequences of distinctive settings? This conception of the national story enables the historian to display two truths now vouchsafed to historians, but often resisted by much of the public: the great extent to which the flourishing of the United States has depended on the exploitation of nonwhites, and the relative weakness, during most of the national history, of egalitarian ideals.

This one-sentence "charter" for a narrative of the United States also acknowledges that the democratic aspirations of the Republic derived primarily—although not exclusively—from England, the specific European country from which virtually all the political leaders of the revolutionary generation directly descended. The declaration of independence impeached the king of England for failing to deliver on what he owed American colonists in their capacity as English nationals, as the king's subjects. To recognize the heavily English foundation of the Constitution of the United States is not to preclude the study of other influences, nor to imply that people today of English descent have any greater personal connection to the constitutional order of the United States than does anyone else. But the reference to England does prevent us from kidding ourselves. Foner is surely correct to begin his *Story of American Freedom* with a section on the complexities of the concept of "The Freeborn Englishman."[24]

Does this vision of the history of the United States lose credibility or appeal if the intended audience is not the American public, but the world? I suspect not. This vision gains much of its appeal from our world-historical situation. Solidarities are being reorganized and retheorized across the planet, and in different directions. I have in mind the proliferation of ethnoreligious nationalisms, the greater standing of human rights organizations purporting to speak for the species and of environmental organizations purporting to speak for the earth, the increasing ordinance of global economic conglomerates, the larger measure of authority exercised by the World Trade Organization, the rise of European identity and the relative diminution of national identity in western Europe, the deterritorialization of identity through the growth of multiple diasporas, the destabilization of ostensibly primordial identity groups by academic theorists, and the breaking down by other academic theorists of the formerly monolithic formation called nationalism into distinctive varieties. The history of the United States achieves some of its world-historical significance in relation to these contemporary transformations, which properly affect our inquiries into the American past. The set of emphases I suggest above may enable more scholars to tell more truths to more people about more of the nation's history as now understood by a global community of professional historians than can other, comparable, one-sentence charters for the national narrative.

Although no single sentence can carry us very far, there are good reasons for forcing ourselves to try a brief formulation. Brevity dramatizes the process by which we define central subjects, how we select certain aspects of an entity's history and deselect others. It encourages us to maintain critical awareness and control over the themes of our narratives. Historians select and deselect with every sentence we write, whether we direct our words to an audience of compatriots, an international learned community, or both, or to any other audience. When we make such choices, as when we make all of the choices entailed by our work, we risk becoming the tools of something, including nations, especially any nation in the destiny of which the historian may wish to play a part, however small. But not all "uses" of historians by nations are equally problematic. Whatever use a historian consciously tries to be to his or her nation, or to any national solidarity, that use is surely best balanced against the imperatives of an international community of scholars for whom the truth is presumably the only client. Hence our two winds of doctrine, if we set our sails right, might yet carry us in the same direction.

NOTES

1. David Potter, "The Historian's Use of Nationalism and Vice Versa," *American Historical Review* 67 (1962): 924.

2. Prasenjit Duara, *Rescuing History from the Nation: Questioning Narratives of Modern China* (Chicago, 1995).

3. Charles S. Maier, "Consigning the Twentieth Century to History: Alternative Narratives for the Modern Era," *American Historical Review* 105 (2000): 807–31.

4. For one discussion of how the history of the United States might figure in a comparative history of national projects in the modern era, see David A. Hollinger, "Authority, Solidarity, and the Political Economy of Identity: The Case of the United States," *Diacritics* 29 (1999): 116–27.

5. David Thelen, "Making History and Making the United States," *Journal of American Studies* 32 (1998): 385.

6. Eric Foner, *The Story of American Freedom* (New York, 1998).

7. Linda Kerber, *No Constitutional Right to Be Ladies: Women and the Obligations of Citizenship* (New York, 1998).

8. Rogers Smith, *Civic Ideals: Conflicting Visions of Citizenship in U.S. History* (New Haven, 1998).

9. Robert L. Middlekauff, *The Glorious Cause: The American Revolution, 1763–1789* (New York, 1982), James McPherson, *The Battle Cry of Freedom: The Civil War Era* (New York, 1998); David Patterson, *Grand Expectations: The United States, 1945–1974* (New York, 1997); David M. Kennedy, *Freedom from Fear: The American People in Depression and War, 1929–1945* (New York, 1999).

10. Thelen, "Making History," 374, 394–95.

11. Ibid., 374, 395.

12. Ibid., 394–95.

13. Michael Kammen, "Carl Becker Redivivus: Or, Is Everyone Really A Histo-

rian?" *History & Theory* 39 (2000): 230–42; Kerwin Lee Klein, "On the Emergence of *Memory* in Historical Discourse," *Representations,* no. 69 (Winter 2000): 127–50.

14. Of several relevant books by Paxton, see esp. Robert O. Paxton and Michael Marus, *Vichy France and the Jews* (New York, 1982).

15. Kennedy, *Freedom from Fear,* cited in n. 9 above. David Thelen, "Re-thinking History and the Nation-State: Mexico and the United States," *Journal of American History* 86 (September 1999): 440–41, and id., "The Nation and Beyond: Transnational Perspectives on United States History," *Journal of American History* 86 (December 1999): 974.

16. Kennedy, *Freedom from Fear,* 855–56.

17. Daniel T. Rodgers, *Atlantic Crossings: Social Politics in a Progressive Age* (Cambridge, Mass., 1998), 508.

18. James T. Kloppenberg, *Uncertain Victory: Social Democracy and Progressivism in European and American Thought, 1870–1920* (New York, 1986).

19. Thelen, "Making History," 380.

20. Henry F. May, *The Enlightenment in America* (New York, 1976); Bruce Kuklick, *The Rise of American Philosophy* (New Haven, 1977); *Victorian America,* ed. Daniel Walker Howe (Philadelphia, 1976); James R. Moore, *The Post-Darwinian Controversies* (New York, 1979). Prominent examples from the late 1960s include David Brion Davis, *The Problem of Slavery in Western Culture* (Ithaca, N.Y.: 1967), and Robert Kelley, *The Transatlantic Persuasion: The Liberal-Democratic Mind in the Age of Gladstone* (New York, 1969). In "American Intellectual History: Some Issues for the 1980s," *Reviews in American History* 10 (1982): 306–17, building on this tradition of scholarship, I sketched an explicit agenda for an internationally oriented approach to the intellectual history of the United States, designed to operate simultaneously with a more nation-centered research agenda.

21. J. T. Merz, *A History of European Thought in the Nineteenth Century,* vol. 1 (London, 1904).

22. I have argued elsewhere for this one-sentence account of the history of the United States; see, e.g., David A. Hollinger, *Postethic America: Beyond Multiculturalism* (2d ed., New York, 2000), 220–22.

23. I take these two issues of the *Journal of American History* to be among the most important published by it in recent years.

24. Foner, *American Freedom,* 3–12.

APPENDIX

Participants in the La Pietra Conferences, 1997–2000

Willi Paul Adams, *Freie Universität Berlin*
Mia Bay, *Rutgers University*
Thomas Bender, *New York University*
Tiziano Bonazzi, *University of Bologna*
Philip Bonner, *University of the Witswatersrand*
Charles Bright, *University of Michigan*
Nicholas Canny, *National University of Ireland, Galway*
William Chafe, *Duke University*
Francesca Lopez Civeira, *University of Havana*
Nancy Cott, *Yale University*
Alan Dawley, *College of New Jersey*
Greg Dening, *University of Melbourne*
Prasenjit Duara, *University of Chicago*
Ellen Carol DuBois, *University of California, Los Angeles*
Mary Dudziak, *University of Southern California*
Colleen Dunlavy, *University of Wisconsin, Madison*
David Engerman, *Brandeis University*
Elizabeth Esch, *New York University*
Ferdinando Fasce, *University of Bologna*
Winfried Fluck, *Freie Universität Berlin*
Eric Foner, *Columbia University*
Dana Frank, *University of California, Santa Cruz*
George Fredrickson, *Stanford University*

Fumiko Fujita, *Tsuda College*
Jun Furuya, *Hokkaido University*
Michael Geyer, *University of Chicago*
Jessica C. E. Gienow-Hecht, *Martin Luther University at Halle-Wittenburg*
Lori Ginzberg, *Pennsylvania State University*
Michael Gomez, *New York University*
James Green, *University of Massachusetts, Amherst*
Carl Guaneri, *St. Mary's College, California*
Patrick Hagopian, *University of Glamorgan*
Christiane Harzig, *University of Bremen*
Jürgen Herbst, *University of Wisconsin, Madison*
Martha Hodes, *New York University*
Dirk Hoerder, *University of Bremen*
Kristin Hoganson, *University of Illinois, Urbana-Champagne*
David Hollinger, *University of California, Berkeley*
Reyaldo Ileto, *Australian National University*
Dolores Janiewski, *Victoria University of Wellington*
Marchelo Jasmin, *Pontifical Catholic University of Rio de Janeiro*
Walter Johnson, *New York University*
Arnita Jones, executive director, *Organization of American Historians*
Robin D. G. Kelley, *New York University*
Linda Kerber, *University of Iowa*
Yukiki Koshiro, *Notre Dame University*
Rob Kroes, *University of Amsterdam*
Karen Kupperman, *New York University*
Michael LaCombe, *New York University*
Lester D. Langley, *University of Georgia*
Alessandra Lorini, *University of Florence*
Erik McDuffie, *New York University*
Molly McGarry, *New York University*
Donna Merwick, *University of Melbourne*
James Mohr, *University of Oregon*
Carl Nightingale, *University of Massachusetts, Amherst*
Mary Nolan, *New York University*
Thomas Osborne, *College of Santa Ana*
Jacques Revel, *École des hautes études en sciences sociales*
Ron Robin, *Haifa University*

Daniel Rodgers, *Princeton University*
Roy Rosenzweig, *George Mason University*
John Rowett, *Oxford University*
Mary Ryan, *University of California, Berkeley*
Nayan Shah, *University of California, San Diego*
Barbara Clark Smith, *Smithsonian Institution*
David Stowe, *Michigan State University*
Victoria Straughn, *La Follette High School, Madison, Wisconsin*
Mauricio Tenorio, *University of Texas / Centro de Investigación y Docencia Económicas (Mexico)*
David Thelen, *Indiana University*
Ian Tyrrell, *University of New South Wales*
Josefina Zoraida Vazquez, *Colegio de Mexico*
Robert Wiebe, *Northwestern University*
François Weil, *École des hautes études en sciences sociales*
Richard White, *Stanford University*
Fanon Che Wilkens, *New York University*
Mari Yoshihara, *University of Hawaii, Manoa*
Marilyn Young, *New York University*

CONTRIBUTORS

Thomas Bender is university professor of the humanities at New York University. His work has focused on cities, intellectuals, cultural history, and questions of narrative synthesis. His books include *Toward an Urban Vision: Ideas and Institutions in Nineteenth-century America* (1975); *New York Intellect: A History of Intellectual Life in New York City, from 1750 to the Beginnings of Our Own Time* (1987), and *Intellect and Public Life: Essays on the Social History of Academic Intellectuals in the United States* (1993). He co-edited *American Academic Culture in Transformation: Fifty Years, Four Disciplines,* with Carl E. Schorske (1998).

Charles Bright is professor of history at the Residential College, University of Michigan. He works on the history of globalization (in collaboration with Michael Geyer), as well as problems in American political history, prison history, and the history of Detroit. His most recent book is *The Powers that Punish: Prison and Politics in the Era of the "Big House," 1920–1955* (1996).

Prasenjit Duara is professor in the departments of History and East Asian Language and Civilizations at the University of Chicago. His work explores problems in social history, nationalism, transnationalism, and the implications of theory for historical questions. His books include *Culture, Power and the State: Rural Society in North China, 1900–1942* (1988) and *Rescuing History from the Nation: Questioning Narratives of Modern China* (1995). He is presently completing a book tentatively titled *Frontiers of the East Asian Modern: Authenticity and Sovereignty in Manchukuo.*

Winfried Fluck is professor and chair of American culture at the John F. Kennedy Institute for North American Studies of the Freie Universität Berlin. His work has focused on American realism, American popular culture, the postmodern period, and the theory of American studies. His books include *Ästhetische Theorie und literaturwissenschaftliche Methode: Eine Untersuchung ihres Zusammenhangs am Beispiel der amerikanischen Huck Finn–Kritik* (1975); *Inszenierte Wirklichkeit: Der amerikanische Realismus, 1865–1900* (1992); and *Das kulturelle Imaginäre* (1997). He is currently working on a history of American culture.

Michael Geyer is professor of history at the University of Chicago. His work has focused on military history and the history of war, contemporary German history, and (together with Charles Bright) on the history of globalization. Writings on the latter include Geyer and Bright, "Global Violence and Nationalizing Wars in Eurasia and the Americas: The Geopolitics of War in the Mid-Nineteenth Century," *Comparative Studies in Society and History* 38 (1996), and "World History in a Global Age," *American Historical Review* 100 (1995).

Dirk Hoerder teaches North American social history and the history of migrations at the University of Bremen, Department of Social Sciences. His publications include *Labor Migration in the Atlantic Economies: The European and North American Working Classes during the Period of Industrialization* (1985); *Creating Societies: Immigrant Lives in Canada* (1999) and *Cultures in Contact: European and World Migrations, Eleventh Century to the 1990s* (forthcoming).

David A. Hollinger is Chancellor's Professor of History at the University of California at Berkeley. He works primarily on the intellectual history of the United States in the twentieth century. His books include *Postethnic America: Beyond Multiculturalism* (1995; 2d ed., 2000); *Science, Jews, and Secular Culture* (1996); and, co-edited with Charles Capper, *The American Intellectual Tradition: A Sourcebook* (1989; 4th ed., 2001).

Akira Iriye is Charles Warren Professor of American History at Harvard University. His main areas of interest are twentieth-century international relations with a focus on nongovernmental actors and, more broadly, the history of globalization. His publications include *China and Japan in the Global Setting* (1992); *The Globalizing of America* (1993); and *Cultural Internationalism and World Order* (1997).

Walter Johnson is an associate professor of history and American studies at New York University. His work focuses on capitalism, race, and resistance, mostly in the nineteenth century and mostly in the U.S. South. He is the author of *Soul by Soul: Life Inside the Antebellum Slave Market* (2000), and is currently at work on a cultural history of the Mississippi River Valley.

Robin D. G. Kelley is professor of history and Africana studies at New York University. His research interests include the history of the African diaspora, twentieth-century black intellectual and cultural history, and U.S. labor movements. His books include *Race Rebels: Culture Politics and the Black Working Class* (1994); *Yo' Mama's DisFunktional! Fighting the Culture Wars in Urban America* (1997); and, with Howard Zinn and Dana Frank, *Three Strikes* (2001).

Rob Kroes is professor and chair of American studies at the University of Amsterdam. He is the author of *If You've Seen One, You've Seen The Mall: Europeans and American Culture* (1996) and of *Us and Them: Questions of Citizenship in a Globalizing World* (2000), as well as the editor of *Predecessors: Intellectual Lineages in American Studies* (1999).

Karen Ordahl Kupperman is professor of history at New York University. Her work focuses on early America, particularly cross-cultural efforts at interpretation and the challenge posed by transplantation of European societies. Her books include *Settling with the Indians: The Meeting of English and Indian Cultures in America, 1580–1640* (1980); *Roanoke: The Abandoned Colony* (1984); *Providence Island, 1630–1641: The Other Puritan Colony* (1993), and *Indians and English: Facing Off in Early America* (2000).

Ron Robin teaches American history and communication theory. He is currently dean of students at the University of Haifa, Israel. His books include *Enclaves of America: The Rhetoric of American Political Architecture Abroad* (1992); *The Barbed Wire College: Reeducating German POWs in the United States* (1995); and *The Making of the Cold War Enemy: Culture and Politics in the Military-Intellectual Complex* (2001).

Daniel Rodgers teaches American cultural and intellectual history at Princeton University, where he is Henry Charles Lea Professor of History. He is the author of *The Work Ethic in Industrial America, 1850–1920* (1978); *Contested Truths: Keywords in American Politics since Independence* (1987); and *Atlantic Crossings: Social Politics in a Progressive Age* (1998).

Ian Tyrrell is professor and head of school at the University of New South Wales, in Sydney, Australia. He has done research on many aspects of American historiography and history, especially regarding social movements. His books include *Woman's World / Woman's Empire: The Woman's Christian Temperance Union in International Perspective* (1991) and *True Gardens of the Gods: Californian-Australian Environmental Reform* (1999).

François Weil is *directeur d'études* at the École des hautes études en sciences sociales in Paris. His research interests include North American historiography, urban and industrial social history, migrants, and the cultural history of genealogy. Among his books are *Les Franco-Americains, 1860–1980* (1989) and *Histoire de New York* (2000).

Robert H. Wiebe died on December 10, 2000. He was a member of the History Department of Northwestern University History Department from 1960 to 1997, when he "officially" retired. His numerous books, which delve widely and deeply into the meaning of the American past, include *The Search for Order, 1977–1920* (1967); *The Segmented Society: An Introduction to the Meaning of America* (1975); *The Opening of American Society: From the Adoption of the Constitution to the Eve of Disunion* (1985); *Self-Rule: A Cultural History of American Democracy* (1996). *Who We Are: A History of Popular Nationalism* is scheduled for publication in 2001.

Marilyn B. Young is professor of history at New York University. Her work has focused on U.S. foreign policy in Asia and Southeast Asia and her books include *Rhetoric of Empire* (1968); (with William Rosenberg) *Revolutionary Struggle in the Twentieth Century* (1980); and *The Vietnam Wars* (1991).

INDEX

Lafeber, Walter, 279
Lagos Renaissance, 128–29
Lam, Wilfredo, 138
land. *See* environmental history
land use and planning, 260, 263, 265
language skills, lack of: barriers to international scholarship and, 321–22, 367, 368; graduate-program requirements and, 326–27; international relations and, 47–48; master narratives and, 212
Laslett, John, 139
Latin America: Amerindian survival in, 199, 208; continental mobility and, 200; and Euro-Atlantic migration system, 214; historiography of, 323; literature of, 38; and Pacific migration system, 200, 202, 217, 218–19; scholars of, internationalism and, 376, 377; universalist principles and, 72. *See also* Mexico
law, international, of American Indians, 108. *See also* legal process
Law, Robin, 151
Layton, Azza Salama, 138–39
Le défi américain (Servan-Schreiber), 299
Lee, Benjamin, 377
Lefebvre, Henri, 32
Leffler, Melvyn, 275
legal process: historical construction and, 28; sovereignty and, 27
Leisler's Rebellion, 115
leisure time, 298, 304
Lenape, 113
Lerner, Gerda, 320, 321, 328
Levi's jeans, 305, 306, 312, 313n8
Levy-Leboyer, Maurice, 318
lexical effect, modernity and, 33
Liang Qichao, 30
Liang Shanding, 36–38, 39–42, 43–44
liberal developmentalism: and nation as basic unit of history, 171; racial, 155, 158, 160–61, 165n165, 167n42
Liberal Tradition in America, The (Hartz), 171
Liberia, 215
liberty, equality, fraternity, 239
Lincoln, Abaham, 251
Linderman, Gerald, 286
Lindeström, Peter, 114
linearity. *See* evolutionism; periodization; temporality
Linebaugh, Peter, 133–34
Lipset, Seymour M., 207
literacy, and mobility, 242

literature: knight-errant tradition of, 37, 40, 44; Manchurian occupation and, 36, 39–42, 44; pastoral thematic of, 36; political control of meaning of, 39–44; racism revealed through, 38; reconstruction of past and, 44; of war, 283–91, 294n50, 387–90; writer as "organic intellectual," 38
Lloyd George, David, 256, 261, 263, 266
local/global events: heterogeneity of, 68; nations as claiming, 32–33
locality: authenticity and, 34–38, 43–44; migration and breakdown of, 236–39
Lodge, Henry Cabot, 277, 281
Lorini, Alessandra, 330
Louisiana: culture of, 208, 209–10; slavery in, 112–13
Louisiana Purchase, 74
L'Ouverture, Toussaint, 158
Lovyse, Lucretia, 112
Lower, Arthur, 323
Loyalists, flight of, 211
Lu Xun, 35, 36
Lüsede Gu (Liang), 36–38, 39–42, 43–44
lynching, 205

McArthur, Douglas, 389
McCloy, John J., 278
McCullough, David, 388
MacDonald, Ramsay, 258
McGerr, Michael, 373
McGrew, Anthony, 53
Machine in the Garden (Marx), 35–36
McMichael, Phillip, 177
McNamara, Robert, 277–78, 288–90
McNeill, William, 7, 236
McPherson, James, 386
Mahan, Alfred Thayer, 80
Maier, Charles, 382
Mailer, Norman, 284
"Making History and Making the United States" (Thelen), 385, 388
Man and Nature (Marsh), 172
Manchuria, occupation of, 36, 39–42, 44
Manifest Destiny, 32, 74–75, 181. *See also* east-to-west movement of history
Many Headed Hydra, The (Linebaugh and Rediker), 133–34
Maoist communists, use of literature by, 41–42
mapmaking, 199
Marcuse, Herbert, 348

Compositor:	Binghamton Valley Composition, LLC
Text:	10/12 Baskerville
Display:	Baskerville
Printer and binder:	Maple-Vail Manufacturing Group